Social Anthropology

of

North American Tribes

Social Anthropology
of
North American Tribes

FRED EGGAN, EDITOR

By

FRED EGGAN • WILLIAM H. GILBERT, JR. • J. GILBERT
McALLISTER • PHILLEO NASH • MORRIS E. OPLER
JOHN H. PROVINSE • SOL TAX

Enlarged Edition

THE UNIVERSITY OF CHICAGO PRESS

Library of Congress Catalog Number: 55–5123

THE UNIVERSITY OF CHICAGO PRESS, CHICAGO 37
Cambridge University Press, London, N.W. 1, England
The University of Toronto Press, Toronto 5, Canada

*Copyright 1937 and 1955 by The University of Chicago. All rights
reserved. Published 1937. Second edition 1955. Composed and
printed by* THE UNIVERSITY OF CHICAGO PRESS, *Chicago,
Illinois, U.S.A.*

ESSAYS IN SOCIAL ORGANIZATION, LAW, AND RELIGION

originally presented to

PROFESSOR A. R. RADCLIFFE-BROWN

upon the occasion of his accepting the chair of
Social Anthropology at Oxford University

FOREWORD

It is particularly gratifying to the authors and editor of this volume that the increasing interest in social anthropology in this country makes it possible to present a new and enlarged edition. Some two decades ago, when the original contributions were being written, it was not at all clear that these pioneer efforts would receive any general encouragement or recognition. Indeed, many comments that we received were highly critical. But particularly since the end of World War II there has been a growing interest in the application of social anthropological points of view and concepts to the study of the social and cultural life of the American Indian, as well as to other regions.

That the roots of this interest are deep in Americanist studies is well illustrated by Sol Tax's "From Lafitau to Radcliffe-Brown: A Short History of the Study of Social Organization." We had hoped to include it in the original edition, but space limitations prevented. In it he traces the development of the various threads which have given rise to the modern study of social organization, both here and abroad, and accounts for some of the differences which are to be found. The editor has prepared an additional chapter, "Social Anthropology: Methods and Results," which attempts to integrate social anthropological and ethnological methods in a productive synthesis and discusses some selected studies on North American social organization which illustrate these methods.

The original volume was prepared to honor Professor A. R. Radcliffe-Brown upon the occasion of his accepting the Chair of Social Anthropology at Oxford University in 1937. We have left Robert Redfield's "Introduction" as originally written. It is still the best brief evaluation of Radcliffe-Brown and his contributions to anthropology; and, while he would undoubtedly write it somewhat differently today, it has stood the test of time. Since then, also, a further volume[1] has been prepared in England

---

[1] Meyer Fortes (ed.), *Social Structure: Studies Presented to A. R. Radcliffe-Brown* (Oxford: Clarendon Press, 1949).

as a tribute to Radcliffe-Brown on the occasion of his retirement from Oxford, and Meyer Fortes' excellent Preface can be read with profit. Since this latter volume also contains an up-to-date bibliography of Radcliffe-Brown's writings, we have omitted this item from the new edition. Radcliffe-Brown's major essays and addresses have recently been gathered together in a convenient volume,[2] but he is still writing as vigorously as ever.

We have rededicated this volume to Professor Radcliffe-Brown. Even though we have not followed his teachings in all respects, we hope that he will be pleased with our progress toward the common goal.

FRED EGGAN

UNIVERSITY OF CHICAGO
CHICAGO, ILLINOIS

[2] A. R. Radcliffe-Brown, *Structure and Function in Primitive Society: Essays and Addresses*, with a Foreword by E. E. Evans-Pritchard and Fred Eggan (London: Cohen & West, Ltd.; Glencoe, Ill.: Free Press, 1952).

INTRODUCTION

ROBERT REDFIELD

This book marks the conclusion of an important episode in the recent history of American anthropology—the immediate presence and participation of A. R. Radcliffe-Brown. The period of five years, during which his influence was directly exerted in teaching American students and guiding their research, is at an end. The circumstance has less finality because his associates in this country know that, just as his work affected theirs before he came to this country to work, so after he leaves will they continue to profit by his stimulating example. Nevertheless, Oxford University will gain what the University of Chicago will lose when Professor Radcliffe-Brown assumes the chair of anthropology at the former institution in the autumn of 1937. These lines are written in the spirit of hail and farewell.

If there is any anthropological generalization that is generally accepted by anthropologists, it is the one about the importance of diffusion in the culture process. What is true of culture in general is no less true of scientific method. Anthropology, as a body of methods and of intellectual interests, is itself a heritage, or rather a number of heritages. As the contact of cultures is favorable to culture change and to the development of civilization, in the same way the meeting of different anthropological traditions may be expected to result in changes in method and viewpoint and to favor the development of anthropology. Professor Radcliffe-Brown brought to this country a method for the study of society, well defined and different enough from what prevailed here to require American anthropologists to reconsider the whole matter of method, to scrutinize their objectives, and to attend to new problems and new ways of looking at problems. He stirred us up and accelerated intellectual invention and variation among us.

The importance of his contribution has been indicated by the amount of discussion that has gone on about him and his work. Few of the American anthropological brotherhood have been entirely indifferent, and many have found it necessary to emphasize their agreement, or disagreement, with his views. One could assemble a small anthology of papers and chapters written recently each with an eye out to Radcliffe-Brown, the writer feeling called upon to define or declare his position in a field in which Radcliffe-Brown appears as leader, adversary, or challenger.

Developments in the field, however, have not been entirely clear, partly because of the fog rolled up by multitudinous pronouncements of the word "functionalism" in a wide range of half-understood senses. As a matter of fact, Professor Radcliffe-Brown does not think or speak of himself as a "functionalist," although he makes frequent use of the word "function." His own use of this word[1] is special and precise: it stands for the activity of an organ as it contributes to the persistence of the organism of which it is a part, and is usually explained by him with reference to an example from physiology. A society is regarded, in some sense, as an organism, and the usages and institutions to be found in the society are described with reference to the role played by them in maintaining the society as a whole. The employment of this conception does not necessarily involve an interest in the development of generalizations as to the nature of society. One might confine oneself to "functional" ethnographic accounts—depictions of unique societies, without comparison, but each presented as an organic whole composed of functionally interrelated and integrating parts. One would then be, in the broad sense,[2] a historian, not a generalizing scientist. Conversely, there is nothing to require a social scientist—one interested in the development of compendent general propositions as to society and human behavior—to adopt the concept of function, and indeed many attempts in the direction of social science get along without it.

[1] A. R. Radcliffe-Brown, *On the Concept of Function in Social Science*, pp. 394-97.

[2] A. L. Kroeber, *History and Science in Anthropology*, pp. 545-46.

Whatever may be left of "function" in American anthropology when the fog lifts, it may now be declared that Radcliffe-Brown's signal contribution is not derived from his use of the concept of function, but rather, quite simply, from his emphasis on a strictly nonhistorical, sharply scientific method in anthropology. The objective of social anthropology is the formulation of general propositions as to society. The social anthropologist deals with classes of societal phenomena; early he names the class with which he deals—sanctions, totemism, Omaha type of kinship system, or whatever; the particular society or institution with which he deals is then of significance only as it represents or modifies the class, type, or declared general proposition. History, on the other hand, has a logical nature essentially different; its nature is "not the dealing with time sequences, though that almost inevitably crops out where historical impulses are genuine and strong; but an endeavor at descriptive integration."[3]

Kroeber, in the paper already cited, goes on to say that, although the historical and scientific approaches should ultimately, and so far as possible, supplement each other, nevertheless, "precisely if they are to cooperate, it seems that they should recognize and tolerate each other's individuality. It is hard to see good coming out of a mixture of approaches whose aims are different."[4] "They need intellectual differentiation, precisely because we shall presumably penetrate further in the end by two approaches than by one."[5]

It was the nature and result of Boas' teaching, as Kroeber ably points out, that the two approaches were, in a sense, mixed. Boas' great strength lay in two aspects of his intellectual nature that are the reverse and obverse of each other: his rigorous and critical analytic treatment of specific, segregated data, and his unwillingness to pursue any single method or point of view. Boas analyzes particular phenomena, without any elaborate conceptual paraphernalia, to see what elements, or events, whether in the present or in the past, bear upon—"explain"—the facts studied. He secures special knowledge of particular fact by critical methods such as a historian would use, and analyzes

[3] *Ibid.*, p. 545.   [4] *Ibid.*, p. 547.   [5] *Ibid.*, p. 569.

phenomena with the rigorousness of the laboratory scientist. But—and this is said in repetition of Kroeber and with awareness that Boas replied to Kroeber on the point[6]—he does not write histories, and he does not prepare scientific systems.

At the time when Boas introduced his methods they were precisely what was needed. They freed anthropological interest from speculative theory, and cleared the ground and laid the foundations for both a critical history and an empirical science. But ambiguity of methodological approach is no longer essential; it is no longer even advisable. With the further development of procedures, on the one hand historical, on the other scientific, and with the confidence achieved by the mastery of ordered fact, it is desirable that the logical character of the objective, the nature of the approach, be made explicit.

"There is no Boas school, and never has been." The work of some of his students has gone off in one direction, and that of others in other directions. Yet a reluctance to clarify the historical and social anthropological ("scientific") approaches has remained, and, more important, no one in America has offered a strictly nonhistorical scientific method, equipped with a self-consistent body of concepts and procedures for getting specific jobs done in relation to ultimate scientific objectives. Radcliffe-Brown has done just that.

It is on this scientific side that emphasis has been needed in American anthropology in recent years. Boas does not write histories, but some of his students do. The development of archaeology, the full realization of its relationship with ethnology,[7] the utilization of procedures by which to infer history from data other than document or buried artifact, have made it possible for American anthropologists to write histories, tentative though of course they are, of American and other cultures. But in the direction of science, such later developments as have occurred have been in the first place exploratory and without system, and second—as in part of the work of Sapir and Mead—with reference to the individual in society rather than with

---

[6] F. Boas, *History and Science in Anthropology: A Reply*, pp. 137–41.

[7] W. D. Strong, *Anthropological Theory and Archaeological Fact*, pp. 359–70.

reference to society alone ("psychological" rather than "sociological").

Radcliffe-Brown has offered an explicit and systematic method for the scientific study of societies. Grant that the method is too systematic to provide in itself a single road to understanding and is too special to represent all interests or to admit all insights. But then let us also grant that it clarifies sharply the distinction between the historical and the scientific approaches in anthropology, and that it affords one procedure and one set of concepts for pursuing the scientific approach.

Too much emphasis has been placed on the question of the validity or the importance of the general propositions issuing from this approach to the study of society. It is said that the generalizations of Radcliffe-Brown are vague. Worse, it is declared that they are commonplace, that these formally guided investigations of special fact yield only the familiar general propositions which common knowledge provides. The effect of these allegations is reduced if emphasis is laid not on the general laws which are achieved by the method, or are hoped to be achieved by it, but on the general formulations, whether substantive or relational, which are offered the student as guides to research. No scientific problem can be attacked at all without some tentative guiding formulation; these are either implicit and undeclared, and correspondingly uncertain and personal, or else they are declared and subject to logical criticism. You cannot have science without concepts. It is in the concepts and in the classification of problems (as, for example, with reference to law and social sanctions[8]) that the more important contribution of Radcliffe-Brown to a scientific social anthropology is to be found. This contribution is called for in American anthropology as a counteremphasis to the analytic and nonconceptualized procedure of Boas. The effort at scientific synthesis arranges the problems in some order, exposes the implicit postulates, and makes it possible to discover if different workers are talking about the same things. The propositions are not to be treated as final but are to be challenged, revised, or abandoned as the investigation into special fact guided by them proceeds.

[8] *Encyclopaedia of the Social Sciences*, articles by Radcliffe-Brown.

The influence which Radcliffe-Brown has exerted on American anthropology is represented in the pages that follow not merely by the extent to which the viewpoints of the seven authors resemble his own but also by the extent to which, stimulated by his teaching, their viewpoints differ from his, being developments out of, or even away from, his own. We are not to assume that the scientific views of the seven contributors are identical with the views of Professor Radcliffe-Brown, any more than we are to suppose that Professor Radcliffe-Brown (who had no part in the preparation of the book) would, if we asked him, agree with everything that appears in the following pages. A teacher is successful to the degree, not that he inculcates, but that he stimulates. And Professor Radcliffe-Brown has stimulated many American anthropologists besides those who have written this book, and caused them to alter and improve their work and methods. His influence will be read between the lines of many American books already written and to be written even by those who do not realize that they write as they do in no small degree because of the work of Radcliffe-Brown.

Certain anthropologists who had been students of Radcliffe-Brown at the University of Chicago conceived this book. The other contributors are also men who have been students of Radcliffe-Brown at the University of Chicago. This restriction of contributors has made possible a book of essays on a single subject and all employing a broadly comparative method. The editor of the book, and the editors of the series of which it is one volume, believe that, aside from the role of the book as a gesture of recognition to a departing colleague and teacher, it is a contribution of no small merit to scholarship in the field it represents.

The occasion which gives rise to the book may excuse the inclusion in this Introduction of a last personal remark. In these five years Professor Radcliffe-Brown's associates in the department have found him always an agreeable and efficient colleague, a generous contributor of time and effort, and a wise and open-minded counselor. Let that go into the record on the testimony of one who knows.

TABLE OF CONTENTS

SOME PROBLEMS OF SOCIAL ORGANIZATION

SOL TAX

SOME PROBLEMS OF SOCIAL ORGANIZATION

SOL TAX

INTRODUCTION

If the general problem of ethnology is to explain[1] the presence and the distribution of cultural phenomena, the task of the student of social organization is to explain: (1) Why every people in the world has made the fact of biological generation one of the important focal points of its culture; why they all have the social ramifications that go under the names of marriage and the family; and why so many of them have lineages, clans, phratries, dual organizations, etc. (2) Why it is that such institutions are so varied in form (if, indeed, they are always variants of the

---

[1] To "explain" seems to mean, in ethnology, to tell how something came to be what it is. This has two aspects, closely related: (1) historical, in terms of unique events, and (2) scientific, in the sense that it involves a universal generalization. Thus, if one wished to explain the couvade, he would eventually want to be able to tell how it came to be in the places where it is. This sounds like a historical question, but if, in some way, he should be able to work out a general law covering the couvade, he would be able to answer the question without recourse to history by indicating the conditions under which the couvade would appear. It seems difficult to indicate these conditions for any phenomena of social organization. Moreover, it is difficult to explain them historically since native peoples do not have much history.

From necessity a species of half-explanation is undertaken. The "historian" says something like: "The couvade has diffused from a point of origin (or even x point of origin) throughout the Old World, and from another place throughout the New World," and leaves unanswered the question of how it originated wherever it did and how it was diffused and accepted by the borrowers. The "scientist" today sees that this is hardly an explanation and offers a rival half-explanation something like: "Every society must recognize the social importance of fatherhood, and the couvade is one means of doing so," or else: "At birth, as at any social transition, the close relatives are, together with the infant, in a dangerous marginal state and must be treated with great care; as far as the father is concerned, the couvade is an extreme manifestation of this"; telling, perhaps, what the couvade does for society but still not answering the question of how it, worth while as it may be, came to be in the places where it is.

As far as kinship is concerned, bare quarter-explanations are current; a set of terms is called "the result of such and such a marriage custom," neither the marriage nor the terms being explained.

same thing and not in reality different). (3) Why institutions which seem most alike occur in some cases in different parts of the world while contiguous peoples often have quite different institutions. (4) Why certain institutions are found to occur in the same tribe over and over again without an absolute correlation being found. (5) Why systems of kinship terminology in particular seem so often to be connected with social institutions and practices, yet the terminology is sometimes found without the institution in question and vice versa. (6) Why some of the most peculiar (to us) forms of kinship systems and social practices are yet found to be distributed so widely. Each of these questions has numerous ramifications, to some of which conclusive answers have been given; in a general sense, however, they are all problems which still confront students of social organization.

The solutions of these problems have been translated, first, into the question of independent invention versus diffusion; second, into the problem of psychological versus sociological causation; and, third, into the choice between *any* kind of natural law and a series of historic accidents. Combinations of these take care of most of ethnological thought, and, indeed, ethnologists not too closely allied with any one theory realize that independent invention and borrowing, psychological and social causes, and innumerable historic accidents, as well, have all, in one way or another, played their parts in the shaping of human social organization. The problem that remains is less to show that any one of these has or has not been instrumental in human history than to show just what part each has played, and each always will play.

The general problem will, perhaps, be best clarified by a discussion of systems of kinship terminology (which, as a matter of fact, now occupy more attention than any other phase of social organization); and this discussion may profitably be limited to a section of California where the Indian tribes vary in their kinship systems and where some of them use the so-called "Omaha" type of system and others the so-called "Crow" type.

In the Omaha type, at its simplest, the father's brother is called "father," and the mother's sister "mother"; their children are all "brothers" and "sisters." The father's sister is called by a special term ("aunt") and the mother's brother by a special term ("uncle"). The uncle's children are called, again, "uncle" and "mother," respectively, and the aunt's children are called the same as one's own sister's children.[2] In the Crow type, on the other hand, the aunt's children are called "father" and "aunt," respectively, and the uncle's children are called the same as one's own brother's children.[3] The two systems are, in a sense, the reverse of each other, but both have in common the overriding of generations—in the one case of the mother's patrilineal lineage and in the other of the father's matrilineal lineage.

Indian tribes representing three distinct linguistic families, all in central California, will form the subject of this discussion.[4] Surrounding a large continuous area of Penutian-speaking tribes are smaller areas of Yukian- and Hokan-speaking groups. A smaller continuous area, including tribes that are Penutian, Yukian, and Hokan, and excluding tribes of each as well, delimits tribes that have, in one form or another, the general features of the Omaha-Crow kinship systems. Thus, of twenty-seven Penutian tribes, twelve (three out of four Wintun, six out of six Miwok, and three out of seven Yokuts) have the Omaha-Crow feature; of four Yukian tribes, one has the Omaha-Crow feature; and of thirty-eight Hokan tribes, five (all Pomo, of which there are seven groups in all) have the Omaha-Crow feature. Thus, eighteen tribes out of a total of sixty-nine tribes of the three language groups use terms for cross-cousins that are otherwise applied between succeeding generations. The rest of the Hokan, Yukian, and Penutian tribes in the region either employ for the cross-cousins the same terms they apply to parallel cousins, or else use special terms entirely. The kinship systems of some of the surrounding groups are not known, but the dis-

[2] For a typical Omaha system see the writer's account of the Fox kinship system in this volume (pp. 247 ff.).

[3] For a typical Crow system see Gilbert's account of the Cherokee kinship system in this volume (pp. 289 ff.).

[4] This discussion is based on material in Gifford, *Californian Kinship Terminologies*, pp. 77–122.

tribution of those that are known is neither continuous nor correlated with linguistic divisions.

Three conclusions are therefore apparent: (1) Since the kinship classifications overlap linguistic boundaries, the problem of kinship systems (not on the terms themselves, necessarily) is not entirely linguistic. (2) Since the Omaha-Crow feature appears in contiguous tribes, it probably represents one problem, either of diffusion or of development due to like conditions or both; it would appear unlikely that in each tribe a different explanation would be found. (3) Since the Omaha-Crow feature seems to be more or less surrounded, where the surroundings are known, by the other two types (*if* one accepts the historical hypothesis), one must suppose it most likely that the Omaha-Crow feature has been spreading from this area to other surrounding Penutians, Hokans, and Yukians; for to suppose the contrary (that more of the tribes previously had the Omaha-Crow feature and that the other types were pushing in from all sides) is to suppose that the Omaha-Crow feature was attacked on several fronts for different reasons—an explanation indeed complex.

More specific conclusions may be reached by a more detailed study of the region. The three Yokuts tribes classify cross-cousins in typical Omaha form; the six Miwok tribes do likewise, with one slightly atypical exception; the Wintun and the Pomo have the Omaha form, too, but the most northern of the former have terminology of a very peculiar sort—intermediate between Omaha and Crow—and the most southern of the latter have a typical Crow type, as have, finally, the neighboring Wappo. Two observations can be made:

1. Not only in tribes of the same linguistic family but in very closely related tribes (most of whose actual kinship terms are identical) can the method of classification be quite different—both where the related tribes are contiguous (Southern and Central Pomo, for example) and where they are not. Thus the Southwestern Pomo do not have the Omaha-Crow feature at all, the Southern Pomo have the Crow type, and the other Pomo, to the north and south, have the Omaha type. On the other hand, all the Yuki except the Wappo designate cross-cousins as

siblings, while the Wappo alone (separated from their brethren and surrounded on all sides by peoples who have the Omaha-Crow feature) are like their neighbors rather than like their linguistic brethren.

2. There are some fine points about kinship systems that need investigation before we can go much farther. What is the meaning of the difference between the Omaha and the Crow types? They seem to be opposites in one sense, alike in another—capable of classifying relatives in entirely different ways, yet existing side by side in the same kind of cultural setting and even, on occasion, apparently becoming mixed.

The comparison in Table 1 of some of the vital kinship terms of the Central Pomo (Omaha type), the Southern Pomo (Crow type of same language group), and Wappo (Crow type of different linguistic family) will serve to clarify such observations.

It is to be noticed that, although the Pomo sets of terms show linguistic relations, their classification is quite different, whereas the Southern Pomo and the Wappo terms are not at all related, yet their classification is almost the same. These three tribes are the closest of neighbors. If one assumes that all the Pomo once had the Omaha feature, can one say that the Southern Pomo, for some reason or other, changed it around and then influenced the Wappo to adopt their scheme? Or might one rather believe that the Wappo, moving away from their neighbors into Pomo and Miwok territory, adopted the general idea of the Omaha-Crow type but bungled it, so to speak, and reversed what the Pomo and Miwok had, and then influenced the Southern Pomo to go with them?

It is difficult to take such guesses seriously, but they are the sort of thing one expects at this stage of the investigation. There is no certain way of knowing that the kinship classification of one people *can* influence that of another; we have even less of an idea of *how* that influence might occur (if it can), and what the factors governing the results are. This suggests the fundamental problem of kinship terminologies—how deeply are they seated in culture? If kinship systems are culture traits that have not much to do with the rest of culture, then perhaps we could imagine them traveling from tribe to tribe like a new tool. But this does not seem to be generally true. Not only are the kinship terms which a people uses grounded as deeply in their everyday

TABLE 1*

COMPARISON OF CROSS-COUSIN TERMS OF THE CENTRAL POMO
SOUTHERN POMO, AND THE WAPPO

Tribe	Father's Sister's Son	Father's Sister's Daughter	Mother's Brother's Son	Mother's Brother's Daughter
Central Pomo	One term, *kegu*, applied by both men and women regardless of anybody's sex or age; *kegu* is the same term as that applied to any nephew or niece		*djute*, term for M B, applied by all *kegu*	*ceki*, term for M y SS, applied by all *kegu*
Southern Pomo	*adjigin*, term for F y B, applied by all M B Ch. Related to Central Pomo term for F y B, *djeki*	*amutsin*, term for F SS, applied by all M B Ch. Related to Central Pomo term for F SS, *mute*	*apakin*, term for o B S, applied by *adjigin*	*apankin*, term for o B D, applied by *adjigin*
			acutkin, term for B Ch, applied by all *amutsin* (none of these terms seems related to those of Central Pomo, corresponding to *kegu*)	
Wappo	*olo*, term for F y B, applied by all M B Ch.	*etsa*, term for F y SS (also o SS), applied by all M B Ch.	*yau*, term for o B S (also y B), applied by *etsa*. *ek'a*, term for o B S, applied by *olo*	*yapi*, term for o B D (also y SS), applied by *etsa*. *ek'abi*, term for o B D, applied by *olo*

*The abbreviations are those used by Gifford, *Californian Kinship Terminologies*, p. 14.

life as any part of their culture (and, indeed, represent an essential part of the transmission of culture itself since they usually reflect the native conception of the biologically generating group that in human society becomes the culture-maintaining group), but they are often the linguistic equivalent of the entire social structure. Yet how, under these circumstances, have the changes that must have occurred in central California (whether by diffusion, migrations, or internal development) occurred?

The Wintun situation has some bearing on this problem. All the Wintun tribes have the Omaha feature with the exception of the most northern tribe. This group is separated by a half-dozen tribes from the Wappo and the Southern Pomo who have the Crow feature. The Northern Wintun are surrounded by tribes which have either (1) the Omaha feature, (2) sibling terms for cross-cousins, or (3) special terms for cross-cousins. Yet this tribe has in some way come to have a very strange kinship system.

While the Omaha-Crow principle of classifying cross-cousins with relatives of the generations above and below is in force here, the choice between the Omaha and the Crow methods is not made. The Omaha way is to group maternal cross-cousins with the generation above, and their reciprocals (the paternal cross-cousins) with that below; the Crow method is to group the paternal cross-cousins with the generation above, and their reciprocals with the one below. Although this is the essential distinction, it goes much farther in the kinship systems, for usually (but not always) the entire line through males is grouped together with the maternal uncle and his son—the females being called "mother"—in the Omaha type, and the entire line through females is grouped together with the paternal aunt and her daughter—the males being called "father"—in the Crow type.

Among the Northern Wintun, however, neither of these alternatives is accepted. Instead, if the woman of the parental generation is older than her brother, her children are "mother's brothers" and "father's sisters" to her brother's children, and the line of descent through both children follows this pattern; while, if the woman is younger than her brother, his children are "mother's brothers" and "father's sisters" to hers, and the lines from then on follow this pattern. This situation seems to represent neither an Omaha nor a Crow type, nor a combination of both, but is perhaps an independent type.

In a very small area in California there are, then, two quite different varieties of the Omaha-Crow principle at work, as well as three non-Omaha-Crow methods of designating the relatives of cross-lines. The problem becomes one not of explaining the Omaha type, or the Crow type, but, first, to explain how it happens that such apparent diversity exists in cultures otherwise very much alike.

It was said above that the problems of social organization resolve themselves into combinations of three sets of alternatives: (1) independent invention versus diffusion, (2) psychological versus sociological causation, and (3) natural law versus historic accident. The California illustration indicates that the solution of the general problem depends not on the acceptance of alternatives—any one of a set or any combinations of several— but rather on the acceptance of all the possibilities given and the determination of what part each plays in the formation of different types of social organization:

1. Both independent invention and diffusion must have played their parts in central California. No tribe has a system utterly distinct from its neighbors or from its linguistic affiliates; yet neither have any two tribes exactly the same system. Distinctive developments of (a) common bases and (b) borrowed elements must have occurred in each tribe. There is no question of invention versus diffusion, but rather of the relative influence of internal and external factors. In what ways have they combined in the various tribes?

2. By the problem of sociological versus psychological causation is meant two different things in current anthropological discussion: (a) The determination of particular social institutions—such as kinship systems—by other social institutions— such as clans or moieties or marriage customs—is termed "sociological" as opposed to the determination of particular social institutions by such psychological factors (cultural though they may be) as notions of classification that crop out in language and social institutions as well. When applied to questions of kinship systems, "psychological causation" is often translated "linguistic causation." That social structures are connected with kinship systems cannot be doubted in California, for in half of the tribes which have the Omaha feature there are patrilineal moieties (which fit the feature); some of them also have the marriage

with the wife's brother's daughter, which also is in consonance with the terminology. But that psychological or linguistic determiners may also be present is just as undeniable, for such features as the notion of age distinctions in certain relationships occur differently in the different linguistic families. Again it seems that the problem becomes one of how each determinant enters the picture.

The problem of sociological versus psychological causation has also the meaning: (b) Are these elements of social organization there to satisfy the needs of the society as such, to help maintain it as a society, or to satisfy the needs of individuals, to help them in their adaptation to one another? The California example as given does not help toward the solution of this problem, since distributions can show only which peoples have what, and not what good is done by what they have.

3. The California example indicates that historical accidents must have occurred; except perhaps in a deep philosophical fatalist sense, it must have been a series of pure accidents that induced the Wappo (with whatever kinship system they happened to have) to migrate southward where they came into contact with Miwoks, Pomos, and Wintuns who, having different kinship systems, gradually exerted influence on that of the Wappo. It must have been partly accidental—what the Wappo were, what they were exposed to, and what they took—but it was not entirely so; for what they could take, or would take, depended partly on what they already had (itself partly perhaps the result of natural causes) and partly on rules of borrowing which are (even if they cannot be stated) some of the laws governing culture. If there were no natural laws governing culture, how could the fact that kinship terms do go together with certain social structures in a number of these tribes, and also in tribes three thousand miles away, be explained?

What has been said about California kinship systems could be repeated for kinship systems in other areas, such as in parts of Melanesia and Africa, as well as in other parts of America. Furthermore, what can be said for kinship in general applies equally well to other problems of social organization.

That kinship terminological systems are somehow connected

with social institutions is a position that, today, is hardly challenged. The question is as to the nature of the connection; that question is now being answered. Using again the Omaha-Crow types of kinship systems by way of example, a statement by Robert Lowie may be quoted:

Among the Omaha of Nebraska the generation lines are overridden—a mother's brother's son is called by the same term as a maternal uncle. This feature is not shared by such fellow Siouans as the Crow or Dakota, but occurs among several Central Algonquian tribes. Since, however, these tribes are neighbors, the peculiarity might be explained through diffusion without recourse to social phenomena. But when the same terminological feature crops up two thousand miles to the west among the Miwok of California as well as in Africa and Asia, one must . . . . look for a common determinant. The latter is to be found in the common stressing of the paternal line, for all the tribes in question have paternal clans and by paternal descent a maternal uncle and his son will always be in the same clan. For the Miwok and Omaha parallels a perfect answer can be given; both permit a man to marry his wife's brother's daughter—the niece is thus elevated in status, becoming a mother to the offspring of her husband's first marriage, whence her brother becomes a mother's brother. Yet the theory is not adequate; there are tribes like the Ojibwa which are also patrilineal but fail to disregard generation lines.

The reverse occurs in Melanesia, in Southern Alaska, among the Crow of Montana, the Pawnee of Nebraska, the Hopi of Arizona and in the Southeastern United States where the paternal aunt's son is reckoned a father and her daughter a paternal aunt. All these tribes are matrilineal, so that the father's sister and her children are always in the same group as herself and her brother. But here too a supplementary hypothesis is required, for there are matrilineal tribes, such as the Iroquois, that do not override generation. For the Melanesian and Tlinkit tribes, at least, nepotic inheritance of widows provides the key: a man inherits his mother's brother's widow, hence her children by the first husband call their cousin father. In Dobu, Melanesia, as Fortune has shown, the father's sister's son is verbally identified with the father only after the latter's death; Malinowski found that in the nearby Trobriands the classification obtains from birth. The steps of the development are therefore clear in this area.[5]

This statement contains a condensed version of the entire theory—with its presuppositions, its proofs, and its conclusions —now held by almost every interested anthropologist in England and America. Lowie himself is not responsible for any of the explanations of kinship offered in these paragraphs. It will be remembered that it was Rivers who first proposed (in recent times) to explain kinship systems in terms of social institutions. Rivers credits the foregoing explanation of the Omaha type to

[5] *Kinship*, p. 571.

Kohler, and the same explanation was later offered by Mrs. Seligman. Gifford, who studied the Miwok, proposed an identical explanation of the kinship system there. Kohler and Rivers are also responsible for the explanation of the Crow kinship type on the basis of marriage with the mother's brother's widow. Of course, the general observation that these kinship terminologies are suited to patrilineal and matrilineal unilateral organizations, respectively, is as old as the notion that terminology is explicable on the basis of social organization. There are the matrilineal clans and the Crow type, and they fit nicely and occur together often enough to make their causal relationship obvious; there are patrilineal clans and the Omaha type, and they correspond in exactly the same way as the members of the other pair do. Each is convincing evidence for the other. But some tribes have the kinship systems without the clans? Yes, but see how the marriage with the wife's brother's daughter fits the Omaha type, and how the marriage with the mother's brother's widow suits the Crow type! Where there are no clans, these are the institutions which have brought on the kinship terminology! The kinship system is sometimes found without either clans or the peculiar marriage? Pass that over; something must have happened (perhaps the social institutions have disappeared, or the kinship terminology has diffused from some place that had the proper institutions), and it need not worry us.

That such explanations have neither coherence nor depth seems apparent; not only do they not take into account all (or even most) of the known facts, but they are haphazard, opportunistic, and particularistic; they are neither based on a general theory to which they may be expected to contribute as parts nor do they spring from—or have support from—knowledge of the intimate psychology or sociology of particular peoples or cultures. They come from the same kind of analytic observations of the presence or absence of cultural traits as do evolutionary theories and Graebnerian associations. Furthermore, as Radcliffe-Brown points out, the explanations hardly explain; if clans and/or the peculiar marriages have brought into being the Omaha or Crow types, then what brought the clans and the marriages into being? Is it actually more reasonable to suppose that the social institutions, rather than the kinship classifications, came first? Kroeber's original position that such forms of linguistic expression and such conditions may be the outcome of some additional factor is certainly not deserving of the complete abandonment that it has suffered. It seems, indeed, a very reasonable position when one takes into account such kinship systems, and their variations, as were described for central California.

To say that the Omaha kinship system fits the Omaha clans and the Omaha marriage between a man and his wife's brother's daughter is simply to say that the Omaha kinship system, clans, and marriage customs are all part of a unified Omaha social organization. To express surprise that the Omaha culture is (or was) an integrated whole is to be naïve in the face of modern ethnological investigations; to explain one part of that social organizations in terms of another is to explain nothing at all. Kroeber, at least in 1909, was cognizant of this when he proposed explaining both the kinship system and the social customs in terms of basic similarities of relationships that at bottom are presumably universal.

What seems to be required is a general theory of social organization, based on facts of sociology or psychology or both, that will take into account not only distributions and correlations but also the everyday facts of life in particular societies. Kinship systems will be a part of the social organization, and explanations of such things as the Omaha-Crow type will be subordinate to a general explanation of social systems. None of the problems of social organization can be solved independently of the others.

Malinowski has one approach to such a theory, derived from the life of one or a few particular societies; his view is enlightening, but the sociology and psychology of his background are necessarily fragmentary, and he neglects the facts of distribution and correlation. His extreme interest in the Trobriand Islands, helpful as it is, keeps him from going far enough. Radcliffe-Brown's interests are much more general, and his contribution consequently greater; he bases his theory on a systematic conception of society (social functionalism), and his explanations are coherent. He takes into account (perhaps more than anybody else) distributions and correlations, but his system is now virtually complete, and should one accept neither the postulates of his system nor the ends to which he assigns his facts, his theory as a whole has relatively little to offer. But *not* lost to the science of social anthropology, as it will eventually be recognized, are dozens of hypotheses, minor theories, principles, and explanations for which his own researches and thought are responsible. And, too, there is the possibility that his system itself will eventually be more widely accepted than it is today.

KINSHIP ACCOMMODATIONS

Recognizing his debt to Professor Radcliffe-Brown, especially, and to Kroeber, Malinowski, Lowie, and many others, this writer may be permitted some synthesized observations which, he hopes, may some day find a place in the science of social organization. Hardly to be designated a "theory," these observations all revolve about the conviction that many of the phenomena of social organization may be partly accounted for by the susceptibility of small communities to the accommodations achieved by individual biologically generated groups.

The general thesis is that all elements of social organization are the result of a complex of social or psychological forces, or principles, acting in particular social situations and tending to create forms of social behavior which, in a small society, may crystallize into institutions. The same forces tend, on the one hand, to crystallize kinship systems and, on the other, to form such institutions as clans and types of marriage. Diffusion is never denied, for where psychological tensions in common social situations are present, the crystallization may come in only one of several societies and be borrowed by others; on the other hand, for like reasons, the same internal developments may occur in different societies independently. It is also not denied that institutions such as clans can secondarily influence kinship terminology, and vice versa; but the fundamental consideration is the causation of both.

The type of explanation presented here is similar to that of

Radcliffe-Brown in certain respects; but in other, equally important, respects, its whole tenor is contrary. The causes presented here and those postulated by Radcliffe-Brown are quite different. He believes that the necessity for social integration is the fundamental cause of all social institutions—that they have a function in keeping the society integrated. He will always admit that individual human nature is active in the formation of all institutions, but for him that is beside the point; what is important is to determine how specific institutions, in particular societies or in all societies, function in the integration of society. Here, on the other hand, the attempt is to see by what psychological and social processes the institutions are originated and maintained; it is understood that one of the processes is that of "accommodation of individuals to each other" which may be translated into Radcliffe-Brown's "integration"; but that is only one of many, and, besides, the interest is in seeing on the basis of what principles such accommodation occurs rather than in determining the value of institutions for that end.

Specifically, there is a number of points of agreement with Radcliffe-Brown; one of his recognized contributions, for example, is his "generation principle"—that there is a tendency to respect members of the generation above, but not so much those of the second generation above. It will be seen that this is perfectly agreeable to the argument to be presented, and there is a large body of evidence in its favor. But the difference in conception and point of view is apparent when one understands that, while Radcliffe-Brown believes that the *raison d'être* for this fact is the social necessity of passing on culture from one generation to the next, it is here argued that the reason for at least a part of this widespread situation is the very commonplace fact that children are small when their parents are old and caring for them—a social situation based on a biological fact—and they obey their parents and respect them for about the same reason that a dog obeys its master. There is agreement on facts, such as the "generation principle," the "sex principle" (that brothers tend to respect their sisters), etc.; but there the similarity ends. Radcliffe-Brown would be the first to deny that he is responsible for the argument that follows; yet he is perhaps the closest to being its "godfather."

The following exposition gives a selective outline of the kinds of forces and tendencies always involved in the introduction and maintenance of social institutions. Following the example previously given, the selection will be in relation to kinship systems, particularly those of the Omaha-Crow types. It is impossible in a short paper, and with the writer's meager experience, to carry through the development of social forms in all their ramifications; nevertheless, this is not intended to be so narrow in its scope as is the material presented. It is intended to be an exposition of a point of view and a method for solving the propounded problems of social organization.

In the type of social organization that will here be considered, the kinship system—including in that term both the kinship terminology and the behavior patterns which accompany it— is one facet of the social organization. Culture always takes account of the biological fact of human generation, and the relationships established in the biological group—the relationships of each individual of the group to every other—are usually made systematic and uniform enough to allow us to speak of them as constituting a "system."

In the present view, the problem of kinship systems is reduced to a problem of choices that individuals must make if they are to live together. In the biological group, with each new generation individual relationships must be established. Since culture is a continuum, obviously some problems of accommodation are solved once for all, but various kinds of situations may still remain as tensions and, in a sense, have to be solved over and over again, no matter how much the solution is aided by precedent. In this accommodation of individuals to one another, the choices that they have are limited not only by cultural precedent but also by a large number of natural limitations and determinations which have helped to make the precedent culture what it is. There is a number of rules or principles—based on psychology or sociology—that seem always to be present, sometimes submerged or in conflict but cropping up again and again to limit or determine the kinds of choices that the individuals can make in their accommodation to one another. Since the same problems of adjustment and the same rules and principles are everywhere present and recur over and over again, the wide distribution of a few solutions may be partly accounted for.

The kinds of forces that are involved in the making of kinship systems cannot be understood unless it is remembered that in a small society there is close and constant contact among the members of the biological group. In a society such as ours there are undoubted complications in the family of parents and children, but in smaller societies there are tensions and conflicts with the uncles and aunts, too, and with cousins. There is some chance that in a primitive group all people who even know that they are related will, at some time or other, have to establish the kind of relationship that must guide their contact. All that is necessary to the argument here, however, is that the family, consisting of parents and children, uncles and aunts, and grandparents and cousins, should have enough contact to make some accommodation necessary, not only at some time in the dark historic past but at the present, with each new generation.

Given friction among people, some of them will solve the problem (perhaps in various ways) and some solution will, in the course of time, spread to other people in like circumstances and will crystallize as a custom. In a small group, with the passage of time an innovation in one generation can easily become the custom of the next; that is what is meant, in large part, by the "sensitivity" of a small group, and it is a most important consideration in this argument.

The rules, principles, or forces that are always cropping up, which reinforce some of the customs and work to undermine and change others, are partly psychological and partly sociological; the purpose here is not to analyze them but rather to describe a selected few of them that seem to be instrumental in making kinship systems, and especially the Crow-Omaha type, what they are.

First, there is a set of rules[6] that seem to be fairly universally followed:

1. *The rule of uniform descent:* If somebody whom ego calls A has children whom ego calls B, then the children of everybody whom ego calls A are called B. Thus, in our society, the children of all uncles are "cousins," the children of all brothers or sisters are called "nephews" and "nieces," etc. This rule is followed consistently in most societies, but not in all. To give but one example—among the Fox Indians the rule is not operative in the cases of the children of people called "grandfather" and "grandmother"; here grandparents are conceived of as being the end of the system and all members of their generation are also called "grandparents"; if, under these circumstances, the rule of uniform descent should be applied (and grandparents' siblings' children be called "parents"), it would conflict with the rule of uniform reciprocals.

2. *The rule of uniform reciprocals:* If A and B are terms used between a pair of relatives, then the reciprocal of every A must be B. This rule has rare exceptions. In Merlav (Banks Islands) the term for "child" has the normal reciprocals "father" and "mother"; yet cross-cousins apply the term "child" to each other. It is possible that, until recently (as in neighboring groups), the father's sister's children were "father" and "father's sister," which have the normal reciprocal of "child," and that other forces have worked to make the relationships equivalent, thereby causing the term "child" to be used by both. It is possible too, however, that the rule of reciprocals is submerged there by other rules.

3. *The rule of uniform siblings:* If the male of a pair of siblings is called A, and the female is B, then whenever a man is called A, his sister must be called B. Rarely broken, this rule often has exceptions where the sister of a "mother's brother" is always "mother's sister" except when she happens to be ego's

---

[6] These rules may be most fluently stated in so far as they apply to kinship terminology, but in each case not only the term, but the entire relationship, is referred to; thus where, later, the word "calls" is used, one may substitute "calls or behaves toward" or "has relationship with."

own mother, and similar cases. This rule may also be modified
by differences in age.

4. *The rule of uniform mates:* If a husband is called A and
his wife is called B, then the wife of any A must be B. Besides
minor exceptions where one's own mother is called by a different
term than the wife of any other "father," there are some important subjugations of this rule. Very often the mother's brother
is called, say, "uncle," and his wife, say, "aunt," while the husband of the father's sister (who is also "aunt") is "brother-in-
law." Variations of this kind occur chiefly in the mates of maternal uncles and paternal aunts; the reasons will be discussed
below.

5. *The rule of uniform ascent:* If somebody whom ego calls
A has parents whom ego calls B, then the parents of all who are
called A are B. This rule is almost as often submerged as followed. Very often, for example, the parents of the people called
"siblings" are alternatively "parents" or "uncles" and "aunts";
in the Fox, as in some other tribes, the parents of grandchildren
are either "son" or "daughter" or else "nephew" and "niece."
Yet the rule operates when nothing seriously interferes.

6. *The rule of equivalence:* Two people who call a third person
by the same term should be siblings to each other. This rule is
often interfered with, yet fundamentally it is operative.

These rules are as purely psychological as anything in culture
can be; they seem to be a striving toward logic. There is another
group of what Kroeber called "principles" determining kinship
systems; but they are rather to be considered as choices that a
people make in their classifications of relatives, and they are
much more cultural in determination. Thus, people may or may
not make distinctions on the basis of sex, or of age, or of generation; they may or may not distinguish relatives before and after
the connecting relative has died. These are descriptive principles, and, although they have been used to classify kinship
systems, their usefulness in analysis is limited.

Two further rules, concerning behavior more particularly, will
be found useful:

7. *The rule of terminological correlation:* (a) Persons toward
whom ego behaves in the same manner he will call by the same

term; (*b*) persons to whom ego behaves in a different manner he will call by different terms; and (*c*) individuals who behave toward one another in the same way will use the same term for one another (and in all cases, vice versa). In most tribes this rule is followed to a large extent; but there are exceptions. Among the Fox, for example, there may be a uniform pattern of behavior between individuals who apply different terms toward one another; this is because another notion interferes—the notion that normal age differences, which amount in effect to generation differences, should be noted in the terminology even if not in the behavior.

8. *The rule of reciprocal behavior:* When there is no reason for the contrary, people behave toward one another in the same way. This applies to human relationships in general, but it has special applications in kinship relationships.

In addition to these eight rules, it will be useful to restate a few of a different kind which Radcliffe-Brown promulgates as "principles":

9. *The principle of the equivalence of siblings:* A group of siblings tends to be considered as a unit; but owing to the combination of this principle with the sex principle, a group of male siblings, on the one hand, and of female siblings, on the other, are respectively especially merged. The reason for this may be partly psychological in that there is something logically in common between offspring of the same parents, partly sociological in that siblings are small children in the same house, to start with, and have a common economic life.

10. *The principle of sex differentiation:* People of opposite sex tend to be more differentiated than people of the same sex. This hardly needs comment; in our own society, for example, while we have a term for "brothers" and for "sisters," we have no term for "brother-and-sister." In Fox society there is one term for "sibling of the same sex" and another for "sibling of the opposite sex."

11. *The generation principle:* Persons of one generation tend to respect those of the generation above (i.e., there is a relationship of sub- and superordination). This is especially clear in kinship, of course, where the children respect and obey their

parents, uncles, etc. Radcliffe-Brown adds as a corollary that alternate generations (grandparents-grandchildren) tend again to behave reciprocally, and, while this appears to be true, it is not necessary to the explanation of the Omaha-Crow types.

12. *The sex principle:* Males tend to respect females. This needs qualifications. Radcliffe-Brown uses it almost exclusively in the context of siblings: a brother respects his sister. I would add that in general there is a kind of "respect" relationship between some or all blood-kin, particularly in the elementary family; there tend to be inhibitions of certain activities and conversation (notably sexual) among the members of the group, and especially between persons of opposite sex.

These rules and principles are purely empirical—the result of observation and analysis—and however they may be explained, they must be recognized as, at the least, important tendencies in human nature and society. If they are rather to be considered "cultural," then they are among the most widespread of cultural traits. At any rate, it is proposed here to use these rules and principles in explaining the genesis, the continuous regenesis, and the reasons-for-being of both the terminological usages and the social customs that usually accompany them.

The Omaha and Crow types are species of systems in which the parallel lines of descent are sharply distinguished from the cross-lines, and in which the relatives of the parallel lines are usually called "grandparents," "parents," "siblings," "nieces," and "nephews," (or "children") and "grandchildren," depending strictly on generation. These parallel lines of descent will be discussed first.

By the principle of the equivalence of siblings, children come to consider their mother and her sister as one, and their father and his brother as one. This may result in their calling their father's brother, "father" (and treating him after the same pattern), and their mother's sister, "mother." Then, by the rule of uniform descent, the tendency is to call their parallel cousins "brother" and "sister"; this latter tendency is not overpowering, however, since children may consider themselves siblings, not because they are offspring of the same parents, but because they grow up as such. Nevertheless, in many places parallel cousins do become "siblings."

If parallel cousins are, indeed, equated with siblings, the rule of uniform descent is usually so enforced that it is almost certain that the offspring of parallel cousins will be equated with one's own siblings' offspring. And so on, so that the entire parallel line will be the same as the lineal. Meanwhile, since the same forces carry over to the next generation, the father's parallel cousins will be the same as the father's siblings (made now almost certain by the reinforcing applications of the rules of uniform siblings and of uniform reciprocals). In the same way, all collateral lines through siblings of the same sex as the connecting relative will be the same as far as relationships are extended.

This merging of relatives has effects both linguistic and sociological. In effect, about half of one's biological group is set apart as "parents," "siblings," and "children" (leaving out of discussion the grandparent-grandchildren generations). This is done independently of any social institutions such as moieties or clans (or *may* be). Now there are many reasons (often economic) why, in some places, the principle of sex differentiation should be emphasized particularly; where it is, the importance of descent from the father or from the mother may be emphasized. When such a conception of differential importance of the lines through males and females comes into conjunction with the merging of relatives as described above, one of two things seems to happen: (1) Everybody in the merged group except one of the parents and his or her siblings of the same sex (and reciprocally the same exceptions) is considered as forming one division. If the mother and her siblings are left out, the group is "patrilineal"; if the father and his siblings are left out, it is "matrilineal." In general, then, all other blood relatives are considered to be in another group, the two groups forming "moieties." These moieties must be exogamous if they are to keep this character. Since the conception of dominance of one of the lines of descent is independent of the rules of kinship here given, it extends beyond any one family, and, no matter whether the dual division starts in one family by a conjunction with the kinship system, or whether it grows up or comes in separately, it must, by intermarriage of the families, be tribal-wide. (2) Everybody in the merged group except one of the parents and his or her siblings and *their entire lines* (through males or females) is considered as forming one division, but the other blood relatives need not all be in the same other division; instead, there is a number of groups, called clans (matrilineal or patrilineal), that extend through the tribe for the same reasons that moieties do. The kinship system does not bring on the clans or moieties, or vice-versa, but both fit because both are partly determined by the same fundamental conceptions (equivalence of siblings, distinction of sexes) and rules (uniformity of reciprocals, siblings, descent, mates, etc.).

We may go on now to the affinal relatives in parallel lines. If we assume that the system is developing as described above, then by the rule of uniform mates, as well as by that of uniform descendants, the father's brother's wife is called "mother," and the mother's sister's husband is considered a "father." In the same way, the mate of any sibling (even though in reality a parallel cousin or even farther removed) is called a "sibling-in-law." In the matter of what the sibling of a sibling-in-law should be called, there is a significant conflict of rules: by the rule of uniform siblings he should be a sibling-in-law too; but, if this should be done, then by the rule of uniform mates the term would have to be applied to *his* spouse too, and then to her siblings, and so on indefinitely. Some systems, therefore, drop the matter entirely and extend no kinship term at all to the sibling of a sibling-in-law. Others utilize the rule of equivalence, however, and apply the term "sibling" to such a relative and usually end the matter there. In other words, the choice is so fine in this case that, of three closely related tribes, one may call this relative "sibling," the other may call him "sibling-in-law," while the third not have a kinship term for this relative.

Meanwhile, for the same reasons that brothers are equated and sisters are equated, brothers may share each other's wives and/or sisters each other's husbands. For other reasons this may or may not occur while the brothers or sisters are all living. If they are living, we have "sororal polygyny" or "fraternal polyandry"; if not, we have the more widespread sororate and levirate. Now these institutions (which fit the kinship terms) do not bring on the kinship system, or vice-versa. Conceptions and rules are again common to both terms and marriages. The father's brother is already "father," the mother's sister already "mother," when the marriage occurs.

However, it would not be surprising if the levirate has some influence in shaping the fine point of the term for sibling of sibling-in-law, for if the levirate were very common it would tend to turn the tide in favor of calling him or her "sibling-in-law," which he or she becomes after the second marriage. But on the other hand it is as fair to suppose that if (for other reasons) these relatives are called "siblings" the sororate and levirate will not be an approved institution, since a relationship would then have to be changed from that of "sibling" to that of "sibling-in-law"—a real revolution in many cases (as among the Fox where, however, the siblings of siblings-in-law are not considered relatives and the sororate-levirate is allowed).

It may be argued that the matter is being over-simplified here in that with the sororate-levirate practices parents' siblings of the same sex are often not called "father" and "mother" but, rather, "stepfather" and "stepmother" (and the reciprocals correspondingly, of course), apparently for no purpose other than to anticipate the coming marriage. But the translation of the native terms into "stepfather" and "stepmother" is unjustified; all that can be said is that the lineal relatives are set off from the collateral by, say, a prefix which is used to set off the step-parents also, among others. Furthermore, it is not intended to argue here that social institutions cannot have some secondary effects on kinship terms, or vice-versa, but that fundamentally an explanation for both sets of phenomena needs to be found.

The cross-lines of descent may now be considered; in them is found the distinguishing features of the Omaha and Crow types. First, however, cross-lines in general classificatory systems may be discussed. By the principle of sex differentiation the mother's brother is usually distinguished from the mother, and the father's sister from the father, as well as the two from each other. By the rule of uniform descent, therefore, one expects the cross-lines to be distinguished, in the first place, from the parallel lines and, in the second place, from one another. In the systems that we are discussing they are, indeed, distinguished from the parallel lines; but at the same time there is a strong tendency to equate the two cross-lines. The reason for this is not so difficult to see, provided that one thinks of the cross-lines as reciprocal. The common type of kinship chart in use—the "ego" chart —sets the cross-lines on different sides of the paper; the people who work with the charts often think in the same manner. But in a sense there is no such thing as a father's sister's son, on the one hand, and a mother's brother's son, on the other; rather, if A is father's sister's son to B, then B is mother's brother's son to A, just as parallel cousins are siblings to one another. So viewed, the merging of the cross-lines means simply the adoption of reciprocal behavior and terminology (thus the one term "cousin" in so many of these systems). The tendency to merge the cross-lines follows simply from the rule of reciprocal behavior as applied to cross-cousins who, in these systems, have no reason for treating one another except mutually the same.

By the rule of uniform ascent, then, coupled with that of uniform mates, if the cross-cousins are equated, so must be their parents. Actually, in cases where the cross-cousins are merged, their parents are too, so that the father's sister's husband is considered a mother's brother, and the mother's brother's wife is considered a father's sister. The pairs of cross-aunts and cross-uncles and their mates are the same, and the cross-lines are equated. This argument could be stated backward just as well, using the principle of uniform mates first and substituting the rule of uniform descent for that of ascent; but it makes no difference, since all the tendencies are present at once, and the kinship system comes into being or changes more or less at once. The point is that in this type of system the cross-lines seem to be fundamentally merged or equated.

In many systems the cross-lines are merged with the parallel lines; where this occurs there is often no distinction of parent's siblings except perhaps as to age; from there on the rules of uniform descent are followed. Sometimes the cross-lines are merged with parallel lines except in the case of cross-aunts and cross-uncles. The rules of descent and/or ascent are here submerged by two tendencies which are always at work when there is only a weak differentiation of male and female lines (which may still be enough, however, to help in the formation of clans): one is to equate all members of the same generation (by the rule of reciprocal behavior) and the other is to differentiate by sex. Usually one or the other of these tendencies dominates, but in some cases anomalies do occur and the cross-lines and parallel lines are merged except for the aunts and uncles.

Now in the Omaha and Crow types of kinship systems the cross-lines are separated from the parallel lines, and they appear at first blush to be quite separated from one another so that one line consists of "uncles" and "mothers" (typically), or "aunts" and "fathers," while the other consists of "nephews," "nieces," and "children." Actually, however, in many of these systems the rule of terminological correlation does not hold strictly in this case, and the distinction between the two lines really depends upon the actual ages of any given set of these reciprocal relatives. So it is, for example, in the Fox system (Omaha type). Where this is the case (and it may be more widespread than the fragmentary literature leads one to suppose), it can be seen that the Omaha and the Crow types may not be as distinct as they appear. If "uncle and nephew" or "uncle and niece" or "parent and child," or even "grandparent and grandchild," actually represent pairs of relatives that behave mutually the same, except where actual age or sex causes a distinction, then the Omaha and Crow types are indistinguishable. However important such an observation may be, the systems of terms must be explained in both cases.

By the sex principle a brother respects his sister; by the generation principle a child respects his parents. The mother's brother and the sister's child thus have a peculiar relationship. From the mother's brother's point of view, he should, out of respect for his sister, respect her child; from the child's point of view, he should respect the uncle as an older man, especially one so closely connected with the mother. The relationship has to be settled one way or the other. If it occurs in a society where there is the female dominance that helps to make matrilineal clans, the mother's brother will dominate and command the respect of his nephew or niece (which fits well with the notion of "clan father" that often appears in such societies). But where there is no such female dominance (in the matrilineal-clan sense), this solution does not usually come. The conflict remains; each of the two respects the other (or should). Radcliffe-Brown has pointed out how the dilemma is solved. When two people respect each other, their relationship is likely to be formal and uneasy, and it may turn into an avoidance relationship entirely, or into a joking relationship; in either case the issue is neatly avoided. Sometimes these ambivalent relationships do result, and sometimes the tension is widespread enough to crystallize them into customs. But even if nothing so definite does crystallize, the relationship remains a peculiar one, and that is the important point.

The father's sister is also in an ambivalent position. To a woman (as Radcliffe-Brown, again, has pointed out) her brother's child is somebody very close, yet, owing to the strain between her and her brother, somebody really far away. It is difficult for her to feel at home in her brother's household. The child, on the other hand, respecting his father who in turn respects his sister, respects his father's sister to such an extent that occasionally this turns into an avoidance (or a joking) relationship. But, again, the fact that this is, in any case, a peculiar relationship is the important point, for these particular results need not come. The society for other reasons may not be susceptible to these peculiar accidents, or else these relatives may simply "muddle along." But, on the other hand, where there is widespread tension, accidents are likely to occur, and in a small community may be taken up and made permanent.

In any event what sort of relationships can be established between cross-cousins, each of whom has a peculiar relationship with the other's parent? Possibly nothing special; they may consider one another as siblings or as cousins. But cross-cousins may find themselves taking cognizance of the peculiarity of their relationship. If a man jokes freely with his mother's brother, how can he, at the same time, carry on a serious relationship with that man's son? (He doesn't know, of course, that his joking relationship results from too much respect or from an equivocal relationship; he naturally thinks that he doesn't respect the man at all.) Some manage, but others do not; the rule, however, seems to be this: If there is a strong crystallization of the behavior between uncles-aunts and their nephews-nieces, the tendency is to do something special about the cross-cousins. The next rule seems to be this: If the relationship of ego to the mother's brother and to the father's sister follows the same pattern, then the children will have a mutual relationship to one another most likely (but not necessarily) of the same kind as to the uncles and aunts. Thus, in Fox, where there is joking between children and both their mother's brother and father's sister, the cross-cousins have a reciprocally mutual joking relationship— in other words, the cousins joke with one another's parents, so joke with one another as well.

If, on the other hand, the relationships with the mother's brother and the father's sister are different, the relationship of the cross-cousins will be an unbalanced one along the pattern of the nepotic (as, for example, where the mother's brother's children obey and respect the father's sister's children). Now, in the latter case (an unbalanced relationship between the cross-cousins), the matter of terminology is often simplified. Since one of the cousins behaves toward the other as he does toward his uncle or aunt, simply apply the rule of terminological correlation and use the term "uncle" or "aunt" for the cousin as well, with its normal reciprocals.

But in the former case (and probably this condition is the more common) the matter is more complex. The tendency is to follow the rule of terminological correlation and thus to apply nepotic terms between cross-cousins; but the behavior is mutually the same between them, and each would have to call the other, say, "uncle," to make the terms fit the social behavior. This, however, would seriously conflict with the rule of uniform reciprocals. So a compromise is often effected. The "uncle-aunt" term is applied to that one of the pair of cousins whose parent has the more peculiar, more equivocal relation with his nephews and nieces, while the reciprocal "nephew-niece" term is given to the other cousin (whose parent has a more definite, even if weaker, relationship with his or her nephews and nieces). It is not clear that this is the most common basis of decision, but it does seem clear that, whatever it is, it is hardly less nebulous than this. With the assumption that this is the general criterion unconsciously adopted, the result in effect is that, if in the society the father's sister has a more equivocal position than the mother's brother, then her daughter becomes "father's sister" to her brother's children, while, on the other hand, if in the society the mother's brother has the more equivocal position, then his son becomes "mother's brother" to his sister's children. Then we have the essential features of the Crow and Omaha types, respectively.

The "decision" in a society (as between the Omaha and the Crow types) is really made on so slender a basis that we see why:

1. Crow and Omaha types are found side by side. The same general conditions produce both, and where there are no crystallizations like clans (as in California), the mother's brother may be stronger in one tribe, while in a neighboring tribe the father's sister may be, thus giving one an Omaha type and the other a Crow type.

2. The two types are found with matriliny and patriliny, respectively, but not necessarily. The Crow type is often found with matrilineal clans, partly because the father's sister has an equivocal position at the same time that the mother's brother (at the head of the child's clan) has his position well established, and partly because the Crow type does fit clans so well; but

whether the clans have helped tip the system in favor of the
Crow type or whether the forces that otherwise made the Crow
type helped make the clans also, one cannot say. The Omaha type
is often associated with patrilineal clans for corresponding reasons.

3. There are such peculiar variations as that of the Northern
Wintun of California. Since a choice between carrying down
either the mother's brother's or the father's sister's line is necessary, it may be made (in the lack of anything in the culture like
clans) by an alternative method, such as on the criterion of the
respective ages of the man and his sister. In Wintun culture it
may be that the elder sibling is more respected or more important in some sense than the younger, and a parent's elder sibling
is in a more equivocal position than his younger sibling. (Why
in this case the rule of uniform siblings is not followed—so that
a pair of siblings, in one case, is father and father's sister and, in
another case, mother's brother and father's sister—is impossible
to determine with the evidence available, but it seems to be part
of the strict bilaterality of the system).

By the rule of uniform siblings, where the mother's brother's
son is "mother's brother," the mother's brother's daughter must
be the same as the mother's sister, usually "mother." The reciprocals must be, likewise, "sister's children" (male speaking)
and "children" (female speaking). By the rule of uniform
descent the lines must be continued in this way as far as relationships are established, and we get the Omaha system. In like
manner the Crow system is formed.[7]

In regard to the affinal relatives of the cross-lines of descent,
it has been said that, where cross-lines are merged, the mother's

---

[7] It may be argued that for no reason at all the father's sister's daughter and
the mother's brother's son are here taken as the basic terms, whereas the "pe-
culiar-marriages" theories have used the father's sister's son and the mother's
brother's daughter as prior. Obviously the choice must be made. But it is
evident that the distinguishing character of the Omaha type is the grouping in
the male line (mother's brother with his son), and of the Crow type in the female
line (father's sister and her daughter); and not to use these pairs as vital elements in the explanation requires a very roundabout treatment of the distinguishing characteristics. As a matter of fact, it doesn't make so very much
difference anyway, because, if the other relationships (father's sister's son, in
one case, and mother's brother's daughter, in the other) conflicted seriously with
the rules of kinship and the principles of sociology and psychology that go to
make up the systems, we should find them different from what they are.

brother's wife and the father's sister's husband are considered as "father's sister" and "mother's brother," respectively. Now very often in these cases, and oftener still in cases where the Omaha-Crow feature is involved, the mates of these uncles and aunts are "siblings-in-law," or something of the sort. This raises a problem. With the mother's brother and the father's sister equivocal relatives, and their children also equivocal, what about the other parents of these children? The mother's brother's wife is in an equivocal position, also, but with this difference: she is not a blood-relative. (Where there is cross-cousin marriage and the spouses of aunts and uncles are actually one's mother's brother and father's sister, no problem of terminology arises.) Not being a blood-relative, none of the inhibitions is necessary, and, if there is any question of how they should be treated, it will very likely be settled by recourse to very free behavior. Thus, if there is joking with the mother's brother, the joking with his wife would be extreme; if there is joking with the father's sister, the joking with her husband would be extreme. But, joking or no joking, there would be a strong tendency to treat the spouses differently from the uncle and aunt. Immediately, however, there is a violation of the rule that people treated different-ly should be called by different terms (if there is a tendency to continue calling them "father's sister" and "mother's brother"). With this conflict one of the tendencies wins; which depends on circumstances. In the Omaha type the father's sister's husband usually is considered a "brother-in-law," since there is here a reinforcing reason for the change: The father's sister's children are called the same as one's own sister's children, so their father (by the rule of uniform ascent) should be called the same as the father of any sister's child, i.e., "brother-in-law." In the same way, in the Crow type, where the mother's brother's chil-dren are called the same as one's own children, the mother's brother's wife is often called "sister-in-law."[8]

[8] There are many variations of this, however. In the Omaha type the logic may extend from the mother's brother's children, by the rule of uniform ascent, to the mother's brother's children's mother (the mother's brother's wife), and she may be called, therefore, "grandmother." This happens occasionally. Among the Fox there is a tendency to call the mother's brother's wife, "sister-in-law," partly because the relationship between cross-cousins is balanced, and,

Since, in the Omaha type, the father's sister's husband is so often called "brother-in-law," and since in most cases a woman can marry anybody whom she calls "brother-in-law" (in fact, this is a preferred marriage), and since this is the closest "brother-in-law" besides her husband's brothers and her sister's husbands, it is not surprising that marriage with the father's sister's husband (usually stated as marriage with the wife's brother's daughter) often takes place. Likewise, since in the Crow type (for reasons stated) the mother's brother's wife is often called "sister-in-law," it is not uncommon or surprising to find that marriage with her is sometimes not only permitted but highly approved. But in neither case is it possible to explain the entire kinship systems on the basis of such marriages; rather, it is apparent that both the marriages and the kinship systems have a complex series of common causes.

It is probable that some of the particular rules and tendencies given here will be found eventually to be unsound, or at least unimportant compared to others uncovered, and it is probable that the explanations that have been attempted on the basis of them will eventually be somewhat modified. The study of social organization is far too complex to hope that even a small part of it can be so summarily dismissed. But we can see something of the importance of the accommodation of individuals of the biological group to one another, the crystallization of these accommodations into institutions, and the development of a more or less definite system of social organization. In this development we must give due place to the accidents of history and to the social and psychological forces that operate, to the processes of internal growth, as well as to borrowing or diffusion. Only when we do this will our observations find a place in the science of social anthropology.

---

therefore, there is a feeling for symmetry of one another's nepotic spouses, and partly because the peculiar relation to the mother's brother is carried to his wife for the same reasons, but without the restraint reserved for a relative, and so she is teased after the fashion of a sister-in-law. Today, although the term is formally "father's sister," the prefix "joking" is usually attached, and in conversation she is often referred to as "sister-in-law."

THE CHEYENNE AND ARAPAHO KINSHIP SYSTEM

FRED EGGAN

THE CHEYENNE AND ARAPAHO KINSHIP SYSTEM[1]

FRED EGGAN

INTRODUCTION

The Cheyenne and Arapaho, along with the related Gros Ventre, offer an excellent opportunity to study certain problems connected with the kinship system, both in its internal relations, its relation to other aspects of social organization, and in terms of wider historical and conceptual problems. These problems may be concerned with the nature of the kinship system at a given period, or with the changes which may occur over a given period of time.

The Cheyenne and Arapaho[2] have occupied a central position in the Plains area in historic times and are considered in many ways to be the most typical tribes of the region. There is some evidence, however, that this central position is rather recent. In early historic times the Cheyenne are reported living in permanent villages in southwestern Minnesota, planting corn and other crops and engaging in a summer hunt. Pressure from the Assiniboine, Ojibway, and Dakota forced the Cheyenne out onto the plains around the beginning of the nineteenth century where they became nomadic buffalo hunters. After crossing the Missouri River, the Cheyenne encountered the Suhtai who spoke a closely related dialect; around 1830 the latter became incorporated into the Cheyenne tribe and contributed several important ceremonies to the Cheyenne ritual.

[1] The following paper represents a revision and condensation of a report on field work carried out among the Southern Cheyenne and Arapaho in Oklahoma during the summer of 1933, as part of a project in North American social organization directed by Professor A. R. Radcliffe-Brown. Funds were provided by the department of anthropology of the University of Chicago, for which grateful acknowledgment is made.

[2] The following brief account of the early history of the Cheyenne and Arapaho is summarized from Grinnell, Mooney, Scott, Swanton, Kroeber, and Curtis (see Bibliography for references).

The early history of the Arapaho is not so well known. While there is indirect evidence that they were once agricultural and resided farther to the east, they are first reported (in 1789) in the northern plains above the Missouri River, from whence they moved southward into the western plains. The most northerly group of the Arapaho remained north of the Missouri River and became known as the Gros Ventre or Atsina; except for a brief sojourn with the Arapaho in 1818–23, their closest associations have been with the Blackfoot.

Sometime after the Cheyenne moved out onto the plains they met the Arapaho; henceforth the two tribes lived in close alliance although each tribe maintained its individuality. Together they controlled eastern Colorado and southeastern Wyoming, but ranged widely over the plains. A division into a northern and a southern group[3] gradually took place in both tribes, but the divisions maintained close associations and kept their tribal unity. No accurate estimate of the size of these tribes is available for the early periods, but in 1890 the Cheyenne numbered 3,654, the Arapaho 2,157, and the Gros Ventre about 850. The earlier populations seem to have been larger.

Both the Cheyenne and the Arapaho are somewhat divergent members of the Algonkian linguistic stock. Kroeber considers the Arapaho language more specialized than the Cheyenne, indicating a more recent connection of the latter with Ojibway and other Central Algonkian languages.[4] The Gros Ventre seems sufficiently differentiated from the Arapaho to indicate a separation of more than two centuries.[5] These conclusions are consonant with what we know of the historical relations of these tribes.

The Cheyenne and Arapaho possessed the typical culture of the western plains, which centered around the buffalo and war. Culturally the two tribes are quite close, as we might suspect from their long and intimate contact, but important differences persisted, particularly in social organization. Differences be-

[3] This division was based partly on facilities for trade and partly on preference.

[4] Kroeber, *The Arapaho*, I, 4–5.

[5] Kroeber, *Ethnology of the Gros Ventre*, p. 145.

tween the Arapaho and the Gros Ventre are less marked in general.

Both the Cheyenne and the Arapaho are divided into named "bands" which occupied definite positions in the camp circle. These bands are difficult to describe or classify; they are not composed exclusively of kindred nor are they exogamous. The feeling concerning descent is bilateral, or even slightly patrilineal at present, but matrilocal residence led to the identification of children with the mother's band, for the most part. Each band was composed of a group of extended households based on matrilocal residence, and as such was a self-sufficient economic unit. But a change of band affiliation was possible, and the family might return to the husband's band or join another one. The Cheyenne[6] in later years had about ten divisions or bands of this character which hunted and camped independently for most of the year under the leadership of a band chief. While definite territories did not exist, each band had one or more favorite spots in which it spent the winter. With the coming of summer the bands joined together and formed a camp circle, preliminary to the annual hunt and tribal ceremonies. The Arapaho[7] band organization has long disappeared; originally the Arapaho were divided into four subtribes (plus the Gros Ventre), and four bands are remembered for one of these tribes which had definite positions in the camp circle. The Gros Ventre[8] "bands" differed from the Arapaho in that they tended to be patrilineal and exogamous, and to occupy more definitely marked-off hunting territories. These patrilineal clans likewise came together in the summer and occupied definite positions in the camp circle.

These three tribes were further divided into a series of societies which had military, social, and ceremonial functions, and which operated only when the tribe was united. The Cheyenne[9] had six societies restricted to males (except for honorary female

[6] Cf. Grinnell, *The Cheyenne Indians*, I, 90–93, and Mooney, *The Cheyenne Indians*, pp. 408–10.

[7] See Kroeber, *The Arapaho*, I, 5–8.

[8] See Kroeber, *Ethnology of the Gros Ventre*, pp. 147–48.

[9] Cf. Grinnell, *op. cit.*, II, 48–87; Dorsey, *The Cheyenne*, I, 15–30; and Lowie, *Plains Indian Age-Societies*, pp. 894–902.

members); these were co-ordinate and followed the same general pattern. Membership was by invitation, but usually a man joined his father's society. The Arapaho[10] had eight such societies, arranged in a graded structure through which successive groups of men passed. The ceremonies of these societies increased in importance, the highest society, composed of the old men, supervising the ceremonial life of the tribe. The women had a single society which paralleled the men's organization. The Gros Ventre[11] system is basically similar to the Arapaho, but each grade was divided into a series of companies which were named and perpetuated.

The Cheyenne had a highly developed political organization in comparison with other Plains tribes. Secular affairs were in the hands of a council of forty-four chiefs, selected every ten years by the retiring group. In theory four were selected from each band, while four were re-elected to serve as head chiefs or executives. The Arapaho had a much simpler system; the government of the tribe was in the hands of four chiefs, apparently representing the earlier subdivisions, and these held office for life. In recent times they were replaced from among one of the graded societies. Little is known of Gros Ventre political organization, but apparently each of the eight or ten clans had a chief, and these chiefs made up the tribal council.[12]

The ritual head of the Cheyenne was the keeper of the sacred Medicine Arrows, but the Sun Dance and other ceremonies were largely controlled by the warrior societies. Among the Arapaho the Sun Dance and other ceremonies were definitely associated with the societal structure; this was probably true for the Gros Ventre as well, though definite information is lacking.

These various aspects of social organization are not independent entities but are related to one another in varying ways. One way of gaining insight into their interrelations is to examine

[10] Cf. Kroeber, *The Arapaho*, III, 153–54; Curtis, *The North American Indian*, Vol. VI, Appendix.

[11] Cf. Kroeber, *Ethnology of the Gros Ventre*, pp. 227 ff., and Lowie, *op. cit.*, pp. 933 ff.

[12] Curtis, *The North American Indian*, Vol. V, Appendix.

them from the standpoint of social structure,[13] which may be defined as the sum total of the social relations of the individuals making up the social group. These social relations are composed largely of social usages—customary ways of behaving—which are abstractable from the actual behavior of individuals. Since these social relations persist, in many cases, from one generation to another, they can be viewed as a structure and analyzed from that point of view.

Among the Cheyenne and Arapaho the most characteristic social relations are those between kindred. Kinship relations not only prevail in everyday life but ramify through the other aspects of social organization as well, so that an analysis of social structure might well start with the kinship system. But while the Cheyenne and Arapaho have been excellently described in most respects, there are no satisfactory accounts of their kinship system. This has not been due to any difficulty in securing material, since the kinship system usually survives the breakdown of other aspects of social structure, but rather to the preoccupation of ethnologists with other problems.

The importance of studying kinship has been apparent since Morgan, but his emphasis on terminology led to linguistic and psychological analyses; the recognition of terminology as a part of the kinship system, and of the latter as an integral and important part of the social organization, is more recent.

One of the important problems facing the ethnologist is to be able to explain the social organization of a given tribe. One type of explanation is historical, and considerable effort has been expended in reconstructing histories of various types of social organization. An alternative method of achieving insight into the nature of social organization is by means of a comparative study of the correlated phenomena in a series of tribes. In order for this procedure to be valid it is necessary to make comparisons within a class or type, to begin with; hence the first problem is adequately to classify social organizations.

Ideally such a classification should be based on the total

---

[13] I am primarily indebted to Professor A. R. Radcliffe-Brown for the conception of social structure which follows.

social structure, but for practical purposes (since the social structure is known in detail for only a few tribes) a preliminary classification may be made on the basis of related criteria. Professor Radcliffe-Brown has suggested that the function of the social structure is to achieve social integration, and hence there is a correlation between the range and complexity of the social horizon and the social structure of the group. On this hypothesis he sets up as indices such factors as the size of the social group, the density of its population, the territorial arrangement, the sex and age divisions, the kinship system, and the various formal organizations which the group may take.

Of these indices, the kinship system has proved the most useful index of social integration; in some cases the kinship system represents practically the total social structure of the group. A kinship system consists of all the social usages—or patterns of behavior—between relatives in a given community and therefore includes the linguistic usages or terminology. These relations originate in the domestic family but are largely socially determined;[14] the kinship system provides rules of behavior which are consistent and which result in a minimum of conflict. The terminology represents one means of organizing these social relations between kindred. From this point of view the social usages, rather than the terminology, represent the most important aspect of the kinship system, and the traditional emphasis on the terms of relationship is not justified. Such a system may be assumed to have some degree of functional consistency, and a fairly close correlation is usually found between the terminology and the social behavior of relatives. Hence in the absence of information concerning social usages some insight into the kinship system may be obtained by a study of the way in which relatives are classified terminologically.

By an analysis and comparison of kinship systems a limited number of structural principles has been worked out which seem to derive from the relations existing in the elementary family and which lie behind both the social behavior and the

---

[14] Compare Radcliffe-Brown, *Social Organization of Australian Tribes*, p. 11, and Linton, *The Study of Man*, chap. vii.

terminology. These principles are found in varying proportions in different kinship systems and may serve as a basis for their classification, as well as for the explanation of the particular correlated features which are found.

The present paper is concerned primarily with the nature of the kinship system of the Cheyenne and Arapaho, and with the relations of the kinship system to other aspects of the social organization. In addition it seems desirable to indicate the significance of the data in relation to various historical and sociological problems, with a view to testing theories or generalizations which have been advanced. The paper may likewise serve to define the type of social integration which is present in these tribes. This is of particular importance since the Cheyenne and Arapaho represent a basic type of social organization for the western plains and thus furnish a convenient starting point for classification and comparative studies.

In the following presentation, description and interpretation will be kept separate, so that the materials may be utilized for other purposes or for different interpretations.

THE KINSHIP SYSTEM

The Cheyenne and Arapaho kinship systems may be conveniently described by an analysis of their terminological structure, the behavior of reciprocals, and the individual life-cycle. The materials for this study were gathered among the Southern Cheyenne and Arapaho[15] on their reservation in western Oklahoma, and supplemented by published materials on these two tribes and the Gros Ventre. The problem of presenting the data for these tribes in compact form is rather difficult, but since the Cheyenne and Arapaho systems are similar in many respects, they will be presented together; Gros Ventre variants will be noted wherever information is available.

[15] The kinship system is still in operation among the older people so that it is possible to get rather detailed and accurate information about the terminology and social usages. Independent accounts were secured from Kish Hawkins and his mother, John Otterby, Coyote Barelegs, and Mrs. Bird White Bear for the Cheyenne; and from Bird White Bear and Jessie Rowlodge for the Arapaho.

TERMINOLOGICAL STRUCTURE

The following diagrams (Figs. 1–3) illustrate the basic terminological structures for the Cheyenne and Arapaho. Kroeber's material indicates that the Gros Ventre structure is essentially the same as the Arapaho.[16] For convenience in analysis English terms will be used, but these terms should be understood in reference to their native meanings which are determined by the applications and the social behavior involved. Table 1 gives the Cheyenne, Arapaho, and Gros Ventre equivalents for the English terms.

The Cheyenne and Arapaho kinship systems are of the "classificatory" type in that collateral and lineal relatives are classed together. The father's brother is classed with the father and the mother's sister with the mother, while separate terms are used for the mother's brother and father's sister. Grandparents are distinguished according to sex, and grandparental terms are extended to their siblings and spouses. In ego's generation older brothers and older sisters are distinguished, while younger siblings are classed together; these terms are extended to both parallel and cross-cousins. The children of brothers are "sons" and "daughters," male speaking, or "nephews" and "nieces," female speaking; the children of sisters are the reverse. All children of sons, daughters, nephews, and nieces are called "grandchildren." For consanguineal relatives, therefore, the Cheyenne and Arapaho have precisely the same basic terminological structure, despite differences in the actual terms used. The Gros Ventre have a similar structure, their terms being cognate with the Arapaho for the most part.

In regard to the system of affinal relatives, however, there are certain important differences between the Cheyenne, on the one hand, and the Arapaho and Gros Ventre, on the other. The Cheyenne classify the father-in-law with the grandfather and the mother-in-law with the grandmother, the children-in-law being classed with the grandchildren, though special terms are available to avoid ambiguity. In ego's generation a man's wife's siblings are classed with his siblings' spouses as "brothers-in-law,"

[16] Kroeber, *The Arapaho*, I, 9–10.

CHEYENNE AND ARAPAHO KINSHIP SYSTEM

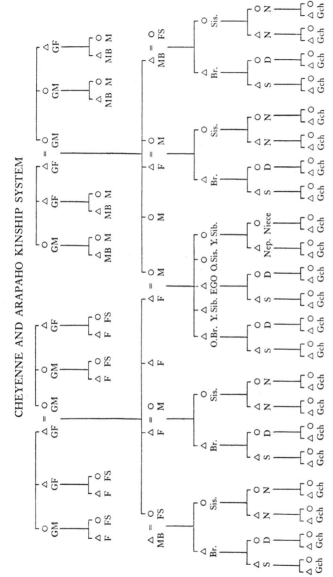

Fig. 1.—Basic terminological structure of the Cheyenne and Arapaho. In this chart the abbreviations *F*, *M*, *FS*, *MB*, *GF*, etc., refer to father, mother, father's sister, mother's brother, grandfather, etc. For the native equivalents see Table 1. Ego = male. When ego = female, the terms remain the same except that her sister's children are "son" and "daughter," and her brother's children are "nephew" and "niece," respectively. △ = male and ○ = female.

CHEYENNE KINSHIP SYSTEM

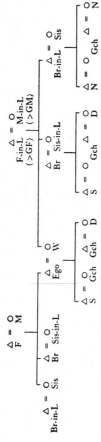

Fig. 2.—Cheyenne affinal structure. Ego=male. Reciprocal terms are used when ego= female. > = "derived from." For the native equivalents see Table I.

ARAPAHO KINSHIP SYSTEM

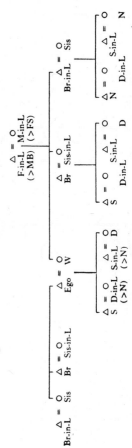

Fig. 3.—Arapaho affinal structure. Ego=male. Reciprocal terms are used when ego= female. For the native equivalents see Table I.

TABLE 1

Cheyenne, Arapaho, and Gros Ventre Kinship Terms

English Term	Cheyenne*	Arapaho†	Gros Ventre‡
Grandfather (GF)	namcím	nεbε'si·wa·'	näbeseip
Grandmother (GM)	nicji'';-ε·'	newa'; neíbeˣᵃ'a	niip'
Father (F)	nihu'';-ε·'	ne·sa'na;nexa'	niiçiną
Mother (M)	na'go';-ε·'	na'a·'; néna'	neiną
Father's sister (FS)	nahań; na·'ε'	nεhéha'; nεheí	nähei
Mother's brother (MB)	naxań	nesha'; nεsi'	nis'
Older brother (O.Br)	na'níha	nä·'sä'hä'ä	nääçahää
Younger brother (Y.Sib)	na·'sima	nä·'häbä'xä'ä	näⁿhäbyⁱ
Older sister (O.Sis)	namhan	nεbiha·'ʰ; nεbi'	nibyᵉ
Younger sister (Y.Sib)	na·'sima	nä·'häbäxä'ä	ną häbyⁱ
Son (S)	na·'; na·ᵃha'	ne·'; ne·hä'	neih'ä
Daughter (D)	na·ts; na·'tona	na'ta·'; nata·ne	natan
Nephew (N)	nats; natsínut	nε'thε' ε'thε	nêt'êt
Niece (N)	na'ᵃham	ną·sεbi	nääçibyⁱ
Grandchild (Gch)	nixa	ne·śią	niisä
Father-in-law (F-in-L)	namcím; tséhemcímit	nεsíthε'	nêsit
Mother-in-law (M-in-L)	nicji'ε·'; tséheγisjimiτu	nεheíhä'	näheihä
Son-in-law (S-in-L)	nixa; tséheγixahaiτu	nεthε'äxʊ	nataos
Daughter-in-law (D-in-L)	nixa	nąsεʙɪ	nääçibyⁱ
Brother-in-law [m.s.] (Br-in-L)	nitówɪ	ya·'; neya·'	nayaą
Brother-in-law [f.s.] (Br-in-L)	nitäm	ne·thε·'bi'	niitibyⁱ
Sister-in-law [m.s.] (Sis-in-L)	nitäm	ne·thε·'bi'	niitibyⁱ
Sister-in-law [f.s.] (Sis-in-L)	naxa'εm§	sä·'; nato'u	natou
"Parents-in-law" (P-in-L)	na'Dowam	na'tanäτɪ	nätänaké (M)
Husband (H)	nąihäm	nä·s	näse (M)
Wife (W)	na'si'im	nätäsihä'ä	nätiçää
"Friend"	ni'sima	bä·'; ne·tεʰᵉi	....

*The Cheyenne terms are derived from field notes. Where two forms are given, the second is usually nonvocative. In the case of father-in-law, etc., where direct conversation is restricted, the second form is used for clearness of reference. The phonetic symbols follow the Smithsonian convention.

† The Arapaho terms listed are derived from field notes. Kroeber (*The Arapaho*, I, 9) gives a similar list, with one or two exceptions.

‡ The Gros Ventre list of terms is given in Kroeber (*ibid.*) except for those taken from Morgan (*Systems*, No. 56) and marked "M."

§ May be used as a general term for "sister," male speaking.

or "sisters-in-law," whereas the wife's sister's husband and the wife's brother's wife are called "brother" and "sister," respectively, and their children classed accordingly. A woman classifies her husband's relatives in parallel fashion. The two sets of parents of a couple refer to each other by a reciprocal term ("parents-in-law").

The Arapaho and Gros Ventre, on the other hand, seem to classify the parents-in-law with the mother's brother and father's sister, and the children-in-law reciprocally, since these pairs of terms appear to use the same stems but different suffixes.[17] In regard to other affinal relatives the Arapaho and Gros Ventre make the same distinctions as the Cheyenne.

The terms recorded by earlier writers reveal essentially the same terminological structure. Morgan[18] recorded a set of terms, furnished by a French trader who had married into the Cheyenne tribe, which agrees except for cross-cousins. Since his informant could not recall a word for "cousin," Morgan assumed they were probably classed as "uncle" and "nephew" or "mother" and "daughter."[19] This, of course, does not take into account the possibility that cousins were classified as siblings.[20] Grinnell[21] classes cousins as "siblings" but his terms are not complete. For the Arapaho and Gros Ventre Morgan[22] gives a Gros Ventre schedule which shows several inconsistencies but indicates that

[17] The differentiation between the term for daughter-in-law and the term for niece is particularly subtle but was quite definite in the minds of my informants. Kroeber (*ibid.*) makes no distinction between these terms for either the Arapaho or the Gros Ventre; Michelson (*Some Arapaho Kinship Terms and Social Usages*, p. 137) found a similar distinction but considers the terms to have different stems.

[18] *Systems of Consanguinity*, Tables, No. 53.

[19] *Ibid.*, p. 215.

[20] Such a classification is suggested by Morgan's classing of the father's sister's son's wife as "sister-in-law." Segar, who knew the Cheyenne in their early reservation days, says: "They regard cousins the same as brothers and sisters and they distinguish them from their own brothers and sisters by calling them their 'far' brother or 'near' brother" (in Perry [ed.], *The Indians' Friend*, *John H. Segar*, p. 862).

[21] *Op. cit.*, I, 157–58.

[22] *Op. cit.*, Tables, No. 56.

cross-cousins were classed as siblings. Curtis[23] classifies the father's brother with the older or younger brother for both the Cheyenne and the Arapaho.

This brief survey indicates a high degree of stability for the basic kinship structures of the Cheyenne and Arapaho over a considerable period, extending back into the pre-reservation period. Further, if the early separation of the Arapaho and Gros Ventre be considered, their terminological structure probably extends back into aboriginal times.

The extensions of kinship among the Cheyenne, Arapaho, and Gros Ventre show some important differences. The Cheyenne and Arapaho extend their terminological pattern bilaterally, as far as can be conveniently remembered. There is no unilateral emphasis, or any marked distinction between the parental groups of relatives in the terminology. The siblings and spouses of relatives are classed as relatives. Among the Gros Ventre this simple extension is modified by a unilateral extension based upon the patrilineal clan—"all the members of both the father's and mother's clan being considered relatives."[24] At marriage a new set of relations is established among the Cheyenne and Arapaho; these are extended to the siblings of the new relatives as well. The use of sibling terms for the spouses of siblings-in-law has been mentioned above. Special terms for stepparents exist, but their use depends on the age of the children at the time of remarriage. Adoption is common; any relationship may be established by the proper procedure, and kinship terms are employed.[25]

The extension of kinship for ceremonial purposes is more varied. The Cheyenne may call a fellow-society-member "friend" or "brother," though the former seems to be preferred.

[23] *Loc. cit.* Curtis is apparently referring to the northern divisions. This classification is characteristic of the Piegan and may therefore be the result of interaction.

[24] Kroeber, *Ethnology of the Gros Ventre*, p. 147.

[25] When children are adopted, "parent" and "child" terms are usually employed, but if a wife's brother's or husband's sister's child is adopted, "nephew" and "niece" terms must be employed "to keep the relationship right."

The Arapaho, who have a series of graded societies, relate the members of alternate societies as "older brother" and "younger brother," while the instructors and novices use "grandparent-grandchild" terms. According to Kroeber,[26] the members of the highest society were also called "grandfather" during ceremonial periods. In the Sun Dance and other tribal ceremonies instructors were called "grandfather" by their pupils in both tribes.

An institution of ceremonial friendship is found among both the Cheyenne and the Arapaho. Two men in such a relationship call each other "friend" rather than "brother," but the relationship is felt to be similar to the latter in many respects, and the children of "friends" often use kinship terms.

A ritual extension of kinship to certain aspects of the natural environment occurs among both tribes, but there is considerable individual variation in such applications at present. There is a general application of kinship terms to the earth, the sky, the sun, and perhaps one or two animals, particularly in ceremonies. Individuals also apply kinship terms to certain objects or animals on the basis of personal experiences.

The various methods of extending kinship for social purposes make it possible for a Cheyenne or Arapaho to be related to a good proportion of his tribe, in one way or another,[27] and to extend relationships beyond the tribe into other groups and to various aspects of nature. These extensions occasionally result in cases where two or more kinship terms are applicable; in such cases the blood-relationship is preferred, even though another relationship, by marriage, might seem closer. In certain cases of adoption the original relationships are kept in order to maintain the system.

This brief survey of the Cheyenne and Arapaho terminological structures shows them to be simple and balanced systems of classifying relatives which are extended in a logical way without any formal limits. Both structures are organized on a strict

[26] *The Arapaho*, III, 160. In both tribes it is also common to call any old man "grandfather," even though no relationship is known to exist.

[27] At a Sun Dance encampment one of my Arapaho informants claimed relatives in practically every family group present.

principle of generation; within the range of consanguineal relatives this principle is not violated. In regard to descent the lineal and collateral relatives are almost completely merged, and there is a definite bilateral character to the structures. In practically all relationships there is a sex differentiation involved, but relative age is important only in one's own generation. Affinal relatives are only partially separated from consanguineal, the Cheyenne and Arapaho differing somewhat in their classification, particularly in regard to parents-in-law and children-in-law. The Gros Ventre have essentially the same terminological structure as the Arapaho, but the extensions are partially determined by clan limits.

KINSHIP BEHAVIOR: RECIPROCALS[28]

The Cheyenne and Arapaho kinship systems have been surveyed from the standpoint of the classification of relatives and the extent to which these relationships are socially recognized; it is now desirable to see how the behavior of relatives is organized in Cheyenne and Arapaho life. The various reciprocal duties and obligations which exist between relatives play an important part in social integration. The basic relationships are those between members of the immediate family, but because of conditions of residence certain relationships of a more distant order are likewise important. In the following pages an outline of the general pattern of behavior prevailing between each pair of relatives is presented.

Parent-child.—The relationship of parents to their children is an important one in Cheyenne and Arapaho life. Parents are primarily responsible for the care and education of their children, but in this regard, as in many others, there is a rather strict division on the basis of sex. A father is responsible for the training of his sons but has almost nothing to do with the education of his daughters, though he must help take care of them through-

[28] The necessity of condensing this paper makes it impossible to give much illustrative material. However, Grinnell, Mooney, Kroeber, and Dorsey supply scattered illustrations of kinship behavior, and Michelson's *Narrative of a Southern Cheyenne Woman* and *Narrative of an Arapaho Woman* are exceedingly valuable in this respect and supplement the material here presented.

out their lives. The mother, on the other hand, is responsible for her daughter's training, particularly in regard to household duties, and with the father's sister teaches her how to conduct herself in the presence of young men, but has little to do with the training of her sons. In particular any disciplinary measures are referred to the father.[29]

Children, in return, are expected to respect and obey their parents; if they do not, it reflects back on the grandparents who are considered to have neglected their duties in regard to their children. A boy is "sort of afraid" of his father, while a girl is careful to obey her mother; the relation to a parent of the opposite sex is more affectionate but never one of familiarity. It is the duty of children to look after their parents when they get old. The relations between parents and children at the various periods of the life-cycle will be summarized in a following section.

The extension of behavior to classificatory parents and children is on the same pattern; these "parents" have the same duties and obligations toward their "children," but their opportunities may be limited by circumstances. The father's brother may become a stepfather; the mother's sister, because of matrilocal residence and the sororate, is very close to her sister's children, so that often there may be little difference in the social position of a mother and her sister. For more distant "fathers" and "mothers" both the Cheyenne and the Arapaho emphasize the extension of attitudes rather than of behavior.[30]

Sibling-sibling.—The relations between siblings are fundamental to many activities in Cheyenne and Arapaho life. Between siblings of the same sex there is a close and intimate bond. Two brothers work and play together, protect each other from danger, and revenge each other. An older brother helps look

[29] Physical punishment is seldom employed. "Someone on earth—whoever gave you your child—is watching you. If you hurt the child he may take it back" (Cheyenne woman).

[30] "For distant 'fathers' the feeling is the only important part—they don't have much to do—they can help you at marriage," explained a Cheyenne informant. An Arapaho, after outlining the attitude of respect for the father, indicated that "it was just the same for distant 'fathers,' when you see them you have that thought."

after a younger brother; the latter should heed his brother's advice. There is no formality between brothers; they may tease one another in a mild fashion but not roughly. Two sisters likewise work and play together and help each other at all times. Frequently they remain together all their lives, holding property in common and often being married to the same man.

The relationship of a brother and sister is modified by differences in sex and age. An older sister will help take care of her younger brother, but an older brother will have little to do with a younger sister. When puberty is reached, their behavior is considerably restricted. A brother is required to respect his sister very highly and is not supposed to be alone with her, gossip, or talk obscenely in her presence. On the other hand, he is vitally interested in her welfare and largely controls her marriage. The sister is subject to similar restrictions but expresses her affection for her brother by looking after his needs and interests.[31]

Among the Cheyenne and Arapaho the attitudes and behavior existing between siblings are extended to all relatives classed as "brother" or "sister," but the intensity of the relationship varies with circumstances. Distant "brothers" might take advantage of their rights in regard to "sisters-in-law" and provoke a quarrel; close "brothers" would ordinarily not do this.[32] Two men who marry sisters call each other "brother," and vice versa. Such men have common duties toward the household and each other's children. Among the Arapaho the "older brothers" in the societies are treated like own brothers; in addition to helping one another during the ceremonies they might play tricks on one another, such as painting the other's horses a different color.

Husband-wife.—The relationship of husband and wife among the Cheyenne and Arapaho is rather hard to define, but certain tendencies seem clear. The social separation of the sexes is

[31] The affection of brothers and sisters for one another is largely expressed in their relations to one another's children.

[32] According to Michelson (*Some Arapaho Kinship Terms*, p. 139), if a younger brother does have intercourse with his older brother's wife and the latter finds out about it, he will do nothing, saying that the younger brother can do what he likes with her.

difficult to overcome, particularly where the marriage has been arranged, and the husband and wife are frequently shy and restrained for a while.[33] The husband also feels a stranger in his wife's camp and may frequently visit his own home. The activities incidental to rearing a family rapidly create new bonds, however. Michelson's Cheyenne narrator remarks: "We had our first child after we had been married a year. It was at that time that I began really to love my husband. He always treated me with respect and kindness."[34] The Arapaho method of allowing the son-in-law to work and live in the father-in-law's household before marriage tended to adjust matters somewhat, also.

The economic and social activities of the husband and wife are regulated by the division of labor. This division is rather strict and is so organized that the activities of each are complementary, not only in household activities but in many ritual activities as well. The men supply the meat food and protection; the women are responsible for the household activities and the moving of camp. In both tribes the wife is included in any ceremonial pledge; among the Arapaho a woman is considered to have gone through the age-societies in accordance with the rank of her husband.[35]

Father's sister–brother's child.—The relationship of a father's sister to her brother's child is one of affection and helpfulness. Before birth she makes a cradle for her brother's child, and later she watches over its welfare. If the child is a girl, she may give it her name and aid the mother in training her. If she neglects her obligations to her brother's children, other women in the family will criticize her, saying: "Your heart is bad—you don't love your brother—you don't help his children."

A father's sister may tease her nieces and nephews in a mild

---

[33] According to Grinnell (*op. cit.*, I, 145), "After a girl had been married .... she might still make use of the protective string for a period of from ten to fifteen days. The husband would respect the string for that length of time but usually not longer." Sexual relations were also surrounded by a number of restrictions.

[34] *Narrative of a Southern Cheyenne Woman*, p. 8.

[35] For the relations of husband and wife in regard to polygyny, adultery, separation, mourning, etc., see the next section.

way; a nephew is not supposed to joke very much in return, but a niece may tease her aunt. The father's sister feels closer to her niece, and they have more in common, than does an aunt and her nephew. Brother's children may take their aunt's property, if necessary. Gift exchanges frequently occur; among the Arapaho the niece is not required to make a return—"everything comes to the niece." The father's sister also has special duties at marriage, death, and other occasions.

Both the Cheyenne and the Arapaho equate the mother's brother's wife with the father's sister as far as social behavior is concerned. While the real father's sister has certain duties which are not shared by the mother's brother's wife or more distant "aunts," similar attitudes are extended to all.

Mother's brother–sister's child.—The relation of a mother's brother to his sister's children parallels, in many respects, that outlined for the father's sister, taking into account the differences in sex. A mother's brother feels a great affection for his nephews and nieces and helps protect and look after them for the sake of his sister. He has duties toward his nephew at various ceremonial occasions and may talk to him if he violates customs but will not punish him.

A mild joking or teasing relationship exists between a mother's brother and his nephews and nieces. The relationship is closest with the nephew, who can take his uncle's property but is expected to make an equivalent return in the future. A niece seldom exercises this privilege but may carry out gift exchanges through the mother's brother's wife.

The father's sister's husband has similar duties and obligations to his "sister's" children; more distant "uncles" feel the same general affection for their "nephews" and "nieces" but have fewer opportunities to express it.

Grandparent-grandchild.—The relation of grandparent to grandchild is likewise characterized by affection and aid. Grandparents usually spoil their grandchildren; if the parents are too harsh with their children, the grandparents will stand up for the latter and threaten to bring them up themselves. In return a grandchild looks up to his grandparents, treating them with deference[36] because of their age and knowledge but being pretty much on a footing of equality. A grandfather often teaches his grandson the stories and myths and the ritual observances. A grandmother aids in the domestic training of her granddaughters but also takes an interest in her grandsons. Both sets of grandparents come together at birth, the father's parents having the privilege of looking after their new grandchild for the first ten days, but the mother's parents normally have more to do with the grandchildren because of conditions of residence.

There is a mild joking or teasing relationship; grandparents may pour water on a grandchild to wake him up early or run him around the camp, and the grandchild may retaliate. Among the Arapaho, in particular, they are considered "sort of equals" who belong together, and special terms may sometimes be applied to grandchildren while they are young. A grandfather may jokingly refer to his granddaughter as "youngest wife" and his grandson as "brother-in-law," while a grandmother may call her grandchildren "husband" and "sister-in-law."[37] These terms do not refer to marriage but are terms of affection; they likewise emphasize equality in terms of generation.

Both the Cheyenne and the Arapaho extend the basic attitudes toward grandparents to more distant "grandfathers" and "grandmothers." An Arapaho summed up the relationship in classifying the sun as "grandfather" because it is "so distant and old and yet so near and attached to us." Ceremonial "grandfathers," however, have to be much more highly respected; among the Arapaho, in particular, there are various restrictions on behavior. It is not permissible to gamble with them, pass in front of them, or take any liberties with them under pain of supernatural sanction.[38] "This 'grandfather' business is dangerous," say the Arapaho.

---

[36] Kroeber (*Arapaho*, I, 18) mentions the custom of young people going around with drinking water for the elders.

[37] Michelson (*Some Arapaho Kinship Terms*, p. 139) states that grandparents may talk vulgarly to their grandchildren, especially the grandsons.

[38] The modern peyote cult conflicts in part with the older ceremonial organization because its requirements involve a disregard for the rules regulating behavior toward ceremonial "grandparents," particularly in regard to passing in front of them.

Parent-in-law–child-in-law.—The relationships between parents-in-law and children-in-law assume a special importance among the Cheyenne and Arapaho. Because of general matrilocal residence a man is in a somewhat different position toward his parents-in-law than is his wife. A man is required by custom to work for his wife's parents; in return a father-in-law looks out for his interests,[39] and a mother-in-law cooks for her son-in-law and makes moccasins and robes for him. A father-in-law may talk with his son-in-law when necessary but is not supposed to remind him of his duties directly. A mother-in-law and son-in-law must honor and respect each other very highly, but must never speak, look at, or be in the same room with each other. If they should accidentally meet, the son-in-law covers his head; if they need to communicate, they do so through the wife.[40]

The relation of a woman to her parents-in-law is not nearly so restricted. A father-in-law must be respected, but he may talk to his daughter-in-law, if necessary, and be in the same room with her. Between a mother-in-law and a daughter-in-law there are no such restrictions; they should treat each other in the "best way," but they may talk freely together. Among the Arapaho they may even argue over the rearing of the children and joke with each other a little. Among the Gros Ventre, Kroeber mentions the restrictions which exist between a mother-in-law and a son-in-law but states that there was "no father-in-law taboo."[41]

Among the Cheyenne a man may publicly present a fine horse to his mother-in-law, who, in return, may make a beaded tipi. They then have the right to talk to one another, if necessary, and the ceremonial exchange is felt to make them less strangers.[42] Among the Arapaho this same custom holds but does not seem so well developed. The daughter-in-law makes moccasins for her father-in-law, who returns dresses or ornaments through his wife.

[39] The Arapaho say: "The father is a closer relation than the father-in-law—you can disappoint a son but not a son-in-law."

[40] This relationship is still maintained to a considerable extent under present reservation conditions.

[41] Kroeber, *Ethnology of the Gros Ventre*, p. 180.

[42] Cf. Grinnell, *op. cit.*, I, 147–48.

The extension of kinship terms to the siblings of parents-in-law and children-in-law is paralleled by an extension of social attitudes and behavior among all three tribes, though not necessarily to the same degree. The relationship of parents-in-law to children-in-law is thus fundamentally the same among the Cheyenne and Arapaho, although the terminology used differs in an important way.

Sibling-in-law–sibling-in-law.—The relationships of siblings-in-law among the Cheyenne and Arapaho, despite the variety of combinations, may all be characterized as "rough" joking relationships. In all of them, likewise, there seems to be a combination of conflict and mutual help. Two brothers-in-law are bound closely together and must work together and help each other. A man is supposed to help his wife's brother—"it is his duty"—and a wife's brother has the right to use his sister's husband's property when necessary. Each must respect the other when he is not present, but when they are together in public, they are expected to joke "roughly" with each other, play tricks on each other, and call each other various uncomplimentary names.[43] Both should take such joking in good spirit and not get angry; in fact, an exchange of presents is essential to a full exercise of this privilege. A man will also make fun of his brother-in-law if the latter doesn't carry out his duties and obligations. Two brothers-in-law may quarrel over the husband's treatment of his wife, and the brother may take her away and force the husband to pay an indemnity. On the other hand, if a wife runs away, the husband has a claim against her brother.

The relationship of two sisters-in-law is parallel in many respects. They are supposed to help each other and exchange gifts; they respect each other but must joke and play tricks on each other when together. A sister keeps watch over her brother's wife and attempts to protect his interests.[44]

The relationship of a brother-in-law and sister-in-law is quite

[43] According to Kroeber (*The Arapaho*, I, 11) they may not talk obscenely to each other. This may be true for the Cheyenne also.

[44] Because of the brother-sister restriction a sister can't say much to her brother's wife in his presence, but the brother's wife is under no such handicap.

the opposite from that of a brother and sister. They may joke "roughly" with each other, make obscene remarks, and indulge in sexual play.[45] In both tribes the levirate and sororate make brothers-in-law and sisters-in-law potential husbands or wives. The Cheyenne recognize this, saying: "The sister-in-law is like a wife." Among the Arapaho, younger sisters might be promised to exceptional warriors before they were mature; "they would let them know that they were their wives and joke with them."[46]

The social behavior outlined is extended to all siblings-in-law, particularly the joking aspect. The spouses of siblings-in-law, however, are classed as siblings and treated as such.

Parents-in-law–parents-in-law.—The relationship of the husband's parents to the wife's parents is one of mutual respect and honor. While they help one another and come together occasionally, "there is something in between them," and they don't talk very much or joke with one another.[47] Their common interests lie in their grandchildren, and they keep up the general pattern of exchange as long as their children's marriage lasts. It is considered bad form to marry any of the children-in-law's relatives; people would talk about such a marriage. This social behavior extends to the siblings of these relatives and to the parents of the spouses of nephews and nieces.

"Friend"-"friend."—The relationship of "friends" takes several forms in the Plains. Among the Cheyenne it was customary to select some nonrelative to pierce the ears of one's child; this might start a reciprocal friendship which continued for several generations. "Friends" usually have little direct contact; they must respect one another and act quite formally, never joking or being familiar with one another—"they are kind of shy." Yet

[45] Informants vary as to the extent to which this was carried, but in the old days sexual intercourse was probably permitted. During the Sun Dance in particular there was a period of license in which such relations took place between brothers-in-law and sisters-in-law (*ibid.*, p. 15).

[46] Michelson, *Narrative of an Arapaho Woman*, p. 596 n.

[47] Michelson's Cheyenne narrator mentions that her mother watched over her conduct after marriage in order to prevent her husband's people from gossiping (*Narrative of a Southern Cheyenne Woman*, p. 7).

in other respects the relationship is like that of "brothers," and their children often use kinship terms on that basis. In the old days this institution was associated with the warpath and the warrior societies.[48]

The Arapaho do not have this institution developed to the same degree as the Cheyenne, and some Arapaho say they have borrowed it from the latter. Former husbands of the same wife, and former wives of the same husband, may call one another "friend," though different terms are used. In the old days if, when on the warpath, a man didn't stop to pick up a fallen lodge-comrade and the latter escaped, he would ever afterward call the man and his brothers "cowards" and joke with them in public; if the man did pick up his fallen comrade, he and his brothers could joke with the fallen man. This relationship is like that of brothers-in-law as far as the joking is concerned.

KINSHIP BEHAVIOR: THE LIFE-CYCLE

In the previous section the general attitudes and behavior patterns prevailing between pairs of relatives have been outlined, but most social activities involve a more complex set of relations. Some insight into the actualization of these attitudes and behavior patterns may be gained through a brief survey of the Cheyenne and Arapaho life-cycles. Since general accounts of the more important events in the life-cycle are available in the literature, it will be sufficient for our purposes to indicate the duties and obligations of relatives at these times.

Marriage and the household.—Marriage is perhaps the most important social event among the Cheyenne and Arapaho[49] and involves practically all the close relatives of the couple. In addition, each gets a new set of relatives—"it is good to get more relatives"—and a whole new set of relationships is established between the relatives of the husband and the relatives of the wife.

[48] See the accounts in Grinnell, *op. cit.*, I, 150, and Mooney, *op. cit.*, p. 416. Grinnell indicates that a sister was often given to a "friend" as a wife.

[49] See the detailed accounts in Kroeber, *The Arapaho*, I, 12–15, and *Ethnology of the Gros Ventre*, pp. 180–81; Grinnell, *op. cit.*, I, 127–58; and Michelson, *Narrative of a Southern Cheyenne Woman*, pp. 5–7, and *Narrative of an Arapaho Woman*, pp. 602–4.

While there are several variant methods of getting married, the duties and obligations of relatives are essentially the same. The regulation of marriage in both tribes is by kinship; blood-relatives, no matter how distant, should not marry.[50] Since the extension of kinship is bilateral, the range of restriction need not coincide with the band, although it may cover the latter more or less completely. Furthermore, it is customary to marry within one's own generation. Among the Gros Ventre, marriage was regulated both by kinship and by clan exogamy—marriage was not allowed with known blood-relatives or in the father's and mother's patrilineal clan groups.[51]

While the majority of marriages in both tribes are elopements at present, the more honorable form is that of purchase. Courtship was formerly a rather difficult procedure, because of the separation of the sexes and the care with which girls were watched by their mother's and father's sisters, but it has become much bolder in recent years, particularly among the Cheyenne. A girl who respected her parents and remained virtuous would be sought after as a wife, and a young man would send his mother, sisters, or father's sisters to ask for her hand. The decision rested primarily with the girl's brother or, if he were not present, with her mother's brother. The girl would usually assent to her brother's decision—"My brother, I have no right to decide—I am your property—I belong to you. If it is all right with you, I am satisfied."[52]

The marriage is validated by an exchange of goods between the families of the bride and the families of the groom. The male relatives of the groom (particularly his "fathers," "older brothers," and "mother's brothers") furnish horses and equipment,

[50] Segar (*Cheyenne Marriage Customs*, pp. 298–301) indicates the range as extending as far as sixteenth cousins for the Cheyenne, but this would vary. Kroeber (*The Arapaho*, I, 16) says the Arapaho were not strict about distant relatives, providing the relationship was not discovered until after the marriage.

[51] Since kinship is extended to clans, the regulation is still essentially by kinship.

[52] This is a Cheyenne statement. Grinnell (*op. cit.*, I, 130) indicates that elopements were rare in the old days, especially if a girl had been given to her brother to dispose of. Michelson (*Narrative of an Arapaho Woman*, p. 602) indicates a similar situation among the Arapaho.

while his female relatives bring dresses, shawls, cloth, moccasins, and food. These are taken to the bride who usually selects her brother (or mother's brother) as sponsor. The latter distributes the horses and equipment among the girl's male relatives, while his wife distributes the dresses, shawls, and other articles among the female relatives. The girl's mother and father's sisters prepare a feast for the husband's relatives, the men eating apart from the women, as usual. The parents, or an old medicine woman, may give advice. The men who have received horses now return other horses, while the women who received dresses, etc., return tipis, quilts, beds, and other household furnishings, and the girl is sent with these gifts to the young man's camp. There his sisters and aunts carry her into the lodge, give her presents, and make her feel at home, while the return gifts are distributed among the groom's relatives in payment for their original gifts. In the meantime the girl's mother and father's sisters have erected a lodge for the couple outside the camp circle; here they reside for a short time before removing to the vicinity of the girl's parents' lodge where a lodge is provided for them in the girl's camp, the first lodge going to the husband's parents.

A variant form of this marriage, more common among the Arapaho,[53] took place when a promising young man would be accepted as a prospective son-in-law and would work for his father-in-law for several years before marriage. The work was considered the equivalent of the "gift" of horses. Among the Gros Ventre, horses were given to the relatives of the bride "for the honor of the act"; sometimes a man would give his daughter to a young man in order to obtain his aid and services. At marriage the man received a lodge and household furnishings, usually from his parents-in-law, and apparently resided near them.[54]

While parents desired their children to have an honorable marriage and usually attempted to arrange one, the young men

[53] Michelson's narrator (*Narrative of an Arapaho Woman*, p. 603) intimates that this was the usual Arapaho marriage, but the other types occur also. Some of my informants indicated that this form was rather rare.

[54] Kroeber, *Ethnology of the Gros Ventre*, p. 180.

preferred to elope with the girl of their choice; otherwise their friends might laugh at them.[55] If a young man could persuade a girl to elope with him, they would usually run off to the camp of his older brother or mother's brother. The brother would consider this an honor, and he and his wife would take charge of the marriage, the procedure being much the same as outlined above.

The general custom of matrilocal residence gave rise to an extended domestic family among the Cheyenne and Arapaho, consisting of a man and his wife, their married daughters and husbands, their unmarried sons, their daughters' children, and any adopted or dependent relatives. The Cheyenne called such a group a "camp" and usually named it after the male head of the family. While each elementary family in the camp occupies a separate lodge, the camp represents an economic unit. The sons-in-law assist in the hunting and work; food is prepared in the mother's lodge, each daughter taking her share to her own lodge where each elementary family eats as a unit.[56] Such an arrangement lasts as long as the sons-in-law carry out their duties.

In former times polygyny was possible, and both the sororate and the levirate were practiced. Younger sisters were potential wives, becoming second wives on reaching puberty or taking their sister's place in case of death. Likewise a brother of a deceased husband might marry his widow. These institutions were not compulsory, but if a wife died, her family would usually want the husband to continue as a son-in-law, and the wife's brother would arrange to furnish a younger "sister" from the camp.[57] If a husband died, his family would want to keep the children close to them, and a younger brother would often take his place. In the old days it was common for households to exchange broth-

[55] At present this is the commonest form of marriage, but modern conditions have disturbed parental control.

[56] Kroeber (*The Arapaho*, I, 12–13) intimates that this is because the daughters do not know how to cook yet. At large gatherings the men of the camp, along with their guests, eat apart from the women.

[57] The Cheyenne say that they do not give distant "sisters" in such cases because they are in a different camp.

ers and sisters in marriage, and for brothers to marry wives who were sisters, real or classificatory. Such marriages were considered a good thing, as bringing the families closer together, but there was no definite regulation.

Divorce seems to be fairly common among both the Cheyenne and the Arapaho. If a wife runs away with a lover, the latter must settle with the husband through an intermediary (usually the latter's ceremonial "grandfather") or be subject to retaliation.[58] If the husband accepts horses and smokes, the incident is closed, but he may demand his wife back and punish her in various ways. A husband has control over his wife, but if he treats her badly, her brothers may interfere and take her away until an indemnity is paid. Where separation is permanent, the children usually remain with the mother's household.

The system of gift exchanges which is instituted at the time of marriage continues as long as the marriage lasts. This exchange, which is practically identical among the Cheyenne and Arapaho, centers around the married couple and follows the rules previously indicated.[59] The initiative comes from the husband's side, in keeping with the view that his side should look after the wife's, and exchanges usually take place between persons of the same sex. When gifts are made across sex lines, the spouse usually makes the return gift. A person who receives a gift is supposed to make a suitable return and may enhance his prestige by returning a larger amount.

Birth and naming.—The birth of a child is an important event among the Cheyenne and Arapaho, and both sets of relatives assemble for the occasion. The women see to the delivery, taking

---

[58] A whole series of customs has developed around this situation. Kroeber (*ibid.*, pp. 13–14) indicates that the husband can't enter the tent where his wife and her lover are because he might harm them. A Cheyenne husband could destroy some of the lover's property. Also, among the Cheyenne, in case a husband did not get full return in the marriage exchange, he had a claim on the wife's family. A chief, however, was expected to ignore his wife's running away.

[59] Male relatives-in-law exchanged similar products; female relatives-in-law exchanged clothing for household furnishings. There is also another important series of exchanges connected with the Sun Dance.

care of the child and putting it into its cradle.[60]   It is the duty
of the husband's sister to make this cradle for her brother's child;
usually she receives a horse in return. The husband's mother and
other female relatives are in charge of the child for the first ten
days; friends who bring presents are repaid by the husband and
his male relatives.

Naming takes place a few days after birth and is in charge
of the husband's relatives. A boy is usually named after the
father's brother or some older male relative; a girl after her
father's sister or grandmother. Among the Gros Ventre[61] a man
might receive his father's name at birth, or take it after the
father's death. It is considered an honor to have one's name
chosen for a child; such a person gives a present to the child and
helps look after it until the child reaches maturity, taking, in
turn, a name from among his father's relatives. The names,
themselves, usually refer to different activities or characteristics,
or to various animals or objects.

The aboriginal beliefs concerning conception are difficult to
discover. The Cheyenne seem to have a belief in spirit children
which enter the mother; these may be long-dead children or old
people who wish to return as a child. Sometimes two spirits
travel together and decide to go into the same mother. Children
belong mainly to the mother because they come from her; a husband "really has no part in the child, but it is his child because
he is the husband."[62]

Training and initiation.—While both sets of relatives contribute to the training of the child, there is some specialization
involved. The husband's relatives usually take charge of ceremonial events; in addition to naming, they sponsor the piercing

[60] Among the Cheyenne the father fastens the afterbirth, the "human part"
of the child, in a tree; among the Arapaho this seems to have been done by a
female relative of the mother.

[61] Kroeber, *Ethnology of the Gros Ventre*, p. 182.

[62] The above statements were obtained from a single informant and could
not be verified as a general belief. Twins had a special position among the Cheyenne, being considered powerful and riding jackrabbits for horses. The Arapaho
had a vague belief that twins were powerful and must be treated alike.

of the child's ears[63] and later his ceremonial haircut. Among the Arapaho these symbolize war activities; among the Cheyenne the father's sisters and other female relatives yell during the piercing. Among the Gros Ventre ear-piercing was not a ceremonial performance.

The mother and her relatives are largely responsible for the behavior of a child around the camp, and particularly for the economic training of girls. A boy had the honored position in the lodge. For a boy there was no particular ceremony at puberty, but sometime after this period he would begin to wear a blanket, avoid his sisters, and act in a grown-up manner. For a girl the period of puberty was an important one. Among the Cheyenne her father might publicly announce the event and give away horses. The girl was painted red and incensed with smoke before retiring with her grandmother to a separate lodge, where she had to remain four days and observe certain restrictions. The Arapaho were not so strict, but a woman was considered "dangerous" during her menstrual periods and the family might move out of the lodge temporarily, except for the mother.[64] In both tribes a "protective rope" was worn by girls after puberty, any violation of which was punished by her relatives.

Among the Cheyenne the first buffalo hunt and the first war party were the occasions to which a boy looked forward. The father celebrated his son's return from his first successful hunt by giving away horses. The return from his first war party marked the achievement of adult status, and if the young man had achieved any notable deed, his sisters and father's sisters would yell and dance, and the youth would receive a new name.

In both tribes individual fasting, as a result of a vow or to obtain power, might be performed at any time after puberty but was not compulsory. Among the Gros Ventre the situation was

[63] A Cheyenne father would invite a "friend" to pierce the ears ceremonially, paying him a horse in return. The "friend" had to be qualified through counting a coup, or else had to delegate the job to someone who was so qualified.

[64] Kroeber, *The Arapaho*, I, 15.

similar, men going out to fast "with the intention of becoming doctors, or receiving miraculous powers."[65]

The age and conditions for entrance into the warrior societies varied among the three tribes. According to Grinnell,[66] boys from thirteen to sixteen years of age might elect to join one of the Cheyenne societies. Usually a boy joined his father's society, and ordinarily he remained in that society, but he might leave and join another. Horses and other gifts had to be given away at the first dance, but otherwise there was no special ceremony. Among the Arapaho[67] the young men around sixteen to eighteen years of age would be formed into a society which performed a dance; this group would then progress through the various dances or societies in order. The Gros Ventre had several companies for each society or dance, which remained as units throughout the series.[68]

Death and mourning.—If a person is sick, close relatives call a doctor and the father's relatives come. When death occurs, the near relatives will wail and mourn. Among the Cheyenne the members of the household give away everything they own, saying: "We have lost one of our flesh—we can accumulate horses and goods again, but we can't bring back our relatives." If a man were killed in war, the female relatives would gash their legs; otherwise they might only cut off their hair. Among the Arapaho mourning was much the same, except that a man's brothers came and took most of his property.[69] Among the Gros Ventre a man might cry on the prairie for a brother, father, or son; a sister would gash herself and cry for a brother, while parents who had lost an only child would give away their property.[70]

[65] Kroeber, *Ethnology of the Gros Ventre*, p. 221.

[66] *Op. cit.*, II, 49. Certain societies selected four girls as honorary members.

[67] Kroeber, *The Arapaho*, III, 151–226. Women had a single parallel society.

[68] Kroeber, *Ethnology of the Gros Ventre*, p. 232. The Gros Ventre had a woman's society.

[69] According to Kroeber, *The Arapaho*, I, 11.

[70] Kroeber, *Ethnology of the Gros Ventre*, p. 181.

Mourning continued for a year or more, the mourners camping outside the camp circle. Finally someone would come and comb their hair and end the mourning; among the Cheyenne a "friend" would usually do this, among the Arapaho some stranger was usually appointed. After mourning was over a surviving spouse might remarry. If a child had been lost, a chum of the same age and sex might be adopted in its place; such a child would use kinship terms for its adopted parents and spend part of its time with them.

In case of murder within the tribe the relatives of the deceased attempted to take revenge, especially the fathers, brothers, and mother's brothers. A murderer was outlawed and had to leave the tribe. Among the Cheyenne the relatives of a murderer might intercede through a chief and pay an indemnity; if successful, the murderer might return and camp near by.[71]

CONCLUSIONS AND INTERPRETATIONS

It is now possible to get some insight into the nature of the Cheyenne and Arapaho social structure by examining the relationship of the various aspects of the kinship system to one another and to other aspects of the social organization. Since rather detailed information on respect and familiarity was secured, an analysis of these relationships will be presented as a basis for further comparative studies. The position of the Cheyenne and Arapaho kinship system in the Plains will be outlined, and an analysis of the types of kinship systems, and their relation to certain historical and sociological problems in the Plains and near-by areas, will be presented.

THE KINSHIP SYSTEM

If we consider the Cheyenne and Arapaho kinship systems as a whole, there is a rather close correlation between the kinship terminology and the social behavior of relatives. The kinship system classifies relatives into socially recognized groups, on the one hand, and regulates their social behavior, on the other; to-

[71] The Medicine Arrow ceremony formerly was performed in order to wipe away the stain of a murder from the tribe.

ward each class of kindred there is a fairly definite relationship, expressed in terms of duties, obligations, and attitudes, which serves to order social life with a minimum of conflict. Within each class of kindred the intensity varies with the "social closeness" of the relative. The Gros Ventre parallels, in both terminology and social behavior, indicate, so far as they go, that this correlation is rather fundamental and that the kinship system of the Arapaho, at least, is relatively stable.

The Cheyenne and Arapaho kinship system is of the "classificatory" type in that there is a merging of lineal and collateral relatives and in its general aspects—terminology, behavior, and extensions—is bilateral. Within consanguineal relationships, the kinship systems are organized on strict principles of generation[72] and sex and, within one's own generation, on the basis of relative age. There is an important distinction made in attitude and behavior between consanguineal and affinal relatives, though certain of the latter are partially assimilated to consanguineal relatives in terminology. In both tribes there is a basic reciprocity to the kinship system, contradictory terms or modes of behavior not being used between relatives. These features result in a definite symmetry to the systems as a whole. Among the Gros Ventre the extensions of kinship are modified somewhat in accordance with the patrilineal clan groups, but the latter seem to have exerted no important effects on the central core of the kinship system.

In certain cases the correlation between the terminology and the social behavior of relatives doesn't hold. There are differences between the Cheyenne, on the one hand, and the Arapaho and Gros Ventre, on the other, in regard to the classification of parents-in-law, without any important differences in the general social behavior of such relatives. Furthermore, there are important differences in the behavior of a man and his wife toward certain of their affinal relatives, particularly the parents-in-law, which seem to be related to the organization of the matrilocal

[72] One Cheyenne informant explained that the kinship system was "just like three horizontal lines."

household situation but which are not expressed in the terminology.

This lack of correlation between the terminology for certain affinal relatives and their social behavior is in contrast to the rest of the system and needs to be explained in one way or another. It is possible to consider these variations, from a historical standpoint, as examples of "cultural lag," and from what is known of Arapaho and Cheyenne history there is some evidence for this view. A comparative study of other Central and Northern Algonkian tribes throws some light on the problem. Certain of the Northern Algonkian tribes classify parents-in-law with the mother's brother and father's sister in the Arapaho manner, while many Central Algonkian tribes classify them with the grandparents in the Cheyenne manner. It is possible, therefore, that the Cheyenne and Arapaho have maintained old forms of classification relatively unmodified, despite the changes incidental to Plains life. It is important to note in this connection, however, that the Arapaho do not seem to be aware of the similarity between the linguistic forms for parents-in-law and the linguistic forms for uncles and aunts and consider them separate terms.[73] The Cheyenne are aware of the linguistic similarities but differentiate these relatives in terms of the form of address (vocative and nonvocative). This difference between the tribes is in accord with the relative length of time they have been in the Plains area. It is also possible that the extended family situation serves to differentiate parents-in-law sufficiently, so that a tendency to maintain a symmetrical terminology does not result in too much conflict,[74] particularly as there are special terms available. These problems will be considered later in relation to the changes which seem to have occurred among some of the Algonkian tribes with reference to social organization.

The possibility of explaining the kinship system of a tribe as

[73] Linguistic authorities such as Sapir and Michelson do not agree on the reconstructions for these terms; hence a linguistic analysis does not throw much light on the situation at present.

[74] A similar situation seems to exist in several tribes in the Plains and adjoining areas, and a comparative study of these might throw some light on the problem.

the result of various social institutions, and, in particular, of various forms of marriage, has long intrigued students of social organization. Lowie[75] has outlined the correlations to be found in North America between the classification of relatives, on the one hand, and the clan and various forms of marriage, on the other, and has suggested a causal relationship between them. Lesser has discussed the Dakota kinship type as it occurs among the Siouan tribes in the Plains area and says: "The system itself shows no emphasis which can be correlated with unilateral descent or group exogamy, but rather direct effect of levirate and sororate marriage, both of which occur extensively among the Dakota tribes."[76]

Such attempts at explaining particular features of a social system by reference to other particular features seem methodologically unsound. In the first place, there are always exceptions which have to be explained. Thus the Cheyenne, Arapaho, and Gros Ventre all use a similar classification of relatives and have the sororate[77] and levirate, while the Gros Ventre alone have unilateral descent and exogamy. Second, a decision has to be made as to which is the causal factor, and in the absence of historical data that decision is not always easy. But, more important, such explanations never explain the presence of the causal factor, which is an equally important question.

In an attempt to remedy this situation Radcliffe-Brown has suggested a systematic comparison of social systems, not with reference to superficial similarities and differences, but with reference to the most fundamental or general similarities and differences which can be discovered. This requires a procedure by which each system may be described in terms of a limited number of structural principles.[78] Certain of these principles

[75] *Primitive Society*, pp. 162–66, also p. 114.

[76] *Some Aspects of Siouan Kinship*, p. 571.

[77] The sororate is not specifically mentioned for the Gros Ventre but can be inferred from some of the myths, and probably was practiced.

[78] "These principles are not to be regarded as causal agents, but any investigation of general causal processes, as distinct from what are sometimes called causes in history, cannot be undertaken without a classification of social systems on such a basis" (personal communication from Professor Radcliffe-Brown).

have been formulated by an analysis of the basic structure of the elementary family and thus have some general significance. It is desirable to see the relative importance of these principles and the forms they take among the Cheyenne and Arapaho, and to evaluate their significance for an understanding of the kinship system.

The principle[79] of the "equivalence of siblings" is one of the basic principles for kinship systems of the Cheyenne and Arapaho type; it is reflected in the classification of a man with his brother and a woman with her sister, and in the strong bonds which are exemplified in their behavior. This principle is especially evident in marriage and the household organization— the sororate and levirate and the matrilocal household all reflect the social equivalence of brothers and of sisters. The important differentiation of sex modifies, but does not obscure, the sibling relationship; a brother and a sister use the same terminology for each other's relatives, for the most part, and there is clear evidence of their strong regard for each other despite the social separation. This is particularly expressed in the control of marriage by the brother and in the mutual obligations toward each other's children. In this connection it is interesting to note that younger siblings are classed together in the terminology regardless of sex, an older sister commonly looking after her younger brothers and sisters without discrimination.

The Cheyenne and Arapaho make a sharp distinction in terminology and behavior on the basis of sex, particularly with reference to older relatives. In practically every aspect of life there is a differentiation according to sex, but this is usually so organized as to provide for co-operation and hence helps hold the family organization together.

Despite the emphasis on sex differentiation, the Cheyenne and Arapaho make no sharp distinction between relatives through the father and relatives through the mother, terminology and behavior patterns being extended bilaterally on the basis of the equivalence of siblings and the distinction of sex, pri-

---

[79] For an analysis of these principles for another type of kinship system see Radcliffe-Brown, *op. cit.*, Part III.

marily. There is a general equivalence of the two parental groups of relatives, both in terminology and in behavior, although certain duties and obligations belong to one side or the other. This relationship is particularly apparent in the system of gift exchange which serves, in part, to bind these two groups together.

Among the Cheyenne and Arapaho the principle of the "relationship of generations" plays an important role in the kinship system. This principle involves not only the cycle of reproduction but the transmission of the social heritage from one generation to another as well. In both tribes the kinship terminology is organized on the basis of generations, with the parental generation maintaining authority over, and exacting obedience from, the children's generation. Between alternate generations, however, there is a different relationship to be found. Grandparents do not have any particular responsibilities for training their grandchildren and exert no rigid authority; they are rather friendly and familiar relatives who are almost "equals." The distinction of sex, so important elsewhere in the system, becomes less significant in these relations, perhaps because of the differences in age.

The principle of reciprocity, which is necessarily involved to some degree in every kinship system, is important among the Cheyenne and Arapaho. For the most part complementary terms and behavior are used by relatives; only siblings-in-law of the same sex and the two sets of parents-in-law use verbally reciprocal terms, and in these instances the behavior patterns are symmetrical also. There is some tendency to reciprocity in marriage through household exchange, but this does not seem to have become organized. The system of economic exchange described above also illustrates this principle.

On the other hand, the lineage principle, which looms large in kinship systems of the Omaha and Crow types where it results in the overriding of the generation principle, plays practically no part in the Cheyenne and Arapaho systems. Here it enters in the organization of the extended household which is based on matrilocal residence, but it is not formally organized in either terminology or behavior. In the Gros Ventre this principle finds formal expression, along with that of the equivalence of siblings, in the formal clan organization but is not apparent in the central core of the kinship system.

These principles are of value to the extent that they furnish insight into the kinship system and indicate further problems which may be solved or hypotheses to be tested. The principle of the equivalence of siblings, for example, seems to underlie not only the classification of relatives but the sororate and levirate and the various extensions of kinship as well. If this is so, the problem becomes, not to explain one of these in terms of the other, but to determine the nature of the "active agent" behind the descriptive principle and the factors or conditions determining the particular forms it takes. Since the relationship of brothers is a very important one throughout the Plains area, a comparative study of this relationship in the various Plains tribes should throw some light on this problem.

Sex differentiation, organized to some extent by most peoples, is highly developed among some of the Central Algonkian tribes such as the Sauk and Fox, Menominee, and others. The use of the "marriage blanket" to prevent physical contact between the newly married couple in some of these tribes seems an extreme form of the more moderate sexual separation of the Cheyenne and Arapaho. Here, again, a comparative study might be very illuminating, in indicating both the variety of forms and the factors which may bring them about. The differentiation of relatives through the father and the mother also takes a variety of forms in the Plains area. Some tribes arrange them in terms of generation and a bilateral extension, others group them in terms of lineages, and still others assimilate them to ego's generation. The kinship system of a tribe such as the Crow can best be understood as in a process of transition from one form to another.

The principle of generations is another one which takes varying forms in the Plains area. In some tribes, such as the Kiowa and Kiowa-Apache, it is highly developed, three or four ascending generations being recognized in the terminology. In other tribes, such as the Omaha and Crow, the generation principle is overridden to a considerable extent, but even so the relationships between generations have much in common. An understanding of the nature of the relationships between various generations seems essential if we are to account for certain shifts in generation such as are found in the Cheyenne classification of parents-in-law with grandparents.

A principle of reciprocity seems inherent in every system, but the precise forms it takes and their correlations need to be studied. Verbal reciprocity looms large in systems such as those of the Mescalero and Chiricahua Apache but gradually diminishes in importance as one moves northward into the Plains area. A comparative study of a series of such tribes would indicate whether there is a correlation of such terminology with symmetrical behavior patterns, as well as give some insight into the nature of reciprocity as such.

The lineage principle gives us a more precise measure of the extent to which unilateral groupings are utilized in the social group. The clan among the Gros Ventre, Crow, Mandan, and Omaha, for example, varies greatly in its significance and relative importance; this can be determined more accurately by seeing the extent to which a lineage principle is involved in the social systems of these tribes. Such a study would, of course, illuminate the correlations with other factors and the conflicts with other principles.

This brief survey suggests the possibility that it may be profitable to deal with observed correlations between various aspects of social organization, not by considering one aspect as caused by another, but by considering them as variant manifestations of some more general factor or principle. Such principles are descriptive, to begin with, and are abstracted from social usages by analysis. But they seem to stand for active forces or factors which are as yet little understood; these factors seem to interact in varying ways in different social situations but often give rise to similar manifestations in widely separated regions. In the Plains area there is a series of tribes with similar patterns of terminology and behavior, though the actual terms used and the behavior content may be quite different. In the case of tribes such as the Cheyenne and Arapaho the similarities are perhaps attributable in part to diffusion, or rather interaction through intermarriage. But the Kiowa-Apache and Kiowa likewise have similar patterns of terminology and behavior, as do the Teton Dakota and some of the northern tribes, though with greater variation. Here the contacts do not seem to have been strong enough to have affected the pattern of grouping relatives, which is, after all, an abstraction of which the Indian is seldom aware. Further, such groups as the Crow Indians seem to be in the process of changing from a more highly organized kinship system to a more diffuse type represented by the Cheyenne and Arapaho systems. It seems likely that the conditions of Plains life (as yet only vaguely defined) favored such systems in comparison with the more highly organized systems which the sedentary village-dwelling Mandan and Hidatsa had developed, and the Crow, in adapting to these new conditions, gradually modified their social structure in the direction of their neighbors, borrowing some aspects and developing others. The development of patrilineal clans among the Gros Ventre has an important bearing on this question. Lowie[80] ascribes this development to ideas borrowed from the Blackfoot, but the accounts of the latter's social organization indicate that the Gros Ventre system is more highly developed, and hence it is probable that borrowing is not the sole factor involved. In this area there are more definite hunting territories and smaller groups; the increase in band solidarity brought about by these factors may well have tended toward a more formal organization of the bands.[81]

Boas has stated that "each cultural group has its own unique history, dependent partly on the peculiar inner development of the social group and partly upon the foreign influences to which it has been subjected."[82] While there is evidence that both of

[80] *Primitive Society*, pp. 125–26.

[81] Lowie (*ibid.*, pp. 157–66) has pointed out that the sib may grow out of types of residence, but in the case of the Gros Ventre this is not likely because the evidence favors matrilocal residence.

[82] *Methods of Ethnology*, p. 317.

these factors may be important in the development of a social system, a precise definition of their contribution is not essential to the problems we have just considered. In dealing with the interrelations found in a social system, or the adaptations exhibited, a borrowed trait is just as good as one which is independently developed. Any information we may get as to the past history of social usages is valuable, particularly where processes of change occur, but a knowledge of this past history is not essential in dealing with synchronic problems.

RESPECT AND JOKING RELATIONSHIPS

The social usages involving restrictions on behavior or privileged familiarity are well developed among the Cheyenne and Arapaho, practically every relative being involved in one category or the other. Thus a man must respect his parents, sisters, and children-in-law's parents, and must "avoid" his parents-in-law, particularly his mother-in-law. On the other hand, he may joke "mildly" with his father's sisters, mother's brothers, grandfathers, and brothers, and must joke "roughly" with his brothers-in-law and sisters-in-law. A woman has parallel respect and joking relationships, except for her parents-in-law where avoidance is not involved.

Lowie has furnished a foundation for further studies of these social usages by reviewing the available data in the light of various theories. He finds ample evidence for a correlation "between social and sexual taboos, and between social license and the possibility of sex relations," but is aware that "this by no means explains all the phenomena."[83] He is skeptical of any all-inclusive theory and sets down as a principle of method:

The regulations in any particular locality should rather be viewed in conjunction with the whole culture, ... whatever interpretations appear from such an inquiry may then be compared with corresponding results from other regions.[84]

The social usages centering around avoidance and joking have attracted a good deal of theoretical attention, particularly in terms of sex. In the following analysis a more inclusive formula-

[83] *Primitive Society*, p. 104.   [84] *Ibid.*, pp. 101-2.

tion of these social usages will be attempted, based on a study
of the social situations in which they occur and utilizing the descriptive principles outlined above. This will furnish a preliminary interpretation, which can then be compared with
others, and eventually may result in a general formulation with
regard to joking and respect.

Respect and joking relationships seem to represent mutually
exclusive forms of social behavior which stand at opposite poles
of conduct.[85] Each of these relationships may vary in intensity.
Thus avoidance seems to represent an intensification of the
respect relationship, while "rough joking" seems to be an extreme form of the "mild joking" relationship. We may state our
problem as follows: Is there any correlation between the categories of joking and respect relationships and the social situations which exist in Cheyenne and Arapaho life, which will throw
light on the classification of relatives in one or the other of these
categories?

Among the Cheyenne and Arapaho (as elsewhere) respect
relationships seem the more fundamental and involve the members of the elementary family as well as parents-in-law. The
parents are responsible for transmitting the social heritage; this
transmission involves authority on the part of the parents and
obedience and respect on the part of the children.[86] The marked
social differentiation on the basis of sex is another factor; the
brother must respect his sister at the same time that he looks
out for her welfare, and vice versa. The relation of a man to his
parents-in-law is more complex. By the general rule of matrilocal residence he must reside in his parents-in-law's camp and
must help support them economically, though to begin with he
may feel an intruder. The mother-daughter relationship is a

[85] Tax has suggested, on the basis of Fox material, that psychologically respect may take two forms: (1) a "teacher-student" relationship in which social
distance is emphasized and (2) a "shame" relationship between blood-relatives of
different sex. Joking represents a release from an emotionally uncertain situation, in part, and involves the psychology of laughter.

[86] The father is primarily responsible for the training of his son and hence
usually exacts more obedience from the son than he does from a daughter; the
mother, vice versa.

respect relationship; this respect is intensified in the case of the son-in-law by the difference in sex. There is a further factor in the rivalry of the mother-daughter and husband-wife relationships; in order that the affairs of the camp may run smoothly, the son-in-law and the mother-in-law avoid each other completely, though manifesting the highest respect for each other. It is significant, in this connection, that the restrictions may be removed when a satisfactory adjustment has been reached by a public exchange of gifts. The relation of a son-in-law and father-in-law is not so restricted. The factor of sex differentiation is absent, and there is the necessity for economic co-operation between the father-in-law and his son-in-law; while there is a reserve felt, there is no avoidance.

A daughter-in-law, on the other hand, has a different relation to her parents-in-law. Normally she is not in close contact with them, unless they should happen to belong to the same band. A daughter-in-law must respect her husband's father because he is of the opposite sex and in the generation above, but there is no avoidance. The mother-in-law, on the other hand, is of the same sex and has an active interest in her son's and daughter-in-law's children; the daughter-in-law may speak freely with her mother-in-law and may argue with her and even tease her mildly—a privilege which is reciprocal.[87] Two sets of parents-in-law are of the same generation, usually, and are related only through the marriage of their children.

All these relationships, centering largely about the domestic household, involve the possibility of social conflict, and in the case of the son-in-law the conflict of interests is inevitable. In certain of these relationships, also, there is a social necessity for avoiding or minimizing conflict if the household organization is to function properly. In these cases the conflict situation seems to be solved largely by suppressing the possibility of conflict.

Joking relationships among the Cheyenne and Arapaho ob-

[87] It is interesting in this connection to note that among the Teton Dakota, who had an extended bilateral family organization, the daughter-in-law avoided her father-in-law and, to a lesser extent, her mother-in-law, to the same degree that a man avoided his mother-in-law and father-in-law (cf. Mead, *Cooperation and Competition among Primitive Peoples*, pp. 391, 394, 401).

tain between more distant relatives in general. Mild joking relationships occur between consanguineal relatives, for the most part, and are not obligatory. Between brothers there is a feeling of equality and an absence of any particular restraint, which results in an attitude of familiarity and which allows mild teasing and joking.[88] Grandparents are in a somewhat similar position, except for the difference in age which introduces an attitude of respect to some extent, but they have no specific duties in regard to the transmission of the social heritage. The father's sister and the mother's brother are in the parental generation, and hence represent authority, but are not directly concerned with the training of their nephews and nieces. On the other hand, their affection for each other manifests itself in their behavior toward each other's children, a father's sister being particularly close to her niece and a mother's brother to his nephew. These relationships involve some conflict in attitudes but no particular conflict in interests. A conflict situation which develops seems to be adjusted by establishing a mild joking relationship which regulates its expression in a socially desirable manner.

These joking relationships take a more extreme form among siblings-in-law, where they become obligatory and involve horseplay, practical jokes, satire, and sexual play. The relationship of siblings-in-law is not affected by differences of generation but is by differences of sex. A man must work in close co-operation with his wife's brother, yet since a husband has control over his wife and a brother over his sister, conflict is almost inevitable. A woman is in a parallel position in regard to her husband's sister; they are supposed to help each other and never show any jealousy in public, but there is a similar rivalry and conflict of interests. A man's relations to his wife's sisters and a woman's relations to her husband's brothers represent apparent exceptions to the general restriction in behavior between members of the opposite sex. But the husband-wife relationship is the one socially recognized exception to the general rule; since sisters are

[88] There is some slight conflict involved between their "social equivalence" and the actual differences in age which give some authority to the older brother.

socially equivalent, the wife's sister seems to be brought into the range of the husband-wife relationship and may actually become a second wife, of course. But here, also, there is the possibility of conflict between the husband-wife relationship and the sister-sister relationship. The relationship of a woman to her husband's brother is parallel; she may marry him if her husband dies, but there is a similar possibility of conflict of interests. The behavior of siblings-in-law of the opposite sex centers around obscene jests and sexual play, in addition to ordinary joking.

The relations of siblings-in-law thus involve fundamental conflicts which are inevitable in view of the household organization and the social relations of siblings and spouses. These conflicts must be regulated in some way if the social order is to operate smoothly; respect as a device for suppressing these conflicts is not possible, since there are no generational differences involved and the factor of sex difference is socially nullified, but obligatory joking seems to serve quite well. Essentially it seems to be a device for organizing hostility in socially desirable ways; such relationships not only make an adjustment to an ambivalent situation but create a definite bond between the relatives as well.

Thus respect and joking relationships seem to be part of a single system of social behavior.[89] We may summarize this brief survey of these relationships among the Cheyenne and Arapaho as follows:

1. *Respect relationship*—where there is some possibility of conflict and the social necessity for avoiding it.
2. *Mild joking relationship*—where there is some possibility of conflict but no particular social necessity for avoiding it.
3. *Avoidance relationship*—where the conflict situation is inevitable, where there is the social necessity of avoiding it, and where generation differences are present.
4. *Obligatory joking relationship*—where the conflict situation is inevitable, where there is the social necessity of avoiding it, but where no differences of generation are involved.

[89] The Cheyenne and Arapaho have also organized the satirical sanction around the relationship of siblings-in-law for purposes of social control, but this involves another system (see Provinse's paper on "The Underlying Sanctions of Plains Indian Culture" in this volume for an analysis of the sanction systems of the Plains).

Some insight into the nature of respect and joking relationships may be gained from this survey. They seem to be correlated with conflict situations and to represent alternate ways of adjusting social conflicts. Respect seems to be the more fundamental relationship, based as it is on the necessity of transmitting the social heritage and on the differentiation of sex. Where respect is not involved, the relationship tends to be one of equality and familiarity, other things being equal. Conflicts are inevitable in any social system, and each social group must regulate them, either by suppressing them or by organizing them in socially desirable ways. The kinship system deals with the conflicts which arise in the elementary family largely by establishing a relationship of authority and obedience among its members, and also by limiting the possibility of conflict in the sexual sphere. With the enlargement of the elementary family through the marriage of the children (or otherwise), new conflict situations arise for which there has been little preparation on the part of the adult individuals concerned. These new relationships are more complex in that they usually involve indirect relationships by way of a third relative and also involve ambivalent attitudes. New relatives are brought into a new social group in one sense and excluded in another, so that they are in an uncertain social position. Where marriage creates a separate household group, these conflicts, except those between husband and wife, may not cause too great disruption. But when larger households are created by marriage, these conflicts must be regulated if the household is to operate efficiently. In systems of the Cheyenne and Arapaho type the regulation seems to be by establishing a relationship of extreme respect or avoidance, on the one hand, or of obligatory joking, on the other.[90] Which of these is chosen depends on several circumstances: the nature of the situation, the generation and sex differences involved, and the social necessity for a solution. Avoidance relationships usually involve generation and sex differences and a situation in which an imme-

---

[90] Where the structural arrangement of the social group is quite different, as among the Western Pueblos, for example, the regulation may be accomplished in quite different ways (viz., Eggan, *The Social Organization of the Western Pueblos*).

diate solution is essential, but since avoidance operates by eliminating social relations, it is not very satisfactory in terms of the social structure. Where generation differences are not involved, obligatory joking relationships are likely to be utilized. The latter furnish a standardized way of behaving in socially uncertain situations as well as a release of emotional tensions. Also they establish bonds between such relatives which gradually bind them together. In regard to the relationships between relatives in different households the same factors seem to be involved, but the conflict situations are normally less numerous and less important, and their regulation is less rigid. The importance of the household structure is evident in these various relationships.

The widespread distribution of respect and joking relationships among the Plains tribes indicates that they are important in this area, but except for Lowie's pioneer account of these relationships among the Crow,[91] there is little comparative material available in the literature. The papers in the present volume will remedy this deficiency to some extent, and the data presented on these relationships among the Kiowa-Apache, the Fox, Cherokee, and Southern Athabaskan groups may be utilized to test and modify the tentative correlations here advanced on the basis of the Cheyenne and Arapaho materials. An adequate classification of these various tribes is essential before comparative studies can take place, however, since the conflict situations vary according to the social structure of the group. There is nothing directly comparable in the Cheyenne and Arapaho system, for example, to the Crow joking relationships between children whose fathers belong to the same clan, since neither tribe emphasizes the lineage principle or has a clan organization. They are comparable in more general terms, however, since this Crow relationship is an example of an indirect relationship through the men of the father's clan who are considered as a unit. When comparative studies between the Plains types have been carried out, the results can be compared with those of other regions, and a more general formulation of respect and joking may then be possible.

[91] *Social Life of the Crow Indians*, pp. 204–6, 213–15.

The nature of social integration is one of the important problems of social life; the possibility of using the type of social integration as an ultimate basis for classifying social structures has been mentioned in the Introduction. If we look at social systems from the standpoint of an "adaptive mechanism," there are two main aspects: (1) the internal adaptation which "is seen in the controlled relations of individuals within the social unity,"[92] and (2) the external adaptation of this social structure to the natural environment. Certain interrelations have been pointed out in considering the kinship system, but it is desirable to consider briefly the whole social organization from this standpoint.

The Cheyenne and Arapaho have a series of social units—the elementary family, the extended household, the band, the society, and the tribe—each of which has a definite organization and definite functions in terms of integration. Each unit has a solidarity based on kinship as well as economic, ritual, or other ties, and on social opposition to other units; at the same time each unit is related to the others in such ways that the whole system continues to exist, and there is a definite cohesion and unity to social life.

The elementary family normally exists as a subdivision of the extended matrilocal family; this group of father, mother, and children usually occupies a single tipi and eats together. Within this group are found the strongest kinship ties and the responsibility for transmitting the social heritage. This group may be enlarged by means of sororal polygyny and is maintained in case of death by the sororate and levirate.

The extended household is the primary economic unit and combines families of orientation with families of procreation by means of matrilocal residence. The household is concerned with subsistence, the men securing meat and hides and the women gathering vegetable products and carrying out other activities. While the families of such a household occupy several lodges,

[92] Radcliffe-Brown, *Andaman Islanders*, p. ix. I am indebted to Professor Radcliffe-Brown for this conception of social integration.

these camp together, and food is cooked in the oldest woman's lodge and carried by her daughters to their own lodges for consumption. The size of the household group varies greatly between the limits of the elementary family and the band, but probably averages somewhere between fifteen and twenty-five individuals.[93] A household is connected by marriage with the households of the husbands and wives of the men and women born in the household; these ties are maintained and strengthened by the series of exchanges which take place and by the duties and obligations of relatives mentioned above.

Such an extended household was well adapted to the rather uncertain Plains life. Several hunters were available for each household, and in case of a large kill there were enough women to prepare the meat and hides. The death of a spouse did not break up the organization, while the household would take care of the children in case of a divorce.[94]

The band among the Cheyenne was composed of a series of extended families, or households, and represented a definite unit. Each band had a name, usually referring to some peculiarity, and each operated as a political and economic unit for much of the year, under the leadership of a band chief. While there were no definite hunting territories, a band usually had favorite winter quarters to which it returned each year.

The band was something of an amorphous social group, difficult to describe in definite terms but operating efficiently under the conditions of Plains life. Because of the general regulation of marriage and residence, the women in a band would normally be born there while their husbands might come from that band or from others. But a man retained his own band affiliation and might rejoin the band in which he was born, or even another one, if the prospects were better. Band affiliation was therefore less of a bond than that of the household.

[93] In 1862 the Arapaho were reported to have had 380 lodges and a population of 2,800 which averages 7 to 8 persons to a lodge. A household would normally have 2 or more lodges.

[94] Grinnell reports this as the native explanation for matrilocal residence (*op. cit.*, I, 91).

Rivalry between the bands was quite strong since the power of a band chief was roughly determined by the number of relatives and followers which he controlled. Mooney states that matrilocal residence led the chiefs to encourage endogamy in order to keep up the strength of the band.[95] From the standpoint of tribal integration, however, it was desirable to enforce kinship exogamy and thus to compel band exogamy for the majority. The camp circle was an objective expression of tribal unity—each band had a definite position in the circle and the whole symbolized one large family.

Information concerning Arapaho bands is scanty since their band system disintegrated at an earlier period, but the available evidence points to an organization similar to that of the Cheyenne. The Gros Ventre had patrilineal clans which were exogamous, but unfortunately we do not know whether they were localized. There is some evidence that the household unit of the Gros Ventre was based on matrilocal residence; if this were so, the patrilineal clans must have been nonlocalized segments. Such an organization would tend to increase the tribal integration by uniting the various local groups more firmly, since the scattered clansmen could maintain their relationships more easily. On the other hand, if the patrilineal clan represented the local group or band, the men would remain in the same group after marriage. The smaller size of the Gros Ventre clans,[96] under such conditions, would make it easier to trace kinship in the local group. Also, more definite hunting territories would lead to a closer local integration and perhaps an increased patrilineal emphasis.[97]

[95] *Op. cit.*, p. 410. The Suhtai generally married among themselves, even after incorporation into the tribe. In recent years, when the "Dog Soldiers" coalesced with one of the bands and thus obtained a place in the camp circle, they tended to intermarry, provided they were not relatives (according to Grinnell, *op. cit.*, II, 63).

[96] The Cheyenne bands average around 300 to 350 members, and the Arapaho were probably about the same. The Gros Ventre clans, on the other hand, were much smaller, averaging only about 100 members in 1885.

[97] The important problem of the relation of the local group to the clan among the Gros Ventre can perhaps be settled by further field work. The correlation elsewhere in America of patrilineal local groups and definite hunting territories is important in this connection.

In olden times, according to some of Grinnell's best informants, the Cheyenne bands were matrilineal and strictly exogamous; each group was supposed to be a body of kindred
descended from a common ancestor, and each group had its own
ceremonies and taboos.[98] While Mooney and other investigators
have denied that the Cheyenne have a clan system, it is probable that the earlier organization was less amorphous. The conditions of Plains life demanded a local group small enough to
subsist by hunting and gathering but large enough to furnish
protection against hostile war parties and raids. The extended
family was adequate for the first condition but was at the
mercy of any war party; the tribe, on the other hand, was too
unwieldy to act as an economic unit for very long. The band
proved an adequate compromise; this is perhaps the most important reason for its almost universal presence in the Plains
area.

The societies of the Cheyenne, Arapaho, and Gros Ventre
were briefly described in the Introduction. Among the Cheyenne
these societies were co-ordinate, and a young man usually joined
the society of his father or other close male relative. The relations of societies to one another were a mixture of rivalry and
co-operation, and during the tribal gatherings they completely
dominated the band organization. In recent times one of the
bands was absorbed by the "Dog Soldier" society which took
its place in the camp circle as a local group, but for the most
part the societies cut across the band system.[99] Among the Arapaho and Gros Ventre the societies were graded on the basis of
age and confined to males, except for a co-ordinate woman's
society. Between the different societies there was a complicated
relationship involving purchase, the ceremonial surrender of
wives, and ritual kinship. Alternate societies seem to have a
close bond in contrast to their common antagonism to the intermediate group, the members of which sell their positions to the

[98] Grinnell, *op. cit.*, I, 90–91. There is no strong evidence for a former clan
system, however, and it is possible that his informants were rationalizing the
past.

[99] The integrative effect of the society system is thus very much like that of
a nonlocalized patrilineal clan system, as far as males are concerned.

lower group and purchase new positions from the higher society.[100] On certain occasions, such as the Sun Dance, there is evidence that alternate societies represent opposition units in much the same fashion that Freshmen and Juniors unite against Sophomores and Seniors in our high schools. "Grandfathers," who are responsible for the ritual training and initiation, were selected from the next highest society, or occasionally from the members of the third higher society; these "ceremonial grandfathers" must be highly respected. The Gros Ventre societies were further divided into a series of co-ordinate companies, each with a name and the privilege of performing the dance of that particular age grade, but the details are not very clear.

The society systems of these three tribes represent segmentary organizations which are relatively independent of the band organization. These societies are primarily associations for men and were concerned with the important activities of protection and war, the tribal buffalo hunt, and the tribal ceremonies. Each society is associated with objects or animals which symbolize these activities. The organization of the Arapaho and Gros Ventre society systems is more complex and highly integrated than that of the Cheyenne, and among the Arapaho, at least, the societies seem to have survived longer than the bands.

The tribal organization of the Cheyenne and Arapaho is compounded of the above elements, but there were additional factors which increased tribal solidarity. The tribe, as we have seen, operated as a unit only during the summer; it was at this time that the tribal ceremonies were performed and the annual hunt carried out. During the period that the tribe was assembled the bands were organized in the camp circle,[101] and the

[100] The use of "older brother" and "younger brother" terms between the members of alternate societies is consonant with this situation. Lowie (*Plains Indian Age-Societies*, p. 951) finds no relationship between kinship usages and societal relationships among the Arapaho, in contrast to the Hidatsa, but my evidence, while incomplete, indicates that the Arapaho system was much the same as the Hidatsa in this respect.

[101] Among the Cheyenne the camp circle was "likened to a big tipi with the entrance facing east," according to Dorsey (*op. cit.*, II, 62). This symbolic conception of the tribe as one large family has many expressions, particularly in the ceremonies.

society organization came into operation. The Cheyenne ceremonies involved the presence and co-operation of the whole tribe and were largely concerned with tribal welfare and growth. The most sacred of these ceremonies concerned the Medicine Arrows on whose condition the welfare of the Cheyenne tribe depends. Murder, for example, would stain the arrows; until they were wiped clean and "renewed," the tribe as a whole suffered. Usually this ceremony was performed annually by the keeper, who was the ritual head of the Cheyenne tribe, as the result of a vow undertaken by some individual. During the ceremony every family had to be represented in the camp circle which was policed by the warrior societies; after "renewal" all the males of the tribe assembled to inspect the arrows which were hung outside the Medicine Lodge.

The Sun Dance was much the same among the Cheyenne and Arapaho though the native meanings varied.[102] Among the Cheyenne the Sun Dance was usually held annually as a result of a pledge and involved the co-operation of all former pledgers and the warrior societies, under the general control of the society of the pledger. Kinship relations were established between the pledger and his instructor, and between the dancers and their sponsors, and a definite system of exchange was involved. Another important tribal ceremony was the *Massaum*, or Animal Dance, which seems to have been primarily related to hunting. The Arapaho had parallel ceremonies, though the tribal symbols often differed considerably. The entire ceremonial organization, including the Sun Dance, the society ceremonies, and the woman's society ceremony, was considered to be a single unit and was called by a special name.[103] The Gros Ventre system seems to have been similar but less highly organized.

The secular activities were in the hands of the council of chiefs, assisted by the warrior societies. This group acted as a unit only when the tribe was united. When the tribe was at war or engaged in the summer hunt, the warrior societies seem to

---

[102] There are excellent accounts of the Sun Dance in Dorsey, Kroeber, and Grinnell (see Bibliography).

[103] Kroeber, *The Arapaho*, III, 151.

have had more authority, but this probably led to little conflict since the society chiefs might also be members of the
council.[104] The annual hunt was formerly an important occasion for the tribe. A successful hunt enabled the collection of
a surplus of hides and meat; during the hunt the warrior societies
maintained rigid discipline and severely punished any infrac-
tions which would jeopardize the success of the hunt.

This brief survey has shown something of the complexity of
the interrelations of the various units of Cheyenne and Arapaho
social organization and some insight into the nature of the bonds
holding these units together. Perhaps the most important factors in holding these various groups together and linking them
to one another are the bonds of kinship; even local solidarity
and ritual relations tend to be expressed in terms of kinship.
Included in these bonds are the ties maintained by the system
of exchange between relatives. The organization of the household and band may be seen in relation to the conditions of Plains
life, particularly in terms of subsistence and protection. The
larger tribal organization is reflected in the camp circle but finds
its integration primarily in ceremonial and symbolic terms. The
band system, which was primarily an economic organization,
dominated most of the year, but when the tribe came together,
the society organization, composed of males, was pre-eminent
and overshadowed the band organization. The importance of
the tribal ceremonies in social integration can hardly be over-
estimated. Today the Sun Dance is perhaps the most important
single factor in keeping these tribes from complete disintegration.[105] The symbolic factors in tribal organization are likewise
important. Mooney is the only writer on the Cheyenne who has
attempted to get at the symbolic basis of Cheyenne social organi-

[104] The Cheyenne council was composed of a body of forty-four chiefs representing the various bands in the camp circle. The Arapaho and Gros Ventre
political organizations are not so well known but seem to have been much
simpler. Dr. Opler informs me that Cheyenne society chiefs resigned upon their
election to the council.

[105] Recently the Sun Dance has stimulated interest in the old organizations,
so that in 1933 the Cheyenne attempted to revive the council of chiefs and increased the membership of the warrior societies.

zation. On the basis of a study of the band system, the camp circle, the society organization, and the council arrangement, he came to the conclusion that "Cheyenne tribal life was organized, not on a clan system, but on a ceremonial geographic basis, as determined by the four cardinal points."[106] This conclusion throws considerable light on both ritual practices and symbolism, as well as on social integration and organization.

KINSHIP IN THE PLAINS AREA

In order to investigate problems by the comparative method it is necessary to classify a series of tribes in terms of their similarities and differences. While there are not sufficient data available to make an adequate classification of Plains tribes in terms of social integration or social structure, a preliminary classification of their kinship systems should be valuable in formulating various problems and in securing some insight into the important aspects of Plains life.

The majority of the tribes in the Plains area are organized on the basis of a camp circle composed of bands. Most of these tribes have a kinship system which is a variant of what might be called a "Generation" type—a type which is found in its simplest form among the Cheyenne and Arapaho. In the eastern Plains, mainly along the Missouri River, is found another type of social organization which is largely based on the village and clan. The tribes in this area emphasize the lineage principle in the classification of kindred and have variants of the Omaha and Crow types of kinship systems. None of these types is restricted to the Plains area, however; as we leave the Plains, a gradual series of changes takes place, leading eventually to systems based on different principles of classification and social behavior. These series are of considerable value in the study of historical and processual problems and in the study of correlated variations.

In the present paper we shall be primarily concerned with systems of the "Generation" type. The Omaha and Crow types (which I consider as two variants of the same type which might

---

[106] *Op. cit.*, p. 411. The points are northeast, northwest, southeast, and southwest.

be called "Omaha-Crow") have been dealt with to some extent by both Lowie[107] and Lesser,[108] and will be considered only incidentally in this survey. The "Generation" type, as found in the Plains area, is characterized by a simple and coherent organization in which generation is emphasized, lineal and collateral relatives are merged, the range of relationship is rather wide but indefinite, the duties and obligations between relatives are organized (largely in terms of familiarity and respect), and marriage is outside the circle of blood-relations. In most of the tribes having this general type of kinship organization, the domestic or household group is an extended family based on matrilocal residence.

The Cheyenne and Arapaho kinship systems represent the simplest, and perhaps basic, form for the "Generation" type in the Plains; the Gros Ventre varies only in that it has organized the range of relationships by means of formal clans and the family and local organizations have been modified somewhat. In the southern Plains, groups such as the Kiowa-Apache and Kiowa seem to vary only slightly from the Cheyenne and Arapaho pattern, differing mainly in their recognition of additional generations above and below the grandparental and grandchild generations and in their greater use of self-reciprocal terms and behavior. Otherwise the kinship systems are surprisingly alike, both in terminology and in social behavior, and the households are also organized largely in terms of matrilocal residence.[109] The terminologies of the Wichita and Caddo in the southeastern Plains suggest a kinship system much like that of the Kiowa-Apache, although the Wichita, in particular, show some variation toward a "Hawaiian" type. The Comanche kinship system is reported to be quite different from the general Plains pattern, which is in keeping with its Plateau affiliations.[110] The Southern

[107] *The Omaha and Crow Kinship Terminologies*, pp. 103–8.

[108] *Op. cit.*, pp. 563–71. Both Lowie and Lesser attempt to explain the kinship terminologies in terms of associated factors such as clans and types of marriage.

[109] See McAllister, "Kiowa-Apache Social Organization," in this volume. I am indebted to Donald Collier for information concerning the Kiowa.

[110] Dr. Ralph Linton is preparing a report on the Comanche.

Athabaskan tribes have been shown by Opler[111] to have two main types of kinship systems which merge into each other. The Lipan and Kiowa-Apache form one type with the Jicarilla, the latter varying somewhat toward a type represented in the Chiricahua and Mescalero systems, in which generation is still emphasized and descent is still bilateral but lineal relatives are set off from collateral ("non-classificatory"), the range of relationships seems narrower, and the terminology and behavior patterns tend to be self-reciprocal. These contrasting types are connected by a series of intermediate systems, however, and all the tribes have an extended family based on matrilocal residence and marry outside of blood-relations.

Another variation on the "Generation" type is found among the Dakota tribes. The kinship terminologies of the Dakota have been considered as a basic type but are perhaps best viewed as variants of the Cheyenne system. The Teton system, which is the best known, differs terminologically in that cross-cousins are given separate terms, but they are treated as if they were siblings. The cross-cousin terms likewise seem fairly recent since Lesser[112] shows that they are derived from the terms for siblings-in-law. The household group seems based on an extended bilateral family, which varies in size and composition, and the larger groupings are somewhat more amorphous than the Cheyenne bands, but the kinship system, aside from the terminological differences, matches the Cheyenne almost point for point.[113] While we know less about the kinship systems of the other Dakota tribes, including the Assiniboine, there is some probability that they had a similar kinship system. In the northern Plains the Plains-Cree, Plains-Ojibway, and possibly the Blood and Sarsi had terminologies which suggest the Dakota type. The Piegan, on the other hand, seem to have had a kinship terminology which was intermediate between the Cheyenne and Arapaho system and the Plateau systems; here lineal rela-

[111] *The Kinship Systems of the Southern Athabaskan-Speaking Tribes*, pp. 620–33.

[112] *Op. cit.*, p. 564.

[113] Cf. the excellent account in Mead, *op. cit.*, chap. xii.

tives were separated from collateral (except for the mother's sister), but all collateral relatives in ego's generation, and in the first ascending and descending generations, were classed as "older" or "younger siblings."[114] Residence tended to be patrilocal among the Blackfoot, and there was some tendency to patrilineal clans which represented local groups, as far as the men were concerned.

To the northeast, the Ojibway, Montagnais, Naskapi, and various Cree groups had kinship systems based on cross-cousin marriage in varying degrees.[115] While these systems still emphasize generation and bilateral descent, the range of relationships is much reduced, the elementary family is isolated in terminology and represents the household group, and the social behavior of relatives is more intensely organized and integrated than in the Plains. Here, again, there seem to be intermediate types; the Plains-Cree and Plains-Ojibway, and perhaps also the Dakota, form a bridge between the cross-cousin marriage systems and systems of the Cheyenne and Arapaho type in which marriage is outside the range of relationships. The variations of the "Generation" type in the Plains, along with a suggested classification of the Omaha and Crow types,[116] are summarized in Table 2.

From this brief survey certain problems emerge more clearly. In the first place, diffusion as an explanation of similarities in Plains kinship is inadequate; patterns of terminology and social behavior do not diffuse very easily. Furthermore, the series outlined above end eventually in kinship systems based on quite different principles, in part at least. Our understanding of the factors determining the choice of alternate principles of classification and social behavior may very possibly grow out of an

[114] Michelson, *Notes on the Piegan System*, pp. 320–34.

[115] Dr. Hallowell has kindly sent me a manuscript dealing with this area, Strong has outlined the Naskapi system (*Cross-Cousin Marriage and the Culture of the Northeast Algonkian*), and Ruth Landes has summarized the Ojibway in Mead, *op. cit.*, pp. 87–126.

[116] The problem of the Crow and Omaha types will be taken up in another paper; the relation between these types and the "Generation" types is an important but difficult problem. For a discussion of the Omaha type see Tax's paper on the Fox system in this volume.

analysis of series which can be controlled in one respect or another. But from the standpoint of the Plains area it is perhaps more significant that tribes coming into the Plains with *different* backgrounds and social systems ended up with *similar*

TABLE 2

A PRELIMINARY CLASSIFICATION OF PLAINS KINSHIP SYSTEMS*

I. *"Generation" type*
  A. *Cheyenne subtype*
    1. Cheyenne
    2. Arapaho
    3. Gros Ventre

  B. *Kiowa-Apache subtype*
    1. Kiowa-Apache
    2. Kiowa
    3. Lipan (?)
    4. Jicarilla (transitional)
    5. Caddo (?)
    6. Wichita (?)

  C. *Dakota subtype*
    1. Dakota tribes
      a) Teton
      b) Yankton
      c) Assiniboine
      d) Etc.
    2. Plains-Cree (transitional)
    3. Plains-Ojibway (transitional)
    4. Blood (?)
    5. Sarsi (?)

  D. *Piegan subtype*
    1. Piegan (transitional)

II. *"Lineage" type*
  A. *Omaha subtype*
    1. Central Siouan tribes
      a) Omaha
      b) Ponca
      c) Kansa
      d) Osage
      e) Iowa
      f) Oto
      g) Winnebago

    2. Central Algonkian tribes
      a) Menominee
      b) Sauk
      c) Fox
      d) Kickapoo
      e) Illinois
      f) Etc.

  B. *Crow subtype*
    1. Mandan
    2. Hidatsa
    3. Crow (transitional)
    4. Pawnee (transitional)
    5. Arikara (?)

* This classification is a revision of Morgan (*Systems of Consanguinity*) and Spier (*Distribution of Kinship Systems*). Dr. Spier's classification was based primarily on the terminology for cross-cousins; the present classification attempts to enlarge the criteria used.

kinship systems. It seems probable that the conditions of Plains life favored a rather amorphous and mobile type of social organization which could vary to meet changing conditions.

Certain of these conditions have been indicated above—the uncertain character of subsistence and the need for protection. Leadership was also of uncertain and varying quality. Perhaps the outstanding adjustment to these conditions in the Plains is seen in the tremendous importance of the relationship of brothers. Everywhere in the Plains brothers formed the most dependable and solid group; among the Dakota "if a man has no brothers or cousins (and this was possible in the days of wholesale death from war parties) he says, 'I am related to nobody.' "[117] Here is a basis for the wide recognition which brotherhood receives in the kinship system. The Cheyenne and Arapaho extend the relationship to all cousins, and fictitiously extend it through the institution of "friends" and by means of common society affiliations. The Kiowa and Kiowa-Apache do likewise, a group of brothers assuming special importance among the Kiowa. We have seen that the Dakota consider cross-cousins as "brothers," even though they are segregated in the terminology, and there is some evidence that the Plains-Cree and Plains-Ojibway likewise attached more importance to the concept of "brothers" than did their relatives to the northeast. The Piegan have carried this principle even farther, so that all collateral relatives, not only in ego's generation but in the first ascending and descending generations as well, are considered "brothers" (or "sisters"). The Crow Indians furnish a crucial instance. Fundamentally, their system of kinship seems to have been in the process of changing from a pure Crow type, such as their close relatives the Hidatsa possess, to a "Generation" type, such as the Cheyenne and Arapaho have developed.[118] Part of this process was the extension of the sibling relationship to cross-cousins. Both the Crow and the Hidatsa also extended the term for brother to the mother's brother and sister's son, though the Mandan preferred to use separate terms.

It is possible, therefore, that the relationship of brothers, because of its importance in Plains life, was one of the factors modifying kinship systems in the direction of a "Generation" type. If this is so, this factor and others may be the important agents in bringing about observed uniformities, and hence it

[117] Mead, *op. cit.*, p. 394.

[118] An analysis of the Crow material suggests that the Crow pattern persists in the nonvocative terminology, whereas the vocative terminology tends to be bilateral in character. The importance of a wide comparative study is clear in attempting to understand such transitional systems.

seems worth while to look for and isolate them, rather than to attribute the uniformity to simple diffusion.

Another important set of problems is concerned with the Northeastern Algonkian tribes. The Naskapi have a functioning cross-cousin marriage system, as do certain of the Cree and Ojibway bands. The Plains-Cree and Plains-Ojibway keep the same system of marriage but marry more distant cross-cousins. The Cheyenne and Arapaho marry completely outside of the range of blood-relationships. Here is a series in which there is a progressive widening of relationships by marriage. Dr. Hallowell has suggested that this may be the result of acculturational influences—undoubtedly an important factor. But in a wider context there is some evidence that the conditions of Plains life encouraged a wider integration and gradually brought it about, regardless of the influence of missionaries or traders. If this may be accepted as a working hypothesis, it has some bearing on the Dakota system. It seems probable that the Dakota kinship system was formerly based on cross-cousin marriage,[119] but that under the influence of Plains life (and contacts) it was shifting to a "Generation" type, as exemplified by the Cheyenne. The use of "brother-in-law" terms plus affixes for the cross-cousins, while behaving toward them as if they were "brothers," is intelligible on this basis.

These few examples indicate that it is possible to gain considerable insight into both the historical and the social aspects of kinship by means of a controlled comparative approach. Working hypotheses can be set up and tested against field work, since it is still possible to get detailed information on kinship for many tribes. Where historical data are available for earlier periods, studies of social change and the factors involved may be made.[120] While such an approach does not answer all the problems we are interested in, it does give us insight and information on many of them.

[119] This assumption has been made before by Rivers and others; in terms of this analysis it seems a useful working hypothesis.

[120] See Hallowell, *Recent Changes in the Kinship Terminology of the Abenaki*, and Eggan, *Historical Changes in the Choctaw Kinship System*, for examples of such studies.

KIOWA-APACHE SOCIAL ORGANIZATION

J. GILBERT McALLISTER

KIOWA-APACHE SOCIAL ORGANIZATION

J. GILBERT McALLISTER

INTRODUCTION

Social organization comprises the segments or groups into which a society is divided, such as family, clan, age, sex, occupation groups, or others. A study of social organization might be approached from several points of view; the method used here is a detailed examination of the kinship system—the terminology, the related behavior patterns, and the further relationships of kindred in the various social units. The procedure will be to present in detail the kinship structure and the life-cycle from the point of view of kinship behavior, and to summarize the social organization with reference to the manner in which the Kiowa-Apache were integrated. This is a logical approach from the point of view of these materials, for, as will appear later, the Kiowa-Apache are like one large, endogamous "band," with a keen feeling of unity. Every Kiowa-Apache was literally related by blood or marriage to every other Kiowa-Apache. Consequently, the family and the numerous ramifying relationships are of utmost importance to these people.[1]

The Kiowa-Apache are a small group of Athabaskan-speaking people now living in southwestern Oklahoma, near the small settlements of Fort Cobb and Apache. This is approximately the same territory that they occupied during the historic period, though their numerous raids carried them over a much larger area, from northern Nebraska to southern Texas and westward into Arizona. The geographical setting is that of the southern plains—a vast prairie crossed by comparatively large rivers flowing east and southeast. There were many kinds of wild animals, the most important of which was the buffalo. When they were

[1] This is a point of view stressed by Professor Radcliffe-Brown, not only in his lectures at the University of Chicago but particularly in his publication, *The Social Organization of Australian Tribes*.

exterminated, the main source of food and shelter for these Indians was gone. Had all plants and animals but the buffalo been destroyed, the Kiowa-Apache life, as well as that of other Plains tribes, might have persisted, and the conflict with white settlers might have been more severe. In aboriginal times there seems to have been an almost never ending supply of buffalo, and even as recently as sixty years ago great herds blackened the prairies.[2] The existence of the buffalo was taken so much for granted by the Kiowa-Apache that there were no buffalo fertility rites, although its social value was recognized in other ways. When the buffalo became scarce, these people had to turn to the smaller animals—deer, antelope, elk, and even rabbits, dogs, and birds for food. Then life was difficult; the men had constantly to hunt and the women to dig for roots and search for berries and fruits.

For as long as the Kiowa-Apache have any authentic tradition, they have been closely associated with the Kiowa, another Plains tribe speaking an entirely different and unrelated language. Communication was carried on by means of the sign language, and most of the old Kiowa-Apache knew a little Kiowa, though very few of the Kiowa had any knowledge of the Kiowa-Apache tongue.

During the time of the annual Kiowa Sun Dance, the Kiowa-Apache functioned as a "band" of the Kiowa, occupying a fixed place on the north side of the camp circle. During this dance the Kiowa-Apache were said to be under the jurisdiction of the Kiowa chief who was leader of the dance and owner of the *Taime*.[3] This chief was obeyed implicitly, for he was said to be in a position of unquestioned authority over both tribes from the announcement to the completion of the dance. Any violation of his orders was a violation of a ritual sanction, and dire catastrophe would befall the offender. The Kiowa-Apache, however, were not subservient to or dependent upon the Kiowa. At

[2] For descriptions of the vast herds roaming the plains in 1872–74, see Thomas Battey, *Life and Adventures of a Quaker among the Indians*, pp. 16–19.

[3] *Taime*: "the great central figure of the sun dance"; an exceedingly sacred object exposed to view only at the Sun Dance (Mooney, *Calendar History of the Kiowa*, p. 240).

the completion of the Sun Dance the two tribes broke up into smaller groups, each following some favorite leader.

Occasionally there was intermarriage between the two tribes, but each tribe remained distinct, and today when the younger people, at least, have a common language (English), there is a surprising formality and stiffness in their relations with each other. Pressure and opposition from the outside is now, and probably was in the past, necessary to bring the two tribes together. More often they oppose each other in various games, and when they assemble for summer dances, each tribal group camps separately. The relationship, therefore, might be called one of "social symbiosis."

Since the Kiowa-Apache were a distinct social entity, they can be considered without reference to the Kiowa. Whatever influence these two tribes may have had on each other through borrowing is certainly of no concern here and can never be more than conjecture. Aside from the Sun Dance and possibly large war parties, at which times they acted together, the two tribes were quite distinct.

At present (1934) the Kiowa-Apache number about two hundred, counting those children who have a parent of another tribe and who, in some cases, live with the other tribe, only occasionally visiting their Kiowa-Apache relatives. Actually there are probably only about one hundred and fifty Indians now comprising the tribe proper. According to the old men, the Kiowa-Apache were always a small group. All estimates made during the nineteenth century, until the measles epidemic of 1892, usually averaged a little over three hundred people. Mooney says, "They have probably never numbered over three hundred and fifty."[4] Inferiority of numbers has been considered the reason for their association with the Kiowa and is the only reason ascribed by the old men of both tribes.

The materials presented here are of a period vividly recalled by the oldest men of the tribe,[5] approximately 1860–80. At that

[4] *Ibid.*, p. 253.

[5] The materials were collected in the field from October, 1933, to September, 1934. This was a research project sponsored by the department of anthropology

time some of the Kiowa-Apache had never seen a white man.
They recall with amusement the first missionary to come among
them—Thomas Battey, in 1872. However, the white man's
influence had already been felt, and the culture was beginning
to disintegrate before the close of the century. For two hundred
years the Kiowa-Apache had had the horse, and its effects upon
the culture were marked. Before its introduction, these Indians
were much less nomadic. Their only domestic animal had been
the dog, which was used chiefly as a beast of burden, either
carrying loads on its back or hauling a travois, on which was
lashed a small tipi or a baby. At that time all who were strong
enough to carry a burden on the shoulders bore loads suited to
their strength. Sometimes, when an enemy attack was feared,
the men carried only their weapons, prepared to fight. In those
days the people had little property and did not make long
marches when they moved; there probably was less warfare.
Also, without the horse, hunting the buffalo was more difficult.
That is a period only hazily remembered now; the present informants lived in a time of increased activity, long marches and
numerous raids, frequent contact with other tribes, larger tipis
and more personal property, when the whole tempo of the culture had been greatly accelerated through the acquisition of the
horse.

The Kiowa-Apache say that they knew nothing of agriculture,
pottery-making, or even basketry. Their receptacles were made
of wood, horn, or hides. A prepared buffalo intestine served as a
water bag. Clothes, moccasins, robes, blankets, and the tipi
were all made from hides, usually buffalo or buckskin. These
people, then, are fairly representative of the Plains Indians. For
an understanding of the former social structure of the Kiowa-
Apache, the kinship system will first be examined.

of the University of Chicago. The present paper is a condensation of the writer's
doctoral dissertation. Of the informants used, Apache Sam Klinekole was by
far the best. Others with whom the writer worked for several weeks each, inter-
spersed over the time in the field, were: Big Ben Chaletsin, Old Man Taho,
Apache Clarence, Erati Taho, and Joe Blackbear. The two principal interpreters were Howard Allen Soontay and Alonzo Chalepah, the latter being fifty-
seven years old and the best living medicine man.

KINSHIP TERMINOLOGY

Kinship terminology is the system of words used in a given community for recognizing relatives. To simplify the analysis, Kiowa-Apache terms will be avoided as much as possible, and English equivalents will be substituted. Consanguineous relationships will be discussed first, followed by those of affinity.

The basic Kiowa-Apache kinship structure is outlined in Figure 1, for a male ego, secondary terms being noted in parentheses under the primary terms. A complete list of all terms with meanings used for designating kin will be found in Table 1. With the aid of the chart it will be noticed that in the first ascending generation there are four terms: (1) *ace*,[6] "father," and anyone whom he calls "brother"; (2) *nade*, "mother," and anyone she calls "sister"; (3) *bedje*, anyone father calls "sister"; and (4) *baye*, anyone mother calls "brother." In the second ascending generation all relatives are known as *soyan*, "grandparent." In the third ascending generation, which is as far as the Kiowa-Apache recognize relationship, the men are called *daran*, "older brother," and the women, *dadan*, "older sister." In ego's own generation distinctions are made between older and younger brother, *daran* and *tlaan*, respectively; and older and younger sister, *dadan* and *detcan*. This applies to both parallel and cross-cousins, which may be surprising considering the difference in behavior and terminology of the parents of cross-cousins. In the first descending generation one's own children and those of a sibling of the same sex are classified similarly and distinguished from the children of a sibling of the opposite sex. Herein lies the only distinction between male and female ego in terminology. A man calls his own son and his brother's son, *jaan*; his own daughter and his brother's daughter, *tceyan*. His sister's children are grouped together and known by the single term *dayan*. Similarly, a woman calls her own and her sister's son *jaan*, her

---

[6] The possessive pronoun "my" has been omitted. Only in the rather rare cases when a Kiowa-Apache addresses a person by a kinship term would he omit this pronoun. A discussion about relatives as presented here without the possessive pronoun would be unintelligible to him. For a phonetic rendering of these terms see Table 1.

KIOWA-APACHE KINSHIP SYSTEM

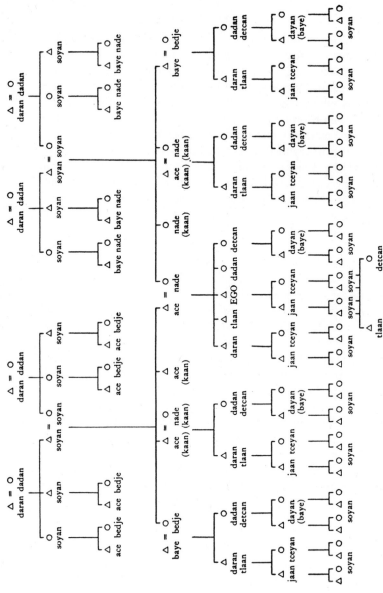

Fig. 1.—Basic terminological structure for the Kiowa-Apache. Ego=male; ○=females; equal sign signifies marriage. Secondary terms are in parentheses. A female ego uses the same terms except that she classes her own and her sister's children together, and has separate terms for her brother's children.

TABLE 1

COMPLETE LIST OF KINSHIP TERMS*

ace [-'à·cé], father, stepfather, anyone father calls "brother," anyone mother calls "husband"

acedatestcinde [-'à·cédàdè·stcį'dé], adopted father

acenadidlin [-'à·cénádídlį̃], stepfather ("he becomes father")

batana [bà·dà·ná], little brother-in-law; sister's husband, wife's brother (m.s.)

baye [-bá·yé], anyone mother calls "brother"; occasionally a man may use this term for a sister's child

bedje [-bé·djé], anyone father calls "sister"; occasionally stepfather

bitcadaca [bìtcàdà·cá·], I follow him about

bitcagoctin [bìlcá·góct'į̃], all relatives, address form ("I am related to them")

cindjaan (-tsìltcà·á(?)], brother's son (w.s.)

cindjaisju [-tsìltcà'íjó(?)], brother's sons (w.s.)

co or *cu* [có·(?)], affectionate term for wife

dadan [-'dà·dą̀], older sister, older female cousin, great-grandmother

daiju [-dà·íjó], sister's children (m.s.)

daran [-dàɣá], older brother, older male cousin, great-grandfather

dayan [-dà·yá], sister's child (m.s.)

denan [dè·ná], man, male (m.s., w.s.); husband, husband's brother, sister's husband, husband's grandfather, granddaughter's husband (w.s.)

detcan [-dè·t'cá], younger sister, younger female cousin, great-grandfather

gotsu [gòtsó(?)], ceremonial grandfather (m.s.) (?)

hactciyan [háctcíyá], old man

hactciyan bitcadaca [háctcíyá bìtcàdà·cá·], father-in-law ("I follow the old man")

icdjanan ['ìcdjá·ná], old woman

icdjanan bitcadaca ['ìcdjá·ná bìtcàdà·cá·], mother-in-law ("I follow the old woman")

ictcinyan ['ìctcį'yá], boy

intcina ['į'tcíná], child, baby

intcina datestcinde ['į'tcíná dàdè·stcį'dé], adopted child

intcina datestcinde sizdjaan ['į'tcíná dàdè·stcį'dé sìstcà·á(?)], adopted son

intcina datestcinde siztceyan ['į'tcíná dàdè·stcį'dé sìst'cè'yá(?)], adopted daughter

itedan ['ìt'é·dá], girl

jaan [-jà·á], son, son of sibling of same sex

kaan [-k'à·á], mother's sister, mother's sister's husband, father's brother, father's brother's wife, stepparent

la [-làh], sibling or cousin of opposite sex; wife's brother's wife (m.s.); husband's sister's husband (w.s.)

latce [-látcé], siblings and cousins of opposite sex

nade [-'nà·dé], mother, stepmother, adopted mother, anyone mother calls "sister," anyone father calls "wife"

nade datestcinde [-'nà·dé dàdè·stcį'dé], adopted mother

nade nadidlin [-'nà·dé nádídlį̃], stepmother ("she becomes mother")

* This is an alphabetical list of all terms and words used by the Kiowa-Apache in making kinship distinctions. The forms in brackets are strict phonetic renderings of the term immediately preceding. The phonetic alphabet used is that recommended in the *Smithsonian Miscellaneous Collections*, Vol. LXVI, No. 6. I am indebted to Dr. Harry Hoijer, of the University of Chicago, for the phonetic renderings and for checking the translation of the terms (m.s. = man speaking; w.s. = woman speaking).

TABLE 1—*Continued*

sise [*-t'sìsé*], sibling or cousin of same sex; wife's sister's husband (m.s.); husband's brother's wife (w.s.)

sisiju [*-t'sìs'íjó*], siblings and cousins of same sex

soyan [*-tsó'yá*], grandparent, grandchild, spouse's grandparent, grandchild's spouse

tcan [*-t'cá*], friend (m.s., w.s.); wife's grandfather, granddaughter's husband (m.s.)

tcana, in-law, including any of spouse's relatives in the first ascending generation, anyone spouse calls sibling of the opposite sex, anyone marrying ego's sibling of the opposite sex, anyone marrying a relative of ego's in the first descending generation

tce [*tcé*(?)], all relatives (nonvocative)

tcetcan [*t'cè'tcá*], woman, female (m.s., w.s.); wife, wife's sister, brother's wife, wife's grandmother, grandson's wife (m.s.)

tceyan [*-t'cè'yá*], daughter, daughter of sibling of the same sex

tedjaisju [*-t'é'tcà'íjó*], brother's daughters (w.s.)

tetcaan [*-t'é'tcà'á*], brother's daughter (w.s.)

tetciyan [*t'é'tcí'yá*], young woman

tlaan [*-t'là'á*], younger brother, younger male cousin, great-grandfather

tlin, wife's sister, brother's wife (m.s.) (?)

xangu, old word for wife (?)

zedan [*-zè'dá*], brother's wife, wife's sister (m.s.); husband's brother, sister's husband (w.s.)

own and her sister's daughter *tceyan*. Her brother's children she distinguishes from her own, also distinguishing on the basis of sex, calling her brother's son *cindjaan*, her brother's daughter, *tetcaan*. Thus, when ego is male, there are three primary categories in the first descending generation, but four when ego is female. In the second descending generation all relatives are *soyan*, "grandchild," the same term as for "grandparent." In the third descending generation great-grandson is *tlaan*, "younger brother"; and great-granddaughter, *detcan*, "younger sister." This is as far as the Kiowa-Apache reckon kinship, going no farther since "old people never live that long." One old informant, who had two great-granddaughters ("younger sisters"), said that, if they had children and he lived long enough, he thought he would call their children *dayan*, for after all they are his "sisters" and his sister's children are his *dayan*.[7] With this same reasoning a great-great-grandson would be *jaan*, "son."

---

[7] This is the manner in which a Kiowa-Apache reasons when asked for the term for some relative which, in his particular case, does not exist. As an exam-

There are, then, but twelve basic categories (thirteen when ego is a woman) into which a man's consanguineous kin are classed. This mode of designating relatives may be termed "classificatory" since lineal and collateral kin are merged. There are some classificatory systems, such as the Hawaiian,[8] which have even fewer categories, merging a larger number of relatives; and other systems, such as the Cherokee, which have more categories, merging fewer relatives.

Though many relatives may be grouped together, there is a feeling of "nearness" or "farness" which is frequently expressed in subsidiary terms or by qualifying the terms given above. A mother's sister may be called *kaan* ("one who holds me") about as frequently as she is called *nade*, but the term *kaan* is never applied to the biological mother. *Kaan* is also used for father's brother, stepfather, and stepmother. Though a stepmother is usually called "mother" (*nade*), this term may be qualified by *nadidlin*, "not my own." Similarly, *acenadidlin*, "father, not my own," is used for a stepfather, although usually he would be called "father." The same qualifying term, *nadidlin*, may be suffixed to "son" and "daughter" to distinguish stepchildren from own children. Usually no such distinction is made, for as the Kiowa-Apache say, "In your own mind you know." Adopted parents or children can also be distinguished: *ace datestcinde*, "adopted father"; *intcina datestcinde sizjaan*, "child, adopted, my son."

Another term for stepfather is *bedje*, the usual term for "father's sister." It is infrequently used, and younger and middle-aged Kiowa-Apache who had never heard of this use tended to be skeptical.[9] The usual term for mother's brother, *baye*, may

ple, when asked for the kinship terms for a father's father's brother's daughter (not, of course, in this manner but from the informant's genealogical tables, in which case the recorder frequently has to ask his informant to assume that such and such a relative has a daughter, or grandson, or whatever relative is in question), the informant will say, "That woman you want to know about, she would be my father's sister, and my father's sister is my *bedje*."

[8] In the Hawaiian system, e.g., there is but one category in the ascending generation, that of parent, no distinction necessarily being made in sex.

[9] Incidentally, this term stirred up one of a number of interesting tribal controversies while I was there. The day after I had been given this term for step-

also be used by a man for sister's children, but not by a woman. Another secondary term is that for younger brother, *tlaan*, used by both man and woman.

There are a number of terms used in ego's generation but not listed in the basic kinship charts in order to avoid confusion. Usually the term for older or younger sibling of the same or opposite sex is used, but the following terms occur: *la*, "sibling of the opposite sex"; *sise*, "sibling of the same sex"; *latce*, "siblings of the opposite sex"; *sisiju*, "siblings." There is some doubt about the existence of a general term for siblings of the same sex.

When it is necessary to distinguish between the grandmother and the grandfather the qualifying "old man" or "old woman" may be suffixed; thus *soyan hactciyan* is grandfather. Grandson and granddaughter are distinguished by suffixing "boy" (*ictcinyan*) or "girl" (*itedan*). "Boy" and "girl" are also suffixed to *dayan* to distinguish sister's son from daughter.

Consanguineous relatives are seldom, if ever, designated by descriptive terms. Usually from the context or the presence of a person, one knows to whom reference is made. Descriptive terms do occur among affinal relatives as noted below.

The basic terminological structures for affinal relatives are shown in Figures 2 and 3. It will be seen that there are but three new categories for a man or woman: *tcetcan*, "wife," or *denan*, "husband"; *tcana*, "in-law"; and *zedan*, "spouse not my own." Two of these three—*tcetcan* and *zedan*, and *denan* and *zedan*—are almost the same. Other affinal relatives, particularly those removed in time, as the third ascending and descending generations, are classified with consanguineous kin.

---

father, a middle-aged Kiowa-Apache came to see me. "Yesterday the old man told you they call stepfather *bedje*. That's wrong; that old man don't know; that's what they call aunt, etc." His reason for coming to me was that he wanted a job, but through him I discovered that there was quite an argument in progress, and all the old men and women were being consulted. Several times after that, when I informally met some old man, he would want to know if I knew what *bedje* meant. The result was that the old people were unanimous in agreeing that the term could be used for stepfather; the younger ones were all doubtful. I give this instance in some detail to indicate how an investigator may be rather carefully checked by the tribe in general. Several times I was amazed at the rather general knowledge of what each informant was telling me, even to minute details. In addition to using all available informants, this served as an excellent check on the data secured.

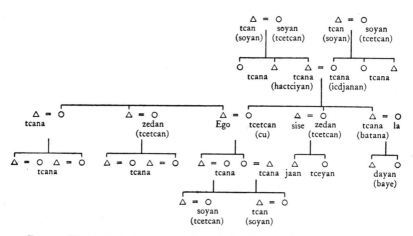

Fig. 2.—Terminological structure for affinal relatives. Ego = male. Secondary terms in parentheses.

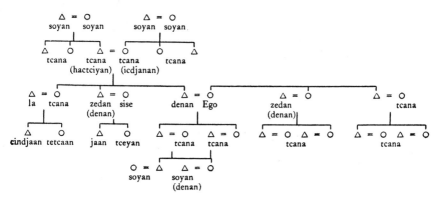

Fig. 3.—Terminological structure for affinal relatives. Ego = female. Secondary terms in parentheses.

A man generally uses *tcetcan* for his wife, but *cu* (or *co*) and *xangu* were also mentioned. There is disagreement over the use of these secondary terms, some informants never having heard of them, other saying they are very old terms, and still others saying they are new terms. There are apparently no such secondary terms for a husband. *Zedan* is used by a man for "wife's sister" and "brother's wife," and reciprocally by a woman for "husband's brother" and "sister's husband." A wife's sister and a brother's wife may also be called *tcetcan*, "wife,"[10] and a husband's brother and sister's husband may be called *denan*, "husband." A wife's brother and sister's husband are called *tcana*; *batana* was given as a secondary term for "wife's younger brother." A woman calls her husband's sister or her brother's wife *tcana*. A man's wife's brother's wife is called *la*, "sister"; and, since the term is reciprocal, a woman calls her husband's sister's husband, *la*, "brother." *Sise* is another reciprocal term, used by a man for his wife's sister's husband and by a woman for her husband's brother's wife. All a spouse's relatives in the first ascending generation are called *tcana*. To distinguish when necessary, the father-in-law may be called *hactciyan bitcadaca*, "old man whom I follow"; and a mother-in-law, *icdjanan bitcadaca*, "old woman whom I follow." A man usually calls his wife's grandfather *tcan*, "friend," but may use *soyan*, "grandfather"; he calls his wife's grandmother *soyan*, "grandmother," but has a right, in fun, to call her *tcetcan*, "wife." A woman calls her husband's grandparents *soyan* but has a right to call his grandfather *denan*, "husband." Spouses of one's own children are called *tcana* by both a man and a woman. The children of a wife's sister are called "own children," since the mother may be called "wife" and the father is called "brother." The children of a wife's brother are called by the same term (*dayan*) as sister's children, since the mother is called *la*, "sister." Similarly, a woman calls her husband's brother's children "son" and "daughter," since their father may be called "husband" and the mother is called "sister." The children of a husband's sister are classified

---

[10] One informant gives *tlin* as an additional term for "wife's sister" and "brother's wife," but as it could not be checked, its accuracy is in question.

with brother's children, since the father is called "brother." In the third descending generation a man calls his grandson's wife *soyan* or sometimes "wife." A granddaughter's husband is called *tcan*, "friend," and seldom, if ever, *soyan*. A woman calls both her grandson's wife and her granddaughter's husband *soyan*. She may also call her granddaughter's husband *denan*, "husband."

It is evident from the foregoing that many affinal relatives are classified together under the general term *tcana*, "in-law." The terms distinguishing those in the first ascending generation were noted. To differentiate those in the first descending generation, where it is possible to have many sons- and daughters-in-law, descriptive terms are frequently used; sister's son's wife is *sitcana cidayan bitcetcan*, "my in-law, my sister's child, his wife." Similar descriptive terms can apparently be used to designate any relative when the classificatory term is confusing; thus younger brother's wife is *sizedan citlaan bitcetcan*, "my spouse not my own, my younger brother, his wife." But it is probably not necessary to use descriptive terms often, for frequently the person can be referred to by name, though there are certain relatives whose personal names can never be used, even in talking about them. This will be noted in the discussion of behavior.

KINSHIP RANGE

Among the Kiowa-Apache the terminology has no defined range, the only limitations being in ego's generation and these not very exact. Siblings are limited to brothers, sisters, and cousins. However, the cousin range may be extremely wide, for a person has many "near" and "distant" father's brothers, father's sisters, mother's brothers, mother's sisters; and parents have "sisters" and "brothers" through marriage; all whose children are "brothers" and "sisters." Then, too, good friends fall into a sibling behavior pattern, and although they do not use sibling terms, their children are considered as "siblings," both in behavior and in terminology. Though there is an attempt to define limits in one's own generation, and to some extent in the immediate ascending and descending generation, the "grandparent-grandchild" generation is "wide open," as the Kiowa-Apache say. Any old person is a grandparent.

For affinal terms one gets his cue from his spouse. There is a fixed number of categories, but the extent to which these terms are applied depends on the number of kin a spouse recognizes, which, in turn, depends on the rather vague pattern mentioned above.

Whatever the reason, and one which comes to mind is the smallness of the tribe, every Kiowa-Apache is related to nearly all the others. If a stranger coming into the group was to take any part in the communal life, he was almost of necessity fitted into the kinship pattern. If he did not become attached to some family, it is impossible to see how he could have continued to exist. Captives were frequently incorporated into the tribe, and hence there probably is no such person as a "pure" Kiowa-Apache. Everyone can trace relationships to Kiowa, Pawnee, Arapaho, Cheyenne, and other tribes. Captive white children became own children, especially if they were young. They grew up as Kiowa-Apache with every right and privilege of a Kiowa-Apache. A captive white woman taken as a wife could, if she were able to adapt herself, attain a position similar to that of any Kiowa-Apache wife. Adult males were almost invariably killed, and there was no mention of one's being taken captive and continuing to live with the tribe, although it might have been possible for such a thing to occur. The father of a sixty-year-old man, one of my informants, was a white man, said to have been a cowboy who "hung around" the tribe for a while. Anyone who had continuous and intimate contact with the tribe was fitted into the kinship system. It is surprising how tenaciously the old kinship pattern and terminology persist, even to-day when relationships are breaking down and the old culture is almost gone. In my own case I acquired certain relatives and only accidentally learned of the importance of that relationship, as will be mentioned under kinship behavior below.[11]

[11] To ascertain more definitely the present range of relationships, a list was made of all the adult Kiowa-Apaches and at least one or two children from each family. This list also included ten persons from other tribes who had themselves

The Kiowa-Apache's range of relationships was wide, and as a consequence, nearly everybody in the tribe, since it was small, was related to everyone else. Frequently, of course, they were related in more than one way. Where a choice was thus open, the most desirable relationship was assumed. This was done, not according to any defined rules or through any agreement or discussion among the parties concerned, but usually by one of the individuals assuming the behavior pattern associated with certain kin. Usually, if any general rules could be made, a respect relationship would be continued or assumed if the new situation demanded it. In one instance a daughter-in-law, through a later marriage, came into the category of "wife" to her former father-in-law. The "daughter-in-law–father-in-law" relationship in all its strictness was maintained, and the man's comment was, "If I talk to her, the news would sure spread out." In another instance a respect relationship existed

---

married Kiowa-Apaches, or whose close relatives had done so. One of these latter was a Kiowa woman whose daughter was married to a Kiowa-Apache, another a girl whose mother (a Kiowa) was now married to a Kiowa-Apache but whose father was of another tribe. This list, which totaled ninety-seven, was checked with three Apaches, with the following results. The oldest informant, a man, claimed relationship to all but three of the group. These three were of those belonging to other tribes, though it will be noted that seven individuals of other tribes had become incorporated into his kin group. A second informant, a middle-aged man, claimed to be related to all but nine of the ninety-seven. The third informant, a middle-aged woman, said that twenty-seven were not related to her. There are several reasons for this large count on her part. First of all, her husband is an outsider, a Sioux (Dakota), so that she has not acquired a large body of Kiowa-Apache relatives through marriage. Furthermore, the women at present are inclined to ignore, if not to deny, that their sister's husband can call them "wife." They have learned that white men laugh at them for this relationship. Where the male informant above claimed her as a "wife" (she was the wife of his cousin), she said he was "no kin." Consequently, she said that his children were not related to her, though he claimed her son as his son. Similarly, the woman ignored a number of relationships which, because of genealogical tables, it was evident that she could have claimed. She was thinking more in terms of close relatives and much in the manner that Europeans count kin ties. Her information, therefore, is to be somewhat discounted and that of the men to be taken as more nearly the norm. However, even considering these discrepancies, and remembering that she married out of the tribe, she claims more than two-thirds of the Kiowa-Apache as kin. If the children of all these adults had been included, the number counted as kin would have been much greater.

between two men. Through a marriage a "grandson-grandfather" relationship came into being. The older man preferred the respect relationship, but the young one familiarly called the older man "grandfather" and began to tease and joke with him. The older man resented the new relationship, but there was nothing he could do about it since the young man had spoken to him familiarly. Probably in the past a younger man would not have been so presuming, and the older man would have had a choice, which would have been for the respect relationship. In another instance a man through a marriage became the brother-in-law of his former grandparent. Not knowing what relationship term to use, the two avoided using any and called each other by personal names. It seems probable that an older person, rather than a young one, and a man rather than a woman, could have chosen the relationship that would be maintained. Similarly, a respect relationship probably took precedence over one of familiarity, and undoubtedly the closer relationship over a distant one.

The last few paragraphs have reached beyond a mere description of kinship terminology, though most of the preceding discussion has been little more than the skeleton outline of the kinship structure with occasional references to wider interests. The more important aspects of kinship, the behavior and its relationship to the terminology, will now be discussed. This will be considered first from the point of view of the individual and his behavior toward different relatives, or rather toward the different categories into which his kin are grouped. It will be seen then what correlation exists between behavior and terminology. Finally, behavior will be considered from the point of view of the whole life-cycle.

BEHAVIOR PATTERNS

The old behavior patterns are falling into disuse with the general disintegration of the culture, so that at present it is difficult to observe the varying attitudes toward relatives. Most of the information here presented was obtained through questions, for only the pronounced patterns, such as avoidance of affinal relatives of the opposite sex, are still visibly continued. When discussing behavior, the Kiowa-Apache use the terms "joke," "tease," "love," "scared," "afraid," and others. These terms vary in meaning, for there are different ways of "teasing," different degrees to which a person is "afraid." When a Kiowa-Apache says that he is a "little afraid of his father," it is different from the "fear" of a brother-in-law, which in turn is different from the "fear" of a mother-in-law. Therefore, when such a term is used below, it must be considered in connection with the other terms used to describe the relationship. The variations in the meanings of these words will become more apparent as examples are given to illustrate the conduct toward different relatives.

Parent-child.—Behavior between parents and children is differentiated not only on the basis of age but also on the basis of sex. A mother and a father are not accorded the same type of love and respect, just as parents do not treat a son and daughter alike. A few generalizations can be made about parent-child behavior, but the analysis will have to be made from the point of view of a father to his son or daughter, or a mother to her son or daughter.

The Kiowa-Apache parent is usually loving, intimate, and indulgent toward his child. His whole life is bound up with that of his offspring and by extension, not only in terminology but also in behavior, directly to many children. Whenever and wherever supernatural aid is sought, the prayers are almost invariably for one's own and one's children's health, success, and long life. One of the important herbal medicines is a "baby medicine," which assures many and healthy children. The ritual life, while thought to center primarily about the individual,[12] is usually indirectly, and sometimes directly, concerned with Kiowa-Apache children. This will become more apparent in the outline of the life-cycle.

When children are small, the parents "tease them, sing to them, make them dance—anything to make them laugh."

[12] This is primarily true only in the visionary experiences.

Kiowa-Apache parents almost court the favor of their children —conduct which frequently conflicts with their position of authority as teachers of the tribal lore. The Kiowa-Apache say:

> Woman sometimes talks to her son. If he listens, the mother is going to try and fix him up, making good moccasins and leggings for him. If he doesn't listen, she may send him to his aunt. . . . . Maybe, after a while, the mother gets lonesome for her boy and calls him back. He says, "No, you scold me all the time. I want to stay with my aunt or my grandpa." Woman gets tired and gets up and goes down where her boy is. "Son, I've come after you." The boy puts his head down. "All right, I'll go back, but you don't treat me good, you scold me; next time I'm going to stay with my grandpa." When the boy gets back, his father says, "Come sit right next to me." The father pats him and gets arrows for him and treats him good.

Most of the time parents try to be "good" to their children; that is the pattern and any parents acting otherwise are "talked about."

A child usually loves and respects his parents but is not intimate with them in the sense of joking or teasing. There is a feeling of formality, of conflict, between the parent and the child generations not noticed between alternate generations. Probably this is due to the superordination-subordination relationship of the two generations, for all authority, all compulsion, so far as the child is concerned, is traced to the parents. Although relatives older than a child, from siblings to grandparents, share to a greater or less extent, depending upon circumstances, in his training, and although an older brother or a grandparent may even be called in to administer punishment, the source of authority seems to be lodged in the parents, particularly the father. Hence the Kiowa-Apache say that a child is "a little bit afraid of his daddy."

The father is most often the one who advises his son. One informant says:

> My daddy treats me good; he gives me good talk and I listen. He says, "Get up early and look after the horses and ponies." If I don't listen to my daddy, the other people will talk about me. If I rastle around right like my daddy says, then the people will talk good about me. Maybe they will let me marry their daughter. My daddy makes arrows for me and arrow bag. He makes bow-string of sinew, and feathers arrows, and puts spikes[13] on them for me. Someday

[13] For many generations the Kiowa-Apache traded for iron to use for projectile points and even the oldest men do not know how flint heads were made.

my friend comes in and I say, "My daddy made this for me." They will know that my daddy is good to me.

Not only does the father give things to his son, but he teaches him how to make weapons and how to use them. Although the father is primarily concerned in the boy's training, all older male relatives are interested, but their share in a child's education depends on their opportunities for contact.

The behavior toward a father's brother or classificatory father is but slightly different from the behavior toward a father. The boy respects him, is a little afraid of him, but ordinarily does not have much contact with him. On his part the paternal uncle seldom gives advice to his brother's son, though he may do so occasionally. The Kiowa-Apache say that these two relatives are not "rough" with each other. The relationship, being a little more distant, is probably a little less formal, though should this potential "father," through deaths, remarriages, or other circumstances, become the mother's husband, the relationship would undoubtedly become more formalized. This difference in attitude may be seen in the use of names. A son would never, under any condition, use his father's personal name, but in order to differentiate between a number of father's brothers, he may use their names. However, he would avoid doing so as much as possible. The father and his brothers can freely use the son's given name but probably use "son" most often.

A woman has little to do with the training of her son. She may advise him, commending or criticizing his behavior, but the actual training is in the hands of the father and other older male relatives. Between mother and child there appears to be a more intimate relationship than between father and child. This is well illustrated by what one informant said:

If your father died and your mother married again and you got a mean stepfather, your mother would probably take your side against her new husband. But if your mother died and your father married again and you got a mean stepmother, your father would probably side with his new wife and not take up for you.

Another informant says, "A boy sure loves his mother; he thinks she is a great thing. He goes to her when he is hungry."

There seems to be less distinction between a mother and her sisters than between a father and his brothers. This may be due to the former practice of polygyny, where two or three sisters married the same man. When this occurred, there was probably little or no distinction made between the several wives, who were all called "mother." They were father's wife, therefore mother. Then, too, a child probably saw his mother and her sisters together about the camp more frequently than he saw his father and father's brothers together since they were usually away hunting or raiding. Also, residence seems to have been matrilocal more often than patrilocal. There is one noteworthy distinction in behavior to actual mother and to her sisters: A child would never use his mother's name, but under certain conditions he might use the name of his mother's sister. There is no restriction upon their use of the child's name.

Aside from talking to his daughter and giving her advice, a man has little to do with her training. The mother and her sisters, or a grandmother, teach a girl to tan hides, make clothes, and cook. The young girls helped their elders about the tipi, carrying water and wood, or they went with them to collect roots, learning the easiest way to dig and how to select the best. Presumably a mother or any of a girl's older female relatives instructed her about marriage, conception, birth, and other sexual matters. Actually there was probably little formalized instruction of this type for either boys or girls; the men deny that their fathers ever taught them about sex.

As the mother is the favorite parent, so the daughter is said to be the favorite child. The son, however, particularly when he grows up, receives the better treatment. His mother and sisters wait on him, cook for him, and make his clothes, and he is accorded much more respect than his sister. He is a potential warrior, hunter, and chief, and they are all "good" to him.

Father's sister–brother's child.—The father's sister is the female counterpart of the father; she is a "stepfather." This is not only indicated by the terminology, where the word for aunt, *bedje*, is also used for stepfather, but is noticed in behavior as well. The respect one has for an aunt is much the same as the respect for a father, with possibly the fear eliminated. The Kiowa-Apache says he is not "afraid" of his aunts, neither is he "rough" with them. He would never tease or joke with them; "you are good to her and she is good to you." If a child is hungry, he might go to his aunt for something to eat. If one could stratify types of behavior, a father's sister would come in between father and mother. A Kiowa-Apache is not so intimate with her as with a mother, nor does he have the fearsome respect toward her that is frequently noticed toward a father. A disobedient child may be sent to his aunt when his parents seem incapable of handling him, and she, presumably, can manage him.

A mother's brother's wife and father's sister are in the same category. The Kiowa-Apache say that there is little distinction in behavior toward these two aunts; possibly they prefer a mother's brother's wife. This seems to mean that they are less formal with her than with a father's sister, otherwise "they are both your aunts, and you behave just alike to them." When it is necessary to address an aunt, the kinship term would usually be used, but when it might become important to distinguish between several aunts, a personal name could be used.

Mother's brother–sister's child.—The relationship between a mother's brother and sister's child is one of friendly intimacy. A nephew "has his heart toward his uncle." One informant says:

I love my uncle, and he loves me. My uncle is like my daddy, but my uncle loves me best. Maybe he catches me and pats me and says, "Nephew, don't act crazy." My uncle doesn't scold, but he talks good. He might make me an arrow and bow. If I shoot funny, my uncle laughs at me, "Nephew, you will make a crack shot."

The mother's brother takes a great interest in the training of a sister's son, teaching him to shoot and taking him hunting. When a boy makes his first kill, or a girl her first piece of handwork, it is frequently the uncle who gives a horse to some old man or woman who then makes public announcement of the child's accomplishment.

If a child is in trouble or wants something, he is more likely to go to his mother's brother than to his parents, for he knows that his uncle will not refuse him. One informant says: "If anything happens, I go to my mother's brother. 'Uncle, I want that pony.' He thinks awhile and then says, 'All right.' Or I may get a gun or arrows from him. My uncle will give me what he can."

A mother's brother and sister's child tease and joke with each other. This, so far as I was able to discover, is not a formalized or standardized type of joking. A woman informant says, "I am not ashamed of my uncle; I tease him and he teases me." If there is any difference in behavior, on the uncle's part, toward a niece and a nephew, it is in the type of jokes. Apparently the jokes with a niece are milder than those with a nephew. The jokes between uncle and nephew are probably less ribald than those between brothers or grandparent and grandchild. This somewhat milder form of joking with an uncle is probably an indication of the respect attitude usually present toward the parental generation. The mother's brother is the most intimate male relative a child has in the first ascending generation; he is much better liked than a father's brother and even more than a father. A child is on terms of near equality with his uncle, as is reflected in the terminology, in which the secondary term a mother's brother can use for a sister's child is the same term, *baye*, that the child uses for him. Reciprocal terms are usually correlated with symmetrical behavior.

A father's sister's husband is in the same category as the mother's brother, and the behavior is said to be the same as that toward an actual mother's brother. Opportunities for expressing this relationship with more distant uncles are often limited, as with all more distant classificatory relatives.

Grandparent-grandchild.—Between alternate generations, the grandparent and grandchild generations, there is a surprising intimacy. Only with siblings of the same sex are the Kiowa-Apache more intimate; and the relationship between a grandparent and a grandchild of opposite sex is probably more intimate than with any other consanguineous kin of opposite sex.

Alternate generations tease and joke without restraint. They are "rough" with each other, say the Kiowa-Apache, by which they mean that a grandparent may tell his grandchild obscene jokes regardless of sex. Around the fire, in the evening, the grandparents tell endless stories, until the grandchildren fall asleep. The glamorous and mythical past of the tribe is reviewed; heroic deeds of ancestors are recounted; the entertaining and often obscene adventures of Coyote are told. This is school for the Kiowa-Apache children, and the child who has not had grandparents to instruct him is thought to be handicapped. To an inquiry about the relative worth of several old men as informants, it was said that one of them "didn't know much because he didn't have any grandparents."[14] A grandparent surpasses a parent, for, as one man said, "My grandpa has a lot more experience; he knows more." All Apaches say that they love their grandparents more than their parents.

Not only do grandparents admonish their grandchildren, but they take an active part in training them. A grandfather will teach a grandson to shoot or make weapons. Similarly, a grandmother will teach a granddaughter to sew, cook, or dig roots. Usually the father's mother makes the cradle at a child's birth. Occasionally a grandparent will give his name to a grandchild, or he may give a horse to the announcer on the occasion of his grandson's first kill.

Sometimes the grandparent may be asked by the parents to punish a child, but despite this fact there is great familiarity between these generations. There is respect for the grandparents but not the kind of respect (fear) that one has for father. This was expressed by one Kiowa-Apache who said, "If a girl or boy doesn't listen to their grandpa, that is wrong, for their grandpa treats them good."

Any disagreement and conflict which may occur between alternate generations are very different from the conflict between parent and child generations. This latter is an ever present, covert feeling of restraint, which the Kiowa-Apache expresses by saying they are "a little bit afraid." With the alternate generation there seems to be much more equality, a free give-and-

[14] It is difficult to understand how an Indian could be without grandparents considering the classificatory system. In this instance the man who made the remark was jealous and discrediting the other's ability.

take, and if a disagreement occurs, it is followed by reconciliation. One informant said, "I have it out with my grandpa, but
I still like him."

This equality of feeling is expressed not only by calling each
other by the same kinship term, but by the reciprocal use of
personal names, which can be used as freely as names are ever
used. The feeling between grandfather and grandson is so intimate that a grandson's wife may be called "wife"; similarly, a
woman calls her granddaughter's husband "husband." The following examples will further illustrate the intimate relationship
between alternate generations.

During my stay with the Kiowa-Apache, I had taken a number of pictures of members of the tribe but never of the oldest
man, one of my informants. He never had had a picture taken,
and he did not want one made. His son and daughter were very
anxious to have a photograph of him, and a number of times
when I had a camera with me they tried to get their father to
pose. He always refused, and if they persisted, he turned his
back on them. One day the old man's grandson was present;
so I asked him to get the old man to have his picture taken. The
boy called to his grandfather, "Come on out and get your picture
taken"; and the old man, grumbling a little, posed for two
pictures.

About the same time I was very anxious to work one more
day with the informant I had found to be the best. The tribe
was having its annual dance, and, since the old man was the
only one with enough interest and energy to lead the dances, he
had to stay and make the others dance. One of the last mornings
I went over to get him, and for more than half an hour I argued
with his relatives. He was willing to come, but they held him.
Finally, when I had given up hope, I said with much disgust to
the old man, "That's a nice way to treat your grandson." For
several months I had been working with the old man, and we
had come to be very friendly, teasing and joking with each other.
Nothing formal had been done about this relationship; but our
behavior had been that of grandfather and grandson, and the
use of the kinship term had followed as a consequence. When I
chided him about his treatment of me, a "grandson," the whole

situation was altered. He then thought he had better come work with me, but his relatives were not going to give in. They told him in no uncertain terms that that was no way to treat the rest of his relatives. The old man was in a quandary, tears coming to his eyes. The situation was amazing to me, for I had no conception of having a claim on the old man. Finally, he thought of a compromise: he would work at the dance all day and at sunset come to my house and work until the morning star came up.

Sibling-sibling; friends.—The most intimate behavior, the closest feeling of unity, is between siblings of the same sex, and between "friends,"[15] who, if they are at all intimate, are considered as "brothers" or "sisters." A Kiowa-Apache says, "A brother is a man's best friend," or "Friends are like brothers; raise up together; go around together when they are children." Usually the association of brothers or "friends" continues through life, and "his head will usually lie in the same place as yours, if you should be killed."

This attitude is not fixed among children but becomes pronounced as the men reach maturity. During childhood an older brother frequently disciplines a younger brother. Upon maturity there is probably less difference between older and younger brothers, and the behavior becomes one of equality. A brother (or "friend") is one person with whom one can tease and joke to extremes. By these extremes a Kiowa-Apache means that obscene jokes and the foulest language can be used to a brother or in his presence. This behavior further expresses itself in sham fights which to spectators may appear real.

Whatever brothers have they will share with one another. "They treat each other right; they don't fuss; they like each other." They may even share a wife, though this probably does not occur frequently. One old man said:

If the unmarried brother comes to visit, the married one tells him to sit down by his wife. Maybe he will say, "Brother, I'm going way down there. I come back tomorrow; you sleep with my wife tonight. It is all right for a brother to

[15] So far as could be determined, a Kiowa-Apache does not have a "friend" of the opposite sex. Intimacy with the opposite sex apparently presupposes sexual relations.

sleep with his brother's wife. If a wife dies, you can get another woman, but if a brother dies, you won't see him any more. Brother, if I die, don't you leave our wife."

The levirate in this form—marriage to a deceased brother's wife —occasionally occurs. It was noted above that a man could call his brother's wife "wife." It is also said that a man may let his visiting "friend" sleep with his wife.

Probably the most frequently heard admonition of an elder to a younger man is "stay with your brother in a fight." An informant says:

If one of your brothers is afoot or surrounded by an enemy, it is your duty to save him or die with him. If a brother is killed and you did nothing to help or save him, you would be disgraced. The story would be told how you did not help your brother; all would talk about it, and the women would laugh at you. They would say, "You gave your brother to the enemy."

This loyalty on the part of brothers is cited as a reason for loving a brother more than a wife.

Though the behavior of siblings is easy and intimate, a man should have a certain respect for his brother. One gets permission before using something belonging to him. "If you catch one of your brother's horses without his knowing it, he might not like it. Get his permission first, ask a brother right." A brother would never refuse. The Kiowa-Apache discerningly remark that "if a fellow tries to work you [obtain something from you], he calls you 'brother' so you won't get out of it."

Brothers generally use kinship terms toward one another, but there is no restraint upon their use of one another's names. Usually a man has the same avoidances as his brothers. A brother's mother-in-law is treated as one's own mother-in-law. Through his brother's marriage a man acquires a whole set of affinal relatives to whom he usually behaves in the same manner as his brother does. Two brothers or two "friends" are as nearly one social personality as can be obtained. At death a living brother further shows his affection by taking one or more of his deceased brother's horses and caring for them better than he does his own.[16]

[16] However, this is not only a demonstration of love, but it adds to the prestige of the one who does it, for the Kiowa-Apache watch and comment on the treatment a man bestows on his deceased brother's horse; for more detail see "Death, Mourning, and Remarriage,' pp. 157 ff.

In the *Manatidie* and *Klintidie*, dancing societies discussed below, a man's partner is his "friend." A man may find this "friend" after he is taken into the group, but usually the friendship has been formed previously. Two good friends may be taken in together and become ceremonial friends. If a man and his partner are not friendly, a change is made and a new partner obtained. These partners, or any real "friends," have the same obligations to each other as brothers, even to sacrificing their lives or sharing their wives. As "brothers" they then have the same relatives, so that in acquiring a partner or a good "friend" one obtains a new set of classificatory relatives since "friend's" relatives are classed as one's own relatives. These fictitious kin are like blood-kin to the children of "friends," who are classified as siblings and consequently would never marry. "Friends," however, never use sibling terms to one another. This former intimate behavior of "friends," considered by the Kiowa-Apache to be as intimate as blood-relationship, together with the classificatory manner of grouping relatives, is now causing legal difficulties in inheritance. Recently an Indian claimed a share in the property of his grandfather's *Manatidie* partner. He claimed this man as his "grandfather" and stated that he should share equally with the real grandchildren. The agency did not recognize this claim, though in many cases such acquired relationships have been legally sanctioned. In the instance cited the man undoubtedly lost because the Kiowa-Apache as a whole dislike him for his avaricious, land-grabbing tendencies and so revealed the fictitious character of the relationship.

The behavior between sisters is much the same as that between brothers—intimate, unrestrained, and loving, but lacking some of the intensity and loyalty of brothers. One informant says, "Sisters love each other. One thing no good, if one gets married, the youngest or oldest, this fellow, it is like he has two wives. Those sisters fuss over the man; but when they are single, they love each other. They can't fix it good like men." However, this was a man's point of view, and he would never admit the woman's claim that sisters love one another more than they do their husbands. Another informant said, "Sometimes a younger sister would want to live with her older sister and then she would make the proposal that she marry her sister's husband, too." It is an accepted axiom that, if a man has several wives, there is little or no trouble between them if they are sisters. In all polygynous unions recorded in the genealogies, the women were sisters.

Sisters tease and joke with one another to the same extent as brothers do. They also help one another in working; together they collect roots, gather wood, or carry water. Each has the same relatives as the others. If they marry unrelated males, each becomes related to the others' husbands' relatives. If women think that a man has mistreated one of their sisters to whom he is married, they may get together and give him a thorough beating. Just as among men, a woman's "friend" is as close as a sister and observes the same behavior.

The relationship of mature brothers and sisters is one of restraint and formality, but avoidance does not occur before adolescence. It would not only be difficult to keep separate the small children before they learned to avoid siblings of the opposite sex, but there would be a conflict with important observances in the child's dancing society, the Rabbits, discussed below. Through observation the children gradually learn to avoid the opposite sex, but sooner or later the parents will enforce the taboos.

An older sister has a motherly attitude toward both a younger sister and a younger brother. She may look after them, prepare food for them, and tease them. An older brother has a fatherly attitude to younger siblings. With the lapse of time a man's attitude toward a brother becomes more and more intimate; but toward a sister it becomes more and more restrained and formal. With maturity "girls don't hardly look at a brother's face; a man don't look at his sister's eyes; they don't sit next to each other. Man can't sit on her bed, nor she on his." They do not tease each other or use obscene words in conversation when the other is present, but they talk to each other and "take each other's words to heart." However, they would not stay in the same room alone with each other.

Regarding the brother-sister relationship, the Kiowa-Apache

say: "If you have a sister, love her as a man loves his daughter." "Brother sort of boss his sister." They refer, of course, to a mature brother, therefore usually an older brother. "The father says to the daughter, 'I love my son; if he sees you running around at night, he can shoot you.' That is why girls listen to their fathers and brothers." "A brother is her boss so that she would be a good girl; men don't want to be laughed at because a sister runs around." "Maybe they only shoot a sister in the leg, but a tough one might kill a sister." Though this is a possibility, no brother has been known to kill or even to harm a sister, but only rebukes her.

Before a girl can marry, her brother's consent must be obtained. Occasionally a brother might arrange a marriage, giving his sister away. At the time of marriage an older brother may admonish his sister "to stay away from him and be a good wife." A man may make his sister go back to her husband or, if he thinks his sister is being mistreated, may take her away from her husband. In connection with this brother-sister relationship, the behavior of brothers-in-law is important and will be discussed below.

These behavior patterns apply to all classificatory brothers and sisters. This includes, in addition to one's own brothers and sisters and cousins, great-grandparents, great-grandchildren, a wife's brother's wife, a husband's sister's husband, and even such distant relatives as a woman's brother's wife's brother's wife, or a man's sister's husband's sister's husband. These last relatives are the aunts (*bedje*) and uncles (*baye*) of a child. Since a child groups them (father's sister and mother's brother's wife; mother's brother and father's sister's husband) together, they should behave to one another as brothers or as sisters.

Though there seems to be no limit to classificatory relatives, even in one's own generation where limits are said to exist, there is more or less intensity in behavior according to the nearness or farness of the relationship, or sometimes according to circumstances. This can be illustrated by what a Kiowa-Apache said about a great-grandparent to great-grandchild relationship. "Maybe to great-granddaughter I will talk a little bit dirty, but

not to my real, full sister." "Sam [male] kind of jokes with
Charline [great-granddaughter]." However, a little later the
same informant said, "When she get older, I can't tease her,
can't use dirty mouth, but treat her like a sister. Don't tease
little sister even if you are twenty and she is five." Though it is
now almost impossible to obtain examples, intensity of behavior
undoubtedly depends to a large extent on opportunities for contact. Behavior seems to be better defined, such as becoming
more formal in avoidance relationships, the more frequent and
intimate the contact.

The basic behavior patterns of all consanguineous kin have
now been reviewed. This behavior is expressed by the Kiowa-
Apache primarily in terms of intimacy or formality. Intimacy,
however, is not necessarily correlated with love or interest, nor
formality with a lack of interest. If this behavior could be strati-
fied, or arranged on a scale, a series probably like the following
would be obtained. This is arranged from the most intimate to
the most formal behavior, from the point of view of a man, toward his consanguineous kin:

> Brother.................Most intimate
> Friends
> Grandchild
> Grandparent
> Sister's child
> Mother's brother
> Son
> Daughter
> Mother's sister
> Mother
> Father's sister
> Father's brother
> Father
> Sister.....................Most formal

This is an assumed average, which would probably vary with
individual cases. I doubt, however, that it would vary were it
arranged by another ethnographer. Again it must be stressed
that this is in terms of patterns of formalized behavior. A man
would be more intimate with a sister's child than with his own
child; custom allows him an easier, joking manner. But from the
observations I could make, at the present time the young men

were much more interested in and showed more affection for their own children. This, then, is merely a convenient way of presenting a synopsized review of the behavior patterns of consanguineous kin.

Husband-wife.—The relation between husband and wife is taken so much for granted, is so commonplace, and varies so much, that the Kiowa-Apache were hardly able to make any generalizations. "Treat your wife right; don't whip her," or "You should love your husband," is about as articulate as they became.

One couple will usually appear affectionate, intimate, loving; another is generally cold, formal, antagonistic. There are couples who seem to vacillate from one extreme to another, being loving and intimate at one time, fighting and quarreling at another. Finally, there are those who seem to be affectionate when alone but rather formal in public. Treating a spouse with respect, reserve, and very little show of affection seems to be the proper pattern, if there can be said to be any set behavior.

This lack of uniformity may be due to the fact that this is the one relationship which could be changed if it was not satisfactory, for separation was not difficult. One could not, however, change parents, grandchildren, or affinal relatives if a marriage was permanent. In all these other relationships the patterns are more fixed.

Behavior may vary according to the type of marriage. If the families made the arrangements, the bride and groom may be almost strangers or, as in one recent case, actually antagonistic. In this latter instance there was little attempt on the part of the man to be considerate or affectionate. In cases of elopement the attitude may be quite different. Whatever the behavior, there is one definitely fixed custom: A man never uses his wife's name, and she never uses his. "Life would be short if I call my wife by her name," is what the Kiowa-Apache believes. As can be seen from the material already recorded, this indicates a formal relationship. However, there are secondary terms of affection— *cu* and *xangu*. Though there is disagreement over the actual terms, there undoubtedly were such terms used only for a wife (or wives), and not for her sister or for a brother's wife. In the summary of the life-cycle additional attitudes will become apparent, and only a few not mentioned there specifically will be reviewed here.

A wife always followed her husband. It is a common sight today to see a woman walking a few paces behind her man (with the children usually trailing along far behind). Though at present husbands and wives may go places together, it is not unusual for them to go separately. Even the newly married of the younger generation may go their separate ways. Usually at any gathering—church, dance, or picnic—the women stay together as do the men. At the only large feasts which now occur, those following a peyote meeting, the men generally eat together and the women eat in several smaller, family groups, though ordinarily men and women eat together.

Formerly there was an economic division between the sexes: the men were hunters, raiders, fighters; the women did practically everything else, even to moving and erecting the tipi. Although women did all the menial labor, their position in Kiowa-Apache life was comparatively high. They might even possess "worship-bundles," and one woman had the important "buffalo medicine" curing power.

In-laws.—For want of a better word, "in-laws" will be used in the sense of the Kiowa-Apache *tcana*. These relationships are most clearly defined, but as in other types of behavior there are found gradations, shadings, and variations.

The most marked restriction is that between affinal relatives of the opposite sex, and the relationship that one hears most about is between son-in-law and mother-in-law, though the avoidances between a man and his daughter-in-law are equally as strict. A man would never touch his mother-in-law, look at her, talk to her, call her name, or be alone with her in a tipi. The attitude is one of utmost respect and avoidance. In a similar manner a woman avoids her son-in-law. Even some of the younger men will not use their mother-in-law's names. When such names were needed in filling out genealogies, they would get some other person to pronounce the name. The Kiowa-

Apache relationship prohibits any type of joking, which differs from the Kiowa. If these in-laws should accidentally touch each other, which apparently occurred occasionally, they would exchange gifts. The following is one of three such incidents related:

A Kiowa-Apache was once starting out on a chase and was in a great hurry. Either someone on the outside called him or he was in a hurry to get something. He hurried to the tipi door. His mother-in-law was on the outside and was just coming into his tipi. At the tipi flap they met head-on. That was very bad. The young man gave a horse to his mother-in-law, and she gave him one. This exchange was made through the wife and daughter. The incident increased their avoidance of each other. The informant does not know whether the man continued on the hunt or not, but thinks the man did.

Apparently there was nothing that could be done to set aside the avoidance. Upon occasion a woman might have to prepare food for a son-in-law. "She cook for me. Inside she will call out, 'Everything is ready for you.' In a little while she comes out, and then you beat it in and eat it quick and get out."

There is one case of a Kiowa-Apache marrying his mother-in-law (deceased wife's mother's sister). Regarding this marriage, the informant said:

I don't like it; I am ashamed. Sometimes I go in and visit this fellow. He was my brother [cousin]. I asked him, "Why you marry your mother-in-law?" This man can't say nothing. At first they were ashamed; they don't go around the camp. They invite them for breakfast or something, but they don't stay long. Someone said to the woman: "You done something wrong." "I don't know why, but this son-in-law is sure stuck on me. He sure is tough. He catches me, but I don't like it, but he always grabs me and says 'I'm going to marry you.' I sure got scared." That is Coyote's way.

When such a flagrant violation of taboos occurred, which is equivalent to incest, nothing was or apparently could be done about it. The Kiowa-Apache say that "they got used to it." The fact that the woman was not wife's mother but wife's mother's sister probably made little difference; anyone whom a wife called "mother" or "aunt" should be avoided just as the actual mother-in-law. There were undoubtedly differences depending upon circumstances of contact.

A relationship of equal intensity is that of father-in-law and daughter-in-law. One informant said, "Don't talk to them, don't be too close, don't touch them." Nor could they use each other's names. They would never stay in the same room together unless other people were present. If they were in camp alone and the daughter-in-law cooked, the behavior would be similar to that mentioned above for mother-in-law and son-in-law. In these instances, when the women announce that the food is ready, they are not addressing their affinal relatives of the opposite sex directly; they say they are "talking to the air." This is the manner in which Kiowa "in-laws" of the opposite sex speak to one another, but the Kiowa-Apache avoid it as much as possible, though with their general disintegration they are beginning to use this "means of communication."

It is surprising to what degree of intensity these affinal avoidances have persisted. One cold, rainy, winter's day, when I was working with an old man, several women entered the front door. They came through the room and passed between the old man and myself, but one woman hesitated at the door. She started to leave again, but it was cold and disagreeable outside. The old man must have noticed her out of the corner of his eye; he certainly did not look at her. He got up and walked to the far end of the room where he stood facing the corner. The woman, his daughter-in-law, hurried through the room, whereupon the old man resumed his seat and continued with the story.[17]

Several times in taking pictures of family groups, the old people, their children, and grandchildren would all be together, but on no occasion would any of the male or female "in-laws" have their picture taken with them. If a younger man wanted a picture of himself, his wife, and children, then the older people would step out.

The relationship of father-in-law and son-in-law is one of respect. There is a feeling of friendship, although a certain formality exists. A father-in-law and son-in-law never joke or use

[17] This incident is doubly interesting. It indicates (1) a flagrant breach of white man's etiquette, of which the Kiowa-Apache are totally ignorant and because of which they are frequently severely judged by white people, and (2) the persistence of their own good manners, which most white people denounce as silly.

each other's name. Another informant said, "Don't hardly talk to him if lots of fellows around; if alone, have right to talk to him."

During his early training a boy is constantly told to be a good man so that his father-in-law and mother-in-law will like him; to be a good hunter and bring meat to his parents-in-law. If both a man's parents and parents-in-law are in the same camp when he brings home fresh meat, he will give the kill to his father-in-law, who will then invite the boy's parents to eat or will give some of the meat to them. A boy was taught that he should work for his parents-in-law; indeed, the secondary term for father-in-law means "old man whom I follow." (Similarly, the secondary term for mother-in-law is "old woman whom I follow.")

The relationship of a mother-in-law and daughter-in-law is much the same as that of a father-in-law and a son-in-law. They have respect for each other, but do not joke or use each other's names. Should the girl call her mother-in-law's name by accident, no serious breach of etiquette occurs, and no exchange of gifts is necessary. They may, however, give presents to each other at any time, and a girl should help her mother-in-law with the work. They talk to each other, but there is a certain amount of restraint. A woman also uses secondary terms for her parents-in-law meaning "old man [or old woman] whom I follow." She is taught to work for her parents-in-law, but there is not the emphasis put on this behavior as in the case of a man, possibly because residence is usually, though by no means always, matrilocal.

This analysis of parent-in-law and child-in-law behavior indicates that a person has respect for affinal relatives of proximate generations. In addition, there are strict avoidances of those of the opposite sex of adjacent generations. The behavior to affinal relatives of the same generation differs somewhat and will now be examined.

Sibling-in-law–sibling-in-law.—The most important relationship between relatives by marriage in the same generation is

between two brothers-in-law. The following quotations, taken
from various informants, will illustrate this relationship:

> A man gives presents to his brother-in-law; he comes to visit you and maybe
> your best horse, your best clothes, your war bonnet—the best thing you got
> you give to him.

> Can joke nice with him, but no dirty jokes; never use his name, not afraid,
> but don't use it.

> If your sister is married, help out your brother-in-law, for someday he may
> be able to help you. If he is afoot and surrounded by an enemy, save him. He
> will do the same for you if he is worthy and brave. Whatever your sister's hus-
> band has, keep your hands off of it. These may be things he values, and he may
> resent your fooling with them. It may happen that, if he did not like what you
> did, he might take it out on your sister by being mean to her. . . . . If you have
> a mind to give your brother-in-law something, do so. If you and your brother-in-
> law treat each other right, there will come a time when they will say that you
> two have one mind.

Before an arranged marriage can be settled, the bride's brother must be consulted. If he objects, the marriage will not take
place. Sometimes a man arranges a marriage, practically giving
his sister away. At the time of marriage an older brother may
tell his sister to love her husband and be a good wife and not
come to him in case there is trouble. A brother may even force
his sister to stay with her husband. Sometimes it seems that a
man is more concerned with the welfare of his brother-in-law
than with his sister's, but this is probably not usually true. It
should be noted that a brother-in-law is the only one of a wife's
relatives who is called by the "in-law" term *tcana* in ego's generation. This will receive further comment below.

The relationship between a man and his wife's sister or his
brother's wife (and the reciprocal relationship of a woman to
her sister's husband or her husband's brother) is one of intimacy.
These are the only persons in the affinal relationship who are
not called *tcana*. The reciprocal term *zedan* is used, which is very
similar to the term "wife." A male Kiowa-Apache has no sisters-
in-law but a distant "wife"; and a female Kiowa-Apache has no
brother-in-law but a distant "husband." These individuals tease
and joke with one another. Thus a man may say to his wife's

sister that he has seen her husband with another woman, or she may tease him about his wife's having another man. Each stands in the potential relationship of spouse, and they can call each other "wife" or "husband," although the Apaches say this is only in fun. As already noted, they might indulge in sexual relations, although this probably did not often occur. If they got married, which might occur, their behavior probably became a little more formalized—at least in public, where husband and wife were expected to be reserved and respectful toward each other. In one sense the behavior of these relatives was more intimate than between husband and wife, for it was permissible for them to use each other's names freely, whereas husband and wife never use each other's personal names.

A sister-in-law–sister-in-law relationship is not nearly so well defined as that between brothers-in-law, though it seems to have been somewhat similar. These women had respect for one another and did not use one another's names. They could joke but only in a mild way. They might exchange gifts but probably did not do so very frequently. There was not nearly the feeling of indebtedness as in the behavior of brothers-in-law. The spouses of brother-in-law or sister-in-law were called "siblings" (i.e., wife's sister's husband is "brother"; wife's brother's wife is "sister," etc.) and were treated as such.

The behavior between parents of spouses is not very well defined among the Kiowa-Apache. At the time of the marriage feast presents are exchanged between the two families. An informant says: "At this feast some would shake hands, some would embrace each other. All these people would be drawn together by the marriage, and they would want to be friendly." Occasionally one family may invite the other over for a meal. If they live at some distance, they may visit each other and are hospitably entertained. During the infrequent contact there is mutual respect and courtesy shown.

The behavior toward affinal kin has now been reviewed. As among consanguineous kin, if it were possible to stratify these relationship patterns, a series like the following might be obtained, from the point of view of a male ego:

Wife's sister..............Most intimate
Brother's wife
Grandchild's spouse
Wife's grandparents
Wife
Sister's husband or wife's brother
Son-in-law
Father-in-law
Wife's brother's wife ("sister")
Daughter-in-law
Mother-in-law..............Most formal

Again this is according to the formal patterns and may vary with different individuals. It merely gives a suggestion as to customary relationships. The position of a wife is peculiar; the outward, formal pattern is one of reserve, with little show of affection or intimacy. In private the behavior between man and wife should be one of great affection and intimacy.

LIFE-CYCLE

The behavior between various pairs of relatives has been outlined. These interrelations can now be approached through a sketch of the life-cycle. This, of course, will be a summary of conditions which are unusual; a Kiowa-Apache normally receives but one name, he joins a group but once, he normally has but one wedding ceremony. These are events that are well remembered by the old men. The daily routine is more difficult to reconstruct, for it was too common, too usual, to be remembered. However, the summer camps, when the Kiowa-Apache now get together for a dance, are probably little different from the annual summer camp about sixty years ago. The change is in things material. The tents are of canvas instead of buffalo hides; the people wear store clothes and shoes instead of buckskins; the beef is obtained from local farmers instead of being hunted; cooking is sometimes done on old iron stoves instead of over open fires; there are no longer herds of horses roaming about and needing care. The social life, however—the visiting, the stories, the gossip, the games, some of the dances—is practically unchanged.

Not all people were normally engaged in the same activities. Unusual events occurred, changing the tempo or completely stopping the routine affairs at some tipis. Births, marriages, deaths, reverberated through the group but affected some families more than others. Meetings of the dancing societies or soldier bands, or certain religious rites concerned all the camp, but different families participated in varying degrees, depending upon the intimacy of relationship to the performing group. Other events, such as wars, the Scalp Dance, or the Sun Dance, affected the whole community almost to the same extent. These varying aspects of Kiowa-Apache life will now be examined.

Birth.—The Kiowa-Apache had apparently no mystical notions about conception. Either a man and woman were fertile and had children, or they did not, which apparently meant that the man was infertile. There seem to have been no charms, prayers, or ceremonies that produced children.[18]. There was only one thing to do: "Live long time [with her husband] and can't make nothing, only way is to get another man." With the cessation of the menstrual flow the woman or her grandfather kept count of the passage of moons, and it was known about when to expect the child. Many taboos surrounded the pregnant woman: she could not eat meat off the leg of beef, "for that meat clings to the bone, and the woman would have a hard time giving birth to the child"; nor could she eat fat, "because that baby has white stuff all over it and makes the birth dry." In addition to a number of other foods that were prohibited, there were certain actions which were harmful: "can't sit with back to sun because afterbirth sticks, they say it burns to you if you do that; don't put no kind of child on your lap because it will cause the

[18] Menstruation, pregnancy, and birth were closely associated with the phases of the moon: "New moon, that's time woman have her blood, or maybe with full moon. Woman says, 'I got monthly: next new moon I didn't have no monthly; she keeps track; maybe nine or ten moons that baby come. It comes with the moon. Great thing when woman see new moon for they say, 'I come with moon.'" Another frequent expression was that "children are made when the new moon comes up." The moon was thought of as female, and in the moon you could see a woman with a newborn baby on a travois. A man or a woman may have prayed to the moon: "I sure need baby," but unless "she sneak around with another man and he fool with her, that's how she get it."

baby inside to sit up so it will be hard to come"; and others. Some foods, such as soup, were helpful; certain actions such as urinating downstream were beneficial.

At delivery the mother was assisted by older women—one of whom was in charge—who were known for their experience and helpfulness. They may or may not have been relatives, but the girl's mother, mother-in-law, and sisters were present at least. Usually female relatives of spouses were brought together at the birth of a child. There were one or two old women who had special medicines for childbirth, "a herb which they gave to the women as a kind of tea in hot water." When the mother was having an unusually difficult labor, a medicine man might be called in to perform a ceremony which would aid in delivery, but before the child was born he would rush from the tipi.

For four days after birth the mother kept to the tipi, and only gradually, as she felt like it, did she assume normal duties.

The umbilical cord was kept and placed in a small beaded pouch; the placenta was buried. Sometimes abortion was practiced, particularly by married women who had a small suckling child. There is some confusion in beliefs regarding the behavior toward twins, but at least in some manner they were set apart. Usually they were thought to have more power.

The paternal grandmother usually made the cradle; if she did not, then the maternal grandmother or some other relative made it. Sometimes the mother got a buckskin belt from her grandmother which she wore to keep her figure in shape.

A few days after the birth a feast was given for the old women who had assisted, and the relatives on both sides of the family were invited. At this dinner four presents were given to the old woman in charge and to each of her assistants, the character of the gifts depending upon the wealth of the family. Either at this time or at another feast given later, each of the old women would pick up the child and pray for its welfare, stressing the wish for long life and good health.

Naming.—Young children as a rule had no names, "because they might die and then the name would have to be avoided." There was no set age or time when names were given. The parents or grandparents would decide that the child ought to have a name. A feast was prepared for "all the people," and some old man who had achieved a reputation for giving good names was called upon to name the child. The old man selected a name himself or gave a family name. In the presence of all the people he prayed for the child who stood before him, and then, raising the child up four times, he announced the name by which he was to be known. The old man who did this was given a horse or other presents. This was one of the very few occasions when an individual was singled out and given social recognition. Names were occasionally changed for various reasons, such as sickness, but usually this was done privately, or more or less quietly, and apparently was not of great social importance. Even though people possessed these formal names, they might not be called by them but by some nickname. The formal names belonged to families and could not be used by another kin group. However, permission might be obtained and compensation made, and the name would then come into the possession of another group. The name of a deceased person was avoided; also words in the language which were identical. After a time, possibly a few years, the name might again be used, being given to some younger member of the family.

Rabbit Society.—Every child belonged to the "Rabbits," or *Kasowe.* Every child was called a "Rabbit," and even today, when the older men become disgruntled with the behavior of some of the younger men, they say, "They are just Rabbits, they don't know anything." The Rabbits were one of the four dancing groups, or societies, of the Kiowa-Apache—the last to cease functioning and consequently the one about which most is known. Since it included every child, boy or girl, and influenced them during the formative years until they became young men and women and were either initiated into another group or because of age and size took a less active part, it was one of the most important social forces in Kiowa-Apache life.

Here only a summary can be given of the procedure. There was no formal initiation into the dance. Parents brought new-born babes to derive the benefits of this "worship," and as soon as a child was able, he participated actively in the dance. There was no set time for the meetings, though they probably occurred more frequently in the summer when the tribe was likely to be together and the necessary "bundle-owner" was available. The meetings occurred as the result of a pledge made by parents when their child was sick or for his future welfare. On the morning of the dance the family prepared a large dinner, and the bundle-owner announced the dance. This was an invitation to the entire camp, but to the youngsters in particular. All the children gathered in the tipi of the people who were giving the ceremony. The sides of the tipi were rolled up, and the parents and visitors sat around outside watching. The bundle-owner sat on the west, and the tipi was filled with children. The child who had been ill, or who was being honored, was seated just before, but with his back to, the bundle-owner. When all the children had assembled, the bundle-owner placed his hand on each of the honored child's shoulders and began to pray:

This boy is sick, he is all right now; so he could step on this earth all right. The grass grows; so he be with it and don't get sick no more. This wild fruit grows; that is the way you going to grow up. These wild fruit gets ripe; may you grow up and be ripe.

The old man prayed a long time, endlessly repeating. After the prayer for the health and long life of the one child in particular, and the Rabbits in general, the dance began. Any two middle-aged men acted as assistants to the bundle-owner, singing and drumming. One of the older boys was selected to be the "bull." The bull had a whip and knife, and if any child did not dance, he not only threatened to whip him but could do so; and at the end of the dance, if a child had not participated, the bull cut his clothing or his hair. "They can't get mad because all the Rabbits jump on them and tear their clothes." The dance could be stopped by a boy's going up to one of the drums and hitting it: "Wait now, I'm going to tell you a story. Way down there I kill rabbit [he hits the drum]; over there I kill a bird [he hits the drum]; over there I pick up a turtle [drum]. There is my witness." He indicates some friend who had been with him. This type of boastful behavior, so characteristic of Kiowa-

Apache, was encouraged. In dancing, the children imitated rabbits, hopping up and down with bent knees and with hands slightly cupped and held up beside their heads in imitation of rabbit ears. (Sometimes they wore rabbit ears attached to their clothing.) Throughout the dancing and feasting there was much horseplay and occasionally obscenity. The children made fun of the old man and poked him with sticks. At times he pretended to be asleep; they hit him, and he jumped up, starting to dance. Whenever dancing the old man always faced west, his back to the group. He wore only a loin cloth, which he pulled aside as he sang the Rabbit song: "When rabbit runs to creek, you see his white buttocks." The big girls and many of the visitors on the outside were embarrassed and ran away, "but the little ones they look up and watch . . . . and laugh." When the dance was finished around noon, a large dish with food was brought in and a prayer said, "so that what they eat will make them live long and be healthy." The food was passed from child to child in a definitely prescribed manner; the first time each took four spoonfuls, but the next time they ate as much as they could. In fact, there was a contest to see which side could eat the most. The old man watched, and when the dishes had been taken out, he announced the winners. The winning side had the privilege of mauling the other side. There was a general scramble until they had all run out of the tipi, so ending the ceremony.

In this group the child had contact with all other Kiowa-Apache children—practically all the people with whom he would be most intimately associated for the rest of his life. A close relationship was thus established with those of his age, including those slightly older and younger in the tribe. As the children were encouraged by their elders to express themselves during the meetings of the Rabbits, everyone could form judgments of the ability and character of the younger members of the tribe. A child was able to form opinions of his associates—opinions which might be helpful in later years. The child also learned social discipline in having to respect the established social forms (the procedure of the dance) and in having to obey the "bull" who was his temporary leader. More important, he learned to respect and obey the old leader, the permanent leader, who owned the most important medicine bundle in the tribe. Though the bundle was never formally introduced in the Rabbit Dance and was in no manner directly connected with the dance, the owner, who was the most respected of the Kiowa-Apache and of whom no one could say evil, regardless of their private opinion, was thus intimately associated with all the children as their permanent leader. The behavior of the old man when he danced undoubtedly affirmed this intimate relationship. He was one of them; his behavior was typical of acts common to the children who had not yet learned Kiowa-Apache modesty, just as small children among white men behave similarly among themselves and without shame. Furthermore, while probably not unusual among children, this behavior was antisocial when committed by an adult and particularly in public. Its being sanctioned in this dance emphasized the unusualness and importance of the meeting. The sacredness of the occasion was stressed by this obscenity. Undoubtedly the Rabbit Dance, establishing such close relationships through a common rite with the same age group and binding them all so intimately with the leader of the most sacred of Kiowa-Apache worships, was one of the most important, if not the most important, of integrating forces for the tribe as a whole.

Until the children were in their late teens, they might continue to participate in the Rabbit Dance. There was no set time or rite which severed their connection with the dance, or announced their entrance into manhood or womanhood, but gradually they began to participate in adult affairs.

Adolescence and training.—No social recognition was taken of menstruation, either the first time or at any other time. The first time a girl menstruated her mother and sisters knew of it, and usually her father, but rarely anyone else. For four days a girl was supposed to stay close to the tipi because she was "ashamed." A woman had more freedom and went about her usual duties but refrained as much as possible from visiting other tipis. Only the medicine men had strict taboos, for they were afraid of blood. No menstruating woman, either relative or nonrelative, could enter a bundle tipi, nor could a bundle-owner eat food prepared by a menstruating woman. Also, at the time of new moon and full moon[19] the medicine men avoided the path to the creek, which had undoubtedly been trodden by menstruating women. Ordinarily a man did not have intercourse with his wife during the usual four days of her period, but he shared the same bed, ate the food she prepared, and continued in every way the regular daily activities and contacts. Presumably the husband was the only one who knew when a woman menstruated.

There was no formal training of children. They learned by watching, by the stories which were told around the fires in the evening, or through experience; and thus they gradually and unconsciously absorbed the culture which was all about them. Listening to the old men, the child obtained a complete review of ideal Kiowa-Apache life. When children were old enough to understand, a father talked to them, instructing them in the "good road, the right way to live."

In addition to the occasion on which a child received a name, or when the Rabbit Dance was being given in his honor, or when he told of his accomplishments during the dance, there was usually another time that a child was singled out for social recognition. This was at the time of a boy's first kill, or when a girl tanned her first hide, made her first pair of moccasins, or accomplished some other woman's task for the first time. Then the grandfather or the mother's brother, if he were wealthy, gave a horse to some poor old man or woman who went through the camp crying out the accomplishments of the young person, usually displaying the kill or the handiwork. A feast may also have been given at that time if the parents loved their child and could afford the display.

Children were continually encouraged to express themselves and participate in tribal affairs. The older male relatives of a boy would take him along on short hunting trips, teaching him to shoot, to stalk, to track. Precocious children seem to have been encouraged, and participation in adult life depended upon

[19] The usual time women menstruate, according to Kiowa-Apache belief.

ability. Usually in his late teens a boy would begin going on raiding and war parties—activities which seem to have concerned him primarily during his twentieth to his thirtieth years. This was a period of intense physical activity and, to an extent, great freedom and license. Around thirty most men were married, and the outstanding ones were asked to join one of the societies.

Marriage.—Bachelors and old maids are practically nonexistent in Kiowa-Apache culture.[20] A wife was almost a necessity. Not only did she care for the tipi, cook, tan hides, make clothes and moccasins, but she bore children. A man without children was a "nobody," whereas a man with a good wife and children amounted to something. Consequently, as noted above, a boy was told to behave so that people would talk about him and let him marry their daughter. Similarly, all girls expected to be married and were told to conduct themselves so that they would be attractive and get a good man. A husbandless woman had little or no place in this culture. The husband-wife relationship was of the utmost importance.

Marriage occurred comparatively late, but sexual experience undoubtedly began early. Theoretically the parents, brothers, and other kin were supposed to watch a girl, some older female relative chaperoning her after she reached maturity. But a boy and a girl interested in each other could find occasions to meet. Frequently the boy would arrange with the girl to slip into her tipi at night. One informant laughingly recalled one such experience. As he was crawling into the tipi, the girl's mother caught him and recognized him. The girl's father invited him in to "marry" the girl, but he ran away. However, he did not intend having his fun spoiled, so he crept back to the tipi door to wait until he was certain the parents were asleep. In waiting he fell asleep, and there they found him next morning, when he again took to his heels.

[20] I can find only one instance in the past of an old maid, and she was a hunchback. There are now two young women who may remain unmarried. One, who is said to be around thirty, is rather fat and exceedingly shy, which behavior is in marked contrast to the usual attitude. The other, twenty years old, has a dislocated hip. Both girls are becoming conspicuous since they have never been "out," and neither has had a sweetheart.

Though this type of courting was probably general, it was not recognized. Supposedly the young men and women remained chaste until marriage,[21] which was an arrangement between families. The bride and groom may not even have known each other previously. The families were interested in the union, for it brought two groups of people into a series of relationships which usually were mutually beneficial. The immediate kin were particularly concerned and had much to say when a spouse was chosen. Aside from the desire to be united with an important family, or to capable young people, the only restriction was a prohibition against marriage within the immediate kin group. This not only prohibited marriages with blood-kin but with close classificatory relations, such as the children of two "friends" who called and considered themselves "brothers" and "sisters."

There was actually no outer restriction, but the Kiowa-Apache were usually endogamous. Even though they were politically and ceremonially associated with the Kiowa, marriage with that tribe was not frequent. On rare occasions marriage occurred with other tribes: Arapaho, Cheyenne, Comanche, or others. When this happened, either the Kiowa-Apache went to live with the other tribe and soon became absorbed by that group, or the spouse from these tribes was absorbed by the Apaches. More often, women were captured from other tribes and taken as wives. The preferred marriage, however, was with a distantly related Kiowa-Apache with good family connections.

The inner boundary of marriage prohibition was the family group; the outer limit was the tribe. But both boundaries might be transgressed without seriously disturbing tribal customs, or without any punishment being inflicted. Even such incestuous unions as those between a man and his father's sister or mother-in-law, though frowned upon, occurred. The couple was shamed, however, and avoided social contacts until the people became accustomed to their marriage. Becoming accustomed to the embarrassing relationship meant that the relatives accepted it by rearranging their kinship ties. Where the conflict was such

[21] Possibly the missionary attitude and the ideal white point of view have influenced informants, so that they are usually inclined to ignore these illicit relationships when talking about marriage.

that adjustments could not be made, avoidance relations were set up. Such an incestuous marriage was a great hardship on the contracting couple, but if they were sufficiently fond of each other, they could eventually live down the social censure. Marriages of this type were exceedingly rare and in the instances mentioned above, of marriage to father's sister and mother-in-law, did not last long. Such marriages would never be arranged by families but were "elopements."

There were at least two types of marriage. The most approved form, but not necessarily the most common, at least until recently, was a marriage which had been arranged by families, the parents choosing spouses for their children. The initiative could be taken by either family, though usually the boy's parents made the advances. A man might express a choice to his parents, who then approached the girl's parents for him.[22] As a girl's older brother had much authority over her, his consent was usually necessary before a marriage was arranged. It was said that, if the brother were on a raid, they might have to wait several months to obtain his consent. If the proposal were accepted, the groom's relatives gathered as many presents as they could and, forming a group, brought them to the girl's parents. The acceptance of these gifts—and usually a feast given for the whole camp in honor of the couple—validated the marriage. Shortly thereafter the girl's relatives, who had accepted the gifts, gathered together an equal or even greater number of presents for the groom's relatives, at which exchange another feast was usually held. The bride and groom had no share in this exchange, which seems to have been a means of bringing the two families into closer relationship. Though the Kiowa-Apache had no fixed rule in the exchange of gifts, the bride's relatives usually gave dishes and other household equipment, and the groom's people gave horses, saddles, weapons, clothing. The girl's parents usually gave a tipi and furnishings to the young couple. Other relatives might give them additional equipment to begin housekeeping, but this had nothing to do with the formal exchange between respective relatives of the newly married couple.

[22] This is sometimes considered as another form of marriage.

Another type of marriage was that of elopement. The boy and the girl would run away, perhaps to some near-by relative. When this occurred, the girl's parents had the right to go to the boy's parents and take whatever they wished, even to the tipi they were living in. Later gifts must be exchanged.

Temporary unions undoubtedly occurred, but the Kiowa-Apache does not recognize them as marriages. In other words, retrospectively at least, a marriage was a lasting arrangement, and for that reason divorce is said to have occurred but seldom. At present innumerable trial marriages occur, lasting from a few days to as much as a year or longer. Only when it appears that a union will be lasting is it reported to the agency. In recording genealogies these temporary unions are generally not remembered, just as none of the old informants remembered how many children had been born to them, as so many had died in infancy. From the materials gathered, every Kiowa-Apache now living has been married more than once; some remarriages having occurred after the death of a spouse. Many Kiowa-Apache indulge in extra-marital intercourse, but so long as it is only a temporary relationship, it has little or no effect upon the marriage. There is little prudery, sentiment, or secrecy connected with sex.

There was no fixed rule regarding residence; the couple lived with, or had their tipi near, one family and then the other. However, matrilocal residence seems to have been most common, but among a roving people place of residence and change of residence may not be very important. Marriage may not have necessitated a change from one community to another for either spouse but may have meant merely a change of dwelling.

Polygyny was practiced but was not very common. Three wives seem to have been the most that any man had at one time. In all polygynous unions noted in the genealogies, the wives were sisters. The formalities observed at the first marriage were not repeated when additional sisters were married. The first wife is said to be the most important. Parents-in-law who had a good son-in-law might give another (usually younger) daughter to the man. Or the young woman might suggest that she also marry her sister's husband because she thought him desirable or because she loved her sister and wanted to live with her.

Divorce was simple when there were no children and the marriage had not lasted long. It meant merely a cessation of relations between the man and the woman, each going back to his or her own relatives. A brother might attempt to force his sister to return if she had taken the initiative, but only if he thought she was at fault. Separation is said to have been very infrequent, but this undoubtedly refers to marriages that had lasted for some years. When it occurred in these cases, it was probably because one of the couple was interested in a third party. In adultery a woman's only recourse was to leave an unfaithful husband, but a man had the right to inflict punishment upon his wife, such as cutting off her hair or the tip of her nose. Her relatives would not interfere. Furthermore, the husband could destroy part or all of the property of a wife's lover. Such actions are said to have frequently resulted in a feud between the men in which each swore to kill the other. It is probable, however, that, aside from the destruction of some of the adulterer's property (a horse or two), few or none of the sanguinary acts were carried out. The woman and her lover could seek sanctuary in a bundle-owner's tipi, where they could not be harmed. The bundle-owner was then asked by the adulterer's relatives, or even the woman's relatives, to take a pipe to the angry husband who could not refuse to smoke. Once having smoked, the husband could not harbor resentment; he was forced to be peaceful, if not friendly, and would probably divorce his wife. Usually when the husband was asked to smoke, he was given presents by the adulterer's relatives.

There is one instance of a woman who sought sanctuary in a bundle-owner's tipi, fleeing from an angered husband who threatened to cut off her nose. As her relatives refused to intercede, the woman remained in the tipi day after day until the bundle-owner of his own accord took a pipe to her husband, in order to be rid of the woman. In case of divorce the younger children would stay with the mother; the older children usually lived with whom they pleased, sometimes staying with the father or his relatives, or at other times with the mother or her relatives.

As noted above, after marriages were once established and the children were growing up, separation seldom occurred. One's position in the social structure had then become relatively fixed, and separation required new adjustments, not only to the family of procreation, but to the families of orientation. Changes of this type were resisted, and social force in the form of public opinion and behavior was so potent that separations were rare.

Even in the present disintegrated conditions, divorce between old couples is frowned upon, though it is very common and relatively unnoticed among the young people. One relatively old couple had been married about twenty-three years and there were six living children when the woman left with another man. Feeling ran very high, but some degree of harmony was restored when the lover gave the deserted husband eighty acres of land. However, after five years the Kiowa-Apache, though ostensibly friendly to the couple, still resent the new marriage.

The disruption of the family was so disastrous that provision might be said to have been made to maintain its integrity even in the face of death. If a man died, his brother should take care of the widow and, if possible, marry her. Similarly, if a woman died, her sister would usually care for the children, and it was considered a desirable arrangement if the widower could marry his deceased wife's sister. In these marriages (forms of the levirate and sororate) very few adjustments had to be made. There was no change whatever in relationships, no new relatives, no change in kinship terminology. The only adjustment which might have been made was between the newly married man and woman, who had been in a secondary husband-wife relationship previously and now became actual husband and wife. However, sexual relations may already have made them intimate, so that often no adjustments were needed. There might have been a change in residence, but that was very insignificant in the life of a nomadic people. In the event that levirate and sororate marriages were not possible, the adjustments were even more complex than ordinary marriages, for the family of the deceased spouse was interested. (This will be discussed under death and mourning customs.)

From this discussion of marriage it should be evident that there were no clans among the Kiowa-Apache nor any clearly defined descent group. Inheritance, succession, and descent follow no absolute rules but do follow certain tendencies which will become clearer as this analysis continues. About the time that a man was married, particularly if he promised to be outstanding in tribal affairs, he was taken into a dancing group or society. There were two such adult groups among the Kiowa-Apache; the *Manatidie* and the *Klintidie*.

Manatidie.—Although it was an honor to belong to the *Manatidie*, one of the two adult male societies or dancing groups, men tried to avoid becoming members. The duties were irksome, the dances were long and arduous, and one had to be brave, which was "dangerous."[23] When it was known that a meeting was going to be held and that new members might be taken in, the young men fled from the camp, but sooner or later the desirable men were caught. Two of the leaders, the *bacaye*, slipped up on a prospective member and dragged him from whatever he was doing, after which he could not refuse to join the group. The relatives of a new member gave a feast to the society and brought presents for the leaders. No women belonged to the group, though the wives of members took an active interest in

[23] Bravery is always stressed; it is one of the greatest virtues of Kiowa-Apache society as well as of other Plains tribes, but one gets the feeling, when talking to the old men, that the pattern requiring the leaders to stand their ground even though they be killed was "expecting too much." This may, however, be a comparatively recent attitude since after the introduction of firearms a man's physical powers and boldness were of little avail. An even later change may be reflected by one informant, a generation younger, who said that it was a great honor to belong to one of the adult societies and that a man might give a horse to get in. This may be his conception of the initiation fees, or it may reflect the attitude of a period when warfare had been suppressed by the government and the societies had ceased to function except in an honorary capacity. Apparently this honorary recognition was of little importance, for as soon as the tribe seems to have been peacefully settled on a reservation, these societies no longer met. None of the old men living belonged to the *Klintidie*, and only the three oldest men (although some younger men claim to belong) knew anything about the *Manatidie*.

the meetings and always went with their husbands, sitting back of them but outside the tipi. They even joined in the singing and dancing, though never mingling with the men. There were between twenty and fifty male members, usually an even number since the members were paired, each having a special partner who was supposed to be his best "friend." These partners sat together, fought together, danced together, painted themselves alike, helped each other in every way; their children were as brother and sister.

There were several officials: the four staff-bearers or chiefs, the two *bacaye*, and the "bull." The four chiefs sat on the west side with their staffs planted in the ground before them. They seem to have been the directors, choosing new members, sending the *bacaye* on errands, and setting the date for a dance. They had to be especially brave in battle, seeking the most dangerous positions, and if they planted their spears, standing by them. They held this leadership for life. The "bull" was the chief of the dance; everyone had to obey him unless he delegated his powers to someone else. His official badge was a whip to which was attached the whole skin of a red fox. The *bacaye* performed what might be considered menial labor, but this was not classed as such in these meetings.[24] They caught the new members, spied on the wives of members during all-night meetings, fixed the fire, and brought water and tobacco. During some of the dances they led the staff-bearers, of whom they "were not afraid."

Meetings were held at any time of the year, usually before raiding or war parties set out. Usually the four chiefs decided upon the time and place, which was kept a secret as long as possible. Sometimes as the result of a vow, or to honor a relative, someone gave a feast. When a member died, permission

[24] The position of "fire chief" in the present peyote meetings is one of honor, yet it is hardly an enviable office. He has to keep the fire burning all night and the ashes neatly placed in the form of a bird's wings; he brings a glowing stick to light the cigarette of any member who smokes; he removes the cigarette butts and keeps the tipi clean; he runs errands for the leader—all of this in addition to the regular singing and drumming, which in itself is no mean task, and, of course, he partakes of the peyote.

had to be obtained from his closest male relative, to whom the whole organization brought gifts, before the next dance was held. There seems to have been only one set time for a meeting—an annual spring dance at which time the four staffs were ceremonially re-wrapped with buck sinew and covered with otterskin. The group then danced through the camp, shooting blunted arrows into the air, and killing, and later eating, any dog that crossed their path. Other meetings were held in a tipi, with the sides rolled up, or in an especially constructed windbreak, where everyone watched the dancing. There was nothing secret about the group; they had many songs and four dance steps, and usually used eight drums. All members had to participate. In the tipi or dance circle, they either sat on the south side, or went by way of the south side to their places on the north side. In leaving, those on the north side went out first, followed by those on the south side, who went around by way of the north side. In dancing they also moved in a clockwise direction, except for the "bull" who took up stations in a counter-clockwise movement at the east, north, west, and south, from which points he supervised the dancing. Members dressed themselves very carefully for meetings. Special designs were painted on exposed portions of the body, and the hair was worn loose except for the scalp lock, to which was attached a long strip of buckskin trailing on the ground. The headdress consisted of turkey "whiskers," eagle feathers, and a deer tail dyed red. They wore short skirts of spotted fawnskin. When they were painted and dressed for the meetings, they were privileged to have sexual intercourse with any woman they met who did not avoid them. She could not object.

Special mention should be made of the four ceremonial staffs, lances, or spears. Two were crook-shaped and two Y-shaped. At regular intervals were placed eagle, road-runner, or goose feathers, taken from birds which were caught without being wounded. As mentioned above, the staffs were ceremonially re-wrapped in buck sinew and otter-skin at each spring dance. They were used in fighting and when once pointed at the enemy had to be used effectively. They could not touch the ground, and if one were accidentally dropped, it had to be picked up by some warrior who could recite a brave deed as he returned it to the owner. However, they could be laid down if they were placed on a row of buffalo chips or the points stuck through a chip into the ground. They were never destroyed but passed on to a successor, who was preferably, but not necessarily, a brother, son, or grandson of the owner. Usually, therefore, these four chieftainships belonged to certain families, being inherited in the male line. When considered in the broad classificatory sense, it was probably not difficult to find a brave and highly thought-of male relative.

Certain duties fell to this society, most important of which were those generally known as "policing." When the camp was moving, the *Manatidie* kept order, allowing no one to break ranks to hunt. During the communal hunts of buffalo, antelope, or deer, they enforced the tribal rules. If anyone disobeyed, they could whip him, kill his horse, or destroy his property. No one could object, for if he did, he was punished even more. If he took his punishment good-naturedly, then the society might later give a dance in his honor or give him presents. The *Manatidie* also seem to have acted as a charitable organization, to whom poor people could come for aid. They never raided, fought, or hunted as a group. Sometimes they had contests among themselves, or sometimes as individuals challenged members of the *Klintidie*, in which case each society cheered for its own members. But there were no organized contests nor any antagonism between these two groups, nor any privileged license with the wives of the other group as is sometimes found on the Plains.

Klintidie.—The *Klintidie* is the other men's society. Only the oldest and bravest men belonged to this group, which was small, usually having ten to sixteen members. As in the *Manatidie*, men did not wish to belong, though it was an honor to do so, and ran away from camp at the time of meetings to avoid, if possible, being asked to join. As the group was composed of older men, they were all married, and their wives, though they did not actually belong to the society, went with their husbands to meetings. The members were paired, and if they did not get along they would change, for partners should be as "blood-brothers."

Apparently, there were a number of individuals, possibly four, who were considered as leaders. One informant said they were called the "dogs." There was another official, the "owl-man," who will be discussed below. The meetings occurred at any time and lasted from one to four days. The time of the dance was announced several days in advance, and all members had to attend or they were publicly ridiculed by fellow-members, who cried out, "You are going to marry your mother-in-law." Usually the dance was held in a tipi.

The leaders wore bands which passed over the left shoulder and under the right arm, trailing on the ground. Two were painted red, and two black. A man could let his partner wear his band. Each man wore a headdress of split owl feathers, and sometimes a bunch of owl feathers was tied to the shoulder. Each had a deer-hoof rattle and an eagle-bone whistle which was blown during the dancing and "when they were mad." A member was never supposed to get angry, even if another man was flirting with his wife, but if his indignation was overcoming him, he obtained relief by blowing on his bone whistle.

The outstanding characteristic of this society was its "contrary" nature. The members talked "backward," as it is usually termed. A command to retreat meant "charge"; to stop meant "to continue." Thus, when they were dancing outside and someone said to them, "Don't dance in that water," they were obliged to go into the creek with full regalia—an event which occurred at one of the last dances held. If during a battle the Kiowa-Apache were losing and everyone was crying out to run, the *Klintidie* had to charge, unless someone noticed their predicament and commanded them "to charge." Only then could they retreat.

In battle they were supposed to be very brave. They would ride up to the thickest of the fight and jump off their pony, slapping it to make it run away. Those wearing the trailing bands would "plant" themselves at a dangerous spot by sticking an arrow through the end of the band. Only another person could release them by pulling out the arrow and telling them to "stay there."

This group is thought of as being intimately bound up with "worship." Smoking, primarily a sacred ritual, and praying were a part of each meeting. In case of general illness or epidemics the dance was held and prayers made. One informant says: "They usually prayed to the medicine bundles which had been given them by their fathers. They prayed to everything: trees, grasses, water, anything that our fathers made. They worshipped with this dance."

The most significant manifestation of the relation of the *Klintidie* to religion is its connection with the owl. Of all animals, including the buffalo, the owl is the most mysterious, the most sacred. "Owl," "ghost," and "spirit" are indicated by the same term. It has already been noted that owl feathers were used as a headdress and were sometimes worn on the shoulder. If an owl hooted, or someone imitated the hooting of an owl the morning after an all-night dance, the *Klintidie* would have to continue dancing for another day. In battle, if someone hooted like an owl, they would have to stand their ground. One of the leaders, probably their most outstanding man, was called the "owl-man" or the "ghost-man." Sometimes during large gatherings he would completely disrobe; he might even have sexual intercourse with a woman publicly. He was privileged to cohabit with any woman who did not keep away from him. But if a woman could not avoid him, she could protect herself by saying, "Do it to me," and then he could not touch her. After a public exhibition of this sort, he would carefully dress himself and then pray for the health and happiness of all. During the meetings of the *Klintidie* this man might arise, remove his loin cloth, pull up his blanket, and back up to each member, exposing his private parts. Women were present. When he took his seat, "he shook out his breech cloth which looked like an owl. When he did that, it meant that they were going to dance four days and nights." This is perhaps another instance of the sacred's being set apart and made awesome by shocking or antisocial conduct.

These several dancing societies are not age-grade associations. It is true that the children belonged to the Rabbits, the middle-aged men to the *Manatidie*, and the old men to the *Klintidie*, but they are not a series of grades. A man could be taken into the last without ever having belonged to the second; or a man could be claimed by the *Manatide* from the *Klintidie*. Though all Kiowa-Apache were Rabbits, some could go through life without ever being asked to join one of the adult groups. However, an important person could hardly escape them.

Izuwe.—Among the women there was but one society, the *Izuwe*, practically unknown today by even the oldest men and women, largely because it was a secret organization. About twenty of the oldest women belonged, and one old man.

The meetings were held in a tipi put up by some man who had been successful on a war party and who, before he left, had asked the old women to pray for his success. When he returned and had erected the tipi, he filled a pipe and held it to the mouth of each of these old women, who smoked in turn and (by implication) prayed for him again. The dances were usually held when a raiding party returned. The tipi was divided by a partition put up near the door, making a small anteroom, so that anyone trying to look through the door could not see what was going on in the meeting. The old man, who was the only male member, sat on the west side, singing and "drumming." The "drumming" was done by rubbing a dried buffalo hide with "something," which made a "washboard sound, zuh, zuh, zuh," from which the organization got its name. The old man covered himself with a blanket, and no one saw how he made the sounds. When he began, the women danced but did not join him in singing. On each side of their heads the women wore feathers which resembled horns, and their faces were painted red with black markings. When a woman died, a female relative (daughter, niece, or sister) was chosen to succeed her. So far as is now known, the novice did not have to give presents or a feast for the society.

Most of the information regarding this group was obtained from one old man whose mother had been a member. When a boy, he and another youngster were peeping in the meeting when a woman saw them and said, "Coyotes, come in." The women sat still. They didn't say anything. Taho (my informant) and his friend went in and sat down. One woman then said, "Our enemy has come in."[25] The old man prayed for them and said, "It is good you came in here; you will live to be old men." The old man "drummed," and the women danced. The boys watched. The women began dancing up to the boys, pecking them and cawing like crows. They did this many times. Finally, they came up and grabbed the boys and threw them down. They stripped their clothes off and sat all over them. The women pecked them all over. It hurt a great deal. What the women did made them (the boys) smell very bad. Finally the boys got mad, fought, got away, and ran home.

This group had nothing to do with the Sun Dance, but during the Scalp Dance they would bite the scalp, wrist, ear, or whatever else the men had brought home to show for their triumphs. It is said that the group had some connection with religion. "People asked the *Izuwe* to pray for the sick"; "this group worshipped nature." Unfortunately, very little is known about them now, so that the many questions which come to mind cannot be answered.

Death, mourning, and remarriage.—Sickness and death were the result of a number of causes. One of the most important was "witching," a power possessed by a few individuals who were greatly feared by the Kiowa-Apache. Natural causes were also recognized. "The sickness kills you, but all kinds of sickness was not 'witching.' You might [also] get killed in war or drowned." Infants and old people "just died," and there was little or no attempt to explain such deaths; it was the death of persons in their prime which concerned them, and the concept of "power" seems to have been associated with all such deaths. A young warrior killed in battle had undoubtedly met an enemy, not necessarily superior physically, but with greater power.

When a person was sick, the medicine man or doctor was

[25] My interpreter, who seldom made any attempt to explain what the old men said, stopped to point out that the woman meant that all men were their enemies.

called in by the family. Usually the charges for curing were very high, and a number of relatives had to contribute. A family that could get together a good deal of wealth could hire a well-known doctor.[26] When a person was very ill and felt he was going to die, he called his relatives to him and gave away some of his ponies or possibly some "medicine" (the right to use some herb) or something else by which he was to be remembered. These bequests were made to any close relative, but a brother was usually singled out to be given ponies. The tails of these horses were bobbed and the manes cut, and they were given exceptionally good care. They were never ridden except into battle where it was a great honor to the deceased owner if they were killed. When a man returned from battle without his deceased brother's pony, the relatives again wailed and lamented. Sometimes they did this when they saw the horse around the camp, for it reminded them of their relative.

The infant mortality rate was extremely high, and the death of a baby was scarcely noticed. A child was mourned by its parents and possibly a few very close relatives. As a person became older, more relatives and friends were concerned. When an adult died, the nearest relatives tore their clothes (sometimes going almost naked and exposing their private parts), gashed their arms and legs until the blood covered them, and sometimes cut off a little finger or shaved the head. Usually women were more demonstrative than men. The extent to which a person expressed his grief seemed to depend upon the closeness of the relationship.

Burial occurred as soon after death as possible—before sundown if a person died during the day, the next day if he died during the night. The body was washed with yucca suds, dressed in the best clothes the individual had, and wrapped in buffalo robes. This was done by any relative, but usually by females. If an outsider helped, which was not likely, she was given a present. Usually dead bodies were avoided as much as possible, being greatly feared. The corpse was removed through the side of the tipi, never through the door, placed on a travois, and taken

[26] Curing rites will be discussed in a later publication.

to some isolated place where a shallow grave had been prepared. Generally only the close relatives followed the travois, but if a stranger attended he was given a present. The corpse was placed in the grave, or in a crevice in the rocks, and stones and cactus put on top to keep the wolves and coyotes from destroying it. Usually one or more of the deceased's ponies were killed at the grave by being pierced in the chest. "Blood would come out, and when the horse was about to die it would wobble, and the widow would grab it around the neck and fall with it. Blood would get all over her." The place of burial was unimportant, with one exception—bodies were never buried near a stream for fear they would be washed out. The grave was seldom, if ever, revisited; in fact, it was usually avoided.

Some of the personal belongings of the deceased might be placed in the grave, such as his shield and weapons, but most of the property, such as the tipi, tipi poles, clothing, utensils, etc., were burned. A medicine man's paraphernalia was destroyed, but never the worship bundles. These descended to the closest male relative, a person whom the owner had presumably trained and designated as the heir. In the absence of a close male relative, a woman might be keeper, as in the case of two of the four bundles at present, though it is doubtful if a woman could perform the rites associated with the bundle. While the shield was buried with the owner, the right to make a similar shield seems to have been inherited. The heraldic tipis were not destroyed but also passed to a brother, son, or other male relative. Certain curing powers, those associated with the use of herbs primarily, were usually passed on, sometimes long before death, to relatives, either male or female. Probably the right to use these herbs was formerly purchased. A man's position in a dancing society was not inherited, but a woman's place in the *Izuwe* was passed on to a female relative.

There were no definite purification rites nor a set period of mourning. Those who had handled the body might wash themselves in the creek, but not if they had cuts. Fat was put upon the cuts, and such persons did not wash until the cuts were healed. When returning from the grave they might get sage and rub it over themselves. Usually cedar or a root called "medicine fat" was put on the tipi fire during the first night. "At night-time they use some kind of root. They break it up and put it in the fire, so nothing bothers them. It is just like you could see the dead. They put this in the fire. You could think of him in your mind." However, cedar and medicine fat were put into the fire at other times, without reference to death. These might be construed as purification rites, or the survivals of such rites, or even as their rudiments, but the old men do not remember anything fixed or compulsory about such conduct.

The day following a death the whole camp moved. The immediate relatives of the deceased lived somewhat apart, probably half a mile, from the others and remained in this semi-isolation for several months. Frequently members of the family would go to some elevated spot and mourn for the departed. "Sometimes they would go sit way up on the hill and feel bad. Somebody might come and talk good to them; make them feel right and bring them back to the group. Maybe if a man or woman died in the spring, they would feel bad all summer and live apart from the main village." There was no rite signalizing the close of a period of mourning, unless the unobtrusive return of the family to the general camp can be construed as such.

There is one important exception to this last statement. To the elementary family, death had serious consequences, disrupting the most important segment of Kiowa-Apache social structure. The spouse was most affected, and his or her period of intense mourning was terminated by relatives-in-law. At a husband's death a woman shaved her head, gashed her arms and legs, and possibly cut off a little finger. She wore very old clothes, frequently only an old cape made from the smoke-blackened flaps of a tipi. In this miserable state she lamented the death of her husband until his relatives "took pity on her." If she had been a good wife and was liked by her husband's people, after about ten days her husband's sisters would call her to their tipi and dress her in new clothes. Similarly, a widower cut his hair and tore his clothes, going about almost naked until his deceased wife's brothers "took pity on him and gave him good clothes." A spouse continued mourning—remaining un-married—for about ten moons, but probably did not remain single this long if levirate or sororate marriages could be arranged. If the remarriage was with a person of another family, it should not occur for at least a year. Remarriage shortly after a spouse's death was an insult to the relatives-in-law; it was an indication that the deceased had not been loved and the proper respect was not being shown. If such a premature remarriage occurred, the deceased wife's sisters would whip the widower and might also whip his bride without interference. Similarly, the brothers would take revenge if the widow remarried too soon. They might even cut off her nose and destroy her new husband's property.

If the woman doesn't say anything to her deceased husband's folks, and they hear about her new man and don't take anything, then they know those people [the deceased's relatives] sure are mad. Some of the relatives of the other man—his brother, father, cousin—will take a pipe to the dead man's relatives, usually his brother's, and give them the pipe. They have to take the pipe; they can't refuse. They smoke and everything is dropped.

The proper conduct was for the spouse to wait a sufficient period, depending frequently upon circumstances, and then obtain the permission of the relatives-in-law to a remarriage. If such behavior were followed, the bonds between a person and the deceased spouse's relatives were strengthened. The new husband and his relatives would give presents to the woman's deceased husband's relatives, creating a bond between her new relatives-in-law and her "former" relatives-in-law. They cannot actually be called "former" relatives-in-law, for neither death nor divorce severed the tie of relationship. A father-in-law continued to call his deceased son's wife "daughter-in-law," and at her marriage he called her new husband "son." Thus the new husband took the place of the deceased husband, acquiring the dead man's relatives. For this reason the widow's relatives-in-law were concerned with her remarriage, and similarly a deceased woman's family was concerned in the widower's remarriage. These remarriages brought together three different groups of people: one's own relatives, "former" relatives-in-law, and new relatives-in-law.

When a member of one of the dancing societies died, that group had to obtain permission from the deceased's relatives before the next dance was held. When asking for permission (which was never denied), the society brought presents to the relatives, and there was general weeping and wailing for the dead. Should the society overlook this courtesy, the deceased's father, brother, or uncle would go to the place of meeting, destroy the drum and possibly other property, and break up the dance. Before the society dared have another meeting, it would have to gather a great number of presents and take them to the angered relative. After the smoking and mourning for the departed and the presentation of gifts, the relatives would be pacified and give permission for the society to meet.

"Something" survived after death, and there was a land of the dead, though these notions are very hazy. "When a man dies, put the body in the ground, but there is something here in the air, because you might hear some kind of noise. You can hear them, but you can't see them. One man he says he knows it; like radio."

"That which survived" was seldom named. The Kiowa-Apache say, "maybe it is *isinsin*"—the word for "spirit" or "owl." Those who talk to the dead talk to the owl; when the dead return, it is the owl returning; when an owl hoots, it is a dead person talking. There are certain men to whom the owl has given power, and these men can understand the hoot of an owl and talk to the dead (a procedure witnessed and described by four informants).

Long ago the land of the dead was visited by a Kiowa-Apache who brought back and gave to the people one of their worship bundles. This place is generally located under the ground, some times specifically located under the waters of "Medicine Lake," a mythical body of water said to be located in the Black Hills region of Dakota. No living Kiowa-Apache has seen this lake, but several of the old men would like to look for it. There is another, but very hazy, belief that "maybe they go up to the sky." This notion may be associated with the "Blue-White Man," whose garments are changeable as the sky, a person so highly revered that his name is seldom mentioned and little is known about him now. He is the donor of the most sacred of the Kiowa-Apache worship bundles. The Kiowa-Apache say he is like the white man's Jesus. The land of the dead is much like this earth, except that there is never a scarcity of food. The man who went under or into "Medicine Water" saw there his dead friends and relatives, and as he sat in a tipi, he heard the ordinary sounds of camp life—the murmuring gossip of women, the scraping of hides, and the barking of dogs.

The Kiowa-Apache are too much concerned with living to be very much interested in the dead. They avoid the subject as much as possible, and their notions, when expressed, are rather hazy and sometimes contradictory. They seem to want to forget the dead. The deceased's name is avoided, at least by the family, and words in the language which are identical with the name are avoided for a time. After the death of a parent, a child will avoid the usual term for mother or father when addressing his classificatory parents and will use the secondary terms. Should a child accidentally forget and call his deceased father's brother *ace* ("father"), instead of the secondary term *kaan*, the family will be reminded of the dead and will mourn again. When a chief dies, all will mourn and avoid his name and similar words. That, say the Kiowa-Apache, is why they have so many synonyms and why their language changes.

CONCLUSION

The outline of Kiowa-Apache culture from the point of view of the kinship system has been completed. Some aspects of their life—such as visions, curing, myth, and ritual have barely been touched upon, but there should be sufficient material for an understanding of the social organization. It must first of all be remembered that the Kiowa-Apache are, and apparently always have been, a small tribe surrounded by peoples speaking unrelated languages. This linguistic isolation was not absolute, for the Plains tribes could communicate with one another when necessary by means of signs. All the Plains peoples were nomadic, without definitely fixed territories, and since most of them were hostile to one another, the fear of attack was ever present. For mutual protection the Kiowa-Apache were drawn together. They were, of course, allied with the Kiowa, but as has already been pointed out, there was no deep feeling of intimacy. Though inferiority of numbers and linguistic isolation aided in binding the Kiowa-Apache together, these were probably not the most important factors integrating this tribe. The structure of the society, the inner factors, the social organization, were more important.

The various segments which comprise any society make up its social structure. These different aspects of the culture are bound together, sometimes intimately, sometimes loosely. Usually they are permanent, coherent groups controlling the life of a people. Among the Kiowa-Apache these segments existed but, with the exception of the dancing societies, were not well defined. There were, for instance, no definitely limited kin groups such as clans which are found so frequently among simpler peoples, particularly those with a classificatory system of terminology. Yet the really important factor integrating these people was kinship. As already noted, every Kiowa-Apache was related to almost every other. By means of the terminology all these people were classified, and with each kin group were associated definite behavior patterns.

Actually, behavior and terminology cannot be considered separately, for a type of conduct frequently takes its cue from the terminology. In the third ascending and descending generations, where these relatives are termed "older" and "younger" siblings, respectively, the informants, none of whom had a mature relative this far removed, did not know how they would act. One old man who had two small great-granddaughters "supposed" that, if they grew up and he lived long enough, he would treat them like "sisters," for he said, "I call them sisters." If they in turn had children, "I ought to call them 'niece' and 'nephew' and behave toward them as I would toward a sister's children. They are sister's children." It seems apparent that the terminology is a convenient way of labeling relatives and associating with each category a general type of behavior. Such a scheme greatly facilitates social contacts, for as soon as one knows how he is related to an individual, he knows how to behave toward him, and since the Kiowa-Apache are almost all related, everyone knew how to act toward everyone else. The whole tribe was bound into one large kinship unit, and however distant or even fictitious these ties may have been, they were, nevertheless, very real to the Kiowa-Apache.

The most important segment or group of the Kiowa-Apache organization was the extended domestic family, the *kustcae*. Several tipis made up a *kustcae*; ideally each tipi housed an elementary family consisting of parents and children. Usually, however, there were several more distant relatives (a grandparent, a mother's or father's sibling) living with the elementary family for varying periods. Children were as much at home in the tipi of their parents' siblings as in the tipi of their own parents. The term "family," then, in the fixed sense in which we usually think of it, cannot be applied to the Kiowa-Apache. The family was a larger unit, very closely knit but, within the bounds of this group, rather variable and fluid. This unit of their social structure, the *kustcae*, or an "extended domestic family," consisted of a group of relatives who lived in several tipis which were located close together, but who did not as a rule eat together. The members of this group were bound by indissoluble bonds of kinship, based in part on matrilocal residence. The wider boundaries of these groups were indistinct and merged into one another. If each Kiowa-Apache family could be represented by one dominant color in the social fabric, there would be centers or splotches of a dominating hue which, though more prominent in one place, could be discerned throughout the fabric. A tiny strand of red or yellow would be found in a dominating splotch of blue. This likening of the social organization to a woven cloth is an old comparison, but there seems to be no better way to visualize the intricate interrelations of Kiowa-Apache family groups, for the core of each kin group is an easily recognized entity, yet merges imperceptibly with others to the very limits of the tribe.

The Kiowa-Apache always camped in relatively large groups

for mutual protection against raiding enemies. Such a camp, made up of several *kustcae*, was called a *gonka*. It was said not to have been a fixed grouping, since its size and importance depended, in part at least, upon the prestige of its leader or leaders. After coming together in the late spring for the annual Sun Dance with the Kiowa, the Apache split up into various groups which might align themselves differently each year. The same people might not remain together even for a winter. Thus, theoretically, there was nothing fixed about the *gonka*, but actually several families probably camped together year after year, clustering about the same leader so that, aside from minor fluctuations, the *gonka* probably remained much the same.

The only clearly defined segments among the Kiowa-Apache were the dancing societies or associations of which there were four: *Kasowe*, *Manatidie*, *Klintidie*, and *Izuwe*. The *Kasowe*, as we have seen, was a children's group to which every boy and girl belonged and was considered by the Kiowa-Apache as a "worship." This rite bound the children close together, gave them a feeling of unity and importance, taught them social discipline by making them conform to the rules of the dance and in co-operating with other children, and intimately allied them with the owner of the most important worship bundle. The *Kasowe* is one of the most important integrating factors in Kiowa-Apache life, not only giving unity to an age-group, but giving the children a feeling of intimacy with the most important ritual of the tribe and thereby establishing a continuity in time. The two adult male dancing societies, the *Manatidie* and *Klintidie*, were of somewhat different nature. They are typical of the Plains soldier bands, having "police" functions in regulating the buffalo hunt and change of camp. Another important function was in encouraging bravery during battle, since certain rules forced members to stand their ground, even in the face of death. The nature and function of the women's society, the *Izuwe*, can no longer be ascertained since it was a secret organization and none of the women living belonged to it. It is now thought to have been a worship group, probably very much like the Kiowa "Old Women" society, to which young men prayed for success before going on an expedition. Perhaps it was a means of encouraging men to do brave deeds and of giving them a feeling of confidence because of the ritual sanction. In these societies all families were represented and bound into a brotherhood or sisterhood; thus, these groups cut across family lines and unified the tribe as a whole.

Other groups among the Kiowa-Apache were not so well defined. The raiding groups were well organized and distinct so long as a raid lasted, but split up as soon as the expedition returned. They can, therefore, be considered only as semipermanent organizations.

More important groupings were those pertaining to the three (now four) worship bundles. These bundles were important factors in establishing a unity in time. These sacred objects very definitely belonged to families and were usually inherited in the male line. The bundles were respected by all Kiowa-Apache, but certain taboos might be observed only by the owner's immediate family. One of these bundles was considered more important and was deeply venerated by all members of the tribe, thus tending toward integrating the whole group. One of the important functions of the bundle-owner was to act as an arbitrator in settling disputes. He would take the peace pipe to an avenging person or persons, and they could neither refuse to smoke nor harbor resentment after they had smoked. All disagreements could be settled in this manner, and it is inconceivable to the Kiowa-Apache that anyone would or could violate a bundle-owner's decision. Sometimes the injured party was given gifts at the time of smoking, but even if this were not done, the disagreement was considered satisfactorily settled. In this manner any disruption from within which threatened the social security could be expeditiously terminated. Thus, the worship bundles integrated the *kustcae* and extended, as the larger kin group did, to the limits of the tribe.

An additional factor which probably aided in integrating the *kustcae* was the occasional ownership of a heraldic tipi. Only one such tipi has been used recently (fifty years ago), though formerly there probably were more. These tipis were painted in a definite manner, sometimes with a design such as a panther, a bear, the rainbow, etc., according to the visionary experience. These tipis belonged to families and were never destroyed at the owner's death, but were inherited in the male line. There was something sacred about them, probably because they were bound up with visions which were the result of supernatural experiences. One such tipi, painted a solid yellow, was associated with the sun; another tipi with four yellow lines about an inch wide encircling it was associated with one of the worship bundles. So far as can be determined now, these tipis were primarily family emblems and undoubtedly tended toward a greater unity and stability of the kin group.

The shields were similar integrating emblems and likewise were the result of a vision. Usually there was a definite number of shields (seven) of each type, and though the owners did not necessarily belong to a certain family, they usually did. This small group of men was intimately bound together through a common ritual. These groups were not continuous in time, probably lasting little longer than the life of the originator, but they tended toward a horizontal integration.

Since families are of so much importance and are integrated by a number of factors, it might be supposed that there would be a definite number, or that certain outstanding families would tend to become stabilized. Here are all the apparently necessary elements for the development of clans, but there was no such segmental organization.

To sum up, Kiowa-Apache integration was of a simple type; there were few groupings, and these tended toward fusion rather than toward apposition. The kinship system was the basis of the social structure and intimately bound together the extended domestic family, with the kin ties extending to the tribal limits. Political and religious interests followed family lines primarily, but again were extended to include the whole tribe. Heraldic tipis were symbols of a family, as were the shield groups, but these latter could include more than immediate kin. Economically, family groups were independent, yet to secure a large number of buffalo (when many hides might be needed for making tipis, etc.), tribal co-operation was desirable. Thus, factors which bound family groups together extended to tribal limits. Tribal cohesion was furthered by the dancing societies which included all prominent men or women, by the Apache's functioning as a band in the annual Kiowa camp circle, by linguistic isolation which distinguished the tribe and set it apart from other Plains peoples, and by inferiority of numbers which practically necessitated mutual agreement and cohesion for protection and consequent survival.

With so many social forces tending toward tribal unity, it is not surprising that the Kiowa-Apache were a closely integrated people. This undoubtedly accounts for the maintenance of their identity through many generations during which time they were surrounded and literally engulfed by unrelated and mostly hostile tribes which far outnumbered them. I think that possibly the unity felt by the Kiowa-Apache as a whole was expressed by the owner, the priest, of one of the worship bundles. He took care of his religion and prayed primarily to it, but he also prayed to the other Kiowa-Apache "worships," for he said, "We are not like white man; we don't kick each other."

AN OUTLINE OF CHIRICAHUA APACHE
SOCIAL ORGANIZATION

MORRIS E. OPLER

AN OUTLINE OF CHIRICAHUA APACHE
SOCIAL ORGANIZATION[1]

MORRIS E. OPLER

THE SOCIAL DIVISIONS

Introductory remarks.—This paper is not intended to do more than define and analyze the place of the several social units in the total social organization of the natives about whom it is written. Since the organization of these people exemplifies a structure based primarily on kinship, much of the paper is necessarily concerned with tracing the range of the genealogical relations recognized as including kin, enumerating the terms which express such relationships, and commenting upon the rights and duties which the nomenclature implies.

One can think of such terms as points of concentration of socially conditioned behavior. Consequently, the intelligent thing to do, if the analyzation of behavior is our task, is to go to these verbal points of crystallization and concentration of social behavior and to test their significance through genealogy and observation under every possible condition; in short, to use them to the fullest measure as mediums through which the native conceptions and social groupings may be revealed. Throughout this paper, then, kinship terminology will be regarded as a means and a technique with which to investigate the facts of social relations which lie behind the terms themselves.

I do not mean to hold up the approach pursued here as a

[1] The field work which provided the material for this study was carried on during the years 1931–33 under the auspices of the Laboratory of Anthropology of Santa Fé, the Southwest Society, the University of Chicago, the Social Science Research Council, the National Research Council, and Columbia University. Thanks are due to these organizations and to Dr. Ruth Benedict, Dr. Harry Hoijer, Dr. Fay-Cooper Cole, Dr. Elsie Clews Parsons, Professor A. R. Radcliffe-Brown, Dr. Edward Sapir, Dr. Robert Redfield, Dr. Sol Tax, Dr. Jules Henry, Dr. John Gillin, Miss Regina Flannery, Edith Nash, and Paul Frank—individuals to whom I am indebted for materials or helpful criticisms.

standard of methodology for the study of social organization everywhere. Naturally an analysis of kinship terminology will be most illuminating when utilized in respect to a people whose basic social unit is organized on the principle of kinship. Undoubtedly the approach is so well suited to the group under discussion because its fundamental social and economic unit is the domestic family. Where the kinship principle is less paramount, where location, vocation, or status exercises more control over social grouping, where a centralized government is invested with many of the functions performed by the family among the Chiricahua, even a complete understanding of the system of relationship may fail to give a satisfactory picture of the total social structure. Useful as considerations of kinship bonds have been in explaining Chiricahua social organization, it will appear from the following pages that much in Chiricahua Apache social life has to be accounted for by recourse to other grounds.

Since the aim of this paper is to provide students with a clear statement of the principles underlying Chiricahua Apache social organization, only the formalized and channelized is considered. The unusual personality or event, so important for an understanding of social psychology or culture change, is left untouched.

The limitations of the task at hand, moreover, root it to one time and place. My data are drawn from the conditions of life which obtained among the Chiricahua Apache immediately before white contact necessitated adjustments and change. Since the Chiricahua were one of the last of the Indian tribes to feel the advance of the white man, it has been possible to gather my accounts from old Indians who actually lived under aboriginal conditions. Information from younger men is admitted only when it clearly bears the hallmark of an earlier tradition. Vast changes have occurred since the youth of my informants, and this paper does not, therefore, present Chiricahua Apache society as it functions today.

The tribe and its location.—The Chiricahua Apache are a Southern Athabaskan–speaking people who formerly ranged through southwestern New Mexico, southeastern Arizona, and the northern parts of the Mexican states of Sonora and Chihuahua. The name of the tribe is derived from the Chiricahua Mountains of southeastern Arizona and was given because one of the three bands of the tribe so often took refuge in this range. As a matter of fact, the name Chiricahua was at first applied only to this one band, but after hostilities with the white man broke out, territorial distinctions were abandoned for the purpose of military alliance, and the term came to be applied to all the hostiles.

Because they have been so many times moved from their traditional territory by the military, the identity and disparateness of the Chiricahua Apache have been somewhat obscured, and they are often erroneously classified. In 1886, after a prolonged conflict between Geronimo, one of the minor leaders of the Southern Chiricahua, and government forces, the entire tribe was removed from Arizona, where it was then stationed. Because of the public interest which attended this event, the tribe is not infrequently called Geronimo Apache. For some twenty-seven years these people were held as prisoners of war, first in Florida, then in Alabama, and finally at Fort Sill, Oklahoma. During their long sojourn in Oklahoma, the tribe became popularly known as the Fort Sill Apache, and reference to them by this name is very common. Since the United States government several times sought to concentrate them on the San Carlos Apache Reservation of Arizona, there is a tendency to confuse them, or to combine them, with the Western Apache (the present inhabitants of the San Carlos and Fort Apache Indian reservations of Arizona). The membership of the tribe is now divided. In 1913 they were released as prisoners of war and given the choice of taking up residence on the Mescalero Indian Reservation of New Mexico or of taking allotments of land in Oklahoma. Less than one hundred chose to stay in Oklahoma. The descendants of this group are now living in the vicinity of Apache, Oklahoma. A larger group removed to New Mexico and now shares the Mescalero Indian Reservation of New Mexico with the Mescalero Apache.

Before the Indian Wars, however, the Chiricahua Apache comprised a separate and distinct tribe. Linguistically and cul-

turally they were closer to the Mescalero than to any other
Apache group. Yet their tongue is a separate dialect of Southern
Athabaskan, and in dress and many phases of material culture
they differed conspicuously from the Mescalero. Before white
contact the Chiricahua and Mescalero Apache were hostile to
each other and raided each other's encampments on occasion.
The differentiation between the Chiricahua Apache and their
Athabaskan–speaking neighbors immediately to the north and
west was even more marked. The Western Apache were agri-
culturists, were organized into clans, and possessed an elaborate
mythology of emergence from an underworld, while the Chiricahua Apache shared none of these characteristics. Linguistically
the Chiricahua are much further removed from the Western
Apache than they are from the Mescalero Apache.

The territory of the Chiricahua Apache tribe is extensive and
is not easy to define accurately. The Rio Grande acted as the
eastern boundary. Occasional journeys and raids brought them
as far north as the pueblo outposts of Laguna, Acoma, and Zuni,
but ordinarily they did not stray much farther north than the
present site of Quemado, New Mexico. The western limits of
Chiricahua country can be roughly indicated, from north to
south, by the present towns of Spur Lake, Luna, Reserve, and
Glenwood in New Mexico, and by Duncan, Wilcox, Johnson,
Benson, Elgin, and Parker Canyon in Arizona. To the south an
undetermined area in northern Mexico was also under Chiricahua control.

Quite as important as any of the easily discernible differences
of territory, language, and customs mentioned above, and no
doubt accountable in terms of their aggregate, is the feeling of
the Chiricahua Apache himself toward his tribe. Within the
Chiricahua tribe as it has been described here, there is a very
real unity. The Chiricahua, though they are divided into three
well-defined bands, consider themselves one people. Hostilities
between two of these bands are unthinkable. And along with this
inner unity goes the practice of opposing one's own tribe to all
others.

The band.—The complete dependence of these Apache on wild
plant and animal life made it impossible for all members of a

tribe to live together. The precarious food supply would soon have been depleted in any restricted area under such conditions. Instead we note a tendency for the tribe to spread out over a large area and to be segmented into social units of graded sizes, all held together by loose bonds and merging one into the other until the tribe is reached.

The unit next in size to the tribe is the band. The Chiricahua band may be thought of as a division of the tribe based on location. Its scattered condition and the vast extent of land it covered left the tribe a particularly useless unit for emergency action. It was the office of the band to step into the breach at such a time. The Chiricahua Apache band really consists of the members of the tribe who live in an area circumscribed enough to permit unity of action at critical moments for defense or offense. The band is, therefore, the largest unit of warfare, though we shall see that a still smaller unit normally acts in matters of raid and aggression. As we should expect in view of its primary function, the band has recognized leaders. These are the most capable and distinguished leaders of smaller units, which, in turn, compose the band.

The boundaries of band territory are not so definite as are the tribal limits nor are they inviolate. Members of one band visit freely within the range of another without causing dissension.

At times of elaborate feasts or important ceremonies the close nexus between band and tribe is plainly revealed. At such times the strict boundaries of the band dissolve. Such an occasion would be a girl's puberty rite and the feast which follows. If a very wealthy man, whose daughter has come of age, is expected to spend much property in celebration of the event, the news travels beyond the band, and people from other bands, if they feel that the occasion warrants the trouble, will attend and be welcomed and entertained.

The ability of the bands to live together in peace is another indication that the band is nothing more than an expedient territorial partition of the tribe. The difficulties encountered when different Apache tribes were placed on one reservation were never felt when bands of this one tribe were brought together.

This territorial unit is of utmost practical importance to the

Apache. It governs most of his immediate contacts. If, when I was attempting to secure the band affiliations of a number of people, the allocation of one were in doubt, the informant would think for a while and then say with conviction, "He must be a *tcíhénè* [a band name]. I always see him with the *tcíhénè*."

The Chiricahua bands were three in number. The most eastern and northern band, whose territories joined those of the Mescalero at the Rio Grande, controlled almost all the Chiricahua territory east of the Rio Grande in New Mexico and has been given a number of names throughout the literature. Those occurring most frequently are Warm Springs or Ojo Caliente Apache, Coppermine Apache, Mimbreños Apache, and Mogollones Apache. The Chiricahua name for this band is *tcíhénè*, which means "red-paint people." In historic times this band has been led by Mangus Colorado, Victorio, Nana, and Loco. From historical records and the accounts of informants the camp sites of the members of this band can be traced to the Datil Range, the vicinity of Rito, Hot Springs, Cuchillo, and the Black, the Mimbres, the Mogollon, the Pinos Altos, Victoria, and Florida mountain ranges. For convenience we might call the *tcíhénè* the Eastern Chiricahua band.

To the south and west of the "red-paint people," ranging through the portion of southwestern New Mexico west of the Continental Divide and through southeastern Arizona, a second Chiricahua band, the *t'cókánénè*, was to be found. The name does not yield to linguistic analysis. This is the band to which the term Chiricahua was first applied. It was this band, often called in the literature "Cochise" Apache after their leader, Cochise, which held Apache Pass, and with which the government had a great deal of trouble during the Indian Wars. The most famous of the strongholds of this band, which might be named the Central Chiricahua band, were the Dragoon Mountains, the Chiricahua Mountains, and the Dos Cabezos Mountains.

The third and southernmost band of the Chiricahua, known in the Chiricahua tongue as *né'nà"í*, or "enemy people," stayed almost entirely in what is now Old Mexico. During the last half of the nineteenth century difficulties with the Mexican soldiery drove them north, where they speedily came into conflict with settlers and United States government forces. After that they were harried from either side of the border until Geronimo's surrender in 1886. Geronimo himself was born a member of this band. Mention of this band in the literature is made under the names of Southern Chiricahua and Pinery Apache. Reference in the literature may be found to their leader, Hǫ˙ whose name has been variously written as Who, Whoa, or Juh. The Sierra Madre and the Hatchet Mountains were familiar landmarks of this band.

From the point of view of the Chiricahua Apache the band was more important than the tribe. This is reflected in nomenclature. There is no true native tribal name for the Chiricahua, but, as we have seen, the bands are named. Most likely this derives from the fact that in aboriginal times, owing to the scattered condition of the tribe and the large area which it claimed, an Apache's meaningful contacts were of necessity limited to members of his band. There were few occasions when tribal unity could be affirmed by a gathering of all tribesmen.

Local division of the band.—The band has been defined as a "social segment the boundaries of which are roughly determined by the possibility of uniting the people within them for emergency action." This definition suggests that the band is by no means the ultimate division of the tribe. In a semiarid country it is not surprising to find that a population dependent on wild plant and animal life is spread thinly over a considerable area by means of graduated social segments.

Within the territory recognized by a band as its own there were favorite places—places easy to defend and difficult to storm; spots where the winter's food supply could be safely cached; comfortable and secluded refuges, often surrounded by mountains and inaccessible country, to which retreat was always possible in time of trouble. The Apache had a complete knowledge of all these sheltered and favorably located fastnesses in his territory. And though the life was nomadic in character, though the men entered upon hunts and raids which took them

away for days, and the women traveled long distances to gather
and prepare the seeds and plants needed for the household use,
the Apache did require a base.

And so we find that the band is subdivided into groups, each
consisting of a number of families. Each group uses a favorably
situated spot, such as has been described above, as a convenient
base. From this place parties are constantly setting out to foray
for food. A whole family often departs on an economic errand.
A body of men may set out from here on a raid for booty or on
the warpath mission of revenge. But as long as their families
are associated with this group, they are powerfully linked to it
and will all drift back.

This subdivision of the band is what I have chosen to call the
Apache "local group." It is the Apache unit, above all others,
which depends on a definite locality. Moreover, the group takes
its name from that of the locality. For instance, the members of
a subdivision of the eastern band of the Chiricahua tribe, who,
when not engaged in other activities, camped around a certain
low-peaked mountain, are called by a term which means literally
"people of the low-peaked mountain." I know of no case where
the local group does not take its name from some geographical
feature of its chosen site.

There is no precise Chiricahua term for local group. The nearest equivalent would be $gò·tàh$. This word is used in two different
senses. The first usage is a rather vague and loose one. Any
group of camps, any settlement of considerable size, is termed
$gò·tàh$. The word is now used to designate the cities and towns
of the white man. It is in this rather general sense that an
Apache would refer to the local group as $gò·tàh$. The same term,
$gò·tàh$, is also used with a different and more exact meaning to
connote the extended domestic family, soon to be discussed.
Then it is always accompanied by the name of the leader of that
social unit.

The local group is composed of families whose members are
related by affinity, or who, though not related, have elected to
live together because of the chance to make a powerful economic
alliance. We have, then, a group of people united by the inter-

marriage of members or by community of interest. Most of the time they camp within easy reach of the same natural landmark. They learn quickly of all ceremonial or social events which occur within the group. Their residence in one general locality makes co-operation for raid or warpath possible.

As might be supposed, therefore, the local division of the band is normally the body present at ceremonies or invited to the social dances. At much advertised and costly events of this nature, individuals from the band or tribe may be present also, but the only group ordinarily represented in force is the local division.

The members of this group, who live together, dance together, and feast together, also co-operate in battle and raid. No one family possesses sufficient fighting men to carry on warfare and raid alone. But one can always recruit from near-by camps enough volunteers whose family larders are also low. Consequently, the local division is found to be the normal raiding and fighting unit. We shall see that, in keeping with this aspect of its services, the local division has charge of the training of the young man for the warpath. The warlike functions of the local division suggest the necessity for leadership. The local division does have its recognized leader whose powers and influence will be discussed presently. It has already been mentioned that the most wealthy and powerful leader of the local groups heads the entire band, should occasion for concerted action arise.

The band is a stable unit. Its territory is extensive enough so that a man, even though he changes residence several times within his lifetime, will still remain within its boundaries. The local group does not share this stability. The local group, as we have seen, depends upon residence in a given place. The members of some of its constituent families are united by marriage, it is true, but this is hardly a serious bond, for there is no social or practical necessity for these families to camp together, and, while the tendency is present, the practice is not always followed.

The families that constitute the local group are there, then, because they consider the particular spot a favorable one for defense or from which to reach a food supply. Or they may wish to associate themselves with the leader of this group who has been extremely successful in raiding, in the hopes that they may share in the good fortune. A family is under no obligations to remain with a local group if it cares to go elsewhere. The leader of the local group has no control over the families beyond his personal influence and prestige.

Under these conditions there is a continual redistribution of family groups within local groups and local groups within a band. For some reason the food supply of the neighborhood may diminish, and the local group melts away. Or an epidemic of deaths may convince most of the families that they would be better off elsewhere. Likewise the death of a leader may bring changes in the group membership. Several instances have been recorded where factional disputes have resulted in the withdrawal of the aggrieved parties to other sections.

The family.—The relation of the individual Apache to the social units thus far treated has been markedly casual. He recognizes his tribesman as one of "the people," as one who speaks, dresses, and thinks much as he does. If a tribesman traveling through his territory needs assistance or shelter, these are freely granted. There is nothing more compelling in one's relation to a member of the same tribe.

The Chiricahua thinks of a member of the same band as a tribesman whose fortunes are a little nearer his own. If the local group of a member of the same band is not too far distant, he may know of him and his family, he may have seen this man or the leader of his band at a social dance. If a common enemy invades the district, both he and the other man may share the duty of repulsing the foe.

It is the same with members of his local group who are not relatives. Since he lives so close to them, he is bound to mingle with them at feasts, ceremonies, and social dances. Since they are his neighbors, they are likely to become his playmates in childhood and his associates in later life. When the co-operation of many men is needed for the enterprise of raiding, it is reasonable that he goes out with his neighbors to seek horses or other plunder. All these social segments have their justification and function. No one of them, however, controls and dictates a body of reciprocal rights, duties, and obligations of an individual to his fellows.

But there is a social unit to which a Chiricahua's attachments are anything but casual. To each of its members he stands in a definite relationship—a relationship which defines his obligations to them and his requirements of them. This group is immediately and intensely interested in him. It supervises his early training. It tests his manhood. It governs whom he may or may not marry. It passes on his marriage choice, if it does not, indeed, choose for him in respect to a mate. If he falls into disgrace, he disgraces this unit. If he is killed, this unit is bound to avenge his death. When he dies, members of the unit risk the defilement of approaching a corpse and accompany his body to a suitable cave or rocky crevice for disposal. This unit, as the steady elimination of other possibilities has suggested, is the extended domestic family with matrilocal residence.[2]

Relationship among the Chiricahua Apache is bilateral, i.e., is reckoned both on the father's and on the mother's side. But residence is matrilocal. The domestic family with matrilocal residence can therefore be defined as the parents, the unmarried sons, the daughters, and the husbands and children of the married daughters. In like manner granddaughters and unmarried grandsons remain as members of the family, while married grandsons live with their wives' families.

The Chiricahua call the extended domestic family gò·tàh, "encampment." The word refers to the fact that all the members of a family camp together, that their wickiups form one cluster. In this respect the family differs from the local group. In the words of an informant:

But within the local group there would be other divisions. All would not live at one place. Some would camp on one side of the mountain, some would camp on the other. Others might camp at any favorable spot near water. These

[2] This name was suggested by Professor A. R. Radcliffe-Brown. The term "lineage" was used until Professor Radcliffe-Brown kindly pointed out that "lineage" imples descent from an ancestor or ancestress whose identity is always kept in mind. The Chiricahua extended domestic family does not possess this quality.

smaller groups or camps are decided along relationship lines. That is, all the relatives and those who marry into a certain family live together.

Each encampment or family is called by the name of its accepted head, usually the oldest man there. To quote again from the native's account: "They [the members of the extended family] are referred to and recognized by means of the name of the leading man in them. We would speak of Naitci *gògò·tàh*, 'Naitci's encampment.'"

It is not difficult to see why a unit with the general features of the domestic family should be the *sine qua non* of Apache society. It was the task of the Apache to wrest a meager subsistence from a semiarid country. He depended upon game and wild plants. A very large-sized group would constitute a severe drain on the natural resources of a locality. A large group, moreover, would militate against easy mobility when a failing food supply necessitated a movement to a more desirable locality. But, on the other hand, the members of the economic unit must not be too few in number. Many of the foods are seasonal. The wild seeds and mescal must be gathered, prepared, and stored when they ripen, and the co-operation of a number of men and women is needed at such times.[3] To keep abreast of the level of subsistence, affairs within the group must go smoothly; there must be little internal friction. Group loyalty must be an active reality. Under such conditions, moreover, the loss of a member is a blow to the safety and unity of the group. The group will feel bound to protect its members, therefore; to plead for them when they stand accused; to avenge them when they are slain.

RELATIONSHIPS BASED ON CONSANGUINITY

Importance of the blood-tie in Chiricahua Apache social life.— The influence of the concept of blood-relationship is so pervasive and omnipresent in the conduct of a Chiricahua's affairs that it would take an entire volume to trace all the ramifications and facets of this fundamental idea. At times of ceremony, feast, want, danger, and death, a Chiricahua may call upon his kin for

[3] For a discussion of Chiricahua Apache food economy see Castetter and Opler, *The Ethnobiology of the Chiricahua and Mescalero Apache.*

assistance, and he is seldom turned away. Even in a matter as subtle as securing a patient for a shaman, as the following quotation will indicate, the influence of the relationship bond is likely to be detected.

> There's a shaman, my relative. And there are some people who have just had a baby. [Note the inference that the baby has come to the entire relationship group.] They are well-off; they have much property. They have horses and buckskin and bring in lots of deer. My relative has nothing like this, though he is a shaman. He is poor. I notice that this wealthy family which has the new baby has lost several babies before this. I go to them. I say, "You people have a new baby. I notice that you have lost several children. My relative is a good shaman. He knows something good to keep the child well. You go to him and ask him, and he'll put up a ceremony for you. But don't tell him who told you about his ceremony."
>
> Those relatives of the little child talk it over. One says, "I'll give a gun for that ceremony." Another says, "I'll give two blankets." Another offers a horse or a buckskin. One of the relatives goes to the man who knows the ceremony. He says, "We have been unable to bring up our children. We need you to help us."
>
> My relative sits there. He just makes some kind of sound in his throat at first. Then he says, "Well, I'll do it. But I need a buckskin with a turquoise tied at the middle of the head, and a yellow horse. Give two other things, anything you want, just so it makes four, a set of four."

There are few contexts in which a Chiricahua Apache's feeling of responsibility toward his relatives and his attachment to them are not operative. In the following excerpt a Chiricahua is addressing a supernatural who has offered him power:

> "There are more things I would like to have from you for the use of my children. . . . . I want you to help me when my family is alone and I am in the mountains. I am worrying and they are worrying. Can you show me how they are?"
>
> "Certainly [replies the supernatural]. I know your children and how much you think of them. I can show you all."

A powerful appeal, when the aid of a shaman was needed, was to address him by name and say, "In the name of all your children, your wife, your whole family, I ask you to help me now." My informant's comment was, "He could hardly refuse you after that."

The Chiricahua Apache's regard for the person and memory of his relative was so intense that an individual had to be very careful that no word or act of his could be construed as an affront. An Apache told me:

If a person dies, his relatives don't like to see anyone wearing red clothes of any kind for the next couple of days. They claim it hurts the one who has lost his relative. If a death occurs near by, others take off their red clothes at once. If your relative dies and you see someone wearing red clothes, you say, "Well, that fellow wore red when I was sad. When his relative dies, I'm going to wear red just for meanness." Fights and bad feeling started just from this in the old days.

Extension of kinship terms in ceremonial or honorary contexts.— The obligations of help and sympathy due a relative are so well understood by the Apache that it is logical for him to use kinship terms when he is afraid or stands in special need, no matter whom he is addressing. Thus Giver-of-Life, a nebulous supreme being, is called "my father" in prayer. The culture hero is referred to as "my brother," and his supernatural mother is termed "mother" or "grandmother" by the suppliant. In prayers and songs the earth becomes "earth woman, my mother," and the sun is named "grandfather."

In order to mollify natural forces and beings which the Chiricahua fear, kinship terms are also addressed to them. Thus the bear is called by the term for mother's brother, and a grandfather term is applied to thunder. To indicate respect and gratitude, one who has aided a person ceremonially is sometimes honored by the use of relationship terms as well. The woman who performed the ceremony at which the child was first placed in his cradle may later be addressed as "mother" or "grandmother" by the child, though no actual kinship tie may exist between the two. In like fashion the woman chosen to assist a girl during her puberty rite may be called "mother" by her charge thereafter.

Outstanding features of the system.—Figure 1 presents an outline of the Chiricahua Apache kinship system in graphic form, and in Table 1 are listed the kinship terms to which the letters used in the diagram refer.[4]

The principal features of the Chiricahua system, most of

[4] For a comparison of the Chiricahua kinship system and Chiricahua kinship terminology with comparable data of other Southern Athabaskan–speaking tribes see Opler, *The Kinship Systems of the Southern Athabaskan-Speaking Tribes*, pp. 620–33.

CHIRICAHUA KINSHIP SYSTEM

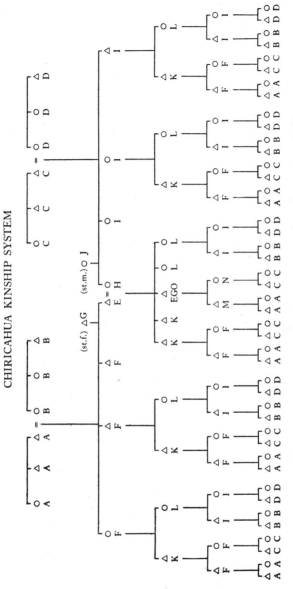

Fig. 1.—Chiricahua kinship system. Ego=male. For the native terms see Table 1.

which we shall have occasion to discuss at length below, may be summarized as follows:

1. All terms except those expressing parent-child relationship are self-reciprocals; a Chiricahua addresses his relative by the same term which that relative has used in speaking to him.
2. There are four separate terms, one for each grandparent, used as self-reciprocals for grandchildren. A grandparent's siblings, regardless of sex, are classified with the grandparent.
3. The mother's siblings are classified under one term. There is a separate term for mother.
4. The father's siblings are classified under one term. There is a separate term for father.
5. There are separate terms for stepfather and stepmother.
6. No terminological distinction is made between siblings, parallel cousins, or cross-cousins. In ego's generation two terms are used self-reciprocally: one which means sibling, parallel cousin, or cross-cousin of the same sex as the speaker, the other which is addressed to sibling, parallel cousin, or cross-cousin of the opposite sex from the speaker. There are no regular terms which indicate age distinctions in ego's generation. Reserve and respect characterize the relationship between siblings or cousins of opposite sex. Upon mutual agreement, cousins of opposite sex (cross- or parallel), but not siblings, may practice total avoidance.
7. Only true children are called son and daughter.

TABLE 1*

CHIRICAHUA KINSHIP TERMS

A	cìnálé	H	cìmá·'
B	cìt'cìné	I	cìɣóyé, cìdài'
C	cìtsóyé	J	cíkà·
D	cìtcó	K	cìkis
E	cìtà·	L	cílàh
F	cìdè·dé·'	M	cíɣè', cìjâ·
G	cìbé·jè'	N	cìɣáfcè'

* The letters (A, B, C, etc.) refer to the relatives in Fig. 1. The terms listed under "I" are used interchangeably for mother's sibling. Either term listed under "M" may be used for son; cìjâ, however, is the more common.

Range of terminological usage.—An acquaintance with some of the common terms of relationship, and some knowledge of the principles underlying their organization into a system, naturally raises the further question of the range over which these terms are used. To begin with one's own generation, this principle can be flatly laid down: all relatives of ego's generation are called either *cìkis* or *cílàh*. The same principle of sex dichotomy, to which attention has been called, is in force throughout this broad range, however. Consanguineous relatives of the same sex call each other *cíɫis*, and those of the opposite sex use the term *cílɑ̨h*. But to say that these terms are applied to all blood-relatives of the same generation is hardly to define their range. The exact termination of blood-relationship is often a moot point.

It is plain that the terms include both father's and mother's siblings' children—that is, all cross- and parallel cousins. They include much more. A simple statement of the range would be that a Chiricahua addresses as *cíɫis* or *cílɑ̨h* the children of anyone whom either of his parents had the right to call *cíɫis* or *cílɑ̨h*. Since his parents addressed cousins as well as siblings by these terms, the range is very wide indeed.

In fact, the range is limited only by memory and knowledge. A Chiricahua may have a number of such relatives whom he has never seen because they live at such a distance. Or such a far-removed relationship may obtain between himself and another that he is not aware of it until some elder who is genealogically minded calls his attention to it. As we shall see, the custodians of the family morals had good reason to investigate any rumors of *cílɑ̨h* relationship between a member of their immediate family and any alleged remote kin.

Quite as broad a range must be allowed for the terms of the second ascending (grandparents') generation. A grandparent term is addressed not only to the grandparent but also to all whom he calls *cíɫis* or *cílɑ̨h*. Therefore, a grandparent, his siblings, and all his cousins, however remote, will be denoted by the same term. All of them will address the child with this same term. Sex is disregarded. The sister and female cousins of a man addressed as *cínálé*, "father's father," will also be called *cínálé*. The range of the terms in the grandchild generation runs parallel, of course, with that of the grandparent generation.

In the first ascending generation the terms are also extended as far as memory will serve. The same is true of the use of terms addressed to the children of siblings and cousins.

Primary and secondary meanings of relationship terms.—It may be asked whether the relationship to everyone in the large group to whom one addresses a given term is precisely the same. The answer is that, while relationships which are expressed by the same term are often of the same order, they dwindle in intensity as the relationship becomes more remote. Thus, while it is theoretically, and often actually, true that one may seek financial assistance from a *cìdài'* of more remote connection than mother's sibling, the overwhelming tendency is to approach a mother's sibling first, if one is living. Contact, location of dwelling, and personal likes and dislikes will modify the traditional behavior pattern in individual cases.

The Chiricahua are quite aware of the distinction between primary and secondary kin who are subsumed under the same kinship term. The younger people advise one of the differences by explaining that so-and-so is *cìƙìs* to them "in the Indian way" if he is a cousin. An informant has often interrupted the recording of his genealogy to warn me that a given relative is not his "real" uncle or aunt. The distinction is neatly made by the native in genealogical work. If he is given a term and asked for the relative to whom he uses it, he will invariably return the name of the member of the immediate family who is addressed by it. Thus, for *cìnâlé*, the name of the father's father would be given and never that of the father's father's sister, though the term might apply equally to her. I have never encountered a case in which an Apache, old or young, was not able to distinguish between his own primary blood-relatives and more remote connections. Very often, however, informants had difficulty in differentiating between primary and secondary relatives of their parents.

Parent-child relationship.—Apache culture attests at many points to the deep devotion of a parent for his child and the affection of the child for his parent. As has been mentioned, an appeal in the name of his children is very difficult for an Apache to disregard. In asking for supernatural power, a Chiricahua will most often plead for something to "help me and my children." In visions where supernatural power is revealed, the recipient's children are often remembered. Thus, in a characteristic story of this kind which I recorded, the power is made to say, "If the ceremony is given to your child, you will not have to ask for any ceremonial gifts; but if it is passed on to other people, then you can ask for gifts." As might be expected from the tenor of this experience, ceremonies, when they are handed down from one person to another, very often pass from parent to child.

One account of a curing ceremony was related by a man who had been restored to health in his childhood through his father's supernatural power. His account of his father's efforts to save him constitute moving evidence of the strong emotional bonds between father and son. The narrative reads in part:

And my father was crying part of the time; I could hear him. He said, "Why not punish me this way? I've lived here many years on earth. I've seen what it looks like. I know how hard it is to live through this world. Don't kill that poor little child. He didn't harm anyone. I love him. Don't let him go. I want him to live to an old age in this world." He said, "If you want to kill anybody in this family, kill me. Take me. I know you can help me relieve this poor child from his sickness, and there's no reason why you should act this way to me." He was angry about this, angry at his own power. I heard him arguing with his power.

From the time of his earliest memories the child is advised, trained, corrected, and punished by his parents. The mother's sister and the maternal grandparents are also much interested in the development and guidance of the growing child, but the greatest share of the responsibility for the child's growth, health, and behavior falls on the parents. Chiricahua parents are equal to the occasion. Some of the parental homilies which I have recorded are especially rich in advice and suggestion for the Apache child.

The child's introduction to the world of Chiricahua ideas comes, most often, through the parents. In her effort to control and advise the child the mother imparts to him the generalized Chiricahua attitude toward owls, the call of the whippoorwill, and the animals and objects she considers objectionable. As the child grows older, the parent advises him concerning the proper behavior before persons popularly considered to be witches, before those who have been bereaved, etc. Still later the mother schools her daughter in the household tasks of cooking, sewing, and weaving baskets, and the father gives his son first lessons in shooting, hunting, and animal lore.

While a Chiricahua parent will exercise corporal punishment if it is deemed necessary, it is not often resorted to. An attempt is first made to frighten the unruly child or to persuade some outsider to intervene. If a child persistently strayed too far from camp, the father might dress himself to resemble the clown who accompanies the Apache masked dancers. Since the child was taught that the clown carries off troublesome children in his basket, the sudden appearance of his father so attired usually had a salutary effect.

Another form of discipline was depicted as follows:

When a child is mischievous, they call an old man who looks fierce. He is no relative. The old man limps in with a sack or blanket in his hand. He acts angry and shouts, "What's the matter?" The father and the mother sit there. They say, "This boy won't obey. He always fights. You can take him and do what you want with him. You can cut off his head or sit on him. We don't care. We aren't going to put up with him any longer." The boy begins crying. The old man says, "So, you won't obey? I'm going to check you off right now." The boy cries louder.

"Now stop that. Listen to me. Come over to me or I'm coming to get you." The child gets frightened. He tries to crawl behind his father, his mother, or his grandmother. But they act as if they have given the old man the privilege to do what he wants with the boy, and they push the boy forward. Then the old man grabs him and struggles with him. He puts him in the sack. The old man sits on the sack and says, "Are you going to behave?" After that the boy is prompt and behaves. If he won't get wood, the mother says, "All right, I'll call the old man." Then he goes for the wood at once.

A favorite device of parents whose boys are unruly is to match these boys against one another and force them to fight. The state of one of these boys, after the combat, has been described in these words:

The boy has had enough. He is bleeding, and his eyes are swollen. He doesn't want to fight any more, and he behaves after that. The parents don't like to strike their bigger boys. They get some other fellow to take it out on him. I saw many boys beaten up at the hoop-and-pole grounds like this. It's just a lesson.

As children grow older, the girl remains in close association with her mother and sisters, sharing with them the domestic tasks of the family. The boy, on the other hand, is expected to spend more and more time away from camp in hunting, raiding, and warfare, until finally, at marriage, he leaves the encampment of his parents to take part in the economy of the establishment of his parents-in-law.

Social relations within one's own generation.—Attention has already been called to the general aspects of the terminology used in address to members of a Chiricahua's own generation, such as the determination of the terms on the basis of sex, the reciprocity of the term used, and the range over which the term can apply. It is now possible to examine the social context surrounding the use of these terms and to note the interaction of the relationships they govern.

As may have been suspected, the practice of calling all relatives of the opposite sex in one's own generation *cílah* is the device through which all persons whom one may not marry are neatly categorized together. What, then, is the attitude of the Chiricahua toward his *cílah?* Does his behavior betray anything that will point to this marriage restriction? Does the same behavior accompany the term *cílah* throughout its range—that is, do the same social relationships obtain between sister and brother as do between cousins of the opposite sex?

The testimony on these points is clear and unconflicting. One informant summed up the relationship in the following words:

A Chiricahua man and woman related in this way hardly speak to one another. Two cousins who call each other *cílah* hardly speak. Cousins, or a sister and brother, could not even go out walking together. They can't joke much. Something holds them apart, so that they don't get too familiar. They aren't lectured about it when they are young. They just sense it and see it; it is taken for granted.

I notice the restraint in my own wife's family. My wife's *cílah* [father's brother's son] doesn't stay long when my wife is around. He has never been known to joke with her. He will with me. She takes the attitude that she wants to serve him when he is around. She acts in a formal way as if she wanted to serve and please him. This man has a sister who is quite free with my wife. They are just reserved to the opposite sex.

This attitude of formality and reserve to those called *cílah* starts when the principals are "grown up a bit." One informant explained:

In the old days those who had the same father and mother hardly spoke to each other. They would sit there and wouldn't say anything. They talked to the father and mother in each other's presence but not to each other. If joking [risqué] goes on when they are both there, one of them has to go away to show respect.

This same Chiricahua said on another occasion:

If you come where your sister is alone, you put disgrace on the whole family. If the mother and father aren't at home and the sister is alone, you must leave the camp. You must stay somewhere else. You must go to the sunny side of the hill or in the shade and sleep until your parents come home. Also, when the whole family is together, you must show respect for your sister. This feeling begins when you are about six or seven years old, when you are just big enough to understand what is being said to you. At that age you can still play with your sisters because, perhaps, you have no other playmates. But after you are fourteen or fifteen, you don't play with your sister any more. In the old days a boy would not even accompany his sister to an Indian dance.

Informants have described to me how they have come home from the hunt, tired and hungry, and have not thought of entering the home because a sister was there alone. "A boy would not stay in the home if his sister was there alone, and it was the same for all those whom he called *cílą̀h*." "A boy would not sleep in a tipi where his sister stayed alone." "A boy is reserved with his sister. He is careful of his language and behavior to her. He acts this way to all *cílą̀h*." These are representative statements of informants on this point.

One old Chiricahua was discussing the respect which an Apache accords his cousin. When asked what a cousin would do to show his respect, his reply was, "A boy shows his respect for a girl cousin by not visiting her." In former days, it is interesting to note, many camps had a separate shelter where a man could sleep if he found his own home solely occupied by a woman of the proscribed relationship.

As might be expected from the atmosphere of restraint, the commission of incest with a *cílą̀h* is of very infrequent occurrence, though it does occasionally take place. One case has been noted in which a young married man was carrying on clandestine relations with the daughter of his father's *cík̇is* (cousin, in this case). A typical Chiricahua reaction to the circumstance is the following:

She was at the mission school in Arizona, and the Indians think that spoiled her. The feeling is high against them. The old Indians use this as an instance of what happens when the old ways of relationship avoidance are violated. When they tried to do as the white man, they got into trouble. When I see a white man go with his sisters or girl cousins, I say, "All right, maybe he won't get into trouble, but the Indian can't do it."

The other case involved two distant relatives, connected through their fathers, who also have the right to call each other cousin. The woman was legitimately married. While her husband was away on some work, she disobeyed the time-honored Chiricahua injunction and went to cook for her cousin. The incest relationship followed. The husband, disgusted and outraged, has remained away, which amounts to a divorce for the Chiricahua. The couple have put a bold face on things. The woman divorced her husband, and she and her cousin have become formally married with the agent's permission.

The old man who first told me of this case was unable to trace the exact genealogical relationship of the two, although he was unusually well versed in such matters. Despite the extreme remoteness of the connection, he was decidedly incensed at the parties to the incest. "He couldn't pull this off when I was young," he said grimly. "A man could be killed for such a thing then. But now we are under the white law."

For a man to have sexual relations with his *cilάh* is considered proof positive that he is a witch. "He must be a witch." "Only a witch would do a thing like that." These are the typical comments that follow a discussion of such incest. The younger people say that the epithet "witch" is directed at the one suspected of intimacy with his *cilάh*, not because the person is thought actually to practice witchcraft, but because "it is the meanest thing that can be said of him." The older people, however, not only called those caught in incestuous relations "witches," but also treated them as they would witches. There is proof that such miscreants were strung from a tree by the wrists and forced to confess their witchcraft as well as their carnal relations. If they did not belong to a powerful family which was willing to plead for them, they might be beaten to death or burned.

This equation of incest with witchcraft is part of a wider

device by means of which Chiricahua society protects itself against aberrant members. Conduct which departs to any great extent from the norm is viewed with suspicion, and, if persisted in, is considered witchcraft. The "queer" Chiricahua, the nonconformist, is consequently suspect. Let him unthinkingly loiter too near an ancient grave, arise too early and be seen facing the east on a hill at dawn, or be caught with any unusual object at the time when a neighbor has contracted some acute sickness, and he is dragged to the nearest tree to explain his conduct.

It is not my intention to describe Chiricahua beliefs concerning witchcraft further than to point out that, by considering the party to incest a witch, Chiricahua society has identified him with all evil power and malevolent forces, and it can, with an easy conscience, proceed to do away with one who has violated the rules essential to the solidarity of the family. It therefore often happens that the members of a family make no attempt to exculpate a kinsman detected in such reprehensible conduct. Not infrequently the father or brother of a girl would dispatch any relative who had thus disgraced the entire family. The slayer answered to no one for his deed.

On one occasion a young man, returning unexpectedly, found his sister and a male cousin in sexual embrace. He ran, crazed with shame and anger, for a gun with which to "kill those two animals." Others, not aware of the cause of his anger, tried to restrain him when he appeared flourishing a weapon, and he is credited with three casualties before the rifle was wrested from him.

It should be added here that the concept of incest is not entirely delimited by the *cilàh* relationship. A Chiricahua is slightly reserved to all relatives of the opposite sex. Sexual relations with a relative of the first ascending generation, such as a distant *cidè·dé*, would be considered as incest and severely punished. Informants agree that such incest is gravely reprehensible, although it is not so grave a misdeed as relations with a *cilàh*.

An additional feature of the behavior patterns in ego's generation is that cousins of opposite sex may practice total avoid-

ance of one another. The relationship as it is established then
has been described in these words:

> J—— and S—— are cousins. They have hidden from each other all their
> lives. When cousins do this, they give presents to each other in the beginning,
> and after that they help each other all the time. They hide from each other
> from that time on just as a man hides from his mother-in-law. Either the man
> or the woman can start it. You can't hide from a sister or an aunt. It is only
> between cousins of opposite sex that this is done, not between two men or two
> women. You cannot arrange with a cousin to use the polite form only;[5] it must
> be hiding or nothing. Of course, if you must speak to your cousin who hides from
> you, you might stand behind a tree, and then you would use polite form in
> talking to her. K—— and Mrs. C—— were cousins and hid from each other.
>
> I had a cousin. Just because she liked me, she wanted me to do it. I had
> been away to school. When I got back, she gave me a saddle and bridle. Then
> she asked me to hide from her. I said no. I told her I had been to school, that
> I didn't want to go the old way, that maybe the government would get after me
> if I did. So she said all right. This was about 1897.
>
> If you hide from your cousin, then anything she has, whether it is money or
> property or anything else, she will give to you. You can't refuse a request from
> a person who hides from you. And it's the same for you if she needs anything.

Other informants have described this cousin avoidance relationship in much the same way. One Chiricahua, after enumerating instances of this mode of behavior, remarked, "They do
it because they love each other very much and wish to show
their respect. After they start it, they are very careful about
what they say about each other, for their relation is one of
respect, like that of a man to his mother-in-law."

As if to emphasize its difference from the *cilǫh*-relationship,
the *cikis* relationship is as close and warm as the *cilǫh*-relation-
ship is aloof and cold. Cousins and siblings of the same sex are
boon companions. The attitude is one of easy, unrestrained
friendship and, if both remain in the same district, of generous
co-operation throughout life.

I have numerous stories of Chiricahua who, upon receiving
warnings from their supernatural power that an enemy was
advancing, hastened to impart the information to a *cikis* and
plead with him to leave the vicinity. In these stories the enemies
always do come and the *cikis* is saved if he heeds the warning,
or destroyed if he does not. Whether or not the supernatural

---

5 For an explanation of polite form, see p. 214.

warnings appear and advise with the rare accuracy that is depicted in the tales, it is significant that the *ciẖis* is so prominently mentioned as a beneficiary of the warning also. I once asked an old Chiricahua Apache if a certain man were his *ciẖis*. "He is the only *ciẖis* I have left," was the answer. "The rest of the world can go by."

Before leaving the question of the use of the terms *ciẖis* and *cilằh*, it should be pointed out that these terms are vouchsafed as well to half-sisters and half-brothers—individuals of the same generation with one parent in common. They are also used in addressing those whose father or mother had at least one parent in common with either of the speaker's parents. The Apache described in this paper do not distinguish between older and younger sibling or cousin.

Nepotic-avuncular relationships.—The familiar Chiricahua Apache relationship pattern of loyalty, economic help, and kindly interest obtains between ego and members of the first ascending generation. Since his mother's sister is a resident of the same camp cluster and a close companion of his mother, his most intimate contacts are likely to be with her. There are no joking or respect relations directed toward relatives of this order, and there are no specialized functions which the parents' siblings have to perform for the benefit of ego. The relationship is generalized and is guided by the feelings of responsibility and interest which have grown up between the individuals involved. Because of the custom of the sororate, matrilocal residence, and the strong bonds between sisters, the mother's sister ordinarily cares for the children at the death of the mother.

A few concrete examples will, perhaps, throw the relationship of children to parents' siblings in its proper perspective. An old Chiricahua informant expressed himself as follows:

Harriet is my brother's daughter. No matter how far away she is, if I am sick she comes and helps around camp. But I have helped her as much as she has helped me. I feel that those related in this way should show a lifelong faithfulness to each other in any emergency and all the time.

This man then cited a case of magnanimity on the part of his wife's paternal uncle. This man lately presented his wife with a steer worth sixty dollars, and "thought nothing of it," when their daughter was ready to celebrate the girls' adolescence rite.

The testimony of a younger Chiricahua supports the statement cited above. He says:

At my uncle's I could borrow money. If he had it, I knew I could get it. Or I could borrow a horse or get in the house, even if he was away, if I needed a place to go. N——, too, goes to his uncle's place [his father's brother's] and takes liberties and uses the house.

One old man mourns the passing of the old relationship thus:

My brother is dead, but he has a boy living. This boy is twenty-five years old. He pays no attention to me. He has no feeling of responsibility. It wouldn't happen so in the old days, because then a boy was dependent on his elders. Now the young men can work, and they disregard the older people.

Grandparent-grandchild relationship.—Because of matrilocal residence, unless two families connected by marriage live in close proximity, the Chiricahua's grandparental contacts are likely to be principally with his mother's parents. Chiricahua grandparents are constantly concerned with the welfare of their grandchildren. They are often left in charge of the children while the parents are foraging for food, and their camp soon becomes the second home of the child. It is not uncommon for a child to sleep at the home of his grandparents as much as he does at his parents' dwelling. Through the medium of gifts of clothing and food, they contribute to the support of their grandchild. The grandparent is the traditional story-teller for the Chiricahua child, and many a bit of counsel and instruction comes veiled in this guise.

In relating something of the life of his father, a Chiricahua informant gave an account of grandparental affection which may be accepted as typical. He said:

My father was left an orphan at about six years of age and was brought up by his grandparent. It was his mother's father who took care of him. This man lived in Chiricahua country. My father lived there with him until he was twelve or fifteen years old. He was with the old man all the time. When he told about it in after years, he said he often wondered why this old man took such an interest in him. He often wondered if he was worth it, worth having so much attention paid to him. My father said the old man was kind to him, was always gentle with him, and used to advise him. He took more pains with him than any other relatives did.

The Chiricahua grandparent is a kind and indulgent friend to the child. He gives toys of his handiwork to the youngster, he shields and "spoils" him much as the grandparents in our own society are charged with doing. One young Apache, complaining that a grandparent had used undue and unjustified pressure to extricate his partner in crime from a scrape, remarked bitterly, "I had no grandparents to stick up for me. Grandparents think too much of their grandchildren." Another informant, discussing the particular obstinacy of a grandparent in refusing to acknowledge that her grandchild was committing incest, said, "Grandparents simply will not admit that such a thing can be, that it could be done by their grandchildren."

There are no separate or additional terms to indicate the great-grandparental–great-grandchild relationship; the grandparent-grandchild terminology is utilized instead. A great-grandparent connected through the father is called *cináĺé* or *cit'ciné* according to sex, and the terms are used as self-reciprocals. In like fashion, the proper grandparental terms are used to those great-grandparents connected through the mother.

MARRIAGE AND DIVORCE

Marriage and marital life.—At puberty a Chiricahua girl is the central figure of a four-day ceremony designed to usher her into the adult world and to insure long life, health, and good fortune for her. After the ceremony and as she approaches marriageable age, she is carefully watched, advised, and trained by the female members of her family.

Every marriage, successful war party, and girl's adolescence ceremony is followed by a feast and a social dance. Even the good fortune or caprice of an individual often inaugurates such an event. The maturing girl, accompanied always by her mother, sister, or her mother's sister, attends these dances and here meets the eligible men of the vicinity.

In the social dancing it is the girl who takes the initiative. All men who desire to dance stand in one designated place. The girl chooses a partner by tapping one of this group on the shoulder, and the man so selected has no choice but to accept the invitation. In this way the girl is able to indicate her preference for a mate, but she can do little more than hope that her obvious interest will awaken a like sentiment in the man. To be sure, her female escort does more than accompany her to the dance grounds. It is no secret that the guardians of the girl have many pointed hints to make about the sensible choice of a partner.

The Chiricahua youth has somewhat more control over the choice of his future wife. If he is of marriageable age and has become interested in a girl, he takes up the matter with his parents and their siblings. It is quite necessary to gain their consent, for one of them will probably act as intercessor for him in obtaining permission from the girl's family, and the bulk of the presents to be given to the girl's parents, when the marriage is agreed upon, must come from them. But if the members of his immediate family disapprove of the girl or are unenthusiastic about an alliance with the girl's family, there is little the young man can do save to look for another and more suitable mate.

In other words, the young people guide their own destinies so far as they can, but in every case their elders are the controlling factor. This is an old Chiricahua's account of the latitude permitted the young people in the marriage choice during his youth:

Sometimes the parents of the boy and girl arrange the match and only tell the principals when all arrangements are made. If a man is industrious, he has more chance to get a match, and the same is true for the girls. Some very ugly Indian men have gotten beautiful girls, not because the girls wanted them, but because the parents of the girl recognized their industry and insisted on the marriage. Old men who are rich sometimes marry very young girls in this way.

One of the oldest and most reliable of my informants told me:

Girls marry at about eighteen or nineteen years. The marriage was arranged by the parents. It wasn't necessary to court a girl. It was just arranged. The boy would often tell the father or a close relative which girl he liked. It is not so easy as we've been making out. Sometimes a girl would run off rather than marry a man. Some girls are forced into marriage.

Yet the Chiricahua parent, like many another, found it expedient to consider the wishes of his child whenever practical. As my informant admitted in the next breath, "After all, the final decision is usually left to the young people. They can be persuaded, but they can't be forced as a general thing. Such marriages do not last."

As soon as the boy's family approved of his choice or decided on a likely mate for him, it acted to accumulate the necessary presents to be tendered the girl's parents. The parents, older brothers and sisters, siblings of the parents, and even more distant kin of the young man contributed property. If the girl was of a very wealthy and respected family, a large and imposing array of presents was needed. If the youth's family was well-to-do, it would brand itself as niggardly and would suffer a loss of prestige unless worth-while presents were offered. For a very beautiful and much-desired girl, the present would be correspondingly large, and an especially industrious and highly esteemed girl might bring her parents considerable wealth.

When the time came to speak, the father or a close relative of the boy would visit the girl's parents. He took with him the gifts which, in later days, consisted of horses, saddles, and guns. If it were the father who went, he might say, as one man told me he did, "I have a boy who likes your daughter pretty well. I am acting as a messenger, and I want to know whether it will suit you to let these two people be united." Then there follows an enumeration of the boy's good points, a glowing account of the presents which have been brought, and a peroration on the desirability of having the families united.

Sometimes, if the young man wished a particularly eloquent representation, he asked someone noted for an agile and persuasive tongue to act as his "go-between." This person received a gift if he succeeded. After consent was gained, the presents were left with the parents of the girl.

A few days after the agreement was reached, the relatives of both the boy and the girl met at the encampment of the girl's family. Here, not far from her parents' home, the girl and her female relatives had built a dwelling for the young couple. During the day the visitors feasted, and at night a social dance took place. Though the wishes of the young people are not entirely ignored, it cannot be overemphasized that marriage among the

Chiricahua is not nearly so much an agreement between individuals as it is a contract between families.

When a Chiricahua marries, he becomes enmeshed in a network of obligations to his wife's family from which he can extricate himself only with the greatest difficulty. His first obligation is an economic one. From his earliest years he has been taught that a man should support his wife's parents and her close kin. Ask any Chiricahua for whom a man should work, and his immediate answer is, "For his mother-in-law and his father-in-law." The following statements emphasize the importance of this principle.

There is something about it so that a man helps his wife's people.

It is usual to live with the wife's people. In the old days the boy had to work for his father-in-law. If a man killed two deer, he would give most of it to his wife's people.

At marriage a man goes to the camp of the girl's parents. We do this because a woman is more valuable than a man. We do it to accommodate the woman. The son-in-law is considered a son and as one of the family. The in-laws depend a great deal on him. They depend on him for hunting and all kinds of work. He is almost a slave to them. Everything he gets on the hunt goes to them. In return he has privileges with the property of his wife's people. He can get anything they have very easily. It is understood that he can call on them for aid. This relationship dates from the time of consent to the marriage.

A man feels under obligation to his father-in-law. He feels that he should hunt for him. Therefore, there was the tendency in the old days to go to the wife's people. A man's parents recognized this obligation too. They often said, "Well, that's what you married for. You'd better go over there."

I have quoted at length from the characteristic statements of so many informants because it is essential to understand how completely a Chiricahua's economic life is identified with the fortunes of his wife's family. So thorough is this identification that no single household stands as an economic unit. It has been indicated that the man, after a successful hunt, brings the slain animals to his mother-in-law's dwelling. He might well do this, for all the food of the extended family, including the provisions of his own homestead, is cooked there. The daughter assists her mother in the preparation of the food and then carries it back to her own camp to share it with her husband, who can never see

his mother-in-law's face. This custom of carrying the food to
the husband has fallen into disuse in late years, and the native
term for the practice is now said in jest to lazy men, in the sense
of, "You want things to be easy, don't you? You want things
brought on a silver platter."

The Chiricahua Apache practiced polygyny. It is difficult to
estimate what proportion of the marriages were polygynous before white influence. Plural marriages have been under the ban
of the authorities for many years and have been the special
target of the missionaries, yet a few cases still persist. The
Chiricahua say that it was a matter of wealth, that all who could
provide for more than one wife were disposed to have another.
I judge that 15 or 20 per cent of the marriages were of this nature
under aboriginal conditions.

Theoretically there was no limit to the number of wives a
Chiricahua could have. Informants have told me that before
their time wealthy men sometimes had three or even more wives.
But no one whom I met had seen a case in which a man had more
than two wives at one time. It is quite certain that, if such cases
did occur, they were extremely rare.

The question of plural marriage throws the economic solidarity of the family into sharp relief. The close economic affiliation
of the son-in-law with the extended family left only one possibility by which plural marriage could operate and yet maintain
the structure of the family inviolate. This was, of course, by
marrying a sister of the first wife or one of the unmarried daughters of the wife's mother's sister—girls whom a wife called *cik̓is*
and who would be living in the same encampment. If the family
had any available sisters or cousins of his wife, no matter how
remote, it would be considered an intolerable insult for a man to
seek elsewhere for a second mate. The second marriage was
attended by no feast or ceremony. There were no additional gifts
given. A second dwelling might be built near the first, or the
two wives might live under one roof, if the household was not
crowded for space.

Many times a second wife was taken at the suggestion of the
first. From all accounts the sisters or cousins lived together

amicably. The wife first married was normally much older than the second and possessed more authority than her younger relative. She generally guided the affairs of the combined household.

When a married woman died, the numerical strength and unity of the family would suffer a double loss if the husband were to marry a woman of another encampment. He would then necessarily leave the encampment wherein he had been living and to the support of which he had been contributing, to reside with his new parents-in-law. A consideration of the lifelong and inseparable bonds of affinity which the young man accepts at marriage will show the impossibility of thus summarily severing his ties of relationship and residence, but for the present it will suffice to say that the extended family has structural safeguards against such economic and social dismemberment.

After the death of his wife, the Chiricahua is less a free man than ever before. Immediately the entire management of his affairs passes into the hands of his deceased wife's relatives. His children are taken and cared for by a sister or cousin of their dead mother. The woman who cares for his children usually becomes, as we shall see, the man's next wife.

The bereaved cuts his hair as a sign of mourning and remains at his former wife's encampment. His immediate wants are administered to by the same woman who cares for his children. He is expected to mourn for a year. During this year the man's conduct is subject to severe scrutiny on the part of his deceased wife's family. Any levity, any undue attention to women of another family, will be counted an insult to the dead and an affront to her family. He is at the disposal of his former wife's kin and is not free to marry whom he will at the conclusion of the year of mourning. He is what the Chiricahua call 'itsádjï·slį̃.

The word 'itsádjï·slį̃ means "he has become 'itsá." It applies to the man as soon as the death of his wife occurs. The word 'itsá does not yield to linguistic analysis. The most useful approximation I have found was given me by an old Apache who told me it meant "belonging to." The concept is that the man "belongs to" any sister or female cousin of his deceased wife during this period of mourning. He is said to stand in the relationship of *'itsá* to her. "He is her *'itsá*" is a common expression.

After the man's hair has grown out and the year of mourning is past,[6] one of those who stands in the relationship of *'itsá* to him will personally approach him and say, "Now you are my *'itsá*. If you are willing, we will get married." It is obligatory for the man to accept. If the dead wife has an unmarried sister, the sister, if she is at all interested in the man, will be the one to speak to him. If no unmarried sister is available, the matter is decided among the female cousins.

It is noteworthy that the choice lies entirely with the dead wife's relatives, who may force him to marry any eligible female of his former mate's generation or may even reject him. In the event that the man has been no great asset to the family, the latter expediency is resorted to as a convenient way to get rid of a loafer and waster. If the year of mourning is well over, and the coolness of the relatives to a man plainly spells to him that they have no intention of asking him to rejoin their ranks, he assumes that he is free and goes back to his own parents' encampment until he can choose another mate.

In case a man is already married to two sisters and one of them dies, he cannot be made to take another sister or cousin of the deceased to wife. He continues living alone with the remaining woman unless he himself feels that he wants another wife. But in such circumstances he is not *'itsá* to his wife's family, and the request comes from him.

When a man marries his *'itsá*, there is no feast, no ceremony at all. As one informant said, "They just start living together." Despite the manifest changes of recent years, the feeling of obligation to marry one's *'itsá* is still surprisingly strong. One case which came up in recent years will serve as an illustration.

A certain woman died. During the following year the husband became interested in a girl not of his wife's family. He spoke freely of his intention of marrying her. Then, at the conclusion

[6] It is considered less reprehensible to marry before the year of mourning is over if the new spouse is one's *'itsá*. In other circumstances marriage before the completion of the mourning period precipitates a scandal.

of a year, his dead wife's sister came to him and reminded him that he was 'itsá to her. The sister became much exercised at his attempt to thwart her rights. She even went to a government official with the matter. He, though not understanding the theoretical merits of the case, took her to be "a woman wronged" and sided with her. Apache public opinion, too, was decidedly against the man, and he found it necessary to harken to old custom. He has recently married his 'itsá.

There existed, then, two streams of influences which encouraged marriage with a sister of one's wife: one, polygyny, and the other, the 'itsá relationship. There is one more point to be discussed in this connection. What takes place if the family of the former wife has no unmarried girl to take her place? In such a circumstance the man does become free. But the year of mourning must first be sedulously kept. There is a final gesture, too, which symbolizes the strength of the family tie that is to be severed. Even though the dead wife's family has no further claim of a tangible nature upon a man, he must, out of courtesy, obtain their permission to marry elsewhere and give them a suitable present. A typical speech which he would make to one of the family, usually to a brother-in-law, is as follows: "I have had a hard time, but now I want to marry again. You have no other girls for me to marry, and now I am ready to marry again." This answer might be returned: "What has happened has happened. It can't be helped. If we had anybody to give you, we'd give you a woman. You have been good to us, and we hate to have you part from us, but there is no help for it. We hope you will get a good girl and be happy."

But even death and this understanding do not entirely abrogate the relationship that has been established. The polite forms and avoidances entered upon at marriage still continue, and since a Chiricahua and his property are always at the command of one to whom he uses the polite form, this family has by no means passed entirely out of his life.

Just as the husband is 'itsá to the relatives of his dead wife who are of her sex and generation, so is the wife 'itsá to the brothers or male cousins of her dead husband. In other words, '*itsá* is a concept which cuts both ways. Precisely every rule and usage which is in force when a man is '*itsá* to his wife's family is equally in force when a woman is '*itsá* to a deceased husband's family. In this case, of course, the tables are just reversed. The woman is at the disposal of her dead husband's family. It is they who choose a mate for her whom she must accept, or they may reject her altogether.

It is the man this time, of course, who approaches the woman and requests marriage. After this formality the man accompanies the woman to her encampment where his brother or cousin had formerly lived. It is also true that the kin of the deceased resent anything in the conduct of the woman that may betray disrespect for the dead or for themselves, even if they have no suitable mate for her.

An incident couched in an informant's own words is illustrative of the last point:

G—— married a Chiricahua man. She was a Chiricahua herself. Her husband died, and she was, therefore, '*itsá* to her husband's family. They did not have an available man for her. T——, the only possibility, was already married. So she married a Mescalero Apache. She went around saying some pretty mean things about the family to which she was '*itsá*. T—— got pretty mad, and said he was going over there and slit her nose.

This illustrates the point that a woman is directly responsible to her dead husband's family. A woman who went around with someone to whom she was not '*itsá* might have her nose cut. It was the right of the dead man's family to dispose of her and watch her conduct. Any of them can warn her of her conduct. If the husband has no brothers, a cousin will marry her. The age of the cousin does not matter. The oldest one does not necessarily marry her. Choice is what counts.

Another woman, even though her husband had no eligible *ci̧ǩis*, so outraged the sensibilities of the entire community by going to live with a man the day after her husband's death that she is considered an outcast today.

As we have seen, the right of any one of several eligible individuals to marry an '*itsá* was not based on age. My data do show, however, a marked tendency to allow the oldest of the unmarried daughters to choose the man if she does not use the polite form to him. This is in keeping with a natural wish of the parent to arrange matches for those in his family whose chances must grow steadily dimmer with advancing years.

With the *'ìtsá* relationship in force, the matter of the care of children at the death of the husband or wife is rather easily solved. If, as has been explained, the woman dies, the children are provided for by a sister or female cousin of the deceased, and in due course of time the household, with this relative of the former wife as stepmother, is formed anew. If it is the husband who dies, the children, of course, remain with their mother. During the year of mourning, when the household has no male head, sustenance is provided by other members of the encampment. At the end of the mourning period, a brother or cousin of the deceased man makes the proper overtures, and a unified household goes on as before. No problem arises when a deceased husband's family has no single men. The children simply remain with the mother in the mother's encampment, and if the mother receives an offer of marriage from a man of another family, the man must, of course, join the household.

The only serious difficulty is encountered when a woman dies and leaves no available sisters or female cousins. The man is then likely to marry out of the encampment. Whether or not he takes the children with him depends on the circumstances. If the new wife has no children of her own and is willing to care for her husband's children, they will come with the father. If they can be cared for by some member of the mother's encampment, they are left behind. The tendency is to retain the children in the mother's group whenever possible. In keeping with their distinct bias for matrilocal residence, the Chiricahua have the feeling that, to be really well trained and properly reared, a child should grow up in his mother's encampment.

Before leaving the general discussion of Chiricahua marriage, a word should be said about the nature of the gifts which are presented to the bride's family. As will be remembered, the gifts represented the collective effort and generosity of the young man's blood-kin. He was under no obligation to return the value of these goods to his relatives at some future time. He was, of course, expected to aid other young kinsmen who might appeal to him in similar circumstances. These gifts have given rise to the statement that the Apache buy their wives. This view has been too long taken for granted and deserves a thorough analysis.

There is no doubt that the Apache parents looked forward to material gain at the marriage of a daughter. A characteristic lecture of a parent to a wayward daughter was expressed by an informant in these words, "We want to rear you well so people won't talk about us; we want to get something out of your marriage, so we want to take care of you." Trustworthy accounts of what transpired between the representative of the boy's family and the girl's father likewise give evidence of considerable haggling over the subject of the presents. One old man frankly told me, "It's not much use asking for a woman in marriage if you can't give a present."

A further circumstance which lends the appearance of wife purchase to the giving of gifts is that no return present of any kind is tendered the boy's family at this time. Add to this that the members of the boy's family have unlimited right to watch the girl's conduct, control her, and even to choose her next mate in case of her husband's death, and a strong argument for bride barter has been made.

But if we are to account for the rights of the husband's family over the wife in terms of the presents they have given, how are we to explain the identical rights exercised over the husband by the wife's family when they have paid no "price" for him? The family of a woman has, as we have seen, the comparable privilege of supervising the conduct of the widower and of allotting a mate to him. Moreover, the woman's relatives can even ignore and ignominiously dismiss him. This last privilege directly refutes any supposition that the man or his family has any property rights over the marriageable females of the family because of the presents given. Even when his wife's family dismisses him and no member of it makes use of her *'itsá* rights, no part of the presents is returned.

But the real refutation of the charge that the gifts are a bride price is that the woman is not property and cannot be treated as property. In the first place, she may divorce her husband and does so for unfaithfulness, brutality, and other reasons to be enumerated later. Moreover, at divorce, no matter by whom instigated, the presents are not returned. Next, the husband has no control over the personal property of his wife. Whatever is accumulated by the woman belongs to the woman. She may share her possessions with her husband, but she is in no wise obliged to do so. I found it impossible to persuade Apache men to sell me anything owned or partly owned by their wives. No matter how certain they were that the woman would part with the object, if she were not at home, it meant an extra trip for me. When both were present, the man took no part in the bargaining. To all appeals that he use his influence to aid the sale, he would return, "It belongs to her." As a final confirmation of the inadvisability of regarding the marriage gifts as purchase, there is the ever present and unanswerable circumstance that a man is much more bound, economically and in every other respect, to the woman and her family than she ever is to him.

How, then, is the marriage gift to be regarded? I look upon it as a demonstration on the part of the man that he has identified himself with the economic fortunes of the encampment of his bride-to-be. Through the gift he says in substance, "Here is property and wealth. It is what you may expect from now on. I am strong and young, and I shall be a valuable addition to the power and importance of your encampment." To my mind it is no accident that, immediately upon the giving of the presents, the polite form begins. From that time the man stands in the relation of affinity to his wife's family, and their property and power are at his service should he need either.

Considerable weight is afforded the point of view presented here by the testimony of an old Chiricahua. When I asked him what a poor man, unable to collect any wordly goods for a present, could do if he wished very much to marry, he told me that a man in such a circumstance would approach the woman's family and say the following: "I am poor, but whatever I am able to accumulate in the way of material things will be yours, for I will be here with you all the time." In this situation the plea of future economic usefulness to the group is plainly equated with the usual presents.

Divorce.—The extent to which a man was identified with his wife's encampment made divorce a most serious step. Yet it did occur as a result of unfaithfulness, incompatibility, sterility, or laziness on the part of either husband or wife. The Chiricahua word for divorce, which can be translated "they walk away from each other," suggests the procedure. When conditions became intolerable, the man just packed up his personal possessions and departed for the encampment of his parents. The Chiricahua Apache were not burdened with possessions, and the division of property was easily decided. A man had only his weapons, his horses, saddles, clothing, and religious paraphernalia, and these he took with him.

If the grounds for the divorce were the unfaithfulness of the wife, the man might cut off the end of her nose before going. There are still one or two women on the reservation thus mutilated. The disfiguration was a very real handicap to the woman in procuring another husband.

When the couple had children, the problem was more complex. Whenever possible the children were left in their old surroundings, in the mother's encampment. If the mother remained unmarried and was not able to support them, the children might stay with a sister of the mother. Sometimes, when there were older boys, the father would take them back to his relatives. Needless to say, in nearly every case very young children remained with the mother. Where the woman was obviously at fault, had been taken in adultery, and was considered unfit as a parent, the father might claim the right to take all the children with him. The mother's relatives, if the case of the man were strong enough, would have to acquiesce. In a few instances which have come to my attention the residence of the children was decided on a basis of riches. Where the man's relatives were wealthy and able to provide for the children without additional strain, and the woman's family was less well-to-do and hardly able to bear the additional burden occasioned by the loss of a man, the children would go with the father. A man who assumes charge of his children at divorce will normally marry again very quickly to provide a home for them. The children, in this case, call the stepmother *cíkḁ́·* and are so called in turn.

At divorce the economic obligations of a man to his former

wife's family are at an end. He is at liberty to marry at any time. The polite forms of speech and avoidances which marked his relations to his wife's family are carried on, however. Therefore, it is always more simple to marry a former wife's sister whenever possible, to escape double obligations of this nature.

When a divorced woman marries again, there is none of the ceremony that marks the marriage of a maiden. There is no feast or giving of presents. The economic rapport has been established in the past. The new husband merely takes his place in the family economy.

Relations of a man and the members of his parents' encampment. —Although a man leaves his parents' encampment at marriage, his interest in its members and its fortunes is not at an end. Because of the tendency for related families to camp near one another, he will not be far from his former campmates. Relatives, even though they are separated by marriage, are often sought out in time of need. But parents do not expect steady support from a married son. They understand that his primary obligations are to his parents-in-law in this respect. The parents look rather to their own sons-in-law for the maintenance of the economy of their encampment. In fact, a young man receives much counsel from his own parents on the subject of the proper respect and economic assistance due his parents-in-law when he marries.

It will be remembered, too, that the parents' home or the homes of the members of his parents' encampment offers a ready haven to a man when divorce or the death of his mate (if remarriage into the family of the deceased does not take place) forces him to seek living quarters outside of the encampment in which he has resided. If his parents are still living he will, in all likelihood, take up residence with them. If his parents are no longer alive, a brother or male cousin (the child of a mother's sister) would invite him to stay with his family. A man might readily place his children in the care of a sister willing to offer them a home, though, because of the restraint between siblings of opposite sex, he would be less likely to live there himself.

TERMS OF RELATIONSHIP BASED ON AFFINITY AND THEIR
SOCIAL IMPLICATIONS

The terms.—Table 2 introduces one of the two systems of
terms which are used to all individuals related by marriage. The
system shown in this table is comparatively simple. There are
only four terms. Two of them express the relationship of an
individual who marries into one's family, and the other two are
used to those into whose family one has married. Each set of
two terms is further subdivided. Of the first set in the table,
the upper term is applied to those members of a mate's family

TABLE 2

Chiricahua Affinal Terms

	First Set	Second Set
Linguistic form used..	To mate's relatives (man or woman speaking)	Relatives of mate to individual (man or woman speaking)
Polite form (3A)......	*kắ'icxéhí*, "one for whom I carry burdens"	*cắ'djiɣéhí*, "one who carries burdens for me"
Regular form.........	*bắ'icxéhń*, "one for whom I carry burdens"	*cắ'iɣéhń*, "one who carries burdens for me"

who are addressed with the polite form of speech, and the lower
term is used to those to whom no special form of speech is applied. Likewise, those of his mate's kin to whom a person uses
polite form address him with the polite form of the second set,
and those who do not use polite form to him employ the other.

Linguistically, the polite form is a special third-person singular or plural form of the verb and is found in every paradigm.
Since there is a regular third-person form, linguists have differentiated between the two by naming the polite form the "3A"
form. Actually, the four terms in the table are taken from
different forms of the verb "to carry a burden." The two terms
in the upper portion of Table 2 are 3A forms, the two lower are
regular third-person forms.

The verb from which the terms are derived is translated today as "carry a burden." That burden, as thought of by the old Apache, was always deer or other game. This is one informant's comment on the general meaning of the word: "The word means to me that in the old days a son-in-law would go out and kill game for the parents-in-law. The word implies to me that the man's business is to hunt in this fashion for me if I am the father-in-law. It is his obligation to do so forever." After reviewing the position and duties of the Chiricahua son-in-law, it seems supremely fitting that he call his parent-in-law "he for whom I carry burdens" and be called "he who carries burdens for me," in return.

A few characteristics of these terms should be noted. No one of them, in the first place, is reciprocal. A man will call his in-law *ká'icxéhí* and be addressed as *cá'djiɣéhí* if the polite form is in use between them, or he will use the regular equivalent if it is not. Again, the terms do not indicate the sex of the speaker or the sex of the one to whom the term is addressed. Finally, there is no separate term for mother-in-law or father-in-law in this set. When *ká'icxéhí* is used in a primary sense and without qualification, it is taken to mean father-in-law or mother-in-law.

In addition to the terms of Table 2 there is another system of affinity terms used only by those who address one another with polite form. They are:

1. Male addressing or speaking of male; female
   addressing or speaking of male . . . . *hàdzì·stì'í*, "he who is old"

2. Male addressing or speaking of female; female
   addressing or speaking of female . . . . *sądjílíní*, "she who has become old"

The use of these two systems overlaps. There is no occasion when terms of one must be used rather than terms of the other except that *bá'icxéhń* and *cá'iɣéhń* can be addressed only to those to whom no polite form is used. For example, a person's *ká'icxéhí* may also prove to be his *sądjílíní* or *hàdzì·stì'í*. In their primary meanings *sądjílíní* and *hàdzì·stì'í* connote "mother-in-law" and "father-in-law," respectively. The sex distinction they make is found useful when a person wishes to indicate definitely one or the other and finds from the context that he can do it in no other way. The comparable term of the other set, *káʾìcxéhí*, does not distinguish between the sexes.

Behavior accompanying the terms.—There are three ways in which a Chiricahua can behave to his relatives by marriage. He avoids them, he uses polite form to them, or he does neither. The rule may be laid down here that both avoidance and polite form necessitate the 3A form of speech. Normally one does not meet, and therefore does not speak to, the relatives whom he avoids, but in speaking of them he uses the 3A form. In an emergency, such as when a quarrel has threatened the family life, and the mother-in-law, who must never be seen, feels impelled to speak to the son-in-law, she might remain hidden from him behind some tree or shelter and carry on a conversation with him in the 3A form of speech.

Another rule which may be invoked is that any of these forms is reciprocal. If a person who has the right to demand either avoidance or polite form of a Chiricahua chooses to request the latter, the person addressed must respond in terms of polite form and can use nothing else. He could not avoid such a person, nor could he neglect to use the 3A form of speech.

Before venturing further, it is necessary to know just what polite form and avoidance mean in terms of behavior. The use of polite form establishes a relationship of utmost dignity and formality between two persons. Before a relative to whom one uses polite form one's demeanor must be reserved and grave. No profanity, coarse joke, or allusion can be indulged in before a person of such a relationship. Even if a third person were to speak smuttily or in terms of sex in the presence of two who use the polite form to each other, they would leave the place at once in confusion. Once, before I was aware of this, I asked an interpreter to question an old man, who stood in such a respect relationship to him, concerning taboos on menstruating women. Although the old man understood not a word of English, my interpreter blushed and haltingly explained that he could not talk to the old man about such things.

A corollary of this attitude is that too great an intimacy with this kinsman is considered shameful. A man could not even see another man unclothed who stood in this relationship to him. This attitude was carried to an extreme in the relationship of individuals of different sexes who used polite form to one another. The Chiricahua crime of crimes would be incest with one to whom the polite form was addressed. One patriarch, after describing the laxness and waywardness which have come upon his people in late years, ended proudly with the statement, "The one thing that has never been violated in my time and even up to the present day is our rule against sexual relations between relatives who use the polite form."

The attempt is made, too, to keep out of all embarrassing positions before this relative. To fall, to lose one's balance, or to be put in a ridiculous position in his presence is the acme of embarrassment. Likewise, if the relative to whom you use polite form is forced into an awkward position before you, it is incumbent upon you to leave the scene at once. It follows, too, that you can listen to nothing derogatory or scurrilous concerning this relative and, of course, cannot start an arraignment of him yourself. It would be considered most impolite and disrespectful to contradict him, moreover.

Finally, the polite form implies that your possessions and even your labor are at the disposal of your relative. It would be impossible for an Apache to refuse anything in the way of property or services requested by an affinity who uses polite form to him. There is a nice balance of mutual regard in this connection. A relative who stands in this relationship to you can refuse you nothing, but, since it is part of the code to be polite and generous in your dealings with him, you make no unreasonable requests.

The attitude and behavior of the parties to the avoidance relationship are identical in every respect with the elements of polite-form relationship with the exception that the principals are prevented from ever meeting face to face. All negotiations between them must be carried on through a third person, usually the wife of the married man; for, of a married couple, only the man avoids any of his mate's relatives. There is a general term, reciprocally used, which can be translated "that one whom I avoid." It is employed in speaking of any person with whom an avoidance relationship has been established.

The avoidance relationship necessitates some manner of warning from others to those in an avoidance relationship who are inadvertently about to come into each other's view. By-standers are most obliging in this respect, and the usual warning, "Do not walk here," is constantly heard. Today, on the reservation, it is not at all uncommon to hear the warning sounded, and to see a man dart out of the rear door of the trader's store as his mother-in-law enters the front.

This might be a convenient point at which to list the affinities whom a Chiricahua Apache avoids, or to whom he uses polite form. It is obligatory for the husband to avoid his mother-in-law, his father-in-law, his mother-in-law's mother, and his father-in-law's mother. With these individuals there is no choice or alternative. There are others with whom an avoidance relationship is usually established, though this is not strictly necessary, and the polite form of speech may take its place. These persons include the sisters and brothers of the mother-in-law and father-in-law. The wife's father's father, her mother's father, siblings of the wife's grandparents, and the cousins of the father and mother of the wife have the technical right to ask for avoidance. In practice most of these request nothing more than polite form, however.

The sisters and brothers of a man's wife may indicate that they wish him to address them in the polite form, but this is a matter of choice. The same is true of the nepotic relatives of his wife—if they are grown at the time of the marriage and wish to do so, they may institute the use of polite form. Very occasionally the wife's sister will avoid her brother-in-law.

The Chiricahua woman does not avoid any of her affinities. At marriage a few of her husband's relatives may use polite form to her, and then she will reciprocate. Siblings or cousins of her husband may do this, and collateral relatives of his parents and grandparents. Her husband's parents and grandparents never make this request, however.

The Chiricahua have their rationalization of this, of course. They say that a man's mother may have to attend her daughter-in-law at time of childbirth, and that it would be impossible for her to see her daughter-in-law at such a time if she addressed her by polite form. This explanation is rather unconvincing, however, for the girl's mother and mother's sister usually aid at such a time rather than the husband's mother. Besides, such an explanation hardly accounts for the lack of polite form to the father-in-law. Another explanation of the Indians is that the husband's father and mother look upon their son's wife as a "daughter," and, since the polite form would not be used to a child, it is not used to their daughter-in-law.

In case the relationship of two people is such that the polite form or avoidance is obligatory, it goes into effect at the very moment of consent to the marriage which establishes the relationship. In those cases where there is a choice of behavior pattern, or where the one possible form is optional, the decision lies entirely with the person into whose family a Chiricahua is marrying. For example, a mother-in-law's female cousin has the right to decide whether she is going to request avoidance, polite form, or nothing at all from a man who is marrying her "niece." In the event that she decides to request avoidance, she will send a messenger to the man to inform him of her intention. After that the man is careful to keep out of her presence and to speak of her only in the polite form.

When one says that a mother-in-law's *cíkis* has the right to request avoidance, he subsumes many women under that short term, *cíkis*. Will all of them ask for avoidance? Theoretically, all have the right to insist on avoidance. In practice the matter is settled along lines of common sense. The primary *cíkis* of the mother-in-law, her sisters, will most likely request avoidance. The man who has married into the family would be considerably grieved if they made no such request. The mother-in-law's parents' siblings' daughters, the female cross- and parallel cousins, might likewise ask avoidance. They would be just as likely, however, to be satisfied with polite form. More remote *cíkis* of the mother-in-law would almost inevitably request polite form only, and, as the relationship became more and more remote, a larger percentage would demand neither polite form nor avoidance.

If a person intends to use polite form to another, the first time he sees that individual, after the consent which gives him the right has been granted, he uses polite form himself in addressing his new affinity. The person so addressed knows immediately that henceforth he is obliged to vouchsafe polite form and all that goes with it to this individual. His answer and all subsequent conversation with this particular affinity are couched in 3A form. A relative who has the privilege, but not the desire, to initiate the use of the polite form or avoidance signifies this by continuing conversation in the usual vein when, for the first time after the consent or union, he meets the man who has married into his family.

Where the polite form or avoidance is an optional matter but is nevertheless requested, it is an expression of approval of the marriage and of the parties to it. "I should be very proud, for many of the prominent men of the reservation use polite form to me," said one Chiricahua.

Another informant told me of an interesting incident which occurred a few days after his marriage. He had gone with his wife to visit some friends. As he entered the dwelling, he came face to face with his father-in-law's cousin. This woman said, "It's too bad we have met face to face. I was going to avoid this man, but now it has been spoiled. Hereafter we will use the polite form." The informant expressed his surprise and pleasure at hearing the venerable lady say that she had intended to avoid him. "I never knew she thought so much of me," he said. In the case of incest noted before, which has resulted in the marriage of a man to his cousin, the members of the woman's immediate family who have a choice in the matter have refrained from requesting polite form or avoidance as a protest against his action.

There are, however, circumstances in which polite form and avoidance are not requested in spite of the right to make the request and even though the marriage is approved. "If I have been very intimate with a girl's brother," an informant explained, "if we have seen each other naked, if he knows me too well and I know him in that coarse way, too, he would not ask me for polite form if I should marry his sister." In other words, the reserve and formality of the polite form cannot be compromised by the specter of past intimacy. The polite form, from first to last, must be maintained on a most lofty plane.

Another such explanation runs as follows:

C—— called my father *cik'ĭs* [father's brother's son in this case]. I call C——'s daughter "cousin." When she married, I could have used polite form to her husband. Then he would have had to use it to me. But I did not want to because we had been pretty intimate. He would have had to act reserved, and it was hard to put him in that position after what had taken place.

The principle of former intimacy plus the principle of age often clarifies other apparently anomalous cases in which polite form is theoretically possible but does not take place in practice.

We have noted that the wife's *cik̆ĭs* (sister or female cousin) has the right to request avoidance or polite form if she wishes. How is it possible to reconcile the right of the wife's sister or cousin to request polite form with the practice of marrying a wife's sister or cousin when another wife is wanted or the first wife dies? One answer, of course, is that neither avoidance nor polite form is obligatory and that there is a greater tendency for married sisters to make use of these rights. But the more important answer by far is that the use or withholding of the polite form depends on the age of the sister or cousin when the man enters the family.

Children and adolescents were not expected to use the polite form. At eighteen or twenty years of age a young person was expected to take his place in the community. After this age period was attained, the individual had the right to use the polite form. In explanation an informant has told me, "A person could not request polite form from another until he or she was old enough to understand the custom, that is, until about eighteen years of age. Just because a girl goes through the puberty ceremony does not make it time for her to ask."

Therefore, if a man entered the family life while any of his wife's sisters and female cousins were still considered minors, there would be no possibility of polite form or reserve toward these individuals. Almost without exception, if Chiricahua are thrown together in the same encampment and do not use the polite form at once, they never will use it; for there grows up a measure of intimacy, of knowledge concerning one another, which obviates the possibility of later restraint. Witness these excerpts from Chiricahua accounts:

I have a sister-in-law. She is only ten years old. Later on, if she tells me about it, I'll have to use polite form to her. But she has grown up while I have been there. I've carried her around and played with her and teased her. I know that she will never tell me to use polite form.

I don't use polite form to my sister-in-law. I never will. She was young when I came over, and now she does not feel like asking me. But my wife's cousin was grown up when I married. I have to use the polite form to her and can never marry her, therefore. Besides, she was married at the time.

The principle is easy to grasp. When the eldest daughter matured, a man from another encampment married her and came to her encampment to live. By the time a younger sister had matured, the household would have expanded enough to require the labor of another helper, and he would take the younger sister for wife if he were planning to marry a second woman. When there were older sisters who used the polite form to him, they were ordinarily married and not eligible mates for him.

The same set of circumstances militates against the use of the polite form by a brother of the wife to his brother-in-law. Where the ages at the time of marriage are nearly alike, however, and no past intimacy interferes, the polite form is ordinarily used.

Avoidance relationships may be terminated by the proper action of one individual concerned and the consent of the other no matter how long the relationship has existed. An informant has described the necessary steps as follows:

A man might have bad luck. One after another of his relatives might die. There might be a certain relative whom he avoids, but who he thinks might give him good advice and encouragement if he could talk matters over with him. So he tells his wife that he does not want to avoid her relative any more. If she thinks it is all right, he rolls a cigarette, takes a few puffs on it, and sends it to the relative with word that, after this, they should not hide from each other. If the relative takes the cigarette and smokes it too, it is all over, and they do not hide from each other after that.

The custom of tendering the cigarette was called "he can walk up to him now."

Either individual concerned may roll the cigarette, but the woman through whose marriage the relationship was made possible must first be approached, if still alive, and her consent gained. A cigarette which is offered may be refused, but never in anger or to show disapproval. One may say, "We have hidden from each other all these years. All this time we have helped each other and thought well of each other. I do not think our relations would be helped by this move. I would rather hide from you for the rest of my life."

Sometimes avoidances and the use of polite form between a man and his deceased wife's relatives were terminated in this manner when the deceased had no available siblings and the man was forced to marry outside the encampment. In case of the wife's death and the severing of relations with the encampment, even the customary obligatory avoidances, such as those with the parents-in-law, may be abrogated. At the death of one's mate, those affinities to whom polite form was never used are no longer considered as relatives. To the others, avoidance or polite form, including all the customary duties and privileges, continues undisturbed unless avoidance is terminated as described above.

Husband and wife relationship.—The terms of the husband and wife relationship have yet to be mentioned. Only those in common use are given here. There is a word *bilnà·c'à·cń,* "he or she with whom I walk about," which can mean either husband or wife. Then there is a special term, *ci'isdzán,* "my woman," used by a husband in speaking of his wife, and another, *cihà·stį·,* "my old man," used by the wife in speaking of the husband.

The relations of the Chiricahua Apache man and wife were of a predominantly economic cast and hardly tinged with much sentiment or display of affection. A man who was too demonstrative to his wife was called "slave" and held up to ridicule by his fellows. The wife was required to follow her husband, whether on foot or horseback. She was expected to stay with the other women and find amusement and enjoyment with them. Few Chiricahua, even of the younger generation, accompany their wives to places of amusement today. Both may go to the same place, a moving-picture show perhaps, but each will go separately with members of his or her own sex. At a social dance no husband would think of dancing with his wife. There is much jealousy over the partners who are chosen, but no thought of branding one's self a "slave" by dancing with one's spouse enters the Apache's mind. At the feast which accompanies a social dance, it might be noted in passing, the men are served separately, and the women fare as best they can later. At home the wife eats with her husband.

The woman has the predominant share of the domestic duties to perform. She makes the home, gathers the wood and water, does the sewing, weaves baskets, shapes pottery, tans the hides, gathers the wild plants, preserves and prepares them, cooks the food, tends to the children, and even has as her prerogative the preparation of the native drinks. The husband's time is spent in hunting, fighting, raiding, and making weapons.

For all her conspicuous round of labor, the Chiricahua woman was less handicapped than the women of most preliterate peoples. There was one man's game, the hoop-and-pole game, which women were not permitted to see. On the other hand, there were tasks of the women from which all men were barred. There were few taboos directed against women as a group.

The Chiricahua Apache women, as well as the men, could be recipients of supernatural power. The "ceremonial woman" was often an important factor in the group, and her prophecies and promises governed many decisions pertaining to war as well as to economy. The Chiricahua woman was extremely influential in family councils. Since her husband came to her parents' encampment as an in-law, she was well protected from any abuse from him by her brothers and father. There was little place in Chiricahua psychology for romantic love in the sense that Western European culture has idealized it, but mutual respect, pride, and affection more often than not marked Chiricahua husband-wife relations.

Introduction.—The importance of the extended domestic family should not blind us to the existence of other social units which contribute to the solution of the problems of Chiricahua Apache life. Thus far we have merely defined and very briefly described these other units. To leave them without further treatment would be to lose the perspective necessary for appreciating the satisfying unity of Chiricahua social organization.

What is needed is some indication of the relative weight and importance of every social unit in each phase of Chiricahua social life. This section is much too condensed to be a full answer to this need, but by discussing a number of the tasks with which the society has to deal, and by showing to what extent each social unit is involved in their solution, some beginning in this direction will have been made, at least. Marriage and divorce have been treated sufficiently to indicate that the family alone controls them, and they will, therefore, not be discussed further here.

Childbirth.—When a child is born, the immediate family alone is concerned. The woman in labor is attended by her mother, her mother's sisters, and the other women of her encampment. Her husband does not attend. Some female relatives of his wife, women to whom he uses polite form, are sure to be present, and it would be unthinkable for him to see under such conditions anyone to whom he uses polite form. If, however, the labor is very difficult, a ceremonial man or woman may assist, and, if the encampment does not contain someone with the supernatural power to aid childbirth, an old man or woman from an outside encampment may be asked to come.

Child-rearing.—The rearing of children is entirely in the hands of members of the child's encampment. The mother, the maternal grandmother, and the mother's sisters are the ones primarily concerned with the instruction of the little girl. At an early age the child is taught the rudiments of the household duties, and as she grows older she is expected to assist in all woman's work.

The little boy is early taken in hand by the men of the encampment, principally by his father, his maternal grandfather, and his mother's unmarried brothers. One of these men will furnish him with a diminutive bow and small unpointed arrows as soon as he is able to handle them. A few years later more serious instruction begins. When the men are repairing or making weapons, they call the youngsters to them and have them watch the process closely and even assist in it. The Apache boy is proud to gain the attention of his elders, and so he learns the everyday tasks of life, and his feeling of consequence grows at the same time. Still later a boy will be delighted by an invitation to accompany his father or an uncle upon a hunt. Such expeditions serve as occasions to teach the boy the lore of the hunter and woodsman.

An Apache child is usually disciplined by the parent. But any close relative reserves the right to scold or punish him. Corporal punishment of children is not unknown, but the authority of the elders is sufficiently heeded to make the need for it infrequent. Often an unruly child is frightened into silence or better behavior. The Apache mother represents the hooting of the owl as a dire warning to naughty children. The Apache equivalent for the bogeyman is an undefined being called *gò·dè*. Its cry (the call of the poorwill) is enough to quiet children at night. Besides the *gò·dè*, the special bugbear of the Apache child is the clown who appears with the masked dancers on ceremonial occasions. The children are warned that the clown is coming with a big basket to take them if they do not behave.

This very sketchy description of the controls used in rearing and disciplining the Chiricahua child is enough to indicate that the authority over the child and interest in the child ordinarily do not pass beyond the boundaries of the extended domestic family.

Girl's puberty ceremony.—As soon after the first menstrual period as arrangements can be completed, the Chiricahua girl is made the central figure of an elaborate four-day ceremony. Not every maiden, it should be noted, has this ceremony performed for her. It is an expensive undertaking and can be consummated only when the girl's parents and relatives can afford it. But, since a girl's health, longevity, industry, and welfare

are believed to be largely dependent upon this ceremony, every effort is made to secure the necessary goods, and, although the rites differ widely in cost and display, some kind of ceremony is held except in cases of extreme poverty.

As has been suggested, the full burden of the expense falls upon the shoulders of the parents and the relatives who are financially able to help. In other words, it is the members of the extended domestic family who are responsible for the well-being of the girl and are anxious to safeguard her health and future.

Usually preparations begin far in advance. The father might begin to store away the necessities several years before his daughter's pubescence. When the time for the ceremony draws near, he has the proper ceremonial paraphernalia ready, such as the drinking tube and the scratcher, the unblemished buckskin robe, the eagle feathers, and the deer-hoof rattle. He then approaches a man who has the right to officiate for the girls at this time and arranges to hire him for the occasion. A fine horse, the proper payment for such services, is put aside. Meanwhile, some woman of the household or encampment is preparing a buckskin dress for the girl.

I do not propose to give a descriptive account of the ceremony here. My purpose now is to indicate a few of the outstanding features which serve to illuminate the relative place and importance of the girl, her parents, the family, the local group, the band, and the tribe in the rite.

The selection of the time for the ceremony and the place at which it is to occur are left to the parents. All the paraphernalia for the ceremonial man and all the food for the feasting are furnished by the parents, although much of it may represent the contributions of other relatives. The parents likewise arrange to have twelve large poles, which are to be used for the ceremonial structure, brought to the grounds.

While the first details of the rite are being enacted, the group of onlookers grows steadily. All the members of the girl's encampment attend and nearly all the members of the local group. A goodly sprinkling of visitors from other local groups and even some travelers from outside bands are to be seen, and their numbers increase as the day wears on. Those whose homes are far away from the grounds build temporary shelters near by and prepare to stay for the whole four days.

The completion of the ceremonial structure is the signal for the distribution of gifts and for feasting. Presents are thrown into the air, and a general scramble takes place. Great pots of food are carried in, and all are served. The women of the girl's family have done the cooking, and they distribute the food. After the feasting the girl is conducted by the ceremonial man through the first of the rites. The rest of this day is devoted to social dancing in which all those present take part. In the evening the rite is continued with the girl dancing to the sacred songs in the tipi and with the masked dancers performing outside for the entertainment of the visitors.

Early in the festivities the leader of the local group to which the girl's family belongs comes forward. He makes a speech, welcoming all visitors and requesting that all refrain from unruly behavior during the ceremony. Throughout the four days the girl not only dances each night in the tipi but is under many restrictions and is dressed in the costume made especially for this occasion.

Just what is the nature of this ceremony? If I were to supply the details, it would be understood as a prayer to the forces which cause all plant life to thrive that they grant the young Chiricahua girl health and vigor. But, waiving for the time the problem of what, in descriptive terms, the ceremony is, one may ask: What does it actually accomplish in the social life, and through which units are its functions realized?

In the first place, the ceremony throws a great deal of light upon the character of the extended domestic family. By a combined effort the family has ushered one of its members past a critical point in her life and assured to itself a woman of strong body and spirit. Second, the family serves notice of its power and wealth through the ceremony. Its members derive a feeling of consequence and importance from the display which their collective efforts have made possible. Moreover, it gives concrete expression to the close bonds within the family. The relatives who respond by aiding to defray the expenses of the ceremony are reaffirming the strong economic unity which has been claimed for the family relationship. Incidentally, the family is announcing to all that one of its young girls is approaching marriageable age.

There is a very real significance in the ceremony for individual members of the family. It gives to the girl a very real feeling of confidence and poise. The father of the girl directs much of the preparation and labor occasioned by the event, and therefore has his moment of public attention. The woman who has lavished so many hours upon the dress that is worn during the rite knows that it will draw inspection and comment from all.

The local group is also actively concerned in the ceremony. Because of the ceremony many strangers and visitors have been attracted to the locality. The local group, in which leadership and police duty are centralized, feels responsible for the maintenance of peace and order. It is represented, as we have seen, by the chief or leader, who talks to the people on the first night and stands guard against excesses and fighting throughout the rest of the period.

The band is represented at the ceremony by members of outside local groups, and the tribe by members of other bands. Though these visitors have no special functions to perform, their very presence is highly indicative of the nature of tribe and band and the relationship of these to the local group. It is evident that the tribe consists of a group of people whose community of interests is genuine, whose ceremonies are open to all, whose hospitality embraces all tribesmen.

The ceremony, then, furnishes a social occasion for all tribesmen who can reach the grounds. It serves as a symbol of the bond which unites all members of the same tribe. Here tribesmen may meet in games and dances. The painting and activities of the masked dancers who perform on this occasion are beneficial to all; the marriageable young people get acquainted; the old renew friendships. The looser, more casual bonds of the tribe as well as the strict, close-knit bonds of the family find expression, therefore, in this one ceremony.

Training of the boy.—Until his marriage the Chiricahua boy remains in the encampment of his birth. The family, quite naturally, is eager to be represented by stalwart, well-trained youths. When the boy reaches the age of fifteen or sixteen and is considered strong enough to withstand strenuous effort without injury, he is expected to pass through a period of physical training intended to test his manhood and, at the same time, to inure him to all hardships. If there are several boys of about the same age in the encampment, they are trained together under the direction of an older male relative.

The usual procedure is to train in early spring or in the fall, but often an icy plunge in winter is required. The boy is awakened before sunrise, made to take a dip in cold water, and then sent with a pack on his back on a long run over rough or mountainous country. The trainer runs along, whip in hand, to strike the legs of any boy who loiters. Often water is held in the mouth so that all breathing must be done through the nose. During this period the boy is thoroughly schooled in the making and handling of weapons. He has to demonstrate his skill in shooting arrows and in hurling stones with the sling. If several boys are in training, one shoots blunt arrows at another who guards himself with a cowhide or buffalo-hide shield. During the day the boys play the games of the men, such as the hoop-and-pole game. Wrestling matches, rough-and-tumble fights, the hurling of large rocks—in short, all imaginable activities of a strenuous nature are conducted to test ability and courage.

Skill in horsemanship is likewise encouraged at this time. The boys are directed to ride horses at full tilt toward a barrier and then to stop suddenly before it. The task which the boys dread most of all is the obligation to stay awake, night and day, as long as possible. This is undertaken to prove that the boys can take their turns with the older men at guard duty and that the camp will be safe in their hands. The youths stay awake as long as they can, often two consecutive days and nights. A relative is present to keep them awake.

There are many other methods of hardening the youths—as many as ingenuity can devise. The training is carried on for several three- or four-day periods, with a few weeks between periods, and continues until the elders are satisfied that a boy is prepared to withstand all the arduous and dangerous tasks of Chiricahua life.

Warpath training.—The training of the young man for general physical fitness is usually in the hands of the extended domestic family, as has been noted, but a few years later, when he is considered old enough for service in war, he goes through another period of training which is in the hands of the local group. The reason for the shift in authority is obvious. The local group is the smallest social unit with enough man-power to carry on hostilities, and it is, therefore, the logical unit to supervise the young man's instruction at this time.

The instruction begins when the young man volunteers to go on the warpath. Not every man is required to do this, and not everyone offers to go. But if a man delays too long, he is labeled a "woman," and he is accepted as one of the weaklings who prefer to stay back with the women and children in time of danger. When a young man has signified his willingness to undertake warpath training, he is often directed by his relatives to go to a shaman whose power is related to matters of warfare. This man performs a ceremony over him and may give him protective paraphernalia such as a designed hat and shield.

Next a war dance is held, and here, before all the people of the local group, the young man is expected to participate. He enters and dances furiously, now leaping in the air, now dropping to the ground, now dodging to the right or left. During this dance the young man represents an Apache warrior avoiding the missiles and arrows of the enemy. The old men sit in judgment on his alertness and agility. They decide whether the enemy has "hit" him or not.

If the boy has performed satisfactorily, he goes again to the warpath ceremonial man to receive further instructions. At this time he is taught the warpath words. On the warpath all the common terms which have to do with raid or battle may not be used by a novice. Instead, circumlocutions of a descriptive kind are employed. A mule, for instance, is called a "tail-dragger" in the warpath language. When the instructor is satisfied that the young man has mastered the terminology, his pupil is ready for the first warpath experience, and the next time a war party is organized he goes along.

The young man who volunteers for warpath service is called "warpath novice" and retains this status until he has completed his first four war parties. As long a period as a year may elapse before the apprenticeship is over. During this time, when the youth is at home, he is addressed and treated like everyone else. He is cautioned, however, that the way he acts at this time will determine his character throughout life. Cowardice and loose morals are especially undesirable during noviceship.

On the warpath, however, the status of the young man takes a sudden turn. He becomes the servant of the older men. Their call means instant obedience. These four war parties act as a training school and a test of character. The boy is expected to watch every move of the warriors with strictest care. He tends the horses, kindles the fires, cooks the food, and stands watch at night. All the irksome and unpleasant tasks fall to his lot.

He is hedged around, moreover, with numerous taboos and restrictions. The warpath language alone may be employed by him. He must not scratch himself except with a wooden stick given to him for the purpose. He must drink water through a reed tube. Certain foods are forbidden. When called he must turn around in a certain prescribed manner. On these first four war parties the novice may not enter into the fight. His office is to observe and obey. On the fifth war party, however, he is expected to be in the very front ranks doing heroic deeds.

From the description it may be seen that, so far as the warpath is concerned, the young man receives his training from any member of the local group, and he is responsible to any member of the local group for his conduct while he is a novice. When a victorious war party returns, war dances, social dances, and feasts follow, and members of the local group attend and participate in all of these. The extended domestic family, which is not powerful enough to defend itself alone, has lent its man-power to the local group and has merged itself with the local group for all war-making activity and the celebrations connected with it.

Leadership and rank.—The war-making functions of the local group imply some organization and leadership. The local groups do have leaders who, in the literature, have been called "chiefs" —a term which is misleading if it is used, as it often is, to indicate absolute or a large measure of control over a group of subjects.

It is difficult to see why these men should be called by any title more suggestive of power than "leader" or "adviser." What strong ascendancy they obtained was secured largely after white contact. The white man came into Chiricahua country seeking "chiefs" with whom to treat. The Indians did the best they could and directed them to the leaders of the local groups. Then the Chiricahua found, to their great discomfort, that the white officials assumed what no Apache would admit—that any agreement with the leader was binding upon the whole group. It became increasingly necessary, therefore, for the Chiricahua to invest their leaders with the right to speak for them. And so the power of the "chiefs," especially of those who were early selected by the whites as likely men with whom to conclude treaties, grew apace. The picture of Apache leadership, rank, and status under aboriginal conditions is quite different, however.

In the extended domestic family the leading man is ordinarily the oldest, as the structure of the family group indicates. The leader of the local group is the most powerful of the leaders of the families which compose the local group. His prerequisites are three: military prowess, wealth, and generosity. The constitution of the local group throws considerable light on the character of this man's position. The constituent families most often associate themselves with a particular local group because the prestige, power, and influence of a leader and his family seem sufficient evidence to them that they will be well protected and enriched if they camp in the vicinity of so distinguished a man and share in his exploits and good fortune.

The head man of a Chiricahua local group, then, can be thought of as a natural-born leader, one who earns the confidence and support of his neighbors. His influence is considerable, but it is of an informal nature. Few can afford to oppose him alone. His wealth is great, plural marriage is possible for him, and his family is somewhat larger, therefore, than the average.

This leader or chief is expected to speak on all important occasions. There is no binding obligation to follow his advice, and, if what he counsels runs counter to the views of the great majority, it is disregarded; but always what he says carries more than ordinary weight, and where opinion is divided or undecided, what the leader suggests is the decisive factor.

Moreover, the leader is expected to use his influence to promote peace in the local group. As soon as news reaches him of an act of violence involving two families of his local group, he hastens to see the principals or the leading men of the families concerned and attempts to force an agreement and settlement before reprisals and a feud break out. Here, again, it is his personal influence and powers of persuasion which count. The families are not forced to accept his recommendations except as they see fit. Likewise, when an Apache is accused of witchcraft, and a menacing crowd is deciding what treatment should be meted out to him, the advice of the leader is listened to respectfully and, more often than not, accepted.

Since the family is such a close-knit unit economically, it follows that those who benefit most directly from the wealth, power, and sagacity of the leader are his relatives. The members of his family bask in his reflected light. These relatives of the leader, these members of his family, form a status group. They are called "good people." Each of them is expected to be better trained and more careful of conduct than the ordinary Chiricahua Apache. A Chiricahua girl of such a family who is caught gossiping is scolded and told that it might be all right for a "trashy person" to act so, but that it is a disgrace for a girl of her family to conduct herself in such a fashion.

The son of the leader can also become a leader. He is recognized as a "good person," the son of a leader, and therefore a man of thorough training and exemplary conduct, and a man with powerful relatives besides. But he is recognized as a leader only if he takes an active part in public affairs and accepts every occasion to talk at meetings, to lead parties on the warpath and raid, and to heal breaches between families. Such an interest in public affairs indicates that he is ready to accept the responsibilities to which his birth entitles him. If, however, he makes no attempt to gain the public eye, it is realized that he is content to lead an ordinary life, with fewer honors and less obligations.

Since the band is composed of local groups, it contains as many leaders as there are local groups. The usual number of local groups for a band is from three to five. Sometimes the exploits of one of these leaders will be so outstanding and his fame so widespread that, if necessity forces the whole band to unite for defense, this man will lead the combined forces.

The place of the leader in Chiricahua society is clearly indicated by what transpires when one is killed. The death of a leader is a severe blow to the local group. Ordinarily a man's death is avenged by his family alone, but when a leader is killed, the entire local group moves to retaliate upon his slayer.

Crime.—Reference has been made to crime and its punishment from time to time, in different contexts. It may be useful, however, to bring these data together, to outline briefly the acts which the Chiricahua consider antisocial, to review the punishments reserved for such acts, and to mention the social groups concerned in securing justice for the injured.

In cases of murder, as has been mentioned, it is the family whose membership has been depleted and whose economy has been impaired. Moreover, it is with the members of his family that an individual has his close personal bonds, and here will be found those who are most incensed at his slayers. In the case of the murder of an ordinary man, one of three things may happen. The leader may succeed in acting as arbiter between the two families involved, in which case a compensation of valuable gifts will bring the matter to a peaceful conclusion. Or, if the murderer has been a troublesome fellow and a constant danger to his relatives, the extended family, rather than be involved in bloodshed on his behalf, may hand him over to the family of the murdered man. He is dispatched by the relatives of the dead man, and no further trouble ensues.

More often, however, the relatives of a slayer will refuse to give him up. Enmity, recriminations, and a deadly feud result. Despite the best efforts of the leader such a feud may run its course. Often several on each side are killed before the leader or other influential men can effect a reconciliation.

The slayer of a leader has little chance to escape or be defended if he is a Chiricahua of the vicinity. The death of a leader is felt to concern not only his family but also the entire local group. The family of the slayer can scarcely hope to offer resistance to the whole local group. If the leader has died at the hand of an outsider, a Mexican, or a member of another Indian tribe, his death is the occasion for a war party of revenge attended by all the men of the local group. The expedition is preceded by a war dance and followed by a victory dance. Much less enthusiasm could be evoked, however, over a war party to avenge the death of a man of ordinary status.

Rape is a most serious offense if it is an unmarried woman who is violated. The offender, if caught, is entirely at the mercy of the girl's relatives, for the girl's chances for a very desirable marriage are considerably lessened, with the consequent loss for the family of economic wealth and a strong additional member. Rape of a married woman is usually settled by presents from the offender or his family.

Theft within the family is unknown because it is unnecessary. If a relative of a Chiricahua has something which the Chiricahua needs, it is a rare case in which he cannot obtain it by asking for it. The Chiricahua have a formalized sentence used in cases of emergency when a favor or property is urgently needed, and a refusal dare not be risked. It is one of the cardinal sins and a certain sign of parvanimity to refuse a request couched in these terms. To a member of the same extended family, when the proper relationship term is affixed to this mode of "pleading in the Indian way," it is well-nigh impossible to return a negative answer.

Theft outside the family rarely occurs and can always be settled by restitution. Of course, the plundering of whites, Mexicans, and Indians who are not Chiricahua Apaches is not considered theft. It is a legitimate part of the economy.

If a Chiricahua has a personal conviction, not shared by the members of the local group generally, that he or a member of his family is being bewitched by a certain individual, he might ambush and slay the person suspected. Such action, if the identity of the slayer is known, might lead to retaliation and the type of feud described above. If, however, there is a general belief that a certain person is a witch, and if he is formally accused by someone, the matter becomes one of public interest. The members of the entire local group gather, hear the evidence against the accused, and determine his fate.

The vindictive attitude and authority of the entire local group in cases of witchcraft are most interesting points. If a man murders another, the slayer has weakened a single family and will be punished by that family. It is unlikely that he will slay again, and he does not usually represent a menace to the entire community. But not so with a witch. The witch's malice is not limited to a single act. His power to injure, to cause disease and death, easily passes beyond any family boundaries. His existence becomes a danger to all whom he meets and knows, to all the inhabitants of the vicinity, to the entire local group. Therefore, it is this local group which takes action against him.

Incest is usually dealt with by the family. The participants have disgraced themselves and seriously lowered the prestige of the family. Ordinarily, before the circumstance becomes generally known, they have been severely punished or disposed of by the family. If the hue and cry of "witch" arises, however, they may be roughly handled by those in the vicinity and may suffer a witch's fate. What happens to them in this case depends largely upon whether their family is a powerful one and is willing to plead and intercede for them.

Economy.—Little needs to be added to what has already been said to indicate that the extended domestic family life is the supreme economic unit. Even when there is an initial union of several families for economic purposes, the undertaking is always reduced to a family basis before it has gone very far.

Thus, men from a number of families may unite for raiding purposes. But once the booty is obtained, it is divided, and each man brings back his share to the family to be added to its resources. Again, women from a number of families might make a joint trip to a locality where the mescal plant is unusually abundant. But when the work begins, the women of one family will be toiling side by side. When the pit for roasting the mescal crowns is dug, they will put their plants together, and when the food is brought back to camp, the surplus provisions of the women of the family will be cached in the same place.

Ceremonial life.—A man's "ceremony" is his personal possession. He is under no obligation to perform it for the public welfare. Usually, then, he uses his power to prevent and cure disease in his own family. If his cures are of a remarkable nature, individuals of other families may approach him and request treatment. In such cases a substantial payment will be asked, but relatives rarely have to pay a shaman for a curing ceremony.

The same partiality to relatives is present when a ceremony is bequeathed or sold. The shaman always desires to leave his power to a relative and will instruct a member of another family in the ritual only if none of his kin is interested in carrying on the ceremony. There is no charge to a relative, but a price is set when an outsider is taking over the rite.

There are one or two occasions when ceremonies are used to benefit a wider group than a family. On the warpath a shaman with the proper power might consent to perform a ceremony to protect and hide the warriors from the enemy, or one might volunteer to make a crude ground drawing which would render the enemy unable to advance beyond it. Also, at the news of an approaching epidemic, a shaman with the right to design and paint masked dancers might be requested to do so and to have them dance to ward off the imminent danger to the entire local group.

Burial.—The dead are buried by relatives. The members of the extended family usually prepare and dispose of the body, but other relatives who live in the vicinity often assist. Non-relatives not only take no part in the burial but are even expected to refrain from watching the funeral procession. The deceased are buried, if possible, on the same day on which death occurs. Burial always takes place during the daytime and as far away from camp as possible. Caves or clefts in the rocks serve as graves. The favorite horse of the deceased is killed on or near his grave, and all his personal property is buried with the corpse or destroyed at the grave.

At the return of the funeral party the dwelling of the deceased is burned, and all who have come in contact with the body are purified by bathing in the smoke of a fire into which a sage, called "ghost medicine," is thrown. All this is done so that the spirit of the dead will not return to give "ghost sickness" to the living—a disease marked by extreme nervousness, faintness, and fear.[7]

Conclusion.—The section just completed, and indeed the entire paper, must not be considered a full exposition of any part of Chiricahua life. It is merely a statement of principles, the most condensed of outlines. Every item of ethnological data, whether it be a ceremony or a man's marriage with his wife's sister, takes on added significance if its relation to the social order is understood. This reduction of a large body of data to the socialized essentials has been undertaken in the belief that, once such an initial step is completed, the descriptive material can be handled more intelligently and meaningfully.

[7] For an extended discussion of "ghost sickness" and its relation to the social setting see Opler, *An Interpretation of Ambivalence of Two American Indian Tribes*, pp. 82–116.

THE SOCIAL ORGANIZATION OF THE FOX INDIANS

SOL TAX

THE SOCIAL ORGANIZATION OF THE FOX INDIANS

SOL TAX

INTRODUCTION

The early history of the Fox is closely linked with that of the Sauk, to whom they are closely related in language and culture. While often allied, the earliest historical records show that they were always distinct tribes, and although in the government records they are always considered together as the "Sac and Fox," the two tribes have always considered themselves as separate, and today they are, in fact, separated geographically and politically.

After a checkered history together in Wisconsin (where their presence was first recorded by the French in the middle of the seventeenth century), Illinois, and Iowa, the two tribes were finally (after the Blackhawk War) pushed west of the Mississippi. In 1842 they ceded their rights to their land in exchange for a cash annuity and for a reservation on the Missouri River in what is now Kansas. The Sauk were in this period far more tractable than the Fox and remained on the Kansas reservation until the early seventies when the reservation was exchanged for one in Oklahoma, where the Sauk still live.

In the middle fifties, however, the Fox, dissatisfied with their Kansas home and with the government's policy, moved back to Iowa where they bought a little land on the Iowa River. Unrecognized by the government, they barely existed by their little agriculture and by begging until, in 1866, the government sent an agent and resumed annuity payments. Since that time, living on their reservation near Tama, Iowa, they have increased their lands and their population and are now well established.

The Fox (also commonly known as the Mesquakie) are a Central Algonkian tribe who had, in historic times, a typical woodland culture. The year for them was divided sharply into two phases. In the summertime (from April until mid-September) they lived in villages of oblong bark houses, growing corn, beans, and pumpkins, with the women tending the crops and making mats and bags of rushes and bark, while the men went off to hunt or to war. In the fall they buried most of their corn to serve them the following spring and summer; then went off on the winter hunt, living a more or less nomadic life until the "great freeze" set in, when they gathered in large encampments. Winter houses were round and made of long poles set in a circle and joined at the top, the whole covered with mats with a bear-skin serving as a door. This duality in life is now gone, although both house types survive, and the women still have their fields of "squaw corn."

Gone also, of course, is war, which was apparently of two kinds. Occasionally there was a "national war" in which the whole tribe participated, but in addition there were frequent war parties initiated by individuals whose dreams or reputation fore-told success. The chief motives for such war parties were re-venge and glory; when the warriors returned, the women met them and they held a Scalp Dance in which the most successful were especially feted. All individuals of the tribe belonged to one of two divisions, *to'kan* and *kic'ko*, which divisions func-tioned in war as competitive parties and in peace as opposing sides in games and certain ceremonies. Now such roads to glory and such warlike competition are ended, but still the dual di-vision functions in its religious and social aspects.

The tribe was also divided into a number of presumably patri-lineal clans which were religious as well as social units. The tribal chieftainship was hereditary in one section of the Bear clan, but it was (even in contrast to that of the Sauk) relatively weak, and the tribal council was politically more important. The clans still exist, though possibly less strong than before, and since the Indians are still largely pagan, they are the chief reli-gious organizations today. The organization of the old house-holds, families, clans, and dual divisions is, of course, almost en-tirely broken down, but the Fox today, on their reservation where they own and administer the land communally, are still a going concern. Their culture has changed in many respects, but replacements rather than losses have constituted the chief process of change, and the society and its individuals seem integrated almost as well today as they were at any time in the past.

Their reservation is located about two miles west of Tama, in central Iowa, and five or six miles east of Montour. The boundaries of the territory, which is now inhabited by some four hundred Fox and a few Winnebago, are quite irregular, the entire area being about five miles at its greatest length and three miles in width. The missionary's home, the church, the government farmer's home and barn, and the little school and the teacher's home, are all located close to the highway and the railroads. From here there is a parting of the ways, and on all sides are scattered the dwellings of the Indians.

The grounds of each household are shut off from the road by a fence and a barbed-wire gate, which serve to keep the horses at home. The house, a small frame building of one or two rooms, stands a few yards back from the gate. Somewhere near by there is usually a wickiup, a round house with a frame of poles and a covering of mats (the old winter house), and very often there is near the house proper a square or rectangular open-air shelter consisting of a raised platform and a roof of branches supported by four poles, the whole having no walls. In the summer the family eats here, sitting on the platform, the food being cooked on an open fire near by. Frequently members of the family sleep on this platform also. This structure is probably a substitute for the old summer house which, with few exceptions, has disappeared from the settlement. There is usually also a barn, a pump, and almost always some fields of corn, some fruit trees, and a little vegetable garden planted with various kinds of beans, pumpkins, and squashes. In all, there are some seventy such "camps," and in each one lives a family consisting of parents and children, sometimes an aged grandparent, and often the young family of one of the children.

There are three cemeteries scattered over the reservation on the summits of hills; the burials are along family lines, for a man will usually be buried where his fathers lie. On a hill, which is said to be the highest spot on the reservation, there is a little clearing, neatly fenced with a bench running around it and forming a circular dance place where the Drum Society holds its ceremonies. In winter, of course, the society must meet in a house. This is the only obvious evidence of the rich ceremonial life in the tribe; the important gens festivals are held in barn-like houses near the homes of the respective clan leaders. In the lower country, near the highway, are the powwow grounds where the annual performance for the benefit of white visitors and the Indian pocket-book is held.

The land is not allotted in the sense that Indian lands elsewhere are; it all belongs to the entire tribe, and the whole community pays taxes to the state of Iowa. Of course, no land can be sold by an individual, yet Indians have definite rights to the farmland that they and their families have been working. Money and other property are inherited according to the state law, and today even wills are made. Personal property, such as tools, clothing, horses, dogs, and other chattels, are not inherited but are divided among the funeral attendants who wash and bury the body; horses, however, are kept by the family, and dogs belonging to the deceased are taken over by his ceremonially adopted substitute. If a person dies of a communicable disease, all his things are burned. Women own their own property and money, and their husbands have absolutely no voice in the management of these.

The old chiefs are gone, and with them the ancient tribal council with its ceremonial functions. The courts of law have jurisdiction in cases of murder, rape, and other major crimes, but for small offenses the only deterrent is public opinion, besides, of course, the displeasure of the Great Spirit, though it is difficult to ascertain just what part the latter plays. Social control, as practiced, may be illustrated by what one Fox Indian says:

If a man is known to have taken something, the owner could go to him and demand or take the stolen goods. If a man steals, they say, "Maybe he needs it." They always know what kind of a man he is. Children are reasoned with and taught when they steal; they are made to fast to make them better. Lying is not punished, but it is followed by loss of luck and reputation. Personal broils are entirely private and individual affairs. A person might hit a man going after his wife but not for something like stealing. Fighters should be ashamed; only dogs fight. It is best to keep the peace and do nothing.

There are among the people certain modes of behavior between relatives and toward strangers, and the culture is active
enough to enforce them. Even political enmities and rivalries
seldom interfere with normal social intercourse, and rarely does
real bitterness and personal feeling rise between members of
opposite factions. As for economic rivalry, there is little opportunity. The land is not allotted, so there is no ownership as
such; no fortunes or great difference in economic status. Where
one finds a family living in a wickiup, it is not due so much to
poverty as to a feeling of conservatism, and the conservative old
man or woman who prefers the old to the new is naturally not
envious of those whose opinions differ.

The native culture has become adjusted to the relatively slight
encroachment of white civilization. If the Medicine Society is
gone, there remain many ceremonies (with at least two new
organizations—the Drum Society and the Peyote cult); if the
main occupation of the men—hunting—is gone, farming has
taken its place, and the Fox have no aversion for work; if war
is gone, there is a rich outside life to relieve the ennui. So the
Indian still has much of his social life intact; he still has his
stories and his ceremonies, his dances and his songs; he has his
work and his play. And he has many new activities: schools,
newspapers and magazines, music and the band, competitive
sports, movies and trips to the city, political life and interests,
and the annual powwow. There are new holidays in addition to
their own: Wednesday and Saturday nights in town, Sundays,
Christmas, the Fourth of July, and others. No sooner has one
occasion passed and been forgotten than another looms ahead.
And all the round of life is still made meaningful in the nexus
of an integrated social organization which (however much it may
have changed) is still typically Fox.

THE KINSHIP SYSTEM[1]

KINSHIP TERMINOLOGY

The Fox have an Omaha type of kinship system. The Fox
terminology is illustrated in Figures 1–4 and Table 1, which

[1] Under the sponsorship of the department of anthropology of the University
of Chicago, ten weeks during the summer of 1932 and a month during the sum-

are self-explanatory.[2] A brief summary of the system is given on page 254.

Siblings.—Brothers refer to one another as *neto·täm^a*, and sisters use the same term for one another. Age distinctions are usually made, however, so that a man calls his older brother

---

mer of 1934 were spent with the Fox. An elaboration of the genealogical and schedule methods was used, the attempt being to get pertinent factual data about all the Indians and to supplement them with statements of informants. Genealogies of practically every Indian were taken, checked against one another, and combined and checked against a few genealogies recorded by William Jones about thirty years before, which were kindly furnished by Mrs. Welpley who worked them out from Jones's notes. In addition a check was made against a family census enumeration made in 1905 by Duren Ward.

The clan to which each name in the genealogies belongs was noted so that the method of descent could be accurately determined. For all living people the translation of the Indian names was obtained, and the circumstances of naming (connected with methods of descent) were noted where possible. A map of the reservation was made, and each household numbered; then separate records for each household were kept to determine the relations of the members and also to note dual-division membership and other data. To check the marriages appearing in the genealogies, and to obtain additional information, a record was made of as many marriages as could be remembered, with information as to the clan of each of the parties and their parents; the tribe of each (tribal intermarriage has occurred); the relationship of the couple to each other, if any; the relationship of the several mates of a person to one another; the number of children born to the couple; the number that were living when the marriage was dissolved (and what became of them); and finally how the marriage was dissolved. "Marriage" includes people who lived together for only a few months.

Records were taken of membership in the various societies revolving about "sacred packs," as well as in other societies, and in secular organizations such as the band and the baseball team. On the genealogies were recorded the adherents to the two factions, so that it is possible to see how they follow family and clan lines.

Meanwhile, the kinship system was obtained (with the help of the genealogies) from some twenty different informants. In cases of disagreements the Indians were sometimes brought together; and in the end, when the theory of the system was worked out, the reason for such errors (which occurred in the descendants of the second ascendent generation when the informant knew of no such relatives) could be easily seen. A few people, but not many, have the theory of the system worked out. Conventional patterns of behavior were obtained from informants and checked by observation; representative ceremonies were actually witnessed at one time or another.

[2] For the spelling of most of the terms the writer is indebted to Dr. Truman Michelson. In the charts relationships are read from ego. Triangles are males, circles females; horizontal lines connect siblings, vertical lines, parent and offspring; equal signs indicate marriage.

FOX KINSHIP SYSTEM

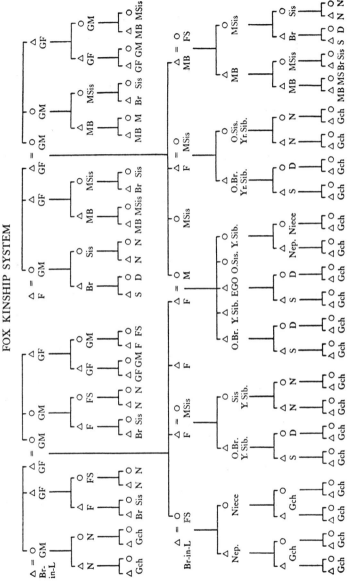

Fig. 1.—Chart of the Fox kinship system. Ego = male. For the native terms and the abbreviations used see Table I and the text.

FOX KINSHIP SYSTEM

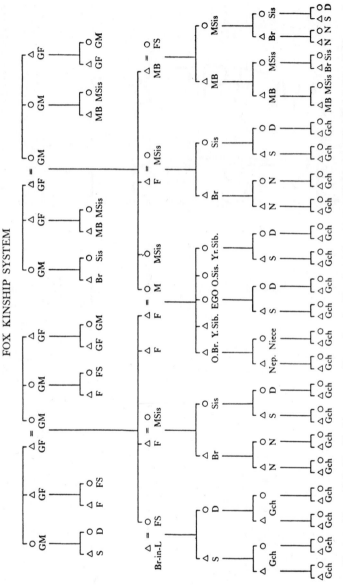

Fig. 2.—Chart of the Fox kinship system. Ego=female. For the native terms and the abbreviations used see Table I and the text.

FOX KINSHIP SYSTEM

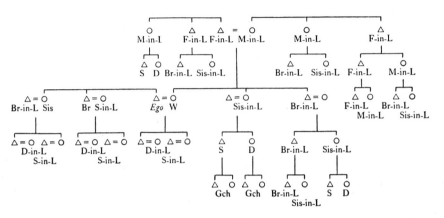

Fig. 3.—Chart of Fox affinal relatives. Ego=male. For native terms and abbreviations used see Table 1 and the text. (Ego's brother's wife = Sis-in-L.)

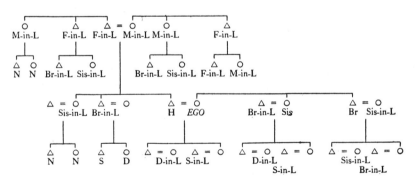

Fig. 4.—Chart of Fox affinal relatives. Ego=female. For native terms and abbreviations used see Table 1 and the text.

nesese, a woman calls her older sister *nemise*, and both call a younger sibling *nesime*. These terms are applied in the same manner to the children of anybody called *no·'s^a* or *negi·^ha* ("father" or "mother's sister") and include, therefore, the parallel cousins.

TABLE 1*

Fox Kinship Terms

neto·täm^a.......sibling of the same sex [Br]; [Sis]
nete'gwäm^a.....sister, man speaking [Sis]
netawäm^a.......brother, woman speaking [Br]
nesese..........older sibling of the same sex [OBr (m.s.); OSis (w.s.)]
nesime..........younger sibling [YSib]
nemise..........older sibling of opposite sex [OBr (w.s.); OSis (m.s.)]
negwi's^a.......son [S]
netane's^a.......daughter [D]
no·'ci'sem^a.....grandchild [GCh]
nenegwa·^ha......son of sibling of opposite sex [N]
ne'cemi·^ha.......daughter of sibling of opposite sex [N]
no·'s^a..........father [F]
negy^a..........mother [M]
negi·^ha..........mother's sister [MSis]
nes'egwis^a......father's sister [FS]
ne'ci'sä'^a.......mother's brother [MB]
ne'me'co.......grandfather [GF]
no·'gome's^a.....grandmother [GM]
nena·päm^a.....husband [H]
ni·w^a...........wife [W]
nita·gw^a........sibling-in-law of same sex [Br-in-L (m.s.); Sis-in-L (w.s.)]
ni·nem^wa.......sibling-in-law of opposite sex [Br-in-L (w.s.); Sis-in-L (m.s.)]
neme'co·m^a.....father-in-law [F-in-L]
nogum^a.........mother-in-law [M-in-L]
nenegwan^a......son-in-law [S-in-L]
ne'semy^a........daughter-in-law [D-in-L]

* This table gives the Fox kinship terms and their primary meanings. The abbreviations (in brackets) are used in Figures 1–4. In addition to the extensions given in the charts, children of any "grandchild" are "grandchildren," and parents of any "grandparent" are "grandparents." Further extensions may be determined by following the rule of reciprocals and the pattern of descent. The terms follow the orthography used by Dr. Truman Michelson.

Parents-children.—Father is called *no·'s^a*, and the term is applied not only to him but to everybody he calls *neto·täm^a* ("brother"); mother is *negy^a*, and the term is restricted to one's own mother. The mother's sister, and everybody whom she calls *neto·täm^a*, as well as the daughter of a *ne'ci'sä'^a* ("mother's brother") is called *negi·^ha* ("mother's sister"). The reciprocals of all these, in all their uses, are *negwiˊsᵃ* ("son") and *netaneˊsᵃ* ("daughter"). These terms thus take care of all parallel uncles, aunts, nephews, and nieces, among others.

Uncle, aunt–nephew, niece.—The mother's brother is called *neˊciˊsäᶜᵃ*, and this term is applied also to his son, his son's son, etc., indefinitely, and in addition to every man to whom the mother applies the term *netawämᵃ* ("brother.") The father's sister is called *nesˊegwisᵃ*, and this term is applied to all whom the father calls *neteˊgwämᵃ*, ("sister"). The reciprocals of both of these terms are *nenegwa·ᵏᵃ* ("cross-nephew") and *neˊcemi·ᵏᵃ* ("cross-niece"), and they are applied to the children of any *netawämᵃ* or *neteˊgwämᵃ*.

Grandparent-grandchild.—Any grandfather is called *neˊmeˊco*, and any grandmother *no·ˊgomeˊsᵃ*; and the reciprocal for both is *no·ˊciˊsemᵃ*, "grandchild." The grandparent terms are also applied, respectively, to the grandparents' siblings and to the great-grandparents and their siblings; the reciprocal follows consistently. Consistent also with the rest of the terminology employed in the cross-lines, the parent's mother's brother's son is called "grandfather," and his son also, etc., indefinitely, the sisters of these grandfathers always being "grandmothers" and the reciprocals of all being "grandchildren."

The system of affinity.—The most common term for "wife" is *ni·wᵃ*, and for "husband," *nena·pämᵃ*, and these terms are not otherwise used. "Father-in-law" is *nemeˊco·mᵃ* and "mother-in-law," *nogumᵃ*, and these terms are applied as well to their siblings. The reciprocal terms in all cases are *nenegwanᵃ*, "son-in-law," and *neˊsemyᵃ*, "daughter-in-law." The father's brother's wife is *negi·ᵏᵃ* ("mother's sister"), and this term is applied to the wife of any *no·ˊsᵃ* ("father") except one's own father; the mother's sister's husband is *no·ˊsᵃ*, and this term is applied to the husband of any *negi·ᵏᵃ*. The reciprocals of these terms in all their applications are *negwiˊsᵃ* ("son") and *netaneˊsᵃ* ("daughter").

The wife of any *neˊciˊsäᶜᵃ* ("mother's brother") is *nesˊegwisᵃ* ("father's sister"), but the prefix *negagadj* ("joking") is usually added to distinguish her from a consanguineous "father's sister." The father's sister's husband is a "brother-in-law." Brothers-in-law apply the term *nita·gwᵃ* to one another, and sisters-in-law use the same term, but brother-in-law and sister-in-law apply the term *ni·nemʷᵃ* to each other. Also, the husband of any *nesʿegwisᵃ* ("father's sister") by blood is *nita·gwᵃ* to a man, *ni·nemʷᵃ* to a woman, and the reciprocals are the same.

Rules of structure.—The Fox terminology is completely systematic and can be reduced to three rules or descriptive principles:

1. *The basic structure:* that one's own siblings, parents and parents' siblings, grandparents, parallel and cross-cousins, and the spouses of one's own and one's parents' siblings and all their reciprocals are as given above.

2. *Succession:* that the offspring of persons called "father" or "mother's sister" are always "siblings"; that the offspring of a sibling of the same sex are always "son" and "daughter," and of a sibling of the opposite sex always "nephew" and "niece"; that the offspring of a son, daughter, niece, or nephew are always "grandchildren"; that the offspring of grandchildren are always "grandchildren" again; that the offspring of a mother's brother are always "mother's brother" and "mother's sister"; and that the offspring of a father's sister are always the same as the offspring of one's own sister. (Note that there is no rule of succession from those called "grandparents.")

3. *Constant reciprocals:* that the reciprocals as given above never vary; each term has its set reciprocal no matter where in the system it is found. It is by application of this rule only that the offspring of persons called "grandfather" and "grandmother" can be determined.

It is by the application of these three principles that any doubts in the minds of the natives themselves are resolved. The first two are, of course, grounded in the minds of the Indians from long experience, and there is never the necessity of applying logic. In cases where the terms for the grandparents' siblings' children must be determined conceptually, however, the third is the guiding principle. The native conception of relationships is that they exist in pairs; mother's brother's son is not a relationship separate from father's sister's son; rather, *neʿciʿsä·ᵃ* and *nenegwa·ʰᵃ* are two aspects of one relationship.

KINSHIP BEHAVIOR PATTERNS

The range of the kinship system is limited only by knowledge and memory, and these differ with different people. Every person, of course, knows his immediate family and, in addition, his parents' siblings and their descendants. Grandparents' siblings are usually known if they live to maturity, and then most of their descendants are also known; beyond that only scattered names are remembered, although there are exceptional individuals who can trace their genealogies through most of the great-grandparent generation. The range is not unilateral; while some people remember more of their father's family, others are equally facile on the other side. Which relatives are best known depends upon circumstances and is not reducible to rule.

The kinship terminology is applied to all known relatives (even in some cases where the genealogical relationship is not traceable) so that the entire tribe is divided into a small number of types of relationship pairs. Each of these types carries with it a more or less distinct traditional pattern of behavior. Generally speaking, the behavior of close relatives follows the pattern in its greatest intensity, that of farther relatives in lesser degree; but there are numerous cases where, for some reason, a pair of close relatives "do not behave toward each other at all as they should."

Underlying all patterns of behavior is a general feeling that there should be good will toward all relatives, by marriage as well as by blood, and a feeling of affection and willingness to help. In addition, between all relatives by blood there is a certain amount of restraint that becomes greater when the relatives are of different sexes. In any pair of relatives these mutual feelings are essential in the behavior of both persons and may be called "equivalent factors." In addition, there are other "differential factors" between the two persons of a relationship pair, as will be seen in the following summary of the behavior patterns:

Brothers.—Besides the equivalent factors, which here emerge in a spirit of comradeliness coupled with what the natives translate as "respect" (a reluctance to discuss any matters of sex or even to joke freely together), there is a differential factor based on actual age. The younger brother should follow his elder brother's advice and to some extent obey him; on the other hand, the elder brother should especially look after his younger brother's welfare. The difference is very informal, however, and hardly more standardized than in our own culture.

Sisters.—What has been said above may be repeated here. Sisters are apparently a bit more ready to tease one another about boys than brothers are about girls, but there are wide individual differences.

Brother and sister.—Between a man and his sister the equivalent factor of restraint becomes very important. Even today sister and brother are never seen alone together, never would think of going together to a theater or dance, and if by chance they are left alone together in the house at night the brother seeks his bed outside. Yet there is no avoidance in any stricter sense. They may see each other, talk together, and work together; there is supposed to be real affection between them, and there usually is.

Differentially, all brothers respect their sisters in the sense that they respect their elder brothers; but they are more deferential toward elder sisters than toward younger. Also, of course, actual age makes a difference, for when the siblings are very young (say under ten years of age), their attitudes are different than when they grow older. A sister is expected to make things (like clothes) for her brother; and the brother tries to find out, through their mother, what his sister would like so that he can bring it to her.

(In addition to bashfulness about sex matters, there is also restraint between brother and sister on religious matters; they do not talk about duties or activities in the religious societies. It might be added that the restraint pattern between blood-relatives, especially of opposite sex, is sometimes carried beyond the family; thus, a very close male friend of a man would not feel free to take his friend's sister out.)

Father and son.—The father-son relationship is much like that between two brothers, except that the differential factor is very much stressed. A son is supposed to obey his father, and if he does wrong, the father is supposed to make him fast "for his own good"—the closest thing to corporal punishment that properly occurs.

Father and daughter.—As far as the equivalent factors are concerned, this relationship is much like that of brother-sister; but the differential factor is reversed, for the daughter obeys and respects her father even as her brother, to some extent, does her.

Mother and son.—The relationship here also is much like that between sister and brother, but since the mother does not have to respect the father in the way that the daughter does, she can help her son when the father is intent upon punishing him. Thus, if he is sent to bed without supper she may (after making him promise to do right in the future) bring him food. Obviously there are wide variations in matters such as this.

Mother and daughter.—The relationship between a mother and her daughter is much like that between a father and his son. It is up to the mother, or other close female relatives, to teach the daughter what she must know, both about household duties and more personal matters. While the father may give the girl good advice about how to behave, his wishes are generally transmitted through the mother, to whom is also intrusted the duty of discipline.

In the case of all these parent-child relationships (as with those of siblings) the pattern extends to all relatives who apply "parent-child" terms to one another, and in the case of the mother-child relationships the mother's sister is just as much equivalent to the mother in behavior as the various fathers are to one another, even though linguistically the latter are all *no·'sᵃ* while the former have different terms. But in these relationships more than in any others among the Fox, the intensity of the pattern depends on the closeness of the actual relationship or on the closeness of the actual social bond, so that a child brought up by its mother's sister would treat her as its mother.

Grandparents and grandchildren.—The equivalent factor of restraint is somewhat lessened between grandparents and grandchildren; there is considerably more intimacy between them than between parents and children, for example. The advice and help of grandparents are sought, and a father's father will, for example, help his grandson in an argument with his son, the boy's father. The restraint is not relaxed to the extent of allowing obscenity (such a thing would be unthinkable); but it is at the same time highly proper to talk over love affairs with a grandparent even of the opposite sex. The differential factor of seeking advice from, not giving it to, a grandparent is present. The grandson will haul water for his grandfather, fill his pipe, etc., as a sign both of his affection and of his respect.

Uncle, aunt–nephew, niece.—Although the previous relationships described are to some extent indefinite, and not so different from those found in our own society, the nepotic relationships are highly formalized and distinctive. Coupled with the other equivalent factors found in blood-relationships is one best described as the "joking relationship." The mother's brother and his sister's children, on the one hand, and the father's sister and her brother's children, on the other, characteristically play light practical jokes on one another, tease one another in public, and, in general, have what the Fox term a "nonrespect" relationship. At any gathering the raillery is usually occasioned by the presence of several pairs of joking relatives. Since these are restrained in their behavior by the same modesty that characterizes other blood-relatives, the joking is always of an innocent sort, with never any bodily contact or obscene reference. As might be expected, the restraint is more marked between relatives of the opposite sex.

There is one differential factor in these relationships: when the nephew and niece are young children, their parents threaten them when they are naughty with the name of their uncle (mother's brother), saying that he will come and eat them up, or something of the sort. This use of the uncle as a bogeyman is very effective, for the children grow to fear the man who sometimes actually does perform such a practical joke (to him) as to pour a pail of water over them as they sleep. Yet when the nephew or niece grows up, he is supposed to forget all this and love his mother's brother. By that time, of course, the uncle can be repaid a little in kind.

Siblings-in-law.—Between all siblings-in-law there is also a pronounced joking relationship, but since they are not blood-relatives, the restraint is absent, and the joking takes on a very ribald character, the keynote of which is, in the case of brothers-in-law, horseplay and obscenity with one jokingly acting as if the other were a woman, or, in the case of a man and a woman, mock love of a verbal nature only and some degree of suggestive obscenity.

Mother's brother's wife and husband's sister's children.—These are relatives who apply terms of consanguinity with the prefix "joking." All aunts and their nephews and nieces joke in the innocent manner, but these "joking" aunts and nephews and nieces joke together in the same way that siblings-in-law do. In addition there is, in this case, the differential factor that exists between uncle and nephew or niece; but when a boy is threatened with his mother's brother's wife, he is afraid of her love, for he is told that she will come and kiss him and make love to him, and this seems to be an effective threat.

Parents-in-law and children-in-law.—No joking is indulged in by these relatives, but neither is there real avoidance. The relationship is like that of parents to children in that children-in-law have duties toward, and respect for, their parents-in-law. But, especially when these relatives are of opposite sex, there seems to be a feeling between them of uncomfortable restraint that keeps them from speaking to one another except on business matters. They would never just sit down and gossip or indulge in small talk.

There are, of course, personal variations in all these relationships. Some people who should joke, for example, do not do so, perhaps because they are "far-away" relatives, or sometimes because one who is a poor teaser is afraid to start anything because he knows the other will get the better of him. Needless to say, there are a few individuals who cannot take a joke as they should. (Nevertheless, the pattern of joking is carried out more uniformly than any of the other behavior patterns, possibly because it is the most positive pattern.)

Some particular points about the kinship system will be discussed later, together with whatever interpretations seem feasible. It may be noted here simply that the foregoing outline shows that the kinship terminology and the kinship behavior patterns are the linguistic and social facets of one coherent system, and they cannot be considered separately until they are first considered together.

SOCIAL STRUCTURES

Besides being the center of the group of relatives already described—which the Fox themselves call the "family"—each Indian is a member of one or more religious societies, one of the two tribal divisions, probably (if he or she is mature) one of the two political factions, and possibly (if a man) the baseball team, the band, or one or another of the various clubs. It may seem as if the oft-recorded fact that the Fox have totemic gentes is being omitted, but although these have special characteristics that distinguish them from the other religious societies, they will be better understood as types of cult groups.

THE FAMILY

Bodies of kindred are, of course, overlapping groups, yet to a Fox Indian his group of relatives is by far the most important social unit to which he is attached. In a population of close to √ four hundred, the size of this group is normally from fifty to a hundred persons, scattered over the reservation in perhaps a dozen households besides his own. The blood tie is considerably stronger than the marriage tie, but this statement should be made with reservations, for when a marriage has lasted for a long time, the affinal ties—whether through habit or through the influence of the children—become strong indeed, and the bond between husband and wife and their children often becomes stronger than that which ties either the father or the mother to his or her family.[3]

What is to one person a group of relatives by marriage is, of course, a group of blood-relatives to his children. It is this group, relatives through the father and through the mother equally, that is, without any doubt, the most important social unit. Genealogies of all the members of the tribe show that, while in some

[3] The difficulty in establishing any firm generalization about the relative strength of consanguineous and affinal bonds by objective means rises from the instability of marriage itself. A great many marriages are of short duration, too short for them to have any effect on the social structure. In 1932 a record of 273 marriages that had occurred in the tribe was taken; of that 273, 67 of the couples were still living together. Of the 205 marriages that had terminated, no less than 105 had ended by means of separation—63 when there were not even any children to show for the marriage. Some people never settle down long enough to have families, and in any interpretive study these and the transitory marriages in general must be treated separately.

(It must not be supposed that the condition described is necessarily a result of recent disintegration. As far back as the genealogies can now be carried, to sixty or seventy years ago when the social organization was probably as integrated as it ever was, the same situation seems to hold. "Easy divorce" is, more probably than not, an old pattern.)

cases (owing to circumstances not to the point) more of the mother's family were remembered, in other cases the reverse was true. Nor is the distinction of cross-lines from parallel lines a difference of social proximity; in all cases the family group most meaningful in daily life is absolutely bilateral.

In addition to relatives brought into the family in the normal course of biological generation, there are additional adopted ones. It must be understood that there are two kinds of adoption among the Fox. In many cases, for various reasons, children may go to live with relatives other than their own parents (for a shorter or a longer time), and for purposes of receiving the child's annuities the foster-parents may adopt the child legally. Whether they do or not, this is often called "adoption." In this case the child is already a relative of the foster-family, and they keep up the old connections so that the question of changed incest groups, for example, does not enter.

What is more often called "adoption" by the Fox might better be termed "replacement" and will be described later. Suffice it to say that, whenever a person has died, no matter what his or her age, some person of approximately the same age, and the same sex, is taken into the family in his place and assumes the kinship relations that the original had. Behavior patterns are extended to people thus adopted, and a person will joke with his adopted mother's brother, for example, just as he did with his predecessor. Records of adoptions of living Indians show that they are never adopted to replace their own blood-relatives.

Relatives feel an affinity for one another that is not found in any social structure other than the family, even the so-called "gentes." They visit one another and stay as long as they please, and where there are personal likes and dislikes, there is also a strong feeling that the dislikes should be submerged. Political factionalism rarely cuts across family lines; when a woman and man of different factions marry, the woman usually changes to the man's faction, although cases of the reverse are known. The personal bitterness that sometimes accompanies burning issues is in such cases allayed, and the children rarely take sides.

Members of the family group are not supposed to intermarry, and it is extremely rare that they do. Eleven cases of inter-marriage of blood-relatives appear in the genealogies, and in all but three of them nobody knew of the relationship until the genealogy was worked out. The three cases have caused much disapproval even though the degrees of relationship would not be considered too close in our culture. The most disapproved case is of a man who married a woman who had previously been ceremonially adopted to take the place of his daughter.

When the clan groups are discussed, it will be seen that marriage within the clan is not only universally practiced but little thought of. This, together with the fact that in ceremonial replacement the adoptee takes the dead person's place in the family but not in the clan, is an indication that the bilateral family is the important social unit.

THE HOUSEHOLD

Since there are no formal rules of residence, and only very slight preferences in favor of matrilocal residence in practice, the household might be considered a group only by virtue of the fact that people have to live together somewhere. In daily life the household is extremely important, of course, for it is usually a group of the closest relatives, and it is the economic unit. Conceptually, however, it is not so important; people come home when they wish or stay with other relatives. Also, in prac-tice its economic unity is tenuous, since if a member of the house-hold has money, he does not necessarily contribute to the com-mon larder; while if he has no money, he may seek sustenance anywhere he happens to be. The household is important because for the most part it contains closely related members of a family.

In 1932 there were seventy-one households: four consisted of a lone man or woman; six consisted of two persons each; eleven consisted of three person each; ten consisted of four persons each; ten consisted of five persons each; six consisted of six persons each; six consisted of seven persons each; nine consisted of eight persons each; six consisted of nine persons each; two consisted of ten persons each; one consisted of twelve persons. Most of them consist of a married couple and some or all of the children of both, or of one or the other by a previous marriage; but in a large number an unmarried brother or sister of the husband or wife, with perhaps a grandchild or some miscellaneous relatives, complete the household. In only one case do two elementary families live together; in this case a man with children by a previous wife married a woman with a married son and family, and all live together. The most frequent cause for any doubling-up (residence of a young couple with the parents of one, for example) is the scarcity of land and houses.

It is not intended here to discuss the religious groups, which Dr. Michelson[4] has so exhaustively studied, except in so far as they are pertinent to the description of the social organization. There are two types of religious societies. The most important consists of a group of members of a "sacred pack," of which there are many, who in the ceremonies are the hosts and, among other distinguishing activities, do not eat. In this type the membership is to some extent hereditary but not fixed as to number, while at the same time there are no particular fixed positions that are always to be filled. Of this type, the sacred packs are all more or less linked to a few "major packs," the members of which constitute what are usually called the "gentes."

In the second type, there are no sacred packs as such; the membership (except in the Peyote cult which, being foreign, follows a different pattern) is relatively fixed, and there are positions to fill. The first type is more important and will be considered first.

The gentes.—How many sacred packs there are in existence among the Fox today no individual knows, but there are certainly at least forty. These packs are classified today into eleven groups, and within each of these groups there is a number of "major packs" and a number of "minor packs." Those persons who are connected with a major pack are connected with all the major packs of its group; but only those connected with the

---

[4] See Bibliography for Dr. Michelson's contributions.

major packs of a particular group can be connected with its minor packs. It thus appears that these groups of packs are the basis of a classification of the people, and how one becomes attached to a group becomes an important point.

The rule is that, if the father belongs to the Bear group or the Wolf group, or one of the others, all his children automatically belong there too. Thus there is patrilineal descent. But each of these groups, which may be called "totemic groups," has a stock of personal names, and if a child is named from the Thunder, for example, he is a member of the Thunder packs, no matter what his father was, in addition to his patrilineal group. This is considered "borrowing," however, and his children, in turn, will always belong to his father's group. Also, people can be taken into the totemic groups in other ways, so that conceivably a man might belong to all of them. It would seem as if these totemic groups are rightly called "gentes" since they are patrilinear in ultimate succession, no matter how much "borrowing" goes on. Yet in daily life clan groupings are conceived of as units without any thought as to how the members became members, for they function as ceremonial societies rather than as hereditary social institutions.

If an Indian is asked to what gens another belongs (and if he understands what is meant), he will think of one of three criteria by which to judge. If he remembers that at the War Chief festivals this person does not eat, he will say he belongs to the War Chief; if he remembers to which gens the person's father was allied, he will answer with the name of that gens; on the other hand, he may simply think of the meaning of the person's name, and if it refers to the Wolf, he will answer that the person belongs to the Wolf gens. Sometimes the answer is that he belongs to two or more gentes. In the native mind today membership in a group of packs is membership there, no matter what the father was.

The basis on which personal names are given is this: If there is no particular reason for giving the child a name from another gens, its father's gens bestows one from its supply of names; if there is any reason for wishing (1) to name it from some other gens than that of the father or (2) to name it into a particular gens like that of the mother, it is done without any difficulty. Of 366 recorded cases of living Fox Indians (1932), 71 were named from a clan other than the father's. Of this number, 10 were illegitimate so that, the father being unknown, the name could not come from his gens; in 2 cases the father was a white man or half-breed without a gens, so that the children were named from the mother's gens. In 16 cases there had been previous deaths in the family, and for a change of luck they decided to name the children from another clan. In 2 cases the mother's sister or the mother's mother adopted the child before it was named, and they took the right to name it from their gentes. In 1 case the child was posthumous, and the stepfather named it. Three children were named by their father's father's mother "out of respect for her old age." The circumstances for the remainder of the cases are unknown except for the statement that "the father gave his permission." (Anent the naming in another clan for "luck," McGee in 1898 quotes the last chief, Push-i-tani-ke, as saying, "When a couple are married and the first child is born, the father has the right to name it, but if it dies, the mother takes the right."[5]

The chief reason for a person's becoming a member of a group of sacred packs, other than by inheritance or naming, is that he is a good singer and knows the songs. He may then be asked to participate as a host in the ceremonies of one of the gentes, and thereafter he is considered a member. As far as the records show, there are three persons who are hosts in more than three gentes.

There is a tradition that the gentes are supposed to be exogamous, and the rule, as it is remembered, is that a man should not marry a woman who belongs for any reason to any of the gentes to which he, for any reason, belongs. This rule is not followed today, and as far as one can judge from the genealogies, it was never followed even if one limits it to purely patrilineal gentes. Certain it is that today there is absolutely no sentiment

[5] *A Muskwaki Bowl*, p. 89. The rule is not so fast now, at least, but the same idea holds.

in favor of gens exogamy, nor is there any statistical preponderance of usage in its favor.

The records of marriages, together with records of the clan
names and the clans of the parents of the parties in the marriage, show that there actually is no clan exogamy. In order to
give every benefit to the notion that there is such exogamy,
only marriages of those whose gens names and whose fathers'
affiliations both mark them as definitely belonging to a certain
clan will be used in the following statistical summary.

For convenience, the largest gens (judged by names) may be
taken. There were, in 1932, 121 persons with Bear names (as
opposed to 100 Thunder, 55 War and Peace Chiefs, 38 Wolf, 39
in three Water clans, 12 Eagle, and one old Pheasant woman).
Of these 121, there were 89 whose fathers were also Bears. Of
these 89, only 42 had been married, but a total of seventy-nine
marriages had been contracted by these 42 Bears. Of these
seventy-nine, twenty-three marriages were with War Chiefs;
twenty-one marriages were with Thunders; ten marriages were
with Wolfs; six marriages were with Water peoples; one marriage
was with an Eagle; seven marriages were with Foreigners; four
were intermarriages among the 42 Bears; and seven were marriages with then deceased Bears.

About one-seventh of all marriages contracted by Bears thus
contradict gens exogamy. Since the Bears constitute one-fourth
of the tribe, however, it might be argued that there is a tendency
to marry out; but when it is remembered that one-half of a
Bear's blood-relatives are normally Bears (and he cannot marry
them), the difference between one-fourth and one-seventh is
accounted for.

The genealogies show that the gentes were hardly more exogamous in the past than they are now. It is significant that
clan intermarriages have occurred among the oldest and most
conservative people living today. To what extent are the gentes,
then, social institutions? They do not regulate marriage, they
have no discoverable juridical functions, their connection with
family lines is tenuous; today, at least, they seem to be social
institutions only in the sense that other cult groups are. It is

for this reason that the term "gens," usually applied to a unilateral kinship group functioning in the regulation of marriage and in secular social life (so that, for example, the kinship terms are often applied throughout gentes, as among the Omaha), should be applied only with reservations to the Fox groups that surround the sacred packs.

There is one group organized about a sacred pack called *mo-wi-ti-a-ki* (the "Little Spotted Buffalo" group or, as Michelson translates it, the "Dirty Little Ani"). It is connected with the packs of the Wolf gens, but one does not have to belong to the major Wolf packs to belong to it, and, indeed, most of the members are not of the Wolf gens. Yet the patterns involved in this group and its ceremonies are exactly like those of the others, the members of which are considered to be in a particular gens. It seems to bear out the conclusion that the gentes vary less from purely religious cult societies than they do from the social institutions that ordinarily bear the name.

Even more significant, perhaps, is the matter of the Buffalo sacred-pack organizations. The Buffalo (or Buffalo Skin) is one of the minor packs of the Bear gens and a major pack of the War Chief, Thunder, and Wolf gentes. The War Chief and Thunder groups hold Buffalo ceremonies twice a year, and the War Chief and Bear gentes, at least, have names in their stocks that refer to the Buffalo. There are "different Buffalo" for each of the gentes, and yet forty or fifty years ago, when there were gens houses in the Fox village (houses in which the ceremonies were held), there was one which was a "Buffalo" house that was, presumably, like those of the gentes proper.

The Singing-around Society (*kiwagamo'ag^{ki}*).—This society has a membership which cuts across family and gens lines and yet is determined, today, largely by heredity. Generally speaking, membership is passed from parents to children, but since a person holds only one membership, he can pass it on to only one child. He (or she) usually chooses his successor during his lifetime, and then both are members of the society, holding one membership between them. In one case an old man, who received his place from his father, has appointed one of his sons to take his place, and that son has in turn since appointed his son (seven years old at the time he was appointed) to take *his* place. In 1932 all three were still living, and one membership was held by three persons. None of the other members of this family can expect in the normal course of events to belong to the society.

There are two other ways in which a person can become a member, however. If a member dies without having appointed his successor, the person who is subsequently ceremonially adopted to take his place will take his place also in the society. The third method by which persons have entered the society is by having become cured through its efforts. In one case where this occurred (some forty years ago) the man is not only a member of the group but is often called by the name of the group.

Of the forty-seven recognized members today, twenty-six are men and twenty-one are women; of these, twelve men and seven women received membership from the father; five men and four women received membership from the mother; one man received membership from his mother's father's brother; one man received membership from his mother's mother's brother; one man received membership from his mother's brother; one woman received membership from her mother's sister; one woman received membership from her brother; one man received membership from a nonrelative because he is such a good singer; one man and four women received membership by replacement of a member by ceremonial adoption; one man received membership because he was cured by the society; and three men and four women received membership by unknown means.

The society "sings around" at the homes of the members of the whole tribe during an epidemic, and it also functioned in the spring of 1934 when a serious drought threatened. Regular meetings are not held, however, and the society has lost most of the social importance it once may have had, chiefly to the Peyote cult.

The Religion Society.—This society, sometimes called the "Drum Society" or "Dream Dance," is a comparatively recent importation (probably from the Potawatomi of Wisconsin). All the positions in the society surround four drums, each of which has a leader and various functionaries. Membership is not strictly limited, however, and positions are available to any who are interested and show the proper religious spirit. Actually, the membership is chiefly concentrated in a few families that are politically allied.

The Peyote cult.—The Peyote cult, which is growing steadily in importance among the Fox, has been in the tribe for about thirty years. Membership is open to everybody, for the cult is mildly evangelistic. Since part of the belief of the cult is that the old religion of the Fox is false, however, people strongly involved in other societies are not likely to become Peyote members. Nevertheless, two Peyote members are in the Drum Society, and some of them take part in the gens festivals. The chief motive for joining the Peyote cult seems to be its curative powers; the peyote is supposed to be somewhat of a cure-all, and when other treatment fails, the patient may take up peyote and thereafter remain a member.

THE DUAL DIVISION

All Fox Indians, male and female alike, are in either one of two divisions called *kic'ko* and *to'kan*. The rule of membership is this: If the father is a *kic'ko*, his eldest child is a *to'kan*, his next child a *kic'ko*, the next a *to'kan*, etc. If he is a *to'kan*, his first child is a *kic'ko*, etc., alternately. In this way the tribe is divided as nearly as possible (by any such methods) into two equal divisions. The divisions used to function in war, but now function mainly in games and ceremonies. Whenever a lacrosse game is played, instead of "choosing up" sides, the *kic'ko* line up against the *to'kan;* and so with all the games, including partnership gambling games (except when members of another tribe are present, when the split may be along tribal lines). In the ceremonies the *kic'ko* and the *to'kan* have dancing or eating contests. In all cases *kic'ko* are placed to the south, *to'kan* to the north; the former are connected with white, the latter with black.

The rule of membership is determined automatically, not by any naming or initiation, and among the first things that a child learns is the division to which he belongs. Yet (today, at least) people do not know the division affiliations of other members of the tribe, unless they happen to remember the side they were once on, or remember what a person's father or next sibling is.[6]

What is to some extent a dual division of the tribe that functions throughout the culture much more than does the foregoing is the division into two political factions. In 1876 the government presented (for purposes of paying the annuities) a new form of tribal roll. Where, previously, only the heads of families were entered on the pay rolls and the number of children was given without specifying their names and ages, the new form required the names and ages of everybody in the family. For "religious reasons" the Indians refused to sign the new roll, and they received no money. By 1881 most of the Indians had signed, but some conservatives refused. It does not appear in the records, but some now say that the more progressive Indians signed and used their annuities to pay the communal taxes; later, when others signed the rolls, they kept their money. This is often cited as the origin of the factions.

In 1881 the principal chief died, and his son succeeded him; the son died within a few weeks. The next son was young and timid, and the council proclaimed Push-e-to-neke-qua chief in his stead. It appears that this man was not of the same family of the Bear clan as the old chief, and, although nothing was said (apparently) at the time, some fifteen years later, when another question of annuities came up, the question of the chieftainship rose as a paramount issue. At that time there were two factions: one unprogressive, opposed to schools, farming, policemen, highways, etc., and also in favor of the old line of chiefs; the other, more progressive, was led by Push-e-to-neke-qua. Today the

[6] One interesting point is that, although the rule of membership given above holds for practically every member of the tribe, it does not hold for one particular group of clans—those related to Water. In these clans all persons are *kic'ko*. There is no rationalization given for this circumstance, but it is affirmed by all; there are not enough cases from these clans to ascertain if it is the name that determines the clan for this purpose or the clan of the father, or both. Interpretations are difficult with such a paucity of data.

same factions exist, with the son of Push-e-to-neke-qua, Young Bear, the leader of one, and the other pretender to the chieftainship, Old Bear, the leader of the other. The latter is still the conservative faction.

It is quite possible that the factions are older than this history. Whenever an important question comes up, the division of opinion follows factional lines, and it is possible that the issues of signing the rolls and succession to the chieftainship simply divided the tribe again in accord with an already present cleavage. The fact remains that the factions are led by two of the three families of the Bear clan, the third family siding with Young Bear as a rule. The other families are also divided without regard to clan.

Each family of the tribe tends to be a unit in political matters, but not so the clans. In ceremonial matters (where the clans are important) factional differences do not enter, and neither of the two factions seems to be more progressive in religious matters than the other. But the members of the Drum Society are nearly all leaders in the Young Bear faction, and there are more members of the Old Bear faction in the Peyote cult (although the leaders of both factions disapprove of peyote).

Marriages between members of the two factions are not uncommon, but in such cases one of the parties to the marriage changes his or her allegiance to suit the other. Women switch more often than men, and there are cases where a woman has changed sides with each of three or four marriages. In 1933 an old woman who, with her family, belonged to one of the factions married the leader of the other faction; now she votes with her husband. In cases of marriage across faction lines, the children (so far as the records are available) do not belong strongly to either faction, since the father's family has one allegiance and the mother's another, and both sides are felt to be equally close. Obviously on such a basis this dual division cannot become a permanent social institution; yet it is extremely important at present, and a great many political and even personal issues are decided along factional lines.

SUMMARY

The bilateral family, cutting across the ceremonial, non-exogamous, and only weakly patrilineal gentes and other cult societies, is the unit in social life to which all allegiances are eventually referred. To consider the traditional dual division, or the factions, or the gentes as of any social significance apart from their connections with the families is to give a false picture of Fox social organization. It is the family that is connected with the kinship system; for the terms and the behavior patterns that go with them are never extended beyond the traceable blood- and affinal relatives—never to all members of the clan or to the dual divisions.

SOCIAL CUSTOMS

MARRIAGE

Courtship.—Ideally, Fox young people are completely chaste before marriage. The parents shower them with good advice, watch carefully the company they keep, and—should an affair look as if it were becoming serious—speak with them about the faults and virtues of the prospective mates and their families. Of course, in these days of automobiles and schools, parental influence is, of necessity, weakened; nevertheless, even now marriage is considered a matter in which parents should have a hand if possible.

In the very recent past there was a definite procedure of courtship. Becoming acquainted with a girl during the course of daily life, a young man took a liking to her. Presumably he received some encouragement; having heard his flute outside her house in the evening, perhaps she came out—managing to evade her mother's watchful eye—and held a tryst with him. But formally the courtship consisted of nocturnal visits to the girl's bedside. In the summer houses, the sleeping benches are about three or four feet from the ground; the young man entered the house, held a lighted match to his face to display his identity (and also to be sure of the identity of the girl) to her and the family, and stood beside the girl's bed to talk to her. This he

continued to do every few nights, and finally—having acquainted his parents with his actions and received their approval—he
proposed marriage. If the girl accepted him, she set an approximate date for marriage ("harvest time," for example). Then the
young man visited her no more in this way, although he might
speak to her in the daytime. They might give each other small
gifts to seal their betrothal, which was not, however, made
public.

Marriage.—When the time came, the young man went to his
fiancée's home again at night in the same way. If she were still
agreeable, he spent the night at her side, remaining chaste, however. In the morning he would stay until the family had seen
him, and then he would leave before breakfast. The next night
he came again; in the meantime, the girl and her parents had
had a last chance to consider; if all was favorable, the young
couple consummated the marriage. In the morning the young
man stayed for breakfast and became part of the girl's household. In a few days he took his bride to his own home, and his
relatives dressed her in new clothes and gave her presents of
drygoods and horses. The latter the bride always gave to her
brothers or, if she had none, to her mother's brothers or to her
brother's children (own or classificatory). Some time later her
family sent a number of gifts, consisting of foodstuffs, to his
family. Then the marriage ceremonies were over. The couple
stayed with the wife's folks, or the husband's, until they had a
place of their own.[7]

Divorce.—Nowadays, legal marriages are often contracted,
but since the cost of a legal divorce is considerable, they are not
usually legally dissolved. Instead, the couple simply separate
and find new mates. Second marriages were probably never sol-

[7] It may be noted that further evidence of bilaterality of the family is to be
found in this procedure; gifts, tending to be of equal value, were exchanged;
residence from the very beginning tended to go back and forth between the two
families. Also to be noted is the conceptual equivalence of a girl's brothers (her
own generation), her mother's brothers (of the generation above), and her brother's children (of the generation below); actually, all are considered on a generational par, and this makes it less difficult to understand why the cross-cousins
(actually on a generational par) are called by terms used for uncles and nephews.

emnized by the exchange of gifts, and they do not seem to be now.

The chief cause for divorce is simply incompatability. If the couple begin to quarrel, they rarely try very hard to make a success of their marriage. Ideally, husband and wife should overlook small faults, even minor excursions into unfaithfulness; in practice they overlook very little, and marriages often break up over minor misunderstandings. Actual adultery is occasionally condoned, but not if it becomes public. There are women who have very bad reputations, of course, and it is noteworthy that now they find husbands only in other tribes.

TABLE 2

MARRIAGES TERMINATED: SHOWING DISPOSITION MADE OF CHILDREN

DISPOSITION OF CHILDREN	MARRIAGES TERMINATED			
	Total	By Divorce	By Death of Husband	By Death of Wife
Total cases.................	205	106	44	55
No children living..........	110	63	21	26
Wife kept...................	45	29	16	....
Husband kept..............	11	....	....	11
Wife's family kept..........	21	10	....	11
Husband's family kept.......	5	....	2	3
Miscellaneous and unknown...	13	4	5	4

In cases of divorce the woman usually takes the children with her, as indicated in Table 2. In this table, information relative to the disposition of the children on the death of one of the parents is also included; in most cases the wife and her family take care of the children, but the father, when living, retains his interest in them.

Preferential marriages.—Although in times past cases of polygyny were more common, in all the genealogies only one case came to light; the preference in such cases was always that the wives should be sisters. The sororate itself is still common knowledge; it is felt to be highly proper now, but in the old days it was, apparently, almost compulsory. In seventeen cases of persons now living, the first and second spouses have been thus related (see Table 3). It is apparent from this table that the levirate is now much more common than the sororate, but that neither is of great importance.

A most interesting form of the sororate was the marriage of a man and his wife's brother's daughter. Although no cases of such a marriage are on record, and nobody remembers the last one, a few of the old people describe the custom in such detail that there can be no doubt of its presence in the old days. In

TABLE 3

RELATIONSHIP OF THE FIRST AND SECOND MATES
(IN PREFERENTIAL MARRIAGE)

MARRIAGE	NUMBER OF CASES	
	Actual Relationship	Classificatory Relationship
Woman married two brothers..............	5	6
Man married two sisters...................	1	1
Man married a mother and daughter........	....	3
Woman married both a man and his sister's son...................................	....	1

the oldtime wickiup there were definite sleeping places on the benches that lined the building, and a married daughter and her husband had their place. Occasionally, if the wife's family liked the young man and wanted to be sure that he would remain in the family (so the informants stated), they took one of their son's daughters, a girl of perhaps eight years, and "put her on the bench"; that is, they had her sleep across the head of their daughter and son-in-law's bed. Thereafter, no matter where the daughter and her husband lived, this little girl—the wife's brother's daughter—lived with them. When she grew up, she would become the man's second wife, and if the first wife died before the child grew up, the husband was expected to await her maturity.

Birth.—When a woman is pregnant, she tells her close female relatives, who tell her what to do. During her pregnancy a woman must be very careful of her health in order to protect the baby. Since there are beliefs that eating scabby fruit will give the child scabs, or eating bologna will injure the child, since it (like the child) is wrapped in skin, or beheading a chicken will cause the baby to be born with a broken neck, etc., there are many things a young woman must learn.

Furthermore, she must be careful to stay away from public places where sorcerers might easily get at the child. Both the father and the mother must be wary of engaging in quarrels— for the baby's sake always—and the father, too, is careful of what he eats and does (for example, he should not touch light-ning-struck trees, snakes, corpses, etc.—innumerable things).

A woman makes preparations for childbirth outside the house in a specially built wickiup. When the labor pains begin, she goes into the wickiup, and the husband notifies women relatives who usually know what is best to do. They cut and bury the umbilical cord and bathe the baby; the mother bathes herself.

The wife in the old days stayed away from her husband in her wickiup for forty days after the birth of the child; nowadays she stays only about ten days. It used to be considered very harmful to conceive a child while still nursing another, so husband and wife did not live together for at least a year—at least, regularly—but beliefs such as this have relaxed very much in recent years.

Puberty.—Even today the puberty wickiup is general. At a girl's first menstruation, she is thrown into the water, with her head covered; then she must be segregated for ten days from everybody except old female relatives. After the ten days she is a woman "and should consider herself as such," but for ten days more she cooks for herself, and at every menstrual period she does the same.

There is no sort of puberty ritual for boys. A boy in the old days was taught to fast, both for the general good of his soul and in the hope of getting a blessing from some spirit. Fasting is still thought important, but with children going off to school it is practically a lost art.

Death.—When a person dies, runners are sent to notify the people, and the same evening there is a ceremony—much like the feasting at the gens festivals—conducted by the gens to which the dead man belonged. It is here that the gens plays its most important part in a person's life. Attendants from other gentes are appointed to sleep that night in the house and to dig the grave the next day. The body is washed and dressed and carried up to one of the three cemeteries, in these days on a truck with a motorcar funeral procession. (The choice of cemeteries follows family lines in general.) A clan marker is later put on the grave. Meanwhile visitors have been bringing gifts to the dead man's family, even while the body is still in the house. The spirit of the funeral ceremony is much like that in our own society.

Adoption.—Ordinary adoption is informal and irregular, but ceremonial replacement follows a definite pattern. Some time about a year after a person has died, his relatives choose some person to take his place. They usually find somebody who is close to the age and of the same sex as the deceased, and presumably somebody of whom they are fond. There is one case in which an old man replaced a child a few months old. The adoption feast, at which a general feast and a religious dance are held and at which the adoptee receives new clothes and many gifts, is usually given by the closest relatives, who furnish the wherewithal, at the home of the nearest relative. Later, the adoptee returns a large amount of foodstuffs as gifts to the family that gave the feast. In collecting the gifts, the host calls on the whole family for help; and, in the same way, the family of the adopted person helps collect the food with which to reciprocate. Occasionally two adoptions are made for one death, when different members of the family (probably disagreeing) each adopts a person. The case of one old man who died some fifty years ago is still remembered because, at his adoption feast, for some reason or other a Wolf gens festival was held—an unheard-of thing—and at night (also a rarity).

In eighty-nine recorded cases of adoptions of this kind, the feasts were made by the dead person's parents in fifty cases; by his children in nine cases; by his nephew or niece in three cases; by his grandparent in three cases; by his grandchild in four cases; by his sibling in eleven cases; by his aunt or uncle in six cases; by his grandfather and uncle in one case; by his husband in one case; and by a nonrelative at whose house the deceased had been living in one case. With the adoption the "ward" takes his place in the family of the deceased although, so far as the records show, never actually in the household. Kin of the dead person then apply to him the proper kinship terms as well as the behavior that goes with them.

INTERPRETATION

In the present-day social organization of the Fox, the kinship system is an integral part of the culture; it represents the classification of all who are considered to be related, and this group of relatives is the most important in social life. The strong family feeling is reflected in the traditional behavior patterns that go with the kinship terms, and it is the group throughout which the kinship terms are applied which functions in daily life. In some other tribes the kinship terms are extended throughout the clans, but not so here; among the Fox the patrilineal clans are not social units in this sense, and the members of a clan do not feel themselves to be a social unity because of kinship. Likewise, one could not interpret the use of the terms "son" and "daughter" for a woman's father's sister's children as meaning "children of women of my clan" and hope to make one's self understand in the language of the Fox. Gentes—clouded in descent and not at all exogamous—exist among the Fox; yet if that is supposed to infer a condition like that of the Omaha tribe, for example, where the gentes are units in the camp circle, they certainly are absent here. In this sense one must insist that the Fox do not have a unilateral social organization, that such a thing is foreign to them actually and conceptually at present.

This fact comes out in many ways. The range of the kinship system itself is a clue, for just as kinship terms are not extended throughout clans, neither are they curtailed in certain lineages. The bilaterality of Fox social organization comes out also in the makeup of the household groups, in the bilocality of residence, in the equal exchange of gifts at marriage, and especially in the adoption into the family of a person to take the place of any relative, but never into the clan. The type of dual organization —an alternation of the children of each family—is indicative in a negative way of the lack of feeling for social groups involving unilateral descent.

About the only social function that clans seem to have had in the old days was the determination of chieftainship, which was in the Bear gens. But there is strong evidence that this actually meant descent in a Fox family that happened to be of the Bear gens. It is conceivable that, before the recent interruption by white contact, the gentes were becoming stronger social units; the fact that all the members of a Water gens were members of one of the dual divisions is an indication of a unity of the gentes that may have been spreading in the culture. On the other hand, the contrary may be true, and it is conceivable that this case was the last survivor of an old system of strong gentes that had broken down. But both historical interpretations are dangerous because (a) the data today are hardly conclusive and (b) a functional interpretation of the anomaly might be possible, if all the facts were known.

It appears that in the last fifty years, at any rate, the gentes have not been socially prominent and, in general, that Fox society has been based on the bilateral group of relatives by blood and marriage. One may wonder, then, how the kinship system can be explained. It is the same kind of kinship system that in many places accompanies strong clans or moieties; yet, as in many other places, it is difficult to explain it in terms of patrilineal clans, unless one adopts the auxiliary hypothesis that clans must have previously existed wherever the kinship system is found. An alternative explanation has been offered on the basis of the marriage of a man and his wife's brother's daughter. It might be well to discuss both of these possibilities in terms of the Fox material presented.

That the classificatory system in general fits clans to some extent was pointed out by Morgan himself, but the hypothesis that it is explicable on that basis was at the same time rejected by him. That a distinction between parallel and cross-lines is reminiscent of the division into clans cannot be doubted, since in a patrilineal society the father, his brothers and sisters, the children of the former, etc., are all in one's own clan while the father's sister's descendants and the mother's siblings' descendants are not necessarily so. Likewise, in a matrilineal society, the mother's sister's female line is in one's own clan, while all others are not necessarily so. Of course, in each case one of the first questions asked is: Why are *both* parallel lines merged with one's own line? The systems could be explained on the basis of exogamous moieties better than on the basis of clans, for then certain relatives in both parallel lines would be in one's own moiety. As a universal explanation of the classificatory system with the distinction of parallel and cross-lines, this has never been seriously accepted, however, since the distribution of moieties is comparatively limited.

The Omaha type, of which the Fox system is an example, seems to fit patrilineal clans particularly well, just as the Crow type fits matrilineal clans. In these cases the lines that are merged consist of relatives who are in the mother's clan, in the Omaha type, or in the father's clan, in the Crow type. Now among the Fox the term for the mother's brother, and his son, and his son, etc., might be considered to mean "male relative of my mother's clan." Indeed, the only male relatives of one's mother's clan besides these are called "grandfathers," and this usage may perhaps be explained on the basis of the extraordinary closeness of the mother's father. There is a strong temptation, therefore, to believe that the formation of patrilineal clans preceded and caused the Omaha type of kinship system. But among the Fox, at least, present-day clans could never have exerted such influence, because the clans are not important enough to effect kinship terminology; and, besides, no Fox Indian ever thinks of his mother's brother as "a male of my mother's clan." Generally, such an explanation of the Omaha type is faulty on grounds of distribution; why do not the Ojibwa (with clans very much stronger than those of the Fox) have this type of kinship system? Also relevant is the simple question of what brought on the clans, if clans brought on the kinship system?

Another answer that has been given is that clans have brought on the Omaha type where both exist, but the marriage with the wife's brother's daughter has caused the Omaha system wherever it, in turn, exists. This theory holds that, if for some reason (unstated) a sororate practice of taking the wife's brother's daughter as a second wife arises, then the natural consequences of that marriage are anticipated in the terminology, and the Omaha type arises. Thus one's child by a first wife will call the second wife "mother" (or "stepmother") and her brother "mother's brother"; but since the second wife is also this child's mother's brother's daughter—and her brother, the mother's brother's son—these relatives are precipitantly called "mother" and "mother's brother." Meanwhile, of course, the wife's brother's daughter would be a "sister-in-law." Now these are the terms of the Fox system (with "mother's sister" substituted for "mother"), and since the Fox also had the designated form of marriage, it would appear that they corroborate this theory.

On general grounds this explanation suffers in the same way as the other, but specifically, among the Fox, it can be shown to be untenable. In the first place, the marriage is barely remembered today, but all evidence points to the fact that it was never very common, and that therefore it could hardly have so affected the kinship system. It appears that the ordinary sororate was fairly common and that the marriage with the wife's brother's daughter was a substitute for it when the wife had no eligible sister. If one looks at the kinship system today, this is understandable, since both the wife's sister and her brother's daughter are called "sister-in-law," and if one is marriageable, so is the other. The question becomes, first of all, why the wife's brother's daughter is called "sister-in-law" (and, reciprocally, of course, why the father's sister's husband is called "brother-in-law" by both a man and a woman). Such terminology fits the marriage and would seem to be a *sine qua non* of it. In order to sustain the theory under discussion it would have to be shown that this part of the terminology is distributed together with the other distinctive features of the Omaha type. The fact is that both features have somewhat independent distributions, even though they often appear in the same tribe.

In considering the terminology applied to the father's sister's husband, and to the mother's brother's wife, it is noteworthy that among the Fox there is a strong tendency at present to think of the mother's brother's wife as "sister-in-law." Now, kinship systems of the Crow type have been explained on the basis of marriage with the mother's brother's wife (or widow)—an explanation comparable to that for the Omaha type on the basis of marriage to the father's sister's husband (or, as it is usually stated, to the wife's brother's daughter). The marriage with the mother's brother's wife, of course, goes together with calling her "sister-in-law." The condition among the Fox becomes interesting, therefore, since with an Omaha type the mother's brother's wife is yet treated like a sister-in-law and is often referred to as one. Whether this is very recent (and the terminology would indicate that it is), or whether marriages have ever been contracted within this relationship, is not known (there are no records of such a marriage, but for that matter there are no records of marriage with the father's sister's husband, either). But it is fair to say that the two relatives have become conceptually equivalent among the Fox. This means (1) that the terminology applied to spouses of uncles and aunts is not completely bound up with the Omaha-Crow types—which rather upsets the explanations on the basis of the peculiar marriages—and (2) that the Fox seem to have been developing a system as completely bilateral as possible, notwithstanding its supposedly unilateral Omaha feature.

The question of how unilateral the Fox kinship system is, is essential to an understanding of the entire question. One has a strong feeling that, even though this type of kinship system is often accompanied by patrilineal groupings, yet the Fox system in practice is as bilateral as any. The "mother's brother and sister's son" relationship is equivalent, and there is practical equivalence in the other cross-cousin relationships in spite of the fact that the mother's brother's daughter is "mother" to her father's sister's children, and the "mother-child" relationship is normally one of superordination and subordination. This is accomplished because it is the relative age of the two that is actually significant. A "mother" (or "mother's sister") normally demands respect of her "children." But if they are the same age, they behave rather as "siblings," and if the "child" is considerably older than the "mother," the respect is actually in the opposite direction. The same is true with grandparents and grandchildren. A good example that is easily affirmed is that of the uncle and his nephew or niece. This is a relationship of equivalence except in the "bogeyman" aspect that has been described. Normally, the "uncle" is the bogeyman to the "nephew," but if the "uncle" is a child and the "nephew" a mature man, the "nephew" is actually the bogeyman. In Fox, at least, all relationships are conceptually equivalent, the nonequivalent behavior being dependent upon relative age alone. It is useless to think of the mother's brother's line as somehow elevated, therefore. The differentiation must still be explained, but not fundamentally on the basis of a unilateral conception. It is for this reason, also, that one cannot think of the Omaha and Crow types as opposite poles of a conceptual scheme. Actually, there may be very little difference between them.

In combination with actual clans or moieties, the Omaha and Crow types assume new and different meanings, and they fit so nicely that one is tempted to explain one in terms of the other. Fox material gives some strong indications, however, that this is an erroneous approach.

EASTERN CHEROKEE SOCIAL ORGANIZATION

WILLIAM H. GILBERT, JR.

EASTERN CHEROKEE SOCIAL ORGANIZATION[1]

WILLIAM H. GILBERT, JR.

INTRODUCTION

The Cherokees of the southeastern United States were a tribe of great importance in early Colonial times. Much has been recorded concerning their merciless wars with the white settlers, yet they remain today a tribe about which little is definitely known so far as social organization is concerned. The various ethnologic observations on the Creeks, Choctaws, Chickasaws, and other Southeastern tribes have been summarized by Dr. J. R. Swanton[2] so that we have today a general picture of the recorded social organization of the Southeastern area. The Cherokees have remained outside of this picture. In 1932 an investigation was made by the present writer of the surviving Eastern Cherokees in North Carolina, and this paper deals with features known, for certain, of this group only. The Western Cherokees of Oklahoma have been exiled from their original home since 1838 and may have developed along different lines.

The purpose of the present paper is to enumerate some of the major features of the Cherokee social organization of today, especially those features which appear to be aboriginal and genuinely non-European, and to treat of one of these features in some detail, namely, preferential mating. Considered under the heading of "General Social Features" will appear such topics as social units, the kinship system, and mechanisms generated for social contacts. Considered under the heading of "Preferential Mating" will be the roles played by the domestic family, the clan, the dance, kinship usages, social sanctions, magical prayer and myth in the drama of marriage, and the provision for social continuance of the tribal culture.

[1] This paper represents a condensation of the writer's dissertation presented to the department of anthropology of the University of Chicago in partial fulfilment of the requirements for the Ph.D. degree.

[2] See Bibliography under J. R. Swanton.

Social units.—The effective social units to be observed among the Cherokees are the band, the clan, the town, and the household. Less important, and perhaps less specifically functional, units today are exemplified in the "company" or *gadugi*, the poor-aid or funeral society, the moiety, the ball team, and the dance team.

The band of Eastern Cherokees has been incorporated in the past under the state of North Carolina. The government of the band is democratic and consists of a legislative council elected at periodic intervals and a chief chosen in the manner of an American president by an assembled convention. The officials of the band dispose of questions of land tenure, aid to the needy, the use made of tribal funds, questions of tribal membership, the leasing of timber rights, and other questions. In all some two thousand people or more owe allegiance to this political organization.

In addition to the band there is the town government. The town has a locally elected chief and assistants, and these political officials hold office under fixed tenures also. The "town" consists generally of a community held together by geographical circumstances—a valley or a closely related neighborhood—and has a unity in terms of other organizations besides the political. The six towns which constitute the Cherokee band are: Birdtown, Yellow Hill, Paint-town, Wolftown, Big Cove, and Graham County.

A smaller social unit, yet one of the utmost importance as a basic division of Cherokee society, is the household in which dwells the domestic family. The Cherokee household is also the basic unit for land tenure. Grants of tenure are temporary and made on condition of cultivation and occupation. The average household consists of the domestic family, with occasionally other relatives such as the mother's or daughter's connections. The father is the head of the household and generally holds the title to the land. The position of the mother as subordinate to the father was apparently reversed in times past when female influence was greater.

The Cherokees are divided into seven matrilineal clans. The names of these clans are: *Aniwahiya* ("Wolf"), *Anikawi* ("Deer"), *Anidjiskwa* ("Bird"), *Aniwodi* ("Red Paint"), *Anisahoni* ("Blue Plant"), *Anigotigewi* ("Wild Potato"), and *Anigilohi* ("Twister"). So far as they are remembered, the names of these clans seem to be totemic and are derived by the natives from various resemblances or occupations. Thus the Wolf clan people were reputed to have been wolf hunters and wolf tamers. They were thought to have possessed some of the qualities of the wolf. Similarly, the Deer clan people were skilled in deer hunting and deer taming. A like property with reference to birds distinguished the Bird clan. The Red Paint clan were noted for their possession of magic in the control of love and other forces. The derivation and meaning of the *Anisahoni*, the *Anigotigewi*, and *Anigilohi* clans are controversial.

In counting the clan affiliations of sample groups it was found that the Wolf clan led with about 30 per cent of the tribe, followed by the Bird clan with 20 per cent. The *Anigilohi* and Deer clans had about 15 per cent each, while far below came the Red Paint, *Anigotigewi*, and *Anisahoni* with about 7 per cent each. Local preponderances of one or two main clans is noticeable. For example, 60 per cent of the town of Yellow Hill consists of Wolf and Bird, 50 per cent of Big Cove consists of Deer and Wolf, and 73 per cent of Graham County consists of Bird and Deer clanspeople.

At one time moieties must have played an important part in the Cherokee tribe as in other parts of the Southeast. Red and white moieties with war and peace functions were distinguished. Today there remains little evidence of survival of this organization. Occasionally opposition groupings may occur in match games and recreations between those who live on one side of a stream and those who live on the other, but of a moiety organization of clans nothing remains.

Ball teams and dance teams are organized groups within neighborhood and town areas. Thus Big Cove has a dance team which practices dances not known to the Birdtown team, and vice versa. Ball teams for playing the Cherokee form of lacrosse are organized by each town for matching engagements. The rivalry between towns is expressed acutely in the ball games in several ways: first, the ball game itself partakes of many of the features of a battle, second, much betting goes on between members of the rival towns, and, third, the conjurers of the rival towns control the outcome of the games by magical processes.

Various forms of economic co-operation exist between neighbors. Of these the most typical are the *gadugi*, or companies, and the poor-aid societies. The *gadugi* consists of a group of a dozen or so men organized as a company with a treasurer, a money collector, a manager or "warner," a secretary, and a chief. Each company elects its officials annually. The most important officials are the chief, who hires out the company, and the warner, who commands the operations of the company and tells the members how long to work and under what conditions.

The *gadugi* hires out its services and divides the profits annually among its members. In addition the members of the *gadugi* work in rotation on one another's farms for four days in the week. White people used to hire these companies for two dollars per day, which averaged about twenty cents per day per member. The members of the company could borrow money from the common treasury in percentages of the money they had earned by the month. At the present time about one-fourth of the people in Big Cove belong to these companies.

The other major form of co-operation among the Cherokees is the poor-aid society. Annually the people of the Raven district in Big Cove meet on August 10 in the graveyard. Here they elect a chief undertaker, a secretary, a gravedigger, a coffinmaker, and two warners. The assembly then combines to clean the graveyard of weeds and to straighten up the tombstones. The officials have various duties. The chief acts as director of poor-aid, and the warners are delegated to look after the attendance. The chief directs the two warners to go around and collect the neighbors who belong to a poor-aid society, and these help any family which needs aid in planting, hoeing, harvesting, or cutting wood. For this service the society expects some payment from the family which it assists in the form of livestock or other property. The chief can command the services of the society with three days' notice during the summer time, while at other times he can command immediate service.

At the death of a person the poor-aid society, in its funeral capacity, is notified, and the chief gives notice to his helpers to get together and dig the grave. The gravediggers consist of a committee of six volunteers, all appointed for one year, who obey the chief. The coffin is made by the coffinmaker and two assistants. Nomination and election of all these officials are generally made from volunteers.

The social units among the Eastern Cherokees vary in importance, but for the purposes of this discussion the clan will be regarded as the center of attention in the exposition of the social organization.

The kinship system.—The Cherokee kinship system is organized predominantly around the social unit of the clan. In order best to comprehend the relationship system let us imagine a Cherokee male informant describing his relatives to us as he knows them (see Fig. 1).

My father I call *gidada*. I also say *gidada* when speaking to my father's brothers, and to any member of my father's clan who is a male. When I speak to my father's sister, or to any female belonging to his clan, I say *giloki*. My father and his clan must be respected by me, and I can never joke with them or be on familiar terms with them. I must defend my father and his clan from all disparaging attacks from others.

My mother I call *gidzi*. I also say *gidzi* when speaking to my mother's sisters or to any woman of my clan who marries someone of my father's clan. I and my mother have always the same clan since I inherit my clan from her. In fact, all of my brothers and sisters inherit the same clan as I do from my mother. I distinguish my mother's brother by the term *gidudji*.

My sister I call *ungida*. She calls me *ungida* too. I call any woman of my own clan *ungida*, except those whom I call *gidzi* ("mother") and *gilisi* ("grandmother"). My older brother I call *unkinili*, and my younger brother I call *unkinutsi*. For protection, my sister looks to me, and I look to my older brother. My sister calls her sister *ungilu'i* and does not distinguish older from younger. All the male members of my clan who are older than I am, I call *unkinili*, except those whom I call *gidudji*, and those who are younger than myself I call *unkinutsi*. I am on terms of familiarity with all of them and can play all sorts of tricks on them. In speaking of ourselves my brothers, sisters, and myself call ourselves *otsalinudji*, "we brothers and sisters."

My son or daughter I call *agwetsi*. I also call the son or daughter of any of my brothers *agwetsi*, but my sister's son and daughter I call *ungiwina'* and *ungwatu* ("nephew" and "niece"). My own children are of my wife's clan, and I have

CHEROKEE KINSHIP SYSTEM

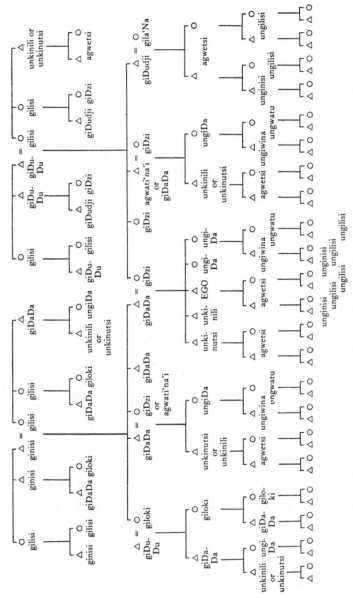

FIG. 1.—Chart of Cherokee kinship terminology. Ego = male. For a female ego the same terms are used except for siblings, where *ungiDa* is used for "brother" and *ungila'i* for "sister." Also, a woman classes her sister's children with her own. The father's brother's wife is called *agwati'na'i* ("stepparent"), if she is of another clan than ego. The terms in the second descending generation follow the pattern.

to respect them. I can joke with sister's children, however, since they are of my own clan.

My son's son I call *unginisi*, but my son's daughter and my daughter's son and daughter I call *ungilisi*. I also call my sister's son's son *unginisi*, but her son's daughter and her daughter's son and daughter I call *ungilisi*. I always joke with and tease both my *ungilisi* and *unginisi*.

My father's father I call *ginisi*, and although I ought to respect him I don't. I call my father's father's brothers *ginisi* also and always joke with and play with them. My father's mother and my mother's mother and their sisters I call *gilisi*, "grandmother," and I can joke and play with them. My mother's father and his brothers I call *gidudu*, and I am on terms of familiarity with them also.

There are also several names which I give to people who are married to my relatives or otherwise related to me. My wife's parents I call *unatsi*, and she calls my parents *djidzo'i*. We have to respect each other's parents just as we respect our own parents. I call my wife's brothers and sisters *agwelaksi*, or "in-laws," and I joke with them a great deal. They call me *agwelaksi* also. My son's wife I call *agidzohi* and my daughter's husband *aginudji*. I have to respect both of these relatives. My mother's brother's wife I call *agilana*, and my father's sister's husband I call *gidudiya*. My brother and I can play the "tobacco joke" on our *gidudiya* and beat him up if he doesn't give us tobacco when we ask for it.

From the foregoing description we can see that the principal means of distinguishing relatives employed by the Cherokees are differences of lineage, generation, reciprocity of relationship, sex, and age. Of these, undoubtedly, the most important is lineage, while sex and age appear to be of less importance.

Four lineages are distinguished, namely, father's matrilineal, mother's matrilineal, mother's father's matrilineal, and father's father's matrilineal. In the father's matrilineal lineage (Fig. 3) all the females are either "fathers' sisters" or "grandmothers," and all the males are "fathers." All men marrying women of this lineage are "grandfathers," while women marrying men of this lineage are "mothers," if of one's own clan, and "stepparents" otherwise. Any child of a man of this line is a "brother" or a "sister." In the mother's matrilineal lineage (Fig. 2) the females may be "grandmothers," "mothers," "sisters," "nieces" (male speaking), or "children" (female speaking). All the women who marry a "brother" of this lineage are "relatives," while the women who marry "mothers' brothers" are given a special term. In the mother's father's matrilineal lineage (Fig. 4) and the father's father's matrilineal lineage

CHEROKEE KINSHIP SYSTEM

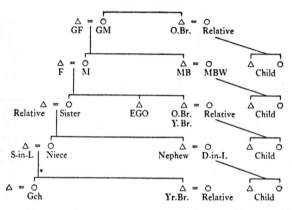

Fig. 2.—The mother's matrilineal lineage. Ego=male. When ego is female, the terms are the same except that the sister's children are "children."

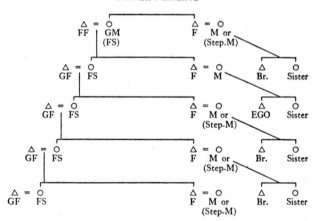

Fig. 3.—The father's matrilineal lineage. Ego=male. The same forms are used when ego is female. The grouping of relatives in accordance with the lineage is well illustrated in these charts; for a description see the text.

CHEROKEE KINSHIP SYSTEM

MOTHER'S FATHER'S LINEAGE

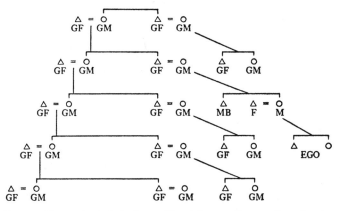

FIG. 4.—The mother's father's matrilineal lineage. Ego=male or female.

FATHER'S FATHER'S LINEAGE

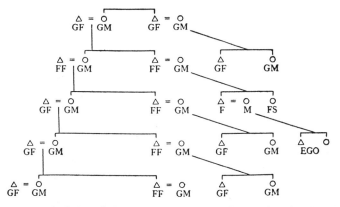

FIG. 5.—The father's father's matrilineal lineage. Ego=male or female. The special term for father's father (*ginisi*) is sometimes replaced by the general word for grandfather (*giDuDu*).

(Fig. 5) all the men are "grandfathers" and the women "grand-mothers." All men marrying into these two lineages are "grand-fathers," and all women marrying into these two lineages are "grandmothers." The four fundamental lineages correspond with the four clans with whom the individual has special relationships. Being a matrilineal system the Cherokee terminology follows the outlines of the Crow type.

The distinctions of generation are most apparent in the terminology for immediate relatives. As Lowie indicates, this might be called "bifurcate-merging" terminology in that one-half of the collateral relatives are merged with the lineal line. This is to say that persons who are parallel cousins are "brothers and sisters," while cross-cousins are given a different terminology. In the case of cross-cousins through the father, the cousins are classed with the father's generation, whereas in the case of cross-cousins through the mother the term "child" is used. Hence generation can be said to be important so far as immediate siblings and parallel cousins are concerned. The grandparent generation is alone distinguished throughout as "grandparents," while other generations are bisected by the lineage principle.

Two important types of relationships occur in the terminology, namely, the complementary reciprocal and the self-reciprocal. Complementary reciprocal terms are terms used between close relatives exclusively and are not used by others. Such terms are used in relationships of the type "father-child," "mother's brother—sister's child." The self-reciprocal terms consist of identical terms used between two relatives. Such would be "grandmother-grandchild," "brother-sister," and similar relationships. In the case of complementary reciprocal terminology, linkages of persons who must remain distinct for certain reasons are secured. In the self-reciprocal terminology a merging of social personalities is desired and, to a certain extent, obtained.

The distinction of the sex of the speaker is often made clear by implication. The male speaker calls his sister's children "nephew" and "niece," while the female speaker calls them "child"; the husband and wife apply different specific terms to each other and each other's parents, and the male and female speakers use entirely different terms for brothers.

The distinction of the sex of the person spoken to is expressed in the following: father and father's sister distinguished; mother and mother's brother distinguished; nephew and niece through a sister distinguished by a man; grandfathers distinguished from grandmothers; husband and wife distinguished; and the use of the term *giloki* ("father's sister") for any female member, and of *gidada* ("father") for any male member, of the father's clan. The distinction of the sex of the person through whom the relationship is traced is expressed in the following: the aunt is a person related through the father; the mother's brother is related through the mother; the mother's brother's wife is related through the mother and brother; and the relationships through the wife are distinguished from the relationships through the husband.

The age of relatives is not distinguished as a rule except by supplementary terms such as "older" and "younger." In the case of brothers, however, the distinction of the older brother from the younger is clearly marked in the terminology. This is a relationship of a complementary type and is to be explained on the basis of the function of the older brother in the family to protect and avenge the younger brother, and to act to some extent like a father or uncle toward him.

The range of the kinship system is extended to include all persons with whom the individual comes into contact. Auxiliary terms such as "second" and "far off" are attached to the commoner terms in designating the remoter relatives—collateral and lineal. In magical prayers kinship terms are extended to the spirits resident in the plant, animal, and inorganic worlds. It is chiefly the matrilineal clan, however, which is employed in tracing relationships throughout the tribe. The four fundamental lineages already mentioned coincide with the four fundamental clans with whom the individual has specific relationships. This can be best described by allowing the Cherokee male informant to continue his account:

My father was of the Wild Potato clan. I must always respect his clan. I must always defend its members from defamation or attack. I am a "brother" of anyone whose father was of that clan.

My own clan is the Wolf, and that is the clan also of my brothers, sisters, and mother. I am free to joke with all members of my clan except those whom I call "mother." I cannot, however, marry a woman of the Wolf clan. Whenever I am traveling, I stay with my "brothers" of the Wolf clan, and when they visit my village they may stay with me. It is important for me to inquire the clan membership of everyone I meet.

My father's father was of the Deer clan. Whenever I find anyone belonging to that clan, I can tease and joke with them as much as I want. I must always try to make fun of them in some remark, and they do the same to me. I am always visiting people of the Deer clan, and I married a girl of that clan. My mother's father was of the Paint clan, and I treat these people the same as I do the Deer clan. I could, in fact, have married a girl of the Paint clan. Deer and Paint people are all "grandparents" to me.

My wife's father is of the Blue Plant clan. I respect him as my father-in-law, but I joke with Joe West, who is also of the Blue Plant clan but who is a "brother" to me because his father is also of the Wild Potato clan. My wife's father's father was of the Wolf clan so she is always teasing and joking with Wolf people. I am a Wolf so that is how she met me. My wife's mother's father was of the Bird clan so she could tease Bird people and could have married one of them.

It all amounts to this: Potato clan people I respect and never marry, Wolf clan people I can joke with but can't marry, Deer and Paint clan people I can tease and marry, but toward the three remaining clans—Blue, Bird, and Twister —I have no general behavior but treat the individuals according to their personal relationships to the Wolf or Wild Potato clan.

It can be seen from the foregoing description that the Cherokee kinship system provides for a means of preferential mating restricted to the relationships with one's father's father's or mother's father's clans. Since the lineages and clan extension of lineages in these cases contain only individuals classified as "grandmothers" and "grandfathers," the Cherokees may be said to have a system which insures marriage with one's "grandparents."

The behavior between relatives in Cherokee society is largely in terms of familiarity and respect. The following relatives must be respected and never directly joked with or treated familiarly: (1) relatives of the first ascending generation such as father, mother, aunt, and uncle; (2) relatives of the first descending generation such as son, daughter, nephew, and niece; (3) respected relatives of one's familiar relatives such as wife's parents or husband's parents; (4) the familiar relatives of one's respected relatives such as son's wife or father's clan brothers; and (5) one's son's child or father's father.

Those relatives who may be treated familiarly include the following: (1) one's brothers and sisters and their wives and husbands; (2) one's cousins who are parallel—related through one's father's brother or mother's sister; (3) one's own clan except the mother and mother's brothers; (4) most persons in the grandparent generation except one's own father's father; (5) all in one's grandchildren's generation except the son's children; (6) one's own affinities and their siblings or spouses and the latter's brothers and sisters; and (7) the familiar relatives of one's own familiar relatives, and the respected relatives of one's own respected relatives (parent's parents and children's children) with the exceptions already noted.

Respect behavior takes the comparatively simple form of an attitude of reverence and regard, and of avoidance of any semblance of equality in contact. It is, then, a simple form of superordination-subordination. Familiarity behavior takes on a more positive and complex aspect with at least three distinct types recognizable. First, there are "sexual" familiarities between persons of different sex standing in the "grandparent-grandchild" relation to one another; second, there are the satirical familiarities between brothers and fellow-clansmen; third, there are indirect familiarities between persons not ordinarily on terms of familiarity.

Intersexual familiarities occur on such occasions as the dance or while visiting. The various familiarities consist of gestures between men and women such as tickling, feinting blows, and exchanging garments; these lead to an extremely close relationship between the parties concerned. In their completed form they are not separable from the familiarities between husband and wife.

The satirical type of familiarity occurs also on the occasion of dances or visits. It has a special form in a magical rite performed at the ball game. At the dance, clan brothers twit one another about various faults and misdeeds, and the persons who are made the butt of jokes and sly digs reciprocate in kind. This familiarity is indulged in constantly between brothers and between men in a "grandparent-grandchild" relationship to one another. A particular form of this familiarity, the "tobacco joke," is directed toward any man who is so rash as to violate a fundamental marriage prescription, such as marrying his father's sister. The tobacco joke consists in the mistreatment of such a man who marries one's father's sister; this person is said to "make himself grandfather" to his wife's brother's children, and these latter gather together where they can catch the father's sister's husband alone and ask him for tobacco, saying that they have diarrhea and need the tobacco to cure it. If the father's sister's husband refuses, or has no tobacco on him, the children of his wife's brother have a perfect right to set upon him, throw him to the ground, and strike, kick, or otherwise maltreat him without effective resistance on his part. This form of familiarity can be indulged in with reference to any man who has married a woman of the joker's father's clan.

Indirect familiarity is a peculiar relationship that can occur only between a father and mother and their children or between a mother's brother and his nephews or nieces. At an early period in his son's life the father will speak to him of matters of the heart. "You must marry my aunt," he tells the boy. The boy thinks at once of the old and ugly person whom he calls "grandmother," and whom he already fears because of her strong teasing, and shrinks in horror from the thought of marrying her as suggested by his sire. As he grows older, however, he begins to tease his grandmother, himself, and this later results in familiarity relations of the intersexual type with other members of his grandmother's clan, some of whom are girls of his own age, and one of which he eventually marries. Another way of indirect joking is for the father to disparage loudly one of his clan brothers in satirical fashion, in the presence of his own son, with the result that the latter is forced to go to great lengths in attempting to defend his father's fellow-clansman from the insinuations and attacks.

Social contacts.—The occasions for social contacts among the Cherokees consist of family relationships, relationships in training, dance contacts, ball games and contests in general, conjuring, and myth-telling.

Relationships within the family take on, in their simplest aspects, the character of a series of pair relationships. Of these the simplest are those of "father-son," "mother-daughter," "father-daughter," "mother-son," "husband-wife," "brother-brother," "brother-sister," and "sister-sister." The simple factors involved in these relationships are degrees of familiarity and respect, education and discipline, or ritualistic avoidance and institutionalized joking or reverence. Included also is the degree of separation in general activities, such as the amount of labor performed in common or in complementary fashion.

The more complex relationships within the family are those of the "father's sister–brother's child," "mother's brother–sister's child," "father's father–son's child," "mother's father–daughter's child," "grandmother-grandchild," "wife's parents–daughter's husband," "husband's parents–son's wife," and "mate's sibling–sibling's mate." The relationships between pairs in this group are affected principally by the emphasis on lineage and generation differences, and especially by the marriageability of persons in certain relationships to one another. All contacts in both these and in the simpler pair relationships are strictly regulated by custom. The social contacts of the individual with his family, or with the community in general, vary with the stage in the life-cycle which he has attained. The contacts appear genetically with the various degrees of unfolding of the personality.

The pregnant mother goes at each new moon to the water's side to pray. The conjurer laves her head, bosom, and face and mutters spells over her. He divines with his beads on a cloth as to whether the expected child will live or not, and how long. In order to facilitate delivery and cleanse the system of the mother, various drinks are administered. Fundamentally, the pregnant mother must be avoided as much as possible. Avoidances take much the same form as the taboos on the woman in menstruation. She must not prepare any meals or go near growing crops or fish traps. She must not eat certain foods or wear certain kinds of clothing, and must not see a corpse or a mask. The father must dig no grave, refrains from playing in the ball game, and must accompany his wife in the various rites preceding delivery. In general, the pregnant wife and her husband will not participate in the dance or in any games or other social contact.

At parturition four women attend. A conjurer must be present if the delivery is difficult, and he resorts to various magical spells in order to induce birth. The placenta is disposed of by the father who crosses two to four ridges and then buries it deep in the ground. The next child will be born within a number of years corresponding to the number of ridges crossed. If the placenta were thrown away in the open, another child might be born almost any time.

The child is given a name some four to seven days after birth. The father's family generally has the task of selecting a name. Sometimes the father's brother will select a ridiculous name for the child as a joke, and the parents will be forced to accept it. Generally, however, the father's sister selects the name for the child. Later on in life new names will be acquired by the child, frequently through the agency of joking relatives and often descriptive of his physical features or misfortunes.

When the child is three to four weeks old, it is carried about sitting astride the mother's back. The grandmother also carries the child; the term *gilisi*, used for grandmother, means "she bears on her back." As soon as the young child is able to walk, it begins to participate in the dances and games of both youths and grownups.

Certain children are raised to be "witches." These are fed on a special diet of a liquid potion of corn hominy for some days, and then certain medicines are administered and prayers said at the end of a given period. These children grow up to be powerful conjurers who may fly through the air, go under the ground, and assume various shapes. They can wish for anything, and it immediately takes place. It is regarded as a terrible calamity to have them in the community, and so they are generally sought out and killed in infancy. Twins are regarded as potential "witches" whose abilities may be even more readily developed.

At the age of four or five years the young boys begin to make bows and arrows and other toys, under the supervision of their fathers or elder brothers. Little girls of this age begin to assist in the household duties. Besides participating in grown-up activities various games occupy the time. Toy bows and arrows are used to shoot crickets or apples in the trees, and the game of the hunter and the deer is played. Instruction, in general, begins to follow the line of the sexual division of labor. The boys are taught magic formulas for success in hunting and for obtaining success in love affairs by the mother's brother, while the girls are taught to make pottery and baskets, and to cook, mostly by their mothers.

The approach to manhood is marked by emphasis on certain activities, such as dancing, hunting, and the ball game. The approach to womanhood is marked by the establishing of menstrual taboos, which place the feminine sex under marked disabilities. The young man must avoid events and persons while training for the ball game, but these prescriptions are largely the results of voluntary activities. Any other limitations on male contacts are the result of their connections with females. The flow of menstrual blood at periodic intervals sets up a dangerous magic for all who might chance to come into contact with it. A female must emphatically be avoided while menstruating; one must not eat anything cooked by her, or touch any object that she has touched, or even walk along a trail over which she has recently traveled. She must not be allowed to wade in the river near where the fish traps are set, or she will spoil the catch. If she should chance to walk through the cornfield, she will stunt and injure the crops. The husband of a woman in this condition is, by reason of his relation to her, compelled to avoid other people.

Entrance into adult status occurs automatically with marriage. The young people meet on various occasions—at the ball game, at the dance, or while visiting relatives, since the family

always take their children with them in their periodic and un-
ending visits to relatives. The friendships of young people often
start in this way; the ripening of intersexual relations then occurs at the dances or other events.

Marriage among the Cherokees is not necessarily a permanent
relationship, nor is it necessarily celebrated by any special ritual.
A man may simply move in with the family of the woman of his
choice and make himself quite at home. He may tire of the
woman later and move off to parts unknown. In other cases he
may take the woman to his own house, and she will stay there
while the family is being raised. Sometimes a young couple will
go out and found a homestead of their own on the mountain
slopes. Often a wedding feast may be given by the groom to
celebrate, and all the relatives on both sides may be invited.
In the past a young woman signified her acceptance of a proposal
by pounding a sack of corn, left at her door by a man, into flour
and then baking it into bread.

The age of consent for legal marriage is fifteen for girls and
seventeen for boys, but marriage at earlier ages frequently occurs, though late marriages are by no means uncommon. The
latter occur in the cases of ugly men who are unable to attract
a wife until they have acquired some knowledge of magic, or in
the cases of the oft-married and powerful conjurers themselves.
Late marriages seem invariably to involve the use of love magic
in attracting female affections.

After marriage the husband farms, looks after the stock, cuts
wood, hunts game, fishes in the river, and visits other villages.
The wife does household chores, looks after the very young children, cooks, sews, washes clothes, and perhaps follows her husband around in his visits. The husband regards with great respect the parents of his wife, and she acts similarly toward his
parents. On the other hand, a man will joke with and treat
familiarly any brother or sister of his wife, and she does the same
with his brothers and sisters. In public meetings of a formal
nature the women always congregate separately from the men.
Thus, in church meetings, men sit on one side and women on the
other. For recreation the married couple play parlor games with

the children in the evening, and various sports out of doors with their adult relatives and neighbors. The basket game is played in the evenings, especially. The only disturbances of life are the periodic menstrual taboos.

As age creeps upward, the importance of disease, and of magic to resist it, becomes more and more uppermost in the individual's attention. When sickness comes, the magical aid of some local conjurer must be invoked to root out the disorder, and often the help of the poor-aid society may have to be called on to tide over the time of incapacity.

When death comes to the family, the local co-operative again functions, this time as an undertaking establishment. Beyond a few unimportant details, immediate relatives are not allowed to take any part in the funeral arrangements or in the burial of the deceased. The corpse is washed and dressed and then lies in state for several days while all relatives and acquaintances come to take their last look. The friends of the family watch the corpse day and night. The coffin, already prepared by the poor-aid society, is brought and the corpse placed inside and borne to the cemetery. An ordinary Christian burial service is generally held at the house of the deceased before interment. In this manner the contacts of the life-cycle are completed.

The contacts involved in training are today almost entirely the result of white influence. The government school among the Cherokees is changing the social order, and the aboriginal training relationships of the past survive only rarely. In this latter type of education it is noteworthy that the mother's brother, or an older member of one's own clan, acted as one's instructor in the lore of the tribe; today the son is frequently indebted to the father for instruction. Training in the aboriginal lore was conditioned by differences of sex and by occupational pursuit. There was a definite system of training involved in becoming a hunter, conjurer, or warrior. Today the transmission of magical prayers is through exchange, purchase, or other reciprocal processes.

The contacts involved in the dances contain more of the aboriginal flavor. There are some twenty-four different dances (see Table 1) still current or still remembered in the village of Big Cove. Of these dances, some eight have fallen into disuse. Following are the names of the dances still practiced or remembered today: Ant, Ball, Bear, Beaver Hunt, Buffalo, Bugah, Chicken, Coat, Corn, Eagle, Friendship, Green Corn, Groundhog, Horse, Knee-deep, Medicine, Partridge, Pheasant, Pigeon, Raccoon, Round, Snake, War, and Gathering Wood. In most of the dances both men and women participate, but only men are allowed to lead and to do the singing and calling for the dances. A few dances are confined to one or the other sex.

It is not possible to describe the various interesting features of the dances in this short paper, but it is important to note that they are intimately connected with all the other major features of the social organization. The basic motive of the dances, as they are at present performed, seems to be the recreational one of a good time and the making of new contacts or the renewal of old acquaintanceships. The names of the dances, their movements—both conventionalized and naturalistic—their singing accompaniments, and their connections with the seasons are to be understood as survivals of a one-time complete annual ceremonial cycle of rituals governing the whole life of the Cherokee Tribe. Hunting methods and habits of certain animals are simulated, methods of sowing seed and tilling the soil are imitated, and other movements are performed which all have lost their major significance so far as present-day economic and practical activities go.

Participation in the dance is symbolic of social contact and solidarity among the Cherokees, and those who have been under an avoidance taboo may return to general social life through participation in the dance. Thus, the woman who has been menstruating or pregnant but is no longer so, the family in whom a death has occurred some time back, and persons under other disabilities may have these avoidances lifted through participating in the dance. Of the dances which are popular today, the Friendship dances, at which the young people get acquainted, are most widely performed. These, and other dances which are specifically recognized as for that purpose, are the vehicles

TABLE 1

DANCES OF THE CHEROKEES

NAME	NUMBER OF SONGS	GIVEN IN EVENING	GIVEN AFTER MIDNIGHT	Gourd	Tortoise Shell	Drum	FUNCTION AND SIGNIFICANCE
1. Ant	1		X	X	X		Imitative of ant colonies
2. Ball	4 and 13	X	X	X		X	Magical attainment of victory in ball game
3. Bear	7		X	X	X		Imitative of animal habits. Occasion for familiarities between sexes
4. Beaver Hunt	4	X				X	Imitative of beaver hunt
5. Buffalo*	2+				X	X	Imitative of buffalo
6. Bugah	7	X		X		X	Imitative of buffoons. Occasion for privileged familiarities
7. Chicken	1+		X	X	X		Imitative of bird habits. Occasion for familiarities between sexes
8. Coat	4		X	X	X		Imitative of taking a wife by paying a coat
9. Corn	4		X	X	X		Imitative of corn planting
10. Eagle	14	X		X		X	Combination of various dances commemorating victory. Joking between men
11. Friendship	44+	X	X	X	X		Many dances, all designed to promote familiarity between sexes
12. Green Corn	7			X	X		Celebrates the harvest of corn and consists of several dances
13. Groundhog	4+		X	X	X		Imitative of hunting groundhog
14. Horse	7		X		X	X	Imitative of horse movements

Instrument columns: Gourd, Tortoise Shell, Drum

* Extinct.

TABLE 1—*Continued*

Name	Number of Songs	Given in Evening	Given after Midnight	Gourd	Tortoise Shell	Drum	Function and Significance
15. Knee-deep	2	…	X	X	X	…	Imitative of knee-deep frog in spring
16. Medicine*	4	X	X	…	…	X	Renewing health. Occasion for familiarities between sexes
17. Partridge	1	…	X	X	X	…	Imitative of quail movements
18. Pheasant*	1+	…	…	…	…	…	Imitative of pheasants
19. Pigeon	3+	X	…	X	X	…	Imitative of hawk hunting pigeons
20. Raccoon	2	…	X	X	X	…	Imitative of hunting raccoon. Familiarities between sexes
21. Round	4	…	X	…	X	X	A woman's dance which culminates an all-night dance at daylight
22. Snake	2	…	X	X	X	…	Imitative of snake
23. War*	2+	…	…	…	…	X	Magical protection and movements of war
24. Wood-gathering	7	X	…	…	X	X	Imitative of woman gathering wood for fire. Begins a series of dances

for privileged familiarity behavior between relatives. Some dances, on the other hand, forbid all familiarity or frivolity of any kind (see Table 1).

Intimately connected with the dance contacts are those of the ball game. This game, a local version of lacrosse, which is practically continental in its distribution, has an importance among the Cherokees by being a basic means of expression of the opposition between rival towns. The captain organizes his team from among the available young men of the town and may enrol some twenty players. He must next secure a conjurer to pronounce the proper magic spells over the team, to help it perform ceremonial ablutions, and thus magically to weaken the other side. The team in preparation for a game is placed under a series of avoidances, most of which are as severe and burdensome as the taboos on a pregnant woman.

In the actual game only twelve players are allowed to participate. Since the game has an almost unavoidable tendency to become a battle royal, two "drivers" are appointed to separate the players in the scrimmages and keep the game going. A small sphere the size of a golf ball is batted about with a racket, the aim being to score over the opponent's goalpost by fair means or foul. A certain number of goals wins the game. The summer is the ball-playing season, and as a rule each town's team plays about three games a year.

The ball game is not only the contest of skill and physical prowess it appears to be. Beneath all this superficiality is the contest between the rival conjurers who are sponsoring the opposing teams, and the side with the most powerful conjurer is the side that wins. The ceremonial and magical preparations for the game are all part of an elaborate strategy worked out by the rival coaches. One indispensable prerequisite to success in the game is the performance of the Ball Dance for several nights previous to the event. The extraordinary nature of the Ball Dance lies in the kinship reference of one part, namely, the woman's dance.

After the ball players themselves have performed a dance, preparations are made for a woman's dance. The male singer or conjurer seats himself in a position facing the town against which his team is soon to play, and takes his drum in hand while seven women dancers line up in a row behind him. Then, as the leader begins to sing and beat on the drum, the women dance forward and backward. The women dance only to the first and last songs of the set, the other songs being merely a vocal accompaniment by the leader. After the completion of each song, the singer will make some derogatory remarks about his fellow-clansmen in the opposing town, saying in effect that their town is bound to lose in the coming game. This amounts to a form of satirical familiarity with one's clan brothers which has the effect of weakening them and their cause. The women dancers may likewise make up derogatory jokes about the persons belonging to their clans who live in the opponent town. After one conjurer gets tired, another may take his place and joke about his fellow-clansmen in the opponent town. These dances continue for many hours and are calculated to insure victory. They end with ablutions.

The ball game just mentioned is not the only form of contest known among the Cherokees. Other and minor forms of games are: (1) a kind of football game played between men and women; (2) a basket game played with dice shaken in a basket; (3) tugs of war between the sexes using grapevines as ropes; and (4) match hunts organized between groups living on opposite sides of streams in which the losers furnish the food for a feast for the winners.

The social contacts brought about by the process of conjuring may be direct or indirect. A person is rated as a conjurer among the Cherokee if he knows "prayers" or magic spells. These prayers consist generally of two parts: (1) practical directions in the use of herbs and chemical extracts to cure disease, induce love, insure hunting success, and the like and (2) an invocation or formula which will compel supernatural forces to aid in achieving a desired result. It was James Mooney[3] who first called the attention of the world to the importance of the sacred formulas of the Cherokees. He obtained a considerable number of the

3 *Sacred Formulas of the Cherokees.*

manuscripts of these formulas written in the characters of the Sequoyah syllabary and in the western dialect of Cherokee by the conjurers for their own use. The wording of these prayers is antique and often refers to situations of earlier times. Yet even today the prayers bear important functional relationships to the social organization. Not only may they be employed to bring about love in an indifferent person, but they are also preeminent in the causation of disease.

It is impossible for us to tell just what are the means whereby the contacts of magic are brought about. It suffices to cite an example. Perhaps the most widely dreaded diseases among the Cherokees are the so-called "simulator" diseases described by Olbrechts.[4] These are diseases produced by conjurers, which are not what they seem when judged from their symptoms but simulate diseases sent by other means. They are meant to fool the patient and make him worse by his undertaking the wrong cure or countercharm. It is said that groups wage battles for months at a time, in which they pester one another by various "simulator" diseases, the latter real or imagined.

The essence of all positive magical prayers, in any case, is the establishment of control over some object through the development of a relationship of familiarity with that object. On the other hand, the essence of countercharms is to set up a magical check or avoidance taboo between the objects involved, and so avoid the dangerous familiarity. Thus the relationships of kinship are carried over into the ideology of magic and religion. We find it difficult in Western culture to appreciate the force which ritual sanctions or magical procedures have in primitive cultures. The violation of some slight taboo, the accidental encounter with an event of ill omen, the knowledge that someone is plotting a magical destruction or death for one's self, or the tendency to rationalize in magical terms the existence of "natural" disorders, will all enter into the category of social contacts involving the use of the supernatural.

Mooney's investigations of the Cherokees in the nineteenth century showed him the folly of attempting to understand the

[4] *The Swimmer Manuscript.*

magical formulas without referring to the mythological background upon which they were built. So he has given us an extensive account of another form of social development, namely the myth-making faculty. The social contacts involved in the transmission of the myths are fast disappearing; the Cherokees themselves refer to Mr. Mooney as the authority for the myths still current. There formerly existed a class of story-tellers who transmitted, from one generation to the next, the legendary lore out of which the ideas of the Cherokees were developed. The story-tellers have disappeared, but their stories linger on, thanks to Mr. Mooney.[5]

In the plots of the stories considerable data can be gleaned concerning the social relationships of the not-far-distant past. The dominant motives of the myths are explanatory in that an attempt is made in various ways to explain the world and its inhabitants. Other motives are interwoven into the pattern, particularly jokester trickery, revenge, love, and family relationships. The jokester trickery consists of practical pranks played between mythical characters which frequently illustrate many of the features of the familiarity relationships between actual relatives.

With the mention of the myth-telling process our account of the essential formal features of Cherokee social organization is completed. One by one the effective social units have been enumerated, the obtrusive features of the kinship system have been noted, and, finally, the outstanding methods of social contact have been presented. It would now perhaps be of some value to turn to one essential feature of the social system, namely, "preferential mating," and see how it ties in with the whole social organization and binds it together into a structure.

PREFERENTIAL MATING

Evidence for preferential mating.—Preferential mating is a term used to express the prescription by law or custom of certain favorable types of marriage which become, by sanction of long social usage, unquestioned and unalterable. Preference in mar-

[5] *Myths of the Cherokees.*

riage is generally expressed for a relative, one not too close or yet too far, marriage with whom will result in the fulfilment of certain obligations. The sororate and the levirate are generally cited as examples of preferential mating, but the form in vogue among the Cherokees lacks a name unless, indeed, we might call it "alternate-generation marriage." The Cherokee man, like Rivers' Pentecost Islanders and the Ungarinyin of Australia, can and does marry his "grandmother."

Let us see how this is done. Considerable difficulty surrounds the collection of reliable pedigrees among the existing natives, and it is especially difficult to ascertain clan affiliations for more than two generations above the contemporary one. A sampling of thirty-five unions in the Big Cove town gave the following results: in twenty-nine cases marriage with a person in a grandparental or great-grandparental clan occurred; in four cases marriage was in the father's clan; and in two cases within the same clan. In this group of thirty-five marriages complete data were obtained concerning the clan affiliations of all four of the grandparents on both sides, a total of eight clan affiliations being needed to verify each union.

In addition, certain data can be gleaned from incomplete pedigrees. In these cases the clan affiliations of one or more of the four grandparents is not known. In these cases the choice of mates shows certain tendencies: (1) a preference may be shown by all the children of one family for marrying persons of only one or two clans or (2) a preference may be shown by persons who marry more than once to marry into the same clan. A study of the clan choices in marriage of the children in twenty-six families showed that in twenty of the families the children tended to marry into the same clan. A study of thirty-five persons who remarried showed that one person married four times, twice into the same clan; six persons married three times and of the six, five married persons of the same clan twice; and of twenty-eight persons who married only twice, at least nine married into the same clan both times. These choices are too great for mere chance.

In studying the clan affiliations locally it was found that there is an average local preponderance of two clans of about 58 per cent. On the other hand, the average percentage of marriages showing a definite choice in clan affiliations is about 60 per cent. This is an interesting correlation and may be interpreted in several ways: (1) the local preponderance in clan numbers may have induced the marriage preference; (2) the marriage preferences may have given rise to the preponderances in clan numbers, or (3) both of these phenomena are results of an underlying principle.

The local preponderances in clan numbers can hardly have given rise to the marriage preferences for the following reason.

TABLE 2

ORDER OF FREQUENCY OF CLAN MATINGS

EXPECTED ORDER	OBSERVED ORDER
1. Deer-Wolf	1. Deer-Wolf
2. Deer-Anisahoni	2. Wolf-Anisahoni
3. Wolf-Anisahoni	3. Deer-Anigilohi
4. Deer-Bird	4. Wolf-Bird
5. Deer-Anigilohi	5. Deer-Anisahoni
6. Wolf-Bird	6. Deer-Bird
7. Wolf-Anigilohi	7. Wolf-Anigilohi
8. Anisahoni-Bird	8. Red Paint-Bird
9. Anisahoni-Anigilohi	9. Anigotigewi-Anisahoni

An enumeration of the heads of households in Big Cove showed the following numbers of clan memberships: Deer, nineteen; Wolf, eighteen; *Anisahoni*, ten; Bird, nine; *Anigilohi*, six; Red Paint, one; and *Anigotigewi*, one. On the basis of the relative clan numbers a certain order of expected matings would occur if local concentration of clan numbers were the most important determining factor in marriage preference. If a comparison of expected order of matings in terms of frequencies of occurrence of clan persons, as based on local clan numbers, were made with the actually observed order of frequency of matings, and a fair amount of coincidence were shown, then it would seem justifiable to assume that local or geographic propinquity governed clan matings. But such a coincidence does not occur as can be seen from Table 2.

It will be observed from this comparison that, with the exception of the Deer-Wolf matings which are unavoidably most numerous because of the immense local concentration in numbers of these two clans, the observed order of matings does not satisfactorily coincide with the expected order.

Another indication that geographic propinquity does not govern clan marriage preference may be noted in the relatively low percentage of marriage within the clan, which was only 6 per cent, and in the similarly low percentage of marriages with the father's clan. If local numbers of clanspeople governed choices in marriage, then in some regions an immense number of Wolf-Wolf matings would occur, or Bird-Bird where these clans preponderated. The inevitable conclusion from this evidence must be that cultural factors operate to restrict and guide marriage choices rather than geographical propinquity.

It would be hard to see how the marriage preferences could have given rise to the local clan preponderances. If clan marriages had been a chance series of permutations, it would perhaps be expected that the numbers of clan members would be locally and generally about equal. With only chance guiding marriages, the possibility of selecting mates from any two of the seven clans would be twenty-nine out of one hundred. Instead, we find that there occurs an average selection of two clans in marriage in sixty cases of marriage out of every one hundred.

It is more likely that the local clan concentration and the marriage preferences indicated are the expression of some common underlying principle. This principle may be the same as that exemplified in the formerly present dual division of society into two moieties. Two groups of clans, one of three clans and one of four clans, constituted the two moieties, and marriage regulations probably acted to limit the choice of mates to members of the opposite moiety. Not only the Cherokees but also the Creeks and other Southeastern tribes are described as having the dual division of society. These were called "red" and "white" divisions and were identified with war and peace functions, respectively. Many of the Southeastern tribes have an organization which would fit a basic eight-clan type divided into two moieties. So far as the Cherokees are concerned, they appear to have lost one of their clans. Moreover, the present-day Eastern band of Cherokees probably does not furnish a representative sample of the clan numbers present in the older tribe before the deportation in 1838. As we have previously indicated, there is no longer visible evidence for moieties.

There is generally an active and a passive party in each case of preferential mating. The active party is the one whose grandfather's clan is the same as the passive party's clan; the passive party is the one who is selected by the active party. There is apparently no correlation of active or passive parties with either of the sexes.

Principles involved.—The operation of the principle of preferential mating can be understood only through its dovetailing with certain other active principles, namely, solidarity, opposition, reciprocity, sanctions, and familiarity-avoidance. Just as the automobile is set in motion only when the gears are in mesh, so also a delicate social organization is to be comprehended only when its activating forces are found in operation. An examination of the roles played by specific social units and by occasions of contact may be expected to exemplify the active principles at work in Cherokee society and their importance in relation to the preferential mating principle (see Table 3 for summary).

First, there is the domestic family. The individuals making up the family are held together in certain ways and kept apart in other ways. The ways in which they are bound together may be called "social solidarity," while the ways in which they are pulled apart may be called "social opposition." Solidarity within the individual family is manifested in the form of a series of pair solidarities, particularly those primary pairs of husband-wife, parent-child, and brother-sister.

The solidarity of the "husband-wife" pair is manifested in the following:

1. Their common attitude of respect toward each other's parental generation
2. Their common attitude of control over the children's generation
3. The fact that both before and after marriage the husband and wife are on terms of privileged familiarity with each other, except during periods in which taboos are imposed to remove disease or uncleanness

TABLE 3

CHEROKEE KINSHIP FACTORS

Factors Illustrated	Type I Relationships	Type II Relationships	Type III Relationships
1. Basic relationship.........	Parent-child	Brother-sister	Grandparent-grandchild
2. Underlying principle	Opposition between contiguous generations	Clan equivalence and generation solidarity	Alternate generation solidarity
3. Secondary pairs of consanguines...........	1. Father-child 2. Mother-child 3. Father's sister–brother's child 4. Mother's brother–sister's child	1. Older brother–younger brother 2. Sister-sister	1. Paternal grandfather–grandchild 2. Grandmother-grandchild 3. Maternal grandfather–grandchild
4. Secondary pairs of affinals.	1. Husband's parents–son's wife 2. Wife's parents–daughter's husband 3. Mother's brother's wife–husband's sister's child 4. Father's sister's husband–wife's brother's child		1. Husband-wife 2. Mate's sibling–sibling's mate 3. Grandchild's mate–mate's grandparents
5. Predominant attitude within pairs...........	Respect and indirect familiarity	Satirical familiarity	Sexual familiarity

TABLE 3—*Continued*

Factors Illustrated	Type I Relationships	Type II Relationships	Type III Relationships
6. Lineage traced............	Two: father's matrilineal and own	One: own matrilineal	Two: father's father's matrilineal and mother's father's matrilineal
7. Terminology..............	Complementary reciprocal in main	Self-reciprocal in main	Self-reciprocal in main
8. Behavior.................	Asymmetrical	Symmetrical	Symmetrical
9. Functioning..............	Superordination-subordination	Satirical sanctions	Clan reciprocity and preferential mating
10. Direction of classification..	Vertical	Horizontal	Vertical and horizontal

4. Reciprocal and complementary rights and duties in marriage
5. The fact that pregnancy and menstrual taboos imposed upon the wife are extended to the husband also

On the other hand, the solidarity of "parent-child" relationships is manifested in:

1. The indirect familiarity relationship which allows of some degree of good fellowship between the generations
2. Mutual aid and protection, the parents first aiding the children, and in their old age being aided by the children
3. The respectful behavior and other duties required of the child toward the father's clan
4. The strong relations between mother and child, both being in the same clan and of the same blood

The solidarity of brothers and sisters is manifested in the following ways:

1. The self-reciprocal terminology between brothers and sisters, and the several collective terms for all siblings or for siblings of one sex taken collectively. Complementary terms between brothers
2. In the clan solidarity which expresses "brother" and "sister" relationships. The clan is an exceedingly solid group
3. In the recognition by the child of the solidarity of the father and his clan and of his mother and her clan

Between the various primary pair relationships just cited there are also in operation forces of social opposition. Particularly strategic in this regard is the opposition between the "husband-wife" pair and the "brother-sister" pair. For in the course of each individual's life he is taken out of his family of orientation's "brother-sister" group and merged with his grandparental clan group in a family of procreation. The sources of opposition are implicit in the very presence of solidarities.

The original husband, wife, and child triangle is seldom found entirely detached from other similar family nuclei because of the bonds wrought by inheritance and marriage. The husband is still bound to his brothers and sisters, and the wife to hers. As a result the child becomes aware of other important individuals of the parental generation—his father's sister and his mother's brother. These are persons of great importance in the training and respect attitudes developed in the child. Strong conflicts develop in the attitudes toward the wives and husbands of one's brothers and sisters, and toward the wife's brothers and sisters. The relations here involve familiarities of the "brother-sister" type and the "grandparent-grandchild" type in combination.

The "parent-child" relationship is a vertical one, and the barrier of opposition between contiguous generations tends to become more developed with the greater age of the relationship. The "brother-sister" relationship is a horizontal one and, extended to the clan, becomes a bond of solidarity that can never be dissolved. The "grandparent-grandchild" relationship is originally a vertical one but on the occasion of marriage tends to be translated, in the form of the "husband-wife" relationship, into a form of horizontal grouping.

All three of the primary relationships are built up on the matrilineal lineage as a basis. The solidarity of the matrilineal lineage is very great and is, perhaps, the most stable fact in Cherokee kinship. It underlies the solidarity of brothers and sisters. The "father-child" and the "grandfather-grandchild" relationships are possessed of solidarity only so far as they touch on the continuity and stability of the matrilineal lineage. The latter, it must be emphasized, holds together the whole system, both in its vertical and in its horizontal aspects.

Each family contains within itself the seeds for its own reproduction and replacement through the translation of the "grandparent-grandchild" relationship into the "husband-wife" relationship. The most important relationships which the individual sustains during his lifetime may be listed in the following order: (1) child to parent, (2) brother to sister, (3) grandchild to grandparent, (4) husband to wife, (5) parent to child, and (6) grandparent to grandchild. The family of orientation includes the first three relationships just cited, and the family of procreation the last three.

Factors of opposition operate most frequently along the lines of generation, sex, age, and lineage within the family. They act to make breaches in the solidarity of the family and help bring about the dissolution of the individual family after the agencies of death and marriage have enacted their role. The breach between the contiguous generations is strong to start with. Age enters into the same role of dividing persons as does generation; the older brother may assume the role of the maternal uncle.

The role of the clan in preferential mating has to a considerable extent been indicated by implication in the discussion on the domestic family. Preferential mating is really an affair between an individual and persons belonging to specific clans and can be called a "clan-individual" relationship. The configurations already established in the individual domestic family are extended to the whole clans which happen to include the persons standing in certain close familial relations to one's self.

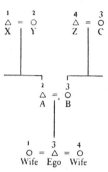

The clan is the exogamous social unit and is also a mechanism for reciprocity. The severity of the ancient laws against marrying within the clan have been relaxed, but a survey of present-day marriages shows that there are still very few marriages of this type. And it does not take much inquiry into the mechanics of the Cherokee kinship system to show that marriage within one's own clan would play havoc with the elaborate mechanism of reciprocity set up by the clan to deal with disturbances in the balance of numbers caused by deaths, births, and marriages.

FIG. 6.—Balance of marriage exchanges between clans. In this diagram of three generations, Arabic numerals refer to clans and capital letters to lineal ascendents of ego, who is male.

The nature of the reciprocity between clans can best be shown by a hypothetical example in which the balance of losses and gains is struck in a typical manner. In the accompanying diagram (Fig. 6) four clans are involved, and some dozen individuals serve as actors in the drama. The following are the steps involved in the process:

1. The original solidarity of clan 1 of ego's paternal grandfather was disturbed by the loss of the grandfather (X) when he married ego's paternal grandmother (Y) of clan 2. X was "lost" in the sense that he went to live with his wife's people and no longer hunted with, or fought in company with, his own clanspeople.

2. Ego's father (A) was brought up as an integral member of clan 2, but he might marry back into his father's clan to redress the original loss of his father to that clan. But the incest regulations will not allow him to marry into his father's clan, hence he marries ego's mother (B) of clan 3, with a consequent loss of one member to clan 2.

3. Ego (male) is brought up in his mother's household as an integral member of clan 3. But the father of ego is reminded throughout his life of the loss suffered by clan 1 (through the marriage of ego's grandfather [X] to ego's grandmother [Y] of clan 2) by the attitude of extreme respect and solicitude which he is compelled to maintain toward clan 1. His whole demeanor throughout life toward clan 1 was as if he owed it something and as if an exchange had been only half-completed.

The only way out of this impasse, and to render justice to the original clan (1) which has given one of its members and received nothing in return, is for ego's father (A) to give ego (of clan 3) to a woman of clan 1 in marriage, and by this act complete the exchange. The way in which this is brought about is by the indirect joking relationship which exists between ego's father (A) and ego; ego's father (A) takes advantage of this privilege and jokes in an indirect fashion with ego. "You must marry my aunt," he says. At first ego does not understand that it is his father's paternal aunt's clan (1) into which he must marry. Later ego overcomes his shyness after the joking by his father on this subject, and begins to joke with this "grandmother" whom his father tells him to marry. In time he will meet a girl of his own generation who is "grandmother" to him and who belongs to clan 1, and he will marry her after becoming acquainted. Then the exchange is completed, and clan 1 has been recompensed for the loss of ego's grandfather (X) through his marriage.

Ego's father (A) does not concern himself about the loss occasioned to his own clan (2) by his marriage to ego's mother (B) of clan 3. But ego's respect for clan 2 will remind him that he should instruct his own children to marry into clan 2 and recompense the balance with that clan. This process can thus be seen to run on indefinitely in the agnatic line, and to act as a process of reciprocity between clans, restoring the balance which is upset by the marriages of the male members of the clans.

In the same way the mother (B) of ego respects ego's maternal grandfather (Z) because her father's clan (4) has suffered a loss by his marriage to C of clan 3, her own clan. So she will compete with ego's father (A) in joking indirectly with her son, telling ego that he must marry *her* paternal aunt (of clan 4). Ego may then become familiar with these "grandmothers" and marry into clan 4 (polygyny has been common in the past). This will complete another exchange. In a family of four or five children half may marry into the father's father's clan, and the other half into the mother's father's clan, and thus a balance is preserved. A girl may likewise marry into her father's father's, or mother's father's, clan, but the element of compensation is not so apparent here since the children follow their mother's line and not the father's.

Regarding those persons of his own generation whom ego may actually marry, the clan affiliation is the prime consideration in marriage, not the actual lineage. Theoretically, in his own generation ego can marry either (1) the father's father's sister's daughter's daughter, (2) the mother's father's sister's daughter's daughter, or (3) the mother's mother's brother's children's daughters. Two persons of opposite sex and different clans may both be *gidudu* ("grandchildren") to the same clan and may, in the absence of other modifying factors, be *gidudu* to each other and so possible mates.

The role that the Cherokee dances play in the drama of preferential mating is quite clear in some points but obscure in others. It is fairly certain that the chief occasion for social contacts with privileged familiarities which ripen into marriages of the preferential type is the dance. But the time of appearance and staging of the dances involve other less understood relationships. The dances originally occurred at intervals which may have corresponded with the cyclical ebb and flow of the tides of human desire for contacts with fellow-humans. One of the most clearly recognizable of these cycles is that connected with the menstrual periods of the female part of the population—regularly the

Cherokee male is seized with feelings of extreme revulsion and a desire to avoid the menstruating female. This feeling takes the form of strict monthly taboos and restrictions on the women which find reflection in many other customs, in the magical prayers, and in the myths of the tribe. Anciently, the Cherokees, as well as other Southeastern Indians, held monthly dances to celebrate the periodic social purification from blood taints and other uncleannesses of the whole community. The monthly dances, of that period at least, constituted ritual sanctions. At the present time the dances have lost this regularity and ritual significance, but have retained their function of bringing men and women together after separation.

The dance today is an expression of neighborhood solidarity in which the whole of each individual family participates. Taking part in the dance causes the individual to be accepted as one with the rest of the community. Those who have offended have their sins pointed out to them, and the general community, by satirical references on the part of clan "brothers" at the dance. This act on the part of clan "brothers" serves as a satirical sanction to correct faults and purge differences from the community. (Similar customs obtain among other tribes of the Southeast). Taking part in the dance reunites a family, which has been separated by taboos because of a death of one of its members, with the rest of the community, thus renewing social solidarity.

The most sociable of the dances are the Friendship dances. Familiarities at these dances consist of such actions as the men's putting their hats on the heads of the females, placing their coats around them, entwining their arms about their necks and shoulders, and various other gestures of ownership and intimacy. These are the dances for getting acquainted, and all the motions of the dance are designed to break down shyness and reserve on the part of the young people. This reserve is broken down, however, strictly along the line of the proper relatives. It is impossible, or improbable, that a young man will tease or joke with a woman of his father's clan, or one of a clan not directly related to him. On the other hand, if he finds a "grandmother" he will tease her to the extreme. In these "getting-acquainted" dances the young men will tease the young women, rather than other young men, because familiarities of the latter type are reserved for other types of dances.

At the Friendship Dance a man may find a wife, and the one way possible for him to proceed is to select her out of his familiar relatives or "grandmothers." Yet the Friendship Dance is not restricted to the marriageables but includes both young and old, from a child hardly able to stand to the doddering old man. This dance is one of the most interesting features of Cherokee life, and its drama may be compared with that of opera in Western culture. The intensely gripping power of this dance, the fascination of its varied rhythms and songs, and its expression of primary desires for sociability—all combine to give it an unusual importance. In fact, this dance was noted by observers as far back as the time of the "deportation." In the renewal of their old-time mating memories and the memories of their spring time of life the old people find their chief consolation as age advances. In the sex glamor of the occasion, which the young people find their chief recreation, and in the general cheerfulness and gayety of the atmosphere of this dance, those who mourn for deceased relatives may find forgetfulness.

The Bugah Dance is a dance performed by masked dancers and is of very special importance from the point of view of kinship. The participants in this dance are "bogeys," masked individuals whose identity is unknown to the spectators. In this dance the "bogeys" perform various clumsy, uncouth, or humorous movements in which they satirize, with appropriate gestures and songs, their joking relatives. Those who may be present enjoy the game of guessing as to which of their familiar relatives the masked joker may be. Not only does the joking take these forms, but later the spectators join in the Bugah Dance and then the teasing takes more open and overt forms. This dance is one of the most widely employed occasions for the display of joking and privileged familiarity between relatives, of the same or different sexes. The "bogeys," who are always men, may even joke and tease one another if they stand in the correct relationships, which further mystifies and delights the spectators.

In the drama of preferential mating it can be seen, from the points already mentioned, that kinship usages play an indispensable role. The Cherokees, as the present writer encountered them, were a cheerful people much given to fun-making. This behavior in the main took the form of privileged familiarity. Although the younger generation is very shy, the youngsters rapidly lose this quality upon approaching the adult estate. On the whole, the average Cherokee is far from being, as the white man has typified the Indian, a stolid, indifferent, unemotional creature who is deaf to all the higher feelings of the white man.

Between absolute avoidance and extreme familiarity there is a whole gamut of relationships between pairs of relatives. We can generalize the opposite poles of behavior as "approach" and "avoidance." Among the Cherokees absolute avoidance is rare and confined to taboo situations involving fear of magical contamination. In this case, although avoidance is recognized as a way of cutting off harmful familiarities, direct kinship situations are not involved. The modified form of avoidance known as "respect" is a characteristic form in Cherokee kinship usages. Respect sharply channelizes, within certain sharply limited areas, the contacts between a pair of relatives. There is superordination and subordination involved and, what is more, a form of implicit social opposition. For complete solidarity or reciprocity is impossible between unequals; one owes and the other is owed. The relationship is a form of adjustment to a potentially overt conflict situation. Without respect behavior, as it exists between parents and children in Cherokee society, it would be difficult to see how preferential mating could be maintained. For preferential mating involves both a plus and a minus, a right way to go and a wrong way to go, and respect is the warning sign which prevents the taking of the wrong road. There can never be any meaningful solidarity without a complementary form of opposition to balance it. In this way equilibrium is maintained in complex kinship systems.

The "approach" pole of behavior involves primarily the acts of privileged familiarity. In the latter the behavior between persons tends to be unrestricted in its freedom (although there are marked degrees between the "gentle joking" of a "sister" and the "rough joking" of a "grandmother") and allows of a fuller measure of contact than any other forms of behavior. Privileged familiarity in Cherokee society is not distinguishable from the so-called "joking relationships." Where the pranks and raillery between relatives exist in a stereotyped form which can be recognized on any occasion as a definite cultural trait, we can speak of them as "joking relationships." These are perhaps never more than condensations of amorphous familiarities within constant forms. Needless to say, joking relationships, as understood here, merge into the respect relationships. Such a case occurs in the case of indirect joking between father and son, and in the joking with the man who marries the father's sister. Joking appears to be allied with potentiality of sexual relations, with social sanctions, and with social opposition.

First, as to potential sexual relations. It has been shown in the section on preferential mating that the relationship of the grandparental clans to ego is one of teasing and familiarity. It might also be noted that obscenities and sexual references abound in this type of familiarity so obtrusively that their meaning is only too clear. Of course, the obscenities occur not only between persons of the opposite sex but also between men. Potentiality of sexual relationships appears in the joking between siblings' spouses and spouses' siblings, and joking expressions are used for these relatives which imply this potentiality. The wife of a brother is called "wife" and like expressions occur. Sibling's mates, it must be remembered, are one's own potential mates because they are presumably in the alternate-generation relationship to one's self as well as to one's siblings.

The social sanctions are involved in the joking relationship through the fact that joking between clan "brothers" serves as a ridicule sanction to cause persons who are erring to repent and "toe the mark." Every fault in a person is held up to view, and a return volley is invited. This type of joking enforces the solidarity of the clan because the children of the jokers are compelled to speak up and to defend their fathers who are thus engaged in twitting one another. It is to be noted in this connection that joking occurs between all types of brothers among the Cherokees and not merely between "brothers" whose fathers are of the same clan, as among the Crow.

The indirect joking between parent and child is allied with social opposition. As has been stated in the section on kinship principles, the parental generation is in a position of social opposition to the generation of ego. Between ego and all persons of the parental generation the relationships are not reciprocal, and the joking of the son by the father is an expression of the social opposition between them. This joking cannot be direct because it is not truly reciprocal. The son cannot joke his father, even indirectly. The joking of the father's sister's husband is not reciprocal either; this man has no comeback when his wife's brother's children attack him. Likewise, the mother's brother, in joking with his sister's children, jokes about some third party in a clan which is familiar to his nephews or nieces.

In the "father-son" joking two objects are achieved: first, the father is enabled to joke with his son whom he cannot ordinarily be familiar with and, second, he can have a bit of fun at the expense of his own father's clan which he must ordinarily respect. The son may attempt a feeble kind of reciprocal joking and tell his father that he should not have married into so unworthy a clan as his own.

In the joking with the father's sister's husband the following functional relationship is involved. The father's sister's position with reference to ego is uncertain—she has qualities of the father, father's mother, and own mother combined; she is of the ascendant generation and, in the case of a male ego, of a different sex; and she is always of a different clan from ego. It can be seen that she is separated from ego by opposition barriers. She cannot be joked since she is of the father's clan; therefore, the uncertainty of the relationship centers on the man who marries her and who is of a different clan from the father's. This man can be joked with by the "tobacco joke." This joke is nonreciprocal on the part of the recipient and can be indulged in only once between the same two parties.

Opposition and privileged familiarity are again involved in

the joking of the Ball Dance. The joking against the opponents consists of a man joking with his fellow-clansmen in the enemy town in the absence of the persons joked. This weakens the opponents by setting up a magical channel of familiarity, as we have already seen. This joking may be against the opponent town as a whole, as well as against the individual fellow-clansmen.

The social sanctions among the Cherokees have already been noted in various contexts in this discussion. They amount to social obligations expressed reciprocally between relatives. They act as means of social control within the group and also control relations of members of opposition groups. Social sanctions include diffuse, penal, and satirical sanctions. The diffuse and satirical sanctions surrounding kinship usages are the only ones of much importance among the Cherokees. In the ritual of the dance and the ball game, and in the theory and practice of magic for the control of disease and other forces, there are miscellaneous sanctions involved. These sanctions are no longer of great power, however, since the mythical background has largely passed away. The sanctions imposed by the United States government and the state of North Carolina, although of an organized type, have not been assimilated. Periodically we find the band government forced to take measures to legalize the *de facto* marriages which have taken place in the community. The passing of blood-revenge and war removed the only potent retaliatory sanctions, those connected with the clan, some generations ago.

Socially the joking between relatives has a special social sanction significance, both positively and negatively. The positive aspect ties up with the joking between persons of alternate generations, which joking will lead to marriage. On the negative side we have the "tobacco joke." Apparently the man who marries one's father's sister is considered an intruder who owes something to his wife's brother's son or daughter. A person can ask for tobacco only once, although he may help others in the same relationship to his aunt's husband to obtain some tobacco at a later time. After one trial of this joke the aunt's husband must be respected—a rather curious relationship, indeed. The father's sister's husband has no comeback at the persecutors, hence the whole thing is not a true reciprocal joking relationship. Indeed, there is no relationship term for one's wife's brother's child. The "tobacco joke" can be played on any man who marries a woman of one's father's clan—for instance, the father's sister's daughter's husband may be asked for tobacco. The feeling of brotherhood between two men whose fathers were of the same clan is so strong that they will always combine to ask a father's sister's husband for tobacco. It must be rather fortunate for one to have a father in the Wolf clan because that clan, being so numerous, must have plenty of men marrying one's aunts!

An explanation for the tobacco joke appears to lie in the Cherokee horror of a man's marrying his father's sister. Such a marriage is the subject of several obscene references, and it is here that the regulatory function enters in, because anyone attempting to marry his aunt would never endure the ridicule. This ridicule has apparently been extended to any man who marries one's father's sister, but instead of being expressed in an ordinary joking relationship it has taken the peculiar form of the tobacco joke. Another type of tobacco joke is expressed with one's sister's husband. One can ask him for a piece of tobacco and, if he brings out his plug, one can keep it all as a joke.

The various forms of the familiarity relationship seem to center most decidedly in the contacts between husband and wife. Familiarity, howsoever it may take place, is concerned with the sexual reference, and with the promotion or prevention of relationships of a potentially sexual type. On the other hand, the respect relationship centers in the attitudes expressed between father and child. A degree of respect is extended to the mother, also, but not to her clan. Avoidance proper, although important in Cherokee society, does not appear in any particular kinship relation but only in a periodic ritualistic form; it is almost entirely obscured by the familiarity and respect relationship.

The purport of satirical joking is not entirely clear. It has a sanction significance in regulating the behavior of one's rela-

tives, and it acts as a social catharsis, clearing the air of violations of the established order. In the Eagle Dance, for example,
the individual dancer sings a song in which he derogates, in no
polite terms, his familiar relatives' accomplishments in war and
peace. Even in the Friendship dances the leading singer will
frequently joke his familiar male relations in a mild manner. It
may be that this satirical joking once linked up with clan revenge. It appears in the Death Song, which disappeared so long
ago that its very existence in recorded literature seems more or
less of a fortunate accident. At some time before 1783 a melody,
purportedly a Cherokee death song, was brought to London and
set to words which give every indication of being entirely
English in origin. A study by H. B. Jones[6] of this song indicates
that an ancient custom existed in which a captive, tied at the
stake preparatory to being burned alive by his enemies, sang a
song in which he satirized the tormentors and predicted the
avenging of his death by his own kinsmen and tribe. This same
custom, noted by Mooney[7] in the myth of the Seneca Peace-
makers, was probably not confined to the Cherokees, but it does
have many of the characteristics of the satirical sanctions just
mentioned. Furthermore, satire between relatives may take
still another form, namely, that of the sending of the *ayeligogi*
diseases upon one another as jokes to try out one another's
skill.

Magic and myth.—The *ayeligogi*, or "simulator" diseases, are
something like syphilis is to the modern physician—they are
great imitators. They are spoken of as "ordeal" diseases and
may be sent to a man by a friend, or even by his parents, to test
his endurance and knowledge of counterspells. On the other
hand, they may represent concentrated hate and revenge arising
from quarrels and must be referred to by euphemisms. Ordinary
treatment fails utterly in cases of these diseases. The principal
aim of the treatment is to find the "source" of the disease and
establish an avoidance relationship in place of the dangerous
familiarity relationship which has developed. The disease situa-

[6] *The Death Song of the Noble Savage.*
[7] *Cherokee and Iroquois Parallels.*

tion has become so complicated that in some cases ordinary diseases may simulate a "simulator" disease.

We cannot enter here into the vast field of interrelationships between disease in general and the social sanctions. It is possible only to note that a violation of many taboos results in disease through the establishment of a dangerous familiarity, and that disease itself can be to a Cherokee only the concrete expression of the resentment of some human or supernatural personage of an offense committed against that personage. The laws of blood-revenge have been sublimated into the laws of conjuring diseases.

When sickness attacks a person, the immediate inference is that a conjurer or conjuring spirit has launched an attack on the patient, which must be answered by a strong counterattack on the part of the patient and his friends. Among other devices designed to ward off the evil effects are those formulas which render the enemy conjurer confused, or make him forget what he is doing, or even make him become actually friendly instead of hostile. A confused state can be induced in the enemy conjurer by magically identifying him with animals such as the rabbit, which hop about witlessly. The conjurer can be separated from his powers and put into a black fog, in which he forgets all his repertoire of magical formulas. Attraction magic is sometimes so strong in its effects that the enemy conjurer can actually be brought around to a friendly attitude and so rendered harmless.

Passing now to another phase of the marriage problem, we find that mating was assisted by the use of love charms. One of the most famous of those cited by Mooney might be included in our present discussion. The title of the formula is in translation simply "Concerning Love."[8] The order of ideas runs somewhat as follows: First the charm-user, a male in this case, sets up a relationship of solidarity with certain benevolent spirits, and a preliminary assertion of the reciter's own attractiveness and charm is made. Then, barriers of avoidance are set up between the woman whom the reciter desires to conquer and the rest of the world of humanity. Blueness and loneliness are to be her lot until she recognizes her true interest, which consists in union

[8] *Sacred Formulas of the Cherokees*, pp. 376–78.

with the reciter of the charm. The latter now begins to set up a bond of familiarity between himself and the woman desired. He names himself and his clan and reminds her that she has been allotted to his clan in marriage from the beginning of the world and that he alone of that clan is suitable for her as a mate. Finally, he creates a barrier of avoidance between himself and the rest of the world. The rest of mankind are compared to noxious animals and are made to appear repulsive and loathsome. The final paragraph ends the prayer with a reiteration of the assertions of the first paragraph—the charms and attractiveness of the reciter and the solidarity by identification which has now developed between himself and the woman of his choice.

It can be seen from this love charm, then, that several of the active principles already discovered in connection with preferential mating are also involved here:

1. Social solidarity by means of attraction magic is evoked through the identification of the reciter's personality with the personality of the desired woman or with the helpful supernatural hypostasis.

2. Familiarity with one's rivals is used as a means of derogating them and elevating one's self (a common practice between clan brothers at the dances).

3. Barriers of social opposition are set up between the desired woman and all possible rivals in the world by means of forces of repulsion or avoidance, and she is made very lonely and blue. In such a state the Cherokee believe that a person is avoided by everyone and that he or she soon pines away and dies. Opposition barriers are set up between the reciter of the formula and his rivals, as he compares the latter to noxious creatures and repulsive elements.

4. A predestined or predetermined marriage prescription with certain clans seems to be intimated. The intense jealousy of other men of his own clan, on the part of the reciter, would seem to indicate his realization of their strong position as possible rivals.

The use of attraction medicine is made most frequently during the night. A young man sings his attraction song in a low voice about midnight, while facing in the direction of the girl's home. She will then dream about him and become lonesome for him unless she has previously fortified herself, on going to bed that night, with counterspells. The next time she meets the young man she is irresistibly drawn toward him, and will then become attached to him by strong and permanent bonds. Thus a strong man-and-wife solidarity is believed to be set up through the agency of the love charms. No man among the Cherokees need be long without a wife with such powerful magic at his disposal.

After he has gained a wife, however, his labors are not over. He may retain her only by a constant use of magic, especially if she be at all attractive and liable to the magical spells of jealous rivals of the husband. In order to retain his wife a man must reaffirm the solidarity existing between himself and his wife in a magical formula, and anoint her breast while she is sleeping with spittle. In this rite he magically unites the essences of his wife's soul and his own soul in a bond of great solidarity, and he repels all rivals in a barrier charm which compares them to noxious creatures. Sometimes, perhaps quite frequently, in spite of a man's best efforts a woman will be attracted away from him by the superior magic of a rival. To remedy this, and to recall the woman, he uses a prayer reaffirming his attractiveness and allying himself with the goddess of fire to reassert the solidarity of the woman with himself.

The rival who is endeavoring to detach a man from a woman makes use of negative love prayers. These prayers are of two types, namely, (1) those designed to separate a man and his woman preparatory to the uniting of the woman to the enchanter through the latter's attraction magic and (2) those designed to render a man unattractive so that no woman will want him. In the case of the spell which separates a man from his wife, each is likened unto a noxious animal and an avoidance relation is magically set up between them. The wife will then leave her husband, or vice versa, unless counterspells are resorted to by the parties thus attacked. In the use of those spells which render a man unattractive, the general purpose is to render more humble some young man who is proud and boastful of his accomplishments with the women. When he is rendered magically unattractive no one will speak with him, joke with him, or dance with him.

In some cases a man's love spells designed to attract a given woman fail to move her. The man's love then turns to hatred and to a desire for revenge. He may practice a spell of unattractiveness on her and, by making her similar to some noxious animal, make her lonesome and repulsive to all men. Or he may continue to ply her with love spells and finally succeed in making her fall foolishly in love with him and go to ludicrous lengths in demonstrating her affection. In this way he attains revenge on her.

The young man who wishes to be popular resorts to various charms to enhance his attractiveness at the dance and to make his singing voice well liked by the people. He may also want to increase his popularity and power in the council. In order to obtain attractiveness he identifies himself with the sun, or with some other great magical personality, while decorating himself with red paint. Ugly men often have to resort to these spells in order to obtain a wife. On the occasion of the dance the possessor of successful attraction magic will, as the leader or singer, act as a power for social cohesion, both through increasing the attendance at the dance and through familiarities within the group. People will always want to dance with an attractive young man and joke with him. Hence the Cherokee feels keenly the necessity for this social attribute. The prayers affirm an attractiveness for all the seven clans, even for the respected clan of his father. A formula inspiring attractiveness while visiting in a strange village is also used on occasion.

Kinship enters into the social relations of the formulas. One such is quoted by Mooney[9] entitled "To Make Children Jump Down," and is designed to assist in childbirth. The wording of the formula is varied, depending upon the supposed sex of the unborn child. The male child is frightened into being born sooner by being told that its grandmother is coming and is only a short distance away. This seems to be related to the idea that the male child is often frightened by an old grandmother's telling

[9] *Ibid.*, pp. 363–64.

him that he will have to marry her when he grows up, shriveled and ugly though she may be. In the same manner the girl child is told that the maternal grandfather is coming. This person is a privileged character in the community so far as teasing of female children is concerned and is greatly feared by the latter.

In general there seems to be some connection between magical powers and the old persons or grandparents. The relationship is quite ambivalent. Two of the most powerful forces in Cherokee cosmology, the fire and the sun, are regarded as "grandparents." The fire is given a variety of names in the formulas: "ancient red," "ancient white," "grandmother," etc. This element is a powerful and magical "grandmother," and one dare not be as familiar with it as one is with the human grandmother. A lack of respect for the fire may result in disease. If one spits on the fire, his teeth are sure to fall out; if he urinates on the fire, worms will attack his bladder. The fire is invoked to protect her "grandchildren" in the house, and bits of charcoal are tied about the necks of the children so that their magical "grandmother" will look after them and not allow them to become lost. "Grandmother fire" is the old woman out gathering wood from which the name for one of the present-day Cherokee dances is taken. Ritual sanctions are closely tied up with the magical kindling of new fire. It must be constantly fed on a special diet of liver, otherwise it will become dangerous and go after its owner causing illness. The sun is also regarded as a "grandmother" and is appealed to in various rites for love attraction and for the cure of certain diseases.

The moon is regarded as a strongly protecting "elder brother" or sometimes as a "maternal grandfather." He is the especial protector of ball players, just as the fire is of the hunter. He has a potent influence over women and is appealed to by the young man when painting up in preparation for the dance.

The magical familiarity of the formulas, linking up with the familiarity of actual social life (the latter, as we have seen, being an integral part of preferential mating), is linked with a familiarity counterpart in the myths. It is possible to conceive of the social relationships described in the myths as typical of the actual relationships to be found among the Cherokees themselves. It is in the projection of various types of homely human relationships into the animal and mythical world that value adheres to the myths. It might be said that the myths, like Aesop's *Fables*, are meaningless without the moral which attaches to them. In the myths we find, for example, that the animals are organized into clans which have blood-feuds between themselves and with men. It is only by making allies of the plants that man can win his war against the animals.

The most important relationships observed between animals are those of jokester trickery, revenge, love, and family relations. Of these we might take the example of the trickster element as most typical. Here are relationships of the familiarity type—the rabbit is a trickster and in the myths he tricks the otter, possum, turkeys, wolf, flint, and the deer, and is in turn tricked by the terrapin and the deer. Other animals also play tricks. The terrapin and the groundhog, for example, are represented as playing jokes on the wolves, who are particularly gullible. The favorite mode of trickery is for the jokester to lure another into a situation in which the latter is made to appear ridiculous or loses something of value. In this way the bear loses his tail, the otter his coat, the deer his sharp teeth, and the possum his furry tail. These jokes would appear pointless without the example of privileged familiarity to indicate their meanings.

The account of the myths concludes the presentation of the drama of preferential mating among the Cherokees. It has been shown that, to understand the events concerned with this principle, several other active principles must be taken into account —reciprocity, solidarity, opposition, and privileged familiarity— and that to accomplish the desired result the activities of the domestic family, the clan, the dance, kinship usages, social sanctions, magical prayers, and myths are controlled. The role of the domestic family was found to be that of establishing relationships of solidarity and opposition, and to introduce the young child to social life. The clan acts to extend family relationships to the whole tribe and to regulate marriage and ritual. The dance serves as the occasion of privileged familiarities which lead to marriage, and to establish and bind social contacts beyond the family proper. Kinship usages of familiarity and respect were shown to be vital prerequisites to the establishment of social attitudes and configurations. The social sanctions enter in diffusely to enforce correct usage and marriage, for any breakdown in the chain of marriages would tend to throw the entire system "out of gear," so to speak. Finally, the wording of the magical prayers and myths refers too frequently to the established order of behavior and mating not to be considered as important factors in the maintenance of the forms of society.

Comparative survey.—Some inquiry should be directed at this point toward the distribution of the Cherokee system of marriage just presented. So far as the clan system is concerned, there is much resemblance between the Creeks and the Cherokees. The Creeks held marriage with either the father's or the mother's clans in disfavor, and although no specifications are laid down, some type of preferential marriage was apparently favored. A Creek could apparently tell by the attitude of any two members of his tribe toward each other, i.e., whether they joked or not with each other, how they were related. Persons who could joke with each other included (*a*) persons having parents of the same clan, (*b*) children and their mother's clanspeople, (*c*) all persons whose fathers belonged to the same clan, (*d*) persons and their father's fathers, and (*e*) persons and those women who had married into the father's clan.

Other usages conform to the Cherokee pattern. It was Creek usage to speak well of one's father's clan at all times while, on the contrary, it was customary to speak disparagingly of one's own clan. How far then, from the meager evidence adducible, can we infer the extension of the Cherokee system? Under present knowledge it is impossible to predict or postulate that any other tribe in the Southeast had a preferential mating system like that of the Cherokee. The Chickasaw terminology and also certain Pueblo terminologies have points of affiliation with the Cherokee, especially in the alternate-generation terms. The seven-clan system is not so far from the basic eight-clan system which seems to underlie the whole of the Southeast, particularly since there is some evidence that in times past there existed a Bear clan among the Cherokees which was absorbed by the Wolf clan. Certainly the Cherokees shared a basic "red" and "white" moiety system with the Creeks. These moieties were probably linked with marriage prohibitions.

Among recorded kinship systems comparable with the Cherokee in marriage prescriptions we might note the Ungarinyin type prevailing in the Kimberley division of northwestern Australia and described by Radcliffe-Brown.[10] Descent is here patrilineal, however, in contrast with the matrilineal Cherokee descent. All persons in a given clan are classified together in kinship behavior, generation levels being ignored in favor of local organization. A man and his brothers, and his and their children, are classified together, as are also the sisters. This is a vertical system since the term includes the generations from father to child with no definite reference to generation levels.

With the Aranda the Ungarinyin shares descent reckoned through four lines, prohibition of marriage with cross-cousins, and type marriages of the second-cousin variety, especially with the father's mother's brother's son's daughter. It differs from the Aranda in its ignoring of generation levels and the balancing of terms on these levels, in classifying all the males of a horde under one term (and also the females), in the persons of one horde behaving alike toward all the members of another, in the type marriage not being with the mother's mother's brother's daughter, or with the father's father's sister's son's daughter, or with the mother's father's sister's daughter's daughter, and in looking to the mother's brother of the father rather than to the mother's brother of the mother. Among the Cherokees a man can marry his father's father's sister's daughter's daughter, his mother's father's sister's daughter's daughter, his mother's mother's brother's daughter's daughter, his father's mother's brother's daughter's daughter, or his mother's father's brother's son's daughter's daughter.

[10] *Social Organization of Australian Tribes*, pp. 89-91.

The systems described are each seeking a way out of an impasse—the balancing of exchanges in marriage between kinfolk and the avoidance of an incest taboo. One must marry a relative, but it must be a relative not too close or yet (presumably) too far away. A network of checks and balances has been consequently developed, resembling in niceties of distinctions and firmness of basic motives the Constitution of the American people.

THE UNDERLYING SANCTIONS OF PLAINS INDIAN CULTURE

JOHN H. PROVINSE

THE UNDERLYING SANCTIONS OF PLAINS
INDIAN CULTURE[1]

INTRODUCTION

In an attempt to clarify the study of law among preliterate peoples Professor A. R. Radcliffe-Brown[2] a few years ago proposed and briefly discussed a set of categories for the classification of the underlying sanctions[3] of social control. With the desire of further examining this proposed classification by attempting to apply it to a preliterate area in North America the present writer undertook a survey of the literature dealing with social control among the Plains Indians. The following pages are a summary of the study.

The reasons for the selection of the Plains area for such a study are obvious ones to most readers: (1) it is the area of aboriginal North America on which fullest data are available and (2) it is an area in which the character of the political development predisposes one to problems of a legal nature, since at certain times of the year the centralized authority of the tribes was exceedingly strong and well defined. It is at once apparent that this annual or occasional emergence of centralized authority should be highly instructive with regard to legal sanctions and political development.

The plan of procedure was to examine the existing literature and attempt to catalogue the data on social control in accord-

[1] Re-written portion of a thesis accepted by the department of anthropology, University of Chicago, 1934, in candidacy for the Ph.D. degree.

[2] *Law* and *Social Sanctions*. To Professor Radcliffe-Brown, who gave freely of his time for consultation during the course of the study, the writer is deeply grateful.

[3] A sanction is defined as "a reaction on the part of a society or of some considerable number of its members to a mode of behavior which is thereby approved or disapproved."

ance with Professor Radcliffe-Brown's classificatory scheme.
Those data are none too plentiful. On only five tribes—the
Assiniboine, Blackfoot, Crow, Dakota, and Omaha—is the material at all satisfactory; a few supplementary instances of the
operation of the sanctions were obtained from the literature on
other of the Plains tribes.[4] It is unnecessary, perhaps, to point
out that in the reports the word "sanction" does not occur.
What does occur are instances of the operation of tribal custom,
covering breaches of tribal regulations and conventions, and the
observations of the investigators. These instances and observations, frequently fragmentary and isolated, furnished the basic
material for the study.

Fully aware of the many difficulties inherent in any attempt
to classify social control mechanisms or social sanctions, Professor Radcliffe-Brown has been careful to avoid too strict definition of the boundaries of his categories, and one does not find
therefore the neatly outlined scheme of classification which
might be expected. Without injustice, however, it is possible to
summarize in outline form the suggested categories; for fuller
discussion the reader is referred to the original articles previously
mentioned.

  I. *Primary sanctions* (those that protect the interests of society as a whole)
      Organized (legal)
        Negative (penal)
        Positive (premial)
      Diffuse (moral or ethical)
        Negative (disapproving)
        Positive (approving)
      Religious (ritual, supernatural)
        Obligatory
          Mediate
            Negative
            Positive

[4] Since the above was written, E. Adamson Hoebel has procured from among
the Northern Cheyenne a number of valuable instances of social control pertinent to the present study. No attempt has been made to incorporate these into
the summary here given. Hoebel's timely study is instructive as to what material may even yet be obtained concerning legal and political features too long
neglected by anthropologists (see *Associations and the State in the Plains*, pp.
433–38).

Immediate
Negative
Positive
Nonobligatory (luck)
II. *Secondary sanctions* (those that protect the interests of the individual)
Retaliatory
Restitutive
III. *Mixed sanctions* (those embodying reactions both of primary and secondary nature)

The principal distinction, it will be seen, is one between primary and secondary sanctions—a distinction based on the interests protected. Primary sanctions protect the interests of the community or society as a whole; secondary sanctions protect the interests of individuals, or groups of individuals less than the whole society, by giving to him, or them, some sort of satisfaction for wrongs suffered. The secondary sanctions, as Professor Radcliffe-Brown points out, are based on the primary ones, not necessarily in the sense that they are subsequent to them in coming into existence, but that they find their authority in the primary ones. This primary-secondary differentiation, it is apparent, parallels the traditional criminal-civil, crime-tort, punishment-revenge, or punishment-satisfaction distinctions so frequently found in modern juridical terminology but is more inclusive in scope in that it allows for the treatment, first, under the primary sanctions, of those diffuse social and religious control forces out of which organized legal control has developed and, second, under the secondary sanctions, of a large class of private wrongs which our modern civil-law terminology does not encompass but which are essential to a thorough understanding of the development of that branch of jurisprudence.[5]

It is to be noted in the foregoing attempt, or for that matter any attempt, to classify the sanctions of social control that two aspects of the problem must be considered: (1) the nature of the attitudes and beliefs aroused by the act calling the sanction

[5] One may justly regret the injection of new terms, but in view of the restricted meanings which so many of our present juridical terms have come to have, some new terminology seems necessary if we are to broaden the scope of our investigation of "law" sufficiently to bring into it the embryonic or rudimentary material of preliterate society.

into operation and (2) the existence and nature of the machinery by which society responds to the delinquent's acts—in other words, their conceptual as opposed to their structural or procedural aspect.[6] The attitudes and beliefs, basic though they may be to the ultimate analysis of social control, are very difficult of analysis at the present time, not only in the Plains where the data are sparse but in our own society where the data are plentiful. For this reason interest here has centered primarily on the procedural aspects of the problem in the hope thereby of avoiding the confusion which a consideration of attitudes would inject into the analysis.

THE PRIMARY SANCTIONS IN THE PLAINS TRIBES

In general, among the simpler societies of the world, the offenses covered by the primary sanctions are much less numerous and differ considerably in kind from those which are the subject of reaction and condemnation in modern society. Characteristic also of these preliterate groups is the absence of any strongly centralized authority for the infliction of penalties, resulting on the whole in the absence or limited operation of organized or legal sanctions and the more frequent application of diffuse sanctions operating in the ordinary course of social interaction. Against these general observations the Plains Indians are of considerable interest, for these warlike, buffalo-hunting nomads had not only extended the jurisdiction of their social control to a degree uncommon in preliterate groups but had also developed a strong and efficient instrumentality for making that control effective.

Organized sanctions and the Plains police.—Any discussion of the organized sanctions in the Plains cannot be separated from the executive machinery through which they were applied—the Plains police. These police, most frequently referred to in the literature as "soldiers" or *akicita*, were selected in a variety of ways. Among the Crow, police duties were associated in irregu-

[6] For the wording of this distinction the writer is indebted to Professor Robert Redfield, of the University of Chicago, whose critical comments during the progress of the study were a frequent source of assistance.

lar order with one or another of the tribal military societies;[7] among the Blackfoot two or three of the military societies were selected to act;[8] likewise, among the Teton-Dakota it appears that an entire society was chosen each year by the head *akicita* to act as the policing unit.[9] The practice differed somewhat among the Eastern Dakota groups where the police officials were chosen without regard to society affiliation,[10] and similar methods of selection are reported for the Omaha[11] and for the Assiniboine,[12] ability and military prowess rather than club membership determining the choice. Among other tribes further variations are reported: among the Hidatsa and Mandan the same society, the Black Mouths, were selected every year;[13] among the Osage the police duties devolved on the gentes.[14] Most of the southern Siouan tribes, the Ponca being a possible exception, followed the Eastern Dakota practice of selecting without regard to society membership. Though military or other societies are often associated with police duties in the Plains such practice is far from universal—a fact which suggests rather strongly that the tribal police power—and hence sovereignty, law, and the state—is but an incident of these associations rather than inherent in them.

Considerable variation is also to be found in the manner in which authority was delegated to these police. Appointments emanated from a head chief, a group of chiefs, a council, or from

[7] R. H. Lowie, *Social Life of the Crow Indians*, p. 229.

[8] Clark Wissler, *Blackfoot Societies*, p. 367. But see also Wissler, *Social Life of the Blackfoot*, p. 26, where he says: "As to whether the men's societies were police by virtue of their own membership, or whether they were individually called out to form an independent body is not certain."

[9] A. Skinner, *Eastern Dakota Ethnology*, p. 173; Lowie, *Eastern Dakota Dances*, p. 141.

[10] Skinner, *Eastern Dakota Ethnology*, p. 173; Lowie, *Eastern Dakota Dances*, p. 141.

[11] Owen Dorsey, *Omaha Sociology*, p. 288.

[12] Owen Dorsey, *Siouan Sociology*, p. 225.

[13] Lowie, *Hidatsa and Mandan Societies*, p. 249.

[14] Lowie, *Ethnology of the Crow and Village Indians*, p. 65.

some other tribally constituted and recognized authority acting for the group as a whole. It stands out clearly, however, that these police, however appointed, were public officials acting openly and impersonally for the public good, and backed up by the highest tribal authority.

The tenure of office is less clear. Among the Crow "every spring" the camp chief appointed one of the military societies to serve as a police force,[15] the office terminating "with the first snowfall."[16] The same seasonal appointment appears to have been made among the Blackfoot.[17] Among the Dakota the information seems to indicate two sets of police functionaries, one set holding office rather continuously during the year, the other set being chosen for special occasions and ceasing to function upon the completion of the service for which appointed.[18] The regulars of the first set held office for life among the Eastern Dakota;[19] among the Oglala they "seem to serve continuously during the year."[20] During the exercise of authority by the special appointees, the authority of the regular *akicita* was suspended.[21] Among the Omaha the hunt policemen, though their office terminated "with the hunt," were apparently available for call whenever tribal affairs warranted some executive action by the Council of Seven. Hence, with the possible exception of the Dakota, Omaha, and Pawnee, the police seem to have functioned only during the summer activities of the tribes.

Some further light is to be obtained by inquiry into the specific occasions on which the police were active. The most important one of these is probably the buffalo hunt. The use of

---

[15] Lowie, *Social Life of the Crow Indians*, p. 229.

[16] Lowie, *Crow Military Societies*, p. 183.

[17] Wissler, *Blackfoot Societies*, p. 367.

[18] Wissler, *Oglala Societies*, p. 10; Lowie, *Eastern Dakota Dances*, p. 131.

[19] Lowie, *Eastern Dakota Dances*, p. 133.

[20] Wissler, *Oglala Societies*, p. 10.

[21] Lowie, *Eastern Dakota Dances*, p. 135. The Pawnee practice resembles the Dakota with the exception that the regular police still exercised their powers in camp even during the term of office of the buffalo-surround police (Murie, *Pawnee Societies*, p. 557).

police during this period is reported for all five groups especially considered in this paper and has been reported generally throughout the Plains.[22]

Police activities in many phases of life other than the buffalo hunt are to be found. On war parties the police acted to keep order while the party was in movement, guarding against surprise attacks, restraining the overzealous, urging on the stragglers, and insuring that no one left the group without proper authority. Such duties are reported for the Omaha, the Eastern Dakota, the Northern Shoshoni, the Kansa, and the Pawnee. Denig's reference with regard to the Assiniboine[23] is ambiguous, Wissler is not specific with regard to the Blackfoot,[24] and no reference is to be found for the Crow. While moving camp, police carried out the orders of the directors or chiefs among the Blackfoot, Dakota, Assiniboine, Hidatsa, Mandan, Comanche, and Iowa; this type of police function is not found for the Crow or the Omaha.

In restraining war parties at inopportune times, specific mention of the police activities are to be found only for the Dakota, Crow, Omaha, and Hidatsa, but it is likely that it existed for a number of other tribes. Argument seems to have been the first recourse on the part of the chiefs and soldiers in attempting to restrain restless braves; this failing, feasts were sometimes given to mollify the warriors, and should these latter still persist in

[22] Some interesting exceptions are to be found, however. For the Sarsi, Goddard reports that "there was no body of men who punished offenses connected with hunting" (*Dancing Societies of the Sarsi*, p. 465), and Lowie records the same absence of the hunt police among the Comanche where the only punishment for advancing ahead of the main body was a reproof (*Dances of the Plains Shoshone*, p. 812; see also Hoebel, *op.cit.*, p. 438 n.). Police bodies are reported, however, among both these groups for other purposes—among the Comanche for regulating the tribe on the march and among the Sarsi "for keeping order during the Sun Dance, and probably at other times when the various bands were camped together. Why, if the police organization was so primarily a buffalo-hunt organization, as is suggested by Lowie and Wissler, it should be lacking among two such eminently buffalo-chasing groups as the Sarsi and Comanche constitutes an interesting problem.

[23] E. T. Denig, *Tribes of the Upper Missouri*, p. 552.

[24] *Blackfoot Societies*, p. 370. Wissler states that "for any occasion the chiefs would call upon one or two of the societies . . . . for police duties."

their intentions, "soldier-killing"[25] was resorted to. During the Sun Dance police were selected for the preservation of order by the Dakota, Crow, Assiniboine, Blackfoot, Sarsi, Iowa, Plains-Cree, and the Kansa; among some of the groups these police also supervised the conduct of the dance ritual.

Though the policing of the buffalo hunt has been frequently remarked by Lowie, Wissler, and others as the primary duty of the police officers, their duties as keepers of the public peace during tribal gatherings appear as important as regulation of the hunt. In fact, if one can judge the relative importance of the police functions by the number of references to each kind found in the reports, police duties in connection with settling disputes, punishing offenders, and maintaining order in camp generally would seem to surpass in importance the police duties at the communal hunt. Police supervision of this kind covered a wide variety of activities ranging from unauthorized absence from the camp or the suppression of horseplay to the compounding or punishment of murder and lesser offenses. During a part of the year, perhaps the greater part, the settlement of such delicts as murder, theft, assault, and similar offenses seems to have been left almost entirely to individuals and their kin—a matter of secondary sanctions, but tribal intercession, through the police or the chiefs, was a frequent occurrence. Presumably it took place when the entire tribe, or the greater part of it, was united for some common purpose. Such societal interference for the prevention of intratribal hostilities is reported from the Blackfoot, Omaha, Crow, Oglala, Eastern Dakota, and the Plains-Ojibway. Nearly all investigators, in fact, ascribe to the police the power to prevent quarrels within the camp.

Regrettably lacking from the reports in most cases is information on the rather crucial point as to how far this police power extended. Did the police have power to carry their orders into effect? Wissler for the Blackfoot states that the headmen must proceed in the settlement of disputes with tact, persuasion, and extreme deliberation and that they are "expected to succeed

---

[25] "Soldier-killing" did not always, or even frequently, extend to the actual taking of life.

without resort to violence."[26] Denig for the Assiniboine denies to the police the right to punish for murder, this being left to the individual.[27] Lowie, on the other hand, citing Beckwourth on the Crow, says that it meant instant death to refuse to abide by the police orders.[28] The use of force among the Dakota also seems quite definite, for the police "see that no one kills another, but in case one does, they either kill him or destroy all his property, destroy his tipi, etc."[29] Among the Omaha the native policemen were empowered to strike those who "quarreled and fought, stole, or scared off the buffalo."[30] The death penalty also was imposed by means of a poisoned staff in the hands of a representative of the Council of Seven on those "who made light of the authority of the chiefs."[31] Though these cases are not numerous, there seems little doubt but that the Plains police did have full power to carry out even the extremest penalties in the execution of the duties of their office.

The punishments inflicted by the police are quite uniform throughout the area. Whipping[32] or clubbing was the most frequent measure resorted to, followed up in more serious cases by destruction of the culprit's personal property—his tipi, blankets, gun, bow, horses, etc. Infrequently, in the case of a particularly stubborn individual, the death penalty was inflicted; Denig reports having seen two killed in his twenty-odd years among the Assiniboine.[33] The severity of the punishment and the rigidity of its enforcement seem to have varied with the seriousness of the offense as measured by the consequences of the act to the welfare of the tribe. If the misconduct at the hunt did not result in a serious deprivation for the tribe as a whole, the

---

[26] *Blackfoot Social Life*, pp. 23–24.   [27] *Op. cit.*, p. 448.

[28] *Social Life of the Crow Indians*, p. 229.

[29] Wissler, *Oglala Societies*, p. 10.

[30] Dorsey, *Omaha Sociology*, p. 363.

[31] Fletcher and La Flesche, *The Omaha Tribe*, p. 213.

[32] The whip is quite generally throughout the Plains the symbol of office of these police officials.

[33] Denig, *op. cit.*, p. 445.

culpability was less than if the act had occasioned dire hardship and want.

Another characteristic of Plains justice is the order-preserving nature of police activity as opposed to the idea of punishment for the sake of social vengeance. This is most clearly brought out by the attitude of the society toward the offender after punishment had been inflicted upon him. Conformity, not revenge, was sought, and immediately after a promise to conform was secured from the delinquent, steps were taken to reincorporate him into the society. For example, among the Assiniboine the police, after inflicting punishment on an offender, waited four days without further action. If during this time the criminal had made no display of resistance or unruliness, they assembled to discuss the case and usually gave presents to the man and reinstalled him in a new lodge.[34] Numerous other similar instances from the Dakota, the Plains-Ojibway, the Mandan, and the Hidatsa are to be found.

This restitution on the part of the soldiers was a completely social act, oftentimes under the direct order of the chief or council. The compensation given was roughly commensurate with the damage suffered through the police action. The important feature is that, were the offender at all amenable to reform, he was given another chance and was provided with those necessities of life that would enable him to make another start. Plains justice was organized, in so far as societal intervention did occur, not to inflict punishment for its own sake but to secure conformity to tribal regulations in order to preserve the integrity of the group.

Unsatisfactory as the recorded data for the Plains tribes are with regard to matters of social control, even the available material is convincing as to the existence of a well-defined legal authority in the area. There seems very little reason, furthermore, for restricting the field of this legal activity to the buffalo hunt, for instances of its penetration into several other phases of life are too numerous to be ignored. The authority is probably a tribal phenomenon, coming into existence with the spring re-

[34] Lowie, *The Assiniboine*, p. 36.

union of the various bands of the tribe and continuing during tribal hunting and military and ceremonial co-operative activity.[35] In summary we find that this police function was invoked most frequently and most rigorously for the following purposes: (1) to regulate the communal hunt; (2) to regulate tribal ceremonies; (3) to settle disputes, punish offenders, and preserve order in camp; and (4) to regulate war parties and restrain such at inopportune times.

One need only glance at the kinds of regulation summarized above to see that each activity in which the constituted police authority concerned itself was something the regulation of which was important to the survival of the society, Plains culture being what it was. The activities group themselves into two categories of social existence: the first three—economic security, the proper relationship of the group with the supernatural world, and the maintenance of peace and order—being concerned with internal affairs; the last, the relationships with other tribes, with external affairs. What social intervention in the affairs of individuals is found among the Plains tribes appears to be directed toward securing a better integration, internally and externally, of the group.

The need for some kind of control has given to the conquest theory of the state such standing as it has enjoyed. But the need for control can arise from other circumstances than those of an invading force subjecting a conquered people. Our Plains data, as McLeod has before now pointed out, would indicate that authoritative and sovereign control can be assumed by a group as a factor of group survival as well as be imposed upon them by outsiders. What would appear to be most fruitful in future investigations on the nature of the state is this need for and development of centralized authority in its relationship to the social structure and to the things that are important in the life of the group.

Before concluding with the organized penal sanctions, atten-

[35] In this connection the possible year-long police function among the Omaha, the Dakota, and possibly other groups warrants further study. Nor is there yet available any good description of what types of control are in effect among the bands during the winter breakup of the tribe.

tion must be called to another type of organized restraint of peculiar interest. This is the specialized development of the satirical sanction—a type of disapproval operating in most societies, including our own, in a very unorganized manner, but applied in the Plains with some degree of formality. Not all or even many of the satirical sanctions in the Plains had become organized, but the fact that any of them were formally applied is but another indication of the tendency to regularize control procedures. The best example is probably the following case from the Blackfoot, reported by Wissler:

> For mild persistent misconduct, a method of formal ridicule is sometimes practiced. When the offender has failed to take hints and suggestions, the head men may take formal notice and decide to resort to discipline. Some evening when all are in their tipis, a head man will call out to a neighbor asking if he has observed the conduct of Mr. A. This starts a general conversation between the many tipis, in which all the grotesque and hideous features of Mr. A's acts are held up to general ridicule amid shrieks of laughter, the grilling continuing until far into the night. . . . . [36]

In another case, among the Omaha, it is reported:

> In olden times members of an unauthorized war party which had lost any of its number, on their return were forced to strip themselves, put clay on their heads and faces, crawl on their hands and knees to the lodges of the principal chiefs, and there cry for mercy.[37]

The latter case presents certain difficulties of classification. One needs, of course, a fuller definition of the word "forced" to know whether the sanction is legally organized, but the difficulty does not end there. Where, when one of the diffuse sanctions of ridicule becomes organized, does one draw the line between that and a penal sanction? When does mockery or debasement become a legal penalty? It is in such cases that the distinction earlier referred to between conceptual and procedural aspects of the problem of social control must be kept in mind.

Other instances giving even more difficulty of classification come to light in connection with the chastity tests for women. For example, the "Owns Alone" ceremony for women over forty years of age was one in which the woman publicly proclaimed her steadfastness to her husband. Should she be challenged by

---

[36] *Blackfoot Social Life*, p. 27.   [37] Fletcher and La Flesche, *op. cit.*, p. 404.

anyone present, she might require her accuser to swear an oath. "If the accuser so swear, the public pelt the woman with buffalo chips and filth, running her out of camp."[38] Or again, in the public ceremony to test the virginity of young girls, "if a young woman is guilty and yet pretends that she is not, any man who knows that she is lying will go up, throw a handful of dirt in her face . . . . or perhaps will drag her forcibly from the place."[39] In these cases the punishment inflicted is probably just as much a penalty as would be subjection to whipping or branding, or some other corporal punishment, and for that reason suggests a penal sanction. But one element is missing. That is some authoritative body or person, representing the entire society, which or who is responsible for bringing about the chastity and virginity tests. The feast is held in public; the men are invited by the woman herald to come and challenge the women assembled for the test, and if found guilty the women are derided and pelted with buffalo chips. But the constituted authority of the tribe—the chiefs and the soldiers—enter the ceremony not as officials in the administration of official duties but as interested spectators, ready to challenge, to ridicule, or throw buffalo chips along with the rest of the crowd.

One finds several other instances of the semiorganized operation of the satirical sanction in the testing of virtuous young men, in the selection of lance-bearers for some of the military societies, in the calling-off of mistresses' names by men on a war party, and in a highly specialized form among the Crow and Hidatsa, in the so-called "joking relationship." All these, however, have but partial organization in terms of tribal centralized authority and must logically be classed as informal diffuse sanctions.

There is yet to be considered under the organized sanctions the positive expressions of approval—those gifts, emoluments, badges, medals, or other rewards or insignia which are tendered an individual in some organized manner, representative of the community as a whole, in recognition of proper conduct. To these the term "premial" has been applied.

[38] Wissler, *Oglala Societies*, p. 76.   [39] *Ibid.*, p. 77.

It is not surprising to find, militaristic and hunt-conditioned as the Plains groups were, that most public commendation came to an individual because of prowess in war and the chase. The chief expression of this approval in an organized way is to be found in the custom, somewhat peculiar to the Plains, of counting coups—the privilege of each individual, whether male or female, to relate in public those meritorious deeds which he or she had done. The term coups ("blows") has come to be applied to these public recitals because it was customary after reciting a worthy performance to strike, or have struck for you, a blow on a drum, a post, or other object. The exploits which warranted a count varied from tribe to tribe in minor details and were ranked in importance; some were of considerably greater value than others in securing tribal approval.

One of the best examples of the formality and regularity attaching to the coup count is found among the Omaha. Here the count was rigorously controlled by the "Packs Sacred to War" group. Until a man's deeds were formally awarded to him by this group, he had no right to assume the honors inhering in his act; such formal bestowal and tribal recognition were essential elements of the award. The Keeper of the Sacred Tent of War, assisted by other leaders, presided at the public ceremony when the honors were bestowed.[40] After being subjected to an oath and presented with a witness stick,

the man claiming the first honor stepped forward and began the recital of his deed, telling how he struck the body of the enemy. He held the red witness stick over the pack and all the people listened attentively to his words. At a signal from the keeper he let the witness stick drop. If no one had disputed his story and the stick rested on the pack, the people sent up a great shout of approval, for the omniscient birds in the pack had accepted his words as true. But if he was disputed and the stick fell to the ground, it was believed that his words had been rejected by the birds. Then the people shouted in derision, his stick was tossed away and the man lost the honor he had sought to gain. If the stick remained on the pack, the keeper granted permission for the man to wear the insignia of the grade to which his deed belonged. . . . . [41]

With somewhat less formality than among the Omaha, the awarding of honors, or the assumption of honors with public approval, is found generally throughout the Plains groups. In

[40] Fletcher and La Flesche, *op. cit.*, p. 142. [41] *Ibid.*, p. 437.

so far as these represent an organized public award, they can legitimately be classed as premial sanctions. There are, however, a number of other types of public acclaim or approval in the Plains which operated as powerful sanctions but the organized character of which is much less clear. The most important of these are the singing of praise songs for returning warriors or hunters, the right of an individual who has distinguished himself to make use of various insignia to proclaim that fact to the world, and awards of various sorts to women for virtuous conduct. The reports are not specific as to just how public, how representative, how regularized, and how organized is the procedure in these cases. A good argument can be made, perhaps, particularly in the case of the awards for virtuous conduct where the matter was given formal consideration by the tribal council, for the inclusion of these forms of approval under the organized sanctions. Yet if one opens up the organized premial category to these cases, a number of other rewards of a semiorganized nature or to which the public as a whole passively acquiesced immediately clamor for admittance. If one sticks to the logic of the classification and draws the line rigidly at the coup count, or at some other distinctly organized proceeding, at once violence is done to closely related types of social control that sociologically should be considered together. This difficulty of classification, insurmountable as it would appear except for purely procedural analysis, is commented on later.

The diffuse sanctions.—These "spontaneous expressions of approval or disapproval by members of the community acting as individuals" were, in the Plains, fairly numerous but are extremely difficult to classify. Ridicule played a very important function. Breaches of marriage and residence rules, of avoidance and respect taboos, were condemned by words or acts designed to bring shame upon the wrongdoer. Among the Crow a man who resisted the abduction of his wife was derided in song; should he later take back this same abducted wife he was told: "Your face stinks," and he was nicknamed the "holder of a crazy woman."[42]

Bravery and proper conduct in war were also strongly con-

[42] Lowie, *Mandan, Hidatsa and Crow*, p. 86.

trolled by ridicule. In an Omaha war dance, after the return from a victorious war party, "laughter and derision greet any mention of cowardice, shrinking or begging for mercy of the opponent."[43] If an officer of the Crow Muddy Hands Society "ran away instead of assisting his fellow tribesman, other people made fun of him and called him a coward."[44] If one of the Crow Big Dog Belt Wearers, whose oath required him never to retreat from the enemy, returned alive to the camp, he was made the "laughing stock" of his fellow-tribesmen, and if he fled in spite of his obligation to make a stand, "he was thenceforth treated as a coward and outcast, regardless of his former reputation."[45] If an officer of the Crow Fox Society failed to live up to his duty not to flee from the enemy, he was "held in contempt and said to be in the condition of a menstruating woman."[46]

Similar applications of ridicule can be found in nearly all the Plains tribes in connection with bravery on the battlefield, and particularly in connection with those members of the military societies whose official duties required of them some brave or rash act, such as staking one's self down before the enemy, planting a lance in the foreground of battle and never leaving it, or refusing to retreat even when repulsed by the enemy. Ridicule was used not only to hold these officers to their obligations but also in selecting them for the dangerous but glorious offices they held. For example, in the selection of the lance-bearers in the Oglala Crow Owners' Society, should the candidate selected refuse the office, he was persuaded, lectured, and given gifts, and if he then still refused, "the members and the crowd join in ridicule and impromptu songs of derision."[47] In inducing an unworthy officer to vacate his office, he was made so ashamed that he withdrew.[48] In the Sotka Society of the Dakota, "if the two virgin singers fall into temptation they are dismissed and publicly defamed."[49] Dismissal from any position of honor in

[43] James, *Long's Expedition*, II, 13.

[44] Lowie, *Crow Military Societies*, p. 183   [47] Wissler, *Oglala Societies*, p. 24.

[45] *Ibid.*, pp. 181–83.   [48] *Ibid.*, p. 65.

[46] *Ibid.*, p. 158.   [49] *Ibid.*, p. 33.

any of these societies was, of course, throughout the Plains a "public disgrace."

Nor were even the most honored exempt from the operation of this sanction if their future conduct should flaunt tribal custom. For example, take the case of Simon, a Dakota brave who had taken so many scalps that no one could "soldier-kill" him—the highest mark of prestige; yet when he turned Christian, cut off his hair, and abjured his Dakota honors,

no one was found so poor as to do him reverence. As he passed through the village, going to his work, he was laughed at, and the children often said, "There goes the man who has made himself a woman." The men who before had honored him as a Dakota brave now avoided him and called him no more to their feasts.[50]

One development of the satirical sanction in the Plains deserves special mention—the well-known joking relationship. Privileged familiarity or some form of joking relationship exists among many of the world's preliterate peoples, but nowhere was it developed quite as distinctively as among the Crow and Hidatsa tribes of the Plains. This relationship existed between individuals whose fathers belonged to the same clan,[51] and the joking privilege was much more than just the liberty to play practical jokes upon, or make obscene remarks to, your joking partner. With regard to it Lowie says:

The basic notion of this relationship in its more serious aspects seems to be that of licensed and unrestricted criticism for an infraction of tribal custom. When a man has committed some reprehensible deed, e.g., married a clan mate, or shown jealousy, it was not the function of his fellow clansmen but of his *makutsati* [joking relative] to reprove him or make fun of him. They would spread the news of the wrongdoing and throw it in the offender's teeth and he was obliged to take all this in good part as the prerogative of *makutsati*.[52]

The practice seems to have begun as early in life as children could be made aware of its possibilities and obligations and to have extended to all manner of behavior: ignorance of technical procedures, poor sportsmanship, improper marriage, cowardice—

---

[50] Riggs, *Dakota Ethnography*, p. 221.

[51] Among the Crow extending to linked clans (Lowie, *Social Life of the Crow Indians*, p. 205).

[52] Lowie, *Mandan, Hidatsa and Crow*, p. 42.

in fact, apparently to anything that was socially reprehensible in the group. Some of the cases indicate that the joking sometimes took a rather inconsequential turn: for the Hidatsa, Lowie records a case where a man was twitted for availing himself of the levirate—a practice regarded as perfectly proper or even obligatory in the society.[53] One cannot be quite sure where the joking of the relationship leaves off and the serious corrective influence begins. Exemption from joking could be obtained by performing brave or great deeds—an interesting case of estoppel.

Among both the Crow and the Hidatsa the impersonal nature of the joking relationship is specific. Though the ridiculed transgressor might feel "like sinking into the ground with shame," he must not resent the fun-poking but must wait for an opportunity to heap shame upon his "relative" when the latter transgressed. Yet the "getting-even" procedure was not in the nature of retaliation, for the requital of the one first joked was not a matter of revenge or personal satisfaction but a distinctly social obligation imposed upon him by the group to which he belonged.

In addition to ridicule other expressions of social disapproval of a diffuse nature were common in the Plains. These expressions were made articulate usually through such words as "disgraceful," "disloyal," "crazy," "without honor," and the like. Any evaluation of their significance as social control factors, in comparison with other mechanisms for the same purpose, is at present impossible. Instances are reported also of other kinds of disapproval, diffuse in nature, such as shunning, gestures, and other physical reactions denoting disgust or disapproval. The Plains literature is practically devoid of any useful material along this line though Fletcher and La Flesche have recorded for the Omaha a list of nineteen terms applied to bad traits of character and bad conduct which, in their words, "may assist toward making clearer Omaha ethics as applied to social life."[54] Such word lists, with as many contextual variations in meaning

[53] *Ibid.*, p. 47.

[54] *Op. cit.*, pp. 603-4. A similar list of terms covering good traits and good conduct is also recorded.

as it is possible to obtain, will probably be necessary before much can be done in classifying, ordering, or evaluating the diffuse expressions of public opinion among the Plains or other primitive groups. We can at present do little more in evaluating the diffuse negative sanctions than to accept Lowie's characterization of the North American Indian generally in this respect, when he says:

> To meet with universal reprobation on the part of one's neighbors; to have derisive songs sung in mockery of one's transgressions; to be publicly twitted with disgraceful conduct by joking relatives—these were eventualities to which no Indian lightly exposed himself.[55]

The diffuse positive sanctions in the Plains, those reactions approving individual conduct, can also be discussed only in the most general terms. That they are important tools for the maintenance of Plains values is easily recognized but the psychological, linguistic, and cultural analysis which is prerequisite for their evaluation is still a future achievement of social science. The values which stand out most prominently are two: bravery for the men and virtuousness for the women. These do not, however, exhaust the possibilities of achieving respect and esteem; generosity, truth, honesty, self-control, courtesy, respect for superiors, industry, and thrift—all were approved and applauded. This approval manifested itself in a variety of ways—through words, glances, smiles, even on occasion through avoidance. The present literature does not even approximate our needs in classifying these spontaneous expressions of approval.

The religious sanctions.—The real force of the religious sanctions as control devices among the Plains tribes is largely obscured by general statements of two types: first, those which emphatically minimize any religious or ritual restraint and, second, those which attribute religious or supernatural influence practically to all regulative procedure. Nowhere does bias play more havoc with understanding than in this aspect of Plains control. Denig, writing generally of crimes and the prevalence of individual revenge among the Upper Missouri tribes, records that these tribes see "in all this no offense to Wakonda, nor any

[55] *Primitive Society*, p. 385.

idea of moral wrong," individual retaliation being the only punishment they expect.[56] Against this can be set the religious restraints among the Omaha where, according to Dorsey and borne out by the later investigations of Fletcher and La Flesche, these extended to a large part of the social activity.[57]

Among the Omaha the following persons and things are listed as sacred: the sacred pipes, the sacred pole, the hide of the white buffalo, the clam shell, the chiefs themselves, the keepers of the sacred tents and pipes, the gentes, subgentes, and all taboos. It is possible to show that the foregoing features constitute almost the whole of Omaha social life. Even violations against the hunt rules and murder were regarded as religious offenses, though the policemen who dealt with the crimes were considered to be of human origin. Whether this greater emphasis on religious sanctions among the Omaha and their comparative neglect by other groups is the true state of Plains religious controls it is impossible to say. The fact remains that it is from the Omaha that most of our examples of religious sanctions must be taken.

Religious sanctions may operate either immediately—that is, may follow automatically from the behavior without the active intervention of supernatural forces—or they may be imposed upon the individual through the mediation of some supernatural agency. The reported cases do not, however, allow us to distinguish in many cases whether some mediating agency is involved or not.

The immediate sanction is best represented by those cases where, for the violation of some taboo, disease or other misfortune results to the offender. The same sanction is reflected in the advice given to scouts in the buffalo hunt, where these are warned that if they do not tell the truth dire consequences, such as being struck by lightning, thrown by one's horse, bitten by a snake, etc., may result.[58] Oaths administered to test the truth of statements are also based on this immediate ritual sanction. In addition to the foregoing examples, all from the Omaha, the sanction is found in connection with the practice reported for the

[56] *Op. cit.*, p. 481.

[57] Dorsey, *Omaha Sociology*, p. 356.　　　　[58] *Ibid.*, p. 367.

Crow by Lowie, and by others for the Plains-Ojibway, Cree, and Blackfoot, of "sexual confession" on war parties; a man who failed to tell the truth at these confessions was likely to be slain on the next war party.

Whether the difficulty previously mentioned of distinguishing between the immediate and the mediate religious sanctions is an inherent one brought about by the native's unclear conception of how nonhuman punishments are inflicted, or is the result of too little inquiry on the part of the investigators, it is difficult to say. Were the facts about many of the immediate sanctions better known, it is quite possible that the intervention of some supernatural agency might be seen. Only a few definite examples of the infliction of punishment by supernatural power are recorded, and these chiefly from the Omaha; the other instances do not admit of analysis from this standpoint.

The active intervention of the gods is shown in the case of two brothers among the Omaha who refused to assume the office of Keeper of the Sacred Tent of War to whom the office had lawfully descended. Shortly after their refusal "both men were killed by lightning, and their deaths were regarded as a punishment sent by the Thunder god for the disrespect shown the office of keeper by their neglect of duty toward the sacred rites committed to their care."[59] Another instance is recorded in connection with the sacred pipes, the life of the keeper of which "would be in danger of the supernatural powers" should he let one of the pipes fall while filling it.[60] The Omahas also "were afraid to abandon their aged on the prairie when away from their permanent villages lest Wakanda should punish them."[61]

Among the Canadian Dakota, if a man failed to carry out his obligation to perform the Sun Dance, "the sun carries this information to the thunders and they will punish him. If he fails altogether in the performance the thunders will kill him," for if the sun "comes to a man and tells him to do a certain thing which the man fails to perform, he will be killed."[62] The

[59] Fletcher and La Flesche, *op. cit.*, p. 403.

[60] *Ibid.*, p. 209.   [61] Dorsey, *Omaha Sociology*, p. 369.

[62] Wallis, *Canadian Dakota Sun Dance*, p. 328.

writer cites one instance of a death resulting from such failure to perform the Sun Dance as directed. Practically no information is available on the positive aspect of the religious sanction, though it is probable that the attainment of a desirable relationship with the gods for acts of a nature opposite to that of sin was much more frequent than the literature would indicate.

The nonobligatory sanctions of Professor Radcliffe-Brown's classification, the so-called "luck" sanctions, are very important in the Plains; they are the motivating influence behind much, if not all, of the vision or guardian-spirit experience, which experience was necessary for the insurance of success in almost any enterprise of vital importance to the individual. Most commonly these sanctions work immediately, the neglect of particular rites resulting in bad, the performance of certain others resulting in good, fortune. The characteristic that distinguishes them primarily from the religious sanction is not their procedural aspect, but their lack of social compulsion from the group as a whole. Hence they might even appear classifiable as secondary sanctions, based on primary group beliefs but carried on purely for individual ends. Until they have become socially obligatory they are important for the individual only in his relationship to the spirit world. Objection to the inclusion of luck sanctions as illogical in Professor Radcliffe-Brown's proposed classification is made in a later section.

The primary sanctions in constituent tribal groups.—Thus far we have looked at the primary sanctions in their relationship to the largest political grouping which occurs in the Plains—the tribe. Very instructive, however, with regard to the operation of sanctions are those group reactions which are to be found in the constituent groups of the larger political whole, ranging from groups based on kinship, such as the elementary family, through larger kin groups and finally to numerous types of nonkinship associations existing for social, military, or religious purposes. In all these we find the primary sanctions operating— group reactions having for their purpose the protection of the honor, integrity, or interests of the group rather than those of any individual member.

In the Dakota family "children are scolded often, they are pushed, or shoved, or sometimes shaken, and they are rarely whipped."[63] If an Omaha girl was disobedient, "she received a blow on the head or back from the hand of the mother."[64] The control exercised by the family group did not cease with the maturity of the child, or even upon its separation from the family group by marriage; the family, as such, was alert to see that it was not injured by an act of one of its members. Particularly is this apparent in the disciplinary actions taken against women who, either through promiscuity before marriage or infidelity afterward, brought disgrace upon the family group.

Larger kin groups—the extended family and the clan—also exercised control of their members within the realm of activity characteristic of those groups. It would be of interest to analyze the sanctions operating in these groups since they controlled their members by reactions similar to those operating for the society as a whole, bringing pressure to bear on them to refrain from doing those things which militated against, or encouraging those things which added prestige to, the family or clan as a whole. Such analysis is precluded, however, by lack of material, since it would entail not only a thorough study of the constitution and control activity of each of the groupings, but also their relationships to one another and to the society as a whole.

The nonkinship groupings afford further opportunity to observe the operation of the social control mechanisms. The Plains tribes had a great variety of such associations, differing in constitution and function. Many of them were so closely identified with tribal control, particularly at certain times of the year, that they were an important administrative body; in such capacity the military societies have been previously discussed. It is of interest also, however, to consider them not as parts of the tribal political administration but as individual units carrying on under their own organization. Many of them had specific functions of a religious, ceremonial, social, or military nature; others embodied all four of these functions. The so-called mili-

[63] Riggs, *op. cit.*, p. 209. [64] Dorsey, *Omaha Sociology*, p. 265.

tary societies are perhaps the most instructive for us, and on them, thanks to the labors of many workers and particularly Wissler and Lowie, we have much valuable data.[65]

Each of these associations was independently organized; so much so in fact that at the time of their selection for any special duty, such as policing the buffalo hunt, it was necessary to deal only with their leaders.[66] Without undue distortion the following general picture of them can be drawn. Usually they were composed of an indefinite number of lay members and one or more of the following officers regularly elected from the membership ranks: leaders, pipe-keepers, lance-bearers, whip-bearers, heralds, food-passers, drummers and singers. Actual direction of the society's affairs were vested in some one of these sets of officers, usually the leaders or the pipe-keepers; police functions were performed by the whip-bearers. In the control of members and officers we find well illustrated most of the control sanctions we have already discussed for the entire community. Penal sanctions were applied for various offenses against the society's regulations—failure to attend meetings, failure to participate in the dances, failure to carry out the duties of one's office. These sanctions were backed up by regular machinery, consisting for the most part of duly elected officials who punished by cutting up the culprit's blankets, by whipping, or by expulsion from the association. Other sanctions operated also: the use of ridicule, the presentation of gifts, the singing of praise songs, and informal approval or disapproval in general conversation.

It is not necessary to report in detail the organization and procedure of control in these associations. It is enough to indicate that the control mechanisms operate in a manner closely paralleling their operation in the tribe as a whole, and to call attention to the fact that in these associations is found a duly constituted and organized authority for the application of the legal sanctions. These miniature societies exhibit the character-

[65] Compiled principally in the *Anthropological Papers*, *American Museum of Natural History*. See in particular Vol. XI, devoted exclusively to Plains societies.

[66] Wissler, *Indians of the Plains*, p. 97.

istics of statehood and organized control as strongly as the tribal whole of which they form a part.

It was this strikingly statelike organization of the Plains associations that led Lowie in his *Primitive Society* to suggest them as forerunners of the state—a suggestion he later abandoned in his *Origin of the State* since he could not reconcile the oppositional nature of the associations, and their decided pull against unification, with the strongly unified and centralized authority necessary for a state. In his search for origins Lowie attempted to make these comparable institutions antecedent ones.

One does not find in these Plains military societies the germs of law and of the state. One finds that the germs have germinated and grown up. They are comparable, not antecedent, to our modern state, and what would appear to be the important problem for study is not the investigation of how one grew out of the other, but what they have in common which might throw light on the nature of law and of the state.

THE SECONDARY SANCTIONS IN THE PLAINS TRIBES

The secondary sanctions, as previously indicated, are based on the general principle of satisfaction for a wrong suffered, a satisfaction secured by some kind, or right, of retaliative action against the wrongdoer. The parties to the action may be single individuals, an individual and a group, or two groups. Thus, secondary sanctions can be seen to extend themselves over a wide range of retaliatory activity, from a mere contractual or tort relationship between two persons to such as assume the proportions of a feud or war and lead eventually into the field of international law. This difference in the individual or group nature of the parties to the satisfaction is not, however, one which affects the fundamental nature of the sanction controlling the settlement; whether an individual or a group is proceeding against an individual or another group, the societal reaction— the sanction—which permits or actively aids the retaliation or restitution is the same.

In fact, in many preliterate groups, and this is especially true of the Plains, it is extremely difficult to determine whether we are dealing with retaliatory actions between individuals or between groups of individuals, for every individual is so closely identified with a family, a clan, a blood-brother, or a band that his actions, whether as an offender or as an injured person seeking satisfaction, usually involve others besides himself. This close identification of an individual with his group is what gives rise to collective retaliation and collective responsibility so frequently found among the simpler groups. This fact is of considerable importance in determining the relative strengths of the conflicting forces and the possible outcome of the conflict, and in throwing light on the oft-observed tendency in primitive societies for an individual to increase the number of his relationships; it does not, however, reflect the nature of the sanction that is operating.

The secondary, retaliatory, restitutive sanctions may be applied by a wronged individual or group with the tacit approval of the community, i.e., supported by a diffuse primary sanction, or they may be applied through some organized procedure of the community as a whole, i.e., through the support of the legal primary sanction. The former is simple individual retaliation or revenge; the latter gives rise to civil law. In the Plains the former type is preponderant—a preponderance that is true of most preliterate peoples in the world. This individualistic nature of Plains justice has been commented on time and again by the various investigators; few have failed to emphasize the nonlegal character of the settlement.

Among the tribes of the Upper Missouri it is said that, since there is no competent judiciary to punish crime, trespass, or insult, "every person is thus constituted his own judge, jury and executioner."[67]   De Smet, McKenney and Hall, Prescott, Larpenteur, and Schoolcraft in other early reports also approximate this statement. Lowie, writing generally of the Plains region, states that "most difficulties were settled by individuals and their kindred," citing adultery and homicide in support of the statement but modifying the latter instance with a statement

[67] Denig, *op. cit.*, p. 480.

concerning the peace-making activity of the chief in attempting to avert a feud.[68] In addition to homicide and adultery, individual redress extended to such other trespasses as assault, theft, and robbery. The manner of satisfaction is retaliatory in some cases, restitutive or compensatory in others.

Despite the preponderance of individual retaliation, enough instances of social intervention are to be found to conclude that civil law was not entirely absent in the Plains. The Omaha murder case, made classic by Lowie's analysis several years ago,[69] where a murderer was banished by action of the Council until the relatives of the deceased forgave him is clearly a case of individual satisfaction, in the settlement of which the tribal authority took a hand. Another mention of societal interference in these individual controversies is found in the following theft case, also from the Omaha:

When the suspected thief did not confess his offense, some of his property was taken from him until he told the truth. When he restored what he had stolen, one-half of his property was returned to him, the rest being given to the man from whom he had stolen.[70]

Dorsey follows the foregoing with the statement that "sometimes all of the policemen whipped the thief"—an application of the penal sanction. Even Denig, whose statements for the most part emphatically deny any civil intervention, states that robbery is seldom attempted since it "would attract the notice and induce the interference of the camp soldiers."[71]

These few cases of intervention do not present a very strong case, it must be admitted. However, another aspect of most investigators' reports raises a pertinent question. Practically all investigators say that the police functioned in settling disputes and compounding crimes. Did these police simply command peace and peace ensued, or did they inquire into the circumstances of the case at hand, determine rights on both sides, and arrive at a satisfactory settlement? If the latter, it would appear that civil law was not unknown to the Plains tribes, at least during such time as the tribal organization included the police

[68] *Primitive Society*, p. 415.
[69] *Ibid.*, p. 416.
[70] Dorsey, *Omaha Sociology*, p. 367.
[71] *Op. cit.*, p. 475.

in an active capacity. It would seem that our investigators' mental images of twelve men in a jury box have obscured a real ethnological problem and precluded the recording of some worthwhile observations. Among the Plains groups the wrongs taken into consideration are not so numerous, the rules of procedure are not so formal or so strictly adhered to as in our own civil procedure, but they do seem to provide on occasion a means whereby an injured individual may obtain redress through the organized intervention of society as a whole.

It is of interest to consider, in connection with the retaliatory sanctions, the problem of composition or compromise for injuries among these Plains tribes. Examples are numerous to indicate that in these groups the law of strict retaliation for wrongs suffered was coexistent with and perhaps relatively less frequently resorted to than indemnification or restitution. Every wrong suffered seems to have been possible of compromise by some substitutive payment, ranging from wrongs involving two individuals up through compensation for damages to tribes as the result of protracted warfare. The one offense in which substitution seems to have been least frequently resorted to was adultery; this is perhaps due to the lack of thorough information or to the offense itself which, by its very nature, makes composition difficult.

The existence of composition for wrongs in lieu of strict retaliation in a society is generally supposed to indicate some advanced step on the part of that society toward an increasing interest in, and social control over, the society's members, and hence is often pointed to as a mark of legal development. The writer is inclined to disagree with this postulate on the basis of Plains data. Numerous as the instances of composition are, they appear to be no more frequently or regularly the concern of the society than is pure blood-revenge or strict retaliation. The willingness to accept compensation for a wrong in lieu of retaliation in kind seems to be no more socially than individually determined. True it is, the society sees to its execution—and it has been proved expedient for survival purposes—but to say that composition is correlated with social intervention, as Hobhouse does, for instance, in his *Morals in Evolution*, seems not to be supported by the facts. After all, it is just as likely that an individual realized that it was wiser in many cases to accept compensation than to exact strict retribution, as it is that society intervened for the purpose and thereby started law on its way. When society steps in, in its peace-making function, it does not seem necessarily to change retaliation to composition for it often, in fact, perpetuates the former. This change from blood-revenge to composition indicates a change in sentiment, but that it indicates any more legal structure is very doubtful.

This is not to deny that society may not foster composition for private delicts. All that is contended is that, before society does step in and compose difficulties between individuals, the individuals themselves had probably already arrived at the idea of composition. A parallel is shown in the present development of international law, as yet largely unregulated by any higher tribunal or court. Should some league or court achieve power to impose its orders on the disputing nations, it would apply those customary practices that have grown up, but it could not be said that the league or court intervention brought them about. For what it may be worth for other purposes the Plains data indicate a great deal of composition for crimes, but these give us little help in indicating any development of politically organized society and hence of law. Whether strictly retaliatory or restitutive in nature, both are found to be regulated but one not necessarily more than the other.

Any survey of social control procedure as brief as the foregoing must leave the reader quite unsatisfied. The writer is frank to admit also that even the presentation of the entire mass of data collected during the survey, of which those data in the preceding pages constitute but a small percentage, would probably not dispel this dissatisfaction. Data for an adequate analysis of Plains social control are yet to be collected.

In spite of this deficiency, and before turning to an evaluation of the sanction categories, one deduction from the material seems worthy of statement even at the risk of reiteration of a viewpoint expressed in the work of others. The material reviewed seems to demonstrate with fair conviction that among these Plains Indians law, even in the most formal and restricted sense in which it can be defined, did exist, not only as criminal law but also, though to a lesser extent, as civil law. Neither of these legal functions can be shown conclusively to have operated for the groups for all times of the year or for the large number of delicts that they do for us, but because law had not yet come to pervade Plains culture as continuously or as fully as it has our own is no more justification for denying its existence than it is for denying the existence of certain plants or animals as evolutionary products because only a few of them are found.

Whether the need for such formal regulation was discovered and evolved in connection with the buffalo hunt, the religious practices of the tribe, or in the conduct of war, it is difficult to say; neither is it possible to do anything more than hazard a guess as to whether or not the device was the result of several independent developments or was hit upon accidentally by one group, elaborated by them, and diffused to the others. Perhaps it was a rationally devised scheme, the brain child of some illustrious leader. All these bits of knowledge appear to be lost in the past; all we have left to work with is the fact that these Plains tribes, archindividualists that they are reputed to be, had developed, when they first became known to us, an organized and formalized means for the curbing of this reputed individualism.

CONCLUSIONS

Some amount of unfairness must result in attempting to evaluate the sanction categories with the limited material that the Plains literature affords. Furthermore, the reduction of the proposed categories to outline form has undoubtedly represented these with a finality and rigidity that is both unwarranted and misleading. With due regard, however, for this unfairness, the sanction categories raise certain problems in connection with the manipulation of social control data which the writer feels impelled to suggest.

As a general consideration, so far as the Plains data are concerned—and the writer believes the same difficulty would be encountered in all attempts to sort similar data—the fitting of the social control material into the proposed categories does irreparable damage to the functional picture of society, since for the sake of the logic of the classificatory device it tends all too frequently to split up closely related behavior that sociologically has meaning only when not separated. For certain purposes such categorical separation may be desirable and legitimate, but for purposes of furthering our understanding of social control it would appear to be misleading. On the other hand, if one is interested in problems more limited in scope than the totality of social control, or even "sanctioned behavior," a scheme as elaborate as the proposed one appears unnecessary.

In addition to the foregoing general consideration, certain more specific misgivings about the terminology and the logic of the classification as it now stands are felt by the writer. With intent only to solicit further contemplation of these logical and terminological difficulties the following paragraphs are written.

The primary-secondary distinction.—The classification of social control activity into these two large categories based on the societal or individual nature of the interest being protected enables us to avoid the use of prevailing terminology which has become so restricted as to preclude consideration under it of certain valuable data. But it requires very little analysis to see that "secondary" as applied to a sanction which supports individual retaliation is a misnomer since the retaliatory acts are not based on secondary sanctions but on primary ones. The secondary sanctions are really not secondary at all, but are primary ones operating in such a way as to permit or assist an individual to obtain satisfaction for wrongs suffered. All sanctions, being social, are by definition primary ones; the individual retaliatory ones are actually no more derivative or secondary in nature than are those applied by the society as a whole since they find their support in a societal reaction just as truly as some kind of action by the society as a whole finds its support there. Our line of cleavage, therefore, is not really upon the primary or secondary nature of the sanction but upon the kind of interest protected by the societal reaction—that is, whether it is a social or an individual interest. Professor Radcliffe-Brown has admitted this terminological difficulty but in view of established usage in dealing with the distinction has followed the traditional practice of distinguishing sanctions when it is not the sanction which is being distinguished but the interests protected by the sanction.

It is important, of course, for some purposes that a distinction be made between these interests since they represent the two large branches of modern law, but the question can be raised whether or not, from either a procedural standpoint or from the standpoint of analyzing social reactions, it is necessary or even logically sound to employ such categories.

The luck sanctions.—In the early part of his discussion of sanctions Professor Radcliffe-Brown rules out of consideration under sanctioned behavior such customary usages as technical procedures, etc., on the ground that, though they may have the authority of society behind them, they are not sanctioned or are not socially obligatory in the same sense as are other social obligations. It is, probably, desirable to draw a line somewhere between the totality of social behavior indulged in by an individual as a member of his group and such social behavior as has behind it a social reaction of a more compelling nature; otherwise social control study would be forced to concern itself with a great variety of usages such as those determining technical procedures, laws of etiquette, and even such things as art patterns, or any other cultural trait or pattern which exerts an influence on individual behavior.

However, the exclusion of social usages of this type raises a question as to the inclusion of the so-called "luck" (nonobligatory religious) sanctions in the proposed scheme for the analysis of social control. That these luck sanctions do exercise control over the individual, and that they are socially determined, is admitted, but that they differ in nature from other social usages simply because they are based more on religious or magical than on practical or ethical beliefs does not make them any more socially obligatory than are the "social usages" which it is proposed to eliminate in the treatment. In so far as a man is no more obligated to make a sacrifice to insure luck in hunting or war than he is obligated to make a regulation bow and arrow for the same purpose, his conduct is not subject to sanction or societal reaction. Hence it would appear that luck sanctions are not properly to be included in a study of social control as such is defined by the other categories of Radcliffe-Brown's sanction classification. For these reasons it would seem that the luck sanctions can properly be neglected except as one is interested in going deeper into the control mechanism and seeing where the social sanctions spring from; but if one does that for the luck sanctions, consistently it would seem he must also do it for the so-called "social usages."

The secondary sanctions.—In the present study it was found to be extremely difficult to classify the material found in the Plains in accordance with the retaliatory and restitutive categories laid down by Professor Radcliffe-Brown under the secondary sanctions. This distinction is in accordance with the familiar but somewhat hypothetical development from a state of unrestrained private vengeance to composition for wrongs suffered. However, when one gets down to actual cases he is immediately confronted by the fact that in any society almost any retaliatory sanction may, and often does, become in any particular case a restitutive or indemnifying one. In other words, nearly always in primitive societies as we now know them an injured person can be bought off by the wrongdoer or his family or friends, and his right of retaliation in such cases becomes restitutive, though the facts of the particular injury and the social compulsion or authority behind his right to some kind of satisfaction remain identically the same. Therefore, though the terms "retaliatory," "restitutive," "indemnifying," etc., may be useful for describing secondarily the nature of the application of the remedy in these cases of satisfaction, they are not useful in their attempt at primary differentiation of the nature of the sanction itself. It is as if we were to devise a different term for the sanction of a penal judgment which operates to inflict a death penalty than we would use for the sanction of a penal judgment which inflicts a fine or imprisonment. The change in individual satisfaction from retaliation to restitution represents a change in attitude of the society with regard to the nature of the compensation to be made, but it does not necessarily represent a change in the basic nature of the compelling force or the procedural mechanism.

In view of the preceding criticisms it is but just to indicate that Professor Radcliffe-Brown has made no unusual claims for the finality of his proposed categories. He is, in fact, largely responsible for the effort put forth in the present study to validate or invalidate them. No one is more aware than he that such categories must be defined and redefined in the light of criticism and more complete data. The categories as they now stand are an attempt to reduce to some order a complex set of social reactions, and as such the categories readily justify themselves. As pedagogic devices for the induction of students into the subtleties of social control they have unusual merit.

THE PLACE OF RELIGIOUS REVIVALISM IN THE FORMATION OF THE INTERCULTURAL COMMUNITY ON KLAMATH RESERVATION

PHILLEO NASH

THE PLACE OF RELIGIOUS REVIVALISM IN THE FORMATION OF THE INTERCULTURAL COMMUNITY ON KLAMATH RESERVATION

PHILLEO NASH

INTRODUCTION

Observers of primitive peoples have frequently mentioned the appearance of religious revivalism in the initial stages of the adjustment of these peoples to white contact. Such revivals are remarkably uniform in doctrine despite the dissimilarity of the cultures in which they appear. Yet careful examination of such doctrines shows that they are not mere importations of Christian dogma, and that their similarity cannot be explained solely on that basis. On the contrary, they usually rest firmly on aboriginal religious beliefs, which have been re-worked and reintegrated in a manner which gives an appearance of uniformity. The uniform aspects of the doctrine are usually assertions about the future in which destruction is assured for persons or objects associated with the whites, and salvation and rebirth are assured for the natives. The ritual of such movements varies widely, from amorphous mass hysteria to elaborate rituals based on aboriginal ceremonialism.

A study of revivalism in three primitive groups[1] led me to the formation of a hypothesis about revivalism and early white contact: *Nativistic cults arise among deprived groups. They follow a shift in the value pattern, due to suppression and domination, and are movements to restore the original value pattern which they do by the construction of a fantasy situation. The nature of this fantasy, which is basic to the cult, is a function of* (1) *the original value*

---

[1] The *Tana Baghat* movement among the Oraon of the Chota Nagpur Plateau in India; the *Vailala* Madness among the Papuans of British New Guinea; the Ghost Dance of 1890 among the Indians of the Plateau and Plains areas of North America (see the accounts by Roy, Williams, Mooney, Nash, and Lesser in the Bibliography).

pattern and (2) *the successive changes in the value pattern under white domination.*

In 1935–36 I had an opportunity to test this hypothesis by the careful examination of a nativistic religious revival on Klamath Indian Reservation which took place between 1871–78.[2] On this reservation, in 1864, members of three tribes were brought together.[3] Two of these, the Klamath and Modoc, were closely allied in language and culture; the third, consisting of two bands of Paviotso, had certain cultural affinities with the Klamath and Modoc but were nevertheless a distinct cultural and linguistic entity. In 1871 the members of these three groups were presented with the doctrine and ritual of the 1870 Ghost Dance. The movement lasted until 1878 on Klamath Reservation. It went through three easily recognized phases, differing in doctrine and ritual, which drew their adherents from different segments of the Indian population.

Here, then, was a situation in which the validity of the hypothesis might be tested. If the hypothesis is correct, those groups which participated most fully in the revival should be those which suffered most deprivation in their contacts with whites. Furthermore, the fantasy situation integral to the cult should be appropriate to shifts in the value pattern which had taken place in the formation of the intercultural community.

The main problem, therefore, was broken down into two problems, concerned with two classes of facts. The first of these was the problem of deprivation.[4] It was necessary to learn what

[2] This project was carried out June 15, 1935–July 20, 1936 as a Pre-doctoral Fellow of the Social Science Research Council.

[3] "Tribes" is used loosely and implies cultural unity, not a cohesive political organization.

[4] As W. Lloyd Warner has pointed out (*Nativistic Religious Movements*, p. 5 n.), my use of the term "deprivation" and its correlate "indulgence" is derived from psychoanalytic terminology. In the psychoanalytic vocabulary deprivation has been used to designate the denial to, or withdrawal from, the individual of satisfactions. In transferring this concept to a sociological context, I have retained this simple meaning, making no effort to distinguish between kinds of satisfactions or the levels within the personality on which their denial is felt as a loss. I do not believe that by thus adopting a psychological term for purposes of sociological analysis I have made an analogy between the individual psycho-

elements within the Indian community on Klamath Reservation had been deprived or indulged during the formation of the intercultural community. To this end informants were questioned and Indian Service records were consulted for observations made and opinions formed at the time. It was felt that acts of aggression committed or condoned represented potential sources of deprivation and indulgence. It was also felt that the introduction of new values, with attendant techniques for acquiring them, represented potential sources of deprivation and indulgence. Specific instances were enumerated in such a way as to make possible an estimate of the most deprived and indulged groups.

The second problem was that of participation in the religious revival. Each phase of the revival had a distinct doctrine and distinct ritual practices. Each phase also constructed in its doctrine a fantasy situation. If the hypothesis is correct, this fantasy should express the restoration of the values denied its adherents, and the mode of participation in ritual experience should be appropriate. All the symbolic aspects of the revival were open to this kind of interpretation. The doctrine, songs, face-painting, and ritual—that aspect of the revival which was common to all its adherents—were an easily reached source of information. The more personal aspects of the revival—autisms in the form of dreams and visions—were also examined, in so far as they could be recaptured.

THE FORMATION OF THE INTERCULTURAL COMMUNITY

CULTURE CHANGE IN THE PRE-RESERVATION PERIOD

The three groups now on Klamath Reservation—the Klamath, Modoc, and Paviotso—were brought together after varied experiences of initial white contact. The general area originally

---

physical organism and society, as Dr. Warner says, or implied a collective reaction. It is individuals who are deprived and indulged, and these terms are used in this distributive sense rather than in a collective sense. It is possible for individuals to identify personal deprivation with damage to a group or collective symbol, and such an identification took place on Klamath Reservation, but this does not necessarily imply that the society was damaged or deprived as a person is damaged or deprived.

inhabited by these peoples embraced the lake district of south-eastern Oregon and its extension in northern California. This general area was the last in Oregon to be settled by whites. The first extensive white settlements in Oregon were at the juncture of the Columbia and the Willamette rivers. This was the goal of the migrations beginning in 1843. About 1850 the valleys of the Umpqua and the Rogue in southwestern Oregon, began to attract settlers. Extensive settlement in northeastern Oregon began after 1858, when the Walla-Walla Valley was opened to emigrants, and continued when gold was discovered in the Blue Mountains in 1861. Settlement in the lake district did not begin until 1863, and in far-eastern Oregon, not until after the Snake Wars of 1866–68.

Within the lake district of Oregon the Indians of the present Klamath Reservation were distributed as follows. The Klamath occupied the drainage basin of Upper Klamath Lake, which lies near the eastern slope of the Cascades, close to the California line. The Modoc occupied the drainage basins of Lower Klamath and Tule lakes. Both of these lakes have rather large drainage areas over which these peoples wandered in the summer, collecting roots and seeds for winter use. In the winter they occupied permanent settlements on the borders of their respective lakes. The Paviotso, now on Klamath Reservation, formerly occupied the area around Silver and Summer lakes in central Oregon—a region which adjoined Klamath territory on the northeast. In addition to these, a group of Paviotso, who originally inhabited Warner Valley in eastern Oregon and Surprise Valley in northeastern California, were associated at one time with Klamath Reservation. The circumstances under which these three Indian groups first met whites, and the degree of change introduced into their lives by contact with white culture, vary widely.

Klamath.—The Klamath had early casual contacts with explorers—Ogden in 1825–26 and Frémont in 1843 and again in 1846—which left no known impress on Klamath culture. Much more lasting effects were felt when the Klamath encountered a body of French-Canadian trappers who introduced them to

European trade goods and took some Klamath with them to The Dalles. Spier places the first encounter at about 1835.[5] The Dalles, both in prehistoric and historic times, has been a meeting place for members of diverse cultures and a great center of trade. As far as can be ascertained at the present time, the Klamath have always had trade relations through intermediaries with The Dalles, but this trade was stimulated after 1835 by actual visits to The Dalles and the introduction of horses as objects of trade. Horses never entered Klamath technology in any vital sense, though they did enter Klamath economy as objects of wealth and units of exchange. Their presence vastly stimulated trade and modified the relations of the Klamath, both among themselves and with other tribes. In order to get horses the Klamath traded slaves at The Dalles. These slaves were principally Indians from Pit River in California (Achomawi and Atsugewi), secondarily Paviotso, Shasta, and Upland Takelma. Some of these the Klamath captured themselves, but in the main they were captured by the Modoc, who traded them to the Klamath who, in turn, took them to The Dalles.

The principal internal effect of this trade was a change in the structure of Klamath society. Prior to the trading period shamans were the richest and most powerful members of Klamath society. But with the increase in trade new values of many sorts entered Klamath culture, together with the enhancement of an old skill—trading—appropriate to acquisition of these new values. This skill was not at the disposal of the shamans. In Klamath culture shamans neither worked nor fought but stayed at home, living in houses others built for them, and on wealth accumulated by fees for curing. The new trade objects, therefore, entered the society in the hands of adventurous, younger men, who traveled with the French-Canadians to The Dalles. These young men learned to speak Chinook jargon; became shrewd traders; accumulated horses as wealth; raided or traded for slaves and kept slaves in their houses; accumulated trade beads, Plains-type clothing, and war accouterments of many kinds; and began to exercise "chiefly" prerogatives which they

[5] *Klamath Ethnography*, p. 7.

learned from other Indians at The Dalles. These were the leading men whom the white administrators first encountered in the
1860's and called "chiefs."

Modoc.—The Modoc shared to a certain extent in these
changes before they had any direct contact with whites. The
changes in Modoc culture were akin to the changes in Klamath
culture but less pronounced. The Modoc did not go to The
Dalles themselves but traded indirectly through the Klamath
and later through the Warm Springs Indians. The Modoc did
not learn to speak Chinook. They acquired horses later than the
Klamath; Plains-type clothing was less common among them;
Modoc "chiefs" never became as powerful or as different from
commoners as the Klamath "chiefs"; and at the same time
Modoc shamans remained more powerful, more aggressive, more
hated and feared among the Modoc than among the Klamath.

The first extensive personal contact between Modoc and
whites came as a result of road exploration in the early days of
Oregon settlement.[6] In 1846 Jesse Applegate and his brother
Lindsay (later the first official of the Indian Service on Klamath
Reservation) explored southern Oregon for a wagon road from
Fort Hall, in what is now southeastern Idaho, to the valleys of
southwestern Oregon, and through them to the Willamette Valley. They were successful in their search. When they returned
in the fall of 1846, they brought with them a small wagon party
which suffered hardship but, nevertheless, successfully reached
the Willamette. From this time on interest in this route, which
came to be known as the South Emigrant Road, increased,
though it never became more than an alternative route. The
bulk of the migration passed over the northern route, but the
volume which passed over the South Road was still very large.

The South Road not only passed through the Modoc summer
range, thus seriously disturbing Modoc life, but also passed
around Tule and Lower Klamath lakes, where the Modoc had
their permanent settlements. The Modoc resisted the encroachment on their territory by raiding and destroying wagon trains.

[6] Applegate, *Notes and Reminiscences*, pp. 12–45.

Such attacks were followed by reprisals, and these reprisals by more depredations.

The result was a long struggle in which many lives were lost, both Modoc and white. As far as the Modoc were concerned, the climax of the struggle was the Ben Wright affair. In September, 1852, when the South Road had been in use about five years, the Modoc attacked a wagon train on the east side of Tule Lake and killed or captured all the emigrants. The citizens of Yreka, a near-by town in northern California, were enraged, and one Ben Wright organized a company of volunteers to punish the Modoc. Wright's plans are not clear, but there is reason to believe that he intended to offer the Indians a steer which had been poisoned with strychnine. A peace meeting was held, but the Indians refused to eat the meat. Wright's volunteers drew their pistols and shot forty-one out of the forty-six Indians present. This attack was remembered bitterly by the Indians. Seventeen years later, when the Modoc were in a peace conference with A. B. Meacham, this treacherous attack was brought up again and used as a symbol around which the Modoc rallied and refused to return to the reservation.

It is not possible to make an estimate of the number of Modoc killed or the extent to which Modoc life was disrupted. The loss to the white community is known.[7] Some idea of the Indian reaction to this situation may be gained from a speech made by Sconchin, in reservation days the head chief of the Modoc. He said:

I thought if we killed all the white men we saw, that no more would come. We killed all we could; but they came more and more like new grass in the spring. I looked around and saw that many of our young men were dead and could not come back to fight. My heart was sick. My people were few. I threw down my gun. I said, "I will not fight again." I made friends with the white man. I am an old man; I cannot fight now. I want to die in peace.[8]

Subsequent to the Applegate exploration there was some military exploration of southeastern and eastern Oregon in 1849, 1858, and 1864, none of which passed directly through the Modoc

[7] Bancroft, *History of Oregon*, II, 477.

[8] Quoted in Meacham, *Wigwam and Warpath*, p. 297.

country. Drew's exploration, that of 1864, had some bearing on Modoc-white relations, for it opened up a shorter wagon road than the one through the Modoc country, and from that time forward the migrations passed through Klamath rather than through Modoc territory. The benefit to the Modoc was small however, for by 1864 the size of the annual migrations had fallen off on the southern route.

By this time the era of settlement had opened for both Modoc and Klamath. In 1863 George Nourse, the first white settler in the Klamath basin, took up land at the lower end of Upper Klamath Lake where Klamath Falls now stands. In the same year one of the Applegates built a ranch near Clear Lake in the Modoc country. From this time on, the Lower Klamath and Tule basins filled up steadily, especially in the Modoc country.

The net effect of this early period of white contact on the Modoc was threefold. The internal structure of Modoc society was somewhat modified by changes in the economic system which followed the increase in trade with the Klamath, and through them with The Dalles. In their personal contacts with whites, which occurred as a result of the opening of the South Emigrant Road and the establishment of Yreka, California, as a trade center for the California and Oregon mines, the Modoc suffered the loss of part of their number in guerilla warfare and a serious disruption of their economic life through the disturbance of their summer wanderings. Sometime during this pre-reservation period a division of opinion arose, and factions were created over the matter of policy in dealing with whites. As armed resistance proved ineffectual, one of the older leaders, Sconchin, decided to accept the new situation. Some of the younger men refused to do so, and over this issue the loose factionalism of aboriginal times crystallized, with Sconchin and Keintpoos, afterward named Captain Jack, opposed as leaders. The conflict thus initiated was not resolved until later years.

Paviotso.—Southeastern Oregon, the country inhabited aboriginally by the Paviotso, was a remote region with little to attract settlers in the early days. Its fringes were visited by Ogden of the Hudson's Bay Company in 1825, by road exploration parties in 1852 and 1859, and by immigrants in 1853. Warner Valley was penetrated by Captain Warner in 1849, and there he was killed by the Indians. This valley was not visited again until Steene reconnoitered there in 1860. Frémont passed through the Silver and Summer lakes district in 1843. This region had no further contact with whites until the movement of miners from California to northeastern Oregon in 1861 brought wagon parties.

Prior to the establishment of Klamath Reservation in 1864, therefore, the Paviotso had experienced very little contact with whites. The Warner Valley group had seen only Warner, Steene, and Drew, and a few California emigrant parties which took the Warner Valley route to the Oregon mines. The Silver-Summer Lake group had seen only Frémont and a few emigrant miners. They had attacked whatever intruders they had seen, but these had been few. Their range had not been disturbed, they had not been attacked themselves, and they had not had sufficient contact of any kind to modify their culture.

CULTURE CHANGE IN THE RESERVATION PERIOD

Establishment of the reservation.—As early as 1858 it was proposed to negotiate a treaty with the Klamath, Modoc, Shoshone, and Bannock, who were then the only remaining Indians in Oregon Territory who had not signed treaties. A site for an agency was selected, but no effort was made to meet the Indians.[9]

In 1864 Elisha Steele, then acting superintendent of Indian affairs in northern California, negotiated an unauthorized treaty with the Modoc. This treaty specified an area, partly in California and partly in Oregon, which was designated as "appropriate" for the Modoc but did not secure a government title to it, nor did it extinguish the Indian title to remaining Modoc territory in northern California. This agreement was never accepted by the United States government. Steele was not authorized to make agreements of this kind, and at the same time he was conducting his negotiations, preparations were under way for a joint council of Klamath, Modoc, and two groups of Pavi-

[9] Bancroft, *op. cit.*, p. 476.

otso at Upper Klamath Lake. The effect of this agreement on the Modoc, however, may well be imagined. It gave them their homeland around Tule Lake, which from this time forward they believed was secure in their possession. Furthermore, it will be remembered that a dispute had arisen among the Modoc over their policy in dealing with whites, and that Keintpoos was the leader of the faction which favored continued resistance. His leadership was not undisputed even within this faction, however. John Sconchin, brother to the man afterward made head chief of the Modoc on Klamath Reservation, was more eager than Keintpoos to continue resistance to white encroachment. At the meeting which culminated in the agreement between Steele and the Modoc, Steele supervised an election in which John Sconchin and Keintpoos were the contestants. Keintpoos was the victor, and Steele recognized him as "chief" of all the Modoc and named him Captain Jack. John Sconchin was jealous and worked against Captain Jack after that, attempting to undermine his authority. Both of these men were younger aspirants to leadership. John Sconchin's brother apparently was not a contestant in this election. He had his opportunity later, when he was selected as head chief by the government.

In this same year, 1864, authorized government representatives arrived at Upper Klamath Lake to confer with the Indians.[10] Invited to this conference were the Klamath, Modoc, and two groups designated as "Yahooskin Snakes" and "Walpape Snakes." It is impossible to learn from the treaty exactly whom the commissioners dealt with as "Yahooskin Snakes." The people afterward designated by that name on the reservation were the Klamath who had their permanent settlements in the Sprague River Valley and had intermarried to some extent with the Modoc. Their habitat has been, and still is, the eastern end of Klamath Reservation, known locally as the "Upper End." They will be designated here as the Upper End Klamath.

The "Walpape Snakes" were the Paviotso who lived originally in the Silver-Summer lake region. At this time the leader of this group recognized by the whites was Panina. He refused to

[10] *Ibid.*, pp. 505-8.

come to the conference, and in October, 1864, a treaty was negotiated between the other three groups and the United States commissioners.

The Treaty of 1864 was a standard agreement which embodied provisions used in negotiating treaties with all the Oregon tribes. It provided, among other things, for the extinguishing of the Indian title to the entire southeastern Oregon region; it set aside a reservation for the exclusive use of these and other undesignated Indian tribes; and it provided for their civilization and eventual allotment on individually owned tracts of land.[11]

The reservation established was slightly larger than the present Klamath Reservation, which has been reduced in size by subsequent land surveys and exchanges. It embraced the nucleus of aboriginal Klamath territory but included no Modoc or Paviotso territory. It is reported that the Klamath signed willingly, but that the Modoc and Paviotso signed reluctantly.

As the commissioners of the federal government returned north from Klamath Reservation, they were fortunate enough to capture the family of Panina. They were held as hostages, and Panina agreed to come to a council the following year. A treaty was negotiated August 12, 1865,[12] and Panina with a few of his followers settled down at the Upper End. Operations began on the reservation a year after the treaty was signed by the Indians. Lindsay Applegate, who had long been associated with the development of the country, was appointed subagent and took office in September, 1865. He visited the Indians and issued rations that fall, and returned in the spring of 1866, when he selected a site for an agency and began construction. The site he selected was near the site of the present Klamath Agency in the heart of Klamath territory. This part of the reservation is known locally as the "Lower End." It represents that portion of Klamath territory in which the majority of the permanent winter settlements were formerly located. There is a natural division between this western part of the reservation and the

[11] The treaty examined was a copy in the files at Klamath Agency.

[12] A letter from L. Applegate to Superintendent Huntington, March 31, 1866 (in *Official Correspondence, Klamath Agency*).

eastern part, here called the Upper End. This terminology will be followed in this paper.

It will be seen that the agency, the permanent Klamath settlements, and the military garrison (Fort Klamath) were close together and formed a compact community on the Lower End. A small town which was growing up at the foot of the lake, Linkville (later Klamath Falls), was peripheral to the Lower End community.

As soon as the agency was established, the Upper End Klamath were added to this community, for they were fearful of raids from the Paviotso in eastern Oregon. The Silver-Summer Lake Paviotso were divided. A portion of them remained with Panina on the reservation, but the remainder were fearful that they would not be fed through the winter and returned to Silver Lake. The following spring (1866) Panina left the reservation with his people, and was gone until July, 1868, when a portion of them returned. A month later the remainder came in, after making peace. In the interim Panina had been killed. The Paviotso had had but little ammunition and had spent most of their time dodging the troops. They had eaten their horses and were reported by the agent to be in a miserable condition.[13]

Although the Silver-Summer Lake Paviotso had given up the struggle and had come onto the reservation, the Snake War was not yet over. Later in that year the Warner Valley Paviotso made an agreement with General Crook. Crook was opposed to the reservation policy and did not insist that this group remove to any reservation. Instead he agreed to take care of them at Camp Warner, in eastern Oregon, until some arrangement could be made for them. They remained there through the winter of 1868, and in the spring of 1869 they made an informal agreement with A. B. Meacham, the new superintendent of Indian affairs for Oregon, to remove to Yainax, on the Upper End of Klamath Reservation.

In the meantime a portion of the Modoc moved onto Klamath Reservation. In September, 1867, Applegate called a council of Indians to inform them that the treaty had been ratified, but

[13] Letter from L. Applegate to Superintendent Huntington, August 21, 1868.

only a portion of the Modoc attended. In October Superintendent Huntington left The Dalles with the first annuity goods, and in November a portion of the Modoc under Sconchin arrived on the reservation to receive their goods. They remained and settled down for the winter at the Lower End near what is now called Modoc Point.

December, 1867, therefore marked the beginning of the reservation community on the Lower End. Both the Upper and the Lower Klamath and part of the Modoc were in close proximity for the first time; the Paviotso had left the reservation. The agency and the fort were close by. Thirty miles away George Nourse had just completed a ferry across Link River at what was shortly to become the town of Linkville.

When the Paviotso returned from eastern Oregon, they settled down in the Sprague River Valley at the Upper End. Once the danger of attack was removed, part of the Klamath also returned to the Upper End, from which they had come originally. A station with a commissary in charge was established at Yainax, and thus a second community within the reservation came into being at the Upper End. It was isolated from the fort and from white settlements, and was then, as that end of the reservation still is, a distinct community which has been more insulated from extensive white contact than any other portion of the reservation.

The Tule Lake Modoc.—From the time (1867) Sconchin's faction separated from Captain Jack's faction until 1869, the latter group remained in the Tule basin. That country was rapidly filling up with settlers who were constantly exerting pressure to have Captain Jack's band removed. They asserted that members of this band stole cattle, frightened the women and children by demanding that meals be prepared for them, etc. To all this Captain Jack replied that he had been swindled out of his reservation in the Tule basin; that he had not known what he was signing when he put his name to the Treaty of 1864; that he desired only to be let alone; and that his friends in Yreka had advised him to stay where he was. One of Jack's Yreka friends to whom he referred was Elisha Steele, who had negotiated the unratified agreement in 1864. Steele supported Jack's complaint of being swindled. He wrote letters to Washington about the matter and also gave letters to Jack and his people in which he repeated Jack's complaint and commended him to the friendly consideration of white people with whom he came into contact.[14]

In 1869, with the change in national administration, came a change in the Indian administration in Oregon. A. B. Meacham was made superintendent. One of his early acts was to make a trip into eastern Oregon. There he met and negotiated with Ocheo, leader of the Warner Valley Paviotso, and persuaded him to settle on Klamath Reservation. This group was among the last of the Paviotso to make peace with General Crook. They were not all willing to be moved to Yainax; a wagon train was sent from Klamath Agency to bring them, and some came but not all. Those who remained through the winter left for Warner Valley in the spring of 1870. The next fall they were persuaded to come back again, and this summer-and-winter alternation kept up until the fall of 1876, when they failed to return at all.

While Meacham was at Klamath he arranged a meeting with Captain Jack, at which he persuaded Jack to move to Klamath Reservation. Jack was reluctant to meet Meacham, but the latter persisted and finally met Jack by going to his camp and walking in uninvited. As an illustration of the role shamans continued to play in Modoc life Meacham's account may be quoted:

We made the opening speech in that council [December 19, 1869] setting forth the reasons for our visit and producing the Treaty of 1864. Here Captain Jack began to manifest the same kind of disposition that has been so prominent in his subsequent intercourse with government officials,—a careful, cautious kind of diplomacy that does not come to a point, but continually seeks to shirk responsibility. . . . . Finding all his objections fairly met he said if he could live near his friend, Link-River Jack (a Klamath) he *would go*. We began to "breathe easy" feeling that the victory was ours, when the Modoc medicine-man arose and simply said, "We won't go there"; when, presto! From exultation every countenance was changed to an expression of anxiety and every hand grasped a revolver.[15]

In spite of this opposition Meacham succeeded. Jack moved to the Lower End, together with all his people, who numbered

[14] Meacham, *op. cit.*, p. 304.   [15] *Ibid.*, p. 320.

forty-three. Three families, totaling fifteen persons and members of another band, remained behind and were brought in by the soldiers.

At Klamath Reservation the Modoc were located, according to their wishes, adjacent to Link-River Jack's group of Klamath. There was friction between the Modoc and the Klamath, and the Modoc and the agent, from the beginning. The Modoc told Meacham that the Klamath were overbearing; they constantly reminded the Modoc that it was their land, their timber, their water, but that it was all right for the Modoc to use it as long as they remembered to whom it belonged. They told him that they had gone to the agent and asked to be moved, and he refused to listen. The Modoc moved toward Williamson River, but it was just as bad there. They went to see the agent three times, and the third time he proposed they should move again. This was too much for the Modoc, and the night of April 25, 1870, they left in a body.

The agent concerned was an army officer, Captain O. C. Knapp, who had replaced Applegate when the administration changed. His story is different, but almost as damning. He said he wanted the Modoc to be on the river, where there was good water, land, and timber. He told them they must move, that they could select their land three miles north on the river, and he would start a farm for them. A week later he visited them and found they had moved only three miles, and had not bettered their location. He insisted they move again. In justification for this order he reported, "That they did not intend to stay after I stopped issuing rations is well known, and I wanted them to be where they could be watched."[16]

It might be supposed that Jack's band was merely restless and regretted its agreement with Meacham if it were not for the fact that Sconchin's Modoc left with the others. They had removed voluntarily to Klamath Reservation and had been as disappointed in their supposed friends, the Klamaths, as Jack's group. They were ridiculed and annoyed in many petty ways. Jack had come on the reservation with only forty-three men, women, and

[16] Letter from Knapp to Parker, May 2, 1870.

children. He left with the entire Modoc tribe, three hundred and seventy-one by the ration issue. There were not sufficient troops at Fort Klamath to bring them back, and there was nothing to be done. Sconchin returned in the late spring with a few families, and others gradually returned until approximately one hundred thirty Modoc were on the reservation. This group settled down at Yainax on the Upper End where they have remained ever since.

At this point the division of the Modoc into two factions was complete. Sconchin's people were united in their acceptance of reservation life, with Sconchin as their acknowledged leader. The same thing was not true of the Modoc who had remained off the reservation. John Sconchin was still anxious to be the acknowledged leader of this group and frequently took issue with Jack. Jack's stand, and the tactics which derived from it, were to remain determinedly in the Tule basin, to avoid conflict with whites, not to confer with representatives of the government, and to wait quietly and peaceably in northern California until his Yreka counselors should be able to get a reservation for him in northern California. John Sconchin and a shaman called "Curly-haired Doctor" were in favor of more active resistance, and the younger men could not be restrained from annoying settlers. The Tule Lake Modoc, moreover, were not as united by close residence as were the reservation Modoc. One group remained throughout this entire period at the foot of Lower Klamath Lake, camping near the Fairchild ranch. They had Fairchild's protection, were unmolested, and caused no trouble themselves. Members of this group, however, had close contact with whites, particularly in Yreka.

The presence of the Modoc in the Tule basin created a problem extremely difficult to solve. They were determined not to return to the reservation, yet the settlers were uneasy and demanded that they be removed. The garrison at Fort Klamath was not strong enough for this task. Meacham blamed Knapp for the whole affair and believed it was still possible to persuade Captain Jack to return peaceably, and that he and his people would stay there if they were separated from the Klamath. His representatives had nearly persuaded Jack to move when an unfortunate incident occurred. Jack's widowed sister had a daughter who became sick. Jack hired a woman shaman who announced that the girl had become sick from dreaming about herself during her puberty dance. The girl died. Jack refused to believe the shaman and insisted that another shaman, a man, had poisoned the girl with his power, so he killed him. A warrant was sworn out for Jack's arrest, and he became frightened and sullen and refused to discuss removal any more.

Meacham was still in hopes that he could settle the matter peacefully. The military order for Jack's arrest was rescinded, and all plans to remove him were suspended while Meacham tried to arrange for a reservation in the Tule basin. Meacham's proposal was rejected by the Office of Indian Affairs, and he was instructed to remove the Modoc to the reservation. Nothing was done immediately, and in the meantime the administration changed. On April 11, 1872, T. B. Odeneal, the new superintendent in Oregon, was instructed to remove the Modoc or find them a new home. Odeneal replied that Klamath Reservation was the place for the Modoc and soon received instructions to remove the Modoc.

Odeneal requested the commandant at Fort Klamath to bring Captain Jack's band to the reservation. His attempt to do so was a failure. Jack and his followers escaped and in an outbreak of violence murdered fourteen settlers.

The issue was now clear cut. Efforts to resolve the conflict peaceably no longer appeared possible. Public sentiment demanded that civil and military authorities capture the rebellious Modoc and avenge the massacre. To do so proved a difficult matter. Jack and his band intrenched themselves in a natural fort in the lava beds south of Tule Lake, from which they were dislodged only after extended military operations involving one thousand regular and volunteer troops and seventy-two Warm Springs Indian scouts. The details of this struggle are not relevant to this analysis. Jack's band was eventually dislodged, dissension grew in his ranks, and the band scattered. Its members were pursued, captured, and imprisoned. The leaders were tried for murder, sentenced, and hanged or imprisoned for life. The remainder of the band were removed to Indian Territory as prisoners of war, where they remained until after the period here under consideration.

The personnel of Jack's followers can be determined with some certainty. Jack himself was a young man, ambitious as a leader. Although he headed the anti-white faction within the Modoc tribe, he did not favor open aggression in resisting whites. According to Meacham's information he denounced the murderers of the white settlers at Lost River for their violence and would have given them up in exchange for peace and lands on Lost River, had he been strong enough. He could not overrule the more violent and the more frightened elements in his band, however, and acts of violence were committed in which he was reluctant to take part. One of these was the murder of the peace commission. A. B. Meacham, General Canby (commanding the military forces in the lava beds), and Dr. Thomas, a clergyman, met several times with Jack and his leading men in an effort to induce them to surrender. The last time they met the Indians became excited and shot and killed Canby and Thomas, and nearly killed Meacham. This was a planned murder. Meacham's eyewitness account shows that Jack was reluctant to give the signal for the attack. When he finally did so, his place was taken by John Sconchin who shot Meacham. Jack shot Canby instead of Meacham. By the time this murder took place Jack's band was badly frightened. The members were convinced that the peace commission was only a device to get them out of the lava beds so that the soldiers could kill them all. Jack's behavior and policy show that he was demanding, but that he wished to avoid violence. He was determined to remain in his homeland but did not want to take the responsibility for resisting authority. He constantly blamed others for his predicament. He said he had been tricked into signing the 1864 treaty and that he had been promised other land, but denied taking part in the murders.

John Sconchin was a rival leader to Jack. As we have seen, he was a younger brother of the chief of the reservation Modoc and had been defeated by Jack in Steele's election of 1864. According to Meacham's information he proposed ever more active resistance to whites and worked against Jack, undermining his prestige with his followers. When the Modoc were first attacked by the soldiers, Jack, John Sconchin, and Scar-faced Charley were living together with thirteen other men and their families on one side of Lost River. On the other side were the shaman, Curly-haired Doctor, Boston Charley, and twelve others with their families. Curly-haired Doctor was a man of great influence, who had proposed more active resistance on numerous occasions. He nearly prevented Jack from going to Klamath Reservation in 1869; he first proposed murdering the peace commission; and on at least one and perhaps two occasions, he used his ritual to insure success against the white soldiers. From the fact that Curly-haired Doctor was living across the river from Jack, i.e., in a different settlement, and from the fact that none of the men in his settlement was of equal prominence, I infer that Curly-haired Doctor was the leader of a small faction within Jack's group. The entire group acted together, but there was a separatism present which, taken together with Curly-haired Doctor's known role in Jack's group, suggests that his group contained the more aggressive, eager elements among the Tule Lake Modoc. Out of fourteen heads of families on Curly-haired Doctor's side of the river, the four who are known included three who had a part in the murder of the peace commission.

After the initial effort to remove the Tule Lake Modoc, which precipitated open conflict, Jack's group was joined by a hitherto independent group of Modoc who were members of a single aboriginal local group, the *a'gáwaskni*, or Hot Creek Modoc. This was the group which had been living near the Fairchild ranch under John Fairchild's protection. When news of the massacre reached Fairchild, he attempted to bring this group to Klamath Reservation for their own protection. On the way this group learned of the threats made by settlers, heard that soldiers were coming, and became frightened and bolted, joining Captain Jack in the lava beds.

It was the Hot Creek Modoc who finally made possible Jack's capture. In the engagement of May 10, 1873, one of their number was killed. None of Jack's close relatives had been killed, and the Hot Creek group accused Jack of putting them in the front of the fighting in order to save his relatives. Eventually they separated from Jack, were pursued, surrendered, and became scouts, leading the soldiers to Captain Jack's retreat.

It is appropriate at this point to summarize the successive roles of the Tule Lake Modoc in the intercultural community. In the early days of white contact this group acted in concert with the rest of the Modoc, actively and aggressively resisting white encroachment. In the latter days of early contact one segment of the Modoc, led by Sconchin, became discouraged by the obvious failure of resistance, and not only accepted the fact of white encroachment but identified themselves with the administrative segment of the white community in such a way as to derive as many advantages as possible. Through the efforts of Steele, Jack found his stand temporarily successful. From this time until Meacham persuaded him to move to Klamath Reservation, Jack pursued a course of passive resistance, in which he was encouraged by Steele and others in Yreka. In pursuing this course, however, Jack had the support of only a small portion of the total Modoc population. Fifteen members remained at Hot Creek, aloof from Jack and the reservation alike, during the entire pre-war period. They had much contact with whites in Yreka and at the Fairchild ranch. Jack had forty-three men, women, and children with him, whereas the total Modoc population was approximately three hundred and seventy-five. When Jack's group moved to Klamath Reservation in 1869, it was ridiculed by the Klamath and failed to get along with either the Klamath or the agent. This might be attributed to Jack's temperament, were it not for the fact that the reservation Modoc had already suffered the same indignities and withdrew with Jack in 1870. When Sconchin returned, he brought with him only one hundred and thirty of the total band. The rest remained with Jack and drifted back later, or went to Hot Creek. When Jack was captured, the total Modoc off the reservation were only one hundred and fifty-nine, showing that some eighty-one must have returned to the reservation in the interim.

Once off the reservation in 1870, Jack pursued his policy of isolation and refused to talk with commissioners, awaiting the support he believed he could get from Yreka. His followers became more demanding, however, were insolent to settlers, and provoked trouble. Jack's tactics of outwaiting the government nearly won him the reservation he wanted, but the administration finally decided against him. Soldiers attempted to remove him forcibly, and his young men broke loose, murdering settlers and eventually murdering the peace commission, and so enraged the public that a peaceful solution was impossible. The frightened Hot Creek band, who scuttled to him for protection, finally brought about his defeat when one of their number was killed. Yet dissension must have been more widespread than merely among the Hot Creek band, for in 1870 there were only fifteen remaining in this group, whereas seventy-five broke away from Jack in the lava beds. Open conflict finally cost Jack and his more aggressive followers their lives and made prisoners of the rest.

Undoubtedly such open aggression was originally provoked by white encroachment. Jack's band contained all the more aggressive elements in the community, both those who favored violence as a means of combating whites, and the frightened, capricious Hot Creek band. But it should be remembered that the Tule Lake Modoc continued for many years to occupy their old lands in defiance of authority, partly because they were encouraged in their stand by their Yreka advisors. In a very real sense the Tule Lake Modoc were the butt of the California-Oregon rivalry which went back to gold-rush days, when California began to draw potential settlers away from Oregon. The Californians accused Oregon of favoring war for commercial reasons— an accusation which had previously been leveled at Yreka merchants by Oregonians. Steele's premature treaty, his offer to get Californian lands for the Modoc, his letters commending Jack to white men, the Yreka merchants' sympathetic attitude toward Jack's stories of ill-treatment on Klamath Reservation, California's reluctance to participate in the Modoc War, and its accusations of commercial motives behind Oregon's participations in the war, were all aspects of a California-Oregon rivalry. The Modoc, and on other occasions other Indians of northern California and southern Oregon, were unfortunate enough to become the butt of this rivalry which was directly related to continued Modoc resistance to white administrators.

The Lower End community.—It will be remembered that prior to 1879 the Lower End Klamath, the Modoc, and, for a time, the Upper End Klamath formed a small community on the Lower End of Klamath Reservation, of which the agency, Fort Klamath, and the white settlement on Link River were all a part. The Upper End Klamath remained near the agency only during the Snake War, 1866–68. After that time they moved to the Upper End, where their descendants still remain.

The Sconchin Modoc were members of the Lower End community from 1867 to 1870, when they withdrew from the reservation with Captain Jack. Those who returned followed Sconchin to the Upper End. The Indian community on the Lower End, therefore, from the beginning of operations in 1866 up to 1870 will be considered as a single joint Modoc and Klamath community.

Fort Klamath supplied work and a cash market for a small amount of Indian produce. The agent and Meacham both complained of the debauchery of the Indians by soldiers and officers of Fort Klamath, although there is no way of estimating the extent of this influence. Link River was a very small settlement until after 1870, was thirty miles away, and had only a rough wagon trail for communication. Its influence on the Lower End community was negligible during the 1866–70 period. The really important modifying influence in this early period was the agency. The formulation and application of an administrative policy made changes in Klamath, and to some extent in Modoc, life which are directly related to the acceptance of the Ghost Dance in 1871.

Administrative policy on Klamath Reservation may be summarized under four headings: (1) provision of food and clothing for Indians unable to exploit their former range; (2) the introduction of democratic political institutions; (3) incorporation of

Indians in the white world as individual farmers; and (4) a campaign against shamanism.

The effectiveness with which these policies were applied varied widely. During the early period on the Lower End the basic needs of the Indians were met adequately, to the extent that there was no greater want or suffering than that to which the Klamath and Modoc were accustomed aboriginally. Two factors appear to be responsible for this situation. First, administrative control was decentralized during this period. The subagent at Klamath corresponded directly with the superintendent for Oregon at The Dalles. His estimates were met adequately and fairly promptly. The problem of transportation was acute, and there were some delays, but not the administrative delays of the later period. Furthermore, the country was not so heavily populated at first, and the Indians continued to collect wild foods in their regular routine, both on and off the reservation. During this early period beef and wheat were issued only to supplement native foods.

When administrators first came to Klamath, they found a number of leading men whom they designated "chiefs" and who signed the treaty as representatives of the tribes. In 1869 this situation was formalized and remodeled when Applegate arranged for the election of chiefs by popular vote. This opportunity arose through the growing age of Lalakes. This man was one of those who had made himself rich trading slaves for horses at The Dalles in pre-reservation times. When the treaty was signed, he was designated head chief. But by 1869 he was very old, and the Klamath came to Applegate and asked for another head chief. Applegate arranged for the election of a chief and eight subchiefs, and a younger man, Allen David, was chosen after a hot contest. At the same time a court was formed, composed of the head chief and all the subchiefs. A sheriff was chosen from among the Indians, and each chief was given a constable, called a "sergeant" by the Indians. Meacham witnessed the first trial in December, 1869. In 1871 John Meacham, then subagent at Klamath, altered the composition of this court. He arranged for the election of a subchief by the former Pit

River slaves and reduced the number of judges to seven, arranging for meetings only once a month. He reported that the Indians were "too much engaged in lawing."[17]

Although the agents have not reported it, the fact is that the chiefs and subchiefs acted as magistrates in their own localities without formal court procedure. This was a prerogative they had never exercised aboriginally, and it greatly enhanced their power and prestige. The court was gradually reduced in power and prestige, however, until in the late seventies it was replaced by the Indian police and a smaller court.

At the same time that the government thus threw the weight of its authority behind the chiefs, it was conducting a campaign against the practice of shamanism. Applegate made no mention of any effort of this kind. Apparently the first agent who attempted to prevent shamanism was Captain Knapp, who arrested, tried, and imprisoned Link-River Doctor for the practice of "spiritual medicine." John Meacham reported an open order against the practice of shamanism and in 1870 declared that the practice had been abolished, but that the belief was as firm as ever.[18] The practice was not abolished, of course; it continued even into modern times. But the campaign was successful in a much subtler way. Klamath and Modoc shamans were believed omnipotent. Yet, after 1869, the Klamath and Modoc saw some shamans shackled, imprisoned, and fined. In at least one instance they saw an agent defy a shaman to kill him by ritual power. In later years (1876) they saw the chiefs, acting independently, sentence a shaman to two years in a dungeon. (This sentence was afterward changed by the agent.) The accounts are not detailed enough to furnish a complete picture of the anti-shamanistic campaign, but the episodes described furnish proof that the prestige and power of the shamans declined somewhat, and that it declined while chiefly power and prestige increased.

The policy of individualization was put into effect in two ways: by encouraging the establishment of one-family farms and

[17] Letter from John Meacham to A. B. Meacham, January 31, 1871.

[18] Letter from John Meacham to A. B. Meacham, November 30, 1870.

by education. The agents at Klamath conceived of education as taking place in the shops and agency farms where Indians were taken as apprentices and in a formal school. By and large these measures were not put into effect at all during Applegate's administration (1865–69), were initiated prior to the Modoc War (1869–72), were interrupted by the war (1872–73), and first became effective after the war.

Applegate was occupied largely with collecting the Modoc and Paviotso, transporting and issuing needed rations, and beginning farm operations in order to make the agency, and ultimately the reservation, self-supporting. As far as possible Applegate employed Indians to work on the agency farm. When a teacher was appointed in 1868, Applegate sent him with some Indian boys into the fields to teach them how to farm. Indians were employed in road-making, rail-splitting and fencing, and farm operations, as far as possible. Applegate asked for a sawmill in 1869, and it was completed the following year. The Indians performed some of the work in the erection of this mill and, after it was completed, cut and hauled logs for it. This was the extent to which the apprentice and formal school system had been applied prior to the Modoc War.

The Indians first began to erect log houses for themselves and to fence and plow their own land in 1869. In 1870 the superintendent of farming reported fifty acres under cultivation by Indians. The Indians depended largely on help from agency employees in establishing themselves on farms. When fighting broke out in the Modoc War, all the employees were sent to the front; hence through 1872 and 1873, operations were at a standstill. (Every year prior to the war small farms were planted for the Indians.) A gristmill was begun in 1871. Construction which was abandoned during the Modoc War was resumed later, and the mill was completed in 1873. Very little of the grain ground in this mill was grown on Klamath Reservation, however, for agricultural operations, with the exception of one year in Applegate's administration, were a complete failure. Year after year crops were planted and frosted, and were replanted and frosted again in the fall, before they had ripened. The yield was small on both agency and Indian farms. When operations were resumed after the Modoc War, all the administrative policies were carried out much more effectively. Buildings were erected for a boarding-school, shops were erected for mechanics, and the sawmill and gristmill were used. Indians supplied the sawmill with logs, and in 1876 three hundred thousand feet of lumber was cut, most of which was sold to Fort Klamath, the remainder being used to build frame houses.

The period of effective individualization on one-family farms began in 1874. In that year, and in each succeeding year until 1877, the agents reported that many Indians were building and living on one-family farms; that they were industrious, planting and caring for their crops assiduously; but that they were much discouraged by the failure of their crops owing to frost.

The first manual-training boarding-school was opened in February, 1874. In September of the same year it was closed for lack of funds. As far as possible Dyar, the agent, replaced it with a day school. The boarding-school was not opened again until the fall of 1875. The average attendance throughout the entire period was twenty-five pupils. In 1877 Dyar's wife supplemented the school with instruction to Indian women in household arts. In this same year Indian boys were taken into mechanical shops as apprentices for the first time.

Thus it will be seen that, prior to the Modoc War, the Indians learned something about agricultural techniques on the agency farms and began to establish individual farms for themselves. During all this period they were dependent jointly on their own efforts at collecting wild foods and on gratuity issues from the agency. After the war they established themselves on individual farms much more extensively but were unsuccessful in their efforts to raise crops, through no fault of their own but owing to the exigencies of the climate. They continued to collect wild foods and receive rations, and about 1875 first became interested in the cattle industry. About the same time they began to learn crafts and engage in small enterprises, selling wood, hay, and lumber to the garrison at Fort Klamath. During the whole of this period formal education and the apprentice system were applied to small numbers, but very ineffectually.

These statements apply to the Lower End community. The Upper End Klamath left this community in 1868, and the Modoc in 1870. Hence these policies were never applied to them, but only to the Klamath who remained.

The Upper End community.—The formation of an intercultural community at the Upper End of Klamath Reservation dates from before treaty days. There had always been Klamath settlements on the Lower Sprague River. Shortly before the treaty was signed a group of Modoc settled down in the Upper Sprague River Valley. Some of the Klamath married into this group, and after the treaty was signed, some members of the Klamath settlements which were left out of the reservation moved east, to the Upper End. Thus, the inhabitants of the entire Sprague River Valley, about the time the reservation was formed, were predominantly Klamath but included some Modoc. Members of this mixed group were designated "Yahooskin Snakes" in the treaty, but they behaved in all respects like Klamath. They did not take part in the Snake War; they moved to Williamson River and lived with the Klamath because they were afraid of Snake raids; and at a time when many of the Paviotso wandered off the reservation rather freely, they remained at the Upper End.

In 1868 the Silver-Summer Lake Paviotso returned from eastern Oregon, where they had been dodging the troops, and found Klamath Reservation a haven of refuge. They were fed and clothed at government expense by a commissary who traveled to Yainax for that purpose.

A year later, 1869, the Warner Valley Paviotso, who had been more active in the fighting than the Silver-Summer Lake group, were induced to settle down at Yainax, and a special resident commissary, Ivan D. Applegate, was appointed to administrate them. Ocheo, the leader of this group, was willing to settle permanently at Yainax, but many of his people were not. Portions of the band remained in Warner Valley where they were fed by the garrison at Camp Warner. Every year, from 1869 to 1876, this band divided and vacillated between Yainax and Warner, and had to be persuaded to come to Yainax every winter. In 1876 the appropriations for their subsistence were withdrawn (no treaty had ever been negotiated with them), and no effort was made to persuade them to return. They settled down in Warner and Surprise valleys, where their descendants are now located. They were members of the Upper End community, therefore, only during three or four months out of every year (from 1869 to 1876).

When the Modoc withdrew from the Lower End in 1870, Sconchin returned to Yainax, bringing some families with him, and in the course of the next few months others drifted back until approximately one hundred and thirty Indians were living at Yainax. Thus the Upper End Indian community consisted, from 1869 to 1876, of about one hundred and twenty Upper End Klamath, one hundred and twenty-eight Silver-Summer Lake Paviotso, one hundred and thirty Modoc, and one hundred and fifty Warner Lake Paviotso.

When these Indians were brought together at Yainax, the nearest white settlers were in the Lost River Valley, fifteen to thirty miles away, and at Linkville, thirty miles away. As time passed, the margins of the reservation were settled, but these points were more distant from the Upper End than from the earlier white settlements. Klamath Agency was, and still is, thirty miles distant from Yainax Station. The Upper End has been, from the beginning, more isolated than any other settled part of the reservation.

Camp Yainax was opened as a permanent administrative station January 1, 1869. During the first two years it was merely a station within the Klamath jurisdiction. While the Modoc complained about their treatment by Captain Knapp, Meacham was still in hopes the Tule Lake Modoc could be persuaded to return if they were given homes separate from the Klamath. He divided the jurisdiction, and from that time to the end of Meacham's administration in 1872, the commissary at Yainax reported direct to Meacham and had separate funds.

Administrative policy was uniform with that adopted at the Lower End. However, it differed in its application. In the early days Yainax was a more compact community, and the commissary had closer and more intimate contact with the Indians, who had much more confidence in him than the Klamath had in their subagent. The Paviotso, in particular, were provided for more amply during the period here under consideration. Their subsistence came from separate funds which were more adequate for their needs.

In the matter of services the Upper End was not so well taken care of. The staff was always very small. Neither teacher, blacksmith, nor physician was provided at Yainax during the first years of its existence. There were only a commissary, a superintendent of farming, and one incidental laborer during most of the period. A school was planned, but none was provided up to 1877. Administrative policy at the Upper End, therefore, was simpler than at the Lower End and, as applied, had a single aim: to teach the Indians how to farm and to encourage them to settle down and work their own farms.

Three periods may be defined. During the three years prior to 1872 agency buildings were erected, the Indians were helped to build thirty log houses, an agency farm was broken and cultivated, and the Indians were helped to construct farms of their own. During this entire period the Indians were permitted to be away from the reservation during the summer months. By and large they supported themselves, though they were helped out during the winter by ration issues. The farms were never successful, even less so than those at the Lower End, and on July 28, 1872, a severe frost wiped out the entire planting. Agricultural operations were virtually abandoned from that time on.

During the spring and summer of 1873 the Indians were not permitted to go off the reservation to collect wild food. There was great anxiety, lest the reservation Modoc be persuaded to join Captain Jack, and settlers would not have permitted Indians in their territory. A small force of cavalry was stationed at Yainax, and an Indian militia was organized. The Indians were on ration issues during this period.

In April, 1874, three hundred stock cattle were purchased for the Indians on Klamath Reservation, and stock-raising proved successful where agriculture had failed. Some of the Modoc had previously had experience with cattle in the Tule basin ranches, and a few of the Warner Valley Paviotso had had some experience. From this small beginning the people on the Upper End gradually entered the cattle business. There were no extensive operations during the period under consideration, but a beginning was made.

At no time was a campaign against shamanism prosecuted on the Upper End. At a late date there was an attempt to interfere with the religious revival, but it was not connected with any anti-shamanistic policy.

Both the commissary at Yainax and the subagent at Klamath Agency reported that the Klamath and Modoc on the Upper End were industrious and anxious to get farms for themselves, but that the Paviotso were not at all anxious to do so and retained many of their old customs. They said that the Silver-Summer Lake band were well pleased with Klamath Reservation, but that the Warner Valley group were undecided as to whether to join their friends and relatives in Warner Valley or not.

In general, the formation of the intercultural community on the Upper End was characterized by independence and absence of restraint, by few contacts with whites, by minimal cultural changes, and by the formation of a compact community rather than the scattered type of the Lower End.

The formation of the intercultural communities on both ends of the reservation was characterized by early and simple beginnings of culture change. Acceptance of white customs and techniques were barely under way in this first ten years of administrative control. Ten years later many more changes had taken place, but in the period under consideration the Indians depended on the collection of wild foods in their original habitat, to a large extent, and had taken over certain superficial characteristics of white culture, but the basic change to dependence on individual enterprise in the form of one-family subsistence farms, with reliance on agricultural and grazing techniques, was common only in the last half of the period, and only at the Lower End. The most notable feature is that the Indians accepted the change eagerly and industriously, only to find that their efforts met with failure, through no fault of their own.

Summary.—Let us now make a résumé of the circumstances under which the various groups on Klamath Reservation met the whites, and were brought together into two communities on the reservation, in order to learn what advantages and disadvantages accrued to the members of the various groups.

The Klamath at an early date began direct trade relations with the whites, which resulted in a shift in the social structure so that the more aggressive, younger men, with no previous background of wealth or social position, derived prestige and wealth through their contacts with whites. Trading was a well-established technique among the Klamath but it was greatly enhanced in the new situation. Thus the position of the shamans as the richest, most powerful, and prominent persons in Klamath culture was successfully challenged by a rising group of younger men. These men were middle-aged when the treaty was signed and were recognized as chiefs by the government. Their position was still further enhanced, their power increased, and their gains consolidated by the introduction of a magistrative system in 1869. At the same time the prestige and power of the shamans were on the decline, through the application of an anti-shamanistic administrative policy.

Early in the reservation period, a division among the chiefs began to take place. Certain of the younger chiefs who had learned to speak English were given jobs at the agency. They became interpreters or farm laborers, supervised the distribution of ration issues, and became herders and teamsters. Both formally and informally they assumed the mediative roles between the administration and the Indians. By thus identifying themselves with the values and techniques of the white community, they estranged themselves to a certain extent from the Indian community but gained in power and wealth, for some of them were paid in money. The other chiefs and the magistrates were never paid a salary.

A small portion of the new values filtered through to the "common" Klamath—those who were neither rich men, shamans, nor slaves. They gradually absorbed certain aspects of the new technology: Plains clothing and iron tools at first; cloth clothing and ration issues later. When the one-family farms were introduced, they were the ones who fenced and plowed land, built cabins, and sowed crops, only to have them destroyed by frost.

Slaves were not specifically mentioned in the treaty. Though their lives were not changed much, they were actually free from that time forward. They had been nominally freed by order of the superintendent in 1869.

In terms of gain and loss, therefore, the Klamath as a whole were better off than either the Modoc or the Paviotso, since they never fought the whites and were not removed, but had the reservation built up around them. Within the Klamath tribe, from the earliest days of white contacts, chiefs and slaves gained, shamans and commoners lost. Shamans, however, were on the losing end from earliest times, while commoners were not seriously deprived until the post-war period, when the effort to raise crops on one-family farms was well under way. Moreover, by the middle of the reservation period, the chiefs were divided into two groups, one of which was gaining values at the expense of the other—agency employees in the mediative roles were gaining at the expense of the more traditional leaders, whose power became more and more nominal as the administration took over more and more functions of leadership.

In terms of the techniques used to gain whatever values were attainable, it will be seen that ritual techniques were on the decline, while secular techniques were in the ascendent. In the early period trading as a skill began to supersede shamanistic practice. And in the later period the skills associated primarily with white culture, in contrast to Klamath culture, were in the ascendent. The ability to speak English and familiarity with agriculture and white crafts superseded trading during the agency period. For the common man the adoption of agricultural skills appeared more desirable than the older hunting and gathering skills or the trading skills, in which he had little part. His adoption of these skills, however, brought failure in the post-war period. By that time only the agency employees had permanently benefited themselves, and these had done so not through the adoption of agricultural techniques but through the adoption of the other set of skills associated with white culture—the speaking of English and the crafts.

The Modoc as a whole suffered more than any other group in their contacts with the whites. They fought them at first, had their homeland taken away against their will, and suffered ridicule at the hands of their supposed friends—the Klamath. The earliest effects of culture contact reached the Modoc indirectly through the Klamath. Theirs was the economic hinterland to Klamath trade relations. Their raids on the Paviotso and Pit-River Indians, especially the latter, furnished most of the slaves which the Klamath traded at The Dalles.

Within the Modoc a division occurred after the first direct white contact. One group, led by Sconchin, proposed making peace with the whites; the other, more divided in leadership, proposed active resistance. Three leaders emerged within the anti-white faction crystallized by Steele's premature treaty. John Sconchin, Sconchin's brother, was personally ambitious, and favored fighting; Captain Jack was equally demanding but favored a more passive course. Curly-haired Doctor, typical of the old, powerful, and aggressive shaman, followed the traditional association of shaman with factional leader and demanded action from Captain Jack. When prevailed upon by Meacham to compromise, this group was dissatisfied and took the reservation Modoc, who were equally dissatisfied, back to Tule Lake. Sconchin prevailed on some to return with him to Yainax. Jack had Yreka advisers, and Meacham was of the opinion that many of them were motivated by a desire to have a Californian reservation for reasons of trade. It thus appears that the leaders of the two Modoc factions appealed to or relied upon separate segments within the white community to maintain their policies and their own positions as leaders. Sconchin relied upon the administration which regarded him as reliable, faithful, and responsible, and regarded Jack as a dangerous desperado. Jack relied upon his friends in Yreka, who regarded him as wronged and badly treated on the reservation, and were perhaps interested in making good their promises of 1864 as well as advancing their own interests.

Jack's group, of course, was not subject to the application of the acculturation policy. It cannot be said that they were more deprived than those who remained on the reservation, although by their selection of the more aggressive of alternative modes of action they became more deprived, as when they were defeated by the military forces in the Modoc War. Similarly, it cannot be said that the reservation Modoc were more or less deprived than Jack's Modoc. They simply chose to accept the less aggressive of alternative courses of action. However, they were subject to the application of administrative policy. They were at the Lower End during the early period of active acculturation but, as far as can be learned, had less part in it than the Klamath. No Modoc, for example, are listed as farm laborers or interpreters during the early period. During the late period of acculturation on the reservation the Modoc were at the Upper End, where aboriginal life was carried out more extensively, where the magistrative system was not introduced, chiefs were not elected, shamans were not persecuted, and where farm individualization did not begin until late in the period now under consideration. The primary difference, therefore, between Modoc and Klamath, with respect to the deprivation or indulgence they experienced as a result of their contact with the whites, was the uniform character of deprivation and indulgence within the Modoc as a group.

The personal contacts between the Klamath and the whites, the values and skills introduced, and the application of administrative policy tended to indulge and deprive, differentially, numerous segments within the Klamath population. In particular, the application of the policy of individualization—the breaking-up of communities by putting individual Klamath families on their own farms—tended to make them individually responsible for their own success or failure. That is, it is not only true that there were wide individual differences in indulgence and deprivation in Klamath society; it is also true that the character of the deprivation, suffered in the late period, was individual in nature. Individual farmers succeeded or failed in their efforts to establish themselves as independent enterprisers.

This was only partly true as far as the Modoc were concerned, and in no instance was the tendency carried as far. The economic changes which produced the basic shift in Klamath social structure were not carried so far among the Modoc. The values and skills introduced among the Klamath were not incorporated among the Modoc. Administrative policy which partially succeeded in individualizing the Klamath was not applied to the Modoc. The deprivation the Modoc suffered was multiple; they lost their young men in the fighting, they lost their homeland as a group, and they were ridiculed by the Klamath because they were Modoc. Most important of all, they were not given the opportunity to learn and apply those skills of individual enterprise—interpreting, mediating, independent farming—in which some Klamath were conspicuously successful. At the time the Klamath were beginning to start farms of their own, the Modoc were still living in three communities, with their own leaders selected in the old manner—informally, by weight of prestige and influence. Their shamans were not persecuted and in the summer they worked their old range, gathering wild food for the winter. Only in the late period, when according to the agents many Klamath were working farms of their own, did the Modoc begin to do the same thing. The ways in which they suffered deprivation were those in which the group as a whole was jointly deprived, and in which the collective symbol "Modoc" was devalued in the eyes of both the white and the Indian community.

In all these things the Upper End Klamath were allied with the Upper End groups generally, and with the Modoc in particular. Both groups were united in opposition to the Paviotso. These latter people consisted of two groups previously described. One, the Warner Valley Paviotso, had suffered severely at the hands of white soldiers in their first white contacts. They were divided in their policies: part of them wished to remain at Klamath; the rest wanted to settle in their homeland. The latter group were encouraged in their desires by the military forces at Camp Warner, who fed them through the summer. They remained at Klamath only during the winter months, where they were dissatisfied and restless. Those members of the group who wished to stay on the reservation were particularly discouraged. There was a constant possibility that another reservation might be given them or that they might be separated from other members of the group if the latter settled down, in defiance of governmental authority, in Warner Valley. This latter possibility materialized in 1876 when a majority of the group settled there and did not return. In the meantime, on Klamath Reservation, the minority who did not want to go to Warner Valley (members of the Upper End community) were free from all the innovations of administrative policy. They had no elected chiefs, no magistrates, no anti-shamanistic campaign, and no schools, and, like the Modoc, they were free to work their old range during the summer months.

The Silver-Summer Lake Paviotso were united, in most respects, with the Warner Valley group. They were not so active during the Snake War; they did not fight, but rather avoided the troops. When they could avoid them no longer, they came to Klamath Reservation for protection. There they were as immune to change as the other Paviotso. All the Paviotso on Klamath Reservation differed from the other Indians there in that they made no effort to become individual farmers during the entire period under consideration.

It will thus be seen that, with respect to two factors in change, the groups on Klamath Reservation were aligned as follows: (1) with respect to initial deprivation the Modoc suffered most, the Klamath suffered least, and the Paviotso were intermediate; (2) with respect to changes introduced through administrative policy and attendant deprivation and indulgence, the Klamath changed most, the Paviotso least, while the Modoc were intermediate.

THE RELIGIOUS REVIVAL OF 1871–78

With the characteristics of the deprived and indulged groups on Klamath Reservation in mind, we may now proceed to that aspect of cultural change which seems most directly correlated

with deprivation—religious revivalism. Between 1871 and 1878
—that is, in the latter half of the reservation period under consideration—the members of all three tribes on Klamath Reservation participated in a religious movement. This movement
was part of a wider movement known in the ethnographic literature as the "Ghost Dance of 1870." It began on Walker River
Reservation in Nevada in 1869. In the course of the next few
years it spread to and was embraced by most of the Indians of
southern Oregon and northern California. As Spier has shown,[19]
this movement and other revivalistic phenomena in the Pacific
Northwest are genetically related. The basic, oldest form Spier
designates the "Prophet Dance." Its Plateau and Basin derivatives, in successive order, have been the Smoholla cult, the
Ghost Dance of 1870, and the Ghost Dance of 1890.

Thanks to Spier's,[20] Du Bois's,[21] and Gayton's[22] work on the
history of the 1870 Ghost Dance, it is possible to compare the
forms this movement took on Klamath Reservation with forms
of the same movement elsewhere. The immediate problem of
this paper, however, is not to compare variants within the framework of the total movement, but to determine to what extent
deprivation and indulgence of various groups on Klamath Reservation determined their acceptance or rejection of the movement as it was presented to them; and to learn to what extent
cultural change on Klamath Reservation determined new forms
or provided new meanings for old forms.

At the outset it may be said that the revival on Klamath
Reservation passed through three phases, which correspond in
a general way to three phases of the movement elsewhere. However, each phase is successively more limited in its similarity,
until, when the third phase is reached, the movement on Klamath Reservation is similar only in its most generalized features
to the third phases elsewhere, and specific forms are seen to be
indigenous to Klamath Reservation.

Dr. Du Bois, referring to the total 1870 movement, has labeled

[19] *The Prophet Dance of the Northwest.*

[20] *The Ghost Dance of 1870 among the Klamath.*

[21] *The Ghost Dance of 1870 in N. California and S. Oregon.*

[22] *The Ghost Dance of 1870 in South-Central California.*

the first two phases of religious activity the Ghost Dance proper and the Earthlodge cult, and has noted that everywhere these two phases broke down into individual dreaming. On Klamath Reservation the phases are not separated terminologically. Instead, the whole revival is described by a single phrase, "Dream Dancing." The Paviotso had no word for the 1870 revival different from that for any religious activity. In order to distinguish terminologically between the three religious phases on Klamath Reservation, I have followed Dr. Du Bois's terminology for the first two phases and have used the Klamath-Modoc term for the last phase.

THE GHOST DANCE

Sometime during the year 1871 a Paviotso from Walker River named Frank Spencer visited the Paviotso on the Upper End of Klamath Reservation. He brought the message that in Nevada they were dancing to bring the dead back, and that on Klamath they should dance too. He lived on Klamath Reservation for about a year, and one big dance and numerous small dances were held in the Paviotso district. These were strictly Paviotso affairs and were not attended by any of the Klamath or Modoc living near by. Everyone danced. Men, women, and children joined in a circle dance—the classic Paviotso ritual form. A single line of dancers moved clockwise around a central fire. Each dancer stepped out with the left foot and on the next beat dragged the other foot. Small dances were held nearly every night, and men, women, and children bathed at sunrise, even through the winter. There were no paraphernalia, no costumes, no instruments. The entire group sang songs, expressive of the Ghost Dance doctrine, to the effect that dead relatives were returning. No one fainted. While Frank Spencer was at the Upper End, he carried the message to the Modoc and the mixed Klamath and Modoc groups. One large dance was held which lasted five nights. The circle dance just described was used, and all painted their faces the same way—a red background with two horizontal black lines on each cheek. They bathed every morning at sunrise. Many people fainted at this dance and were revived by two men, who dipped bunches of white sage in water and sprinkled them, praying and singing. Sometimes those who fainted were carried around the circle on a blanket. None of those who fainted had visions.

The Klamath and the Modoc were told that Old Man Coyote was bringing back the dead and the animals that used to be in the region. The songs they sang mostly told about the dead and the "message," and were partly borrowed from the Paviotso and partly original. In all, four dances of five nights each were performed at the Upper End. There was one large performance in the Paviotso district, besides the many small performances: one of mixed Klamath and Modoc, just described; another attended mostly by Modoc; and a fourth southeast of the reservation attended by the Yahooskin only.

The spring of the year the fighting broke out in the Modoc War (1872). Doctor George, a shaman from the reservation Modoc, carried the Paviotso message to the Tule Lake Modoc. A dance ground was prepared at the mouth of Lost River, and the circle dance, as described, was performed. Doctor George, however, introduced some innovations. He had the dancers paint their faces with three horizontal stripes in red, white and black, he stretched a rope of twisted tule around the dance ground and declared that no one who wanted to interfere would be able to cross it, and he erected a pole to the east of the central fire.

Doctor George was specific in his promises and personally ambitious in his role as proselyter and prophet. He said that a Paviotso messenger had told him that all the dead Modoc were coming back, that one who was a headman like a "chief" was coming back and he wanted everyone to dance.

There are different kinds of rules, and unless we do it the right way we are dead and gone. If we are to do as they tell us, we must dance and sing. I will give you a dream so that you can meet them. Even if you are not dead, you just lie down and you will know all about it. All the Modoc are coming back. Put up a long pole, put a fire to one side of it, and dance. If some of you fall down, you must go and meet the dead.

Doctor George told the dancers where to get the pole, told them to come together under it, and showed them how to dance.

One doctor fell down as if he were dead. He went back to meet the dead people coming. He got up and told the people, "Now I have been there, and I saw everyone that is coming back. If any of you fall like I do, you will meet the people coming back. You must sing like me and believe, or you will be turned to rock. The dead are coming back when the grass is about eight inches high. White people will die out, and only Indians will be left on earth. Whites will burn up and disappear without leaving any ashes. Deer and other animals will all come back. A good many of you have relations who have died. They will all come back, and people will never die any more. Those who will come back have died once, but they will never die any more. You must think of nothing but the dead people coming back."

Doctor George said that he had been back himself to meet the dead and that others could, too, if they would lie down. These people were called "dreamers." Doctor George told them, "Whenever you dream, paint your face red and white. Do as your dream tells you. If you don't obey your dream, you will turn to rock."[23]

The Tule Lake Modoc performed the five-day dance only once, after which Doctor George returned to the reservation. The only further interest in the revival which the group showed was in connection with the Modoc War. At the time of the first engagement in the lava beds, Curly-haired Doctor attempted to repeat Doctor George's exploit. He stretched a rope of twisted tule around the Modoc battleground and declared that white soldiers would be unable to cross it. Although the Modoc successfully defended their stronghold, the soldiers did cross the rope, and from that time on the Ghost Dance was discredited in the Tule Lake group.

Certain points in the Ghost Dance doctrine, as this group accepted it, are of interest. It was specifically mentioned that the Modoc dead were returning. Throughout accounts of the movement there are numerous and repetitive references to the dead, to various people's relatives, to the necessity of thinking constantly of the dead, etc. This is not the case in accounts of other Klamath Reservation groups. Communion with the dead was not emphasized at all among the Upper End Klamath and the Paviotso, for example, although it appeared in one known instance among the reservation Modoc. At Tule Lake more threats were directed against nonbelievers or against believers who failed to perform the ritual properly. The ritual was said

[23] From information gathered by Dr. David Rodnick.

to be powerful and dangerous; it was said that the dead would return and that the ritual must be performed, not only to bring back the dead, but to protect the living from the dead.

The doctrine was specific in its promises and threats. The dead, it was said, would return when the grass was a certain height. Unbelievers would be turned to rocks. One woman, who did not participate, lost one of her children during the ritual. The boy's death was said to be a punishment, and it was predicted that she would turn into a bird. The threats were partly directed toward whites; they were to be burned up. Any who tried to interfere would be unable to cross the rope of twisted tule.

This doctrine, therefore, was specific and aggressive toward both whites and unbelievers, and even believers. It was attended by great excitement and considerable autism. None of these things was true of the Ghost Dance among other Klamath Reservation groups. The dead appeared more prominently, and the collective symbol "Modoc" had a role here which similar symbols did not occupy among the other groups.

The role of Doctor George as an innovator should be taken into account. This man afterward became a shaman but was not yet a shaman in 1871. He became one of the best-known and most powerful shamans the Modoc remember. He was killed about 1906, after a patient died, and was the last shaman to be so killed.

He was an aggressive, ambitious man. The pole he used was aboriginally a symbol of shamanism, erected to the east of a shaman's house and decorated with stuffed birds representative of the shaman's spirits. In the Ghost Dance at Tule Lake, Doctor George used this pole somewhat as a shaman uses his. He had the dancers hang furs and blankets on it, he put it on the east side of the fire, he told the dancers where to find it and how to put it up, and he oriented a dance around it. The fact that one who was not a shaman should use such a symbol in a shamanistic way shows that, in spite of the absence of an anti-shamanistic campaign on the Upper End, the barrier between the ritual practices of shamans and nonshamans was already breaking down. This was a prime characteristic of the entire revival on the Upper End, as will appear in later phases.

The specificity of promises and threats may account in part for the failure of the Ghost Dance to continue at Tule Lake. After the initial enthusiasm, it was tested and rejected. Had there been no opportunity for testing the doctrine, it might, perhaps, have continued. The fact, however, that abandonment of the doctrine coincided with a more direct and aggressive mode of response, namely, fighting, suggests the possibility that in this situation the two responses were mutually exclusive.

The inclusion of the collective symbol and the doctrinal stress on the dead, coupled with extremely aggressive elements in the doctrine, are consonant with the damage to the collective symbol suffered by contact with the whites. The Modoc have suffered; many have died at the hands of the whites. Now it is asserted that the Modoc dead will return, and coupled with their return will be a general destruction of the whites. Yet there is danger in this retaliation for the Modoc. To protect one's self it is necessary to believe, to think constantly of the dead, and to perform the ritual according to the rules laid down by those who have had dream contact with the dead.

The pole introduced by Doctor George is somewhat similar to poles used elsewhere in the Ghost Dance. However, since the context in which Doctor George used the pole is reminiscent of Modoc shamanism, and in view of his shamanistic ambitions, I am inclined to attribute this form to his personal invention rather than to regard it as an importation from outside. Thus, it will be seen that Doctor George employed some of the paraphernalia of shamanism to advance his position within the community, using them in a ritual but nonshamanistic way, and using them before he had experienced the supernatural contact appropriate to becoming a shaman.

Frank Spencer, the Paviotso who brought the Ghost Dance message from Walker River to Klamath Reservation, never visited the Lower End. Sometime during the first year of the revival a Klamath named O'Toole brought the news to the Lower End at the same time that the Upper End Klamath told their friends on the Lower End about it. One big dance was organized at Williamson River Flat, across the river from the home of Allen David, then head chief. Forty or fifty families participated, mostly Klamath with a few Modoc. They set up their summer houses in a large circle on the flat. The dance ground was inside the circle of houses, set off by a canvas wall and open at the eastern end. In the center of the circle formed by the canvas wall a large fire was built, around which they danced five nights. The dance form was the circle dance already described. The dancers had their faces painted with similar designs but in different colors: two or three horizontal lines on the right cheek in various combinations of red, white, and black. Some dancers lost consciousness, but none had visions. Those who fainted were carried around the circle, sung and prayed over, and brushed with white sage by two men, just as on the Upper End. In the morning after each dance the entire community—men, women, and children—bathed in the river. The songs they used were all in Klamath and were the same as the ones sung by the Klamath at the Upper End.

The leaders in organizing this dance were Lobert, O'Toole, Frank Chilks, and Allen David. Lobert was a shaman, O'Toole, who brought the message from the Upper End, was a "commoner"; Frank Chilks was a "commoner"; while Allen David was head chief. This mixture of two commoners, a chief, and a shaman reflects the general participation in this phase of the revival on the Lower End. The only notable absences were of agency employees. Interest in the Ghost Dance was general, participation was wide, and excitement was minimal. No threats or promises were made, no visions were experienced, and the doctrinal emphasis was on the beneficent aspects of the expected change. The songs said: "Soon all people on earth will live together," or "The message will resound; everyone on earth will hear it."

The attitude of all the groups on the reservation had the common characteristic of mild skepticism. The only Klamath Reservation group which wholeheartedly accepted the personal meanings of the doctine was the Tule Lake Modoc. The dances described were all that were held and covered a period of about a year. Sometime during that year a delegation of men from both Upper and Lower Ends traveled into Nevada to learn something about the Paviotso prophet. They were dissatisfied with what they learned and gave an adverse report.

It can be seen that, as far as the Paviotso were concerned, the Ghost Dance was a religious revival in a strict sense: an increase in religious activity accompanied by the enhancement of well-established religious symbols and practices. Their participation was both collective and individual. That is to say, there was one mass ceremonial, followed by much home and family ritual, individual dreaming, and spontaneous personal ritual participation.

The reservation Modoc and the Upper End Klamath responded to the stimulus in much the same way. They had mass ceremonials, no individual performances, and a moderate amount of fainting. The Klamath had no visions, but they sang about both the dead and the "message." The Klamath on the Lower End participated less fully than the Modoc and the Klamath on the Upper End, and had only mass ceremonials, moderate fainting, and no visions, and sang only about the "message."

With these differences in mind, therefore, it may be said that the Klamath and the reservation Modoc responded in much the same way, emphasizing the joint or group aspects of the ceremonial. For neither of these people was the Ghost Dance a revival except in the loose sense; for the dance forms, the "message," some of the songs, face painting, and modes of participation were foreign to aboriginal Klamath and Modoc ritual. They were dancing to an imported message, with imported forms. Their participation implied no discernible anti-white feeling, merely a generalized apprehension about the future, which was approached by the Modoc with some slight concern and by the Klamath optimistically.

THE EARTHLODGE CULT

The Ghost Dance was introduced to Klamath Reservation in 1871, and interest in it lasted about a year. On November 28, 1872, the first attempt was made to bring the Tule Lake Modoc onto the reservation by force. By this time Frank Spencer had left the reservation and the initial excitement had died down; and a short time later, at Tule Lake, the failure of Curly-haired Doctor's magic rope brought an end to Ghost Dance activity off the reservation.

No further revival activity took place on Klamath Reservation until 1874, sometime within a year after the termination of hostilities. At that time a new message and dance were brought onto the reservation from northern California. The bearers of this new message were Henry Jackson and Pit-River Charley, two former slaves of the Modoc and Klamath, respectively. By birth they were Achomawi or Atsugewi of the Pit River region in northern California, but had been captured as young men in pretreaty times and brought up in the homes of Klamath and Modoc Indians. After the treaty they continued to live on Klamath Reservation. Just after the war they returned to California to visit their relatives. They arrived at the time of the Earthlodge-cult excitement there and visited dances at Falls City and Alturas. Henry Jackson had been a Modoc slave and still lived at Yainax; he and Pit-River Charley roused interest around there. Charley then went to the Lower End, where he lived, and became a leader in the construction of three dance houses there. Under the leadership of these two men the movement progressed simultaneously in the two places.

The doctrine of the Earthlodge cult, throughout its wide distribution as well as on Klamath Reservation, was fairly close to that of the Ghost Dance. It was asserted that the dead would return, that the date of their return was near at hand, and that on the day of their return whites and unbelievers would be destroyed by an earthquake. Dancing, it was said, would hasten the approach of the dead. Dancers were encouraged to faint and dream of the returning dead. The leaders frequently went into trances in which they met the dead and, when they regained consciousness, reported how near the dead were. Many people met and talked with their dead relatives who were then on the march, or had visions of the land of the dead where everyone was happy.

This news came to the Upper End in the winter. The mem-

bers of this community were exhorted to build a semisubter-
ranean house in which the faithful might take refuge on the
anticipated day of destruction. Four such houses were built:
one on the Upper End and three on the Lower End. The first
one was used by Modoc and the Upper End Klamath; the other
three were used by Klamath only. These houses were patterned
after a type which was standard throughout the southern range
of Earthlodge-cult distribution. This type was a house of log
and earth construction—circular, with a depressed floor, one
main support, and a corridor entrance on the south. All but the
Upper End dance house corresponded to this type. The Upper
End house was somewhat modified in accordance with Klamath-
Modoc usage in house-building. It was also of log and earth
construction, was nearly circular but had a slight east-west
elongation, had four main supports, and had a corridor entrance
on the east. All four dance houses were larger than any built
previously on Klamath Reservation.

In the middle of each house, whether it had four posts or only
one, a fire was built. A circle of dancers stripped to the waist
stood around this fire, either lifting their heels off the ground
rhythmically while they sang or flexing their knees in time to the
music while they twisted and turned colored handkerchiefs over
their heads. Sometimes they moved in a circle, as in the Ghost
Dance, but they never joined hands. They continued to dance
five nights in order, bathing each morning at sunrise, but they
no longer painted their faces. Those who fainted were not revived, in order that they might dream of the dead.

No estimate is possible of the number of performances held.
As time went on, dreaming became increasingly common, not
only in the dance houses but also at home, until it became en-
demic, and the features by which the Earthlodge cult may be
distinguished merged imperceptibly with the third phase of the
revival.

Some idea of group participation, however, may be gained
from informants and by a study of the distribution of dance
houses. The Paviotso knew of the Earthlodge cult but did not
participate in it. There was only one dance house in Modoc

territory, whereas there were three of them in Klamath territory. Some discount must be made for the more diffuse nature of the Klamath settlements. Since there was only one dance house for each principal area of Klamath settlement, and there was also one dance house for the principal area of Modoc settlement, I see no reason to suppose that the Klamath were much more active than the Modoc.

Only one song was remembered which can be positively identified as belonging to the Earthlodge cult. The words to this song are not Klamath-Modoc, and I was told that Pit-River Charley brought it up from California.

Sometime during the year 1874, a delegation composed of members from both Upper and Lower End Modoc and Klamath, but no Paviotso, visited Falls City, California, and journeyed as far east as Fort Crook in order to learn the truth of the Earthlodge "message." This delegation witnessed dances at Falls City and Fort Crook; they believed and carried what they heard back to Klamath Reservation, making the doctrine even stronger.

Several points of comparison between Upper End and Lower End practices are worthy of consideration. Most outstanding are the basic differences in doctrine. On the Upper End the anti-white element was strong, whereas it was absent on the Lower End. Coupled with the anti-white doctrine was the need for protection from the disaster, even by the Modoc. To avoid destruction one must believe and accept the protection of the Earthlodge. On the Upper End the return of the dead was asserted as imminent and predicted for a specific time; this was not the case at the Lower End. And at the Upper End the return of the dead was associated with a wide destruction and was both hoped for and feared, while at the Lower End, in doctrine at least, only the favorable aspects of the dead's return were mentioned. In the Earthlodge cult, therefore, as in the Ghost Dance, the basic difference in attitude of the Upper End and Lower End groups persisted: the Upper End was apprehensive about the future, aggressive toward whites, surrounded itself with ritual precautions to ward off the danger of its own aggressive assertions, and accepted specific promises and threats which eventually failed to materialize. In this case, however, the failure of the promises did not lead to a rejection of the doctrine, for dreaming became more widespread, and the abandonment of the Earthlodge dances was not due to any rejection of doctrine but to a preoccupation with personal autism. The people of the Upper End were told, when the dead failed to return and the earthquake did not arrive, that they had not believed strongly enough. The important fact, then, is not that the doctrine was rejected, but that the focus of religious interest was shifted from a world-event to the self. This situation contrasts with that of the Tule Lake Modoc during the Ghost Dance. There, by a specific event, the Ghost Dance doctrine was tested, failed, and was rejected. No such single event marked the end of the Earthlodge cult at either the Upper or the Lower End. It is only possible to say that the trend of the entire revival was in the direction of greater preoccupation with the self, and that at this time the individual, as a symbol, was coming into the focus of sociological as well as of ritual attention. This, it will be remembered, was the period in which many Indians began to live on and cultivate their own farms. Administrators were interested in inducing Indians to do so; and many Indians were interested in achieving this status.

For the Earthlodge cult as a whole the outstanding appeal was the possibility of personal communion with the approaching dead. Both ritual and doctrine favored this sort of autism, and it was freely experienced. The role of the leaders stimulated it, for their own trances and pronouncements about the dead were followed by many trances and similar visions by the dancers. The appeal to the leaders—personal aggrandizement of previously declassed individuals—should not be overlooked. Pit-River Charley and Henry Jackson had both been slaves. At the Klamath Marsh dance house the large center post was called "Charley." Both these men directed the dancing, led the songs, and experienced frequent trances, after which they reported their conversations with the dead.

The personnel of the Earthlodge cult contrasts with the preceding and subsequent movements in an interesting way. The men who were active in the Ghost Dance and the Dream Dance were by and large the same, whereas the leaders, delegates, and remembered participants of the Earthlodge cult were not so active in either of the other two phases of the revival. The participants in the Earthlodge cult were not all former slaves by any means, but they were principally men who were not prominent in any other way and included only one chief and one shaman. The others were commoners, with a sprinkling of former slaves. The situation was favorable, of course, to men who wished social recognition and had never received it. The ritual was brought in by former slaves who as leaders occupied a role in the ritual which exacted a great deal of personal deference. The Ghost Dance, preoccupied principally with doctrine, did not offer this opportunity, and the Dream Dance, as will be seen, favored the symbolic rather than the real aspects of deference.

The Earthlodge cult differed from the Ghost Dance in many respects, one of which is particularly significant. In the Ghost Dance there were many beliefs and practices which emphasized the joint or communal aspect of the ceremony. Men, women, and children were all required to take part. The dance ground was inclosed, and none of the participants was permitted to leave during the five-day ritual. At the Upper End, Old Man Coyote, identified in part with the culture hero, was said to be at the head of the returning dead. In the dance ritual all joined hands. Face painting was uniform. At the Upper End also it was specified that the dead were Modoc dead. It will be seen that these communal symbols were stronger at the Upper End than at the Lower End, but that in both groups many group symbols were emphasized which were not emphasized in the Earthlodge cult. Not only had the doctrinal stress shifted, but the force of the collective symbol had been to a certain extent dissipated. All the foregoing characteristics of the Ghost Dance were either indifferently observed, had no force, or were subject to individual variation during the Earthlodge cult.

The forms of the Earthlodge cult were derived from more diverse sources than the Ghost Dance. Those that were imported came from northern California and were uniform with practices there. The dance houses were either of the type used throughout the northern-California distribution of the Earthlodge cult or were a combination of this type with the two types of winter houses used by the Klamath and Modoc. The dance form, unlike that of the Ghost Dance, was not foreign to Klamath-Modoc culture but represented an old form. The colored handkerchiefs are an importation from northern California, where they were used in the Earthlodge cult and allied movements. Those songs used which are still remembered are probably from northern California. Face painting, used only at the Lower End, is non-Klamath and may have been brought with the ritual from northern California, or carried over from the Ghost Dance.

It will be seen that, with the progression from the Ghost Dance to the Earthlodge cult, a shift had taken place in the character of revivalism. In doctrine, practice, personnel, and symbolic appeal the religious interest had moved from the group symbol toward the individual symbol. With reference to differences between the Upper and Lower Ends, the two movements were much the same, although the basic differences of attitude toward whites and apprehension about the future were still there. The Upper End resisted the whites and was apprehensive about the future, whereas the Lower End accepted the whites and was optimistic about the future.

THE DREAM DANCE

During the summer of the first year of the Earthlodge cult, dreaming became more and more common. People began to dream at home as well as at Earthlodge dances. Dream content underwent a change which was different at the two ends of the reservation. Formerly dreamers had experienced visions of the returning dead or had seen the dead engaged in old-time activities. At the Upper End dreams now began to conform to a stereotyped form in which the dreamer saw his dead relatives, who were dancing with their faces painted and sang for him. Such dreamers woke up in the night and sang the songs they had heard in the dream. They sang them with their families in the

morning; and at gatherings, which were held frequently, groups
of people sang their dream songs together, performing the dance
steps they had seen, and painting their faces like the dead.
Dance steps, face painting, and songs were subject to wide individual variation. Each one had his way, and it was compulsory
for him to do exactly as he was shown in his dream. Those who
did not became sick. Many sick people came to the public dream
dances for help. They were carried around in a blanket, in the
same way as fainters in the Ghost Dance. One of the Upper
End Klamath described one of these episodes:

My cousin, a young boy about my age, was sick, and I went to see him. He
said, "I'm glad you're here. I'm going to a good place, where there's no more
sickness. I'm sorry for you people. I'm tired. I'm sorry. There are lots of bad
things going on here. Now I'm going out. I'm glad you came." I was standing
away from him. He called me "cousin" and said, "Don't stand far out. Come
close. I love you and you love me. I'll still love you when you're dead. Stay
away from trouble." I cried. "Don't be sorry," he said.

That night four men held that sick boy up in a blanket and carried him
around to every house in camp. They gave him a piece of meat—one swallow—
at each house all the way around. Then they took him to bed. He said, "Good-
bye, everybody," and died right there.

Doctor George was active in the Dream Dance. During the
winter he held a Dream Dance in an ordinary house which was
an earthlodge but not a dance house. Here they danced five
nights and bathed in the morning after the last night. They did
not paint their faces or form a circle, but they stood in place
and danced up and down on their heels, as in the Earthlodge
Dance. Several people sang their dream songs, but Doctor
George was the principal one. Statements conflict as to whether
George was a shaman at this time or not. At any rate he devoted
himself principally to helping the sick, whom he rubbed with his
hand.

Doctor George derived his power from his dreams, which were
very strong. The exact nature of his dream could not be learned,
even from his wife and son, and it may never have been revealed. However, he had many dream songs which are known
all over the reservation today. There are several versions of
them, all of which follow the basic theme: "I am a big horse; I
drag the earth behind me."

Doctor George planted a pole outside his winter house, on the east side. It was like the pole he used during the Ghost Dance at Tule Lake, and was like a shaman's pole except for the decorations. Sometimes they danced around this pole in the daytime, and at night they danced inside the house. He told those who came to his dances, especially the prominent men, that they should put up poles in front of their houses, too.

Doctor George's dance was the only phase of the revival on the Upper End that attracted the attention of the administration. The blacksmith and one other white man from Yainax drove to George's house early one morning, when the Indians were dancing around the pole, and tried to arrest him. The blacksmith had a long black beard. When they tried to take Doctor George away, one of the Indians, an old man, caught hold of the blacksmith's beard. They had to turn George loose in order to make the old man let go, and George got away. The white men gave up and drove back to Yainax, but after that the Indians were more secretive and there was no more trouble.

Mose Brown, former leader of the "Yahooskin" (mixed Klamath and Modoc of the Upper End) had a Dream Dance. He became sick, and a group of men came and sang dream songs for him. They stayed two weeks, and he got a dream and sent men out to do as his dream said. Seven men went out, each dressed with one white feather down his back and white paint on his forehead. The seven went out on horseback, and the rule was that they should kill one deer. His son, Harrison, not understanding the ritual meaning, went along and shot two deer. They told him not to cut them up but to pack them in. When he got in, they dressed him like the seven men and put the deer on his back, with the deer's head over his, and he approached his father from the east. The son knelt down, and his father examined the deer's head, first on one side, then on the other. Harrison then let the deer fall to the ground over his head and went out. This was what his father had dreamed, and from this time on he grew better. That night Harrison dreamed the deer was chasing him, and again the next night. He was frightened, but he didn't know what to do and was afraid to say anything about it. His father, however, was getting better, and in time the dream passed away.

These episodes, quite different in character, are probably from different periods in the growth of the Dream Dance, but it is not possible to place them accurately. The Dream Dance lasted for at least three years on the Upper End, and the end point of its change was not reached until several years after that. As these isolated examples indicate, dreaming was incorporated more and more into the context of shamanism. Certain points in the process of incorporation may be pointed out. Dreaming was aboriginally associated with sickness and shamanism. During the Dream Dance phase of the revival, dreaming of the dead was added to other kinds of dreaming as one of the causes of sickness. The first cures were attempted by carrying the patient around the circle of dancers. Doctor George's Dream Dances were largely oriented around his own cures. Other dreamers went in groups to sick persons' houses and sang for them in the twilight —a time of day traditionally associated with the dead. In time these dreamers came to be called *do'deik'álgat'k'*, a word whose basic meaning is "dreamer" but which was aboriginally applied to the novice shaman. Dream doctors began to use some of the techniques of shamanism, such as rubbing with ashes and blowing water, but did not attempt to suck out disease. For a time it was said that dream doctors could see disease but could not cure it. They began to diagnose other kinds of dreams besides dreams of the dead. In one instance, it is said, a dream doctor told a patient: "You have been dreaming of something; a bear, perhaps. You should see a shaman." Nightmares, and bad dreams generally, came to be included in the category of ways in which sickness could be caused. The end point in this development came when an accredited shaman devised a cure for a sickness caused by dreaming, which involved sending out his spirits to drive in the dream, so that he could catch it and it would no longer trouble the patient. This was a complete amalgam of aboriginal shamanistic practices with Dream Dance elements and took place at a relatively late date, probably ten to fifteen years after the inception of the Dream Dance.

It will be seen that, while the line of demarcation between the Earthlodge cult and the Dream Dance on the Upper End is uncertain, so that no single point of transition can be isolated, yet each in its entirety was different and can be recognized as a phase in the total revival. The Earthlodge cult had a doctrine in the form of a belief about an impending world-event, a fairly uniform group ritual, and regular meeting places, and the personalized features of the ritual and doctrine were associated with the dead who were thought of as returning. The Dream Dance had no doctrine in this sense. Its symbolism was not concerned with any specific world-event. The ritual was highly variable in its earlier phases and became uniform in its later phases only in so far as it was incorporated into prerevival shamanistic practices.

The highly personalized features of the Dream Dance were associated with the dead, but the dead were no longer thought of as returning. Participants in the Dream Dance had visions of them in the land of the dead. They thought of them with dread and regarded such dreaming as dangerous. These dreams were accompanied by feelings of anxiety which could be removed only by acting out the dream. Dreams which were forgotten, or were not acted out properly, made people sick. The curative aspect of the Dream Dance was introduced as a means of removing the symptoms which followed such dreaming. The Dream Dance was a much more hysterical phenomenon than either the Ghost Dance or the Earthlodge cult. It contrasted with these earlier movements which, aside from the Tule Lake version, were accepted without much excitement and with a certain skepticism. The Dream Dance was characterized by great excitement, by much sickness, and by an aimless anxiety which was not directed toward any particular event or placed in time. Most important of all, the attention of Dream Dancers was not directed toward any doctrine, or object of ritual, but toward the self. The participant's own dream experiences, symptoms, anxiety, ritual performance, power, danger, or death were the object of attention. In terms of the development of the total revival, therefore, the Dream Dance was a further step in the progression away from group symbolism and participation toward an individual symbolism and participation.

The Ghost Dance represented a sharp break with Modoc and Klamath ritual tradition. The Earthlodge cult was more in accord with this tradition, and the Dream Dance was still more consonant with it, and in the course of its development became incorporated into it. At the same time the aboriginal distinction between the ritual experience of shamans and the ritual experience of nonshamans was broken down. Participants in the Dream Dance, particularly the strong dreamers, began acting like shamans; and shamans who participated in the Dream Dance acted more like ordinary men. Doctor George's pseudo-shamanistic cures and paraphernalia were an extreme development of this equalizing tendency. As the Dream Dance grew older, the traditional gap between shamans and nonshamans widened again as ordinary people ceased dreaming, and shamans incorporated Dream Dance symbols and practices into their rituals.

The personnel of the Dream Dance at the Upper End cannot be known in its entirety, of course. Those whose names are remembered are men who were also active in the Ghost Dance but who were less active in the Earthlodge, and include three chiefs, or former chiefs, and Doctor George, who either was already a shaman or became one soon after the Dream Dance was given up.

It is of some interest to know that Mose Brown, or Mosenkasket, as his name was sometimes written, had been the chief among the Upper End Klamath. He was ambitious politically and tried to oust Lalakes as head chief in the early days. He was prevented by the agent and not long after was deposed as chief of the Upper End Klamath, Lelu being given his place. The symbolism of deference in his dream is understandable in this context. It was not typical of the Upper End and resembled much more closely the dreams of men at the Lower End, as will be seen. By and large, however, the Upper End participated as a unit, with the exception of the Paviotso, who took no part at all.

At the Lower End the Dream Dance had a somewhat different form. It lasted about three years, and the process of transition from the forms of the Earthlodge cult to the Dream Dance forms can be more clearly recognized. Individual dreaming and home rituals were as common as at the Upper End, but the symbolic content and subsequent ritual behavior were quite different. The aspects of sickness and curing did not appear at all. Their place was taken by dreams in which the self was at the focus of attention but in an entirely different role from that characteristic of the Upper End. Some samples will illustrate the difference.

David Allen dreamed he was a shaman and saw himself preparing to smoke like a shaman, and dancing like a shaman. He was given two songs and later he gave a dance at which he danced like a shaman and sang his songs.

Jason Howard dreamed that God called him up into heaven and told him to go back to earth and learn to write, and he would take him back into heaven, and Jason could do God's writing for him. He had a song about that, and a second song about "people from heaven coming back." Jason stayed in his house, and people came in and danced and sang his songs in the evening. Jason was neither a chief nor a shaman.

Chon-chon, a shaman, had a dream in which he received a dance step, a face-painting, and a song. He built a special house and held a dance in it. Men and women stood shoulder to shoulder and stepped to the right, dragging their left feet. This man's song was: "Everyone's father is coming back and will be a big chief." In his dream he was told to ask while he was performing his dance, "Do you believe what I say?" and the dancers should answer, "Yes."

O'Toole, who brought the Ghost Dance from the Upper End, had a dream and was given many songs and told to perform a ritual. O'Toole built a special earthlodge with a corridor entrance to the east. He stood just inside the door, and everyone that came in to dance had to shake hands with him and call him "big chief." After all had come inside, O'Toole went into the crowd and showed people how to dance, paint their faces, and sing his songs, of which he had several. O'Toole said he saw dead people walking around among the crowd.

Lobert, a shaman, had a dream and built a big earthlodge with a pole in the center which went up through the smoke-hole in the roof. It was a smooth pole, with no decorations. Lobert dreamed that those who came to his dance should try to climb this pole and get up onto the roof. Those who were successful would get to heaven. He dreamed a face-painting, a dance step, and many songs. Lobert also wore a headdress and buckskin clothes, which he decorated according to his dream. Some informants said that Lobert used colored handkerchiefs. [These and the costume are reminiscent of similar practices used in the final phases of the 1870 revival in northern California. Lobert's was said to be the first Dream Dance at the Lower End, and its close similarity to the Earthlodge cult confirms this opinion.]

It will be seen that, with the exception of Lobert's dance, these performances conform closely to a single type in which the dreamer sees himself in some self-enhancing role. In some cases this role involved the acceptance of values and skills associated with white culture; in other cases it involved the acceptance of values and skills associated with Klamath culture. But in all cases it was only secondarily connected with the dead, it involved the acceptance or rejection of no particular doctrine, it was highly individualistic, and the rituals were subject to wide individual variation, which revealed dissatisfaction with the present and some concern about the future, but involved none of the vague dread and anxiety typical of the Dream Dance on the Upper End. Moreover, on the Lower End people did not become sick and connect their sickness with dreaming, as on the Upper End.

Lobert's early ritual contained elements which must be regarded as specifically Christian in origin. The use of the word "heaven" may have been injected by modern interpreters, but the notion of personal salvation, and of heaven as upward, are basic to the original ritual. There had been little missionization up to this time, but L. S. Dyar, the agent at Klamath, had been preaching for some time and reported wide interest. Mr. Harer, the commissary at Yainax, had also been preaching, but no effects of his work appeared in the Dream Dance there.

It is appropriate to inquire whether, aside from the increasing individualism of the Klamath, there is any sociological basis for the identification of some dreamers with white values, such as writing, and the identification of other dreamers with Indian values, such as shamanism or becoming big chiefs. Looking over the examples used, we find that, out of two shamans, one wanted everyone to try for personal salvation in a Christian heaven, and one asserted that everyone's father would be a big chief. Of the two commoners, one wanted to do God's writing, and one wanted everyone to call him "big chief." The head chief of the Klamath visualized himself as a shaman.

It will be remembered that at this time the magistrative power of the old-line chiefs was on the decline. Allen David was one of these. He has been described as a handsome, grave, dignified man; a great orator, a man of influence among the Indians, and a valuable man to the administration. He was one of the old-line chiefs who had been created by the administration, and who were being replaced in power and influence by the men in mediator roles—the interpreters and agency employees who supervised ration issues. Shamans had been persecuted but had not been removed from the scene by any means. Many commoners had attempted to become individual farmers but had never succeeded in raising a good crop. It is evident that, sociologically speaking, the various segments of the Klamath population were in great confusion in their identification with white and Indian values, but that one small group, the agency employees, were in a superior position while others were, in varying degrees, deprived through their contact with white culture. The dreams, and the rituals based on dreams which are still remembered, follow this cleavage fairly closely. None showed real opposition to white values. Commoners tended to desire mediative roles; shamans wanted personal aggrandizement as "big chiefs." Chiefs wanted ritual enhancement, one of them as a shaman. These categories are necessarily somewhat forced, for the complete picture is a conglomerate which reflects the inchoate structure of Klamath society in this preliminary period of change. The only group which was clear cut in its identification, and which had clearly benefited by contact with white culture, was the small group of agency employees, none of whom had any part in any phase of the entire revival.

During the latter half of the Dream Dance the agency belatedly recognized that a revival was going on and attempted to put a stop to it. Some of the agency employees, notably Dave Hill and Blow, made an effort to prevent Dream Dances, but they were unsuccessful as long as public sentiment was strongly behind the dances.

The Dream Dance at the Lower End came to a close with the acceptance of Christianity in 1878. The Klamath had been visited by a missionary as early as the tenure of Lalakes as head chief; Lalakes and a number of others were baptized at that time. Soon after the Modoc War a missionary preached in the open fields at Klamath Agency. In 1878, at the close of the Dream Dance at the Lower End, Agent Nickerson organized a Methodist church and the Indians built a church house. The response was immediate. Many Indians joined this church at once, although the greatest interest came a few years later under the administration of Emery.[24]

CONCLUSIONS

The religious revival of 1871–78 may now be placed in the total situation of change. It will be seen that all the peoples, on or near Klamath Reservation, who participated in the revival were in a preliminary period of change in which acceptance or rejection of white values was still tentative. Within every tribal group there was a division of opinion which was expressed in separate forms. Thus, the Paviotso were divided over their choice of residence; the Modoc were divided into localized factions on the basis of resistance to, or acceptance of, the fact of white conquest; and the Klamath, within a general framework of acceptance of white values, were divided as to what aspects of white culture were acceptable and confused by their lack of success in applying white skills. In all cases except the Paviotso, resistance to white encroachment, in the form of defiance of governmental authority, had brought retribution in one form or another. Owing to the lack of co-ordination between military and civil Indian policy, the Warner Valley Paviotso were able to waver in their choice of residence for seven years. The Tule Lake Modoc had been defeated in war. The Klamath, except for the shamans, accepted white encroachment and white values and skills without resistance. Yet, in the later period of revivalism, all the Klamath groups except the agency employees were losing, or had already lost, whatever benefits they originally derived from accepting white values and adopting white skills. In particular, they had been encouraged to assume responsibilities as individuals which, through no fault of theirs, they had been unable to meet; and at the same time the older mechanisms

[24] Cf. Kirk, *A History of the Klamath Indian Methodist Mission.*

for dealing with these responsibilities were in process of disintegration. Joint settlements were being divided; the responsibility of leadership was first centralized in the hands of a few men and then withdrawn; rituals of all kinds were in abeyance; a conscious effort was being made by the administration to decentralize all forms of leadership and responsibility and to put them into the hands of the heads of individual households, living on one-family farms, and tilling the soil as individual, responsible, American farmers. This process, which began as early as 1869, got well under way after the Modoc War, and by the time of the Dream Dance had brought failure to the Klamath farmers three years in succession. We know, therefore, that all members of the Indian community were in conflict with one another over acceptance of, or resistance to, white culture as it was presented to them, and we may well believe there was conflict in their own minds.

During this early and tentative stage of acculturation these people were presented with a doctrine and ritual which they accepted and reinterpreted. The doctrine embodied symbolisms of many kinds: assertions about the future; identifying symbols embracing group and self; demands for action; fantastic symbols of power. The ritual was foreign and was gradually modified in accord with local tradition. Subsequent to the revival, the Paviotso and Modoc returned to older, more stable ritual forms, while the Klamath accepted Methodist Christianity. But in all three groups the return to stability in the ritual life, in whatever form, coincided with acceptance and success in secular affairs connected with white values and techniques.

The basic problem presented at the outset of the investigation was defined as the relation between deprivation, experienced in the formation of the intercultural community, and participation in the revival. The response to deprivation by revivalism was only a portion of the total response, represented in individual cases by such other aspects of change as fighting, the adoption of agricultural skills, the decline of ritualism, etc. In order to define more clearly the relations between revivalism and deprivation, the relation of revivalism in the various groups under consideration to other aspects of change should be examined.

The Paviotso resisted white contact from the outset, but when their resistance met with effective counterresistance they pursued a passive course, merely dodging the soldiers as long as possible. In so doing they suffered much deprivation, but when it became too severe they returned to Klamath Reservation as a refuge. The Warner Valley group were unable to decide between their old home and Klamath Reservation and vacillated between them. All the Paviotso were subject to minimal cultural changes of all kinds. They quietly resisted all efforts to put them on farms, and they were regarded as too low in the cultural scale to be amenable to the introduction of democratic institutions. Their participation in the revival was minimal. Their doctrine contained no overtly aggressive assertions, either against whites or against themselves. They experienced no autistic visions and produced no hysterical symptoms. The revival ran its course in a short time and left no permanent residues. Its form was thoroughly in accord with their passive resistance to white culture. It contained no specific assertions about themselves or whites but was merely a revival of old forms and practices. It was anti-white only in the sense that it was nonwhite.

The Tule Lake Modoc represented that portion of the Modoc tribe which had selected the most aggressive course of action in the intercultural situation. They both resisted the whites and demanded concessions from them. They suffered extreme deprivation initially, although no more so than the reservation Modoc. Their participation in the revival was brief. Its symbolism, as accepted by them, was extremely aggressive and specific in its assertions. It contained both anti-white and anti-self elements, and was accompanied by hysterical symptoms and autistic fantasies. In both ritual and doctrine, the group symbol "Modoc" was enhanced to the detriment of the symbol "white." The course of the revival was principally an increase in ritual activity, accompanied by nonritual acts which were extremely aggressive, both against the self and against the outside world, and justified in the name of the collective symbol. This was in accord with the inclusion in this group of the aggressive and dissatisfied elements in the Modoc community. A quick test and rejection of the aggressive aspects of the ritual coincided with the outbreak of physical aggression—a course of action subsequently followed by retaliation and failure to get the desired end.

The reservation Modoc suffered deprivation in the initial period, particularly damage to the integrity of the collective symbol. It will be remembered that in the beginning this group followed Sconchin, who chose to accept government support of his position. After the initial resistance they chose a passive course of action, accepting the fact of white conquest and relying on governmental authority to retain what advantages had accrued to them in the early period of culture change. When they were offered the revival doctrine, they accepted the self-enhancing symbolism, gradually increasing the anti-white doctrine and simultaneously increasing the self-punishing aspects of the doctrine until the collective symbolism was abandoned and specific fears gave way to general anxiety. This general anxiety was relieved by the production of physical symptoms which were, in turn, relieved by pseudo-shamanistic treatment. The whole affair was concluded by incorporation of revival elements into aboriginal shamanism.

The members of this group were divided in their allegiance and experienced difficulty in making up their minds to remain on the reservation during the Modoc War. At one time they withdrew in a body but went only as far as Lost River, explaining to the agent that they had been afraid of the Klamath and had gone to Lost River to escape the work of Klamath shamans. Their choice of a course of action was evidently a source of emotional conflict, which may easily have been responsible for the generalized anxiety of the post-war period of revivalism.

This hypothesis is confirmed by the action of the Upper End Klamath, who participated in the revival in much the same way as the Modoc, but who produced no autism in the early phases, and only partially shared the anxiety phase of the revival. During the Dream Dance the Upper End Klamath rituals corresponded more closely to those of the Lower End Klamath.

Members of the latter group resisted the first white encroachment but were receptive to white culture when it was presented to them in an acceptable form at the hands of traders. During the early period of culture change which followed their trade contacts at The Dalles, Klamath society underwent a change in the status hierarchy on a basis of identification with white values and skills. Changes in this hierarchy corresponded closely with participation in the revival. By the time of the revival only one small group had received unequivocal benefits from identification with white values and acceptance of white skills. This group consisted of the agency employees. The other groups—chiefs, shamans, commoners, and slaves—all participated. However, they persisted in their basic attitude of faith in the future, in so far as it was identified with white culture.

The basic relation is therefore clear. Acceptance or rejection of white culture did not determine acceptance or rejection of the revival doctrine, but success or failure in gaining the ends anticipated in the acceptance or rejection of white culture did determine acceptance or rejection of the doctrine. Participants in the revival were people who in some measure had failed to derive the satisfactions they anticipated in following a particular course of action. In this sense they were deprived, and this, it appears, is the basic relation between deprivation and revivalism.

It will be seen that deprivation, in this sense, was experienced within the context of acceptance or rejection of white culture, and was experienced as damage to the integrity of both group and individual symbol. Both these aspects of deprivation were reflected in the doctrine and ritual of the revival. The Paviotso neither accepted nor rejected white culture but took a passive attitude of disinterest. The symbols of white aggression, values, and skills did not appear in any overt form in their doctrine. The Tule Lake Modoc resisted white encroachment and rejected white culture in an aggressive way. The Ghost Dance at Tule Lake was an aspect of aggressive resistance which was expressed in the symbolism of doctrine and ritual, used as an aggressive weapon against the whites, and rejected when it proved ineffectual. It has been pointed out that the Modoc experienced cultural changes secondary to those of the Klamath and were immune to the effects of reservation policy. The deprivation they suffered, therefore, was widespread and uniform throughout the population, and was associated with the group symbol. The level on which deprivation took place was reflected in the Ghost Dance doctrine.

The reservation Modoc were subject to the same initial deprivation as the Tule Lake Modoc. They suffered additional damage to the group symbol at the hands of a non-white group—the Klamath. Before the war they engaged in a revival with strong group and anti-white symbols. During the war they were undecided about their course of action and later produced a revival which was oriented around symptoms of anxiety. Thus in their revival they reflected the damage to the group symbol at the hands of the whites, but not at the hands of the Klamath, and later they produced symptoms appropriate to their conflict over alternative modes of action. The fact that no anti-Klamath doctrine appeared fixes the character of the revival as an anti-white movement. There was an anti-Klamath reaction, nonritual in its nature, which, aside from the flight to Lost River, took the form of gossip and hostile anecdotes which are remembered to this day.

The Upper End Klamath and the reservation Modoc accepted the earlier doctrines in much the same form, except that the Klamath were less aggressive in all their manifestations—in the matter of anti-white doctrine, autism, hysteria, and assertions of danger in the ritual. During the Earthlodge cult they accepted the aggressive, anti-white, and antiself doctrines in the same way as the Modoc—elements which the Lower End Klamath deleted. This was not in accord with the character of Upper End Klamath experiences. In all phases of the revival except the Earthlodge cult, the Upper End Klamath combined elements characteristic of both Klamath and Modoc, but in this instance they pursued a course very close to that of the Modoc. The circumstances which determined their choice are only partially known. In this instance the fact that there was only one dance house on the Upper End, at which joint Modoc and Klamath rituals were held, must be taken into account.

The Lower End Klamath were receptive to white culture from the beginning. They were not removed, engaged in no armed conflict, and were eager and willing to accept the ways of white culture whenever they were shown them. At an early date they identified their future with the symbols of white culture. In the revival, as in their other reactions to white contact, they preserved this optimistic outlook. In both the Ghost Dance and the Earthlodge cult they deleted anti-white doctrines and specific aggressive assertions about their own future in its relation to the anticipated world-event. Even after they had attempted to become individual farmers and discovered that their attempt had failed to reward them, they did not express pessimism about their future, only confusion about which of the available roles they should select.

It will be seen, then, that:

1. Deprivation on Klamath Reservation occurred both as a result of initial attack and as a by-product of acculturation.

2. When both these aspects of deprivation are taken into account, it is seen that deprivation coincided closely with participation in the revival.

3. Deprivation through acculturation occurred primarily as an incongruity between values and the techniques for attaining them. Skills were introduced which brought no rewards, and values were introduced without appropriate skills for acquiring them.

4. Deprivation occurred, therefore, in groups which accepted, as well as those which rejected, the symbols of white culture.

5. Hence the basic fact of deprivation was the denial of satisfactions anticipated and sought for by resisting or accepting the symbols of white culture.

6. The groups which suffered the most aggressive attack initially accepted or produced ritual symbols which either (a) threatened aggressive retaliation against the whites, (b) named the agency of retaliation as an impersonal cosmic event, (c) protected themselves from destruction by the performance of ritual and belief in the doctrine, or (d) engaged in self-punishing ritual practices.

7. The only group which had extensively taken over white values and skills—the Klamath—produced fantasies which ex-

pressed (*a*) their acceptance of the roles defined by white administrators, and (*b*) their dissatisfaction with the benefits attached to their own roles.

8. The only group which had unequivocally benefited by identification with, and acceptance of, white skills and values—the Indian employees at the agency—not only took no part in the revival but attempted to suppress it.

9. The course of the revival as a whole followed a progression from enhancement of group symbols, group participation, and attention focused on doctrine to enhancement of personal symbols, individual ritual, and attention focused on the self.

In view of these facts the hypothesis set forth in the introduction to this paper should be modified as follows: *Nativistic cults arise among deprived groups. Deprivation may occur within the framework of either acceptance or rejection of values and skills associated with white culture. Revivalism, however, is only one aspect of a total response to white culture. Revivalism is that portion of the response which expresses in ritual symbolism the basic attitudes of acceptance or rejection of white culture, feelings of loss or damage, aggressive retaliation in response to deprivation suffered, and self-punishing assertions and practices in proportion to aggressive retaliation.*

FROM LAFITAU TO RADCLIFFE-BROWN

A SHORT HISTORY OF THE STUDY
OF SOCIAL ORGANIZATION*

SOL TAX

* Originally written as Part I of my Ph.D. dissertation, "Primitive Social Organization with Some Description of the Social Organization of the Fox Indians" (Chicago, 1935). I have made no substantive changes nor any attempt to carry the history beyond 1934. I have made a few editorial changes, including some to take into account the passage of time (deaths of persons, etc.) since this history was written.

FROM LAFITAU TO RADCLIFFE-BROWN

SOL TAX

I. FORERUNNERS

Reporting his experiences in eastern North America, John Lederer, an early English adventurer, wrote in 1672 concerning the Tutelo, an eastern Siouan tribe:

> From four women, viz., *Pash, Sopoy, Askarin* and *Maraskarin*, they derive the race of mankind; which they therefore divide into four Tribes, distinguished under those several names. They very religiously observe the degrees of Marriage, which they limit not to distance of Kindred, but difference of Tribes, which are continued in the issue of the females: now for two of the same tribe to match, is abhorred as Incest, and punished with great severity.[1]

This, to my knowledge, is the first mention in modern ethnological history of three phenomena—clans, matriliny, exogamy—peculiar to the study of what in anthropology is called "social organization." A fourth, that of kinship terminology, remained unbroached until forty-two years later,[2] when Joseph Françoise Lafitau, a French Jesuit missionary, described the kinship system of the Iroquois—hitting by chance on the archetype of the "classificatory system," which was to become a catch phrase in the infant science a century and a half later:

> Among the Iroquois and the Hurons, all the children of a Cabin regard their mothers' sisters as their mothers, and their mothers' brothers as their uncles; in the same way they give the name of father to all their fathers' brothers and that of aunt to their fathers' sisters. All of the children on the side of the mother and her sisters and of the father and his brothers they regard as equal to brothers and sisters, but as regards the children of their uncles and aunts—that is to say, of their mothers' brothers and their fathers' sisters—they treat them only on the footing of cousins although they may be as closely related as those whom they regard as brothers and sisters. In the third generation the grand-uncles and grand-aunts become grandfathers and grandmothers of the children of

---

[1] *The Discoveries of John Lederer*, pp. 10–11.

[2] Although Andrew Lang says that Nicolaus Damascenus, who lived in the first century A.D., described the classificatory system of kinship terminology for the Galactophagi (article, "Family," *Encyclopaedia Britannica* [12th ed.], X, 160). I am dealing only with modern researches, however.

445

those whom they call nephews and nieces. This continues always in the descending line according to the same rule.[3]

Such interesting observations remained, however, unnoticed and unused. Early explorers brought back, during the seventeenth and eighteenth centuries, many more accounts of strange customs relating to marriage, the family, and such institutions as clans; oddly, kinship terminologies were rarely recorded, if, indeed, noticed.[4] Almost a century passed before Lafitau's observation was repeated in print. In 1823, James Edwin, who led an expedition into the West, described the kinship system of the Omaha in these words:

The designations by which the Omawhaws distinguish their various degrees of consanguinity are somewhat different from ours; children universally address their father's brother by the title of *father*, and their mother's brother by that of *uncle*; their mother's sister is called *mother* and their father's sister *aunt*. The children of brothers and sisters address each other by the titles of brother and sister . . . . a man applies the title of We-hun-guh, or sister-in-law to his wife's sister . . . . he also calls his wife's brother's daughter Wahunguh, and may in like manner take her to wife. . . . . A man distinguishes his wife's brother by the

[3] *Mœurs des sauvages amériquains comparées aux mœurs des premiers temps*, I, 552–53. Liberties have been taken with the translation; the French is: "... parmi les Iroquois, & parmi les Hurons, tous les enfans d'une Cabane regardent comme leurs mères, toutes les sœurs de leurs mères, & comme leurs oncles, tous les frères de leurs mères: par la même raison, ils donnes le nom de Pères à tous les frères de leurs pères, & de tantes à toutes les sœurs de leurs pères. Tous les enfans du côte de la mère & de ses sœurs, du père & de ses frères, se regardent entr'eux également comme frères & sœurs; mais par rapport aux enfans de leurs oncles & de leurs tantes, c'est-à-dire, des frères de leurs mères, & ses sœurs de leurs pères, ils ne les traitent que sur le pied de cousins, quoiqu'ils soient dans le même degré de paranté, que ceux qu'ils regardent comme leurs frères & leurs sœurs. Dans le troisième Génération cela change; les grands oncles & les grandes tantes redeviennent grands-pères & grandes-mères, des enfans de ceux qu'ils appelloient neveux, & niéces. Cela se continuë toûjours ainsi en descendant, selon la même regle."

[4] Lewis H. Morgan says: "It is a singular fact, but one which I have frequently verified, that those Americans who are most thoroughly versed in Indian languages, from a long residence in the Indian country, are unacquainted with their system of relationship except its general features. It does not appear to have attracted their attention sufficiently to have led to an investigation of its details, even as a matter of curiosity. Not one of the number have I ever found who, from his own knowledge, was able to fill out even a small part of the schedule. . . . . The same is also true of the returned missionaries from Asia, Africa, and the Islands of the Pacific . . . ." (*Systems of Consanguinity and Affinity of the Human Family*, p. 135).

title of "Tahong," or brother-in-law, and his son also by the same designation. He calls the wife of his brother-in-law "cong-ha" or mother-in-law. A woman calls her husband's brother "Wish-e-e," or brother-in-law, and speaks of his children as her own. . . . . Men who marry sisters address each other by the title of brother. All women who marry the same individual, even if not previously related, apply to each other the title of sister.[5]

Edwin at the same time went further and described some of the behavior patterns in the relationships, notably the parent-in-law avoidance. Yet, for all these preliminary observations, again decades were to pass before kinship systems were to obtrude themselves upon the scientific world.

Meanwhile, such an important concept as that of the totemic clan was crystallizing. Albert Gallatin, the great American statesman, who in 1842 founded the American Ethnological Society of New York and who may be called the first ethnologist in America (if not, indeed, in the world), redescribed exogamy, as occurring in the Southeastern tribes, and gave currency to the phenomenon. Moreover, he first adapted to use the Ojibwa term "totem." This is especially noteworthy because there was no chance observation in his case but rather a study of the literature; moreover, he suggested comparisons of a number of tribes. He writes, concerning the Choctaws, Cherokees, Creeks, Natches, and others:

Every nation was divided into a number of clans, varying in the several nations from three to eight to ten, the members of which respectively were dispersed indiscriminately throughout the whole nation. It has been fully ascertained that the inviolable regulations, by which these clans were perpetuated amongst the southern nations, were, first, that no man could marry in his own clan; secondly, that every child belongs to his or her mother's clan. Among the Choctaws, there are two great divisions, each of which is subdivided into four clans; and no man can marry in any of the four clans belonging to his division. The restriction amongst the Cherokees, the Creeks, and the Natches, does not extend beyond the clan to which the man belongs.[6]

And again: "Whether the *Totem*, or family name of the Chippewaya, descends in a regular manner, or is arbitrarily imposed by the father, has not been clearly examined."[7]

[5] *Account of an Expedition from Pittsburgh to the Rocky Mountains*, p. 329.

[6] *Archaeologia Americana*, p. 109.

[7] *Ibid.*, p. 110. Gallatin obtained his Ojibwa information from *Tanner's Narrative*, p. 313.

Comparative ethnology in the subject of social organization could now begin. An early explorer of northwestern Australia, Sir George Grey, after making independent observations of the tribes of that region, proceeded to compare his discoveries with those reported by Gallatin:

One of the most remarkable facts connected with the natives, is that they are divided into certain great families, all the members of which bear the same names, as a family, or second name: the principal branches of these families, so far as I have been able to ascertain, are the Ballaroke, Tdondarup, Ngotak, Nagarnoek, Nogonyuk, Mongalung, Narrangur. But in different districts the members of these families give a local name to the one to which they belong, which is understood in that district, to indicate some particular branch of the principal family. . . . .

These family names are common over a great portion of the continent. . . . .

These family names are perpetuated, and spread through the country, by the operation of two remarkable laws:

1st. That children of either sex, always take the family name of their mother.

2nd. That a man cannot marry a woman of his own family name.

But not the least singular circumstance connected with these institutions, is their coincidence with those of the North American Indians, which are thus stated in the *Archaeologia Americana.* . . . .[8]

Grey then quotes fully from Gallatin's statements and remarks that animal and vegetable crests and family names are common to both. He wondered about the origin of these institutions though he did not speculate on them. Grey showed himself a worthy precursor of modern ethnologists, for, in addition to his general observations, he published genealogies, with data on clans and marriages.

Yet, one cannot say that the science of social organization and kinship was launched. While it is true that Henry Schoolcraft brought together considerable information on the American Indians, including some on clans,[9] one need merely catalogue the ethnological developments that took *no account* of such observations to see that the study of society in these respects was, prior

[8] *Journal of Two Expeditions in North-West and Western Australia,* II, 225–27.

[9] In *Historical and Statistical Information Respecting the Indian Tribes of the United States,* he says: "That feature of the organization of tribes which consists of their being associated in clans, or what has been more appropriately denominated the *totemic tie* . . . . is designed rather to produce fraternity and the means of at once recognizing it, than for any practical operations upon their simple theory of government" (Part I [Philadelphia, 1851], p. 193).

to 1860, embryonic. To see what was being done in ethnology, one can examine two sets of evidence: the general books on that subject and the journals of the anthropological and ethnological societies. The first general treatises were concerned with the natural history of mankind, including biological, linguistic, cultural, and sociological phases of life. Thus Prichard, for instance, surveyed peoples all over the world, and included such vague items on social organization as: "The Rejangs [Sumatra] live in villages under the government of magistrates subject to a king of the whole country. They are separated into clans, or tribes, or kindred."[10] And, although Van Amringe the next year published considerable material on topics such as the position of women and the relations of sexes in different parts of the world, there is nothing remotely selective or interpretive about it.[11] In the next decade the accumulating knowledge about clans, totemism, and kinship still failed to penetrate works such as Latham's *Descriptive Ethnology* (1859).[12] Theodore Waitz, too, in his great work, *Anthropologie der Naturvölker*, devotes a few pages to social organization, mostly to the matters of chastity and romantic love and the degradation of women-as-property among primitive peoples; on such things as kinship there is nothing, and on social structure only this:

> In passing from sexual and family relations to the social condition of uncivilized nations, but little can be said that is generally characteristic. Families generally live near each other independently under their own chief, gradually forming little societies, without any form of government, until internal dissensions or external attacks compel them to unite and submit to the sway of one or more individuals who have proved their prowess or their wisdom. Such peoples may, however, remain for a long time without any organization, oscillating between a state of perfect independence and one of despotism. It is an erroneous view to consider this oscillation among rude nations as degrees of social development, instead of attributing it to its natural cause.[13]

[10] Prichard, *Researches into the Physical History of Mankind*, V, 72.

[11] Van Amringe, *An Investigation of the Theories of the Natural History of Man*.

[12] J. F. McLennan (*Studies in Ancient History*) attributes to him the discovery of clans and exogamy.

[13] From Vol. I, edited and translated into English by J. F. Collingwood as *Introduction to Anthropology*, pp. 301–2.

This paragraph is labeled, in the Table of Contents, "Societies: Clanship," so that, while it is unsatisfactory to argue from negative evidence, it seems clear that Waitz's concern with clans bears little relation to the problems that have since beset anthropologists.[14]

Evidence for the view that the study of social organization was not crystallized before the middle sixties is even more conclusive (if equally negative) when the journals are examined.

The anthropological societies always combined physical and social studies of man. From the beginning there was, too, no dearth of accounts of different native tribes. But never in this period was there even a general discussion on any topic relating to social organization. In fact, although the *Journal of the Ethnological Society of London* began publication in 1848 and the *Journal of the Anthropological Society of London* in 1863, it was not until 1866 that there is any discussion on any of the general topics that later occupied the attention of students of kinship. Then there appeared in the *Anthropological Review* a summary of a paper on marriage and exogamy read by E. B. Tylor before the British association. Before 1865 there was nothing of the sort.[15] What happened in the middle sixties was a mushroom

[14] Compare this, for example, with Tylor's *Researches into the Early History of Mankind*, where information on clans, exogamy, and rules of descent (pp. 279–86), marriage by capture (pp. 286–88), parent-in-law taboos (pp. 288–91), and couvade (pp. 291–302) is collected and dealt with in quite modern fashion.

[15] The early societies and their publications may be tabulated thus:

1843–71....	Ethnological Society of London	Journal Transactions	1848–71 1861–70
1860——...	Société d'Anthropologie de Paris	Bulletins et Mémoires	1860——
1863–71....	Anthropological Society of London	Anthropological Review Memoirs Transactions Journal of Anthropology	1863–70 1863–69 1863–70 1870
1873–75....	London Anthropological Society	Anthropologie	1873–75
1871——...	Anthropological Institute of Great Britain and Ireland (since, "Royal" prefixed)	Journal	1871——

In the first volume of the *Journal of the Ethnological Society*, there were four ethnographic articles, all of which included some data on marriage and the family. So with succeeding volumes. But there was nothing general in the early numbers. Typical is the contrast between two articles of William Ridley: the first appeared in the *JES* in 1856 (IV, 289–93) on the Zamilaroi tribe and in-development of the study of social organization which in the course of a few years saw the fruition of the first great stage of ethnological history.

II. HISTORICAL EVOLUTION

It appears that four relatively independent factors combined to give us what might be called the "historical evolutionary school" of anthropology. First, there was the intellectual temper of the century—the materialistic philosophy, which saw Comte and Spencer seeking a positive science of society—together with the encouragement and analogy of the progress in biology that culminated with Darwin. Second were the researches into classical and protohistorical times by men like Bachofen and Maine, culminating in their evolutionary interpretations of ancient and contemporary society. Third, there were the accounts of curious customs brought back from other continents by the growing number of travelers that became the stimulus and the subject matter of those historians to whom they suggested evolutionary sequences, the first of whom was J. F. McLennan. Fourth was the influence of the out-and-out ethnography of Morgan and the interest in kinship—which led to his evolutionary explanation of it—of which it was the beginning.

These four factors were not entirely independent; in a general way, the first was a condition of the other three, but to what extent and in what way, it would be fruitless to inquire. If one is speaking of the theory of social evolution itself, it can be said that Spencer alone conceived the entire framework; but if one is thinking of the development of the theory in respect to social

---

cluded the names of the sections and the marriage and descent rules, as well as a vocabulary *without* kinship terms, and throughout no apparent evidence of further interest. Another appeared in 1872 in the *JAI* (II, 257–91) on "Australian Languages and Traditions," and this contains kinship terms, marriage rules, descent, classes, etc., *plus* comparisons, reference to Morgan's terminology, etc.

In Vol. II (1863) of the *Transactions of the Ethnological Society of London* appears Bailey's article on the "Wild Tribes of the Veddahs of Ceylon," which includes a good discussion of cross-cousin marriage; but this is hardly comparable in theoretical scope to Lubbock's article in Vol. VI (1868) on "The Origin of Civilization." So it is in all the publications; theory appeared *after* 1865.

organization particularly, Spencer properly takes the place—merely part of the background—that has been assigned to him. Again, if one is thinking of the genesis of the science of social organization, Bachofen, Maine, and McLennan may be lumped together as having independently contributed much the same thing, while Morgan stands apart for his distinctive contribution.

Maine, Bachofen, McLennan.—Sir Henry Maine published *Ancient Law* in 1861, the same year that Bachofen's *Das Mutterrecht* appeared, and there was a great deal else in common between them. Both were jurists; both drew their source material from Indo-European protohistory and history; both adopted a strictly historical point of view, purporting to show that there was a development of domestic rule and the family from earlier stages to the family as we know it. But there are striking differences as well, for while Maine was willing to limit his conclusions to the so-called "Aryans," Bachofen felt that he was making a universal generalization; and whereas Maine's conclusions were that, underlying the Indo-European family system, there was a patriarchal family, Bachofen contended that mother-right preceded the patriarchate everywhere.

Maine (1822–88) was primarily a comparative jurist, an authority on Roman law. He was never an evolutionist in the sense that some of his contemporaries were, for he neither delineated a series of "stages" of human history nor believed that there is evidence to warrant such procedure. "So far as I am aware, there is nothing in the recorded history of society to justify the belief that, during that vast chapter of its growth which is wholly unwritten, the same transformations of social constitution succeeded one another everywhere, uniformly if not simultaneously."[16] Nevertheless, he believed that all societies whose histories are known were once organized on the model of the Hebrew patriarchate, hence his "patriarchal theory," which he attributed, however, to Plato (*Laws* iii. 680) and Aristotle (*Politics* i. 2).

In 1852 Maine began a series of lectures in which he laid the

[16] Maine, *Dissertations on Early Law and Custom.*

foundation for his *Ancient Law*, the work which made him immediately famous. His interest throughout was in jurisprudence, which he attacked from the historical point of view, and only incidentally did his *Ancient Law* contain material bearing on the evolution of the family. Here he wrote: "The rudiments of the social state, so far as they are known to us at all, are known through testimony of three sorts—accounts by contemporary observers of civilizations less advanced than their own, the records which particular races have preserved concerning their primitive history, and ancient law."[17] And, although he made use of all three sources, his chief dependence was on the last. But he did not study ancient law to discover the "rudiments of the social state" so much as to determine the meaning of law in general. McLennan especially set out to disprove the patriarchal theory; and in 1883, in refuting a posthumous work of his antagonist, Maine became, perhaps, more of an evolutionist than he had ever been, denying theories of original promiscuity and "the horde" and claiming that matrilineal descent must have come later as a result of a disproportion of the sexes. By 1883, of course, the argument on such matters had passed its climax; the decision, if any, had gone against Maine. In any event, Maine's influence in the history of ethnology was comparatively slight, owing perhaps to his conservatism in a very extravagant era.

J. J. Bachofen, a Swiss, was a student chiefly of classical antiquity. The traditions and the mythology of the Greeks and Romans were the chief sources of his theories, for he saw in them definite evidence of the importance of relationship through females. In the Orestes myth, for example, the mother-child relationship is sacred. Bachofen noted also that Herodotus had described the Lycians as having a sort of matriarchate; and it appeared to him that the Spartans had traces of such an organization. These were the sources for Bachofen's theory. Later (*Antiquarische Briefe* [1880]), he discussed the Nairs of India as a living example of the matriarchate. He was convinced from such

[17] *Ancient Law*, p. 116.

evidence that matriarchal preceded patriarchal organizations of society, and his theoretical endeavors were spent in explaining how and why the change came about. To do so, he set up an evolutionary scheme: first, there was no marriage, or some sort of communal marriage; then the women, morally revolted by this state of affairs, established their own rule; but, since motherhood is very material, in the course of history the spiritual, creative influence of the father came to be recognized, and mother-right was overthrown. Bachofen was really the first of the family-evolutionists, and, on the Continent especially, his influence has been inestimable.

John Ferguson McLennan wrote:

> It was in the spring of 1866 that I first heard of *Das Mutterrecht* and then I found that I had been anticipated by Herr Bachofen in this discovery. No two routes, however, could be more widely apart than those by which Bachofen and I arrived at this conclusion. I was led to it by reasoning on the exigencies of my explanation of the origin of the form of capture. To Bachofen the fact seems to have revealed itself as everywhere underlying the traditions, and especially the mythologies, of antiquity which his prodigious learning comprehended in all their vast details.[18]

Indeed, that sums up the difference. McLennan's *Primitive Marriage* was published in 1865, four years later than *Das Mutterrecht*. Both were concerned with the evolution of marriage and types of descent, and both saw in human history a single line of development. But, except that he was anticipated by Bachofen and except that in the German-speaking world Bachofen probably had more influence (on Freud, for example), McLennan played a more important part in the history of the study of social organization. McLennan not only set forth an evolutionary scheme of the development of society, but he used much ethnographic evidence and introduced a terminology ("exogamy," "endogamy," for example) that has survived. Besides the questions of descent, totemism, and class, he drew attention to the importance of marriage regulations, marriage by capture, female infanticide, etc., and worked them into his theory of social evolution:

[18] *Studies in Ancient History*, p. 391 n.

Whether the system of kinship through females only prevailed universally at first or not, it must have prevailed wherever exogamy prevailed—exogamy and the consequent practice of capturing wives. Certainty as to fathers is impossible where mothers are stolen from their first lords, and liable to be re-stolen before the birth of the children. And as exogamy and polyandry are referable to one and the same cause—a want of balance between the sexes—we are forced to regard all the exogamous races as having originally been polyandrous.[19]

And:

At the outset of our argument we saw that if the system of kinship through females could only be shown to exist, or to have existed, it must be accounted a more archaic system of kinship than the system of relationship through males . . . . and that to prove its existence on such a scale as to entitle it to rank among the normal phenomena of human development would be to prove it the most ancient system of kinship. We now submit that we have amply established our proposition. . . . . We have seen (further) that polyandry must be accepted as a stage in the progress towards marriage proper and the patriarchal system. The lower forms of polyandry we have found to be accompanied by the system of kinship through females only. We have seen polyandry change its form till it allowed of kinship through males, and then die away into an obligation on the younger brothers in turn to espouse the widow of the eldest brother.[20]

McLennan, like Bachofen, postulated an original state of promiscuity, for, he argued, the father would then have been unknown and this fact would account for tracing descent through females, which he found to be prevalent. Following the state of promiscuity, or possibly substituted for it, came the family based on polyandry, which could also explain the origin of matrilineal descent. Polyandry, he argued, was connected with female infanticide, making women a scarcity. The very scarcity of women, again, led to the capture of girls from other tribes and finally to the rule that only women of other tribes were fit wives (exogamy). Originally, of course, the exogamic groups were matrilineal.

McLennan thought that he could see survivals of descent through females, of totemism, even of promiscuity, in classical and Indian lore; but his chief evidence was the survival of all these and of marriage by capture reported from living tribes in all parts of the world. McLennan was the first student of social

[19] *Primitive Marriage*, reprinted in *Studies in Ancient History*, p. 124.

[20] *Ibid.*, p. 123.

organization to use ethnographic materials as the basis for his argument.

Of all topics which are today lumped together as "social organization," McLennan missed only one of importance—that of kinship systèms. That was to await Morgan; and only after the American introduced the subject a few years later, did McLennan include it in his discussions. Then he attacked Morgan, an attack apparently sufficiently convincing to keep the subject of kinship terminology from its proper sphere for many years.

Morgan.—With Lewis H. Morgan historical evolution reached its climax, while at the same time the subject matter of social organization was finally rounded out. Morgan's great contribution was his virtual discovery of the variety of kinship terminologies; his use of them to reconstruct the history of society, while at the time it seemed most important, must now be considered comparatively insignificant. Since Morgan's positive influence in the study of kinship has been greater than that of Bachofen, Maine, and McLennan together, his work deserves some detail.

While engaged in what was perhaps the first explicit ethnographic research in America, Lewis Morgan observed the peculiar kinship system of the Iroquois;[21] believing that it was unique, he thought little about it. In 1858 he discovered that the Ojibwa (of quite different linguistic stock) had the same system; this curious fact led him to investigate further, and he soon came to believe that it was universal in America. Aided by the United States State Department, he sent a questionnaire to government agents and missionaries all over the world, requesting them to send him the kinship terms in use. In addition, Morgan himself collected terminologies of a number of American Indian tribes.

It is apparent that Morgan was at first interested in tracing racial history; he believed that the fact that the American Indians, even though now linguistically and physically divergent, had the same kinship system was proof that they are genetically related. He sent out the questionnaires to see if he could dis-

---

[21] *The League of the Iroquois* was published in 1851.

cover to whom the Indians as a whole were related and whence they came. While languages change, he pointed out, ways of reckoning relationships remain constant. "We may . . . . be able to . . . . re-associate nations and races, whose original connection has passed from human knowledge."[22] It is evident from such a statement that (1) Morgan was at this time thinking in terms of nonevolutionary historical reconstruction; (2) he was, from the beginning, convinced that systems of kinship terminology remain the same after other things (such as language) have changed; (3) he was already using a circular argument that was to stay with him: that kinship terms can be used to reconstruct history because they remain constant, we know they remain constant because they are widespread among people who once were one and who have otherwise changed, and we know they were once one because the kinship systems are the same.

Morgan, when he set out to collect kinship terms, was not an evolutionist. He wrote that "the children are of the tribe [meaning 'clan'] of the *mother*, in a majority of the nations; but the rule, if anciently universal, is not so at the present day."[23] By "anciently universal" he meant at some period after the clans had diverged from the common ancestor; had he had the evolutionary notions he developed later, he would not have questioned the universality of such rules. Although it is easy to make much of a stray statement, the whole tenor of Morgan's writing at this time was nonevolutionary.

When the schedules were returned to him, he began to organize the material; and then it was that he worked out the theory that was to bring him fame.[24] While waiting for the government to publish his work, he became afraid that he would be anticipated and read a preview before the American Academy of

[22] *Circular in Reference to the Degrees of Relationship among Different Nations*, p. 14.

[23] *Ibid.*, p. 13.

[24] Some account of the friends who influenced Morgan in the working-out of his theories is contained in his biography, *Lewis Henry Morgan: Social Evolutionist*, by Bernard J. Stern. There is excellent material in this book, but to a student of social organization possibly valuable interpretations are lacking.

Arts and Sciences.[25] Although the Preface to *Systems of Consanguinity and Affinity of the Human Family* was dated January, 1866, the work was not published until 1870.[26] *Systems* completed the plateau of historical evolutionism, and at the same time it rounded out the subject matter of the science of social organization.

Systems is a contribution that ranks with any in ethnology, both because it bares a tremendous amount of factual material and because it draws inferences from it that, fallacious as the gross argument may be, contain a number of ideas that have found a permanent place in the science. If for nothing else than that Morgan began the practice of recording terminologies systematically, he should be remembered; but even to the detail of getting the terms in relation to a speaker, and in the first person, he has been followed to this day.

The first great result of his schedules was that he saw an important distinction between two general types of systems: the one that he found in America,[27] which he now called "classificatory," and the one that typifies the Semitic and Celtic languages —where all relatives are carefully distinguished by the terms "father," "mother," "sister," "brother," "son," "daughter," "grandfather," "grandmother," "grandson," "granddaughter," and combinations of these terms, so that a type of cousin would be called "my mother's sister's daughter," for example, or "my father's sister's granddaughter"—which he called "descriptive." The terms "classificatory" and "descriptive" have caused confusion, but most of the confusion was in the minds of writers later than Morgan, who was himself aware that English, for example, has nondescriptive features (such as the term "cousin" or "uncle") but who nevertheless appreciated the distinction that is, in fact, there. It may be that the distinction is overrated in importance, but that remains to be proved.

[25] *A Conjectural Solution of the Origin of the Classificatory System of Relationship.*

[26] "Smithsonian Institution Contributions to Knowledge."

[27] Cf. Lafitau's description of Iroquois, pp. 445–46 of this paper.

Within the classificatory systems, Morgan made a further distinction. He found that some systems (like that of Hawaii) made no distinctions whatsoever except on the basis of generation and sex, so that the siblings of both the father and mother are all called "father" and "mother," and their children all "brother" and "sister," and *their* children all "son" and "daughter," and so on; this he called the "Malayan system." On the other hand, the systems in America and in parts of Asia make a distinction between parallel and cross-lines, i.e., between the father's brothers' and mother's sisters' lines as one group, and the father's sisters' and mother's brothers' lines as another. These systems he called the "Turanian" (in Asia) and the "Ganowanian" (in America).

Morgan's first problem was to explain the differences. He first noticed that, broadly, the classificatory system is of value to a small tribe, for it tends toward unity, while, on the other hand, such a system would be harmful to a society such as ours, where the inheritance of property is so important. Such an observation, which in modern days would be termed "functional," was to him of minor importance; for he recognized that kinship systems cannot always be tied functionally with the social structure, since—although Morgan's first assumption is that kinship systems cannot be made out of whole cloth but must always fit the societies in which they grow—he believed that kinship systems change very slowly and "it is rendered not improbable that they might survive changes of social condition sufficiently radical to overthrow the primary ideas in which they originated."[28] Kinship systems must always have originated in a social system of a type that would produce such a terminology, but the kinship terminology is likely to survive after the social system has passed; therefore, he thought that one can reconstruct social systems from the kinship terminologies and *at the same time explain the variations in kinship terminology that we now find.* So he reconstructed history in the first place to explain the terminology, but more important, as an end in itself, with the terminology as the proof of the history.

[28] *Systems*, p. 15.

Anyone who supposes that Morgan reached such conclusions without an argumentative tussle has not read *Systems*. One must read his arguments with the knowledge that (1) he was, from the beginning, interested in reconstructing history, and that alone, and, further, that (2) he was convinced, without raising the question or trying to prove it, that kinship systems must arise in connection with social systems (and cannot be diffused as traits in themselves). The latter and the point that kinship terminologies can survive the causes that gave them rise are all that he assumed; and it may be said here that both those assumptions have today a tremendous body of evidence in their support.

With that background, Morgan asks: Can the classificatory system (he does not try to account for descriptive systems because he considers them natural and logical in the societies in which they are now found) be accounted for (1) by causes and institutions now operative in different societies (and if the answer is "Yes," the matter loses historical importance, for it might then have grown up again and again), or (2) can it be accounted for by any supposed antecedent condition of society? If so, the classificatory system "must be treated as a transmitted system from the earliest epoch of its complete establishment, and its origin would be contemporaneous with the introduction of the customs, or the birth of the institutions, from which it sprung" (*Systems*, p. 474).

The first essential for historian Morgan was to answer the first possibility in the negative, and he proceeded to do so in the following way: by analyzing the social conditions in societies today that *might* account for the growth of the classificatory system and showing that they are insufficient. First, he pointed out, there are two possible external causes that suggest themselves: (*a*) the use of the band of kin for mutual protection; this would tend to draw the relatives together, but, since it would not account for the peculiar *way* they are drawn together as exemplified by the classificatory terminology that we find, it cannot account for the system; (*b*) clan (he calls it "tribal") organization will account for some parts of the system (such as, in a patrilineal society, the merging of the father and father's brother who are in the same clan, and of the father's brother's children and one's own siblings, since they are all in one's own clan), but it would not account for other parts of the system, such as the merging of one's brother's son with one's own son in a matrilinear society, where they may be of different clans. Second, he went on, there might be *internal* causes that would originate the classificatory system again and again; such are polygyny, or polyandry and the levirate, which can explain parts of the system (the parallel lines) but not all of it; another reason why Morgan rejected these internal causes is that the number of people in any society affected by these customs is not great enough to account for the origin of the terminology. Such customs have, however, he pointed out, helped to perpetuate the kinship terminology that arose earlier and from other causes. So Morgan rejected the possibility that these kinship systems could have arisen over and over again from one cause or another. And, of course, if they could have arisen but once, they are useful in tracing history.

Although it is difficult to prove that Morgan's conclusion must be rejected, the tendency is to believe that classificatory systems have arisen independently (and, of course, a much greater complexity and lack of uniformity are now recognized). If Morgan was right, however, and the theory of several independent origins of the classificatory system is discarded, the next question is, Must one accept Morgan's alternative—are all the peoples with classificatory systems historically connected? Yes, but not necessarily genetically related, for (*a*) the peoples *may* have had a common ancestry, with both the social organization and the kinship terminology that go with it, and, diverging, have kept the terminology, or (*b*) the peoples may *not* have had a common source, but the kinship terminologies may have diffused independently with or without the concomitant social organization that gave it rise. Morgan accepted condition *a* without considering *b*. Morgan believed in unilinear evolution in the sense that he thought that at one time all people were one, had a uniform culture, of course, and, before or after diverging, gradually changed their cultures in somewhat the same direction. The Ganowanian family came to America "with the blood stream." (Morgan, no doubt, was confused about culture and biology, but, fortunately, it does not hamper his argument.) Morgan 's next step was to postulate the kind of social organization that would give the Malayan type of kinship; then the kind that would give the Turanian and Ganowanian types. But he could not explain the latter in terms of their social organization alone, but on the basis of that plus the fact that it was a modification of the Malayan. That is the reason why he had to have an "evolution"; for, if he could explain each separately, they might have been independently developed without causal connection. This is the secret of his evolutionary scheme—this, rather than the fact that he tried to start from the opposite of monogamy and work up, as some have cynically said.

What sort of social organization must have existed back in the days when all the people who now have the classificatory system were one and when that system originated? That became Morgan's problem. But, first of all, which kinship system was older, the Malayan or Turanian? Morgan's answer was that the Malayan was older, for the Turanian could be explained only as an outgrowth of the other. Specifically, then, what kind of social organization could possibly demand the Malayan type of nomenclature? Morgan's answer was "the communal family." If a group of brothers married a group of sisters, and they all lived together with their children, one would expect them to use the Malayan terminology.[29] What kind of family life, next, could account for the Turanian and Ganowanian families? Morgan

[29] Because, of course, all the men of the generation above would be either one's own father or stepfather (mother's husband)—and in this case it would be impossible to tell which—and thus called "father"; all the women of the generation above, either one's own mother or stepmother, would thus be called "mother"; reciprocally, and for the same reasons, all relatives of the generation below would be called "children"; all relatives of one's own generation would be full siblings, half-siblings, or step-siblings and would thus be called "brother" or "sister." A condition much like this was reported from Hawaii and served as Morgan's model and proof. It should be noted that Morgan's position was *not* that a person would be ignorant of his mother's identity, as has been claimed; rather that a stepmother would be called "mother" because of the similarity of relationship, as, indeed, is the case among so many peoples.

had rejected simply "clans" as an answer, but he now argued that, *given the Malayan kinship system*, if clans are organized and the "consanguine family" described earlier is consequently broken up, the Malayan system will be modified to suit new conditions, and the Turanian system is the result.[30]

For the later stages of the family—from the clan type to our own simple bilateral type—some of Morgan's evidence was historical, but more was based only on logic and the presence of various social institutions (such as polyandry) in native tribes. But the assumptions that Morgan made, such as that of the dependence of kinship terms on social structure and the lag of terminology in social change, are historically more important than the exact sequence of evolution that he set up.[31]

Morgan's later works, *Ancient Society* and *Houses and House Life of the American Aborigines*, brought together considerably more material and clarified his point of view; the former added little to his argument, while the latter was concerned chiefly with the development of ideas of property. The influence of *Ancient Society* has been greater than that of *Systems*, partly because it is a smaller volume; but, while the theory in *Ancient Society* is largely outmoded, the raw material in *Systems* is of inestimable value.

Morgan completed the foundations of historical evolutionism;

[30] The mother's brother comes to be distinguished from the father's brother because they are in different clans, and the mother's sister from the father's sister for the same reason. But in a matrilineal society, for example, a man would still call his brother's child "child," even though they might be in different clans, because kinship systems are conservative and there was no strong reason for changing the Malayan in this respect.

[31] As given in *Systems* (and changed only slightly in *Ancient Society*), Morgan's series is as follows:

1. Promiscuous intercourse
2. Intermarriage of brother-sister
3. The communal family
4. The Hawaiian custom
5. Malayan form of classificatory system
6. The tribal organization (clans)
7. The Turanian and Ganowanian systems of relationship
8. Marriage between single pairs
9. The barbarian family
10. Polygamy
11. The patriarchal family
12. Polyandria
13. The rise of property: lineal succession of estates
14. The civilized family
15. Overthrow of classificatory system of relationship and substitution of descriptive

and no great constructive additions were made after 1870. Argument on the subject was, however, just beginning, and for twenty years it consumed the energy of the growing science as tag does that of children—with by-products absolutely essential to healthy development.[32] Space does not warrant a detailed account of what happened in those twenty years. Historically most important was McLennan's answer to Morgan, for his claim that "the classificatory system is a system of mutual salutations merely"[33] seems to have been convincing enough to delay the study of kinship for thirty years.[34] Aside from McLennan, the most important participants in the discussions were Sir John Lubbock,[35] C. S. Wake,[36] W. Robertson Smith,[37] A. W.

[32] The evolutionary arguments have consumed chiefly English energy, although both on the Continent and in America there have been and still are stray exponents. In England, it is fair to say, at one time all anthropologists were believers in social evolution of the unlinear type; in France it was never so strong; in Germany it was, in many quarters, bitterly opposed; in America it was current until Boas, who had never been an evolutionist, became the strongest influence.

[33] *Studies in Ancient History*, p. 273. On p. 277, nevertheless, he tries to explain the Malayan type on the basis of early marriage customs.

[34] Until Rivers revived it.

[35] Lubbock lectured in 1868 on the origin of civilization, refuting Bachofen and McLennan on (as now considered) minor points. His "Origin of Civilization and the Primitive Condition of Man" appeared in 1870; in it he presented his own scheme of promiscuity–individual marriage–exogamy–matriliny–patriliny, differing slightly from that of his predecessors, mostly on the causes of the changes. In 1871 he gave Morgan's work a rousing welcome in the first article of the first *Journal of the Anthropological Institute*, utilizing much of the data in *Systems* for constructive hypotheses. As late as 1911 (*Marriage, Totemism, and Religion*), he maintained his evolutionary position.

[36] In 1873, refuting McLennan, Lubbock, and Morgan, Wake ("Marriage by Capture") denied original sexual communism. Later ("Marriage among Primitive Peoples," pp. 197–207) he was one of the first to make use of Morgan's tables in *Systems* to counter Morgan's argument. He also used Ridley's Australian material here, also on kinship terms. In 1878, after reading *Ancient Society*, he supported the view that the father must always have been recognized ("The Origin of the Classificatory System of Relationships Used among Primitive Peoples"). A year later he came out definitely for patrilinear priority ("The Primitive Human Family").

[37] A strong supporter of McLennan; *Kinship and Marriage in Early Arabia* is dedicated to the proposition that "male kinship has been preceded by kinship through women only."

Howitt and Lorimer Fison,[38] Baldwin Spencer and F. J. Gillen,[39] and in America J. W. Powell, W. J. McGee, and others.[40] Sir E. B. Tylor was somewhat aberrant; although none of his work looks like the typical evolutionary discussion of logic and conjecture, he nevertheless contributed to the side of the argument which claimed priority for the matriarchate when he showed, by statistical means, that, on the assumption that there was a unilinear evolution, the distribution of traits such as parent-in-law avoidance and the couvade is explicable only if they are considered survivals from a matriarchal condition.[41] Toward the nineties, however, the interest of the evolutionists was shifting to psychological, rather than historical, problems.

Westermarck, in 1889 and 1891, rather smothered all arguments;[42] while still not abandoning all evolutionary disposition, he gathered such a mass of facts to show the improbability of the schemes established that, practically speaking, nobody again cared or dared to entered the lists. Nevertheless, Frazer un-

[38] Howitt began his Australian researches in 1865. In 1880, in a book called *Kamilaroi and Kurnai*, he first pointed out that the classificatory system and exogamy are two sides of the same thing. In 1873 he began to collaborate with the Rev. Mr. Fison. In a joint article in the *JAI* in 1882 ("From Mother-Right to Father-Right") they showed how (but not on the basis of observed change) maternal descent could change to paternal in Australia. Both believed that promiscuity underlies group marriage in Australia, and Howitt's book in 1904 (*The Native Tribes of South-East Australia*) and his article in 1907 ("Australian Group Relationships") devote considerable time to discussions of group marriage, the latter in answer to Andrew Lang. Chiefly because of Howitt's and Fison's work, Australia became the stamping ground of the theorists.

[39] In *The Native Tribes of Central Australia*, they support Morgan's, as against McLennan's, view of kinship terminology (p. 56). Their work on Australia was as important to later discussions as Howitt's was to earlier.

[40] Powell wrote long theoretical discussions in the early Bureau of American Ethnology reports as well as in the *American Anthropologist*. McGee is an example of a pre-Boas American; his "The Beginning of Marriage" (1896), while refuting the theory of original promiscuity, is evolutionary. He was supported by H. Solotaroff in 1898.

[41] "On a Method of Investigating the Development of Institutions," etc., Tylor makes out his best case with the levirate.

[42] A preliminary paper on *The Origin of Human Marriage* appeared in 1899. His *History of Human Marriage*, in three volumes, was first published in London, in 1891.

blushingly supported Morgan's notion of origin as late as 1910, and, as late as the twenties, Hartland[43] and Briffault,[44] resuscitated similar arguments. One may write finis, however, to the attempts to set up "from promiscuity to monogamy" series on the basis of ethnographic data and date it 1890. In the span of thirty years the historical evolutionary school had run its course; and, whatever else one may say of it, it cannot be denied that in those same thirty years cultural anthropology had grown from nothing to maturity. Practically all our elementary concepts about social organization—and its terminology—were developed by these evolutionists, and to try to evaluate their contributions would be as if a bullfrog were to try to evaluate a tadpole. Since we, at the present time, *with* all the concepts developed by the evolutionists, find it difficult, if not impossible, to synthesize the materials we have on social organization, who can say that it was unfortunate that the first ethnologists were beset by a false formula?

III. PSYCHOLOGY

Attempts to explain the phenomena of social organization in terms of individual psychology have been connected historically with (*a*) the evolutionists, (*b*) the psychoanalysts, (*c*) the American historians, and (*d*) the functionalists.[45] Since psychology is but a phase of the latter two and since they are of great importance in contemporary anthropology, the Americans and the functionalists will be treated separately in other sections.

Evolutionary psychologists.—To find the origin of a cultural institution, such as exogamy, for example, is, in the first place, a historical problem; but it is, at the same time, a "scientific" problem, for to establish a "law" as to how such an institution can *ever* start is to solve the historic problem also (except as to the exact time and place). All the evolutionists did both the his-

---

[43] *Primitive Paternity;* also *Primitive Society.*

[44] *The Mothers.*

[45] Wundt, the German psychologist, contributed little to the study of social organization. Bastian might also be considered here, but his work was of such a general type that it has made no impression on the study of social institutions particularly.

tory and the science at the same time, but some of them used theoretical notions in order to establish their history (Morgan's implicit generalization that kinship systems must be growths in social organizations, for example), while others used evolutionary history (notions of "survivals" or "primitive peoples") as a means of establishing their generalizations. It is on the basis of this difference that a distinction can be made between "historical" and "scientific" evolutionists.

From the very beginning, the English evolutionists were biased on the side of psychology as the basis for their scientific explanations of social institutions. On the other hand, the French evolutionists (notably Durkheim) opposed what they called "sociology" to psychology. The development of scientific evolutionism and its branches would play a very essential role in any complete history of social anthropology, but it happens that the subject matter involved was chiefly religion and mythology, so that its history in a paper on social organization is comparatively unimportant. In fact, it is only on borderline problems such as incest and totemism-and-exogamy and the esoteric phases of the transitions of birth, puberty, marriage, and death that the scientific evolutionists enter this paper at all.

James Frazer, especially, and Ernest Crawley are the most renowned of the evolutionary psychologists. The latter's most important work, *The Mystic Rose*,[46] denies the historical approach entirely and attempts to explain customs such as marriage-by-capture not as survivals from previous social states but rather as answering a psychological need.[47] Frazer's only work on social organization, *Totemism and Exogamy*, really deals with the religious phenomenon of totemism, and only incidentally with exogamy. More historically minded than Crawley, he took up one by one the theories of the older evolutionists, discarding

[46] Shorter works: "Sexual Taboo: A Study in the Relations of the Sexes"; "Exogamy and the Mating of Cousins."

[47] Designed to obviate the dangers attendant on getting married. The idea is that all human relationships are fraught with great mystic danger, and especially when there is anything unusual about them—more especially when physiological functions are involved. The danger must be gotten around: hence, such weird customs as marriage-by-capture.

most of their historical hypotheses; as far as exogamy is concerned, however, he finally did approve of Morgan's idea—that exogamy was consciously originated by a few people who disapproved of brother-sister marriage. Actually, Frazer's contribution to the study of social organization has been slight, and, in fact, the same may be said for the other English psychologists: the study of religion is apparently better adapted to their type of theory. Those who have here been called "evolutionary psychologists" have been, however, the backbone of English anthropology. Excepting for the specialized groups of Rivers, of G. Elliot Smith, and of Malinowski and Radcliffe-Brown, they still constituted English anthropology in the 1930's. The last outpost in anthropology of social philosophy—armchair speculators —their broad vision and power of analysis kept them the most influential force in the science.[48]

Psychoanalysis.—Psychoanalytic theory is related to the study of social organization at two important points: (1) the origin of the family, incest, etc., and, indeed, of culture itself, and (2) the psychology of family relationships. Both of these have been dealt with by Freud and others, but the former especially in *Totem and Taboo.*[49] Freud is a specialized kind of evolutionist, apparently holding that all of culture originated with a single act of patricide which resulted in changing a horde of ape-men into a human society, with its complexes and its incest taboo. The psychology of familial relationships has been dealt with by the psychoanalysts for western Europe, and, following the lead, for one matrilineal society by Malinowski. Roheim[50] has given to Australian social organization, meanwhile, a psychoanalytic interpretation which has had very little influence, however, in anthropological circles. Although psychoanalysis is as old as any

[48] Prominent are R. R. Marett, Carveth Read, H. Ling Roth, and F. R. Somerset (Lord Raglan).

[49] Sigmond Freud, *Totem and Taboo*. The theory of the origin of culture set up here is amply discussed in Malinowski, *Sex and Repression in Savage Society*.

[50] *Australian Totemism*.

of the dominant schools of ethnology, its application to social organization generally is still a matter for the future.[51]

IV. DIFFUSIONISTS

Replacements in the ranks of the aging evolutionists were rendered virtually impossible by four developments which occurred at the turn of the century: (1) the diffusion to America of the German geographical-psychological interest and the inauguration of scientific ethnography there, which lost America to the evolutionists; (2) the development of sociological functionalism in France, which kept the French from feeling a keen interest in the sort of psychological-evolutionary theories that were current in England; (3) the rediscovery of kinship terminologies by Rivers, which resulted in a stimulation of interest in the internal structures of tribes; and (4) the growth of the *Kulturgeschichte*, which more definitely drew the Germans from evolutionism and —more serious—took Rivers and his followers in England farther from it.

This short section will be devoted to the fourth development, together with a further minor departure in England itself: the advent of the Heliolithic school.

Kulturgeschichte.—The German-speaking world had had its social evolutionists; Bachofen himself wrote in German, and Lippert, Kohler, and, of recent years, Muller-Lyer, were to be reckoned with. Nevertheless, there was, contemporaneous with them, another strain, quite different, which had its origin in the kind of "natural history of mankind" that was current in the fifties and sixties. World ethnography was its first keynote— world ethnography, with its resultant interest in museums, on the one hand, and in geography, on the other. From the description of the tribes of the world came (*a*) somewhat psychological analyses of what was common to them, and the relations

---

[51] Ernest Jones in 1924 explained the famous paradox on incest psychoanalytically: the reason why there is a "universal horror of incest" and yet strong laws against it is that inclinations toward incest are present but repressed ("Psychoanalysis and Anthropology").

of the various differences to environmental factors; from the museums was born an interest in cultural traits and their distribution—which, coupled with the old desire to trace history, led directly to (b) the *Kulturkreise* theory and the *Kulturgeschichte* school.

In social organization, at least, the German historians have one thing in common with the evolutionists: they seem prone to crystallize social complexes into unvarying forms. So, for example, the "matriarchate" has become for them something almost as definitive and unvarying as a milk bottle. Moieties and clans, "secret societies," and totemism are treated in much the same way. Treating phenomena of social organization so, the Graebnerites[52] can handle them in tracing their histories quite as if they were boomerangs and spear-throwers. Since, in addition, these anthropologists have an iron-clad *Methode* for tracing histories, they have been quite successful from their own point of view in dealing with the very treacherous subject of social organization. If there were any way of checking the historical reconstructions that they have established, outside that prescribed by the *Methode* itself, they might perhaps be useful to others; unfortunately, however, the *Kulturgeschichte* people have dealt solely with peoples without recorded history, so that neither the method nor the results can be adequately checked.[53] Actually, these German historians have had practically no influence on the study of social organization outside their own circle —with one prominent exception: Rivers and his followers, who, however, were influenced not by the *Methode* but by the simple notion that clans and moieties, as well as kinship systems, can be diffused and confused.

Heliolithicists.—Quite independent of the German historians,

[52] Following geographer Ratzel, Graebner and Foy founded the school; Graebner's great methodological work was *Methode der Ethnologie*. Chief adherents to the school, which traces history through culture circles (*Kulturkreise*) which correspond in space today to layers marking periods of the past, are Father Wilhelm Schmidt and Father Wilhelm Koppers.

[53] The conception of the matriarchate employed by the Graebnerites is severely criticized in J. H. Ronhaar, *Woman in Primitive Motherright Societies*.

research in Egypt and Mesopotamia gave impetus to another group of diffusionists. The only thing in common between the two is the belief that independent invention is next to impossible, so that common cultural forms must be traceable to a common origin. G. Elliot Smith apparently was the first to postulate that there was a migration of the "Children of the Sun" from Egypt through southern Asia and Oceania to America, taking with them a number of important culture traits. W. J. Perry,[54] however, is more important in this history because he dealt at length with social organization. Perry bore out the evolutionist contention that mother-right preceded father-right, but to him there was nothing evolutionistic about it. An archaic culture with maternal clans was spread over the world until supplanted (in most places) by the migrating Children of the Sun from Egypt, who brought with them, along with sun-worship, dual organization and patriliny. In the matter of a scientific conclusion, a theory of some sort, one can ask, "Is it useful?" and the promulgator must, to satisfy his critics, use it to help solve some problem. In the matter of history, however, the only question is, "Is it true?" because if it is not true, it certainly cannot be useful (as, say, a "case in point" of something or other). This section is not intended to be critical so much as interpretive, but one is bound to observe that highly questionable and wholly unverifiable "history" cannot have much influence outside the circle of those with faith.

v. RIVERS

To most anthropologists today, Rivers is the founder of the modern study of social organization. Mrs. Seligman is his direct disciple; Radcliffe-Brown, his pupil, owes to him his interest in kinship and to some extent its direction; he changed the views of Lowie and Kroeber in America; and the pupils of all of them in the British Commonwealth and in America are indirectly indebted to him. Only Malinowski in England (and not his pupils) was somewhat free from the point of view of Rivers, and, of

[54] *Children of the Sun.*

course, his contributions, in both method and theory, also have some foundation in the work of Rivers. In Germany, Rivers is probably considered an offshoot of their own dominant school; but he did not receive from Germany, nor did they take from him, those contributions for which most Anglo-Saxon anthropologists honor him. In France, up to the 1930's there was no specialization in the field of social organization; but were there such an interest, it is inconceivable that the followers of Durkheim would not be, to some extent, followers of Rivers.

River's first great contribution was to ethnographic method; he it was who, almost single-handed, made research into the social organization of tribes what it is today. When he accompanied the Torres Straits expedition from Cambridge, he was a psychologist, interested in making certain tests; as a psychologist he needed to know how the subjects he was testing were related, so he obtained their genealogies. Presently he realized how much of the social organization of a tribe he could uncover by the genealogical expedient.[55]

Publication of the Torres Straits expedition included the first somewhat scientific accounts of native societies ever written— by W. H. R. Rivers.[56] These he followed with a study of the Todas of the Nilgiri hills of southern India, where he brought to bear his genealogical method, with results that gave to ethnology a report unparalleled many years after for completeness and accuracy.[57]

Rivers' second great contribution was a direct result of his first. Having accurately obtained kinship terms as well as social structures by the use of genealogical records and having done this, moreover, for a large number of different tribes, it was not long before Rivers saw the connection between the system of terms and the clans, moieties, and marriage customs. He says

[55] W. H. R. Rivers, "A Genealogical Method of Collecting Social and Vital Statistics."

[56] *Reports of the Cambridge Anthropological Expedition of Torres Straits,* Vol. V: By Rivers—*Genealogies, Kinship; Regulation of Marriage;* Vol. VI: *Genealogies, Kinship; Regulation of Marriage; Social Organization.*

[57] *The Todas.*

that "the terminology of relationships has been rigorously determined by social conditions and . . . . systems of relationship furnish us with a most valuable instrument in studying the history
of social institutions."[58] This sounds very much like Morgan,
and Rivers, indeed, gave Morgan every credit for the initial discovery. To Rivers it was a tragedy that anthropologists followed McLennan and not Morgan, for doing so caused them to
miss even the facts of kinship: "Those who believe the classificatory system is merely an unimportant code of mutual salutations are not likely to attend to relatively minute differences in
the customs they despise."[59] Rivers himself gave credit for
"having been the first fully to recognize the social importance
of these differences"[60] to J. Kohler;[61] perhaps it does rightly belong there, but it was certainly Rivers who did the major share
of the research in linking kinship terms to social institutions and
Rivers whose work brought kinship terms again into anthropology.[62]

Rivers started his career as an evolutionist. In 1907 he published an article in which he argued that the classificatory system
originated with group marriage when dual divisions or clans had
already evolved.[63] In 1911, however, after having done his major
research in Melanesia, while attempting to work up the material
he came to the conclusion that migration and diffusion must be
brought in to explain the distribution of types of social organization in Melanesia; he accepted, therefore, the main tenets of
Graebner's method.[64] The change in point of view was very con-

[58] Rivers, *Kinship and Social Organization*, p. 1. This is the thesis of the entire book. Note that Rivers made both of Morgan's points—(1) that kinship
systems originate to fit social institutions and (2) that (this is implicit) kinship
systems survive the institutions and can, therefore, be used in reconstructing
history. That the type of history was different will soon appear.

[59] *Ibid.*, p. 19.

[60] *Ibid.*

[61] Kohler, *Zur Urgeschichte der Ehe.*

[62] Lowie and Kroeber and their followers, for example, were influenced by
Rivers alone.

[63] "On the Origin of the Classificatory System of Relationships."

[64] *The Ethnological Analysis of Culture.*

scious with him; in the Introduction to his *History of Melanesian Society* he describes how, after writing half the book, he changed his opinion but not the book, since he felt he could reconcile the two positions and thereby also make the book a valuable study in method. Rivers did neatly reconcile the evolutionary and Graebnerian approaches, for he theorized that the progressive evolution was, at a certain point, disturbed by migrations and contacts, when it was not only confused, but stimulated.[65]

Nevertheless, Rivers' contribution was not his history, but rather (1) his ethnographic procedure, which is followed today by most trained ethnologists; (2) his recognition of the importance of kinship terminology in social organization; and (3) his method of inferring the social history of a tribe from elements of the kinship system, a method which engaged the attention of a prolific school of anthropology at least through the 1930's.

Brenda Seligman is Rivers' most ardent disciple; she has carried his methods from Melanesia to Africa, where, in small areas, she has tried to interpret both peculiar kinship systems and marriage customs, together, on the basis of inferences from both, with a grasp of the details of her subject which foreshadowed the work of the mid-century British structuralists.[66]

VI. AMERICAN HISTORIANS

The history of the study of social organization in America can be divided into four phases: (1) the period of evolutionism, from the time of Morgan to about 1900, indistinguishable from that in England; (2) the era of historical indeterminism, from about 1900 to 1915, when kinship terminology was considered a separately diffusible linguistic phenomenon; (3) the kinship phase, from 1915 to 1935, where the emphasis on the relation of kinship terminology to social institutions is dominant; and (4) the recent period of dynamic structuralism in which kinship structures are

---

[65] *The History of Melanesian Society.*

[66] See especially "Marital Gerontocracy in Africa"; "Bilateral Descent and the Formation of Marriage Classes"; "Asymmetry in Descent." Later, influenced by Malinowski, Mrs. Seligman became more "functional," less historical, and wrote a general theoretical study, "Incest and Descent."

seen in a time dimension under acculturation. This paper stops with the third period; Eggan's (below) treats the fourth.

In 1895 Boas, who had been trained in Germany, published his famous broadside against the evolutionists.[67] On pages 27–28, the development of anthropology in Germany was outlined; Boas belonged to the group that had developed contemporaneously with the evolutionists and was never itself evolutionistic. Boas had left this group and come to America before *Kulturkreise* theories developed, so that he was still in the geographical, psychological, middle-of-the-road-historical state when his influence began to be felt in America; he had never been an evolutionist and, indeed, considered those who were "a new school." Now, after considerable training in ethnography, he wrote the case against the "new school," which had its adherents in America as well as abroad. Never, thereafter, did evolutionism seriously raise its head in America.

The keynote in the study of social organization specifically, in the second phase, was sounded by John R. Swanton in 1905. He demolished the evolutionary theories with data from the American Indian tribes, by showing that, as far as history can be safely reconstructed, maternal descent was spreading from the Tsimshian to the other (more patrilineal) tribes of the northwest coast when the white man came; he pointed out his refusal to believe, furthermore, that the matrilineal Iroquois and Cherokee and Hopi and Tsimshian, for example, were more primitive than the patrilineal tribes. Besides showing the importance of the possibility of diffusion, he warned that so-called "vestigial" characters might really be functional.[68] American anthropologists were not going to be hasty in accepting any conclusions; there were to be no rules of method except painstaking research in the minutiae of recorded and reasonably reconstructed history; every theory would have to stand the test of common sense.

With such a point of view it is not surprising that ethnograph-

[67] *The Limitations of the Comparative Method of Anthropology.*
[68] "The Social Organization of American Tribes."

ic, rather than theoretical, work characterized this period. Every American anthropologist had his turn in the field, and all brought back better or worse accounts of the social organization and the kinship terminology, with comparisons pointed toward historical relationships of the "traits" or of the tribes. Kinship systems were hardly noticed, although usually partly recorded, as much for their linguistic value as for their ethnologic.[69]

The problem of kinship terminology was first dealt with by Kroeber, in the *Journal of the Anthropological Institute*.[70] For Morgan's general distinction between "classificatory" and "descriptive," Kroeber substituted an analysis of eight "principles" underlying the classification of relatives, and he suggested that kinship systems be described according to which principles are adopted. This suggestion has to a large extent been followed in America. Kroeber, at the same time, claimed that the principles made use of in any system become a matter of the psychology of the people, and two relatives may be called by the same term simply because they are conceived to have something in common according to one of the principles in use in the whole system. Since all language consists of classifications of phenomena that are conceived to belong together, Kroeber argued that kinship terms must be conceived as parts of the language, not of the social organization.

On the whole it is inherently very unlikely in any particular case that the use of identical terms for similar relationships can ever be connected with such special customs as the Levirate or group marriage. It is a much more conservative view to hold that such forms of linguistic expression and such conditions are both the outcome of the unalterable fact that certain relationships are more similar to one another than others. On the one hand this fact has led to certain sociological institutions; on the other hand to psychological recognitions and their expression in language.[71]

[69] The best of the studies are Francis La Flesche and Alice Fletcher, "The Omaha Tribe" (BAE-R 27, 1911) (and, long before, as good a study as any later: J. O. Dorsey, "Omaha Sociology" [BAE-R 3, 1884]); Swanton's work on the northwest coast and on the southeastern tribes; Lowie's Crow studies.

[70] "Classificatory Systems of Relationship."

[71] *Ibid.*, p. 83.

Kroeber maintained this point of view for many years, even after his colleagues in America came to believe the contrary.

Lowie especially was impressed by the work of Rivers; in 1915 he accepted the importance of the relations of kinship terms to social organization, with reservations to account for diffusion.[72] The next year, possibly afraid that he had been too hasty, he emphasized diffusion very much more.[73] But when Gifford,[74] Swanton,[75] Sapir,[76] and even Kroeber[77] began to take the sociological view seriously, Lowie in 1917 became its strongest American adherent and, since then, has always been willing to theorize on the origin of kinship terminologies and social structures in terms of each other as well as external factors.[78]

Year after year more evidence is amassed to prove to American anthropologists that kinship systems are related to social institutions such as moieties and clans, the levirate, and cross-cousin marriage; and, today, the tendency is to link particular features of terminology with particular institutions where they are found to exist. But, unlike Morgan, the Boas students never assume, because a terminological features is found without its concomitant institutions, that therefore the institution must have been present once; and, unlike Rivers, they do not explain an anomalous system on the basis of the combination of two systems in contact when there is no evidence of such contact. Diffusion is never denied any more than it is asserted by rule; nor is internal development and the lag of one element of culture behind another. American anthropologists, in short, refuse to accept any broad principle as a basis of historical reconstruction.

[72] *Exogamy and the Classificatory System of Relationship.*

[73] "Historical and Sociological Interpretations of Kinship Terminologies."

[74] Especially in *Miwok Moieties.*

[75] "The Terms of Relationship of Pentecost Island."

[76] "Terms of Relationship and the Levirate."

[77] *California Kinship Systems.*

[78] See especially his last chapter in *Culture and Ethnology;* his reviews in the *American Anthropologist* of Rivers' articles on kinship in Hastings' *Encyclopaedia of Religion and Ethics;* "Family and Sib"; "The Avunculate in Patrilineal Tribes"; "A Note on Relationship Terminologies"; "Hopi Kinship"; and his article on "Kinship" in the *Encyclopaedia of the Social Sciences.*

VII. FUNCTIONALISTS

Apparently, Malinowski first employed the term "functionalism" for a school of ethnology, and the term gained currency chiefly as applied by himself and others to himself and his followers. Malinowski himself, nevertheless, often included in his lists of adherents to his doctrines and methods anthropologists like Lowie and Sapir (for examples), who differed from him on important points; always he included Radcliffe-Brown, who differed on very important points. One can establish the following similarities and differences:

1. Malinowski, Lowie-Kroeber-Sapir *et al.*, and Radcliffe-Brown are at one in that, as opposed to the evolutionists, Graebner, or Elliot Smith, they desire to study culture as it is lived rather than as cold traits useful for some purpose or other; they are all concerned with discovering the inner workings of a culture and in theorizing on the relations of the parts.

2. Malinowski and Lowie-Kroeber-Sapir *et al.* are at one in their interest in studying the relations of individuals to one another, in their desire to explain social phenomena psychologically; they are opposed in this to Radcliffe-Brown.

3. Malinowski and Radcliffe-Brown are agreed that social institutions—indeed, all parts of any culture—have functions in maintenance of something, and their prime interest is in figuring out the various functions. The Americans, though not denying the fact that some culture traits have discernible functions, yet refuse to make a rule about it and certainly do not spend all their time looking for functions.

4. Malinowski and Radcliffe-Brown are agreed that, to find functions and to make universal generalizations, history is not necessary and that doubtful-reconstructed-history is pernicious. The Americans deny the possibility of determining functions without history and insist on the danger of any generalization about culture that has not taken account of the historical nexus of the cultural elements involved; furthermore, they insist that probable-reconstructed-history is better than no history.

5. Malinowski and Radcliffe-Brown are *not* agreed on what they mean by "function" or "functionalism"; and the Americans are not particularly interested in that argument. Malinowski considers anything a "function" if it "does something" for (*a*) another part of the culture, (*b*) the individual, or (*c*) the tribe. Radcliffe-Brown carefully distinguishes between "function for the individual" and "social function" and professes interest only in the latter. Also, while Malinowski is satisfied to find a series of unrelated or relatively unrelated functions for cultural phenomena in one tribe or generally, Radcliffe-Brown has an elaborate and highly systematized science worked out, so that there is a grand function, subfunctions, and innumerable minor functions that fill in the hierarchy.

6. As far as kinship specifically is concerned, there is little in common between any two of the three, as will be seen.

Since Malinowski is most prone to use the term, it is fair to reserve the word "functionalist" for him and his followers. Radcliffe-Brown prefers the term "comparative sociology" for his type of theory, and it may be shortened to simply "sociology" if the term is understood in this context. By the mid-thirties the adherents of Malinowski's functionalism who had published were Raymond Firth,[79] E. E. Evans-Pritchard,[80] and Reo Fortune.[81] Lloyd Warner seemed to be the only prominent disciple of Radcliffe-Brown. In both cases there were dozens of students doing field work after the pattern of their respective teachers, but no additional young theoreticians had developed.

Malinowski's most important statements on the subject of kinship and social organization appeared in two articles in 1930.[82] Although written in general terms, the data are drawn almost exclusively from the Trobriand Islands. The type of theory which Malinowski proposes does not suffer by such an extension as much as would that of Radcliffe-Brown, for example. Sociological parenthood and marriage—really, the simple active family (no matter on what fictions it is based), such as there is in the Western world, the Trobriands, or anywhere else—is to Malinowski the initial situation of kinship, from which all clans and other structures are derived. Viewing a tribe in its everyday life, Malinowski believes, peels off the camouflage of clans and moieties that has beset anthropologists; it is then seen by what psychological processes and for what social needs these extensions have come into being.

A. R. Radcliffe-Brown deals with kinship quite otherwise.[83] Following Rivers in his adherence to the doctrine that kinship terminology is closely related to social institutions, he goes much

[79] "Marriage and the Classificatory System" (for example).

[80] "The Study of Kinship in Primitive Societies."

[81] *Sorcerers of Dobu.*

[82] "Parenthood: The Basis of Social Structure," in Calverton and Schmalhausen, *The New Generation* (New York, 1930), pp. 138–68; also, "Kinship" in *Man*, No. 17 (1930), pp. 19–29.

[83] His most important publication on kinship is *The Social Organization of Australian Tribes.* The material here is chiefly from unpublished lectures.

further in some respects: kinship terms are to him only parts of the kinship system, in the first place, because patterns of behavior accompany them and both must be considered together. Furthermore, the kinship system is inextricably bound to the entire social structure—being, in fact, the subjective aspect of the structure itself. Since this is so, there obviously cannot be any significant lags of one or the other, any more than the convex side of a lens can, when the lens is moved, lag behind the concave. The problem is never dependent upon history, therefore; for at any point in time the whole functions as of itself. The problem to Radcliffe-Brown is to determine the functions of the various parts of the whole in maintaining the social structure. This can be determined by analysis for any one tribe, but only by comparison of the results for each tribe can the general function of any institution (wherever it is found to exist) be determined. By "function" is meant specifically what the institution does for the maintenance of the societal structure itself; culture is conceived of as acting *through* individuals but *for* society.[84] That takes care of the functional aspect; the structural problems are related to the functional as anatomy is to physiology, but in kinship there are special problems of form. There are certain universal principles inherent in the nature of human society and in the way that both the race and the culture carry on that are always acting upon the structure. The principles which will be dominant are determined by still other factors in the culture, but the principles, as they work themselves out in each society, determine the kinship structure. In this scheme there is no room for cause-and-effect hypotheses; a kinship system is neither the cause nor the result of a social institution or a marriage practice; rather, both must be considered results of functional needs and structural principles more basic than either.

VIII. RECAPITULATION

Although, before 1860, many stray facts about the social organization of native peoples had reached the literature, they

---

[84] The influence of Émile Durkheim, freely acknowledged by Radcliffe-Brown.

achieved no kind of order until the social evolutionists, chiefly in the following decade, used them to trace the history of human society. Discussions about that history have been largely abandoned since about 1890; but anthropologists with evolutionary tendencies continued in diminishing degree to be concerned with the psychological foundations of the various stages and their development. Since the end of the century there have been several coincident developments: The geographic interest of nonevolutionary Germany gave rise to the *Kulturgeschichte* school in Germany that affected Rivers and his followers in England. Independently there developed in England a school positing a single Egypt-centered diffusion, which school gained few professional adherents. From France, "sociology" spread to Radcliffe-Brown, who, combining it with the Morgan and Rivers interest in kinship, came to lead one branch of the functionalists, the other being soon started under the guidance of Malinowski. Radcliffe-Brown and Malinowski were the influences which, combined with the American interest in detailed historical changes, were destined to mold the developing study of primitive social organization in the coming generation.

SOCIAL ANTHROPOLOGY: METHODS
AND RESULTS

FRED EGGAN

SOCIAL ANTHROPOLOGY: METHODS AND RESULTS

FRED EGGAN

INTRODUCTION

The occasion of a new edition of this volume offers an opportunity to take account of the progress which has been made since 1937 in the application of the methods of social anthropology to the study of the societies and cultures of North American tribes. These methods were introduced to American anthropology by Radcliffe-Brown during the years 1931–37; since then social anthropology has come to be the dominant anthropological discipline in England and has had an important influence on American ethnology, as well. Indeed, some of us have come to believe that we need to adopt the structural-functional approach of British social anthropology and to integrate it with our traditional American interests in culture process and culture history.

The contributions of Radcliffe-Brown have been well summarized by Redfield in his original Introduction (p. ix): "Professor Radcliffe-Brown brought to this country a method for the study of society, well defined and different enough from what prevailed here to require American anthropologists to reconsider the whole matter of method, to scrutinize their objectives, and to attend to new problems and new ways of looking at problems." This new method was scientific or generalizing, rather than historical, and was concerned with the formulation of general propositions as to society or societal phenomena rather than with "descriptive integrations." It concerned itself with such concepts as social structure and social function and involved assumptions as to the nature of society and culture which were alien to the thinking of American ethnologists. It is not surprising, therefore, that these new procedures and points of view have made slow headway in the United States and are only now beginning to secure the recognition that they merit.

The earlier edition, in addition to Redfield's Introduction, contained a series of studies on the social organization and kinship systems of a number of North American tribes—Cheyenne and Arapaho, Kiowa-Apache, Chiricahua Apache, Fox, and Eastern Cherokee—as well as a theoretical analysis of problems of social organization, a study of sanctions in the Plains, and an analysis of religious revivalism among three tribes on a single reservation. While the subject matter varied considerably, the contributors shared a common interest in problems of social structure, a common set of concepts, and a broadly comparative method which gave the volume a certain unity. For the new edition we have attempted to add historical perspective, and to bring the study of social anthropology up to date, so far as it concerns the North American Indian.

I have elsewhere[1] discussed the development of cultural anthropology in the United States in some detail, comparing and contrasting its growth with that of social anthropology in England. In the period of evolutionism (1870–1900), Lewis H. Morgan, single-handed, created the study of kinship systems, as Tax points out; but with the advent of Franz Boas a sharp break was made in the past. Boas outlined a program[2] involving detailed studies of individual tribes in their cultural and regional contexts and a formulation of general laws of cultural growth, but he condemned the "comparative method" then practiced as inadequate for his purposes. In its stead he proposed the "historical method" and set down the requirement that only those phenomena can be compared which are derived psychologically or historically from common causes. These strictures, valuable as they may have been at the time, had the effect of predisposing most of his students against the use of the comparative method—except for linguistics when genetic relationships could be assumed.

In the "formative period" (1900–1915) of American ethnology the major attention of the early Boas students was devoted to the collecting, ordering, and interpreting of the cultural data on

---

[1] Eggan, "Social Anthropology and the Method of Controlled Comparison."

[2] Boas, "The Limitations of the Comparative Method of Anthropology," pp. 270–80.

the "vanishing" American Indian, as well as to further clearing the intellectual air of speculative theories. Tax calls this the "era of historical indeterminism" and notes that kinship phenomena were considered to be separately diffusible linguistic phenomena. Swanton's 1905 paper, "Social Organization of American Tribes," was not so much a summary of the subject as then known as a further demolishment of evolutionary theories. Kroeber, in "The Classificatory Systems of Relationship" (1909), rejected sociological explanations in favor of psychological or linguistic ones, a choice which had far-reaching effects on American cultural anthropology.[3]

In the following period, which might be called the "classic period" (1915–30) of American ethnology, historical and regional interests were dominant. The concept of the culture area was used to order the growing body of cultural data, and distributional studies were utilized to provide an outline of chronology. Sapir's "Time Perspective" (1916) set the keynote for this period, but it was Wissler who provided the synthesis and the interpretation.

The American Indian[4] was a notable achievement in many respects, organizing as it did a whole series of regional studies into a single frame. But this frame was mainly taxonomic and an outgrowth of museum experience, as Wissler himself points out.[5] Turning to the dynamic factors underlying the culture area, Wissler found them in the relation of the underlying ecological pattern to the culture center; in *The Relation of Nature to Man in Aboriginal America* (1926) he came very close to stating this relationship in causal terms.

Tax, with specific reference to studies of social organization, calls this period the "kinship phase," in which there was a growing concern with the relations of kinship terminologies to particular social institutions, such as clans and marriage practices. Lowie early developed a moderate sociological and functional

---

[3] See, for example, Eggan, *Social Organization of the Western Pueblos*, pp. 11 ff.

[4] Wissler, *The American Indian* (1st ed., 1917; 2d ed., greatly expanded, 1922; 3d ed., 1938).

[5] *Ibid.*, Preface to 3d ed., p. v.

position, influenced by Rivers, and was followed by many American ethnologists. The shadows of classical evolutionism still loomed large, however, and sociological interpretations made slow progress. As late as 1938 Wissler could still state that "anthropologists find classificatory systems the more interesting, possibly because they appear so senseless"; and joking and avoidance relationships "deserve careful study because they promise to be survivals of more archaic forms of social and marriage systems."[6]

During this period, also, chronology tended to become an end in itself, and some ethnologists became so preoccupied with time sequences that they did not pay much attention to culture as such. The mechanical treatment of material culture was extended to social organization and ritual, and culture came to be viewed as a mere aggregation of traits brought together by the accidents of diffusion. Ruth Benedict's dictum that "until we have abandoned the superstition that the result is an organism functionally interrelated, we shall be unable to see our cultural life objectively or to control its manifestations,"[7] indicates the temper of the times. The reaction against this mechanical and atomistic conception of culture came from both without and within. By the end of this period, Dixon, Spier, and Radin had attacked both the theory and the procedure, and Benedict had modified her earlier position.

This reaction on the part of American ethnologists came at the beginning of the depression, and the following decade was a period of transition and reorientation for cultural anthropology in the United States. As a result of the depression, the center of gravity shifted from museums to universities, and interests turned from historical inquiries to social science and a concern for contemporary problems. There were new developments in the directions of acculturation, applied anthropology, personality and culture, ecology, and class and caste in modern communities. There were the pioneer studies by Redfield and his associates of Yucatecan

[6] *Ibid.* (3d ed.), pp. 170, 172.

[7] Benedict, *The Concept of the Guardian Spirit in North America*, pp. 84–85.

communities. And there were the contributions of Malinowski and Radcliffe-Brown.

Malinowski, as a result of his sojourn in the Trobriands during World War I, had developed a superior type of field research which emphasized the complex interrelations of cultural life. Radcliffe-Brown, as a result of his experiences in the Andamans and in Africa and Australia, had developed an interpretation of ritual and myth and a conception of social structure which laid the theoretical basis for the modern development of social anthropology. The major portion of this development has taken place in England, where social anthropology has emerged as the basic discipline concerned with society and culture,[8] but there has been a considerable "feedback" into American anthropology, both before the war and particularly since.

Linton's *The Study of Man* (1936) was perhaps the first major volume to show definite evidence of the impact of structural and functional points of view—culture and society are clearly differentiated, and such concepts as social system, status and role, integration and function, are intermixed with the more usual cultural categories, though Linton's own interests soon went in other directions. Lowie's *Social Organization* (1948) presents a recent survey which incorporates a great deal of modern social anthropological thinking. And Murdock's *Social Structure* (1949), though he deprecates the influence of functional anthropology on his own thinking, makes a major contribution to comparative sociology: "We have found that sex behavior and the forms of social organization in our own society exhibit the same regularities and conform to the same scientific principles as do comparable phenomena among the simpler peoples of the earth."[9] If, as Redfield suggests, one measure of the importance of Radcliffe-Brown's contribution is the amount of discussion that has gone on about him and his work, then that contribution is increasing.

Social anthropology today stands on a broader base than that

[8] Evans-Pritchard, *Social Anthropology*, and Fortes, *Social Anthropology at Cambridge since 1900*, both discuss this development in some detail.

[9] Murdock, *Social Structure*, p. 322.

provided by Radcliffe-Brown; but, as Fortes[10] has recently pointed out, the guiding ideas in the analysis of social structure have come from Radcliffe-Brown. My own views[11] are that we need to develop a still broader base for cultural anthropology in the United States by adopting the structural and functional points of view of British social anthropology and integrating them with our traditional ethnological interests in culture history and culture process. As I look at the two developments, our strengths and weaknesses are complementary, and, if we can find a way of relating the two, the resulting synthesis should be highly productive. This process has, of course, been under way for some time but has been obscured by misunderstandings and disputes over terminology and method. The following sections are in part an attempt at clarifying some of these issues, as well as a presentation of some of the results achieved so far in the systematic study of North American societies and cultures.

METHODS AND CONCEPTS

Looked at in the abstract, there are major differences between British social anthropology and American ethnology as to methods and points of view. The British social anthropologists tend to think of themselves as sociologists concerned primarily with the social structures and institutions of primitive societies,[12] or they utilize social structure as a frame for the organization and interpretation of cultural phenomena;[13] most American ethnologists consider culture as the major concept and point of departure and subordinate social structure to it, if they utilize this concept at all, preferring to operate with concepts of culture pattern and cultural form.[14] There is also an expressed difference in ultimate objectives: the formulation of general propositions as to

[10] Fortes, "The Structure of Unilineal Descent Groups," p. 25.

[11] See Eggan, "Social Anthropology and the Method of Controlled Comparison."

[12] See Firth, *Social Anthropology;* and Evans-Pritchard, *Social Anthropology,* pp. 10–11.

[13] Fortes, "The Structure of Unilineal Descent Groups," p. 21.

[14] Kluckhohn, "The Study of Culture."

society versus descriptive integrations or processes of culture growth, though here the distinction is not so clear-cut.[15] But when the actual studies made by British and American anthropologists are examined, while there are differences in emphasis and selection, there is also a considerable area of common ground. If we can define and enlarge this area of agreement, anthropology as a whole will advance. Kroeber[16] has pointed out the importance of differentiating the scientific and historical approaches to anthropology, so that they can supplement one another more effectively. Both approaches were implicit in the work of Boas; but, as Redfield notes above (p. xii), none of Boas' students has emphasized the scientific side to any great extent. Science requires concepts for the formulation and solution of its problems, and it is here that Redfield sees the more important contribution of Radcliffe-Brown to a scientific social anthropology:

> This contribution is called for in American anthropology as a counteremphasis to the analytic and nonconceptualized procedure of Boas. The effort at scientific synthesis arranges the problems in some order, exposes the implicit postulates, and makes it possible to discover if different workers are talking about the same things. The propositions are not to be treated as final but are to be challenged, revised, or abandoned as the investigation into special fact guided by them proceeds.[17]

I have elsewhere[18] pointed out that we have made some progress in developing concepts, formulating problems, and establishing procedures for gathering and analyzing our data. In the field our primary data are derived from the observation of individuals behaving in social situations—the concepts of the individual, society, and culture are interrelated, and to get from one to the other requires analysis and abstraction. We can separate conceptually the groups of individuals who have adjusted their

[15] Evans-Pritchard, for example, thinks of social anthropology as essentially historical in character (*Social Anthropology*, pp. 61–62).

[16] Kroeber, "History and Science in Anthropology."

[17] Redfield, Introduction, p. xiii above.

[18] Eggan, *Social Organization of the Western Pueblos*, pp. 4 ff. Much of what follows is a revision and expansion of what I wrote there, but put in a broader context.

mutual interests sufficiently to co-operate in satisfying their social and personal needs, and identify the social relations which develop through recurring social interaction. These relationships of individuals and groups make up the social structure: the network of continuing social relations which gives organization and stability to social life.

The conventional attitudes and behavior patterns by which this mutual adjustment and co-operation of individuals is carried out can also be separated and treated as a unit. These social usages fall into patterns which make up the culture of the group, along with the material products of individual and group activity —it is this patterned quality of culture which makes prediction possible for the members of the social group. These two aspects of social behavior—social structure and cultural pattern—cannot exist independently of one another in human society: society and culture are mutually dependent, and social relations are carried, or exemplified, only in cultural behavior. Social institutions partake of both aspects: they are composed of individuals organized through recurring social relationships into a social structure, with a set of attitudes, beliefs, and behavior patterns through which the structure is exemplified and the institutional ends achieved. And concepts of personality structure and development have obvious relationships to both society and culture and can be fully understood only in both contexts. As Hallowell remarks, while they may "be conceptually differentiated for specialized types of analysis and study . . . . it is being more clearly recognized than heretofore that society, culture, and personality cannot be postulated as completely independent variables."[19]

While the concepts of society and culture are interrelated, they differ in certain important respects. Social structures, since they require sufficient adjustment of individuals to one another to enable co-operation for group ends, have a limited number of forms. Contradictory behavior between individuals beyond a certain point leads to social disorganization—or to social change; and, as Murdock has recently shown, social structures tend to

[19] Hallowell, "Culture, Personality, and Society," p. 600.

change in predictable ways.[20] Culture patterns have a greater variety of possible forms, since there is apparently less adjustment required as to beliefs and practices within the minds of individuals; but the larger organizations or configurations of culture may well be limited to a considerable extent in terms of types. We do know that these patternings or organizations have an important influence on innovation and borrowing and hence on cultural change.

A further reason for the conceptual separation of social structures and cultural patterns is that they may vary independently of one another. Similar social relations may be derived from objectively and historically different cultural behavior; and, conversely, similar behavior patterns may support diverse types of social relations in particular societies. This suggests the importance of studying both social and cultural change and of seeing them in relationship to one another rather than considering them as a unit. The social structure may or may not change in type with particular changes or modifications in cultural content and organization. The relative independence of cultural form and social structure also suggests that similar social structures may recur in widely separated areas, characterized by objectively different cultural elements and patterns. This opens up a whole new field for comparative research, provided that we do not have to restrict our comparisons to genetic relationships.[21]

It seems probable also that the processes of borrowing and invention play different roles with regard to social structure as compared with cultural phenomena. We often find social forms persisting, despite the partial or even complete replacement of their cultural content. Social relations are more abstract and more difficult to grasp than are cultural forms, and, as Murdock notes, social organization seems "singularly impervious to diffusion. . . . . Traits of social structure appear to be borrowed, in general only under conditions in which the same traits would be inde-

[20] Murdock, *Social Structure*, p. 250.

[21] Compare Spier, "Historical Interrelation of Culture Traits," for a discussion of the general Americanist position.

pendently elaborated even in the absence of culture contacts."[22] Social structures are no more subject to ready borrowing than are linguistic structures, whereas cultural elements, like linguistic vocabulary, may be more easily taken over. The patterning or configurational aspects of culture may offer parallel resistances to borrowing, as Benedict has demonstrated.[23]

The concept of integration likewise has a somewhat different meaning with reference to social structure and to culture. Social structures may differ in terms of the number of individuals bound together and in the character and complexity of the ties uniting them with one another. Cultural integration, on the other hand, refers to the degree to which beliefs, attitudes, and behavior patterns are mutually adjusted and form a system without contradictions or loose ends. This process takes place in the individual but may be generalized for the group. Social integration and cultural integration not only are measured by different criteria but can vary independently of each other.[24]

If we look at societies in terms of the problems of adjustment or adaptation which they face, we can get further insights into the nature of social structure. There is growing evidence that social systems have tasks to perform and that some types of structure are more efficient than others for particular purposes. In the long run, these differences in efficiency are of very considerable significance for social and cultural change—and for survival. Thus bilateral structures are flexible and adjust easily to new conditions but find difficulty in providing social continuity and in transmitting property and position. Unilateral structures, on the other hand, provide efficient mechanisms for both but are slow in reacting to changed conditions. Here, as in the biological world, specialization in structure brings about efficiency in adjusting to certain conditions but a relative inability to deal with change.

These problems of adjustment and adaptation vary in terms

[22] Murdock, *Social Structure*, p. 196.

[23] Benedict, *Patterns of Culture*.

[24] Radcliffe-Brown has been more concerned with the concept of social integration; Malinowski with that of cultural integration.

of such factors as population size and density, techniques for exploiting the environment, and ritual attitudes and practices. Social structures which will integrate and organize small and scattered populations may be inadequate for larger and more concentrated populations. New agricultural techniques may require new organizations of individuals to be effective, or new groupings may be needed for co-operative action. Whether there are similar differences in the effectiveness of various methods of establishing ritual relations with nature or of dealing with the supernatural is not yet clear. But the concept of efficiency or effectiveness is important not only for giving us some insight into the factors responsible for social and cultural change but also because it allows us to formulate hypotheses as to differential development under variant conditions.[25]

The role of the individual in relation to a society and its culture is an ambiguous one. Individuals are essential to the maintenance and perpetuation of both society and culture, but these latter are independent of any particular individual or set of individuals. The psychological processes by which the social heritage is transmitted from one generation to the next tend toward stability; major changes come about at crises when there are conflicts which the society cannot resolve with its own resources. At such times individual personalities loom larger and may bring about far-reaching changes in both social structure and culture.

The individual needs a certain degree of both cultural integration and social integration, though there are apparently wide limits for both. Cultural integration is perhaps the more essential for the personality structure, which may be one reason for the considerable development of the field of "personality and culture" in the United States in recent years. But the parallel processes of socialization of the individual and his integration into social groups are likewise important; suicide is in part a phenomenon of social isolation, as Durkheim long ago pointed out, and the significance of class position for adjustment to American life has been recently emphasized by Warner.

[25] See, for example, the discussion in Eggan, "Cheyenne and Arapaho Kinship System," pp. 89 ff., above.

The problems of personality structure and development thus have complex relationships with both social structure and culture; it is probable that they will not be completely solved until the social and cultural systems of various groups are more adequately known. And beyond these is the problem of the nature of human nature.

In the foregoing brief survey I have been more concerned with social structure than with the concept of culture, because the latter is more familiar to American anthropologists. With Kroeber and Kluckhohn's[26] review and critical analysis of the various definitions of culture since Tylor and with Kluckhohn's account[27] of recent developments in the theory of culture and in the methods and techniques for its study, we have a comprehensive view of this central concept of anthropology. For Kluckhohn, culture is an abstraction from observed regularities in the modes of response of a given society and represents their distinctive way of life. He thinks of culture as a historically created system: "that cultures have organization as well as content is now generally recognized." Indeed, he considers that the greatest advance in modern anthropological theory is "probably the increased recognition that there is something more to culture than artifacts, linguistic texts, and lists of atomized traits."[28] He goes on to discuss in considerable detail the advances which have come from the recognition of form or structure in culture, and he makes an important distinction between explicit and implicit culture, the latter being the common denominator underlying a multiplicity of cultural content.

One of the important problems facing the student of anthropology is to "explain" the social structure and culture of a given social group.[29] One form of explanation, as we have seen, is historical and attempts to work out the sequences of events leading to certain end-results. The data and forms of culture seem to be

[26] Kroeber and Kluckhohn, *The Concept of Culture: A Critical Review of Definitions.*

[27] Kluckhohn, "The Study of Culture."

[28] *Ibid.,* p. 89.

[29] Cf. Tax, "Some Problems of Social Organization," p. 3, above.

more amenable to tracing through time and space, and much of our ethnological research has been in this direction, though Herskovits states that "culture exhibits regularities that permit its analysis by the methods of science."[30]

An alternative method of achieving insight into the nature of society and culture is that of generalizing science, which utilizes the comparative study of correlated phenomena in a series of tribes or in the same group at different times or under different conditions. Generalization requires repeatable units which can be readily identified; and social structures, which have a limited number of forms, readily lend themselves to classification and comparison. The discovery of covariation and correlation of social phenomena may lead to tentative hypotheses which, when adequately tested and verified, may be considered generalizations.

Generalizations do not have to be universal in order to be useful. If we can formulate the conditions under which social or cultural phenomena correlate or covary, such information will be exceedingly useful for the organization of further research. Ultimately we may hope for the discovery of universal "laws," but at the present state of our knowledge we can be content with more limited generalizations. Depending on our problems, either culture or society may be central in our analysis, and we may utilize either historical or generalizing methods—or both together.

The crucial problem with regard to generalization, whether broad or limited, is the method of comparison used. Radcliffe-Brown has said: "It is only by the use of the comparative method that we can arrive at general explanations. The alternative is to confine ourselves to particularistic explanations similar to those of the historian. The two kinds of explanation are both legitimate and do not conflict; but both are needed for the understanding of societies and their institutions."[31] In the United States, for reasons which we have noted briefly earlier, the com-

---

[30] Herskovits, *Man and His Works*, p. 625.

[31] Radcliffe-Brown, *Structure and Function in Primitive Society*, pp. 113-14.

parative method has long been in disrepute. But Ackerknecht, in a survey of the comparative method,[32] emphasizes the importance of comparison for cultural anthropology and sees signs of a renaissance: "In whatever form the comparative method may reappear, it will express the growing desire and need in cultural anthropology to find regularities and common denominators behind the apparent diversity and uniqueness of cultural phenomena.[33]

In England the comparative method has had a more continuous utilization and development. Nadel, in his theoretical analysis of the comparative method,[34] points out that while social anthropology cannot experiment, the comparative method is the equivalent of the experiment, in that the artificial induction of variations is replaced by the observation of variable phenomena. "We study variations, found and looked for in the data of observation, and correlate them so that from them general regularities may emerge."[35] He notes that comparison needs further refinement in the form of planned selection and rigorous checks and controls in order to approximate to the experimental method, and he offers the method of concomitant variations as a means to that end. He goes on to discuss the various differences in approach and scope of interest in the applications of the method of covariation, particularly in primitive societies. "Thus the comparison with primitive societies may throw into relief salient features which, in advanced societies, are often obscured, and suggest hypotheses of correlations otherwise not as readily seen. No wonder, then, that anthropology has become almost a laboratory for the quasi-experimental approach to social phenomena, which all students of society have been ready to utilize."[36]

The particular adaptation of the comparative method to social anthropology which Radcliffe-Brown has made is well illus-

[32] Ackerknecht, "On the Comparative Method in Anthropology."
[33] *Ibid.*, p. 125.
[34] Nadel, *The Foundations of Social Anthropology*, chap. x.
[35] *Ibid.*, p. 222.
[36] *Ibid.*, p. 228.

trated in The Huxley Memorial Lecture for 1951,[37] where he shows that Australian moiety divisions are instances of certain widespread general tendencies in human societies. He thinks of social anthropology not in relation to "society" or "culture" but as concerned with the "process of social life," of which society and culture are certain aspects. For him "the unit of investigation is the social life of some particular region of the earth during a certain period of time"; and he is interested in discovering the general forms of social life and dealing with them in terms of continuity and change.[38] The general task of social anthropology is to "formulate and validate statements about the conditions of existence of social systems . . . . and the regularities that are observable in social change."[39]

The systematic comparison of world-wide instances, while an ultimate objective of social anthropology, is rather difficult to carry out in terms of our present limited knowledge of social systems. My own preference is for the utilization of the comparative method on a smaller scale and with as much control over the frame of comparison as it is possible to secure. It has seemed natural to utilize regions of relatively homogeneous culture or to work within social or cultural types and further to control the ecological factors so far as it is possible to do so. Above all, it is important to control the historical framework within which comparison takes place. While I share Radcliffe-Brown's vision of an ultimate science of society, I think that we first have to cultivate more intensively what Merton has called the "middle range" of theory, and I suggest the method of controlled comparison as a convenient instrument for its exploration, utilizing covariation and correlation and avoiding too great a degree of abstraction.

This is in no sense a new method that I am proposing, but it is one that I have utilized and tested extensively in my own researches over the last two decades, both among the American Indian and in the Philippines. It involves the conception of so-

[37] Radcliffe-Brown, *The Comparative Method in Social Anthropology.*
[38] Radcliffe-Brown, *Structure and Function in Primitive Society*, pp. 4-5.
[39] Radcliffe-Brown, *The Comparative Method in Social Anthropology*, p. 22.

cial life as a system subject to forces for both continuity and change, and it utilizes the concepts of both social structure and cultural type. The structural approach gives an added dimension to the perspectives in which social life is usually viewed; functionalism enables us to see sociocultural units as wholes. Comparative study of social phenomena should be made, in the first instance, between phenomena which belong to the same class or type or, alternatively, between phenomena derived from the same historical source. Comparison need not be limited by the strictures laid down by Boas and followed by many of his students. The historical framework which we develop is both a legitimate end in itself—as a portion of culture history—and a means to more adequate comparison. The failure of British anthropologists to utilize historical data or inferences as to history is an unnecessary handicap—the dangers of "conjectural" history with modern controls has been greatly exaggerated. For some of our best insights into the nature of society and culture come from seeing social structures or cultural patterns over time. Here is where we can distinguish the accidental from the general, evaluate more clearly the factors or forces operating in a given situation, and describe in general terms the social and cultural processes involved. Not to take full advantage of the possibilities of studying social and cultural change under relatively controlled conditions is to do only part of the job that needs to be done.

Such an approach as here sketched is not the only road to theoretical understanding. Murdock's multidisciplinary attack upon the problems of social structure, utilizing the "postulational method" and a statistical analysis of the data from a large number of societies, is an alternative method that gives important results. And some British social anthropologists have given up comparative studies in favor of intensive investigations of one or two societies and the development of hypotheses on the basis of these investigations, which are to be tested on other societies: "If the studies are systematic and each is used to test the conclusions reached up to that point and to advance new hypotheses which permit verification, each will reach .... a deeper level of investigation which in its turn will lead to a clearer definition of concepts."[40] Evans-Pritchard prefers to call this method "experimental," but his emphasis on intensive studies of selected societies for the solution of limited problems is in accord with what we have proposed.

Kroeber, in a recent commentary, has stated: "All science or disinterested intellectual inquiry ultimately seeks knowledge of process. This must be preceded, however, by description of the properties of the form and substance of the phenomena, their ordering or classification upon analysis of their structure, and the tracing of their changes or events."[41] To our thinking, these are the essential tasks that we face. The possible rewards are contained in Radcliffe-Brown's statement: "It will be only in an integrated and organized study in which historical studies and sociological studies are combined that we shall be able to reach a real understanding of the development of human society, and that we do not yet have."[42]

With this brief theoretical background, we can now turn to some of the results which have been achieved by the application of these methods and points of view to the problems of social anthropology among North American tribes. The details as to procedure and analysis are presented in the preceding papers and in readily accessible sources. The sixth edition of *Notes and Queries on Anthropology* provides an excellent section on the methods and techniques of social anthropological research; and Radcliffe-Brown's Introduction to *African Systems of Kinship and Marriage*[43] provides a detailed discussion of these important topics. I have discussed my own adaptations and modifications in *Social Organization of the Western Pueblos*.

RESULTS AND PROSPECTS

The progress made in the application of social anthropological methods to the study of North American tribes has been pri-

[40] Evans-Pritchard, *Social Anthropology*, p. 90. In a later statement ("Religion," p. 9). however, he re-emphasizes the comparative method.

[41] Kroeber, "Critical Summary and Commentary," pp. 273-74.

[42] Radcliffe-Brown, *The Comparative Method in Social Anthropology*, p. 22.

[43] Radcliffe-Brown and Daryll Forde (eds.), *African Systems of Kinship and Marriage*.

marily in the realm of kinship and social organization, with such
notable exceptions as Redfield's *Folk Culture of Yucatan* and related studies, Steward's ecological studies of the Great Basin and
Southwestern tribes,[44] and various others. Despite Morgan's
pioneer studies of kinship, we still do not have an adequate classification of social structures comparable to that for cultural
types, though preliminary surveys have been presented recently
by Driver and Murdock and should soon be available.[45] And
Morgan's *Systems* is becoming increasingly important as a historical base line against which to measure change.

The social anthropological interpretation of myth and ritual,
on the other hand, has continued to lag behind, though there are
a few exceptions here. There are large amounts of data collected
in texts, but, except for the Navaho, little attempt has been
made to give us the meaning and significance of rituals for the
participants and for the tribe. One detailed interpretation of the
Sun Dance would enable us to revalue the whole literature. The
rich field of totemic phenomena, cut off from study by Goldenweiser's critique, needs to be re-examined in terms of modern
social anthropological conceptions. Frederica de Laguna's recent paper[46] on the Tlingit is an indication of what may still be
done in this important field. The interrelations between ritual
and social structure and the mediating role of myth represent the
new frontiers of social anthropological research. It is here that
we will find many of the answers to the questions we are beginning to ask about values.

The brief survey of research which follows is largely confined
to developments in kinship and social organization, though I

[44] Steward, *Basin-Plateau Aboriginal Sociopolitical Groups;* "Ecological Aspects of Southwestern Society."

[45] Presented at the 1952 meeting of the American Anthropological Association. Driver's paper, "Economy, Residence, and Descent in Aboriginal North
America," is in press, and Murdock's "North American Social Organization" is
in process of revision. I have therefore not made use of them in the present paper
to any great extent.

[46] Frederica de Laguna, "Tlingit Ideas about the Individual," pp. 172–91;
also Catherine McClellan's "Interrelations of Social Structure with Northern
Tlingit Ceremonialism."

have tried to place these in their larger setting and to indicate their relationships to other aspects of culture and environment. Since I hope to publish a comprehensive survey of social structure in North America some time in the future, I have felt free to select a more limited range of topics for discussion, many of which have grown out of the papers originally presented in this volume. Though there are new directions to research, there are few sharp breaks with the past, and my debt to my predecessors and colleagues will be clear.[47] I have sometimes attempted to put their contributions into a somewhat different perspective, in order to formulate new problems for further investigation.

Perhaps the most important concepts guiding the analysis of social structure today are the structural principles worked out by Radcliffe-Brown from the analysis of kinship systems, notably the lineage principle and the principle of the unity and solidarity of the sibling group.[48] These principles were exemplified in several of the original papers and have been an important guide in further research.

Tax, in his theoretical discussion of the Fox social structure (pp. 277–82), has presented an alternative theory as to the development of Omaha-type terminology, based on the modern conceptions of the Fox as to the character and extensions of their kinship terminology. In the present-day social organization of the Fox, while the kinship system is an integral part of the culture, the patrilineal "clans" are neither exogamous nor composed solely of relatives; and Tax could find no clear evidence in his genealogies that they ever were. He therefore rejected the conception of any effect of the clan system upon the kinship terminology and attempted to develop an explanation for the Fox situation in other terms (see also above, pp. 25 ff.).

More recently, however, Margaret Fisher has edited William Jones's notes on the Fox, the marriage data in which demonstrate clearly that the Fox clans were exogamous in the middle of the nineteenth century but that exogamy was breaking down

---

[47] I include graduate students in this category.

[48] Radcliffe-Brown, *Structure and Function in Primitive Society*, chap. iii.

toward the end of the century. Some of the reasons for this breakdown are indicated in her historical summary of Fox history[49]—it is literally amazing that there is any Fox culture left! This suggests that the Fox formerly had a social structure more like that of their neighbors and that the present Fox social structure can be interpreted as in process of change from a more typical "Omaha" structure, based on the lineage principle, to a more bilateral structure, brought about in part by the acculturative processes to which they have been subjected during the last century. The basic Fox kinship structure still corresponds to a lineage pattern, except for grandparent-grandchild extensions, and there is economy in interpreting it in that framework. Furthermore, we now have considerably more evidence of change in American Indian social structures under conditions of acculturation than we had when Tax made his original study, and the changes involved have parallels elsewhere.

We also have considerably more data available on the Omaha and their neighbors and can carry Lowie's preliminary analysis of Omaha kinship terminologies[50] a step further. Thanks to J. O. Dorsey's pioneer account, we have a reasonably complete set of terms to work with for the Omaha, as well as several good accounts of Omaha life over the last century or more. We also have considerable data on other Central Siouan tribes, some of whom are closely related to the Omaha, as well as on Central Algonkian tribes who occupy adjacent regions and participate in the same sociocultural life. In an earlier paper (see above, p. 93) I presented a preliminary classification of "lineage" type systems for the Plains, and I have elsewhere discussed the relationship of these tribes to the earthlodge culture complex of the eastern Plains or Missouri River region.[51] It seems clear that all these groups were organized on the lineage principle, though the patterns of descent varied between north and south. The

[49] William Jones, *Ethnography of the Fox Indians*, pp. 77-78, and Introduction.

[50] Lowie, "The Omaha and Crow Kinship Terminologies."

[51] Eggan, "The Ethnological Cultures and Their Archeological Backgrounds," pp. 41-42.

Omaha and their neighbors were organized in terms of patrilineal clans, which, in turn, were divided into subclans or lineages. These clans were organized into a moiety structure, perhaps originally exogamous, which was reflected in the organization of the camp-circle and in the organization of the world of nature. But the permanent earthlodge villages were organized in terms of matrilocal residence and an extended matrilocal family. Fortune is explicit on this point: the earthlodge, which was inhabited during the agricultural periods, was organized in terms of matrilocal residence, whereas the tipis used during the hunting periods were organized on the basis of patrilocal residence.[52]

It is possible that this dual organization and residence are a result of the reversal of cultural values brought about by the horse and that co-operative buffalo-hunting activities brought about a greater emphasis on the patrilineal line—or, alternatively, that the adoption of intensive agriculture and the earthlodge complex led to an emphasis on matrilocal residence which facilitated the joint cultivation of agricultural plots by the women. Throughout the Prairie Plains the earthlodge was occupied by a group of women matrilineally related via matrilocal residence, whatever the formal pattern of descent; and this suggests a functional relationship between the composition of the extended household and the activities in which the members were engaged. That matrilocal residence is relatively old among some of the Central Siouans, such as the Osage, is attested by historical evidence.[53]

Comparative study of the Central Siouan and Central Algonkian groups will aid in testing these alternatives, since tribes such as the Winnebago were outside the earthlodge area. The differential effects of this type of acculturation on the matrilineally organized village-dwelling tribes of the region will likewise be important. Groups such as the Pawnee apparently responded to these influences by shifting from a clan toward a more bilateral type of organization, and similar changes took

[52] Fortune, *Omaha Secret Societies*, p. 24.

[53] Nett, "Historical Changes in the Osage Kinship System," quoting Vissier, *Histoire de la tribu des Osages* (1827).

place among the Wichita[54] and the Crow. The Mandan and Hidatsa made other types of adjustments but were so seriously decimated by epidemics that they did not have the same opportunities.[55]

Murdock, following Leslie White, believes the Omaha type of social organization represents a mature form of the patrilineate, and he characterizes the Omaha proper as "Neo-Omaha" on the basis of neolocal residence, with matri-patrilocal alternatives.[56] But if Fortune is correct, the variations in residence followed a regular alternation seasonally, a fact which escaped early observers and gave rise to confusing statements. Murdock further derives "Omaha types" from "Dakota" or "Fox," though in the case of the Omaha tribe he suggests that the occurrence of sororal polygyny may reflect an ultimate matrilocal derivation. The Fox proper he places in the "Fox type" of social organization, which includes groups in transition from one rule of descent to another and with asymmetrical cousin terms. Because of residence, the Fox are "Neo-Fox" and are derived from "Neo-Omaha" as a consequence of the loss of exogamy through adopting neolocal residence patterns: "The non-exogamous patrisibs of the Fox point to a former Omaha structure."[57] We are in essential agreement with Murdock with regard to these conclusions, though I believe he has misinterpreted the nature of the residence patterns among the Omaha. Since he assumes that when any social system in comparatively stable equilibrium begins to undergo change, "such change regularly begins with a modification in the rule of residence,"[58] the character of the residence patterns among the Omaha and related tribes becomes of crucial significance for his interpretations.

The parallel distribution of matrilineally organized village-

[54] Cf. Schmitt and Schmitt, *Wichita Kinship: Past and Present*.

[55] E. Bruner has recently made a field study of the Hidatsa; see also Bowers, *Mandan Social and Ceremonial Organization*.

[56] Murdock, *Social Structure*, pp. 239–41. I put his specialized types in quotation marks.

[57] *Ibid.*, p. 234; see also pp. 232 ff.

[58] *Ibid.*, p. 221.

dwelling tribes in the Prairie Plains offers an important problem for historical and functional research. Both Caddoan- and Siouan-speaking tribes are represented, and most of them participated in agricultural activities centered around the women inhabiting the earthlodge, which has a long archeological history in the region. The villages were organized in terms of matrilineal lineages and clans, and frequently these were grouped into moiety organizations as well. All had variants of Crow-type kinship systems which were consonant with the matrilineal lineage pattern.

A comparison between these Omaha- and Crow-type social structures in the Missouri River region will be of importance in determining the structural and functional significance of particular rules of descent and their relative ability to stand particular types of acculturation. The lineage segments inhabiting the earthlodges were apparently small "corporate" groups controlling houses and agricultural plots in the fertile and easily worked bottomlands along the streams; the larger clan groups regulated marriage and controlled ceremonies and sacred bundles, as well as having other associations. In both groups, also, there were societies whose membership cut across the clan and moiety structures, as well as a centralized political and religious organization. Such complex and highly structured social systems seem specialized for social purposes and find difficulty in adjusting rapidly to new conditions of social and cultural change or to new environmental situations.

The various Southeastern tribes,[59] the Creek, Choctaw, Chickasaw, Cherokee, and Seminole, most of whom spoke Muskogean and were part of the Creek Confederacy at various times, offer an opportunity to see what happens to matrilineal lineage systems under conditions of recent acculturation from white sources and further to combine functional and historical methods and points of view. All these groups participated in a similar culture and were organized in terms of matrilineal clans and phratries and/or moieties and lived in "towns" in extended matrilocal families. A class system cut across the clan and "town" sys-

[59] See Swanton, *Indians of the Southeastern United States*, for details.

tems, and there was an elaborate ceremonial system with calendric observances throughout the year.

During a preliminary study[60] of the kinship terminologies of these tribes, I found a considerable number of variations from the normal Crow pattern, which seemed to form a regular series. It was possible to formulate a series of hypotheses by which these apparent variations might be explained in terms of different degrees of white acculturation incident to the removal of these tribes to Oklahoma in the early nineteenth century and their subsequent life. I was fortunate enough to find historical documentation for the Choctaw case and further evidence in the historical records of the other tribes to make the hypotheses worth pursuing. In the meantime Gilbert's study of the Eastern Cherokee (see above, pp. 285 ff.) provided further confirmation of the hypothesis by giving a base line against which the Western Cherokee in Oklahoma might be measured.

Spoehr became interested in these problems soon afterward and carried out extensive field researches in Florida and Oklahoma during 1938–39. These studies not only provided new data on Seminole social structure but confirmed the hypotheses which had been proposed and provided further demonstrations of the processes by which the changes had come about, as well as the acculturational factors involved. Since the Seminole had split off from the Creek during the eighteenth century and part had stayed in Florida while the rest were removed to Oklahoma, he had an excellently controlled situation, which is about as close to "laboratory" conditions as we can get in social anthropology. Not only was he able to determine the differential developments in the two Seminole groups and the factors—acculturational and ecological—which were responsible, but he was able to use the more conservative Seminole data to throw light on early Creek organization. By a detailed genealogical and social investigation among the various Oklahoma groups, he was also able to work out the stages by which Crow-type kinship systems were progressively modified toward bilateral types, and the concomitant variations in other aspects of social organization, which he

[60] Eggan, "Historical Changes in the Choctaw Kinship System."

shows are in functional relation with the changes noted in the kinship systems. On the basis of these results he is able to propose a number of new hypotheses for further investigation. Spoehr's studies are the best controlled and most detailed comparative studies of social and cultural change which we have for American Indian tribes, and this brief mention does not do them justice—they need to be read.[61]

These studies of Southeastern tribes also contribute further to our knowledge of matrilineal lineage systems of Crow type and their strengths and weaknesses. In contrast to the village tribes of the Missouri River region, the Creek, Choctaw, and other Southeastern tribes lived in a somewhat dispersed pattern around "town" squares, and the considerably larger populations increased the problems of social integration. The various dual organizations, warfare and games, the class structure, and the confederacy itself may all be seen as integrative devices for the maintenance of tribal or supertribal unity, though they had other functions as well.

In terms of an ultimate interest in systematic general "laws," the Southeastern tribes would seem to support Radcliffe-Brown's suggestion that "any marked functional inconsistency in a social system tends to induce change."[62] The kinship systems—and social structures—of the Southeastern tribes seem to have partially recovered their internal consistency by means of a series of similar changes. Here is also an instance where structural-functional and historical points of view are both essential—neither by itself can lead to these results.

In the Southwest I have attempted to organize and compare the complex social structures of the various Western Pueblos—Hopi, Hano, Zuni, Acoma, and Laguna—for the purposes of preliminary classification and interpretation.[63] In general, these Pueblos appear to conform to a single specialized type of social

[61] Spoehr, "Camp, Clan, and Kin among the Cow Creek Seminole of Florida"; "Kinship System of the Seminole"; "The Florida Seminole Camp"; "Changing Kinship Systems."

[62] Radcliffe-Brown, "Kinship Terminologies in California," pp. 533–34.

[63] Eggan, Social Organization of the Western Pueblos.

structure, based on matrilineal lineages and clans, and with a Crow type of kinship system and with cross-cutting society or ceremonial organizations. The variations which are present I have tried to account for in historical terms, either as events in the past, such as the Pueblo Rebellion and its aftermath, or as aspects of Spanish and American acculturation.

The relationship between the Eastern and Western Pueblos and the considerable differences between their social structures offered a problem which I attempted to solve by an accultural-tional hypothesis, following the lead of Parsons but going considerably further into the realm of conjecture. Murdock, on the other hand, classifies the Tewa in his "Eskimo type" of social organization and states that "the non-exogamous patri-sibs and patri-moieties of the Tewa are obvious survivals of a previous patrilineal organization."[64] The key to this problem may lie in what I have called the "Keresan bridge," the group of Keresan-speaking Pueblos which adjoin Zuni on the west and the Tewa and Tiwa on the east. Here there is some evidence of variation from lineage to bilateral organization, and I have interpreted it as in that direction, though further evidence may reverse it.

Recent studies by Dozier on the Hopi-Tewa of Hano have both confirmed and greatly expanded our knowledge of the social structure of this little-known pueblo and the changes which have gone on since the Hano people migrated to First Mesa around 1700 and settled among the Hopi. He has shown how the mi-nority Hano group has maintained its cultural individuality, while being assimilated biologically, through the structural de-vice of strict matrilocal residence. He has also shown how Hano kinship terms, identical with or obviously related to the New Mexico Tewa, have been reorganized in terms of the Hopi model and fitted to quite different principles of organization, as well as correlated to different patterns of behavior.[65]

[64] Murdock, *Social Structure*, p. 227. Hill's forthcoming study of Santa Clara and Dozier's comparative studies of Tewa and Hano may help us decide which is the better interpretation.

[65] Dozier, "Resistance to Acculturation and Assimilation in an Indian Pueblo"; "Kinship and Linguistic Change among the Arizona Tewa"; *The Hopi-Tewa of Arizona*.

For Zuni, recent investigations by Roberts and Schneider of current kinship patterns suggest that I considerably underestimated the amount of acculturation which has gone on in this pueblo. The preliminary evidence which Roberts has assembled from genealogies indicates that the situation Kroeber described was more typical than I had thought. There is still a core or nucleus of kinship terminology which conforms to the Crow type, but there is a further invasion of the kinship structure by the self-reciprocal grandparent-grandchild terminology and a considerable amount of random variation.[66] Whether conservative families show similar trends is not yet clear, but the general breakdown of marriage at Zuni suggests the degree of change. I would therefore support the original analysis, but in terms of a much greater degree of acculturation than is to be found among the Hopi. In general, we have probably considerably underestimated the amount of Spanish acculturation; and Adair's account of the American period makes clearer the influences of agency and school, particularly with regard to water and land.[67]

For the non-Pueblo Southwest we now have a number of studies of the Southern Athabaskans to supplement Opler's and McAllister's pioneer accounts,[68] particularly Goodwin's study of Western Apache social organization.[69] Opler's preliminary survey[70] of kinship terminologies established two basic types: Jicarilla and Chiricahua, which corresponded in part with Hoijer's linguistic classification. More recently Bellah[71] has reviewed all the Apache kinship systems from a structural-functional standpoint, utilizing the Parsons-Levy categories, with

[66] Schneider and Roberts, "Zuni Kinship Terms." Research on these problems is still in process.

[67] Adair and Leighton, "People of the Middle Place: A Study of the Zuni Indians." Adair has prepared the first part on Zuni culture of this volume.

[68] See Opler, above, pp. 173 ff., and bibliography in Bellah; McAllister, above, pp. 99 ff.

[69] Goodwin, The Social Organization of the Western Apache.

[70] Opler, "The Kinship Systems of the Southern Athabaskan-speaking Tribes."

[71] Bellah, Apache Kinship Systems.

very interesting results. He notes that the seven tribes studied are in the same general region, speak closely related languages, and have much of their culture in common, so that they "were in all likelihood a homogeneous group in the not too distant past."[72] By comparing their kinship systems, he isolates the differences and attempts to account for them in terms of differences in the environment and in culture contact. He criticizes certain of Opler's conclusions and some of Murdock's theorems, though, in general, his data support Murdock. He questions Opler's conception of Chiricahua as a basic type—"the results of this research lie in the opposite direction: that Chiricahua is probably one of the more divergent systems"[73]—but he does not present the reasoning behind this conclusion. He also demonstrates that the apparently random character of certain distinctions are actually "related to systematic structural differences and are not decided by 'minor or irrelevant factors,' "[74] as proposed by Opler and followed by Murdock.

This is an important study, despite Bellah's illusion that structural-functional types of analysis are not in present use, but it needs a historical dimension to give it further validity. Kroeber early suggested the use of linguistic criteria to test Opler's kinship classification by utilizing kinship terms from Northern, Pacific, and Southern Athabaskan;[75] and Hoijer is at present engaged in a large-scale linguistic comparison which will serve as a basis for establishing types and variants in each region. If we can establish time relationships for the splitting-off of the Southern Athabaskan tribes by means of lexico-statistic or other techniques, we shall be in a position to gain additional insights into the development of their social systems. We shall then be able to compare Pueblo and Southern Athabaskan social structures in a partially controlled framework, in which it may be possible to isolate the effects of the introduction of agriculture

[72] *Ibid.*, p. 4.

[73] *Ibid.*, p. 63.

[74] *Ibid.*, pp. 133–34.

[75] Kroeber, "Athabascan Kin Term Systems."

and other traits on various aspects of social structure, as well as to see the correlative influences of Navaho and Apache groups on Pueblo life.

Turning, now, to the Plains, there has been a considerable amount of research in recent years, and the Plains area is ripe for a new integration which will be more satisfying than the older ones. Through the work of Strong, Wedel, and others, recently summarized by Lehmer,[76] we have an adequate outline of cultural development in the archeological horizons firmly anchored in stratigraphy and radiocarbon dates and buttressed by the testimony of many sites. I have elsewhere discussed the interrelations of archeology and ethnology for the interpretations of cultural development in the Plains.[77] For theoretical understanding of Plains culture we need to center our attention on social structure and see its interrelations with ecology, on the one hand, and political and ritual activities, on the other. We can then see more clearly the nature of the social and cultural processes by which tribal groups entering the Plains from neighboring areas (as practically all of them did) came to develop similar sociocultural types.

In a preliminary survey of "Kinship in the Plains Area" (above, pp. 89–95) I classified the majority of the Plains tribes as having a social structure centered around the band and the tribal camp-circle, and with a "generation"-type kinship system based on the principle of the equivalence of siblings. In terms of the data then available, the matrilocal extended family appeared to be the major type; but more recent studies indicate that a bilateral extended family centered on a group of siblings was equally important, being found particularly among the Teton Dakota and the Kiowa.

Recent studies of the Comanche, Gros Ventre, Blackfoot, Teton, and Wichita, among others, enable us to enlarge our understanding of Plains institutions. The Comanche, while a

[76] See Lehmer, "The Sedentary Horizon of the Northern Plains," for details and references.

[77] Eggan, "The Ethnological Cultures and Their Archaeological Backgrounds."

"typical" tribe in most respects, never developed a tribal super-structure of camp-circle, chiefs' council, and soldier societies. Wallace and Hoebel suggest that this may be a result of their Shoshonean background,[78] but Colson proposes an ecological explanation: the larger band groupings and the larger and more dispersed buffalo herds made the summer hunt less crucial for survival.[79] In either case the Comanche data indicate that social institutions are not so readily borrowed as are cultural practices. Regina Flannery's monograph[80] on the Gros Ventre indicates that they do not have patrilineal clans, as suggested earlier, but their broken-down condition makes it impossible to clarify all the questions as to their social system. For the Blackfoot Confederacy we have a series of studies which throws new light on the social organizations of these interesting tribes. Hanks and Richardson's account of Northern Blackfoot kinship[81] indicates different subsystems for men and women, the former age-graded and the latter generational. In addition, there are kinship extensions based on the matrilineal lineage, though the basic orientation is toward the patrilineal.

Goldfrank outlines the changing configurations in social and religious institutions among the Blood during the Reserve Period and shows the importance of history in such a process: "The full import of the material collected in the field became clear only after it was analyzed in the light of the historical records. . . . . In every analysis of the acculturation process, history has been the key to an understanding of the past changes in social structure."[82] With Lewis' study of the Blackfoot[83] during the period of white contact as a framework, the comparative study of the variations among the Piegan, Blood, and Northern Blackfoot can be seen in better perspective, and it is hoped that the original

[78] Wallace and Hoebel, *The Comanches*, p. 235.

[79] Colson, review of *The Comanches*, pp. 13–14.

[80] Flannery, *The Gros Ventres of Montana*, Part I: *Social Life*.

[81] Hanks and Richardson, *Observations on Northern Blackfoot Kinship*.

[82] Goldfrank, *Changing Configurations*, p. 2.

[83] Lewis, *The Effect of White Contact upon Blackfoot Culture*.

plan of the Columbia group to make such a study can be carried out.

More recently the Schmitts have been studying the Caddoan tribes of the Plains: the Caddo proper, Wichita, Pawnee, and Arikara; their joint monograph on the Wichita,[84] utilizing genealogical data from a wide age-range, reconstructs the kinship system of 1850-75 and demonstrates the steps by which it has changed to the modern reservation system. The older Wichita system is based on the "generation" principle, but certain features suggested a derivation from a still older matrilineally oriented system. Comparison with Caddo, Pawnee, and Arikara developed a series of probable changes in Caddoan kinship which parallel those worked out by Spoehr for the Southeastern tribes; Iva Schmitt is now testing this working hypothesis among the Pawnee.

Murdock[85] classifies most of the Plains tribes that he includes in his study as subtypes of "Hawaiian" and derives them from "Normal Hawaiian" social structures; the Teton are, however, put in "Yuman" and derived from "Patri-Iroquois." The Schmitts have postulated changes for the Wichita which are contrary to this assumption.[86] The Arapaho probably belong ultimately with the Northern Algonkians, who have a cross-cousin marriage system and an Iroquois- or Dakota-type cousin terminology, whereas the Cheyenne derive from the sedentary earthlodge culture of the Prairie Plains, according to archeological evidence, and very probably had a lineage organization before moving onto the Plains. Hence some variation in derivation is probable.

Ecological studies in the Plains region by Wedel[87] and others have demonstrated the significance of climatic variations for subsistence economies and population concentration and have indicated the kinds of studies we need for the future. Collier, in

---

[84] Karl and Iva Schmitt, *Wichita Kinship: Past and Present.*

[85] Murdock, *Social Structure*, chap. viii.

[86] Schmitt and Schmitt, *op. cit.*

[87] Wedel, "Some Aspects of Human Ecology in the Central Plains."

his field study[88] of local groups in the Northern Plains, found two types of large bands, as well as the "camp" based on extended kinship and the temporary hunting camp. Each of these was related to the annual cycle of subsistence, as well as to social conditions prevailing in the region. In the Plains area as a whole the annual cycle of the buffalo, involving periodic aggregation and dispersion, was reflected in the human cycle of camp-circle and dispersed band. We have noted Colson's suggestion that differences in the cycle of the buffalo in the Southern Plains may have been related to the Comanche's simplified social patterns— she also suggests that we need more studies on the level of the band in the Plains as a whole.[89]

For such problems as the nature of "respect" and "joking" relationships, which were described in detail for a number of tribes in the original edition, we now have considerable additional data for Plains tribes. Hassrick[90] has analyzed Teton Dakota kinship organization in terms of a gradient of respect and familiarity; and Karl and Iva Schmitt[91] have done the same for the Wichita. Radcliffe-Brown[92] and Murdock[93] have presented theoretical discussions of joking relationships; Radcliffe-Brown suggests that they are one special form of alliance, comparable to that formed by gift-exchange, intermarriage, or ritual kinship. Murdock, on the other hand, is more concerned with avoidance relationships and offers an explanation based on psychoanalytic inferences as to relations within the family. It is clear that my own tentative explanation of joking and respect relationships (above, pp. 75–

[88] Collier, "Field Notes."

[89] Colson, *op. cit.*, p. 13.

[90] Hassrick, "Teton Dakota Kinship System."

[91] Schmitt and Schmitt, *op. cit.*

[92] Radcliffe-Brown, "On Joking Relationships."

[93] Murdock, *Social Structure*, pp. 272 ff. Murdock's emphasis on cross-sex patterns and behavior has led him to neglect joking and avoidance relationships between relatives of the same sex. His "distinct impression from general reading that the relations between brothers-in-law are commonly characterized by reserve and respect, especially by a marked tendency to avoid mentioning matters of sexual import" (p. 279), is certainly not true for the Plains tribes or for the Northern Algonkians and many other groups.

81) is incomplete and needs to be modified and supplemented. There are enough data now available for the Plains to make a reformulation worth while—I would agree with Lowie's principle of method that "whatever interpretations appear from such an inquiry may then be compared with corresponding results from other regions."[94] As we shall see below, joking and respect relations play a somewhat different role in systems based on cross-cousin marriage, and it is perhaps premature to present a definitive explanation until we have a better understanding of the whole range of the phenomena involved.

We also have a number of specialized studies of Plains Indian life which give new perspectives on several problems. Provinse's pioneer study of law and sanctions in the Plains (above, pp. 341–74) suffered from a dearth of case studies as to the application of sanctions to particular offenses, as well as from a perhaps too narrow definition of legal phenomena. These deficiencies have been remedied in large measure by Hoebel's study of Comanche law-ways,[95] Richardson's analysis of law and status among the Kiowa,[96] and Llewellyn and Hoebel's profound interpretation of Cheyenne law.[97] Hoebel has a monograph on primitive law in press which will put these and other studies in new perspective.

Various studies of warfare[98] and trading relations[99] in the Plains region have thrown additional light on their changing patterns and significance for organization—both intratribal and supertribal. Particularly significant in this respect is Mishkin's re-evaluation of the role of the horse in Plains culture,[100] in which he calls attention to its importance for economic activities and for social ranking, as well as for warfare, though economic determinism is overemphasized in his account.

[94] Lowie, *Primitive Society*, pp. 101–2.

[95] Hoebel, *Political Organization and Law-Ways of the Comanche Indians*.

[96] Richardson, *Law and Status among the Kiowa Indians*.

[97] Llewellyn and Hoebel, *The Cheyenne Way*.

[98] Smith, *The War Complex of the Plains Indians*; Secoy, *Changing Military Patterns of the Great Plains*.

[99] Jablow, *The Cheyenne in Plains Indian Trade Relations*; Lewis, *op. cit.*

[100] Mishkin, *Rank and Warfare among the Plains Indians*.

In the general field of social and cultural change we have just begun to exploit the rich resources furnished in ethnohistorical documents, mostly filed away in government reports or manuscript collections. The historians who once exploited these materials for historical ends have largely disappeared, but the latter offer an important challenge to the cultural anthropologist. Philleo Nash's study of religious revivalism on the Klamath reservation (above, pp. 377–442) indicates what can be done with documentary data in a relatively controlled situation to test and reformulate hypotheses as to the nature and significance of nativistic cults. Mooney's account of the Ghost Dance of 1890[101] for a long time stood alone, but now we see the Ghost Dance as an example of a class of reactions to acculturative situations. Nash's revised hypotheses can be tested against the revivalistic cults that are still springing up on American Indian reservations, as well as on the "Cargo Cults" and other movements that have developed in Melanesia and New Guinea in the wake of the war.

These brief observations may call attention to the major new developments in the study of Plains society and culture. Plains Indian society, despite its lack of lineage and clan, still has a social structure. This structure is "horizontal" or generational in character and has little depth. The extended family groupings in terms of matrilocal residence or centered around a sibling group are amorphous but flexible. The bilateral or composite band organization, centered around a chief and his close relatives, may change its composition according to various circumstances—economic or political. The camp-circle encompasses the tribe, provides a disciplined organization for the great communal hunt, and a center for the Sun Dance and other tribal ceremonies which symbolize the renewed unity of the tribe and the renewal of nature. The seasonal alternation between band and tribal camp-circle is related to ecological changes in the environment, and particularly to the behavior of the buffalo. It is for these reasons that I believe an understanding of Plains social structure to be essential to the larger integration.

The working hypothesis proposed earlier (above, p. 93) that

[101] Mooney, *The Ghost Dance Religion and the Sioux Outbreak.*

"tribes coming into the Plains with *different* backgrounds and social systems ended up with *similar* kinship systems," can be tentatively extended to Plains social structure as a whole, despite the variations noted. That this is in large measure an internal adjustment to the uncertain and changing conditions of Plains environment—ecological and social—rather than a result of borrowing and diffusion is still highly probable.[102] Here is a hypothesis that can be applied to neighboring regions as well as to the Plains.

So far we have considered a limited number of problems and regions. We could examine with profit the discussion of Mesoamerican social organization by Guiteras Holmes;[103] the nature of the social systems of the Yuman tribes of the Lower Colorado River;[104] the sociocultural systems on the Northwest Coast, including the significance of the potlatch;[105] the changes in Iroquois social structure since the seventeenth century, as worked out by Basehart;[106] the re-evaluation of the Californian data in the light of the discovery by Gifford of the importance of patrilineal lineages in various areas; and many others.

But space permits the discussion of only one additional problem, and I have selected the problem of cross-cousin marriage in relation to the social organization of various regions in northern North America. In general, we have overlooked or ignored the significance of cross-cousin marriage; we will find that cross-cousin marriage provides a social structure which can stand alone or can combine in varying degrees with lineage structures such as clans and moieties. Radcliffe-Brown[107] has shown its

[102] Compare Murdock, *Social Structure*, p. 192, where he notes that traits of social organization show practically no tendency to yield distributions of the normal type exhibited by culture traits and complexes generally.

[103] Guiteras Holmes, "Social Organization."

[104] Spier, *Yuman Tribes of the Gila River;* Kroeber, *Handbook of the Indians of California.*

[105] Barnett, *"The Nature of the Potlatch"*; Codere, *Fighting with Property.*

[106] Basehart, "Historical Changes in the Kinship System of the Oneida Indians."

[107] Radcliffe-Brown, *The Social Organization of Australian Tribes.*

importance in aboriginal Australia for the understanding of forms of social structure; Lévi-Strauss[108] has more recently made it central to his theoretical analysis of kinship structure and marriage exchange; and my first published paper[109] was on the possibility that cross-cousin marriage was practiced among the ancient Maya, a suggestion for which there has since been some additional support.

Rivers is responsible for the modern theoretical study of cross-cousin marriage systems. As a result of working with such systems in Melanesia and India, he came to the conclusion not only that a "close connection exists between methods of denoting relationship or kinship and forms of social organization, including those based on different varieties of the institution of marriage," but that the terminology was "rigorously determined" by social conditions and could therefore be used to reconstruct past social institutions.[110]

The latter conclusion, in particular, has proved unacceptable to American anthropologists, as Tax's discussion shows (above, pp. 477–79), and even today there is considerable ambivalence shown toward the first portion. Thus Murdock, while accepting the influence of customs of preferential marriage on kinship terminology when they apply to all or most marriages, in his hypothesis concerning changes in social organization allots no place "to the influence of such factors as preferential marriage customs."[111] We can test this assumption against the data for the Northern Algonkian-speaking tribes.

Rivers,[112] on the basis of Morgan's schedules, had suggested the possibility that cross-cousin marriage formerly existed among some of the Northern Athabaskans, the Cree, and some of the Dakota; but this suggestion was not taken seriously until

[108] Lévi-Strauss, *Les Structures élémentaires de la parenté.*

[109] Eggan, "The Maya Kinship System and Cross-Cousin Marriage."

[110] Rivers, *Kinship and Social Organization,* p. 1.

[111] Murdock, *Social Structure,* pp. 123, 222.

[112] Rivers, *op. cit.,* pp. 49–55.

Hallowell[113] pointed out that kinship terms recorded in early documents reflected cross-cousin marriage among the Ojibwa, Ottawa, and Algonkin, and Strong[114] found cross-cousin marriage in full operation among the northern bands of the Naskapi. This latter discovery stimulated Hallowell and others to carry out further researches in the field, as well as to examine the existing literature more carefully, with the result that cross-cousin marriage was discovered to be widespread among the Northern Algonkian peoples north of the Greak Lakes and the St. Lawrence River.[115]

Strong's preliminary account of the northern bands of the Naskapi suggests that we have here a relatively new type of social structure for North America: *a bilateral band held together by cross-cousin marriage*. These bands were small, from 30 to 50 members, and composed largely of kindred. The family patterns were varied, though patrilocal extended families were common, and there was a constant shifting of families. Each band had a huge area in which to hunt and fish and depended primarily on the migrating caribou, with food being generally shared. There was no concept of definite hunting or trapping territories, such as are found to the south, nor was there much to inherit except hunting gear, which passed down in the paternal line. There was also no trace of any lineage or sib-organization, chieftainship is vested in the oldest or wisest man of the group, and shamanism is the result of individual predisposition. The Caribou God is the major deity, controlling hunting activities; and rites for the caribou are the most important rituals, though the black bear is also important.

Each of these northern bands is apparently held together

[113] Hallowell, "Was Cross-Cousin Marriage Formerly Practiced by the North-Central Algonkian?"

[114] Strong, "Cross-Cousin Marriage and the Culture of the Northeastern Algonkian."

[115] See Hallowell, "Cross-Cousin Marriage in the Lake Winnipeg Area," for a summary up to 1937. For a general orientation to the peoples, culture, and environment of the Northern Algonkian region see Johnson (ed.), *Man in Northeastern North America*.

largely by the practice of bilateral cross-cousin marriage. This marriage was considered most correct, and over a third of the cases in the Barren Ground band were of this type. Further, the kinship system exemplifies this marriage system, so to speak, since there are no affinal terms and there are all of the expected equivalences with regard to terminology, particularly the equation of siblings-in-law with cross-cousins. With regard to kinship behavior, there exists a complex joking relationship between cross-cousins, involving also the privilege of sexual relations with the sisters of male cross-cousins, which is consonant with the terminological differentiations and with the marriage expectations. There is no evidence of any conscious organization of cross-cousin marriage in terms of two or more intermarrying families, but this marriage practice may be a convenient way to avoid incest restrictions in small and isolated groups. Strong suggests that the relative isolation and small numbers played some part in maintaining the custom of cross-cousin marriage.[116]

The Naskapi bands immediately to the south, such as the Davis Inlet band, do not practice cross-cousin marriage at present, nor do their kinship systems show the correlative terminological correspondences, except in a few instances. Thus all cousins are classed with siblings, except for the mother's brother's daughter, female speaking; and the sexual joking and exchanges are limited to siblings-in-law, who are not equated with cross-cousins, except in the case mentioned. Here we have a relatively controlled situation, in which the variant factors seem to lie in the greater degree of acculturation in the more southern bands. Strong's conclusion: "The presence of cross-cousin marriage among these people, coupled with the recorded traces of the institution to the south and west, seems to indicate that it was an early ingredient of the Algonkian culture which has been able to persist only in the far north where other cultural contacts and white missionary influences have been relatively slight,"[117] forms an important working hypothesis, even though later discoveries modify the statement as to persistence.

[116] Strong, *op. cit.*, p. 278.
[117] *Ibid.*, p. 288.

The Montagnais and other Algonkian peoples to the south, in contrast to the northern Naskapi, live in a forested environment with a richer supply of sedentary game; Father Cooper has called attention to the importance of migratory or nomadic versus sedentary habits of fauna with reference to land tenure.[118] Here the population density increases from around one person per 300 square miles to perhaps one person per 25 square miles, and there is a correlative increase in band size and a reduction in the size of the hunting territories.

Speck's numerous studies[119] of land tenure in this region have conclusively demonstrated that these Northern Algonkian peoples did not hunt promiscuously but that a small family or group of families hunted and trapped each winter over particular districts. The boundaries of these districts were clearly known, and trespass was forbidden. The same family group continued to exploit a given district year after year, even practicing conservation of game, and the occupance and hunting rights in a particular territory usually passed from father to son, though, in the absence of sons, a son-in-law might take over.

Hallowell[120] has discussed the variability of the family hunting territory in the Northern Algonkian region in terms of the factors regulating the size of the territory. He finds that ecological factors are particularly important in this connection, and he believes that sound ecological hypotheses will enable us to describe the factors controlling the size of Algonkian hunting grounds as well as the "basic dynamics of the hunting territory as a whole."[121] His comparative data for the Berens River band in the Lake Winnipeg area shows larger groupings involving one or more married sons (or sons-in-law) or two married brothers and their families, when the father is dead, as additional units.

Cross-cousin marriage has been reported by a number of investigators from the Montagnais area, but it is apparently no

[118] Cooper, *Temporal Sequence and the Marginal Cultures.*

[119] See Speck, "The Family Hunting Band as the Basis of Algonkian Social Organization."

[120] Hallowell, "The Size of Algonkian Hunting Territories."

[121] *Ibid.*, p. 44.

longer a working system. Thus Flannery's account of "Cross-Cousin Marriage among the Cree and Montagnais of James Bay" shows that cross-cousin marriage is traditionally permissive and somewhat preferential but is dying out at the present time. The kinship system is consonant, in that cross-cousins are separated from parallel cousins and siblings; but she notes that the young people, under missionary or other white influence, have come to consider both types of cousins as closely related to them.[122]

The patrilocal extended families in this Northern Algonkian region, if they were to avoid marrying among themselves, would have to marry into neighboring families, for the most part. There is no evidence that particular extended families systematically intermarried—the exigencies of survival in this region would make that difficult—but it is clear that cross-cousin marriage once operated as an important integrating mechanism for the band. Flannery finds in these groups no evidence of a sib system and no property to conserve in the family through cross-cousin marriage. She proposes, as a tentative working hypothesis, that cross-cousin marriage may be the result of the extension of the incest taboo to parallel cousins through proximity of association, whereas cross-cousins, being reared in different families, would be free to marry.[123]

Looking at the Northeastern Algonkians as a whole and following up Hallowell's ecological hypothesis, Arch Cooper has suggested that the social gradient is related to the ecological gradient: in general, as one goes from the barren grounds in the north, with their migratory animals, to the richer forest regions of the south, with their sedentary animal populations, there is not only an increase in population density and band size and a reduction in the size of the band territory but a further differentiation of the band in terms of extended family units, with a preference for patrilocal residence and patrilineal inheritance, and a correlative differentiation of band territory into family

[122] Flannery, "Cross-Cousin Marriage among the Cree and Montagnais of James Bay," p. 31.
[123] *Ibid.*, pp. 32–33.

hunting units with boundaries and rules to trespass. Band integration was apparently supported and maintained by summer gatherings, a more complex ritual, and political organization, and by cross-cousin marriage.[124] The degree of interrelationship of these various factors seems promising enough to warrant further investigation, particularly in view of Hallowell's and Speck's studies noted earlier.

Hallowell's own field investigations among the Cree and Ojibwa-Saulteaux of the Lake Winnipeg region[125] have added a further dimension to our knowledge of cross-cousin marriage systems among the Northern Algonkian peoples. Not only did he find cross-cousin marriage still practiced in the area, but he was also able to show how the system operates. The kinship pattern of all the bands studied was of similar type, with the characteristic terminological equations of cross-cousin marriage. The kinship system not only defines the social status of individuals in such a way that only persons of the same generation are potential mates, but it divides this generation into "siblings" and "cross-cousins." The Saulteaux have, in addition, a patrilineal clan organization which places strangers not otherwise related and of different clan in the category of "cousin," those of one's own clan and generation being classed as "siblings."

With small communities and a low areal density, most marriages will be between individuals who are "cross-cousins" to one another, real or classificatory, and the original family lines will become more and more linked. Hallowell's genealogies confirm this theoretical picture rather closely in certain instances, and he found some families and clans which had intermarried over several generations. He also points out that in such situations the marriage of *first* cross-cousins cannot be viewed as an independent trait but rather "as an integral part of the operation of the social system as a whole."[126] He also shows clearly how aberrant marriages are brought into the proper kinship positions.

[124] Arch Cooper, "Ecological Aspects of the Family Hunting Territory System of the Northeastern Algonkians."

[125] Hallowell, "Cross-Cousin Marriage in the Lake Winnipeg Area."

[126] *Ibid.*, p. 100.

On the western side of Lake Winnipeg reside Saulteaux, who were originally identical in language and culture but who have had considerably more contact with whites than the more isolated Berens River groups. Here blood relationship is now a bar to marriage, and first cousins cannot marry; kinship terms have as yet not recrystallized into new patterns, but cross and parallel relatives tend to be merged, with cousins grouped together against siblings, and only the diminutive of "cross-cousin" conveying the sense of "sweetheart." The number of Anglicized synonyms and the trends toward English patterning are apparent.

"If," Hallowell concludes, "it can be assumed that the fundamental social organization north of the Great Lakes and the St. Lawrence River was once essentially similar to that in the Lake Winnipeg area, then the problem of contemporary variants in northern Algonkian kinship systems and marital practices may profitably be attacked in terms of this hypothesis." He states the hypothesis as follows: "*It seems to me that northern Algonkian kinship systems are . . . . intelligible as variants of a basic pattern that has undergone modification as the result of acculturative processes and differences in local conditions.*"[127]

In the meantime, Ruth Landes was carrying out field studies among the Ojibwa of southern Canada in the region of Rainy Lake, Ontario, and her published reports[128] give us a comprehensive account of Ojibwa social organization. During the summer the Canadian Ojibwa live in small villages of from three to fifteen closely related families; but during the winter they break up into individual family groups, each of which exploits its own hunting grounds. According to Landes, genealogies show no stress on matrilocal, patrilocal, or independent residence, and apparently individual preferences were the deciding factor.[129] Here, as among the Saulteaux, there were patrilineal exogamous clans with totemic names the members of which regarded one

[127] *Ibid.*, p. 108; italics are mine.
[128] Ruth Landes, "The Ojibwa of Canada"; *Ojibwa Sociology; The Ojibwa Woman.*
[129] *Ojibwa Sociology*, p. 76.

another as relatives. These were linked into larger phratry units, but there was no clan localization nor any special clan possessions beyond the regulation of marriage.

Within the village, kinship is the basis for social conduct, and there are definite behavior patterns between particular relations. The kinship system is "bifurcate collateral," and bilateral in character, and the classification of relatives is in accordance with cross-cousin marriage. The terminology was identical with that of the Cree.[130] Siblings of the same sex aid one another, and brothers and sisters must respect one another very highly, but cross-cousins are the "vital relationship," being involved in courtship, sex, and joking behavior; after marriage the respect relationship between potential parents-in-law and children-in-law becomes one of avoidance. These two intermarrying groups are the most important sets of relatives, so far as the Ojibwa are concerned.

Within the village the bilateral kinship obligations are not infringed on by clan obligations, except after the death of a spouse, when mourning and subsequent remarriage in terms of the sororate and levirate are controlled by the clan of the deceased. Clanship operates primarily in terms of "nonrelatives," defining the position of Ojibwa in other villages for hospitality and other purposes, and serving as an integrating mechanism for the whole tribe. This relatively clear division of function and the lack of corporate possessions for the clan, coupled with its absence among other Northern Algonkian peoples, suggests that the clan system may be relatively recent among the Ojibwa. A comparative study of Central Algonkian clan systems will throw light on this problem.

Landes notes, however, that though cross-cousin marriage is practiced among the Ojibwa to the north and east of the Manitou reservation on Rainy River, at Emo, at the present time, cross-cousin marriage is forbidden as part of a blanket taboo on marriage between all relatives. She states that "this seems a recent development, a consequence of contact with the Dakota

[130] For the Indian rationale of cross-cousin marriage see Father Rossignol's "Cross-Cousin Marriage among the Saskatchewan Cree."

Sioux."[131] The two populations are closely related, and the kinship terms and behavior patterns are the same except that cross-cousin marriage does not take place.

Landes' *Ojibwa Sociology* was in press at the time Hallowell presented his hypothesis, noted earlier, and she makes no attempt to explain the shift in cross-cousin marriage practices as possibly due to acculturative pressures from white society, but so recently that the kinship system has not yet readjusted to the change. This is a hypothesis that can be tested, however, and someone should visit the Rainy River reservations in the near future to affirm or deny it.

A more immediate opportunity to test this hypothesis was provided by the Red Lake Ojibwa, who are closely related to those at Emo but who have been subject to greater white acculturation on their reserve in northern Minnesota. Landes mentions that the Minnesota Ojibwa at Red Lake, Cass Lake, and Leech Lake do not practice cross-cousin marriage, nor do they make the terminological identifications with the marriage, although they have the same terms.[132] To examine this situation further, we sent a group of graduate students to Red Lake in 1947–48. Here Elizabeth Bott[133] found a patrilineal clan system, much like that at Emo, and utilized mainly for hospitality when visiting. She also found a kinship system in which the terminology was exactly like that at Emo, but without any joking between cross-cousins—only with siblings-in-law. Here a cross-cousin of the opposite sex was said to be "just like a sister—or brother," and marriage with them is viewed with horror. Relatives are counted as far as third cousins, and marriages should take place beyond that range.

Even so, she found a number of cases of marriage with close kin, all of which caused a furor. Upon investigation, most of

[131] Landes, "The Ojibwa of Canada," p. 104. In *Ojibway Sociology*, p. 55, however, she suggests that the cross-cousin marriage prohibition is the consequence of influence from the Minnesota Ojibwa.

[132] Landes, *Ojibway Sociology*, p. 55.

[133] Letter of July 23, 1948; see also Bott, "A Comparison of the Social Organization of the Emo and Ponemah Bands of Ojibwa Indians."

these turned out to have been instigated by Ojibwa who had come from Canada not too long ago. Today residence is generally patrilocal, and property is usually inherited in the patrilineal line; there is a more settled and concentrated pattern of life than among the Canadian groups. It seems clear that Red Lake is one step further away from cross-cousin marriage, in that the *behavior* patterns have been modified in accordance with the changes in marriage, though the terminological patterns are still largely the same. Of significance in this connection is the restriction of the sexual joking patterns to siblings-in-law, who are still potential mates under the sororate and levirate. We can predict that siblings-in-law will soon be differentiated from cross-cousins terminologically, as well. This separation of siblings-in-law from cross-cousins is an important marker in the breakdown of cross-cousin marriage systems, as we have noted for the Naskapi and as we will see later also.

The Canadian, Emo, and Red Lake Ojibwa form a relatively controlled series with respect to the degree of modification of their original kinship system and the probable degree of white (or Indian) acculturation. Hallowell's hypothesis allows us to see them as variant expressions of similar acculturative processes rather than as unrelated sets of traits. Landes' hypothesis that the restriction on marriage with cross-cousins at Emo is the result of influence from the Minnesota Ojibwa is not clear from the historical data available and needs further investigation. There are a large number of Ojibwa groups in both the United States and Canada; the study of these will give us further variants, depending on local conditions. Hallowell mentions, for example, that inquiries among the Plains Cree and Plains Ojibwa to the west in Alberta indicate that marriages of first cross-cousins are rare but that marriages of second cross-cousins have a high incidence, partly as a result of white religious pressures and partly perhaps as a result of influences from the Plains.[134]

[134] Hallowell, "Cross-Cousin Marriage in the Lake Winnipeg Area," pp. 109–10, n. 29.

Mandelbaum,[135] more recently, has studied the Plains Cree, who occupied the transitional area between the forests and the plains. Their migration into this region was relatively recent, and their social organization was intermediate in many respects between that we have described earlier and that of the Plains proper. The Plains Cree were organized into large bilateral bands which were loose territorial units, oriented around a chief and his relatives and with variable residence. The kinship system is organized in accordance with the logic of cross-cousin marriage, for the most part, and this marriage custom is reported as still practiced in some of the bands, though not compulsory.

Morgan[136] also compiled a Plains Cree kinship terminology which reflects cross-cousin marriage in its terminological equations (though Morgan was unaware of this marriage practice), and a comparison of the two is instructive.[137] The modern system is more "classificatory" than that recorded by Morgan, in that there is a greater tendency to equate the father with the father's brother, and the mother with the mother's sister, but both give a number of terminological equivalences indicative of cross-cousin marriage. There are differences also in the terms for children of cross-cousins, but the significance of these is not entirely clear. Mandelbaum also lists a series of alternate terms for certain relatives-in-law, some of which have almost completely supplanted the "cross-cousin" terminology. One of Mandelbaum's informants reported that cross-cousin marriage was practiced by the more easterly bands but not by the westerners.

These differences suggest the influence of another series of factors concerned with the adjustment to Plains life which I have described in an earlier article in this volume (above, pp. 89–95), as well as those of white acculturation. As the Cree and Ojibwa groups moved out onto the edge of the plains, they found that they had to adapt to new conditions in regard to group activities

[135] Mandelbaum, *The Plains Cree.*

[136] Morgan, *Systems of Consanguinity.*

[137] I am indebted to George Fathauer for a preliminary comparison of these kinship terminologies while he was holding a research assistantship at the University of Chicago.

for which their old social organization and political system were inadequate. Part of this shift to a broader-ranged and more flexible system is reflected in the changes in the kinship system, as well as in the development of warrior groups and in the shift in band composition and leadership—here both the comparison of the Plains Cree with their eastern relatives and the comparison of the Plains Cree at earlier and later periods lead to similar conclusions. The series of alternate terms listed byMandelbaum for certain relatives, on the other hand, is more probably due to the decline in cross-cousin marriage and the consequent need to distinguish relationships which were formerly functionally merged. This shift in cross-cousin marriage is related to the factors of white acculturation mentioned earlier, in all probability; correlatively, while "rough joking" continues between male cross-cousins, a much milder joking relationship occurs between a man and his female cross-cousins. Mandelbaum gives no data which would suggest a shift from first to second or more distant cross-cousins for marriage purposes, though this may well have occurred in part.

It is even *possible* that the Algonkian-speaking Gros Ventre and Arapaho of the high plains may represent the last stages of this process of adjustment to Plains conditions. While both groups have wide-range "generational"-type kinship systems and marry outside the range of known relatives, there are a few terminological equations, or partial equations, which are reminiscent of cross-cousin marriage, notably that of daughter-in-law and niece and, correlatively, aunt and mother-in-law, or uncle and father-in-law (above, p. 45). These by themselves are not particularly significant, and I did not so interpret them originally. But the Arapaho and Gros Ventre were in the Northern Plains in the late eighteenth century, and there is some probability—even if low—that they once had a cross-cousin marriage system which was modified and gradually given up as they adjusted their social structures to the new conditions of Plains life.[138]

---

[138] Regina Flannery's recent study of the Gros Ventre unfortunately provides no evidence for or against this historical hypothesis in the portions so far published.

The Northern Algonkian data indicate that cross-cousin marriage was important in this northern region and vindicate Rivers as against his critics, both in terms of the presence of cross-cousin marriage and in regard to its close connection with terminological systems. They also demonstrate the virtue of considering the social structure of a group as a social *system* and not as a series of independent customs or traits. Hallowell, who has done this in admirable fashion, notes that "without an understanding of how cross-cousin marriage works in terms of the social system considered as a whole, intertribal comparisons cannot mean very much."[139]

These Northern Algonkian tribes are organized primarily in terms of kinship, which is everywhere bilateral in character. Technically, most of the kinship systems are "bifurcate collateral," setting off the elementary family from collateral relatives; but Hallowell has shown that, while this is true formally, from a *sociological* standpoint the systems are equivalent to a "bifurcate merging" pattern.[140] This, of course, makes considerable difference with regard to where they are classified in the current classifications. The custom of cross-cousin marriage makes it possible to characterize the kinship system further. The essence of cross-cousin marriage is that it creates multiple bonds between a limited group of relatives and maintains these from generation to generation, rather than tying nonrelatives together in an expanding system. Thus it intensifies relationships locally but tends to isolate each local group from its neighbors, though never completely, of course. Everybody with whom one has social relations, including marriage, is normally a relative; strangers are potential enemies unless they can be brought into this system and treated as "relatives."

The Naskapi represent perhaps the simplest form that a cross-cousin social structure can take: the kinship system and the marriage practices comprise the essential system, and aboriginally probably each small band formed a tightly knit and semi-independent unit. The Montagnais farther south apparently

[139] Hallowell, "Cross-Cousin Marriage in the Lake Winnipeg Area," p. 105.
[140] *Ibid.*, p. 109, n. 17.

had a more complex variant, with partially patrilocal extended families tied together in part by marriage and in part through summer band organization and band activities. In some regions there were apparently incipient "lineage" organizations centered around hunting and trapping territories, though there is evidence that these were stimulated in part through the fur trade. The Ojibwa in historic times have spread westward and to the north and south under pressures of various kinds. They maintained their kinship system and cross-cousin marriage, with its intense local integration, but either added or borrowed a patrilineal clan system. This clan "grid" operated among the Ojibwa to maintain a "nation-wide" and even "international" integration on the basis of the clan relationships—expressed in kinship terms. I have suggested that this clan system is recent, since it has not affected the central social structure and has no localized or "corporate" features beyond the regulation of marriage and remarriage.

The Cree are important in this connection as a control group. They enjoyed a comparable expansion but did not develop a clan system or any other means of large-scale integration beyond linguistic and cultural similarities. Many of them engaged in the fur trade, often as middlemen, and this economic bond was apparently important; but considerable deculturation has taken place. An intensive comparison between the Cree and Ojibwa would be rewarding in connection with an analysis of the role of Ojibwa clans.

The virtues of Hallowell's hypothesis as to the basic social organization of this region and its variation in terms of acculturative processes and differences in local conditions are many. It puts the social structure of the region in perspective and makes it possible to formulate problems in sociocultural dynamics more adequately than otherwise. It also orders a great deal of apparently random social and cultural behavior with economy and finesse. And it has the further virtue of being testable by additional field work and by further historical research.

One problem of some importance is that of classifying kinship systems or social structures based upon cross-cousin marriage. As we have seen earlier, Murdock believes that customs of primary preferential marriage influence kinship terminology, and his statistical coefficients validate this belief. But in his theoretical formulations he considers kinship terminology to depend upon residence and descent patterns primarily and allots little influence to preferential marriage customs.[141]

On this basis Murdock sets up eleven major types of social organization; of the groups we have considered, he classes the Naskapi as "Normal Yuman" and the Ojibwa as "Bi-Dakota," neither of which is directly derivable from the other.[142] Utilizing sources similar to those of this paper, he characterizes the Naskapi as bilateral in descent but patrilocal or, alternatively, bilocal in residence; and the Ojibwa as patrilineal in descent and bilocal, or neolocal, in residence, and with bilateral kindreds. The "Yuman" type is not considered stable but in transition to a more definite descent pattern—it is characterized by Iroquois cousin terminology and the absence of exogamous unilinear kin groups. The "Dakota" type, on the other hand, is stable and widespread and includes, by definition, all patrilineal societies with Iroquois cousin terminology. Iroquois cousin terminology is thought to develop on the basis of unilinear descent, though it is also influenced by unilocal residence. On this basis Murdock apparently attributes the Naskapi cousin terminology to the influence of patrilocal residence and the Ojibwa cousin terminology to patrilineal descent.

But Strong states that, for the northern Naskapi, "post-marital residence may be either patrilocal or matrilocal" and that "a constant shifting of families from group to group within the band, or from band to band, makes any generalization impossible."[143] Furthermore, granted that the Ojibwa are "patrilineal" in descent, which may be true formally but not sociologically, the Cree are reported by Landes to have identical kinship termi-

[141] Murdock, *Social Structure*, p. 222.

[142] *Ibid.*, pp. 231 ff.

[143] Strong, "Cross-Cousin Marriage and the Culture of the Northeast Algonkian," p. 286.

nology and by Hallowell to have a similar social system, except for patrilineal clans. Only the Montagnais would seem to have strong tendencies toward patrilocal residence, and even here there are many exceptions.

In this whole Northern Algonkian region the kinship systems and social structures appear to have a common pattern, so far as the central structure is concerned. There are variations, to be sure, but the similarities outweigh the differences. In this region, also, there are no uniformities in either descent or residence patterns. There is, however, uniformity with regard to the practice of cross-cousin marriage throughout the region in the present or recent past, and I would suggest that there is a definite relationship between cross-cousin marriage and the kinship systems in this area. Murdock, in his preliminary study of "North American Social Organization," states that among the northern Naskapi "patrilocality has given rise to preferential cross-cousin marriage and Iroquois cousin terminology."[144] How this comes about is not clear, and in any case the evidence as to residence makes it improbable. Murdock elsewhere makes some theoretical suggestions as to cross-cousin marriage which involve unilinear descent,[145] but these likewise do not fit this region.

For purposes of classification of social structures it seems to me that we have to class the Northern Algonkian systems together as variants of a single type related to cross-cousin marriage. The Northern Algonkians have basic similarities in language and culture, and they inhabit a region with a generally similar ecology, in which they make a bare subsistence living. It would be surprising to find radically different social structures here. This is Hallowell's conclusion as against Murdock's. Looking at the further variations which have been noted, Hallowell's hypothesis that these are "intelligible as variants of a basic pattern that has undergone modification as a result of [white] acculturative processes and differences in local conditions" seems to hold for the cases examined, except possibly for

[144] Murdock, "North American Social Organization."

[145] Murdock, *Social Structure*, p. 320. The suggestions in "The Positive Gradient of Kinship" may well be significant otherwise, however.

the Plains-oriented groups, where the acculturative situation and processes may be of a different character. This hypothesis allows us to place the instances in a single frame of change and to control the comparative situation in a variety of ways, none of which involves so-called "conjectural" history or the reconstruction of institutions which may never have existed.[146]

The changes which have gone on under recent acculturative influences need further investigation, but the apparent results are relevant for the "Evolution of Social Organization" which Murdock has formulated and applied to his sample of 250 societies.[147] The Naskapi, who are now "Yuman," "are shown by both internal and distributional evidence to have been Hawaiian at one time. For the Ojibwa, who are Dakota in type, Hawaiian is a probable, though alternative, derivation." The Cheyenne and Arapaho, on the other hand, "are still Hawaiian and show no survivals of any other structure."[148]

That all the Northern Algonkian tribes were derived from a common type is probable and that this type is "Hawaiian" is possible. That Ojibwa was first derived from a "Normal Dakota" type and, in turn, from "Normal Guinea" or "Normal Yuman" or, alternatively, from "Iroquois" via "Yuman" seems a bit too complicated, however. Looking at the changes that have taken place in recent times, the shift in the northern Naskapi bands under acculturation has been from a "Normal Yuman" to an apparent "Hawaiian" type. Among the Northern Saulteaux, Hallowell reports a shift under strong white acculturation to cousin terms on the English model—from "Bi-Dakota" to "Eskimo," in Murdock's terms. And among the Minnesota Ojibwa the basic terminology has remained the same, although

---

[146] See, for example, Paul Radin's reconstruction of a former practice of marriage with the daughter of a sister among the Winnebago, of which he says there is "absolutely no question" that it was once permitted (*Method and Theory of Ethnology*, p. 35, n. 7).

[147] Murdock, *Social Structure*, chap. viii and Appendix A. Murdock states that he hopes interested specialists will try out the method on societies which they know well, especially where there is actual or inferential evidence against which to test the conclusions.

[148] *Ibid.*, p. 347.

the behavior patterns are different. But there has been one major change in all these groups: the development of a series of alternate terms for affinal relatives as the discrepancies between marriage theory and marriage practice become great enough to bring about a change.

The foregoing changes, if correctly interpreted, are not theoretically possible in terms of Murdock's Table A, though this is not necessarily a definitive test. Nor would I agree that the Cheyenne and Arapaho have always been the same. For the Arapaho I have suggested the possibility, at least, that they may have shifted from a cross-cousin system of Northern Algonkian type to their present system. The Cheyenne almost certainly once resided in earthlodge villages and very likely had matrilineal descent and matrilocal residence patterns before moving out onto the Plains, though we do not have any clear evidence as to their kinship system at that time.

The Northern Algonkian data also suggest that Steward's generalizations[149] as to the economic and social basis of primitive bands need some modifications and additions. He has done this, of course, himself as a result of his studies of *Basin-Plateau Aboriginal Sociopolitical Groups*, but the Northern Algonkian data add another dimension by emphasizing the probable role of cross-cousin marriage in producing bilateral or composite bands. It is of interest here that cross-cousin marriage in a variety of forms appears scattered throughout the Great Basin, often among the more isolated groups. Steward does not consider it of any great importance in terms of the social structure of the region, and it is not tied in with the kinship system to the same extent as among the Northern Algonkian groups, but there may well be important parallels between the two regions. Cross-cousin marriage may bring about a social system which is *structured* enough that residence patterns and descent patterns can vary considerably without necessarily changing the essential character of the system in its local aspects. If this should be so, we would need to consider cross-cousin marriage as more important than we have in the past, and for these kinds of systems we might

[149] Steward, "The Economic and Social Basis of Primitive Bands."

have to revalue the significance of descent and residence patterns. The various marriage practices of the Basin area might well be considered from the standpoint of the structures they create.

For the Northeastern region generally, Hallowell[150] has postulated a constellation of psychological characteristics making up the typical personality structure of the individuals concerned and has extended it tentatively to other Eastern Woodland groups such as the Iroquois. Beyond this core of personality characteristics a considerable amount of variation has been reported, and it may turn out that these variations are intelligible in terms of the variations noted in social structure and family organization, on the one hand, and the degree and types of acculturation, on the other. It is significant, for example, that the Ojibwa now feel that the Canadian Indians are different from those of the United States, despite close relations in blood, language, and culture.[151]

Cross-cousin marriage, in bilateral or unilateral form, occurs in several other regions of North America: the Northwest Coast, the Athabaskan area, possibly among some of the Eskimo and Aleut, and in California and the Great Basin, as well as in Central America and in tropical South America. In each region, as Hallowell points out, we have to see how cross-cousin marriage works in terms of the social system as a whole: "To discuss it as a 'culture trait' divorced from the social context of which it is a part . . . . can only lead to superficial and inept comparisons, if it does not involve an actual distortion of fact."[152] But once such a series of studies has been made, we will then be able to isolate the essential role of cross-cousin marriage more adequately. We can also see the variant combinations into which cross-cousin marriage can enter.

Among the Haida on the Northwest Coast, for example, there

[150] Hallowell, "Some Psychological Characteristics of the Northeastern Indians"; "Culture, Personality, and Society."

[151] Landes, *Ojibwa Sociology*, p. 1. She refers to the "conventionality" of this distinction, but it may have a psychological basis.

[152] Hallowell, "Cross-Cousin Marriage in the Lake Winnipeg Area," p. 105.

is a complex social structure organized on the basis of matrilineal exogamous moieties, cross-cousin marriage, and avunculocal residence. According to Murdock, "Each avuncu-clan comprises the inhabitants of a particular village—a group of matrilineally related adult males together with their wives, their unmarried or recently married daughters, and their young sons who have not yet left to join the household of a maternal uncle."[153] Among the neighboring Tlingit a similar structure is found, except that the village is characteristically composed of two intermarrying local segments of the matrilineal moieties— or two "avuncu-clans," in Murdock's terminology. Some of the southern Tlingit have three matrilineal phratries, and the Tsimshian have four. Here is a series of increasing complexity, and a study of the differential role of cross-cousin marriage in each would be of great interest. For the northern Tlingit the "ancestral lines are ideally conceived as ever-intertwining and the marriages between them as ever renewed or perpetuated. . . . . The individual or self is perhaps never ideally complete, unless it is the product of the correct ancestral lines, is mated again to the paternal line, and procreates children of the same ancestry."[154] Frederica de Laguna points out that this ideal is never completely achieved, because of the advantages of having grandparents and affinal relatives in several different local clans —here may be a clue to the more complex social structure among the southern Tlingit and Tsimshian.

The complex rights to land, property, and privileges are organized in terms of lineage, clan, and moiety and are mediated through the potlatch. The kinship systems are organized in terms of the matrilineal lineage and cross-cousin marriage. Ideally, there is no need for affinal terms, but, as noted, the ideal situation is not completely achieved. Here avunculocal residence

[153] Murdock, *Social Structure*, p. 72. Note that Murdock uses "clan" in a special sense, but the meaning is clear.

[154] Frederica de Laguna, "Tlingit Ideas about the Individual," p. 175; see also Catherine McClellan, "The Interrelations of Social Structure with Northern Tlingit Ceremonialism," for an account of the way in which Tlingit ceremonialism serves to strengthen and reaffirm basic social groupings.

further complicates the situation, and the nephew may inherit his maternal uncle's house and marry his widow as well as his daughter. The kinship terminology takes this into account, classifying the father's sister and the father's sister's daughter—who may also be the mother's brother's wife and the mother's brother's daughter—together. But there is no line of father's sisters such as we find in the normal Crow type, so that the kinship systems of this region should be given a separate name to avoid continuing this confusion. Murdock, following Spier in the utilization of cousin terminology for major classification, lists the Haida and Tlingit as "Avuncu-Crow"; but, pending a more detailed comparison of "lineage" type systems, with and without cross-cousin marriage, we might better call these northern Northwest Coast systems "Tlingit type" or "Haida type" to distinguish them from the ordinary Crow-type kinship systems.

In these complex Northwest Coast structures, cross-cousin marriage serves to tie together the local clan and lineage segments into a highly integrated unit. Each village has its own territory and fishing or hunting rights; but without a wider integrating mechanism, there would be little tribal unity. This latter is provided by the matrilineal exogamous moiety—or phratry—system which encompasses every individual (and extends to neighboring tribes as well), regulates the co-operative and competitive aspects of social life, and provides continuity and a corporate character.[155] In these tribes the lineage pattern implicit in cross-cousin marriage social structures is given explicit expression in terms of rules of descent, succession, and inheritance. Through avunculocal residence males are brought up under the guidance of their maternal uncles and succeed to the latter's position as chief of the house, or of the village. The typical household is composed of males related through the female line, and in the ideal case the women may be similarly related, though of the opposite moiety. Under these conditions

[155] McClellan, *op. cit.*, p. 76, notes: "Kinship, real or putative, rather than territorial considerations, governs this pan-Tlingit dual organization, and a host of reciprocal obligations and kinship observances weave back and forth across the dividing axis."

group activities are facilitated, and lineage segments can act corporately to achieve particular ends. When we examine Northwest Coast society from this structural standpoint, we shall have new insights into its operation.

Unilateral cross-cousin marriage in its two forms provides somewhat different basic structures from that of bilateral cross-cousin marriage. For North America we have few good examples of matrilateral cross-cousin marriage, though Lévi-Strauss's reworking of the Miwok data[156] in terms of this marriage type suggests that it may have been important in some of the California tribes. In the Northern Athabaskan region there are two tribes reported as favoring unilateral cross-cousin marriage—the Chipewyan and the Kaska. The Chipewyan, neighbors of the Cree in the region of James Bay, have a kinship system that corresponds in part to the custom of marrying the father's sister's daughter, though the available data are incomplete. The Chipewyan have family hunting territories, like the Cree, but practice matrilocal residence, so that a man characteristically helps his father-in-law.

The Kaska, who practice matrilateral cross-cousin marriage, are located to the east of the Tahltan, who in turn adjoin the Tlingit. Through interaction with the Tlingit, the Tahltan have essentially the same general social structure, though cross-cousin marriage is not specifically reported. The Carrier to the south reflect the Tsimshian pattern, and cross-cousin marriage is specifically mentioned. The Kaska are divided into two matrilineal moieties, which regulate marriage and the organization of potlatches, but whose importance otherwise is slight. The kinship system, according to Honigmann, "corresponds to the Crow type."[157] Residence is generally matrilocal,[158] and a man is ex-

---

[156] Lévi-Strauss, *op. cit.*, chap. xxii.

[157] Honigmann, *Culture and Ethos of Kaska Society*, p. 128.

[158] Residence patterns among both Northern and Southern Athabaskans seem strongly matrilocal, in the absence of strong influences to the contrary, so that I do not attempt here to account for the differences between Chipewyan and Cree in this respect or to utilize the residence pattern in explanation of the kinship system among the Kaska.

pected to help his father-in-law; with an industrious son-in-law a man can retire from active hunting and look after the near-by trapping lines.

Father's sister's son and mother's brother's daughter are preferred marriage mates, and marriage between father's sister's daughter and mother's brother's son is prohibited.[159] The kinship terms given show a rough fit with this pattern of marriage, but structurally it is impossible for exogamous moieties and matrilateral cross-cousin marriage fully to adjust to each other.[160] The key to the significance of the marriage pattern seems to lie in the relation of matrilocal residence to the hunting and trapping operations. It takes a man about two years to adjust to the terrain and routes of a new territory, and there are statements that they find this adjustment a difficult one. However, matrilateral cross-cousin marriage would facilitate this process, since a man would be working for his mother's brother in the latter's capacity as father-in-law and would, in turn, be supported by his sister's son. These two employed reciprocal terminology before marriage and could joke with one another; after marriage there was respect and reserve coupled with mild joking, but no evidence of submission. This pattern is breaking down with the increased value of trap lines and the tendencies to have a son inherit.

The moiety pattern of the Kaska is very likely derived from the northern Northwest Coast via the Tahltan, since the moieties are called "Crow" and "Wolf," respectively, and regulate marriages and potlatching. The Kaska moieties are nonlocalized, however, and the constituent groups feel only vaguely related. Matrilateral cross-cousin marriage here seems to strengthen the mother's brother–sister's son relationship in a way comparable to avunculocal residence on the coast but is apparently not thoroughly integrated with the moiety structure, since the "incompatible" systems operate together without too much

---

[159] Honigmann, *op. cit.*, p. 129.

[160] Matrilateral cross-cousin marriage requires three or more intermarrying units to operate properly, since brother and sister exchange is forbidden by rule. This can easily be seen by drawing diagrams.

conflict. I would guess that the actual regulation of marriage is in terms of matrilineal lineages and that marriage with the mother's brother's daughter has not been on an extensive enough scale to order the intermarrying groups into a series which conflicts with the moiety grouping for ceremonial occasions.

The Chipewyan apparently used patrilateral cross-cousin marriage to obtain similar results, but in somewhat different ways.[161] This marriage type brings about the exchange of husbands, or wives, in successive generations, so that brother and sister exchange occurs over time but not in the same generation. Hence a man is aided here by his son-in-law, and the latter is supported, in turn, by the man's son's son. Thus in ideal cases there is a continual shifting back and forth between a few localities, but the integrative pattern is more amorphous than with bilateral cross-cousin marriage. Whether the Chipewyan ever practiced this marriage pattern systematically is not clear from the available evidence, though the kinship accommodations suggest that it was more than an occasional occurrence.[162]

The hypothesis advanced by Hallowell also furnishes a basis for evaluating variations in the social structures and kinship systems of the Dakota tribes, though I am not sure that Hallowell would want to go that far. Morgan presented extensive schedules for these Siouan-speaking groups; and, on the basis of the derivation of cross-cousin terms from the terms for siblings-in-law, Rivers suggested that these and other features pointed to the former prevalence of cross-cousin marriage.[163] Much later Lesser made a comparative study of Siouan kinship[164] for the purpose of analyzing the types of kinship systems which occurred—Dakota, Omaha, and Crow—and discovering possible

[161] I am indebted to George Fathauer for suggestions as to the role of the son-in-law in explaining the Chipewyan practice.

[162] Flannery ("Cross-Cousin Marriage among the Cree and Montagnais of James Bay," p. 32) records unilateral cross-cousin marriage from Rupert's House in the vicinity of James Bay; and Michelson found it on the west coast of James Bay and in Labrador, inland from Fort George.

[163] Rivers, op. cit., p. 52.

[164] Lesser's full study has unfortunately never been published, but a summary is presented in "Some Aspects of Siouan Kinship."

functional relationships and explanations. He finds an empirical correlation of the Dakota type with a sibless band organization, of the Omaha type with patrilineal clans' and moieties, and of the Crow type with matrilineal clans and phratries; and he considers the Dakota type to be the direct result of the levirate and sororate, both of which are common. He also sees the Dakota system as the basic type, with Omaha and Crow as later variations brought about by particular types of marriage, descent, and/or residence.

There is no statement in the literature that the Dakota tribes ever practiced cross-cousin marriage, but in view of Morgan's data and the intermediate position of the Dakota between the Ojibwa and the Plains tribes I originally suggested that "the Dakota kinship system was formerly based on cross-cousin marriage, but that under the influence of Plains life (and contacts) it was shifting to a 'Generation' type as exemplified by the Cheyenne" (above, p. 95).

Since then, Hassrick[165] has published his detailed account of the Teton Dakota kinship system, which shows that cross-cousins, while differentiated terminologically, behave as if they were "siblings," though less intensively. With regard to the terminology for cross-cousins, he says that there seems to have been a shifting of either terminology or the mode of behavior, since the terms are derived from the sibling-in-law terms plus the suffix -si, meaning "stop" or "go away." Hassrick thinks there has been a shift in behavior patterns, since he finds no evidence of cross-cousin marriage or joking behavior between cross-cousins in recent times.[166] But he finds strong indications that "the Dakota have shifted the emphasis of their system from a lineal and collateral to an affinial organization," with "good terminological evidence of former cross-cousin marriage."[167] He further suggests that "the entire shift may have been the result of a changing economy, for the system indicates an adjustment to the new Plains environment. The increased dependence upon

[165] Hassrick, "Teton Dakota Kinship System."

[166] *Ibid.*, p. 344.

[167] *Ibid.*, p. 346. He uses "lineal" to refer to ancestral affiliation.

the buffalo, and later the introduction of the horse demanded a dispersed mobility, and produced a larger population."[168] On the modern reservation there is another change going on, involving the breakdown of the old band organization and a greater emphasis on the conjugal family, and these are accompanied by "the return of cross-cousin marriage."[169]

These tentative conclusions receive considerable confirmation at the other end of the Dakota series—among the Santee or Eastern Dakota, who remained along the Mississippi River and in southern Minnesota while their linguistic and cultural relatives expanded into the Plains. Later they participated in the great massacre of 1862, which led to their imprisonment and removal to the Santee reservation. Some were brought back to their old territory by missionaries, and from these and their descendants Ruth Landes has constructed a rather detailed account of their former social life.[170]

The Santee resided in villages considerably larger than those of the Ojibwa. Each village was a kinship unit, for the most part, and closely identified with its land; trespass rules were kept. Each village was economically self-sufficient and hunted under the leadership of a shaman. Summer hunts for buffalo also occurred, sometimes in co-operation with other groups. The village was also the war-making unit; the village chief was normally a "peace chief," and a shaman was the war leader.

Each village was also normally "exogamous," since marriage was outside the range of kinship; residence was variable but probably patrilocal for chiefs, since chieftainship went in the male line. Marriage required intervillage co-operation, as did games, which expressed intervillage rivalry and usually ended in quarrels. There was one exception to village solidarity of significance to the present problem—the *berdache* were exiled from the village in a kindly but mournful spirit.

[168] *Ibid.*, p. 347.

[169] *Ibid.*

[170] Landes, "The Santee or Eastern Dakota." This account has unfortunately never been published but contains a great deal of valuable data on shamanism and political organization as well as on kinship and marriage. The field research was probably done around 1935.

The kinship system was a wide-range "classificatory" system based on generation principles, differing from that of the Ojibwa in not having the cross-cousin marriage equivalences, and conforming to the Teton system terminologically. But among the Santee the cross-cousin relationship is a courting, flirting relationship, in which there is unmerciful teasing and hostility. Landes notes a tendency to divert this courting relationship to siblings-in-law, who are identified in behavior and use the same basic linguistic terms. The Santee have forbidden the marriage of relatives "throughout historical time," but they consider the cross-cousin almost like a sibling-in-law, though cross-cousins are counted as "siblings" so far as their children's classification is concerned. Specifically, Landes says that male cross-cousins joke and play sexually and can humiliate one another in public without holding offense. Female cross-cousins have a similar relationship, but cross-sex cousins are more hostile and personal in their relations. Siblings-in-law have parallel relationships, but their behavior is bolder and, when of cross-sex, more exicted.

The exiling of the *berdache* from his native village is intelligible in these contexts. His homosexual tendencies made him act like a "cross-cousin" or "sister-in-law" to the men of the village, and he was apparently expelled from the village because of feelings that the village should be exogamous. In the new village he is a stranger and can have sex relations and even marry. He jokes with everyone, calling them "cross-cousins" or "siblings-in-law." In general he is the village clown and prostitute, and stories about *berdache* deal with their sexual exploits.

Marriage was not allowed between relatives closer than fourth cousins, and it was felt to be wrong and dangerous for close relatives to marry. The proper form of marriage involved parental selection, with exchange of property between the family groups; but elopements resulted when the couple took matters into their own hands or were too closely related to marry in the regular fashion. Residence was often matrilocal, though there was no general rule. Women owned the houses, and there was a marked avoidance of the mother-in-law, though the avoidance might break down after a while if the son-in-law was a good provider.

Mourning for a deceased spouse was violent, and remarriage was in terms of the sororate and levirate, but without the controls exercised by the surviving spouse's clan, as among the Ojibwa. This interesting account gives us a picture of Eastern Dakota social structure which is similar to Ojibwa in many ways but differs in village size and organization, and in the important matter of cross-cousin marriage. If we assume that the Santee once had cross-cousin marriage but gave it up for various reasons, including increase in population density and village size and the necessity of co-operation for communal buffalo hunts and for protection against enemies, part of this picture becomes more intelligible. For with the abandonment of cross-cousin marriage, the common status of "cross-cousin *and* sibling-in-law" is divided into two separate statuses. Since the joking and sexual behavior was still consonant with the "sibling-in-law" relationship, it apparently retained the old terms, whereas the "cross-cousin" relationship was no longer a marriageable one and a suffix meaning "stop" or "go away" was apparently added as a temporary marker. Hence Landes found that, while cross-cousins and siblings-in-law joked with one another, there was always tension involved, particularly with cross-cousins of the opposite sex, who thought in sexual terms but "had to repress part of it." There was considerable hostility expressed, sometimes in rape and sometimes in "eat-all" feasts of bear fat or muskrat fat. The stories of sexual and other exploits emphasized siblings-in-law more than cross-cousins, part of a tendency "to reduce the mating connotations to the vanishing point" and to heighten the mating tendencies of siblings-in-law as expressed through the sororate and levirate.

But this state of affairs involves serious contradictions, which the Teton Dakota have apparently solved in behavioral terms. They maintain the same terminological patterns, but the behavior between cross-cousins approximates to that of siblings, whereas the sibling-in-law behavior remains the same. The further stage in this process would apparently be to shift the terminology of cross-cousins to siblings, in keeping with the general Plains patterns, but the Teton Dakota were on the Plains for only three or four generations before being put on reservations. A test of this hypothesis can perhaps be made with the intermediate Dakota groups, the Yankton and Yanktonai, about whom we at present know relatively little.

This brief analysis suggests that in relatively well-controlled situations it may even be possible to infer the former presence of an institution such as cross-cousin marriage with a considerable degree of probability, even in the absence of the institution in the ethnographic and historical records. In this connection I should emphasize that the foregoing interpretation is mine and not Ruth Landes'—she nowhere in her paper suggests the possibility of former cross-cousin marriage among the Santee, and her evidence is all the more convincing for that very fact.

There is one further suggestion that might be made with regard to the usefulness of Hallowell's hypothesis. Archeologists are beginning to believe that Iroquois culture developed in the region of the Great Lakes and St. Lawrence rather than being imported wholesale from elsewhere. In the light of the parallels between Iroquois, Ojibwa, and Dakota kinship terminologies I should not be too surprised if early Iroquois social structure should turn out to be based on cross-cousin marriage. Lafitau's description of Iroquois kinship (quoted by Tax, p. 445) indicates an Iroquois-Dakota-type terminology as early as 1724, and Basehart[171] has traced the developments from that foundation among the various Iroquois groups. Archeological researches and ethnohistory may jointly give us an answer; while there are hints in Iroquois culture which suggest the possibility of a former practice of cross-cousin marriage, these are not of sufficient import to warrant such a working hypothesis at the present time.

SUMMARY

There are essentially no "conclusions" to this survey of certain of the results of the application of social anthropological methods, concepts, and points of view to North American tribes; nor have we considered all the areas or problems which might be

[171] Basehart, *op. cit.*

involved. This is primarily a report of "work in progress," and I have attempted to exemplify, if only indirectly, the significance of structural and functional concepts when put in the frame of history. The evidence presented here, incomplete though it may be, demonstrates that changes in aboriginal Indian social structure have been continuing throughout the historic period, not only as a result of direct acculturative processes, Indian or white, but also as a result of internal readjustment to new conditions of social and cultural life. With Murdock, I believe there is clear evidence of determinism in social structure, though I believe it is more complicated than his analysis provides. His conclusion that "the evolution of social organization is always channelized by the characteristics of the existing structure, which regularly limits the possibilities of change and in some instances also predetermines its direction,"[172] is an important working hypothesis, even though I have queried some of the details of his interpretation in terms of my own analysis. As he himself points out, the limitations involved in his selection of kinship data make a comparable analysis of other kinship terms desirable for a complete demonstration.[173]

This review of North American data suggests two major types of social structure,[174] with a third type which may be of equal importance or subordinate to the others in classificatory significance. One type is based on unilineal descent and organizes kindred in terms of the lineage principle. Such social structures frequently have "corporate" features and a complex organization and represent essentially specialized adaptations to relatively stable conditions. The other type is bilateral in character and emphasizes generation and the unity of the sibling group. These structures are usually shallow in depth but wide-ranging and provide a more flexible adaptation to fluctuating or

[172] Murdock, *op. cit.*, p. 250.

[173] *Ibid.*, p. 130.

[174] Compare Radcliffe-Brown, Introduction to *African Systems of Kinship and Marriage*, where a fourfold classification of social structures is proposed.

changing conditions. Between these two types we find various combinations, with possibilities of change in either direction. Systems based on cross-cousin marriage may represent a third major type—or, alternatively, important subdivisions of the first two mentioned. Such systems have an implicit or built-in structure which is bilateral and tightly knit, separating relatives from nonrelatives and making a sharp distinction between parallel- and cross-sex relationships, but which can also lead to unilineal emphases. The latter, in turn, can be merely a "clan grid," bringing nonrelatives into the kinship structure, or a highly integrated system such as is found among the Tlingit and Haida.

The neglect of the phenomena of cross-cousin marriage in American cultural anthropology is difficult to understand in view of the fact that it is now forty years since Rivers wrote *Kinship and Social Organization* and suggested the possibility that it was practiced by several of our northern tribes. Even the field researches of Strong and Hallowell demonstrating its actual occurrence in certain of these regions failed to stir anybody's imagination as to its possible significance. I have tried to remedy this deficiency in part by calling attention to the potential importance of Hallowell's conclusions as a working hypothesis for ordering the variations among all the Northeastern groups, except the Eskimo, in a single controlled framework of change. I have also extended this hypothesis on a more tentative basis to the elucidation of variations in the Dakota groups and even to the Iroquois. For cross-cousin marriage systems in northern North America I consider Rivers' conclusions as to their occurrence to be reasonably demonstrated, and we owe him an apology for our long neglect.

I have also emphasized the importance of controlling the comparative framework in as many directions as possible, so that variations in one set of factors or phenomena can be matched with other changes. Murdock has done this on a large scale with selected social phenomena and with important results. I see the two approaches as complementing each other, and conflicting results as setting up problems to be solved. It is gratifying to find him saying: "Historical and comparative tests lead to the same conclusion. The sociologist or functional anthropologist who suspects the one, and the historian or historical anthropologist who suspects the other, may each exercise his private choice. The social scientist, presumably, can accept both and take comfort that they are in complete agreement."[175]

I have also tried to build on the framework of analysis of social structures provided by Radcliffe-Brown. His lifelong efforts to develop social anthropology have involved the necessity of providing a large-scale framework of concepts, classifications, and tentative generalizations with which to attack scientific problems. Because his mind has ranged so widely, we can concentrate on more limited problems. By clarifying, with Kroeber, the relations between science and history, he has helped to make it possible for us to see the two in their relationship and to utilize both for further insight into the nature of society and culture. Steward has recently suggested: "For those who are interested in cultural laws, regularities, or formulations, the greatest promise lies in analysis and comparison of limited similarities and parallels. . . . . The most fruitful course of investigation would seem to be the search for laws which formulate particular phenomena with reference to particular circumstances."[176] The preceding survey suggests some of the possibilities of such a search in the field of kinship and social organization.

[175] Murdock, *Social Structure*, p. 352.

[176] Steward, "Evolution and Process," p. 325.

BIBLIOGRAPHY

BIBLIOGRAPHY

The following abbreviations are used:

AA	American Anthropologist
AAA-M	American Anthropological Association, Memoirs
AES-M	American Ethnological Society, Monographs
AES-P	American Ethnological Society, Publications
AMNH-AP	American Museum of Natural History, Anthropological Papers
AMNH-B	American Museum of Natural History, Bulletin
BAE-B	Bureau of American Ethnology, Bulletins
BAE-R	Bureau of American Ethnology, (Annual) Reports
CU-CA	Columbia University, Contributions to Anthropology
FMNH-PAS	Field Museum of Natural History, Publications, Anthropological Series
ICA	International Congress of Americanists
JAFL	Journal of American Folklore
JAI	Journal of the Anthropological Institute (now the Journal of the Royal Anthropological Institute)
JES	Journal of the Ethnological Society of London
SI-CK	Smithsonian Institution, Contributions to Knowledge
SI-MC	Smithsonian Institution, Miscellaneous Collections
SWJA	Southwestern Journal of Anthropology
UCPAAE	University of California Publications in American Archaeology and Ethnology
UW-PA	University of Washington, Publications in Anthropology

ACKERKNECHT, E. H. On the Comparative Method in Anthropology (in R. F. Spencer [ed.], Method and Perspective in Anthropology, Minneapolis, 1954).

ADAIR, J., and LEIGHTON, D. People of the Middle Place: A Study of the Zuni Indians (manuscript, 1954).

APPLEGATE, LINDSAY. Notes and Reminiscences of Laying Out and Establishing the Old Emigrant Road into Southern Oregon in the Year 1846 (The Quarterly of the Oregon Historical Society, 22, 12–45).

ATKINSON, J. J. Primal Law (London, 1903); with an introduction by Andrew Lang on "Social Origins."

BACHOFEN, J. H. Das Mutterrecht (Stuttgart, 1861).

BANCROFT, HUBERT HOWE. History of Orgeon, II (The Works of Hubert Howe Bancroft, San Francisco, 1886).

BARNETT, H. G. The Nature of the Potlatch (AA, n.s., 40, 1938, 349–58).

BASEHART, H. Historical Changes in the Kinship System of the Oneida Indians (Ph.D. thesis, Harvard University, December, 1952).

BATTEY, THOMAS. Life and Adventures of a Quaker among the Indians (Boston, 1903).

BELLAH, R. N. Apache Kinship Systems (Cambridge, Mass., 1952).

BENEDICT, R. The Concept of the Guardian Spirit in North America (AAA-M, 29, 1923).
———. Patterns of Culture (New York, 1934).
BICKNELL, A. D. The Tama County Indians (Annals of Iowa, 4, 1899, 196–208).
BLAIR, E. H. (ed.). Indian Tribes of the Upper Mississippi and the Great Lakes Region (Cleveland, 1912).
BOAS, FRANZ. The Methods of Ethnology (AA, n.s., 22, 1920, 311–21).
———. History and Science in Anthropology: A Reply (AA, n.s., 38, 1936, 137–41).
———. The Limitations of the Comparative Method of Anthropology (in his Race, Language, and Culture, New York, 1940).
———. Race, Language, and Culture (New York, 1940).
BOTT, E. Field Notes, 1947–48.
———. A Comparison of the Social Organization of the Emo and Ponemah Bands of Ojibwa Indians (M.A. thesis, University of Chicago, 1949).
BOWERS, A. W. Mandan Social and Ceremonial Organization (Chicago, 1950).
BRIFFAULT, R. The Mothers (New York, 1927, 3 vols.).
BRUNER, E. Field Notes on the Hidatsa, 1952–1953.
BUSBY, ALLIE B. Two Summers among the Musquakies (Vinton, Iowa, 1886).
CASTETTER, EDWARD F., and OPLER, MORRIS E. The Ethnobiology of the Chiricahua and Mescalero Apache, No. III (Ethnobiological Studies in the American Southwest, Bulletin of the University of New Mexico, Albuquerque, N.M., 1936).
CODERE, H. Fighting with Property: A Study of Kwakiutl Potlatching and Warfare, 1792–1930. (AES-M, 18, 1950, 1–136).
CODRINGTON, ROBERT HENRY. The Melanesians (Oxford, 1891).
COLLIER, D. Field Notes on Northern Plains Social Organization (1939).
COLSON, E. Review of E. Wallace and E. A. Hoebel, The Comanches, Lords of the South Plains (Man, No. 8, 1954).
COOPER, ARCH. Ecological Aspects of the Family Hunting Territory System of the Northeastern Algonkians (M.A. thesis, University of Chicago, 1942).
COOPER, J. M. Temporal Sequence and the Marginal Cultures (Catholic University Anthropological Series, No. 10, Washington, 1941).
CRAWLEY, A. E. Sexual Taboo: A Study in the Relations of the Sexes (JAI, 24, 1894, 116–25, 219–36, 430–46).
———. The Mystic Rose: A Study of Primitive Marriage (London, 1902).
———. Exogamy and the Mating of Cousins (Anthropological Essays Presented to E. B. Tylor, Oxford, 1907).
CURTIS, E. S. The North American Indian (Cambridge, 1909–11, Vols. V–VI).
DALL, W. H. Tribes of the Extreme Northwest. In Department of the Interior, United States Geog. and Geol. Survey of the Rocky Mountain Region (Contributions to North American Ethnology, 1, Washington, 1877).
DAVIDSON, D. S. (ed.). Twenty-fifth Anniversary Studies (Publications of the Philadelphia Anthropological Society, 1, Philadelphia, 1937).
DEACON, A. BERNARD. The Regulation of Marriage in Ambrym (JAI, 58, 1928, 325–42).
DE LAGUNA, F. Tlingit Ideas about the Individual (SWJA, 10, 1954, 172–91).
DENIG, EDWIN T. Tribes of the Upper Missouri (BAE-R, 46, 1929, 393–628).

De Smet, Father. Life, Letters and Travels of Father Pierre-Jean De Smet, S.J., 1801–1873 (New York, 1905, 2 vols.).

Dorsey, George A. The Arapaho Sun Dance (FMNH-PAS, 4, 1903).

———. The Cheyenne, I: Ceremonial Organization (FMNH-PAS, 9, 1905, No. 1).

———. The Cheyenne, II: The Sun Dance (FMNH-PAS, 9, 1905, No. 2).

Dorsey, J. Owen. Omaha Sociology (BAE-R, 3, 1884, 211–370).

———. Siouan Sociology (BAE-R, 15, 1897, 213–44).

Dozier, E. P. Resistance to Acculturation and Assimilation in an Indian Pueblo (AA, n.s., 53, 1951, 56–66).

———. The Hopi-Tewa of Arizona (UCPAAE, 44, No. 3, 1954, 259–376).

———. Kinship and Linguistic Change among the Arizona Tewa (manuscript, 1954).

Driver, H. E. Economy, Residence, and Descent in Aboriginal North America (manuscript, 1954).

Du Bois, Cora. The 1870 Ghost Dance (Anthropological Records, 3, No. 1, 1939, 1–151).

Durkheim, Émile. La Prohibition de l'inceste (L'Année sociologique, 1, 1897, 1–70).

Eggan, Fred. The Kinship System and Social Organization of the Western Pueblos with Especial Reference to the Hopi (Ph.D. thesis, University of Chicago, Chicago, 1933).

———. The Maya Kinship System and Cross-Cousin Marriage (AA, n.s., 36, 1934, 188–202).

———. Historical Changes in the Choctaw Kinship System (AA, n.s., 39, 1937, 34–52).

———. Social Organization of the Western Pueblos (Chicago, 1950).

———. The Ethnological Cultures and Their Archeological Backgrounds (in J. Griffin [ed.], Archeology of the Eastern United States, pp. 34–45, Chicago, 1952).

———. Social Anthropology and the Method of Controlled Comparison (AA, n.s., 56, 1954, 743–63).

Evans-Pritchard, E. E. The Study of Kinship in Primitive Societies (Man, 29, 1929, No. 148, 190–94).

———. Social Anthropology (London, 1951).

———. "Religion" (in The Institutions of Primitive Society: A Series of Broadcast Talks, Oxford, 1954).

Evans-Pritchard, E. E., et al. The Institutions of Primitive Society: A Series of Broadcast Talks (Oxford, 1954).

Fathauer, G. Social Organization and Kinship of the Northern Athabascan Indians (M.A. thesis, University of Chicago, 1942).

Firth, Raymond. Marriage and the Classificatory System of Relationship (JAI, 60, 1930, 235–68).

———. Social Anthropology (Encyclopaedia Britannica, in press, 1955).

Fison, Rev. Lorimer. See Howitt and Fison.

Flannery, R. Cross-Cousin Marriage among the Cree and Montagnais of James Bay (Primitive Man, 11, 1938, 29–34).

———. The Gros Ventres of Montana. Part 1. Social Life (Catholic University Anthropological Series, No. 15, Washington, 1953).

FLETCHER, ALICE C., and LA FLESCHE, F. The Omaha Tribe (BAE-R, 27, 1911).

FORTES, M. Social Anthropology at Cambridge since 1900: An Inaugural Lecture (Cambridge, 1953).

——. The Structure of Unilineal Descent Groups (AA, n.s., 55, 1953, 17–41).

FORTUNE, R. Omaha Secret Societies (CU-CA, 14, 1932, 1–193).

——. Sorcerers of Dobu (London, 1932).

FRAZER, J. G. Totemism and Exogamy (London, 1910, 4 vols.).

FULTON, A. R. The Red Men of Iowa (Des Moines, 1882).

GALLATIN, ALBERT. Archaeologia Americana (Transactions and Collections of the American Antiquarian Society, 2, Cambridge, Massachusetts, 1836).

GAYTON, A. H. The Ghost Dance of 1870 in South-Central California (UCP-AAE, 28, 1930, No. 3).

GIFFORD, E. W. Dichotomous Social Organization (UCPAAE, 11, 1916, 291–96).

——. Miwok Moieties (UCPAAE, 12, 1916, No. 4, 139–94).

——. Clans and Moieties in Southern California (UCPAAE, 14, 1918, 155–219).

——. California Kinship Terminologies (UCPAAE, 18, 1922, 1–285).

GILBERT, WILLIAM H., JR. Eastern Cherokee Social Organization (Ph.D. thesis, University of Chicago, Chicago, 1934).

GIRAUD-TEULON, A. Les Origines du mariage et de la famille (1874).

GODDARD, P. E. Dancing Societies of the Sarsi (AMNH-AP, 11, 1916).

GOLDENWEISER, A. A. Totemism: An Analytic Study (JAFL, 23, 1910, 1–115).

——. Remarks on the Social Organization of the Crow Indians (AA, n.s., 15, 1913, 281–94).

GOLDFRANK, E. Changing Configurations in the Social Organization of a Blackfoot Tribe during the Reserve Period (AES-M, 8, 1945, 1–73).

GOMME, G. L. On the Evidence for Mr. McLennan's Theory of the Primitive Human Horde (JAI, 17, 1887, 118–34).

GOODWIN, G. The Social Organization of the Western Apache (Chicago, 1942).

GRAEBNER, FR. Die melanesische Bogenkultur und ihre Verwandten (Anthropos, 4, 1909, 726–80, 998–1032).

GREY, GEORGE. Journals of Two Expeditions in North-West and Western Australia (London, 1841, 2 vols.).

GRIFFIN, J. (ed.). Archeology of the Eastern United States (Chicago, 1952).

GRINNELL, GEORGE B. The Cheyenne Indians (New Haven, 1923, 2 vols.).

GUITERAS HOLMES, C. Social Organization (in S. Tax [ed.], Heritage of Conquest: The Ethnology of Middle America, pp. 97–118, Glencoe, Ill., 1952).

HALLOWELL, A. IRVING. Recent Changes in the Kinship Terminology of the St. Francis Abenaki (ICA, 22, 1928, 97–145).

——. Was Cross-Cousin Marriage Formerly Practiced by the North-Central Algonkian? (ICA, 23, 1930, 519–44).

——. Cross-Cousin Marriage in the Lake Winnipeg Area (Publications of the Philadelphia Anthropological Society, ed. D. S. Davidson, 1, 1937, 95–110).

——. Some Psychological Characteristics of the Northeastern Indians (in F. Johnson [ed.], Man in Northeastern North America, Andover, Mass., 1946).

——. The Size of Algonkian Hunting Territories: A Function of Ecological Adjustments (AA, n.s., 51, 1949, 35–45).

——. Culture, Personality, and Society (in A. L. Kroeber [ed.], Anthropology Today, Chicago, 1953).

HANKS, L. M., JR., and RICHARDSON, J. Observations on Northern Blackfoot Kinship (AES-M, 9, 1945, 1–30).

HARRINGTON, JOHN P. Tewa Relationship Terms (AA, n.s., 14, 1912, 472–98).

HARTLAND, EDWIN SIDNEY. Primitive Paternity (London, 1909, 2 vols.).

———. Primitive Society (London, 1921).

HASSRICK, R. Teton Dakota Kinship System (AA, n.s., 46, 1944, 338–47).

HERSKOVITS, M. J. Man and His Works (New York, 1948).

HOBHOUSE, L. T. Morals in Evolution (London, 1915).

HOEBEL, E. A. Associations and the State in the Plains (AA, n.s., 38, 1936, 433–38).

———. Political Organization and Law-Ways of the Comanche Indians (AAA-M, 54, 1940, 1–149).

HOLLIS, A. C. The Nandi—Their Language and Folklore (Oxford, 1909).

———. A Note on the Masai System of Relationship and Other Matters (JAI, 40, 1910, 473–82).

HONIGMANN, J. J. Culture and Ethos of Kaska Society (Yale University Publications in Anthropology, No. 40, New Haven, 1949).

HOWITT, A. W. Kamilaroi and Kurnai (Melbourne, 1880).

———. The Native Tribes of South-East Australia (London, 1904).

———. Australian Group Relationships (JAI, 37, 1907, 279–89).

HOWITT, A. W., and FISON, REV. LORIMER. From Mother-Right to Father-Right (JAI, 12, 1882, 30–46).

IVENS, W. G. Melanesians of the Southeast Solomon Islands (London, 1927).

JABLOW, J. The Cheyenne Indians in Plains Indian Trade Relations, 1795–1840 (AES-M, 19, 1951, 1–100).

JAMES, EDWIN. An Account of an Expedition . . . . to the Rocky Mountains in the Years 1819, 1820, by S. H. Long (London, 1823, 2 vols.).

JOHNSON, F. (ed.). Man in Northeastern North America (Publications of the R. S. Peabody Foundation, 3, 1946, 1–347).

JONES, ERNEST. Psychoanalysis and Anthropology (JAI, 54, 1924, 47–66).

JONES, H. B. The Death Song of the Noble Savage (Ph.D. thesis, University of Chicago, Chicago, 1924).

JONES, WILLIAM. Fox Texts (AES-P, 1, 1907).

———. Mortuary Observances and the Adoption Rites of the Algonkian Foxes of Iowa (ICA, 15, 1907, 263–67).

———. Notes on the Fox Indians (JAFL, 24, 1911, 209–37).

———. Kickapoo Ethnological Notes (AA, n.s., 15, 1913, 332–35).

———. Ethnography of the Fox Indians, ed. M. W. Fisher (BAE-B, 125, 1939, 1–156).

KING, W. ROSS. The Aboriginal Tribes of the Nilgiri Hills (Journal of Anthropology, London, 1870).

KIRK, CLAYTON. A History of the Klamath Indian Methodist Mission (MS, 1936).

KLUCKHOHN, C. The Study of Culture (in D. Lerner and H. D. Lasswell [eds.], The Policy Sciences, pp. 86–101, Stanford, Calif., 1951).

KOHLER, J. Zur Urgeschichte der Ehe (Stuttgart, 1897; reprinted from Zeitschrift für vergleichende Rechtswissenschaft, 12, 1897, 187–353).

KROEBER, A. L. The Arapaho, I: General Description (AMNH-B, 18, 1902, part 1).

KROEBER, A. L. The Arapaho, III: Ceremonial Organization (AMNH-B, 18, 1904, part 3).
———. Ethnology of the Gros Ventre (AMNH-AP, 1, 1908, part 4).
———. Classificatory Systems of Relationship (JAI, 39, 1909, 77–84).
———. California Kinship Systems (UCPAAE, 12, 1917, No. 9, 340–96).
———. The Matrilineate Again (AA, n.s., 19, 1917, 571–79).
———. Zuni Kin and Clan (AMNH-AP, 19, 1917, 39–204).
———. Philippine Kinship Terms (AMNH-AP, 19, 1919, 69–84).
———. Handbook of the Indians of California (BAE-B, 78, 1925).
———. History and Science in Anthropology (AA, n.s., 37, 1935, 539–69).
———. Athabascan Kin Term Systems (AA, n.s., 39, 1937, 602–8).
———. Critical Summary and Commentary (in R. F. Spencer [ed.], Method and Perspective in Anthropology, Minneapolis, 1954).
———. (ed.). Anthropology Today: An Encyclopedic Inventory (Chicago, 1953).
KROEBER, A. L., and HOLT, CATHERINE. Masks and Moieties as a Culture Complex (JAI, 50, 1920, 452–60).
KROEBER, A. L., and KLUCKHOHN, C. The Concept of Culture: A Critical Review of Definitions (Papers of the Peabody Museum, Harvard University, 41, 1950).
LAFITAU, P. JOSEPH FRANÇOISE, de la Compagnie de Jésus. Mœurs des Sauvages Amériquains (Paris, 1724).
LANDES, R. The Ojibwa of Canada (in M. Mead [ed.], Cooperation and Competition among Primitive Peoples, pp. 87–126, New York, 1937).
———. Ojibwa Sociology (CU-CA, 29, 1937, 1–144).
———. The Ojibwa Woman (New York, 1938).
———. The Santee or Eastern Dakota (manuscript, no date).
LANDTMAN, GUNNAR. The Kiwai Papuans of British New Guinea (London, 1927).
LANG, ANDREW. The Origin of Terms of Human Relationship (London, 1908).
———. Primal Law (see J. J. ATKINSON).
LATHAM, ROBERT GORDON. Descriptive Ethnology (1859).
LEDERER, JOHN. The Discoveries of John Lederer (Cincinnati, 1879; republished from original edition of 1672).
LEHMER, D. The Sedentary Horizon of the Northern Plains (SWJA, 10, 1954, 139–59).
LERNER, D., and LASSWELL, H. D. (eds.). The Policy Sciences (Stanford, Calif., 1951).
LESSER, ALEXANDER. Kinship Origins in the Light of Some Distributions (AA, 31, 1929, 710–30).
———. Some Aspects of Siouan Kinship (ICA, 23, 1930, 563–71).
———. The Pawnee Ghost Dance Hand Game: A Study in Cultural Change (CU-CA, 16, 1933).
LÉVI-STRAUSS, C. Les Structures élémentaires de la parenté (Paris, 1949).
LEWIS, A. L. Notes on Polygamy (Anthropologia, 1, London Anthropological Society, London, 1873–75).
LEWIS, O. The Effect of White Contact upon Blackfoot Culture, with Special Reference to the Role of the Fur Trade (AES-M, 6, 1942, 1–73).
LINTON, RALPH. The Study of Man (New York, 1936).

LLEWELLYN, K. N., and HOEBEL, E. A. The Cheyenne Way (Norman, Okla., 1941).

LOWIE, R. H. The Northern Shoshone (AMNH-AP, 2, 1909, 165–305).

———. The Assiniboine (AMNH-AP, 4, 1909, 1–269).

———. Social Life of the Crow Indians (AMNH-AP, 9, 1912, part 2).

———. Some Problems in the Ethnology of the Crow and Village Indians (AA, n.s., 14, 1912, 60–71).

———. Social Organization (American Journal of Sociology, 1914, 68–97).

———. Dance Associations of the Eastern Dakota (AMNH-AP, 11, 1916, 101–42).

———. Dances and Societies of the Plains Shoshone (AMNH-AP, 11, 1916, 803–35).

———. Historical and Sociological Interpretations of Kinship Terminologies (Holmes Anniversary Volume, Washington, 1916, pp. 293–300).

———. Military Societies of the Crow Indians (AMNH-AP, 11, 1916).

———. Plains Indian Age-Societies: Historical and Comparative Summary (AMNH-AP, 11, 1916).

———. Societies of the Hidatsa and Mandan Indians (AMNH-AP, 11, 1916).

———. Culture and Ethnology (New York, 1917 or 1929).

———. Notes on the Social Organization and Customs of the Mandan, Hidatsa, and Crow Indians (AMNH-AP, 21, 1917, 1–99).

———. Review of Rivers' articles on Kin; Kinship; Marriage, Introductory and Primitive; Mother-Right (*in* Hastings' Encyclopaedia of Religion and Ethics) (AA, 19, 1917, 269).

———. Family and Sib (AA, n.s., 21, 1919, 28–40).

———. The Matrilineal Complex (UCPAAE, 16, 1919, 29–45).

———. Primitive Society (New York, 1920).

———. The Avunculate in Patrilineal Tribes (AA, 24, 1922, 94–95).

———. Origin of the State (New York, 1927).

———. A Note on Relationship Terminologies (AA, 30, 1928, 263–68).

———. Hopi Kinship (AMNH-AP, 30, 1929, part 7).

———. (article) Relationship Terms (Encyclopaedia Britannica, 14th ed., 1929, and later printings).

———. The Omaha and Crow Kinship Terminologies (ICA, 24, 1930, 102–8, reprint).

———. Kinship (Encyclopaedia of the Social Sciences, 8, 1932, 568–72).

———. Social Organization (New York, 1948).

LUBBOCK, SIR JOHN. On the Origin of Civilization and the Primitive Condition of Man (Transactions of the Ethnological Society of London, n.s., 6, 1868, 328–41).

———. On the Development of Relationships (JAI, 1, 1871, 1–29).

———. On the Customs of Marriage and Systems of Relationship among the Australians (JAI, 14, 1884, 292–300).

MCALLISTER, J. GILBERT. Kiowa-Apache Social Organization (Ph.D. thesis, University of Chicago, Chicago, 1935).

MCCLELLAN, C. The Interrelations of Social Structure with Northern Tlingit Ceremonialism (SWJA, 10, 1954, 75–96).

MACFARLANE, A. Analysis of Relationships of Consanguinity and Affinity (JAI, 12, 1882, 46–64).

McGee, W. J. The Beginning of Marriage (AA, o.s., 9, 1896, 371–83).
———. A Muskwaki Bowl (AA, o.s., 11, 1898, 88–91).
McLennan, Donald. The Patriarchal Theory (London, 1885).
McLennan, John Ferguson. Studies in Ancient History (London: 1st series, 1876; 2d ed., 1886).
MacLeod, William C. The Origin of the State (Philadelphia, 1924).
Maine, Sir Henry J. Ancient Law (London, 1861).
———. Dissertations on Early Law and Custom (New York, 1883).
Malinowski, B. Baloma: The Spirits of the Dead in the Trobriand Islands (JAI, 46, 1916, 353–430).
———. Crime and Custom in Savage Society (London, 1926).
———. Sex and Repression in Savage Society (London, 1927).
———. Kinship (Man, 30, 1930, No. 17, 19–29).
Man, E. H. On the Aboriginal Inhabitants of the Andaman Islands (JAI, 12, 1882, 327–434).
Mandelbaum. D. The Plains Cree (AMNH-AP, 37, part 2, 1940).
Meacham, A. B. Wigwam and Warpath or The Royal Chief in Chains (Boston, 1875).
Mead, Margaret (ed.). Cooperation and Competition among Primitive Peoples (New York, 1937).
Meek, C. K. A Sudanese Kingdom: An Ethnographical Study of the Jakun-speaking Peoples of Nigeria (London, 1931).
Michelson, T. Notes on the Piegan System of Consanguinity (Holmes Anniversary Volume, 1916, pp. 320–34).
———. The Owl Sacred Pack of the Fox Indians (BAE-B, 72, 1921).
———. How Meskwaki Children Should Be Brought Up (in E. C. Parsons [ed.], American Indian Life, New York, 1922).
———. The Autobiography of a Fox Indian Woman (BAE-R, 40, 1925, 291–349).
———. The Mythical Origin of the White Buffalo Dance of the Fox Indians (BAE-R, 40, 1925, 23–289).
———. Note on Fox Mortuary Customs and Beliefs (BAE-R, 40, 1925, 351–496).
———. Notes on the Fox Society Known as Those Who Worship the Little Spotted Buffalo (BAE-R, 40, 1925, 497–539).
———. The Traditional Origin of the Fox Society Known as the Singing Around Rite (BAE-R, 40, 1925, 541–615).
———. Contributions to Fox Ethnology (BAE-B, 85, 1927).
———. Buffalo Head Dance of the Thunder Gens of the Fox Indians (BAE-B, 87, 1928).
———. Contributions to Fox Ethnology, II (BAE-B, 95, 1930).
———. The Narrative of a Southern Cheyenne Woman (SI-MC, 87, 1932, No. 5).
———. Notes on the Fox *Wapanowiweni* (BAE-B, 105, 1932).
———. The Narrative of an Arapaho Woman (AA, n.s., 35, 1933, 595–610).
———. Some Arapaho Kinship Terms and Social Usages (AA, n.s., 36, 1934, 137–39).
Mishkin, B. Rank and Warfare among the Plains Indians (AES-M, 3, 1940, 1–65).

MOONEY, JAMES. Cherokee and Iroquois Parallels (JAFL, 2, 1889, No. 4).
———. Myths of the Cherokees (JAFL, 1, 1889, No. 2).
———. Sacred Formulas of the Cherokees (BAE-R, 7, 1891).
———. The Ghost Dance Religion and the Sioux Outbreak (BAE-R, 14, 1896).
———. Calendar History of the Kiowa (BAE-R, 17, 1898).
———. Myths of the Cherokees (BAE-R, 19, 1900).
———. The Cheyenne Indians (AAA-M, 1, 1907, part 6).
MORGAN, LEWIS H. Circular in Reference to the Degrees of Relationship among Different Nations (SI-MC, 5, 1862, art. 10).
———. A Conjectural Solution of the Origin of the Classificatory System of Relationship (Proceedings of the American Academy of Arts and Sciences, 7, 1868).
———. Systems of Consanguinity and Affinity of the Human Family (SI-CK, 17, 1870).
———. Ancient Society (New York, 1877).
———. Houses and House Life of the American Aborigines. *In* Department of the Interior, United States Geog. and Geol. Survey of the Rocky Mountain Region (Contributions to North American Ethnology, 4, Washington, 1881).
MURDOCK, G. P. Social Structure (New York, 1949).
———. North American Social Organization (paper presented at 1952 meeting of the AAA in Philadelphia).
MURIE, JAMES R. Pawnee Indian Societies (AMNH-AP, 11, 1916).
NADEL, S. F. The Foundations of Social Anthropology (Glencoe, Ill., 1951).
NASH, PHILLEO. Revivalism and Social Change (MS, 1937).
NETT, B. R. Historical Changes in the Osage Kinship System (SWJA, 8, 1952, 164–81).
Notes and Queries on Anthropology (6th ed., revised and rewritten by a Committee of the Royal Anthropological Institute of Great Britain and Ireland, London, 1951).
OFFICIAL CORRESPONDENCE, Klamath Agency, Oregon.
OLBRECHTS, F. M. The Swimmer Manuscript (BAE-B, 99, 1932).
OPLER, MORRIS E. An Analysis of Mescalero and Chiricahua Apache Social Organization in the Light of Their Systems of Relationship (Ph.D. thesis, University of Chicago, Chicago, 1933).
———. An Interpretation of Ambivalence of Two American Indian Tribes (Journal of Social Psychology, 7, 1936, 82–116).
———. The Kinship Systems of the Southern Athabaskan–speaking Tribes (AA, n.s., 38, 1936, 620–33).
PARSONS, ELSIE CLEWS. Laguna Genealogies (AMNH-AP, 19, 1923, 136–292).
PERRY, D. W. (ed.). The Indian's Friend, John H. Segar (Chronicles of Oklahoma, 11, 1933, No. 2).
PERRY, W. J. Children of the Sun (New York, 1923).
PRICHARD, JAMES COWLES. Researches into the Physical History of Mankind (London, 1847, 5 vols.).
PROVINSE, JOHN H. The Underlying Sanctions of Plains Indian Culture: An Approach to the Study of Primitive Law (Ph.D. thesis, University of Chicago, Chicago, 1934).
RADCLIFFE-BROWN, A. R. Three Tribes of Western Australia (JAI, 43, 1913, 143–94).

RADCLIFFE-BROWN, A. R. The Regulation of Marriage in Ambrym (JAI, 58, 1928, 343–48).

———. The Social Organization of Australian Tribes ("Oceania" Monographs, No. 1, Melbourne, 1931).

———. The Andaman Islanders (Cambridge, 1933, 2d ed.).

———. (article) Law: Primitive (Encyclopaedia of the Social Sciences, 10, 1935).

———. (article) Sanctions, Social (Encyclopaedia of the Social Sciences, 13, 1935).

———. On the Concept of Function in Social Science (AA, n.s., 37, 1935, 394–402).

———. Kinship Terminologies in California (AA, n.s., 37, 1935, 530–35).

———. The Comparative Method in Social Anthropology (The Huxley Memorial Lecture for 1951, Royal Anthropological Society of Great Britain and Ireland, London, 1951).

———. On Joking Relationships (in his Structure and Function in Primitive Society, London, 1952).

———. Structure and Function in Primitive Society: Essays and Addresses (London, 1952).

RADCLIFFE-BROWN, A. R., and FORDE, DARYLL (eds.). African Systems of Kinship and Marriage (London, 1950).

RADIN, P. Method and Theory of Ethnology: An Essay in Criticism (New York and London, 1933).

RAGLAN, LORD. Incest and Exogamy (JAI, 61, 1931, 167–80).

READ, CARVETH. No Paternity (JAI, 48, 1918, 146–54).

REDFIELD, R. The Folk Culture of Yucatan (Chicago, 1941).

RICE, S. A. (ed.). Methods in Social Science (Chicago, 1931).

RICHARDSON, J. Law and Status among the Kiowa Indians (AES-M, 1, 1940, 1–136).

RIDLEY, WILLIAM. The Kamilaroi Tribe of Australians (Journal of the Ethnological Society of London, 4, 1856, 285–93).

RIGGS, S. D. Dakota Grammar, Texts and Ethnography (U.S. Geographical and Geological Survey of the Rocky Mountain Region, 9, 1893).

RIVERS, W. H. R. A Genealogical Method of Collecting Social and Vital Statistics (JAI, 30, 1900, 74–82).

———. Reports of the Cambridge Anthropological Expedition to Torres Straits, Cambridge, 1904, 1908, 5: 122–53, 233–48; 6: 64–102, 120–26, 169–85).

———. On the Origin of the Classificatory System of Relationships (Anthropological Essays Presented to E. B. Tylor, Oxford, 1907).

———. The Ethnological Analysis of Culture (Report of the British Association for the Advancement of Science, 1911, 1–10).

———. The History of Melanesian Society (Cambridge, 1914, 2 vols.).

———. Kinship and Social Organization (London, 1914).

———. Descent and Ceremonial in Ambrym (JAI, 45, 1915, 229–33).

———. Social Organization (London, 1924).

ROHEIM, GEZA. Australian Totemism (London, 1925).

RONHAAR, J. H. Woman in Primitive Mother-Right Societies (The Hague, 1931).

ROSCOE, JOHN. The Bakitara or Banyoro (Cambridge, 1923).

Rossignol, Rev. M. Cross-Cousin Marriage among the Saskatchewan Cree (Primitive Man, 11, 1938, 26–28).
Roth, H. Ling. The Signification of the Couvade (22, 1892, 204–42).
Roy, Sarat Chandra. The Oraons of Chōtā Nāgpur (Ranchi, 1915).
———. Oraon Religion and Customs (Calcutta, 1928).
Sapir, Edward. Terms of Relationship and the Levirate (AA, n.s., 18, 1916, 327–37).
———. Time Perspective in Aboriginal American Culture: A Study in Method (Memoir 90, Geological Survey of Canada, No. 13, Anthropological Series, Ottawa, 1916).
Schmitt, Karl and Iva. Wichita Kinship: Past and Present, pp. 1–72 (Norman, Okla., 1952).
Schneider, D., and Roberts, J. Zuni Kinship Terms (manuscript, 1954).
Schoolcraft, Henry Rowe. Historical and Statistical Information Respecting the Indian Tribes of the United States (Philadelphia, 1851, Part 1).
Scott, H. L. Early History and Names of the Arapaho (AA, n.s., 9, 1907, 545–60).
Secoy, F. R. Changing Military Patterns on the Great Plains (AES-M, 21, 1953, 1–112).
Segar, J. H. Cheyenne Marriage Customs (JAFL, 7, 1898, 298–301).
Seligman, Brenda Z. The Relationship Systems of the Nandi, Masai, and Thomga (Man, 17, 1917, No. 46, 62–66).
———. Marital Gerontocracy in African (JAI, 54, 1924, 231–50).
———. Studies in Semitic Kinship. Part 2: Cousin Marriage (Bulletin of the School of Oriental Studies, 3, 1924, Part 2).
———. Asymmetry in Descent (JAI, 58, 1928, 533–58).
———. The Bari (JAI, 58, 1928, 409–80).
———. Bilateral Descent and the Formation of Marriage Classes (JAI, 58, 1928, 349–76).
———. Incest and Descent (JAI, 59, 1929, 231–72).
Semalle, M. R. Review of Morgan's *Systems* (Bul. et Mém. de la Société d'Anthropologie de Paris, ser. 2, 4, 1869, 173–78).
Sibree, Rev. James, Jr. Relationships and the Names Used for Them among the Peoples of Madagascar, Chiefly the Hovas; etc. (JAI, 9, 1879, 35–50).
Skinner, Alanson. Eastern Dakota Ethnology (AA, n.s., 21, 1919).
Smith, M. W. The War Complex of the Plains Indians (Publications of the American Philosophical Society, 78, 1938, 425–64).
Smith, Maurice G. Political Organization of the Plains Indians, with Special Reference to the Council (University of Nebraska Studies, 24, 1924, 1–84).
Smith, W. Robertson. Kinship and Marriage in Early Arabia (Cambridge, 1885).
Solotaroff, H. On the Origin of the Family (AA, o.s., 11, 1898, 229–42).
Speck, F. G. The Family Hunting Band as the Basis of Algonkian Social Organization (AA, n.s., 17, 1915, 289–305).
———. Kinship Terms and the Family Band among the Northeastern Algonkian (AA, n.s., 20, 1918, 143–61).
Spencer, Baldwin, and Gillen, F. J. The Native Tribes of Central Australia (London, 1899).
Spencer, R. F. (ed.). Method and Perspective in Anthropology: Papers in Honor of Wilson D. Wallis (Minneapolis, 1954).

SPIER, LESLIE. The Distribution of Kinship Systems in North America (UW-PA, 1, 1925, No. 2, 71–88).

——. The Prophet Dance of the Northwest and Its Derivatives: The Source of the Ghost Dance (General Series in Anthropology, No. 1, 1925).

——. The Ghost Dance of 1870 among the Klamath of Oregon (UW-PA, 2, 1927, No. 2).

——. Klamath Ethnography (UCPAAE, 30, 1930).

——. Historical Interrelation of Culture Traits: Franz Boas' Study of Tsimshian Mythology (in S. A. Rice [ed.], Methods in Social Science, pp. 449–57, Chicago, 1931).

——. Yuman Tribes of the Gila River (Chicago, 1933).

SPOEHR, A. Camp, Clan, and Kin among the Cow Creek Seminole of Florida (FMNH-PAS, 33, No. 1, 1941, 1–28).

——. Kinship System of the Seminole (FMNH-PAS, 33, No. 2, 1942, 29–114).

——. The Florida Seminole Camp (FMNH-PAS, 33, No. 3, 1944, 115–50).

——. Changing Kinship Systems (FMNH-PAS, 33, No. 4, 1947, 151–235).

STERN, BERNHARD J. Lewis Henry Morgan: Social Evolutionist (Chicago, 1931).

STEWARD, J. H. The Economic and Social Basis of Primitive Bands (Essays in Anthropology Presented to A. L. Kroeber, Berkeley, 1936).

——. Ecological Aspects of Southwestern Society (Anthropos, 32, 1937, 87–104).

——. Basin-Plateau Aboriginal Sociopolitical Groups (BAE-B, 120, 1938, 1–346).

——. Evolution and Process (in A. L. Kroeber [ed.], Anthropology Today: An Encyclopedic Inventory, Chicago, 1953).

STRONG, W. D. Cross-Cousin Marriage and the Culture of the Northeast Algonkian (AA, n.s., 31, 1929, 277–88).

——. Anthropological Theory and Archaeological Fact (Essays in Anthropology in Honor of Alfred Louis Kroeber, Berkeley, 1936, pp. 359–70).

SUMNER, W. G. Folkways (Boston, 1907).

SWANTON, JOHN R. The Social Organization of American Tribes (AA, n.s., 7, 1905, 663–73).

——. The Terms of Relationship of Pentecost Island (AA, n.s., 18, 1916, 455–65).

——. Aboriginal Culture in the Southeast (BAE-R, 42, 1928).

——. Social Organization and Social Usages of the Indians of the Creek Confederacy (BAE-R, 42, 1928).

——. Social and Religious Beliefs and Usages of the Chickasaw Indians (BAE-R, 44, 1928).

——. Some Neglected Data Bearing on Cheyenne, Chippewa, and Dakota History (AA, n.s., 32, 1930, 156–60).

——. Source Material for the Social and Ceremonial Life of the Choctaw Indians (BAE-B, 103, 1931).

——. Indians of the Southeastern United States (BAE-B, 137, 1946, 1–943).

TAX, SOL. The Social Organization of the Fox Indians (MS, Department of Anthropology, University of Chicago, 1933).

——. Primitive Social Organization with Some Description of the Social Organization of the Fox Indians (Ph.D. thesis, University of Chicago, Chicago, 1935).

TAX, SOL, *et al.* (eds.). Heritage of Conquest: The Ethnology of Middle America (Glencoe, Ill., 1952).

TYLOR, E. B. On a Method of Investigating the Development of Institutions; Applied to Laws of Marriage and Descent (JAI, 18, 1888, 245–72).

———. Researches into the Early History of Mankind (London, 1865).

VAN AMRINGE, WILLIAM FREDERICK. An Investigation of the Theories of the Natural History of Man, etc. (New York, 1848).

VISSIER, P. Histoire de la tribu des Osages (Paris, 1827).

WAITZ, THEODORE. Anthropologie der Naturvölker (first volume translated by J. F. COLLINGWOOD as Introduction to Anthropology, London, 1863).

WAKE, C. S. Marriage by Capture (Anthropologia, 1, 1873–75, 73–78).

———. Marriage among Primitive Peoples (Anthropologia, 1, 1873–75, 197–207).

———. The Origin of the Classificatory System of Relationships Used among Primitive Peoples (JAI, 8, 1878, 144–80).

———. The Primitive Human Family (JAI, 9, 1879, 3–19).

———. The Nature and Origin of Group Marriage (JAI, 13, 1883, 151–61).

WALLACE, E., and HOEBEL, E. A. The Comanches, Lords of the South Plains (Norman, Okla., 1952).

WALLIS, W. D. The Sun Dance of The Canadian Dakota (AMNH-AP, 16, 1921, 317–80).

WARD, DUREN H. Meskwakia (Iowa Journal of History and Politics, 4, 1906, 179–89).

WARD, PAUL. Sovereignty: A Study of a Contemporary Political Notion (London, 1928).

WARNER, W. LLOYD. Discussion of "Nativistic Religious Movements" (Proceedings of the Seminar on Racial and Cultural Contacts, University of Chicago, 1935–36, mimeographed).

WEBSTER, HUTTON. Totem Clans and Secret Associations in Australia and Melanesia (JAI, 41, 1911), 482–508).

WEDEL, W. R. Some Aspects of Human Ecology in the Central Plains (AA, n.s., 55, 1953, 499–514).

WESTERMARCK, EDWARD. The Origin of Human Marriage (1889).

———. The History of Human Marriage (London, 1891).

WILLIAMS, F. E. The Vailala Madness and the Destruction of Native Ceremonies in the Gulf Division (Anthropology Report No. 4, Territory of Papua, 1924).

———. Sex Affiliation and Its Implications (JAI, 62, 1932, 51–82).

WISSLER, CLARK. The Material Culture of the Blackfoot Indians (AMNH-AP, 5, 1910, 1–108).

———. The Social Life of the Blackfoot Indians (AMNH-AP, 7, 1911, 1–64).

———. Societies and Ceremonial Associations in the Oglala Division of the Teton Dakota (AMNH-AP, 11, 1916, 1–99).

———. Societies and Dance Associations of the Blackfoot Indians (AMNH-AP, 11, 1916, 363–460).

———. The American Indian (1st ed., 1917; 2d ed., 1922; 3d ed., 1938, New York).

———. The Relation of Nature to Man in Aboriginal America (New York, 1926).

———. North American Indians of the Plains (AMNH-Handbook Series, No. 1, 1927).

INDEX

INDEX